THE
DECADE
IN TORY

THE
DECADE
IN TORY

An Inventory of Idiocy
from the Coalition to Covid

RUSSELL JONES

unbound

First published in 2022

Unbound
Level 1, Devonshire House, One Mayfair Place, London W1J 8AJ
www.unbound.com
All rights reserved

Text design by PDQ Digital Media Solutions Ltd

Cover photographs:
© World Economic Forum / swiss-image.ch/Photo by Remy Steinegger,
bit.ly/3pmkSDC
© Simone Fontana / Flickr, bit.ly/3PnTX5c

A CIP record for this book is available from the British Library

ISBN 978-1-80018-171-7 (hardback)
ISBN 978-1-80018-172-4 (ebook)

Printed in Great Britain by CPI Group (UK)

1 3 5 7 9 8 6 4 2

They were careless people, Tom and Daisy—they smashed up things and creatures and then retreated back into their money or their vast carelessness, or whatever it was that kept them together, and let other people clean up the mess they had made.

F. Scott Fitzgerald, *The Great Gatsby*

Contents

Part 4: A Perpetual Vortex of Agitation

Part 1
The Wrong Walk
to Freedom

2010
Take Up the Cudgels

Settle in, imbibe whatever sedative or chemical agent does the trick for you, and let's rewind the clock to those halcyon days of 2010, when we all still thought things couldn't get any worse. Remember how that felt? Me neither, but honestly, there was a time when we still thought 'rock bottom' was the shambolic, incoherent and unrepresentative backroom scramble to assemble a working government while the global economy collapsed around us.

'This is it,' we said. 'This is as bad as it will ever get.'

Oh, to be that naïve again.

But truthfully, things in Britain had reached a terrible new low: the banking system had gone into meltdown; unemployment had spiked at over 2.5 million;[1] the Eyjafjallajökull volcanic eruption presented unprecedented challenges to both airlines and newsreaders; Cadbury had been sold off to the Americans;[2] and the Vauxhall Insignia had inexplicably become Britain's ninth-bestselling car.[3]

This madness could not go on.

It was obvious Labour couldn't go on either. Britain's voters had grown tired of looking at the miserable face of Gordon Brown, and the moment had arrived to replace him with a more even distribution of misery.

By comparison with what came next, there wasn't much wrong with Brown: he was just fundamentally ill-fitted to the presentational part of being prime minister. In an era of retail politics, he emanated the exact aura you would get if you told Squidward to perform an interpretive dance about an abattoir in Croydon.

Brown's prodigious despondency would have been bad enough on its own, but his entire party seemed to have given up. Nearly one in three Labour MPs decided not to stand for re-election in 2010.[4] It was a knackered party, sullied by Iraq, mired in the controversy of the expenses scandal, and cursed by being in the driving seat when the global financial crisis hit.

Public debt was enormous. In Labour's last year in charge, Britain owed an eye-watering 62 per cent of our gross domestic product (GDP), which we can all agree sounds terrible, because by now we've been told it was terrible for well over a decade, and it has become an immutable truth that it was the terrible-est thing ever.[5] So it might be a shock to learn that, as a percentage of GDP, in 2010 we owed less than we had during 190 of the previous 300 years.[6] It was half the average debt Britain ran during practically the entire Victorian era, to which Tories are obsessed with returning. Or in Jacob Rees-Mogg's case, remaining in for ever.

Nobody would suggest the economy didn't need to be improved, but public finances are nothing whatsoever like your domestic finances, and even if they were, nobody raises an eyebrow if you borrow four or five times your annual income to invest in a place where you're going to live. Whereas Britain, home to us all, owed a comparatively tiny two-thirds of what it earned in a year and had a century to repay it. Just like repaying any large loan, as long as people kept getting a wage and paying tax, gradually reducing the debt wouldn't be a problem. All we had to do was keep people working, so tax receipts could slowly increase.

In fact, prior to bailing out the banking sector in 2007, state debt as a percentage of GDP had been lower than when Labour inherited the country from John Major, and almost 12 per cent lower than when Thatcher left office.[7] The interest we paid on our debt was half that paid by Thatcher.[8] Even in the dying months of the Brown administration, the deficit between what we earned and what we spent was only 4 per cent higher than under the previous Tory government led by Major – and Major hadn't had to bail out the entire banking industry.[9]

Unhindered by truth, Tories insisted Labour had failed to rigorously regulate American banks,[10] which a brief search of the atlas reveals are actually located in America, and therefore not technically Westminster's remit. But Tory leader David Cameron was only too keen to explain that our non-existent crisis was something we should panic about, and that the panic was all caused by Labour profligacy.

He was slightly less keen to explain that in 2007 – just as banks were teetering – he had personally endorsed a paper published by the Tory party that argued for even less financial regulation.[11] 'We see no need to continue to regulate the provision of mortgage finance,' it boldly declared, arguing that the 'regulatory burden should be measured and reduced year on year'.[12]

It went on to say that 'from its first days in office, a Conservative government should challenge the public and press assumptions that encourage excessive regulation'.

As it turned out, from its first days in office, the Conservative government mostly challenged the documented fact of stated Conservative policy. You won't be remotely surprised to hear the report was authored by John Redwood, a ceaselessly muddled beta-version humanoid and 'the nastiest man in politics', in the words of his ex-wife.[13]

But facts, schmacts: the Labour extravagance story was well told, and with few exceptions, Britain's news media swallowed whole the myth that the collapse of the entire global economy was brought about by Gordon Brown opening a Sure Start centre in Hartlepool. The press then regurgitated that myth, lavishly and spectacularly, all over your living room carpet, until the tale of Labour's financial mismanagement stank up the whole country. What had been a real-life failure of the not noticeably left-wing, privately owned international banking system was recast as the fault of a reckless left-wing state, extravagantly wasting money on fripperies such as feeding children.

Gordon Brown was incapable of correcting the story, not least because he was too busy calling members of the public bigots.[14] Yet even without that, Brown simply didn't have the presentational skills to persuade anybody to give him a hearing.

By contrast, David Cameron's time at Eton had imbued him with smooth eloquence and polished manners, to which he added lacquered hair and what appeared to be a varnished face, and then launched himself upon the public with a series of meticulously planned impromptu speeches. He insisted our historically unremarkable debts were historically unique, but that Tories would fix it all with something he called Progressive Conservatism.[15]

It turns out Progressive Conservatism is exactly the same as regular Conservatism, except that while you're shitting on people's lives from a great height you have the decency to peek down between your knees and tell them how bad you feel about it.

Alongside his compassion, Cameron urged us all to join his Big Idea about Society, which he imaginatively named the Big Society. This concept promised to solve the problems of our economy by getting people to do for free things that other people currently got paid to do.[16]

When it became clear this would cause a complete loss of income for millions of people and therefore a collapse in the tax revenue on which repaying our debts was dependent, Cameron insisted his party was focused on more important matters. They'd cut £6 billion of wasteful spending, recreate vocational school training, make local councils pay people to recycle, and turn the UK into a low-carbon economy; all of which sounds lovely, and all of which was proven to be complete bollocks.[17] Famously, he also ordered Tories to stop 'banging on about Europe' – advice they would surely have taken to heart, if they'd had one.[18]

Cameron hugged hoodies,[19] hugged huskies,[20] and if the election had been delayed a few weeks more it's a fair bet he'd have got round to hugging Hannibal Lecter, if only to secure those bits of the psychopath vote not already covered by his backbenchers.

Nobody can pretend the Tories didn't promise hardship, but nobody can pretend they showed us the full panoply of thumbscrews in their lair. Much of the campaign centred around a debate over that £6 billion of cuts, which Cameron suggestively promised would hurt us just enough to titillate,[21] but which transformed into an excruciating and disfiguring £81 billion of cuts the moment voters had entered George Osborne's Red Room.[22]

—

Election day loomed, and Cameron did the first and probably last really hard work he'd ever attempted: he mastered the art of jabbing random bits of air with his thumb whenever he wanted to emphasise something, which for some reason Britons think of as a key prime ministerial trait, and he perfected his habit of walking swiftly out of shot the moment he'd finished a sentence, so people gained the impression he was a man on a mission, rather than just a slippery bullshitter avoiding follow-up questions.

It was a fearsome combination of skills, which he deployed with enough panache to very nearly persuade the public that he looked like a potential prime minister, rather than his true calling: assistant entertainments manager at a City hedge fund. A new Tory government seemed inevitable – like death.

Unfortunately for Cameron, in the midst of this well-laid plan, up popped the Liberal Democrats, who had cleverly positioned themselves as all things to all people, vaguely suggesting they'd deliver Scandinavian levels of public services but with American levels of taxation, a combination that constitutes Narnian levels of fantasy.

Their sunny, harmless leader, Nick Clegg, appeared to be a Cabbage Patch doll of Colin Firth that somebody had sculpted from memory, and his inoffensive manner presented no threat whatsoever to wavering voters who feared the fetishised cruelty of the Tories, but were equally unsure about another five years of Gordon Brown morosely shuffling around TV studios looking like he'd just learned how to smile from a book.

To shy and guilt-ridden Tory voters, the Lib Dems presented themselves as: a bit shit, but at least we're not Labour.

In wavering Labour areas, Lib Dems announced that they were: the only party that could prevent a Tory candidate from winning.

It was a great strategy for a party whose highest ambition had always been to come no better than third in everything, but it all went horribly wrong when, on 6 May 2010, voters accidentally gave Nick Clegg some actual responsibility, and he had to decide whether to be Labour or Tory.

Nick chose to be Tory.

And this is an important point to remember: Nick Clegg decided, not us. Voters had been offered a choice between a deflated scrotum, a polished turd, and an innocuous tea boy from the HR department who could promise anything he wanted because he knew nobody would give him power. And in the last recorded sensible decision made by a British electorate, we decided we didn't really want any of them.

But due to the vagaries of our electoral system, this meant we accidentally handed Nick Clegg the authority to choose our next government on our behalf; which is how David Cameron, a sort of irritated glans in a shiny suit, became the sixth person since the war to start the job of prime minister after not winning a general election. He was by no means the last.

—

A coalition government was rare in British politics, but to some extent, every government is a coalition.

For example, despite rumours to the contrary, Labour is not a socialist party: it is an alliance of socialists, social democrats, trade unionists, vague progressives, hard lefties, drippy moderates, wet liberals and virulently awful gobshites, thrown into a hessian sack and hosed down with cat's piss while they ineffectually fight to the death.

On the other hand, the Tories are an alliance of one-nation Conservatives, patrician demagogues, tax-loathing wide boys, mindless libertarians, thoughtless nationalists, soulless xenophobes and virulently awful gobshites, thrown into a velvet bag and hosed down with Château Lafite while they ineffectually fight to the death.

But now we had a *genuine* coalition drawn from diverse groups of awful gobshites, and it was something of a novelty, which the assembled press reported with all the hostile cynicism and meticulous scrutiny usually reserved for that bit at the end of the news about a cat that can play a banjo. All of this lent a strange ambience to Cameron's unsettlingly homoerotic meet-cute with Clegg in the rose garden of 10 Downing Street.

And then the new almost, sort-of, more-or-less government set about its project.

Clegg would make sure everybody in Cabinet had enough biscuits and destroy his party for a generation; Cameron would watch as much Netflix as humanly possible and walk tersely off camera after every question; and his pet sadist, George Osborne, would drag the unsuspecting country into a pub car park and kick the bejesus out of us.

Osborne was the political heavyweight of the outfit, having benefited from the experience of two – count them, two – real-world jobs prior to entering politics. In his first role, he was a part-time data-entry clerk, responsible for filing the names of dead people at an NHS morgue. In his second job, he folded towels at Selfridges.[23]

And then he became an MP and Chancellor of the Exchequer. And I'm sure, with a CV like that, we can all agree he richly deserved it.

Osborne announced to Parliament that his first Budget would restore 'sanity to our public finances and stability to our economy',[24] and then immediately buckled us back into the recession from which we had only just wriggled free.[25] He did this with the full support of the masochistic Lib Dems, including Nick Clegg, who during the election had warned of 'Greek-style unrest' if a party with a narrow electoral mandate attempted draconian cuts.[26] He then voted for an average 19 per cent cuts across government departments.[27]

The results were catastrophic. After the deep decline during the 2007 banking crisis, the economy had begun a recovery, and grew 2.1 per cent in the months before the Tories came into office – that's very close to the growth rate immediately before the crash.[28] But austerity sucked all the money back out of the economy, terrified the public into stopping spending, put the willies up every potential investor, and plunged us straight into a recession again. It set the country back years, and Tory policies meant the UK experienced the slowest recovery from a recession since records began in 1830.[29]

The official title of Osborne's Budget was 'Responsibility, freedom, fairness: a five-year plan to re-build the economy'.[30] In Labour's last year in office, public-sector debt was 62 per cent of GDP.[31] It climbed to 79 per cent by the end of those five years of rebuilding, for which Osborne took no responsibility whatsoever.[32]

And as for the promised fairness? The gender-equality charity the Fawcett Society said the Budget was 'blatantly unfair'[33] and had a 'grossly disproportionate and devastating' impact on women.[34] The BBC reported, 'The cuts to the welfare benefit are regressive, in the most basic sense of costing families in the lower half of the income distribution more.'[35] Even Theresa May told Osborne his cuts would widen inequality in Britain,[36] and that women, disabled people, older people and ethnic minorities would face being 'disproportionately affected'.[37]

But what about that long-oppressed group: financially secure, upper-middle-class white men? Brace yourself, Marjorie: they did rather well. Changes to corporation, inheritance and capital gains taxes that began in 2010 saved them an estimated £70 billion in a decade,[38] by the end of which even right-wing libertarian wackadoos the TaxPayers' Alliance were complaining. They found the poorest tenth of families now paid 47 per cent of their income as tax, while the richest tenth paid just 33 per cent.[39]

The poorest tenth might protest this wasn't in keeping with the fairness promised in the Budget, but the poorest tenth wasn't conspicuously over-represented around David Cameron's Cabinet table: 23 of his 29 ministers were white male millionaires.[40]

So that's the rich made richer, and the poor made poorer: so far, so Tory. But what about the middle? Well, there were 15 per cent pay cuts across the public sector for anybody who was greedy enough to earn more than £25,000,[41] which wasn't even the nation's average wage, and 500,000 public-sector employees were unceremoniously sacked.[42] Widespread protests began across the nation, private investment dried up, the economy and productivity tanked,[43] and it became common, once again, for Britain to be referred to by foreign diplomats as 'the sick man of Europe'.[44]

The coalition had been in office just three months.

—

Picture, if you will, a 75-foot, acid-spitting incubus, festooned from head to toe with the bones of its victims and fattened up with essence of vitriol mined from the very foothills of Purgatory. Now imagine that – with enormous care – you can pack that hellish incarnation of depravity neatly into the body of a small, bald, nondescript halfwit, but you have to instruct him to always speak quietly, lest the monster burst out and rampage across the face of the earth, yea, even unto the end of days.

Iain Duncan Smith isn't really called Iain Duncan Smith. Only two generations earlier his family name was Smith – the double-barrelled affectation is new, as is the rogue letter 'i' in his first name, added after his christening.[45] Like many a leading Tory in today's party – and I'm looking at you, Jacob Rees-Mogg and Boris Johnson – he is not a person but a persona, and one that is barely capable of sustaining its own weight.

His strange combination of pride, stupidity and brittleness is evident in what Ian Smith – or, as I guess we'll have to keep calling him, Iain Duncan Smith – allowed to be claimed on the Conservative Party website: that he'd been educated at Italy's prestigious Università di Perugia, when in fact he'd been at the town's rather less prestigious Università per Stranieri, a language school, which he attended for just three months.[46] Smith did not obtain any qualifications.[47]

His impressive educational achievements didn't stop there, or start there either: while working at Marconi, he attended six separate courses at their Dunchurch College of Management and gained, yet again, not a single qualification.[48]

As leader of the Tories in the early 2000s, his approach to policy was reportedly described by colleagues as 'illogical' and 'messy',[49] and him as 'a political handicap'.[50] He was so unthinking that he was once persuaded to approvingly pose in front of a spoof advertising campaign claiming, 'It rained less under a Conservative government', and didn't question it for a second.[51]

If he were any thicker, he'd set.

But the Tories placed in him their hopes and dreams for the elderly, the sick and the unemployed, and IDS launched into his role as Secretary of State for Work and Pensions by implementing four prodigiously senseless policies.

First: he would extend the pension age, which he declared would 'reinvigorate retirement' by making it start later, so you would lack the vigour to enjoy it.[52] This would also have the effect of forcing older people to remain in jobs they desperately wanted to leave, thus making those jobs unavailable to the record numbers of younger people seeking jobs they desperately wanted to start.[53]

Second: he would transform people who didn't have a job into powerless feudal serfs, by forcing them to work for any benefits they got.[54] This turned 'benefits' into 'wages' in all but name. However, benefits were only one-third[55] of the legal minimum wage,[56] and you don't need three months of failed education at an off-brand Italian language school to work out that this would undercut the wages of people who already had jobs, driving down earnings for everybody, especially for low-skilled people whose jobs were now being done for starvation wages by resentful chemistry graduates.

It's fine: we can probably just blame all that on Bulgarians.

Third: Iain Duncan Smith would force people with disabilities or debilitating illnesses to take up jobs that they wouldn't get paid for and often weren't physically capable of doing. If they didn't do these jobs, they could be stripped of 70 per cent of their benefits.[57] His department reclassified people with incurable diseases such as multiple sclerosis and Parkinson's disease as 'able to work soon',[58] and used this as justification for cutting their benefits by 25 per cent, leaving them surviving on £73 per week.[59]

Half a million people suffering from everything from amputated limbs to terminal cancer were subjected to this cut.[60] Almost 8,000 of them, apparently, had irrecoverable, chronic conditions, such as cystic fibrosis or motor neurone disease, yet were reclassified as 'likely to recover'.[61]

Iain Duncan Smith is either Jesus Christ incarnate, healing the blind and leprous, or he's a thermonuclear moron.

For the last of his four policies, IDS would abolish Britain's plethora of benefits and tax credits, and merge them into a single, simple payment scheme called Universal Credit.[62]

Universal Credit would relieve stress for people claiming benefits, according to IDS, but not according to *The Lancet*, which by 2020 had linked a sharp increase in mental health problems among the unemployed to the introduction of Universal Credit; it also found one-third of claimants had become clinically depressed.[63]

IDS claimed Universal Credit would be relatively quick and easy to roll out, taking only three years. We can all forgive the slight delay he announced after the first couple of years, and at least there had been a solitary pilot scheme to prove, well, literally nothing, since it selected only the simplest claimants, who had no dependants or complicated living situations,[64] and even then, only one of those claimants turned up to the launch of the scheme.[65]

But that first delay was followed by another rescheduling; and then a further minor change to the timeline; and then a postponement to address unforeseen issues; and then a deferral for additional amendments. Before you knew it, there had been eight separate delays, and that three-year delivery window had become thirteen. At the time of writing, full and final implementation is still – you guessed it – three years in the future, just as it was at launch, and just as it probably always will be.[66]

But as we know, projects often take longer if you do them on the cheap: Universal Credit would cost a mere £2 billion to implement, claimed IDS, which unfortunately soon became £15.8 billion.[67] That's the equivalent of £3,600 per hour, every single hour since Henry VIII was on the throne – and what's that between friends?

Tragically for IDS, none of those friends worked at the National Audit Office, which found the cost of running Universal Credit could be higher than the system it replaces (thus nullifying its entire reason for existing),[68] and that was before IDS announced costs had jumped by a further £1.4 billion.[69]

Finally, we move on to his reassurance that nobody would fall through the cracks. He might have failed dismally by every other criterion he set for himself, but he surely wouldn't fail on that. Surely not.

Well, unfortunately, lots fell through the cracks. Fell to their deaths, in fact. In 2019 the *British Medical Journal* found 120,000 deaths linked to Universal Credit and associated austerity.[70]

—

Yet at the time, it was hard to find many people calling for anything except more and more of that austerity, which in the hands of the Tories appeared to be defined as fiscally ineffectual meanness combined with condescending judgement about the poor.

Tory MP Nicholas Winterton objected to having to travel on standard-class trains because of 'the type of people you get there',[71] while newly appointed Conservative peer Howard Flight worried aloud that giving poor people benefits would only 'encourage breeding'.[72] He was forced to apologise for saying what he thought, but not for thinking what he said.

However, the fact that he was forced to apologise at all was deemed a success for Cameron's project of modernising the Tory party, as evidenced by the deluge of cutting-edge Tory MPs entering Parliament that year.

Surely the most modern of these was Jacob Rees-Mogg, who is what happens when a Dalek has hate-sex with a pendulum, and styles himself as the 'honourable member for the 18th century'.[73] He'd come a long way since his earliest foray into politics 13 years earlier, when he was selected to stand in the largely working-class Scottish seat of Central Fife and thought it wise to take his nanny with him on the campaign trail, so she could chauffeur him around council estates in a Bentley.[74] He was 27 years old.

We also welcomed Sajid Javid, who had been global head of trading at Deutsche Bank Asia, responsible for collateralized debt obligations,[75] the dangerously exotic financial instruments that were a major cause of the 2007 crash.[76] The US Senate reported that Deutsche Bank had caused 'material damage to ordinary people and the wider global economy',[77] and this obviously made Javid the ideal man to be put in charge of all the country's money as a minister in the Treasury.[78]

Inexplicably, the effortlessly terrible Andrea Leadsom also became an MP, and it's tempting to wonder if she got the job because her local party were temporarily befuddled by her queasy resemblance to a melted waxwork of Margaret Thatcher.

She was joined by Matt Hancock, a human spork who had spent the preceding years delivering an eerie premonition of his future competence: in opposition, he had been George Osborne's adviser, providing all the insights and judgement needed to thoroughly bugger up our economy for a decade.[79]

Behind them lurched Gavin Williamson, who had been demoted sideways into politics after his Mr Fumble-Thumbs act went down badly at the pottery he managed; he marketed their range of commemorative tableware for Charles and Camilla's wedding with the wrong dates on.[80]

The most bearable of the new intake was Rory Stewart. Despite having the demeanour of someone who phones in sick because he went out in the wind and got a runny eye, he had in fact been an accomplished academic, celebrated charity worker and distinguished diplomat, and was quite clearly in the wrong party at the wrong time. He had never voted Tory in his entire life, and then somehow became a Conservative MP, which makes you wonder if he did it for a dare, or maybe he just got pissed and accidentally ticked the wrong box.[81]

Speaking of alcohol, Mark Reckless, another newbie (and a perfect example of nominative determinism), missed a vote on the Tories' first Budget because he got shitfaced and 'a bit lively' in a House of Commons bar.[82]

Fellow new MP and the world's smallest intellectual giant Liz Truss had previously worked at a charity dedicated to improving public services,[83] where she wrote a report claiming A levels 'stymied original thought'.[84] She then had the extremely original thought of improving public services by becoming an MP in a party that was relentlessly destroying them. She had managed to win her seat even though her own local Conservative Association campaigned to deselect her weeks before the election.[85]

And finally, we welcomed Priti Patel, a prototype Nurse Ratched who had become an MP following a lucrative career with British American Tobacco, when they were lavishly funding Myanmar's incredibly brutal military dictatorship.[86] We can only speculate why Patel decided to move into politics, but if you were to suggest it was because it afforded her the opportunity to fuck up even more lives, few would argue.

—

Unmanageable debt that would take half a lifetime to bring under control was apparently an urgent crisis for the nation, but a glorious and freeing opportunity for its students: thus, the new government raised the limit on tuition fees from £3,290 to £9,000.[87] A typical student leaving university after three years of fees and maintenance loans could now expect to begin adult life owing £43,000,[88] yet earn an average of £13,400.[89]

The UK's state debt at the time was 74 per cent of our annual income, and therefore an unparalleled calamity. Students' debt would be 320 per cent of their annual income, and therefore 'a very progressive package', in the words of Universities Minister David Willetts.[90]

The stated rationale of raising tuition fees – namely that this would provide better funding for universities – would have been more believable if the Tories hadn't simultaneously cut university funding by 40 per cent.[91] It's always possible there was a logic behind all this, but that human ingenuity has not yet developed tools sophisticated enough to track it.

But as the old adage goes: Give a man a fish, and you feed him for a day. Teach a man to fish, and you can leave him with a lifetime of debt and make billions off his repayment plan.

And of course, the Liberal Democrats, who had campaigned on a pledge to oppose any rises in student fees, voted for this policy. The title of the first Lib Dem election broadcast had been 'Say goodbye to broken promises',[92] and you may now commence bleak laughing. In April 2010, Nick Clegg was said to be the most liked politician in Britain; by November he was the most despised.[93] Student protests broke out across the country, and even the *Telegraph* reported that 'their cause was justified'.[94]

Policy changes to education often take years to show results, but in 2019 the Organisation for Economic Co-operation and Development (OECD) found England's higher education was now costlier than anywhere in the world except the USA,[95] and that the net returns of getting a degree in England were lower than in almost every OECD country.[96]

During the same decade, the average salary of the head of a British university[97] tripled to £253,000.[98]

But Tories weren't just applying their novel 'make it cost a fortune but produce worse results' method of improving education to universities: in 2010, startled halibut Michael Gove scrapped building projects for 719 primary and secondary schools, on the grounds that they were a waste of money.[99] You'd think simply saying 'cancel something' would be easy, but Gove still managed to bungle it: at least 25 schools were told they had been spared the axe, pressed ahead with spending, and then had to be told they were going to remain crumbling wrecks because Gove couldn't do sums.[100]

Ian Liddell-Grainger had reached his limit: you don't become a Conservative backbencher to scrap school improvements inefficiently. As he proudly states on his own website, he is 'prepared to take up the cudgels on behalf of other people'.[101] He threatened to majestically march along Downing Street in protest, and then majestically didn't.[102]

Chastened by Liddell-Grainger's powerful threat to very nearly meander halfway along a street while people wondered who he was, Gove redoubled his efforts to cause maximal havoc with minimal thought: he announced the free school programme, which encouraged parents, charities or businesses to set up their own schools and largely define their own curriculum. That curriculum could be anything they wanted, as long as it included one period each of English and maths per week.[103] You could be funded to teach levitation, or indoor hang-gliding, or care of magical creatures; Michael Gove didn't give a flowery tartan fuck, he just coughed up the money.

And man alive, what money.[104]

To give this a little context, the government's original promise was that the new free schools would be cheap, at £3 million each.[105] Slight underestimation. Setting up the Nishkam School in west London cost the taxpayer £45 million.[106] A staggering £18 million was simply to buy the site. The land for the Bobby Moore Academy in Newham was a comparative bargain at only £392,000, but then the taxpayer ponied up another £37 million to put a building on it. Research confirms that it isn't made of solid gold bricks.

Meanwhile the Harris Westminster Sixth Form looks so much like a multistorey car park that its own Wikipedia page describes it as an '8 storey uninspiring building'.[107] Somehow, converting this pre-existing, drab, yet perfectly functional office block into a school cost us an eye-watering £49 million.

Furious gonad Toby Young was a cheerleader for the policy, and bravely put your money where his mouth was by setting up the West London Free School. Sadly, the building he had his eye on was occupied by 20 charities and voluntary groups,[108] plus a school for severely disabled children.[109] But Toby went ahead anyway, because he is a man in a terrible hurry to reach the kingdom of 'I Was Proved Right', yet never seems to get there. And most unexpectedly, all that hurrying didn't apply to publishing the cost of this vanity project: it took nine years for the government to declare the public had been squeezed for £30 million for his school – ten times the cost we were promised.[110]

By 2022, over 500 free schools had opened, and another 220 are on their way, at a cost of at least £4.8 billion; of those, 13 per cent have already closed.[111] An estimated £150 million of funding has been wasted on free schools, some of which never even made it to opening day,[112] and £900 million on lawyers.[113]

And the schools that did make it to opening day squandered a fortune. The National Audit Office said the policy was 'a waste of money' after it found more than half of all free-school places were in areas where they were 'not needed'.[114] Each of these areas already had schools. Each of those schools already had spare capacity.

To give you a sense of how much money is being wasted on pointless vanity projects and favours for pals in business and the media, here's a simple way to get a handle on those vast numbers.

One thousand seconds is 16 minutes.

One million seconds is 11 days.

One billion seconds is 31 years.

So, when we talk about £4.8 billion being wasted, what we mean is: £1 per second for 150 years, two months, three weeks and four days. That's £3,600 per hour, every single hour since Abraham Lincoln was elected president.

There were 40,898 people reliant on food banks in 2010.[115]

The argument for free schools is that they produce better results, and it's true, they often do, but this is largely because they get to choose which pupils attend, and then get to spend more money on each of those carefully selected kids. The annual education budget in a normal local authority school is £4,767 per child. In a free school it's 62 per cent higher, at £7,761 each.[116]

19

The Conservative Party's central credo celebrates value for money, the power of the free market, and self-attainment; it rails against top-down decision-makers 'picking winners' and throwing public cash at them. Also: it backs free schools.

—

But if you need somebody to pick winners and use taxpayer money to ensure nobody else gets a chance, the Tories are the very guys for you.

Starting in 2010, working-age welfare dropped by 71 per cent, while spending on older people rose 10 per cent.[117] I've got nothing against older people, and my plan is to become one myself one day, but Britons over 65 have, on average, five times more net worth than those between 25 and 35.[118] The Intergenerational Foundation, a politically independent research group promoting fairness across different generations, reported that austerity had been most harmful to working families with children, while wealthy pensioners and older homeowners had actually benefited.[119]

At first glance it does seem unjust, but if you make a closer analysis of the situation, you'll find that for every 10 years older a person is, the likelihood they'll vote Conservative increases by 8 per cent.[120] And that's certainly not a pattern George Osborne intended to interrupt with a sudden dose of fairness.

Local councils also suffered unfairly. The minister for local government, Eric Pickles, was reported to be passionate about localism, and the *Telegraph* reported he was 'determined to reverse the presumption that Whitehall knows best'.[121] He then sat at a desk in Whitehall, and imposed cuts on local government.[122]

To be fair, he did prove Whitehall doesn't know best. So there's that.

What Pickles appears to have meant by his much-vaunted 'localism agenda' was that your local council would be handed all the responsibility and blame but none of the money. Research by the University of Cambridge found comfortable, Tory-voting constituencies in Hampshire, Bedfordshire, Somerset and Wiltshire suffered the smallest cuts to local government grants.[123] The cuts to (predominantly Labour-voting) post-industrial cities in the North of England and inner-London boroughs, which had the greatest need, were at least three times as severe.

David Cameron had proclaimed 'we're all in this together', but some of us were in it three times deeper than others, and without a paddle.[124]

And what sacrifices was Mr Pickles making in service of austerity? He heroically claimed public funds for a second home in central London, which Pickles said he needed because he lived an unsurmountable 37 miles from Westminster, a commute that he claimed took him four hours, even though the regular train service takes around 90 minutes.[125] Maybe he was jogging to work, although a cursory investigation suggests otherwise.

When pressed on this – and honestly, who doesn't want to press on Eric Pickles? – he said he needed the second home to ensure he could get to work on time. A bit like people with just one house do.

—

Yet due to the Chancellor's austerity, 1.3 million fewer of us had jobs to go to,[126] and it turned out many people had no homes either. This was something the Conservatives were determined to fix, by deploying the most important tool in a house-builder's arsenal: a thesaurus.

Tories had realised that people who read – or worse, wrote – *Daily Mail* headlines hated the idea of social housing, which was full of awful people with ghastly manners. But those same Tory voters wanted there to be more affordable housing (ideally built somewhere else), because affordability was something desired by striving people with lovely grandparents.

So the government decided to redirect our focus away from 'social' housing and towards 'affordable' housing, which would have been terrific if the two things cost the same amount. But their definition of affordable homes allowed rents of up to 80 per cent of market value, whereas social rents were set at 50 per cent.[127]

'Affordable' suddenly meant 'less affordable'.

Naturally, some people were able to tighten belts and pay an additional 60 per cent to a landlord, but for those who couldn't afford it, homelessness beckoned. That doesn't necessarily mean the very visible homelessness of people sleeping rough (although that increased 250 per cent in five years from 2010).[128] But for every desperate person sleeping in a doorway, there were over 100 'hidden homeless' – 280,000 people sleeping in cars, sofa-surfing, or shoved into decrepit B&Bs in dying, jobless towns.[129] This included 136,000 children.[130]

Two houses for Eric Pickles, though. And billions for Toby Young's fad. So it's not all bad news.

—

You'd already be justified in having doubts about the government's priorities, and if those much-hugged huskies could talk – or if the somewhat less willingly hugged hoodies could talk in a way David Cameron could comprehend – I'm sure they'd have raised some concerns too.

First, the huskies: having promised in May 2010 to lead the 'greenest government ever',[131] by October Cameron had cut the budget for the environment department by 30 per cent (compared with an average of 19 per cent across all departments).[132] Natural England, the government's advisory body responsible for protecting the natural world, had to cut a quarter of its staff.

If it had continued to be properly funded, perhaps it could have found time to advise Environment Minister Caroline Spelman that for every £1 spent on flood defences, £9 is saved in property damage,[133] but it's not certain she'd have listened, let alone understood. Tories cut the budget for flood defences by 15 per cent,[134] which, Spelman claimed, meant '145,000 extra homes' would be protected from flood risk by 2015.[135] By 2015, 5.5 million households were at flood risk,[136] because it turns out climate change doesn't read factually tenuous press releases.

With the greatest respect to teenagers in hoodies, I doubt they read them either, but unlike the weather or Spelman, they are at least sentient, so must surely have been aware of the collapse in the support they received. Spending on youth services in England and Wales was slashed by 70 per cent.[137]

Seven hundred and fifty youth centres closed, and some areas – Trafford, Luton, Slough – lost absolutely all their funding. Every penny – gone. Expenditure on youth justice – preventing reoffending or keeping kids out of the justice system in the first place – was cut by 45 per cent.[138]

Prior to the election, David Cameron had spent as much time telling youths to stop stabbing one another[139] as he spent creepily offering to glide over and hug them,[140] yet youth services, which had been a vital tool in the fight against knife crime, were simply swept away.[141] Lo and behold: a 30 per cent increase in people injured by knife crime in just six months.[142]

—

Such crime is, of course, the remit of the Home Secretary, and as you would expect from the self-styled 'party of law and order', the Tories took it seriously.[143] In opposition, their Shadow Home Secretary had been Chris Grayling, but Cameron took a long hard look at him, said 'nope', and gave the job to Theresa May.

Compared to everybody that came after her, Theresa May was a good Home Secretary; compared to everybody that came before her, she was fucking dreadful.

Both May and jazz-funk Justice Secretary Ken Clarke protested the 20 per cent cuts to the criminal justice budget, but Osborne had the whip hand, and we ended up losing one in every five of our prison, probation and court staff,[144] plus 21,732 police officers.[145]

To be fair to May, some of those terrible decisions were imposed upon her by George Osborne. But to be equally fair to May, she was capable of being truly monstrous without anybody else's help.

Upon taking office, she implemented the hostile environment policy, which aimed to reduce illegal immigration by making life hell for anybody whose melanin levels made the Tories worry about local house prices.[146] She commissioned vans to drive around areas suspected of being excessively brown, with 'Go Home or face arrest' written on the side,[147] which was such a dick move that even Nigel Farage described it as 'nasty [and] unpleasant'.[148] She had adverts placed in buildings used by faith groups cordially inviting them to go back where they came from.[149] She introduced the benign-sounding Right to Rent policy, which charities, campaigners and even groups representing landlords said unlawfully discriminated against tenants based on race.[150]

The hostile environment scheme was found to have been 'incompatible with human rights'.[151] The UN Human Rights Council said the policy 'stoked xenophobic sentiment'[152] within the UK, and Britain's Equality and Human Rights Commission found it was illegal, ineffective and inhumane.[153] It was implemented by the Tory party, so you'd expect inhumane, but ineffective too? All that hatred, and it didn't even achieve its goals – unless, of course, its goals were simply to satisfy racists, in which case: job well done!

Theresa May's dictum that we should 'deport first and hear appeals later' also boggled the mind.[154] The England and Wales Court of Appeal described the Home Office-designed appeals process as 'Byzantine' in their criticism of its vast, unnecessary complexity.[155]

The labyrinthine system May and her henchmen designed led to lunatic outcomes, such as that of Paul Tate, a disabled 53-year-old British-born man who uses a wheelchair, and who had never travelled abroad, yet was held for four months in an immigration removal centre because somebody suspected he might be an American.[156] US authorities were unable to provide any records of him being a US citizen, mainly because he's from Bangor in Wales, but nevertheless, he was denied bail on the grounds that 'he says he's a British citizen but has done nothing to prove it'.[157]

Tricky, since Theresa May had abolished the ID cards scheme that would have made proving it possible.[158]

Meanwhile Chris Grayling, the minister who had been deemed even worse than May, was given the job of minister for employment.

He was responsible for Jobcentres and getting more people into work, so obviously, his first act was to make 10,000 people redundant from – yes – Jobcentres.[159]

—

Those 10,000 people were all real. It's easy to forget that we aren't simply talking about abstract numbers, or soulless mathematical models. The story of Paul Tate, battling to remain in the country where he was born, illustrates how easy it is to forget that, hidden behind each statistic, and crushed beneath each of these cruel failures, there are actual human beings suffering terrible consequences.

A worse economy meant you were poorer. If you were poor to start with, this meant genuine, grinding poverty: hunger, fear, being unable to heat a home (if you even lived in one), being unable to clothe your kids.

If you were one of the millions unemployed, the safety net to prevent you falling into such terrible poverty was made more fragile, and finding reliable work became harder. If you still had a job, you were paying more taxes but, like everybody else, getting worse services.

If you were a victim of crime, the chances of anything being done were surely not helped by over 20,000 police officers disappearing from our neighbourhoods. If you were ill, hospital and GP waiting lists were beginning to spiral again, causing pain, anguish and in some cases, death.[160]

The environment was being eroded, and not simply in the hard-to-grasp sense of ice caps melting, or jungles in South America vanishing. The streets where you lived crumbled; the buildings where your kids were educated were decrepit; the transport network was useless.

If you were a student, you faced a life being even more indebted. If you were a minority, you faced a life being even more persecuted. If you were a woman, you faced a life with less money, less security and fewer opportunities. If you were disabled, you faced a life of yet greater hardship.

And yet millionaires became richer. Billionaires became more common.[161] Wealth inequality, which had fallen steadily since the Second World War, suddenly turned around and started to climb again: the richest fifth of Britons now owned close to half of the nation's wealth, the poorest fifth just 8 per cent.[162] Money was splashed around, but not for the little people, and seemingly not to repay the nation's debts either: the servicing of public debt – the amount we chose to repay – was the lowest for 300 years.[163]

So, for all the pain, our debt rose a further 6 per cent in the first year under the coalition,[164] as money that should have been paying off what we owed was instead hurled into bizarro schemes, such as extra cash for the wealthiest people in Chalfont St Giles, or a spare school for Toby Young to play with.

Even with the largesse shown to our desperately struggling millionaires, the Office of National Statistics reported earnings were down 8.5 per cent compared with Labour's last year in office.[165] Yet as an indication of the depth of compassion found in compassionate Conservatism, Cameron's adviser Lord Young dismissed it as a 'so-called recession', and said we had 'never had it so good'.[166]

He resigned in that special kind of unforgivable disgrace that lasts less than a year,[167] and then he was back as an adviser again,[168] telling the Cabinet the recession was a 'good time to boost profits' by exploiting the low wages caused by the Tories' own austerity.[169]

He wasn't the only Tory MP living down to their reputation: Conor Burns, MP for Bournemouth West, was awarded the brilliant-sounding Golden Dolphin prize for his 'stoic support of the Young Britons' Foundation';[170] rather less brilliant is the news that the Young Britons' Foundation wanted to scrap the NHS, encouraged its members to use sub-machine guns, and suggested the waterboarding of prisoners could be justified.[171]

Meanwhile, Christopher Chope sought to encourage the trend towards poverty by introducing a bill to scrap the mandatory minimum wage,[172] and then, alongside David Davis and blank-eyed error magnet

John Redwood, he attended celebrations for 'Climate Fools' Day' as part of an ongoing battle against the fundamental laws of physics and the survival of human civilisation.[173]

—

Yet as 2010 staggered towards its end, the scale of the damage being done to society remained largely unchallenged.

Labour couldn't oppose; it was too focused on finding a replacement for Gordon Brown that could cause the most Shakespearean levels of fratricidal damage. They found it in the surprise win for Ed Miliband over his brother David. The outcome was so shocking that Ed has continued to look vaguely startled ever since. Nevertheless, once elected he polled well, despite wandering around for years looking like somebody embarrassed to receive the award for Sexiest Supply Teacher. But the long internal war to be Labour's Next Defeated Leader meant there was practically no national opposition to the Tories from within Parliament.

Meanwhile the print media could hardly be expected to hold the Tories to account, given their almost constant irrumating support for Conservatives. Of Britain's 15 main national newspapers, only one backed the Labour Party.[174] The rest vocally supported the Tories or their Lib Dem partners in the coalition.

Thankfully, we could rely on the BBC to balance things out by flexing its renowned leftie muscles. The corporation's controller of global news output, Craig Oliver, joined the Downing Street operation as David Cameron's director of communications.[175] Andrew Neil, editor of the right-wing *Spectator* magazine, fronted both of the BBC's two leading political discussion programmes, *This Week*[176] and *Daily Politics*.[177] The editor of these programmes, Robbie Gibb, was brother of Conservative MP Nick Gibb, and later became director of communications at Theresa May's Downing Street.[178]

Sure, Nick Robinson, the BBC's chief political correspondent, had been national president of the Young Conservatives[179] and then president of the Oxford University Conservative Association,[180] but those sympathies were balanced out by his deputy, James Landale, an old-Etonian close contemporary of David Cameron who was also offered – and declined – the Tory communications job.[181] Meanwhile, a report by the University of Cardiff found from 2007 to 2012 (both in and out of office), Conservative politicians received 50 per cent more airtime on BBC *News at Six* than Labour politicians did.[182]

So if the tsunami of unmitigated failure that started in 2010 has been a revelation to you, nobody should be especially surprised.

2011
Fornicating Hippies

Regardless of the pain inflicted on the nation, the government had ended 2010 on a high, and I'm not just talking about Michael Gove.

It was free from serious scrutiny, much caressed by a friendly media, largely unopposed by a weakened Labour Party, and had entirely subsumed the Lib Dems. The 2010 public protests, though large, had been non-violent, and had therefore been completely ignored. Few household-name MPs had been discovered doing anything seriously scandalous, and the sheen hadn't yet chipped from the dewy, pearlescent brow of our new prime minister.

The government was strutting around the place, preening and clucking at its own smartness, but like any turkey, it just about made it to the second week of January before it started to absolutely stink.

At the 2010 election, David Cameron had pledged that on his watch no employee of a bank that had been rescued by the state would receive a bonus of more than £2,000.[1] So imagine the nation's surprise when the Royal Bank of Scotland, recipients of £45 billion of our money, slipped their boss a £963,000 bonus.[2] The mathematicians among you will notice this marginally exceeds £2,000, but Cameron said he would 'not go to war' over such a minor discrepancy, possibly because *Downton Abbey* was about to start.[3]

Coincidences happen all the time, so it is surely mere happenstance that in January 2011 it was found there were more Tory MPs actively on the payroll of the financial sector than the total number of Lib Dem MPs in Parliament.[4] If it was a coalition government, the junior partners were apparently the banks. More than a quarter of Tory MPs and peers were currently or recently employed by the financial sector they were meant to be policing.

A second coincidence happened almost immediately, when it was revealed that David Cameron's £1,000-per-head fundraising ball was being sponsored by the banking sector,[5] and that half of pre-election donations to the Conservative Party had come from the City of London.[6]

You wait years for a coincidence about unseemly relations between banks and the Tory party, and then three come along at once: George Osborne had thrashed out a vicious-sounding £2.5 billion levy on the banks, who immediately used their safe word.[7] The banking sector felt, in the words of Barclays chief Bob Diamond, that the time for 'remorse and apology' was over;[8] struggling, persecuted people like him wanted and deserved their piffling little £17 million in pay and bonuses.[9]

Thankfully, the Tories were there to lend a hand. Even as Osborne imposed a swingeing 0.13 per cent levy on banks, he also cut corporation tax by 3 per cent,[10] which sounds similar if you say it fast enough, but is actually a cut 23 times bigger. We can't have big finance helping to resolve these issues simply because they caused them.

Oh, and there were 61,460 people reliant on food banks in 2011.[11] That was an annual increase of 50 per cent.

—

But the noisome stench of favours for the banking sector had barely been wafted out of the window before another gust of rancid putrescence leaked from Downing Street. Andy Coulson, Cameron's chief press secretary, resigned as more and more revelations about tabloid phone hacking began to emerge.[12] Only two years earlier, Coulson had told a House of Commons committee investigating his role as editor of the *Daily Mirror*, 'We did not use subterfuge of any kind,' and denied any knowledge of phone hacking.

Now, as evidence began to suggest he knew full well what had been going on, he declared, 'I stand by what I've said about those events,'[13] yet he must have known he was about to be exposed over his deception about his previous duplicity regarding his earlier subterfuge – and apologies to Christopher Nolan if that's the plot of his next movie – because he ran for the hills with his arsehole blinking like a Chilean miner.

Yet his resignation didn't stop the story. Within days it emerged that Coulson, a man with a 20-year record of publishing literally any salacious rumour he fancied, hadn't even been subjected to proper security vetting for his job in 10 Downing Street.[14] Perhaps minimum levels of due diligence seemed like a lot of effort to a PM who was spending hours watching his favourite hyperreal crime drama, *Midsomer Murders*.[15]

So when it transpired that while working for Cameron in opposition,[16] Andy Coulson was also still being secretly paid by the *News of the World*,[17] it began to seem reasonable to wonder if the Tories might be marginally improved by having a leader who wasn't such an entitled, indolent, vacuous dink. Or at least by taking the remote control away from him.

Cameron, on a roll after his empty and already broken promise of being the greenest government ever, had followed up with a crusade to 'rip off the cloak of secrecy' from the actions of his government, so 'you'll be able to hold [us] to account'.[18] And this was going swimmingly, right up until transparency was actually required, at which point, due to a tragic design flaw, things became awfully opaque when you asked questions about the PM's close relationships with people being investigated for hacking phones.

In January it was revealed that the *News of the World* had illegally accessed the voicemail of the murdered 13-year-old Milly Dowler, a disclosure that was met with universal revulsion.[19] Few of us had expected the Murdoch tabloids to be organs of profundity or sticklers for the truth, but this was beyond the pale, as well as being frankly mind-boggling: what conceivable purpose did hacking the voicemail of a dead child serve? None: it was simply symptomatic of a culture that recognised no boundaries, no decency, and no compunction to follow the law.

The list of hacking victims sprawled across society, and included actors, models, sports personalities, musicians, TV presenters, royals and their households, members of Parliament, senior police officers and Boris Johnson, the then Mayor of London.[20]

Police believed the newspapers had targeted the phones of rape victims, the families of British soldiers killed in Iraq, victims of the 7/7 London terror attacks, and the parents of the murdered eight-year-old Sarah Payne.[21]

Given the quantum levels of entanglement between politics and the press, it was certain that the scandal wouldn't remain on Fleet Street; thus began the slow, grinding inevitability of revelation.

Jeremy Hunt, a demonic pixie with ministerial responsibility for regulating the media, had allegedly maintained what was called 'improper contact' with the *News of the World*'s owners.[22] Hunt was supposed to be impartially judging whether Rupert Murdoch should be allowed to buy yet more of our media landscape, yet his office sent hundreds of messages to News Corp, privately suggesting they find legal holes in the regulator's objections to the purchase.[23] Hunt said he made a 'very, very determined effort to show that I behaved with total integrity', and such was his commitment to transparency that, when a journalist spotted him hobnobbing with the Murdochs outside one of their drinks parties, Hunt 'ripped off the cloak of secrecy' and nobly hid behind a tree.[24]

He wasn't the only one disquietingly close to the Murdoch syndicate. Michael Gove, himself a former Murdoch journalist and a shite in sheep's clothing, attended parties at the home of Rupert Murdoch's daughter, Elisabeth.[25] George Osborne had personally met up with Murdoch executives 16 times in just the few months since the election.[26] This included five meetings with Rebekah Brooks, who had been editor of both the *News of the World* and its sister paper, the *Sun*, and was now chief executive of the parent company.

While you could argue that meetings in 11 Downing Street were all above board, it's hard to put an 'official business' spin on the news that Cameron and Rebekah Brooks went horse riding together, shoulder to shoulder and jodhpur to jodhpur. If that remains insufficiently sleazy and elitist for your tastes, wait until we get to the bit where the actual police force responsible for investigating this fetid swamp regularly loaned Brooks a horse, and she and Cameron took turns on it.[27]

I can't remember the last time the police offered to loan me a horse. It's been years.

Investigative journalists wrestled to grasp the extent and depth of intimate entwinement between the prime minister and a bunch of habitual crooks and liars who hacked the voicemail of a murdered 13-year-old girl, and who were literally, until 2007, making secret payments to one of Cameron's most senior advisers.[28] The earliest rumours about this latest round of phone hacking had emerged before Christmas 2010, so reporters asked if Rebekah Brooks had met with the prime minister over that Christmas period.[29] No, came the response, following those much-vaunted transparency principles: he did not have Christmas dinner with Rebekah Brooks.

That's not what we asked, said the media: did he meet up with her over Christmas?

'Oh look, a spaceship!' said the office of the prime minister, transparently, and then ran inside and shut the door.

It would be wrong to blame the Tory party for the malign, biased, untruthful and often illegal actions of much of Britain's absolutely terrible print media. But it would be right to say the Tory party has long been its main political beneficiary – you could go as far as to say 'instrument' – and that as a result the Conservatives have done as little as humanly possible to impose basic decency on their tabloid friends. This time, however, the calls for action could not be brushed aside. Cameron announced the Leveson Inquiry into the ethics of the British press, and half the Tory party ran to one of the few remaining libraries to look up 'ethics' in a dictionary.

From the beginning it was intended that the Leveson Inquiry would be in two distinct parts. Part One was to be held immediately, but Part Two was intentionally delayed to allow the completion of ongoing police investigations. On the day the first report was delivered to Parliament, Cameron guaranteed Leveson Two would go ahead, telling the House of Commons, 'We remain committed to the inquiry as it was first established ... It is right that it should go ahead, and that is fully our intention.'[30]

It didn't go ahead.

Who the hell knows how many people walked away scot-free, but at least Andy Coulson wasn't one of them: he was convicted of perjury relating to his role in hacking voicemails and got 18 months. He served just five. The *News of the World* was closed for ever on 10 July 2011, but please don't feel too sorry for the *NOTW* journalists: I read in their paper that all unemployed people live in five-bedroom houses and get £50k in benefits. And anyway, a week earlier the domain name for its near-identical replacement, the *Sun on Sunday*, had been registered, so I doubt they were out of work for long.[31] Meanwhile, Rebekah Brooks was quietly handed £10.8 million as compensation for resigning from her job,[32] which is 21 times what the average Briton earns in a lifetime.[33] Murdoch still owned 27 per cent of Britain's print media, he continued to back the Conservatives, and David Cameron said it was time to move on.[34]

—

'Moving on' was one of the rare things people of Scotland agreed with David Cameron about, and in increasing numbers: in May the Scottish National Party (SNP) got its first ever outright majority, as the country ran elections to the Scottish Parliament in Holyrood.[35] Cameron said he would 'treat the Scottish people with the respect they deserve', which had historically meant 'not very much', and was exactly the kind of thing that made them want to separate from England in the first place. The election marked a sea change in the campaign for Scottish independence, and little that's happened since appears to have slowed that cause.

Meanwhile, Nadine Dorries (a long-running experiment to prove any one of us could be a better MP than the ones we've got, and so could our pets) brought forward a proposal for legislation to start sexual abstinence classes in schools. But only for girls, who, if I correctly recall from my high-school biology classes, are only half of the problem. This followed hot on the mandatory high heels of her 2009 motion opposing women wearing comfortable shoes in the workplace.[36]

The rest of the UK left Nadine to it and pressed on with tackling reality. As part of the coalition agreement, Nick Clegg had demanded the Tories agree to two major planks of Lib Dem policy: reform of the House of Lords, and a referendum on changing the voting system. In May 2011, the referendum took place, and almost nobody noticed.

The voting system for UK general elections is first past the post (FPTP), which applies the relatively simple concept that the candidate who gets the most votes wins. On the face of it, this sounds eminently fair and rational; and it probably would be if there were only ever two candidates.

But if there are lots of candidates in a seat, the vote gets split. This leads to the phenomenon whereby an MP detested by the majority of constituents can not only win the seat but can go on to become virtually irremovable from office. All it takes is their opposition being divided between a multitude of other, smaller parties. This is a commonplace occurrence: in 2005, not a single MP was elected with a genuine majority of local support.[37]

That's unrepresentative at a constituency level, but at a national level the effect is worse. The uneven distribution of votes across the country meant that to elect each Tory MP required an average of 38,000 votes. Labour MPs each needed 31 per cent more votes: 50,000 for each member elected.[38]

But you have to feel bad for the Green Party, who got over 1.1 million votes in 2015, and ended up with just one MP.[39] FPTP is profoundly unrepresentative.

At the 2010 general election the (sadly now defunct) Voter Power Index[40] calculated the value of votes using a formula that considered multiple factors, including the number of voters not being represented by their MP's views, and the difficulty in removing an MP. It produced some shocking results. 'One person, one vote' is the cry of democracy around the world, yet in the ultra-safe Merseyside constituency of Knowsley, the relative inability of each vote to make any difference to the outcome meant each constituent had the equivalent of 0.002 typical votes.

Lib Dems wanted the introduction of the more representative alternative vote (AV) system, which would allow voters to rank candidates in order of preference, increasing the chance of voters being at least partially represented by whoever won, and, by a wonderful coincidence, benefiting the party that was everybody's second choice anyway: the Lib Dems.

By 2011 AV was one of the five – yes, really, five – different voting systems used in various UK national, local and regional elections and, not without good cause, many people felt it was time to sort this nonsense out once and for all.[41] To that end, Lib Dems asked for a referendum: cos they always make things better.

Cameron had agreed to have a vote, as the price of forming the coalition, but despite this, he opposed the change to the voting system and spearheaded the 'No' campaign. It's hardly surprising he didn't want to mess around with a winning formula. You may have never kissed a Tory, but you've still probably spent most of your life being fucked by them. Since the Second World War the 60 per cent of us who don't vote Tory[42] have spent 62 per cent of our lives under Tory governments:[43] the opposite of the result you'd expect democracy to produce.

FPTP is a dogshit system, but dogshit works just fine for the Conservatives.

Cameron claimed AV would lead to more coalition governments,[44] and you have to say that's a bold move: using yourself as an example of a godawful thing people should avoid more of. The 'No' campaign went on to claim, falsely, that a new voting system would cost £250 million.[45] And of course, the moment – practically the exact atomic instant – the polls closed, and there was no point in continuing the pretence, the 'No' campaign admitted the figure was 'made-up'.[46]

It all sounds eerily familiar.

The AV referendum was our chance to Take Back Control. To give the British voter a chance to dictate British interests. A way to prove our democracy works, and to finally restore power to Westminster. But ironically, the Tories persuaded us that all that stuff wasn't important. Only 42 per cent of us even trudged out to vote. The 'No' campaign won by a landslide. Everything stayed the same, and your vote probably still means bugger all.

—

After a year in office, the government had become quite the experts at needlessly smashing up things that people had worked a lifetime to create, so understandably they were peeved when, in August, a bunch of amateur freelancers in cities across the country began to do the same thing.

The trouble started in London, after police shot and killed Mark Duggan during a botched arrest. Within hours pent-up anger overflowed and all hell broke loose. There were riots across London on the first night, and the next night the trouble spread to Manchester, Birmingham, Bristol, Liverpool, and a dozen other towns and regions.[47] It was the worst civil unrest in decades: five people were killed, over 180 police officers injured, 3,000 people arrested, and at least £200 million of damage was caused. Yet outside of Tottenham, the riots were nothing to do with Mark Duggan. There were deeper, more complicated causes.

Everywhere suddenly sold out of ladders, as columnists across the nation mounted the highest horses they could find and raced to apportion blame. Yet there was very little agreement. Depending on who you asked, the unrest was caused by gang culture, or by unemployment, by criminal opportunism, or by social exclusion.

Looting a branch of Sports Direct was 'entitlement culture' according to the *Daily Mail*'s take on rioters, which almost seemed to regret that 'nobody even shot them for it'.[48] Meanwhile, in a startlingly rare instance of noticing what the hell is going on, the *Telegraph* blamed 'moral decay at the top'.[49]

If right-wing newspapers couldn't even agree, how was the varnished skin tag occupying Downing Street expected to know what opinion he should have? Fortunately, a survey asked whether the public thought 'the Government's response to the economic crisis was helping fuel the rioters', and only 36 per cent of the public said no.[50] Finally, the government knew what the right solution was, and could leap into... inaction.

Nick Clegg said, 'We've all got to know that our homes, our shops, our communities can be kept safe at times like this,' and then reassured a grateful nation that the huge cuts to policing would go right ahead as planned.[51]

Cameron rushed in front of a camera, said, 'More police officers are needed on the streets,' and asserted that people asking him not to cut 20,000 police officers from the streets were 'missing the point'.[52] He then rushed off camera again before anybody had a chance to join up these two statements to form a small but powerful collection of high-grade gibberish.

Ed Miliband called for an inquiry and said society should avoid seeking 'simplistic answers',[53] but instead, Cameron delivered very nearly the most simplistic answer it is possible to supply: two words. He glared with an almost erotic petulance at the cameras, made his mouth go as tight as a gnat's chuff, and declared that we all now lived somewhere called 'Broken Britain'.

When asked to define Broken Britain, he characterised it as: 'Irresponsibility, selfishness, behaving as if your choices have no consequences, children without fathers, schools without discipline, reward without effort, crime without punishment, rights without responsibilities,[54] which is such a good description of Boris Johnson's premiership that it's tempting to wonder if one of Cameron's pair of £25,000 sheds is in fact a TARDIS.[55]

—

Riots are not lovely things, but looking for people to blame for them is a lovely way to keep everyone distracted from the slow-motion horror stories being deliberately enacted with everybody's full knowledge.

Eric Pickles, the multi-homed star of 2010's most inexplicable train journey, made a grand comeback in July, as a leaked letter from his office to the PM predicted the government's planned cuts to the housing benefit cap would make 40,000 additional families homeless.[56] That's half the size of the British Army. Plus their kids.

In one of those casual uses of benign language that disguises genuine evil, these were described as 'homelessness acceptances', as though the families were signing for an Amazon delivery. Yet making somebody homeless doesn't make them vanish from reality; they would still require temporary housing, social care, new school places for their kids, and all the other urgent services people in crisis need. None of this is cost-free, so Pickles' letter went on to explain that the housing benefit cap would probably end up losing money, rather than its intended plan of saving some.

Of course, Pickles 'flatly denied' he had warned Cameron that it would increase homelessness,[57] even though the entire letter was printed in the *Guardian*.[58] His explanation was that he, personally, hadn't written to the PM: the letter was signed by his private secretary. Totally different.

So his explanation was ignored, and the letter was ignored, and the policy remained in place, and everybody blithely moved on to the next stupid, destructive debacle.

—

During the summer of 2011, the nation's most intransigent Jobcentre Plus receptionist, Theresa May, granted permission for the UK Border

Force to use what was euphemistically described as a 'more risk-based approach' to checking the passports of EU citizens.[59] What this amounted to was: let's just chance it and do fewer checks on almost everybody coming into the country.

This was a continuation of a policy implemented – with May's approval – in 2010, by the head of the Border Force, Brodie Clark.[60] The impetus behind it was, naturally, to cut costs, because the Border Force budget had been slashed by 20 per cent by a government that kept bleating on about how deeply concerned it was about immigration.[61]

Nobody noticed for a while, but in the early summer of 2011, in between advertorials promoting retirement timeshares in Spain, headlines appeared in the *Daily Mail*[62] and *Daily Express* bewailing the multitude of EU nationals suddenly flooding our borders,[63] and Theresa May, in the words of the committee that ended up investigating this shit show, 'panicked'.[64]

By November, Theresa May had lurched into the House of Commons to make a statement best summarised as: Oh my God, it's all gone wrong, who can I blame?[65] She alighted on Brodie Clarke and suspended him on the spurious basis that he'd applied her policy to all immigrants, and not just to those lovely European people that we all liked so much.

It's axiomatic in politics that if you've got yourself into a pickle, you should launch an inquiry. The things take an eternity to complete, giving you years to dodge any awkward questions with 'we must await the outcome', and by the time the truth does emerge – if it ever does – the media is already in high old fizz about the next scandal you're frantically trying to cover up. Multiple rolling inquiries are an excellent signifier of congenital bunglers desperate to avoid discovery.

Theresa May launched three simultaneous inquiries into the Brodie Clark business,[66] and then, a few days later, just in case the can hadn't been kicked far enough down the road, she added a leak investigation too.

The inquiry she had (quite ludicrously) asked sodding MI6 to conduct was quietly dropped the moment journalists had been suitably impressed by the James Bondness of it all. The results of a second inquiry have never been published, nor was the outcome of the leak inquiry. A decade later the Home Office still refuses to reveal their findings.

The last of the four reports was eventually squeezed out into the nation's recoiling palm; it found ministers 'must be clearer on their requirements in respect of standards, policy and decisions'.[67] Basically: Theresa May hadn't given proper instructions, got found out, and Brodie Clark lost his job.

Clark launched legal proceedings for constructive dismissal, but the matter was settled out of court, with the understanding that the details of the matter should never be disclosed. This wasn't good enough for the Home Affairs Committee, which still remembered that time in aeons past (less than a year earlier) when David Cameron had promised to 'rip off the cloak of secrecy' from the actions of government.[68]

So MPs launched a fifth investigation into the matter, but the Home Office, despite promising to release all the evidence, then utterly refused to do so.[69] You could say this wasn't in keeping with the 'transparency agenda', but I think we can all see right through it. The chair of the Home Affairs Committee could too: he called the departure of Brodie Clark 'totally unnecessary' and said Theresa May's decision-making over the policy was 'wrong'.[70]

Theresa May, scourge of immigration and stout defender of our borders, had been in office barely a year, and had managed to abolish the ID-card scheme designed to track immigrants, destroy the records of identities so it was harder to tell who was here legally, and close the Office of the Identity Commissioner.[71] And now, through a combination of vandalism and innate negligence, she had weakened our capacity to check people coming into the country. And all this was going on while she was commissioning vans to drive around immigrant communities telling them to 'Go Home'.

Yet despite the secrecy clause in the out-of-court settlement, the UK Border Agency's accounts reveal Brodie Clark was paid off with a sum of £225,000 without admission of liability or wrongdoing on either side. That was eight times the average salary at the time, but a small price to pay to avoid Theresa May having to face mild embarrassment about her graceless, relentless, bungling ineptitude.[72]

—

As rolling austerity caused the economy to tank, unemployment soared past 2.5 million,[73] which was the highest level since the Tories had previously been in charge,[74] and you can't say they're not sticklers for tradition.

Within Whitehall, ideas for creating jobs were flying around like shits in search of a fan, although nobody seemed to consider perhaps stopping hoovering all the money out of the real economy and then handing it to rich banker friends so they could hide it in the Cayman Islands.

Steve Hilton, the prime minister's biggest 'thinker' and the Barefoot Cuntessa of Downing Street, weighed in: he reckoned the way to create 2.5 million jobs was to abolish maternity leave.[75] This might have had some effect, if somebody had desperately wanted to employ 2.5 million exhausted new mothers at the time, but sadly, there weren't even that many expectant people in the country. Uncompetitive Britain clearly hadn't been procreating enough, and official figures showed the waiting time for babies on the NHS was still doggedly stuck at nine months. Bloody socialists.

Undeterred, Hilton proposed the government could simply ignore employment laws until employment spontaneously happened, which led to Number 10's permanent secretary having to 'explain that if David Cameron breaks the law he could be put in prison'.[76] Such minor details barely impinged on the blue-sky world in which Hilton lived. After all, this was the man who had, while the Tories were in opposition, advocated privatising the M25 and suggested the nation should buy 'cloud-bursting' technology to increase the number of sunny days we get.[77]

Cameron paid this dolt £276,000 a year. But then again, he did wander around with no shoes on, and that's a sure sign of being a genius; or of having the mind of a three-year-old.

For the rest of us, average incomes finally began to increase again, by a modest but very welcome 2.8 per cent.[78] However, the banks, who by 2011 had been given £456 billion of public money (that's £3,600 per hour, every hour since the pre-historic era in which dogs were first domesticated), were now refusing to lend money to people who wanted to buy a home.[79] This caused a surge in demand for rented properties, and the cost of rent soared by 5 per cent in just six months, wiping out any wage increases, and once again predominantly affecting poorer and younger people.[80] One in every five of those younger people was unemployed: almost a million of them; but the government refused to see any connection between this and people being angry.[81]

(The rise in rents also affected the dozens of Tory MPs who were landlords, but they didn't complain very much.)

Unsurprisingly, people started sleeping in tents on the street. Slightly more surprisingly, they did it on the steps of St Paul's Cathedral, called themselves Occupy London, and set about peacefully requesting a small degree of sanity and honesty. It didn't seem too much to ask.

The Occupy movement suggested the rich should stop avoiding tax at a time when almost half the planet lived on £3.70 a day, yet £23 trillion was hidden in tax havens (that's an impressive £360,000 per hour of tax avoided every single hour since the Norman Conquest in 1066).[82] They suggested we look after health services, education and employment, because these things tend to help humans. And they suggested we stop terminal levels of pollution because, without wishing to overstate matters, terminal things tend to help humans rather less.

These do not seem to be especially contentious ideas. They seem eminently sensible, and in some cases the absolute bare minimum required to continue the medium-term survival of human civilisation. Nobody sane could dispute them. To launch into a tirade about these rational, moderate, entirely achievable goals, you'd need to be a sociopathic, attention-seeking, fact-averse maniac in the pockets of the banks, who is willing to let thousands die in support of your bananas, evidence-free, much-disproven theories.

Enter Boris Johnson, who called them 'fornicating hippies'. He called them 'an eruption of boils', and 'bivouacked crusties'. He demanded judges find 'the cojones' to put a stop to it all.[83]

And then he called for the top rate of tax to be cut.[84]

—

People were starting to call 2011 'the busiest year for news ever',[85] which in retrospect is hilariously naïve. At the time, we were all busy shitting ourselves inside out at the news that the Institute for Fiscal Studies had predicted Osborne's cuts would push 3 million children to poverty within the year[86] and cause the sharpest fall in average incomes in 35 years.[87] As winter approached, a quarter of us were now unable to pay our fuel bills,[88] and a report found being too poor to heat our homes was now killing more Britons than road accidents.[89]

Swings and roundabouts, though: that lovely cut in corporation tax was announced, which must have been a relief for all those corporations freezing to death in poverty.[90] Osborne insisted the measures would actually increase the amount of money corporations paid, because (to paraphrase very slightly) 'something, something, stardust and magic'. In 2010, with the higher rate, the Treasury collected £43 billion in corporation tax. It fell billions below that each subsequent year, and by 2015, when Osborne's miracle was meant to pay off, we still hadn't recovered to 2010 levels, and we were another £11 billion out of pocket.[91]

Not that anybody mentioned billions. The government only liked to talk about billions when it was spending money on things the public liked, such as…

Sadly, the end of the previous sentence doesn't exist.

But when the government was furtively giving away huge wodges of cash to people the public hated, they preferred to talk about pennies. 'The extra 1p cut in corporation tax will help firms increase investment,'[92] said the head of the Confederation of British Industry (CBI), and went on to claim vulgar largess to rich corporations would allow them to focus on 'growth potential'.

The tax cut went ahead. Growth in jobs didn't. Unemployment kept on climbing to 2.62 million.[93] That lowly penny was next seen hanging around with a swarm of its friends, until they merged into a supercluster, and became the average £2.6 million salary for top bosses.[94] That's 145 times the average UK income. Meanwhile, it was revealed that donations to the Conservatives from those very same valiantly struggling heroes in the finance sector had quadrupled in five years.[95]

—

All that lovely new money handed by George Osborne to the richest of the rich showed how useful it is to have friends in high – oh, who are we kidding? – medium places, as the hitherto obscure figure of Adam Werritty could attest.

The friendship between Werritty and Liam Fox predated the coalition government. As far back as 2002, Werritty had moved, rent-free, into the taxpayer-funded flat of Fox, who was then shadow health secretary. In 2005, Fox used MP's expenses with which he paid Werritty.[96]

Werritty then became chairman of the right-wing thinktank Atlantic Bridge, which listed its official London office as No. 341 Portcullis House, House of Commons. This was Liam Fox's room.

All of this was vague and unofficial, but absolutely nothing got better when Liam Fox became the Secretary of State for Defence in 2010.

Despite having no security clearance,[97] Werritty visited Fox at the Ministry of Defence (MoD) 22 times over the next 16 months.[98] He was present at 40 of Liam Fox's 70 ministerial engagements,[99] and went along on 18 overseas trips,[100] even though he had no official role whatsoever.

So far, so weird, but then it emerged Liam Fox also blocked civil servants from attending meetings where Werritty was in attendance, so nobody knows what was discussed. It could all have been above board, and there's nothing to suggest otherwise. Nothing whatsoever. All absolutely fine.

In 2009, Werritty arranged and attended a meeting between Liam Fox and the British Ambassador to Israel, allegedly with the intention of enlisting UK support for an Israeli attack on Iran.[101]

In 2011, as news of this strange entwinement and covert war-mongering emerged, Fox denied Werritty was his adviser. But in the words of the BBC's Nick Robinson: 'His business cards stated he was an adviser, he booked hotels as an adviser, he fixed meetings with people who believed he was an adviser. Finally, he raised funds from people who thought that too.'[102]

This last bit is worth mentioning because, in the midst of the scandal, the moneygrubbing never stopped: the Fox/Werritty combo persuaded a billionaire donor to cough up £104,000 to Atlantic Bridge, as well as giving them free office space and letting them both fly around on his private jet, because Atlantic Bridge was set up as a charity, and charities always have private jets, right?[103]

In October, Fox resigned in disgrace over the Werritty business, and Atlantic Bridge was dissolved after the Charity Commission figured out what was going on.[104]

—

The following month, 2 million public-sector workers went on strike in protest at changes to their pensions.[105] For decades, there had been an implicit trade-off for comparatively low-paid teachers, Jobcentre workers and other civil servants: their salary might be low, but they had a pretty decent government-backed pension to make up for it.

But now the government wanted to renegotiate those pensions, and renegotiating meant reducing. Sure, teachers got a shitty salary and lousy working hours, but at least their promised pension was now about to be stolen, so they'd all die in penury. And that can score as much as 51 in Scrabble, so for God's sake, focus on the positives.

The government imposed a deadline for talks about the pensions, which was too short for any proper discussions to take place, then announced that if agreement wasn't reached, the cuts would just happen anyway. So workers went on strike, demanding proper talks.

Across the UK, 62 per cent of schools closed,[106] which led Cabinet Office minister and maths prodigy Francis Maude to declare: 'What today has shown is that the vast majority [of public sector workers] do not support today's strike.'[107] In Scotland, only 2 per cent of schools remained open.[108] Perhaps Mr Maude's difficulties with sums were a result of a really important missed day at school, an eventuality that clearly worried the PM, who asked, 'How can it possibly be right for our children's education to be disrupted by trade unions acting in that way?' temporarily forgetting he had already closed schools twice in 2011: once for a royal wedding that none of the pupils were invited to and once for a referendum that he didn't even want.[109]

And then, with the decisive rigour and Churchillian pugnacity that made him such a great leader, over the course of 24 hours Cameron said the industrial action was a 'damp squib';[110] then that it was 'obviously a big strike';[111] and then that industrial action would 'achieve nothing';[112] and then he backed down on the deadline he had imposed and agreed to continue talks.[113]

—

The year had kicked off with Nadine Dorries being a halfwit, and it ended with her swapping the remaining half for a trip to Australia, where she was to take part in *I'm a Celebrity... Get Me Out of Here!*. She hadn't informed her party or her constituency about this, probably due to her absolute certainty that they would definitely approve.[114]

They didn't.

Frankly, you can't blame them: it's hard to justify a jaunt on reality TV when you're a serving MP, assuming you overlook the £40,000 fee and complimentary business-class flights. It just goes to prove that you can't buy class, but you can rent crassness by the hour.

Dorries' unhinged explanation was that she was only participating to highlight her pro-life views.[115] It was a bold tactic: surprisingly few anti-abortion campaigners have the courage to make their point by pocketing a load of cash, donning a swimsuit and standing under a shower of cockroaches, merrily gnawing on a kangaroo bollock.

Fellow Tories lined up to put the boot in. Louise Mensch said Dorries had 'demeaned the role of an MP'. Follicular fire hazard Michael Fabricant said she had 'let down her colleagues', which was at least a public service, because now her colleagues finally knew how the rest of us felt. And backbencher Claire Perry said Nadine Dorries was 'not fit to be an MP', and yet Nadine Dorries is still an MP, and has since been promoted to Cabinet rank.[116]

I mean, promoted to Cabinet. Rank.

—

In November, the homeless charity Shelter calculated 35,000 people faced losing their homes before Christmas, a rate of two per minute.[117] But these things weren't as important to David Cameron as laying the foundations for the crisis that would dominate the decade.

The 2007 crash had hit every major nation, and across the Eurozone there was a series of rolling political battles over debt. European nations wrestled and haggled until they finally had a workable rescue plan, and then at the last minute, in swept David Cameron to pointlessly veto the whole bloody thing.[118] It scuppered a strategy that would have helped the 450 million people living in the EU, including everybody in Britain. It infuriated all our major international partners, and it plunged the politics of the entire continent into a monumental crisis. Newspapers reported Cameron had 'cast Britain adrift in Europe', at a time when, with the fruit-loop exception of the *Daily Express*, they all still considered this to be A Bad Thing.[119]

But it caused a practically orgasmic spasm of delight among the tiny group of maniacal Eurosceptics who had been dementedly humping the leg of the Tory party for a generation. Now, 18 months into his tenure, and with Labour ahead in the polls, Cameron apparently felt an appeal to the 7 per cent who then supported the UK Independence Party (UKIP) might replenish his electoral position and bolster his flagging levels of smug self-esteem.[120] A knee-jerk act of petty vandalism against the plan to rescue a continent was just the ticket.

Everyone was cock-a-hoop. The Little Englander corps of the Tory backbench were cock-a-hoop. The *Daily Express* was cock-a-hoop. And even Nigel Farage was both a cock and an absolute hoop.

Cameron had clearly hoped his act of sabotage would bring the Eurosceptics onside. Instead, it emboldened them. Having fucked up the continent and, unwittingly, his own future, he rushed on camera to hilariously claim he would not 'undermine the UK's position in Europe's single market', and then whoosh! – he dashed off camera again, charging away to meet his fate.[121]

2012
Badgers Moved the Goalposts

Michael Gove is, in the words of his Cabinet colleague Chris Huhne, 'the politest man in the House of Commons',[1] but Huhne might have been surprised and delighted by the revelation that Michael Gove was also, when nobody was looking, the politest woman too.

In early 2012 it was revealed that Gove had, for a couple of years, been using a private email account set up in the name 'Mrs Blurt' to engage in discussions that he didn't want to be subject to Freedom of Information requests.[2] You can be sure these emails were all totally benign, since they included discussions between Mrs Blurt and his/her/their special adviser, Dominic Cummings, who we all know to be the most ethical man in Britain.[3]

The Information Commissioner investigated the esoteric nature of Gove's alter ego, and in February 2012 ruled that all the Mrs Blurt emails must be made public.[4] Gove, sticking rigidly to his government's much-vaunted transparency agenda, spent £12,540 of public money to get legal advice about how he could keep his aberrant behaviour secret.[5] In the end, it turned out he couldn't.

But by the time the legal process had played out, by some unhappy chance an unidentified person described as 'staff' had systematically deleted more than a hundred official emails relating to Gove's department, so to this day nobody knows what was said.[6]

'Many individuals routinely delete emails so as to maintain order in their inbox,' said Gove's department by way of explanation.[7] And who are we to argue with such an honest-sounding response? After all, it's not as if Gove had a habit of writing down secret plans and then hiding them from the public.

A week later, newspapers revealed secret plans to privatise state schools, which Gove had written down and then hidden from the public.[8]

The rationale behind the proposal to sell off schools was that the government needed the cash because, Gove's memo explained, the 'massive expansion of free schools and academies is costing too much money'.[9] Those would be the free schools that were Gove's idea. And that massive expansion of academies? Oh yes, that was a Conservative policy too, introduced by Gove in 2010.[10] But Michael and Mrs Blurt were, as has been noted, two of the politest people in the House of Commons, and they would never be so rude as to point out this glaring hypocrisy.

—

Fortunately, Gove's plan for a fire sale of many of your children's futures didn't make it past his top-secret drawing board. The same cannot be said for his plan to remove the requirement for teachers to be qualified.[11] By 2020, that meant 72 per cent of secondary schools could fill their classes with teachers who might have no idea what they were doing, but who were cheap.[12] That's your kids having their futures harmed by a deliberate removal of basic standards of teaching, but it barely made the news in March 2012, because Peter Cruddas had monopolised events.

Cruddas, estimated to be worth $1.3 billion, was the co-treasurer of the Tory party, and one of its main fundraisers.[13] Donations to political parties are supposed to be given with no strings attached, otherwise it becomes tricky to distinguish them from naked corruption, but Cruddas occupied the exceptional zone where somebody is bright enough to make a billion quid, but apparently not bright enough to understand that he shouldn't allow the *Sunday Times* to secretly film him selling privileged access to David Cameron for huge piles of cash in donations.

'£200,000 to £250,000 is Premier League,' Cruddas blithered into the hidden camera. 'You can ask him practically any question you want.'[14]

Probably not a second question, though, cos Cameron would have already marched off in a huff.

Cruddas resigned the moment the story appeared but had a swift change of heart, and launched a legal action against the *Sunday Times* for libel. And won. The court found the articles about him had been defamatory, and awarded him £180,000 which, embarrassingly for Cruddas, isn't even Premier League.[15]

Further relegation beckoned for Cruddas when the *Sunday Times* appealed the decision, and the Court of Appeal found a central allegation to be absolutely true.[16] Cruddas, they ruled, really had been selling access to the prime minister. Most of the £180,000 damages had to be repaid, knocking poor old Cruddas down into Conference National League (Division Three).

He basically vanished from front-line politics until 2020, when he suddenly reappeared to join the massed ranks of pals being given a life peerage by Boris Johnson. The House of Lords Appointment Commission said they could not support his candidacy due to the 'historic concerns' about his time as treasurer,[17] but Johnson, blithely ignoring the documented, legally binding ruling by the Court of Appeal, said the details of Cruddas' history were 'untrue'.[18] Which was itself untrue. A brief squabble ended when the honours watchdog was overruled by Johnson: the first time this had ever happened in the whole of English history.[19]

This is unrelated, so please don't read too much into it, but the previous year Cruddas had given £50,000 to Boris Johnson's leadership campaign.[20] And that's barely 'Sunday morning five-a-side' league.

—

In March Steve Hilton, the brains behind the idea to 'remove all the Libyans from Libya and replace it with a giant solar farm to power Britain',[21] announced he was taking an unpaid sabbatical to go off to California, where he'd seem normal. He was going to 'study how governance could be improved',[22] which must have come as a surprise to David Cameron, who'd been paying Hilton to know how to do that for the previous five years. Although frankly, Hilton's suggestion that we 'replace the Commonwealth with a new union of countries based on their shared love of techno music' should have alerted the PM to the fact his brains trust was going a bit HAL 9000.[23]

Before leaving, Hilton put his final thoughts in a memo, presumably having already learned that anything he said aloud would be drowned out by a chorus of exasperated sighs. In essence, he said we should cut everything in half, especially the number of civil servants.[24] The Whitehall slaughter should include energy scientists at the Department of Energy, farming specialists at the department responsible for food, and people who know about economics at the Treasury.

Why should a government waste time with experts when it could have the kind of blue-sky thinking that suggests, as Hilton did, sending the Royal Family on training courses in Silicon Valley to bring them up to speed with the latest contemporary thinking?[25] And with that, Hilton wafted out of the door, followed by the breeze of a thousand relieved exhalations.

Days after Hilton's departure, and after much fanfare and many gratuitous leaks to friendly papers, the Chancellor delivered his Budget to the House of Commons, sipped his traditional whisky, and sat down with a satisfied leer. His first attempt at a Budget had crashed the economy for a decade.[26] His second had increased our debts,[27] added to unemployment, precipitated riots, and undermined national security at our borders.

But this time, it was perfect. Nothing could go wrong. Third time lucky.

It was a monumental disaster. At a time when a quarter of us couldn't afford our fuel bills, Osborne cut to 45 per cent the top rate of tax for people earning more than £150,000 and shoved £42,500 into the pocket of anybody earning a million quid.[28]

Tories claimed the tax cut would reduce tax avoidance, and therefore bring in more money. But if the problem was tax avoidance, Osborne could have simply closed the loopholes that allowed that tax avoidance, rather than trusting rich people – who had already proven that they regularly avoided tax – to suddenly have a fit of honesty.

Cameron's ex-Cabinet secretary Gus O'Donnell said the cuts would 'have a very large cost' to the economy. He explained that not only did the evidence show the optimal rate of the top tax bracket was 48 per cent, but that ministers had been shown that evidence and had ignored it.[29]

O'Donnell's statement was a blow to Osborne, but it was nothing compared to the visceral flagellation that was about to come.

While rewarding wealthy tax avoiders, the Chancellor was simultaneously removing tax relief for people over 65. He claimed this was a 'tax simplification',[30] but it looked and felt exactly the same as a £259 tax increase on your poor old nana, and was therefore quickly dubbed 'the granny tax' in 96-point Helvetica on every front page.[31]

That was just the start of a rolling PR disaster: Osborne had also cut tax relief for charitable donations, which would lead to charities getting less money, and managed to unite the Labour Party, the Church of England, David Davis and Cate Blanchett in opposition,[32] and once you get Galadriel involved, you're basically toast.[33]

Tax was slashed for the rich but raised on things the government blithely assumed poor people liked to do, such as eating pasties while being miserable in caravans. As a sop to the mob, there was the traditional crowd-pleasing attack on the financial sector, behind which another sleight of hand took place. Osborne boasted of how much sadism he would inflict upon the quivering banks without mentioning how much the banks liked it.

'Just you wait,' he said, 'I'm going to mercilessly thrash the banks by very slightly increasing their levy to 0.105 per cent.'[34]

'Mercy!' cried the banks. 'And whatever you do, please don't simultaneously slash our corporation tax bill by 19 times as much.'[35]

But Osborne slashed their corporation tax by 19 times as much anyway, the vicious bastard, and how the banks laughed.[36]

Yet the public didn't pay much attention to this empty, performative nonsense, because we were too busy having a conniption fit about Greggs and learning what was eventually voted Word of the Year: omnishambles.[37]

The tabloids might love the Tories, but they love blood more, and Osborne's Budget was spurting like the Russian royal family. The headlines were merciless, and journalists demanded to know the last time this bunch of privately educated millionaires had eaten a pasty.

Being the more dastardly of the two, Osborne chose to vanish for a few days so he wouldn't have to answer the question. The more docile Cameron awoke from his slumber, and confidently announced he had recently bought a Cornish pasty at Leeds train station and had enjoyed it very much; it was a plausible story for very nearly a minute, until it was discovered there was nowhere at Leeds train station that sold Cornish pasties.[38]

Inevitably, the pasty tax went through a U-turn[39] and then the charity tax went through a U-turn.[40] For a while, Osborne's career seemed likely to go through a U-bend, but fortunately terrified and obscure figures from the backbenches were pushed blinking into the sunlight to mouth heavily scripted, servile praise of Osborne, such as David Ruffley's 'one man's U-turn is another man's listening, caring government'.[41]

Charities and pasties were saved, but what about that other desperately struggling group: millionaires paying top-rate tax? Thank the Lord, they were fine: the tax cut for them stayed in place.

But the Tory majority in the Commons meant the tax increase for your granny went ahead.[42]

—

Having heroically leaped to the defence of the strong and powerful, the Tories resumed attacking the old and poor and cancerous, with a bold new strategy for the NHS, which they claimed would improve patient satisfaction and reduce administration costs. The result was a record drop in patient satisfaction,[43] and administration costs rising 180 per cent.[44] And I think we can all applaud their efforts and say job well done.

Health minister and Leslie Nielsen impersonator Andrew Lansley announced: 'We need to take steps to improve health outcomes, bringing them up to the standards of the best international healthcare systems.'[45] A fine ambition, assuming you were not aware that the NHS was already the best-rated health system on earth.[46]

Two separate studies by the Commonwealth Fund compared the NHS to health services in 10 similarly wealthy nations. We were in top position for care and equity, and in the top three for survival rates, access to treatment and administrative efficiency. Taken overall, the reports concluded that the NHS was the best healthcare system in the world. Twice.[47]

Yet the reports found we spent less per person than any of those other countries – $3,129 each, compared to $7,538 in the lowest-ranked but most expensive USA.[48]

It was a nationalised service providing great outcomes with world-beating efficiency and the lowest cost on the planet. In short, exactly the kind of thing that disproves the core beliefs of Conservatives, and therefore it could not be allowed to continue. Clearly, we needed to follow the USA and privatise stuff, pronto.

Among the Tories who argued for the privatisation of the NHS, or who have financial connections to private healthcare businesses, were: distressed hedgerow Boris Johnson,[49] Vulcan dolt John Redwood,[50] a Rosa Klebb tribute act called Priti Patel, the constitutionally slack-brained Liz Truss, sentient teaspoon Matt Hancock, and a fat-necked rugby-club boor by the name of Dominic Raab, who had the gall to say 'it certainly wasn't anything I wrote' about a pamphlet that he wrote, arguing for more NHS privatisation, in which he was listed as one of the authors.[51]

Because he wrote it.

Last but not most, Andrew Lansley was having his palms warmed by thick wads of cash from private healthcare: he took a £21,000 donation to his private office from John Nash, chairman of private-health provider Care UK.[52] Mr and Mrs Nash have given almost £300,000 to the Conservative Party, and the Tory party promised to 'open up the NHS to new independent providers'.[53]

Ninety-six per cent of Care UK's £400 million income came from being one of those 'independent' providers to the NHS'.[54]

Nash did nothing illegal. A donation is not the same as a bribe, so let's be perfectly clear about that. They are very different things. However, the non-Tory half of the coalition government seemed very sensitive to the optics of the thing.

'Donations from private individuals in no way influence policymaking decisions,' asserted Lansley's spokesman. Meanwhile his coalition partners the Lib Dems called the donation 'a staggering conflict of interest'. You decide.[55]

Having entered government promising 'no top-down reorganisation' of health, Tories now embarked on a shake-up that was, in the words of the chief executive of NHS England, 'so big you could see it from space'.[56] That reorganisation, the Health and Social Care Act, is 637 pages long,[57] including 200 pages of explanatory notes.[58] To put that into context, the entire act that created the NHS in 1946 was just 98 pages and needed no explanatory notes whatsoever.[59]

Given the scope of the changes, their description by one insider as 'unintelligible gobbledegook' and the later admission that not even the Cabinet understood a bloody word of it, Lansley's reforms are something of a challenge to explain; in essence they can be broken down into these broad concepts.[60]

The Tories argued that the NHS, the most efficient large health service on the face of the planet, wasn't efficient. So, to make it more so, they would forcibly inject into it a swarm of squabbling competitive providers,[61] the management and appointment of which have reduced efficiency in every other health service. This, Tories maintained, was not privatising large parts of the NHS: it was simply making large parts of the NHS privatised,[62] and that's a totally different thing.

The Tories also claimed there were too many managers in the NHS[63] and vowed to get rid of them. Instead, doctors would now do all the managing.

With doctors now managing, who would do doctoring? Would it be a sudden influx of new staff? Well, there was bad news on that score too: Lansley's cautious estimates in 2011 blithely predicted 24,500 staff would be lost,[64] and by 'cautious' I mean 'wrong'. We lost 160,000 nurses alone by 2019, and that's not even counting losses from other areas of the NHS.[65]

Moving on: the government argued that hospitals and NHS services were cooperating with one another too much, and that this was ineffective. In future, cooperation would be deterred,[66] and the few remaining managers (or newly transmogrified doctors) would have to spend their days engaged in obligatory rivalry rather than collaboration.

Finally, Tories contended that a single, unified NHS was too complicated. To make things easier, they introduced quite literally hundreds of cross-pollinating health groups, service bodies, management institutes, delivery vehicles and administration faculties, which they described in a brain-mangling document hilariously entitled 'Understanding the New NHS'. Apparently, it was a simplified guide, although its organisational diagram and explanation sprawled across 14 aggressively impenetrable pages.[67]

To this day, if you query a Tory about funding for the NHS, they'll reflexively bark that expenditure has continued to increase since 2010. And, broadly speaking, it has. But we are living longer, so the number of older people suffering with complicated, expensive and incurable conditions has also increased. Those patients need lots of time-intensive, hands-on care, and the cost of new drugs to treat them has also continued to rise. Despite the efforts of previous governments, NHS spending hasn't kept pace with demand, or with international standards. So how did the Tories do after 2010?

Well, in 2009 the annual increase in spending was 6.9 per cent, in a race to bring Britain's health budget closer to international norms. Then, in 2010, investment in the NHS went off a cliff, fell steeply each year since, and by 2019 it was down to 1.5 per cent.[68] That's still technically a rise, but it's the lowest growth in funding over a decade that the NHS has ever received, during a period of the highest growth in demand; plus a 180 per cent increase in the cost of administrating this chaos, effectively wiping out every penny of cash increase.[69]

Less money, more patients, fewer doctors, worse management and greater organisational confusion: it's a recipe guaranteed to piss off the patients, or, as we were now instructed to call them, customers. Customers know best, so in future, customers would make their own informed choices about their own care.

Let's role-play that, shall we?

'Doctor, I would like treatment for this boil.'

'Ooh, that does look nasty. I prescribe 637 pages of unintelligible gobbledegook,[70] and I'll see you when you've finally understood it enough to make your own informed choices about which commissioning body will fund the cure. That will be about five years from now, by which time your leg will be gangrenous.'

Frankly, it doesn't take a genius to predict it would be a disaster, which is fortunate, because we didn't have a genius: we had Andrew Lansley. In 2010, 70 per cent of us were satisfied or very satisfied with the NHS. After the first year of the fulsome dirty protest that he performed upon our nation's most beloved institution, Lansley had pushed satisfaction levels down to 58 per cent.[71]

It was a failure so vast and noisy that even the glazed polyp in 10 Downing Street couldn't fail to notice, although it did take him a couple of years. A Downing Street staffer was reported to have said Lansley should be 'taken out and shot', not that you'd have known this at the time.[72] The PM cheerily defended the chaos as it rolled on.

When challenged by Labour's Angela Eagle, our 'modern Tory' prime minister modernly replied, 'Calm down, dear, calm down and listen to the doctor,' which was so patronising, condescending and gauche that even that clattering gobshite Cameron realised his error and apologised.[73]

Meanwhile an anonymous Tory MP was quoted as saying George Osborne 'kicks himself for not having stopped [Lansley's reforms]'.[74] If Osborne really believes what he preaches, he should outsource that kicking to enthusiastic private contractors. Form an orderly queue.

So where did all of this leave us? Well, the admin cost alone of the Tories pointlessly beating the NHS with the world's shittest book on management theory was £4 billion.[75] That's £1 per second for 126 years. Or, if you prefer, £3,600 per hour, every hour since the first Sherlock Holmes story was written.

Yet even though the Tories have since tried to wash their hands of the whole debacle, they didn't lift a fucking finger to fix it: this idiocy was still fragmenting the NHS when the pandemic struck.

Lansley was sacked, which was the least Cameron could do: if he could have done less, he would have.

In fact, he did do less: because no sooner had Lansley been sacked than he was handed a seat in the House of Lords, a slight downgrade from the original idea of shooting him.[76] He now sits in the Upper House alongside his generous sponsor, John Nash, who was ennobled Baron Nash in 2013.[77] Between 2010 and 2017 the business he co-founded, Care UK, had received over £780 million in NHS contracts.[78]

The poor, struggling office of Andrew Lansley was also £21,000 better off.

—

In June, things finally seemed to be going right for our regular guest star Eric Pickles. He launched a shiny new scheme to 'break the cycle of deprivation' in all the families his government had worked so assiduously to make more deprived.[79] And sure, it's easy to carp, but at least Tories had noticed, and – bless – they'd decided to have a go at helping.

Pickles' new scheme, backed by £450 million, was labelled the Troubled Families Programme, and it was only slightly undermined by the fact that £450 million equates to £6.75 each, and was therefore unlikely to make much of a dent in the cycle of deprivation.

But the biggest embarrassment for Pickles was that his announcement coincided with the news that the prime minister had suffered his own family-related troubles. The colossal phallus had managed to accidentally abandon his own eight-year-old daughter in a pub, and got all the way home before a brief exercise in counting his offspring revealed his sums didn't add up.[80]

Well, we could have told you that, David. £6.75 each? Are you kidding?

—

As part of the coalition agreement that put Cameron into Downing Street, the Lib Dems had insisted on two key planks of their manifesto. The first of these – reform of the voting system – had been ritually murdered in 2011, and now it was time for the second bit of casual, cynical butchery, this time over reform of the House of Lords.

It was quite reasonable for Nick Clegg to assume things would all go swimmingly. Not only had the Lib Dem manifesto promised to 'replace the House of Lords with a fully elected second chamber',[81] but the Tories had also offered something similar: 'a mainly elected second chamber to replace the current House of Lords'.[82] The Labour Party were in favour, and 74 per cent of the public wanted a fully or partly elected upper chamber.[83] It was an open goal.

The legislation would hugely improve democracy and accountability in Britain and put an end to the dishonest abuse of the honours system. It had smoothly passed its first hurdle in the House of Commons and was just about to become law, when suddenly, out of the darkness in the backbenches, loomed a harrowing antique dildo going by the name of Jacob Rees-Mogg, who mooed out an objection.

Since the changes would affect the bishops who sit in the House of Lords (he argued), the legislation would surely need to be debated as a 'hybrid bill'.

The Speaker blew the dust off the rules of Parliament, riffled through the cracked and creaking parchment, and discovered a hybrid bill is one of myriad arcane procedures that have grown like fungi on the rotting corpse of our body politic. It is described as a bill that 'would affect the general public but would also have a significant impact for specific individuals or groups',[84] and correct me if I'm wrong, but that is exactly the same as any other legislation in almost every conceivable way.

But Rees-Mogg wasn't interested in the finer points of hybrid legislation: he was interested in introducing a delay, the first of many. Behind the scenes, Tory backbenchers had started to mount a rebellion. After all, you don't become a Tory MP to improve democracy or stop the wholesale procurement of parliamentary privilege.

If one objection stopped progress for a few minutes, they said to themselves, how much progress could be stopped if we just talk and talk and talk? There is a time limit on debates in the House, and if the MPs filibustered for long enough, time would run out, and the bill would inevitably fail.[85]

So they set about yapping. Amendments were forwarded. Points of order were raised. Motions were suggested, extremely slowly debated, and then rejected in favour of new, even more stridently sluggish proposals. Interminable speeches of heroic tedium were ground out as the clock wound relentlessly down, and hope faded.

It was a staring contest, and in the end, Cameron blinked. He conceded enough to please the rebels, who then immediately demanded yet more concessions. But the amendments were enough to infuriate the opposition and incense the Lib Dems. Labour refused to back the mutilated bill, and when it finally came to a vote, 91 Tories voted against the measure, and over a dozen abstained.[86]

Cameron briefly toyed with the notion of trying again, decided it was all too much trouble, and abandoned the whole idea.[87] Parliamentary reform was killed stone dead for another generation, and it was beginning to look like the Lib Dems had sacrificed the trust of their voters and the future of their party in return for two lost promises and the lion's share of the blame.

—

And there was plenty of blame going around in July, when the International Monetary Fund, in recognition of the sterling efforts of George Osborne to stop anybody from spending anything, downgraded their forecasts for Britain's economy. It had already been a pretty weak prediction, just 0.8 per cent growth[88] (compared to the 2.1 per cent Osborne had inherited from Labour).[89] Now the IMF cut that to just 0.2 per cent.

The nation needed a boost, and thankfully along came the 2012 London Olympics.

The prelude to the games had gone surprisingly well. A Labour government and Labour London Mayor had won the Olympics, and then Tessa Jowell, a Labour minister, had led all the planning. Sebastian Coe, the Tory peer and former Olympic gold-medal winner who had become chairman of the bid committee, praised Labour for their organisational skills in bringing the games to London, and organising a workforce of 70,000 to staff the event.[90]

And then the Tories took over.

As incoming Mayor of London, Boris Johnson had attended the closing ceremony of the previous games in Beijing. He'd been there less than 24 hours before the Chinese media condemned him for being 'rude, arrogant and disrespectful.'[91] It probably didn't help that he rocked up to the closing ceremony looking like a horny Honey Monster crammed into a suit he'd borrowed for an appearance at a tribunal, then shoved his hands in his pockets and launched into a preposterous skit about 'wiff-waff coming home'.

'Unlike the Chinese,' observed China's *Titan Sports* newspaper, 'the British seem to like to laugh about their stupidity.'[92]

They weren't wrong.

After this inauspicious start, the incoming Tory government, true to form, spent the subsequent years deploying their traditional tactic of privatising as much as possible, including outsourcing security staffing for the games to G4S for a fee of £248 million.[93] As the London games drew closer, US presidential candidate Mitt Romney raised concerns about our preparedness.

'There are a few things that were disconcerting,' he said, focusing particularly on 'the stories about the private security firm not having enough people'. Fortunately, Johnson was able to set him straight with his usual combination of understated candour and pinpoint accuracy.

'I hear there's a guy called Mitt Romney who wants to know whether we're ready,' Johnson boomed at a Hyde Park crowd. 'Are we ready? Are we ready? Yes, we are!'[94]

We weren't.

With a contract to supply 13,000 personnel, G4S fell at least 3,500 short. Even the staff who did turn up called the arrangements 'a shambles', as G4S were unable to provide their staff with uniforms or passes, or even confirm that their own employees had jobs.[95] Nobody knew where they were meant to go or what they were meant to do, and something like 16 million visitors were about to turn up, asking where the toilets were.[96]

The army was drafted in as an emergency measure, deploying 18,000 troops on the streets of London when it became increasingly clear that even the government's unfulfilled contract for 13,000 staff was less than half those required. The military's chief planner for the games described it as 'a national strategic shock' and said the armed forces would take two years to recover from their involvement.[97]

When asked earlier in 2012 what the government should do to improve the UK business outlook, G4S chief executive Nick Buckles replied, 'Continue to focus on traditional Tory values around encouraging a meritocracy,'[98] and because of all that lovely merit, G4S kept their £57 million management bonus.[99] Nick Buckles took home £1.9 million in 2012, up from £1 million the previous year.[100]

There were 128,000 people reliant on food banks in 2012.[101] That's an annual increase of 109 per cent.

For a few days, the G4S scandal threatened to undermine a great event, but to the rescue rode Boris Johnson again, to boost the Olympic spirit and finally recover from his embarrassing fiasco at the Beijing closing ceremony. He did this by donning a ludicrous helmet-and-suit combo, clutching a pair of union flags, and getting himself stranded for several minutes halfway down a malfunctioning zip wire, dangling in mid-air, repeatedly bellowing 'Team GB'[102] while the world's press gazed on, slack-jawed.

The start of the games finally took people's minds off the combination of majestic ineptitude and degrading comedy. *The Times* described the opening ceremony as 'a masterpiece'. The *Telegraph* said it was 'brilliant, breath-taking, bonkers, and utterly British'. China Daily described it as 'a dazzling ceremony designed to highlight the grandeur and eccentricities of the nation that invented modern sport'.[103]

Tory MP Aidan Burley called it leftie crap.

This is the same Aidan Burley who, the previous year, had attended a Nazi-themed stag party where the toast was 'to the ideology and thought process of the Third Reich',[104] so most things probably seemed quite leftie to him. But still: bit harsh, Aidan. Bit harsh.

He went on to say it was 'the most leftie opening ceremony I have ever seen',[105] seemingly forgetting the previous one took place in a literal communist state. 'Thank God the athletes have arrived!' he tweeted. 'Now we can move on from leftie multicultural crap,' and then, when the BBC asked him about his criticism of multiculturalism, he replied, 'I wasn't having a go at multiculturalism.' Words are so difficult sometimes, aren't they, Aidan?

Faced by the uncomfortable fact that the biggest cheers of the entire ceremony came during celebrations of multiculturalism and the NHS, the Tories were quick to distance themselves from the comments: as renowned wordsmith Boris Johnson said, in a phrase that will chime down the ages: 'It wasn't global Brito-pap.'

If you're asking yourself: 'What the spangly yellow fuck does "global Brito-pap" mean?', don't worry, you aren't alone.

Cameron was a little clearer: Aidan Burley's comments were 'idiotic', he said. 'We all celebrate the NHS.'[106] This, it turned out, wasn't strictly true: Danny Boyle, the Oscar-winning director behind the opening ceremony, later confirmed the Tories had asked him to remove the NHS celebration completely.[107]

The Olympics were supposed to inspire a generation to take up sport, but it didn't quite work out that way. Subsequent Tory cuts to sport facilities, both in and out of schools, meant within four years of the Olympics ending, 1,295 swimming pools, grass pitches, sports halls and athletic tracks had closed, and almost half of children left school unable to swim.[108]

By 2019 it was even worse: 2,488 school pitches and 677 public tennis courts were gone, and only 1 per cent of sixth formers from poor backgrounds did sport in school.[109]

So probably not the matchless social and political success the government had hoped for. But for a moment, national spirits had been lifted enormously, and were lifted yet higher when George Osborne emerged from his dungeon to attend the Paralympics, to be met with cataclysmic jeers from the 80,000-capacity crowd.[110]

—

In September, reports appeared of a contretemps between Tory Chief Whip Andrew Mitchell and police at the entrance to Downing Street. Officers had asked Mitchell to enter the heavily guarded street via the pedestrian gate rather than the main gate, which was a sufficiently gross personal insult to Mitchell's pride that, according to the official police log made by two officers present, he said, 'Best you learn your fucking place. You don't run this fucking government. You're fucking plebs,' and, 'You haven't heard the last of this.'[111]

He was right about that last part.

Mitchell denied saying 'pleb', though admitted swearing at the police and treating them with disrespect; but by the time his hybrid apology-cum-denial seeped out from between his gritted teeth, few people cared whether the incident was real or not: it *felt* true, quickly became known as Plebgate, and would not go away.

The chairman of the Police Federation said, 'It is hard to fathom how someone who holds the police in such contempt could be allowed to hold a public office,'[112] not realising that holding people in contempt is a feature of the Tory party, not a bug. But then suddenly, as if by magic, Mitchell did not hold a public office at all: he resigned, still pleading partial innocence.

That would normally be the end of the matter, but nothing was normal any more, so there was an epilogue. It emerged that a member of the public who had independently written an eyewitness account supporting the police version of events was, in fact, an off-duty police officer who hadn't even been there at the time. He ended up getting twelve months in prison for lying to police, which is seven months more than Andy Coulson served for lying to the entire country.[113]

But that wasn't the end of the matter either: there was a postscript to the epilogue. Andrew Mitchell sued the *Sun* for libel, claiming their account of events had damaged his career, and it's fair to say the case didn't go spectacularly well. The High Court found against him, described his behaviour as 'childish' and ruled that 'Mr Mitchell did speak the words alleged or something so close to them as to amount to the same, probably including the politically toxic word "pleb"'[114]

It was reported that his costs could reach £2 million, which is a hell of a lot to pay for expressing your true feelings about the lower orders, and being too proud to enter via a side gate.

—

Somehow, despite the generous donations by Andrew Mitchell and the expenditure generated by 16 million Olympics fans each wanting to spend a penny, the economy was still in the shithouse. We had re-entered a recession once again, and where we had once worried about a double-dip recession, we now faced the prospect of a triple-dip[115] for the first time on record.[116]

You could blame it on the international banking crisis, but as the name suggests, the international banking crisis didn't just affect Britain. And this was a problem for the government, since it meant we had other countries to compare ourselves to. Most other wealthy nations had implemented a stimulus package to kick their economies up the arse, and it had worked: the USA had growth of 2.25 per cent.[117] Britain, by contrast, stuck our economy in the arse with a massive dose of horse tranquilliser in the form of austerity, for no reason more rational than groundless ideological fervour, and we were flatlining.

Our recovery was the feeblest in recorded history.[118] It was slower than the USA, Canada, France and Germany, and much slower than Japan, right until the moment a tsunami hit their nuclear power station. That terrible disaster saved Osborne from yet more embarrassing comparisons with his own godawful economic plan, but his relief didn't last long: the UK fell behind Brazil in the global economic league table.[119]

Unemployment was starting to recede, but half the new jobs being created were part time. Unemployment was no longer the primary jobs crisis: it was now *under*-employment. Those wanting more hours but unable to find them had increased 113 per cent in two years,[120] and now, in addition to the almost 8 per cent of adults who had no job,[121] a further 10 per cent had a job that offered too few hours to pay the bills.[122] In Thatcher's recession, which was then debated as a national crisis of unparalleled severity, we spoke of the unemployed as 'one in ten'.[123] But in 2012, one in six of us lacked enough work to house, heat and feed ourselves.

Keen to avoid the sense of personal responsibility that was his party's founding philosophy, David Cameron alighted on a new set of people to blame for the consequences of his own policies. In his conference speech in October, this self-styled 'one nation Conservative'[124] divided the nation into two categories: strivers and skivers.[125]

Strivers worked for what they had, achieved things all on their own, and were to be praised and given tax cuts. Skivers, meanwhile, were sucking the life out of the economy by living on handouts, taking drugs, vandalising their neighbourhoods, and getting everything handed to them on a plate. They deserved benefit cuts. It stands to reason.

Cameron's none-too-subtle message was: Tories are all strivers, and look how rich it made us; to which one can only respond with the words of George Monbiot: 'If wealth was the inevitable result of hard work and enterprise, every woman in Africa would be a millionaire.'[126]

Let us, therefore, take a quick detour into the striving history of George Osborne and David Cameron, so we can see how much they achieved without anybody's help.

Osborne strove so hard that before he was even born, he'd managed to move into the womb of a woman who was married to a multimillionaire aristocrat.[127] And Cameron had, by the sweat of his oh-so-smooth brow, succeeded in being the Queen's cousin[128] and issued from the loins of a multimillionaire[129] stockbroker who was busy running a fund for tax-avoiding entities.[130] There was no dumb luck involved, and nothing was provided for them: it was striving, striving all the way.

After the hard work they put into being born to wealthy people, they wanted us to believe they both toiled relentlessly to save enough money to go to Eton and St Paul's: at the age of 13, apparently, they alone were earning enough to pay the £44,000 per annum attendance fees.[131] They were strivers, so nobody else paid: certainly not the state, which listed their private schools as charities (and therefore made them tax exempt),[132] and which got other, poorer people to pay the tax Cameron's dad was helping people to avoid.

And don't pretend it was all easy once George and Dave reached school. Oh no. Cameron, for example, had to battle to stay away from the bad influence of privileged children in tiny class sizes. But he succeeded in working hard and not idling his days away smoking pot, except for that time he was almost expelled from Eton for smoking pot.[133]

After overcoming the obstacle of being at some of the most exclusive and expensive private schools on the planet, Cameron and

Osborne moved to Oxford University, which is so egalitarian that after 33 years of social progress since Cameron left, over 60 per cent of its intake still came from the 7 per cent who are privately educated.[134]

Our future PM, although the child of a multimillionaire, was deemed so poor that he had to have his [trigger warning] entire university education paid for by all the rest of us. Can you imagine the horror? It was such a dreadful burden that he made sure your children will never have to experience it. He even got a special grant, called an Exhibition, which left him with the additional problem of having to walk around with another few quid in his massively deep pockets.[135]

Yet he still laboured on. While at Oxford, the two men avoided disreputable, antisocial behaviour, like heavy drinking and smashing up restaurants, interrupted only by their membership of the Bullingdon Club, which is famous for antisocial behaviour, heavy drinking and smashing up restaurants.[136]

Once they entered politics, they stood on their own two feet, except for that time Cameron claimed £21,000 in a year of public money to pay his mortgage.[137] Or the claim of almost £100,000 in expenses for the house and paddock at George's Cheshire home – because we all know it's impossible to be Chancellor without having access to a team of horses.[138]

It was this sort of vigorous self-reliance that lent Cameron and Osborne the moral certainty needed to cut the tax paid by them and their friends and neighbours, while slashing the income for people who were too idle or sick or cancerous to be born into extreme privilege.

—

The government now set about helping all those poor, unemployed young people by hitting them with a thesaurus until their definition of 'job' transformed into 'apprenticeship', thus allowing unscrupulous employers to avoid paying the minimum wage. But at least the training was boosting the competitiveness of Britain's information and knowledge economy: it mostly consisted of filling supermarket shelves and making sandwiches.

When asked in Parliament, 'What is the value of an apprenticeship making sandwiches?', Matt Hancock, then the Under Secretary of State for Skills, declared: 'I am in favour of sandwiches';[139] and I'm sure that was a relief to the 126,000[140] apprentices whose income was barely half the absolute minimum amount required to stay alive, and not even enough to buy the sandwiches they were making.[141]

But beyond the traditionally contentious subject of 'do you, or do you not, approve of sandwiches', plenty of people were concerned that the government's apprenticeship scheme was focusing on the wrong things. Elmfield Training, a private company, won a £37 million government contract to place apprentices, declared an immediate profit of £12 million, and paid its CEO a dividend of £3 million.[142] Meanwhile the apprentices were earning £4.30 per hour stacking shelves at Morrisons, the supermarket that ended up taking one in every ten apprenticeships created in 2012.

There are two questions arising from this. The first is hard to answer, but easy to guess: what happened to all the people Morrisons would otherwise have employed on a full wage? How does intentionally undercutting wages help to boost growth? Are they mad?

The second is: what became of the CEO of Elmfield Trading? Well, he managed to crash the company only a year later, somehow turning a £12 million profit into an £11 million debt to over 180 suppliers, while paying himself and associated people another £1 million. He was banned from trading for six years.[143]

—

Miraculously, sandwich enthusiast Matt Hancock didn't end up being the most ludicrous figure as the year drew to its close. Owen Paterson, the climate-change sceptic[144] who had somehow ended up as the environment secretary in 'the greenest government ever',[145] had ignored scientific advice about the necessity of killing badgers, and ignored common sense by expecting 5,000 of the famously elusive nocturnal creatures to be shot by marksmen wandering randomly around Gloucestershire in the middle of the night.

The problem, Paterson insisted, was not his sterling native stupidity, but cheating. 'The badgers have moved the goalposts,'[146] he squawked, and then raced off to become even more ridiculous by voting against same-sex marriage.

He was far from alone. The Tories have long claimed their introduction of equal marriage demonstrates their modern, liberal attitude. But this boast is mildly hampered by the awkward reality: 117 Tories voted for it, and 127 against.[147]

Bob Blackman opposed the changes on the basis that a marriage is 'between one man and one woman.'[148] Blackman had pursued an 11-year affair with a married local councillor, which, if my maths is correct, made his marriage one man and *two* women.[149]

David TC Davies (not to be confused with the more famous David Davis, or indeed with Top Cat) called gay marriage proposals 'barking mad' and said, 'Parents would prefer their children not to be gay.' When challenged on whether his attitude made him a bigot, Top Cat offered an unconventional defence: he couldn't be homophobic, he said, because he had once punched an openly gay boxer.[150]

Some objected to same-sex marriage on the principle that they rejected any innovation whatsoever, such as Gerald Howarth, who joyfully – hell, let's say 'gaily', since he's so averse to changes in definition – declared, 'I am not a Tory moderniser.'

You can say that again. He described gay soldiers as 'appalling,'[151] and when debating same-sex marriage warned Parliament about 'the aggressive homosexual community who see this as but a stepping-stone to something even further,'[152] but declined to explain what, in the depths of his fetid imagination, was meant by 'something even further'.

The rest of the objections were pretty much what you'd expect: a combination of predictions that same-sex marriage would lead to brothers marrying brothers (Sir Roger Gale);[153] that you should classify same-sex marriage alongside incest (Philip Hammond);[154] and that allowing same-sex marriage would ruin 'normal marriage' (Bob Stewart).[155]

And that makes a lot of sense: as we all know, the courts are awash with divorce petitions listing 'my neighbours are gay' as the primary reason for the collapse of a marriage.

2013
Mad, Swivel-Eyed Loons

Despite the best efforts of half the Tory party to make love illegal and defend the right of bigots to be incensed by anything they don't understand, the same-sex marriage act finally made it into law in 2013. In a not overcrowded field, this was one of David Cameron's proudest achievements, and he capped it by delivering a mid-term review of the government he led.[1]

He didn't get off to a great start, by refusing to accept questions from any female reporters,[2] then declaring 'the economy is rebalancing', as our national debt reached 95 per cent of our GDP (up from 62 per cent in Gordon Brown's last year).[3] Dictionaries across the land had to update their definition of 'rebalancing' to accommodate an extra million children living in poverty,[4] while the number of millionaires grew by 41 per cent.[5]

As a result of inflation and pay freezes, the average worker in 2013 earned the same as in 2003, wiping out 10 years of hard-won improvements.[6] At the lowest end, a further 1.4 million working people had dropped below the living wage since Cameron moved into Downing Street.[7]

One in five working people earned less than the amount required for the most basic standard of living. For the millions more on Jobseeker's Allowance, which included at least 490,000 people personally made redundant by the government,[8] the weekly income of £74.70[9] was one-sixth of the average wage.[10] They weren't all stoned slackers, surely?

Privatising things was, the Tories had told us, the key to solving this, as it would make everything cheaper. Yet in January, fares on our privatised rail services rose a further 4.3 per cent,[11] double the rate at which earnings were rising.[12]

Since the Tories had privatised rail 20 years earlier, average rail fares had increased 66 per cent relative to incomes. The cost of a single ticket from London to Manchester had increased by 208 per cent.[13] Regularly commuting on public transport in the UK was now far more expensive than driving to work: £2,191 for an average rail season ticket, compared to £1,441 for annual fuel costs.[14] Enticing people away from public transport and into cars was literally the opposite of what the environment demanded from the 'greenest government ever'. It was also costing 8 per cent of the average commuter's annual income.

And how had the owners of those privatised franchises coped in these troubling times? You can relax – the Tories had got them covered: direct public subsidies to the rail service had doubled since rail was in supposedly inefficient public hands.[15] Between privatisation and 2012, Virgin's West Coast Main Line received £2.5 billion in taxpayer subsidy, 20 per cent of which was handed straight to its shareholders in the form of dividends.[16]

Obviously, not much detail of the rising debt, rising inequality and skyrocketing poverty made it into Cameron's half-term review, which mostly focused on how much he loved his Tamagotchi, or as the rest of us called him, Nick Clegg.

Among those battling heart-breaking poverty was Andrew Bridgen, who in January took to the airwaves to plead for more money for MPs like him.[17] His job, he wailed, only paid £65,738, which he was forced to top up with £7,773 each month for six hours work as director of a vegetable processing firm. That's barely £1,295 per hour, and who among us could scrape by on that? Thankfully, the taxpayer came to his aid: in a single year, he claimed expenses of £25,000 for staying in hotels in London, even though he had a flat of his own in Westminster: he said he had ditched it when his marriage broke down.[18]

Poor Andrew Bridgen. I'll start organising the telethon; you call Bono and get the charity single underway.

Meanwhile, Christopher Chope clearly didn't get Cameron's memo about how everything was 'rebalancing'. His mask, which had never been particularly securely attached, slipped completely in January as he explained to Parliament where catering staff in the Commons dining room fitted into his hierarchical view of humanity. It was 'absolutely fantastic', he bragged. 'Three servants for each person sitting down.'[19]

Yep. Servants.

Let's hope he didn't order the lasagne: that same month, news broke that Ireland's Food Safety Authority had found horsemeat in a range of ready meals, pies, nuggets and burgers widely sold in Britain.[20] This was a crisis for Britain's lovers of fine cuisine, but doubly so for Owen Paterson, the arch-Thatcherite Secretary of State for Environment, Food and Rural Affairs.

Paterson was already struggling with the 'environment' bit of his remit, but most people had expected that: for years, he had expressed unstinting support for fracking, and unstinting loathing for wind farms.[21] On taking office, he spent 14 months declining offers to be briefed about climate change from the government's chief scientific adviser,[22] and then cut funding for Britain to adapt to climate change by over 40 per cent.[23] He had his beliefs, and no amount of factual information was going to make a dent in them.

But not many people had placed a bet on his small-state, anti-regulation ideology being so severely challenged by a fatty lump of formless mince. No, not you, Mark Francois.

The reason the scandal was uncovered by Ireland's food safety regime, rather than by Britain's, can be expressed in two words: Owen Paterson. Paterson believed the invisible, yet all-powerful 'market' would fix every problem, but he also believed the market could be annihilated in seconds by the mere presence of a food-standards officer with a clipboard and a reflective tabard. Anybody who got in the way of the market's operations was, in the view of Paterson, harming the 'wealth creators' who had made such a splendid job of creating wealth that Britain hadn't had a pay increase for a decade.

He believed Europe-wide inspection regimes were the cold, dead hand of leftie naysayers, beating the hell out of British entrepreneurial spirit; those inspectors, who had conned us into thinking they were just ensuring unscrupulous suppliers hadn't been slipping fetid bits of Shergar into your Scotch egg, were actually detestable agents of a bloated liberal quangocracy.

'Release the Kraken!' Paterson howled, and set about demolishing the UK's food standards framework. Within a couple of years of him taking charge, the budget for food sampling was cut 70 per cent, we lost over 800 inspectors, and as a result we were no longer capable of ensuring we were eating healthy food.[24]

This wasn't simply about horses. Gnawing on leg of Dobbin might be anathema to Britain's traditions, but the real scandal was deeper: the more traditionally British beef being processed was often described by those handling it as 'green' and 'putrid', and we in Britain no longer had the capacity to test it.[25] Paterson had cheered Cameron's 'bonfire of red tape', and only then discovered that the tape had been preventing him from dancing off a cliff in a libertarian frenzy.[26]

Thus, we ended up with the world-standard hypocrisy of a hard-line Eurosceptic, rigid in his certainty that Britain works best alone, taking an emergency flight to The Hague to announce that 'it's clear that Europol is the right organisation to coordinate efforts' to solve the problem.[27]

We were still only in January.

—

In 2010, before entering government, George Osborne had made a speech at the University of London, laying out eight benchmarks for economic competency, 'against which you will be able to judge a Conservative government'. The first item on his list was 'we will maintain Britain's AAA credit rating'.[28]

In February, Britain lost its AAA credit rating.

We then slid back into recession for the second time since Osborne took hold of the economy. Enoch Powell once said, 'All political lives end in failure,' but it seemed Cameron and Osborne were in far too much of a rush to wait to the end.[29]

The fundamental inadequacy of their politics was that (despite having enough cash to fritter away on free schools and nocturnal orienteering games with woodland creatures) Osborne was still choosing to make smaller debt repayments than anybody had for the previous 300 years;[30] as a result, debt was still rising.[31]

It no longer appeared, to any objective observer, that solving a debt problem was the government's major focus. Instead there was an ideologically driven agenda to use the banking crisis as cover to dismantle the 'post-war settlement': the consensus that arose after the Second World War, which had been the background to British politics ever since. The settlement established the world we all knew: a mixed economy that was safer than overreliance on one insanely risk-obsessed sector; industry regulation to prevent abuses; a government that helped out in hard times and was repaid in taxation when the nation was flourishing again; and a welfare state.

This model created the world that almost anybody born since 1945 took for granted (and taking it for granted is probably the crux of the problem). The Thatcher government had applied an axe to these norms and ended up widely loathed; the Blair government had attempted, albeit inconsistently, to regain many of our traditional standards. But now, it seemed, Osborne had had enough, and decided it all had to go.

The result of this obsession was that spending money on smashing stuff up became more important than sensible cost-saving choices, more urgent than building for a future, and a greater imperative than repaying our debts. Annihilation was the whole point. And so money was burned, the future began to dry up, and debt continued to rise.

The global credit-rating agencies couldn't help but notice, because the Tories kept going on TV to gleefully boast of the bone-deep cuts they were making to the staggering nation, and yet the bank balance didn't seem to be getting any better.

In a panic, Osborne leaped from TV studio to TV studio, insisting everything was going fine, and we should delay judging him until the end of his first five years as Chancellor.

At the end of his first five years as Chancellor, the credit rating was still AA, and had sunk yet further to be listed as 'negative'.[32]

—

For light relief, in April the government ventured away from the sleaze, ineptitude and squalor of its Westminster operation, and selected a delightful nature reserve outside Glasgow to announce its new policy of charging 5p for plastic bags.

'Interesting place for a visit,' said one of the attending police officers. When asked why, he said, 'Because of what the locals use it for.'

The government had selected a dogging site.[33]

Yet thanks to the Tories, you could now be completely fucked by total strangers in the comfort of your own home: the bedroom tax was introduced on 1 April, because taxing people for having a spare room sounds exactly like an elaborate and not especially funny joke.

The rationale was that there were people unnecessarily using up capacity in the nation's shrinking social housing stock by having a room they didn't need. Moving those tenants into smaller homes seems, at first glance, like a practical and efficient way to free up space needed to accommodate Iain Duncan Smith and Eric Pickles' growing army of homeless families.

The trouble was, 96 per cent of those affected by the new tax had nowhere else to go: smaller homes simply didn't exist.[34] Practically every tenant targeted by the bedroom tax therefore ended up penalised by the government for living in a home the government had told them to move into, and which it was now impossible to move out of.

Few readers will be shocked to hear that the main proponent and defender of this cruel, pointless, ineffective and preposterous policy was, once again, the morbid egg that answers to the made-up name of Iain Duncan Smith.[35] You might wonder how he sleeps at night, but fortunately I've looked into it for you, and have the definitive answer: he sleeps in a coffin lined with money, floating on a lake of orphans' tears.

Concurrent with the bedroom tax, IDS introduced a cap on housing benefit, which would mean, according to his own department's impact assessment, almost everybody would lose out. The average cost to households would be £83 per week, but 17 per cent of them would lose more than £150 per week.[36] And obviously, everybody affected was already on incomes low enough to require benefits, so it's an absolute certainty this only impacted people already too poor to keep a roof over their heads.

All this harm was enacted so we could cut the amount the state spent on welfare; yet the rocketing cost of Universal Credit meant any money IDS saved was instantly swallowed whole by one of his other dazzling innovations. Tories continued to assert that we simply *had* to impoverish thousands because we were skint; yet when Margaret Thatcher died that same month, she was granted a state funeral, and without blinking an eye, they magicked up £3.6 million to pay for one.[37]

All that money, and she was still dead; but there were 347,000 living people reliant on food banks.[38] That's an annual increase of 169 per cent.

If the gross inequality of it sounds like a sick joke, you'll at least have been warmed up for the news that 'Ding Dong! The Witch is Dead' entered the top 10 in the week of Thatcher's funeral.[39] Many still contend George Osborne missed a trick: he could have buried her in Liverpool, installed a dance floor on her tomb, and charged £10 a go. The national debt would have vanished in no time.

—

But the debt kept on rising, despite the government's repeated attempts to destroy anything valuable that might help to repay it. The next thing to be improved into calamitous failure was our legal system.

The reforms were introduced by weapons-grade bungling expert

Chris Grayling, and he really lived down to our expectations. He might have had the cranium of Homer Simpson, but he more than made up for it by having the competence of Chief Wiggum and the ethics of Mr Burns.

Following his impeccable work as employment minister, during which unemployment rose to 3.4 million while he bewilderingly sacked 10,000 of the people responsible for finding them work, Grayling had been promoted to Lord Chancellor.[40] He was the first non-lawyer to serve in that office for 400 years, and after his tenure, you can see why everybody since Elizabeth I had asked for qualifications.[41]

The right to equal and full access to the law can be traced back to the ancient cultures of China and Athens, is codified in Magna Carta, and is the basis of legal systems throughout the civilised world. It is an absolute fundamental.[42]

Grayling passionately believed in that system, in much the way lions passionately believe in antelopes. The cuts he introduced with April's Legal Aid, Sentencing and Punishment of Offenders Act (LASPO) meant 113,000 litigants per year were no longer provided with legal services.[43] They could still turn up to court, of course, and a legal system still existed. But without a lawyer to guide defendants through their case or represent their interests, fair and equal access to law was effectively gone.

Supporters of the government argued lawyers were overpaid and therefore the cuts were valid. And certainly, there have always been a very few high-profile barristers who become extremely wealthy. But the average salary for a legal-aid lawyer in 2013 was £27,000, which was less than the starting salary for a manager at Aldi.[44] And no disrespect to Aldi, but they aren't exactly Clarence Darrow.

The rates paid for legal-aid services are not vast. There are fixed fees for specific activities, adjusted to match the wealth of local areas. For example, a solicitor can claim £131.40 for attending a police station in Hartlepool. That's the entire fee, even if the solicitor is there all day. The rate for writing a solicitor's letter is £3.38.[45] Nobody was bleeding the system dry.

The cuts disproportionately affected people needing advice to work through the Tories' nightmarish Universal Credit application, or Iain Duncan Smith's cruel and arbitrary 'fit to work' programme. In 2011, before LASPO was implemented, 91,000 people used legal aid to get advice for benefits cases. After LASPO, it was down to just 478.[46]

And the cuts didn't stop there. Over the decade, a further 40 per cent was slashed from the overall budget for the justice system.[47] In 2019, only a third of people appearing in UK courts had any legal representation.[48]

And then the great sell-off began. Between 2010 and 2019, half of magistrates' courts were closed and £223 millions' worth of them were sold.[49] The practical effect of this is that thousands of lawyers, witnesses, defendants and litigants must now travel for hours to reach a courtroom. For many of those people, it will be a one-off event. But for lawyers, staff and expert witnesses, this may be a daily occurrence. Needless to say, with the huge cuts to income and the added expense of hours of daily travel, the number of solicitor firms offering to do legal-aid work dropped by nearly 30 per cent.[50]

In 2018, the Law Society campaigned for a judicial review of the cuts.[51] The government responded by announcing plans to abolish judicial reviews.[52]

But back in 2013, Grayling had barely warmed up. Having contributed to record unemployment in his first job and gutted the judicial system in his second, he now set about the prison and probation services.

His first move: ban books in prisons. Education has long been seen as a cornerstone of rehabilitation, but seemingly the government didn't care about cutting reoffending or building a better society, just about being performatively cruel. It's a lesson Priti Patel has taken to what I suppose we must call her heart, but Grayling got there first. Thankfully, in 2015 the ban was ruled illegal by the High Court.[53]

Legal aid, already cut to the bone for the general public, was abolished completely for many categories of prisoner.[54] The effect of this was that if you happened to be in prison, and therefore had zero income to fund your own legal representation, legal services were effectively unavailable. You might assume that an innocent person ending up in prison is a rare event, but in 2020 alone there were 1,336 overturned convictions.[55] That's more than the entire population of Wormwood Scrubs.[56] Thankfully, in 2017 the ban on legal aid for prisoners was also deemed illegal and stopped.[57]

Undeterred (but definitely still turd), Grayling introduced fines for simply pleading guilty.[58] Under his plan, if somebody entered a guilty plea at a magistrates' court, they would be fined £150. But those convicted at a Crown Court would have to pay £1,200. Over 100 magistrates resigned in protest, on the basis that Grayling's innovation skewed justice: the fines incentivised innocent people to plead guilty, simply to avoid the risk of a later fine they couldn't afford to pay. The policy was ditched by Michael Gove because it was dysfunctional, purposeless, sensationalist twaddle, all things of which Gove is normally such a fan.

After he left the Ministry of Justice, the National Audit Office produced a report on Grayling's tenure. It found his policies aimed at cutting costs and reducing reoffending had led to reoffending rates 'increasing significantly' and at a cost that was £467 million more than predicted.[59] A report by the British Sociological Association called his reforms an 'unmitigated disaster'.[60]

He was promoted to Leader of the House of Commons.[61]

—

In May, voters were invited on a tour of the mind of Nigel Farage, an experience not dissimilar to being trapped inside an empty wardrobe with a live rat. Farage had been the leader of UKIP, stood down before the 2010 general election, counted to 10, and then stood as leader again as soon as polls closed.

Don't question his methods: he has an unimpeachable common touch and is unquestionably a man of the people, as demonstrated by the following exchange between him and a journalist, on the event of Nigel winning his seat as an MEP.

'From now on,' said the journalist, 'it's going to be endless lunches, lavish dinners and champagne receptions. Will you be corrupted by the lifestyle?'

'No,' replied Nigel. 'I've always lived like that.'[62]

During the brief interregnum between the leadership of Nigel Farage and the leadership of Nigel Farage, the small, quixotically deranged UKIP had been led by Lord Pearson of Rannoch, who must have assumed he had the election sewn up, right until the moment he opened his mouth. At the launch of his party's epic, psychotropic 486-page manifesto, he informed the BBC that he hadn't even read the whole thing.[63]

And frankly, that's a shame, because it's a dazzlingly entertaining document. It includes plans to force Britons, under risk of arrest, to dress more smartly at the theatre, and to turn the Circle Line into an *actual* circle.[64] It would introduce a compulsory uniform for taxi drivers, and have every train in the country repainted in what it describes as 'traditional colours',[65] unlike the current trains which, as we all know, only exist in shades of pleurigloss[66] and octarine.[67]

Having wised up to the electability issues connected with printing details of their derangements in glossy brochures and distributing them to the media, UKIP welcomed back Farage, hid most of their best maniacs, and precipitated the first slithering of tiny pebbles that eventually became an avalanche that overwhelmed our country.

In May's local elections, the Tories, after less than three years in charge, retained the support of just one voter in four. Yet UKIP had leaped to 25 per cent, chomping at Cameron's heels, and making the pressure for a referendum on Europe impossible to resist.[68]

UKIP, and especially Farage, appeared to have come from nowhere, but this is a misreading of the situation. Wind the clock back to the late 1990s and consider the story of the British National Party (BNP).

For as long as it had existed, the BNP was home to the extreme right and fascists. It was founded by John Tyndall, a neo-Nazi former member of the National Front, who said that between the National Front and the BNP there was 'scarcely any difference in ideology or policy'.[69]

However, the entire far-right grouping was steeped in the imagery and reality of violent, racist thugs. This clearly deterred many people from lending their support, but in 1999 Nick Griffin became leader and, in ways that will seem queasily similar to the strategies employed by both Cameron and Farage, attempted to detoxify his party.

Griffin gracelessly stumbled a few steps closer to the typical attire and speaking style of a mid-ranking politician, and mostly disowned his party's connections with thuggery. Suddenly, from a starting point of as little as 0.06 per cent of the vote, the BNP started winning council seats and even elected a few MEPs; in some constituencies, they gained the support of 16 per cent of voters.

The BNP's rise seemed unstoppable, right until the moment Nick Griffin appeared on BBC *Question Time* in 2009, and was brutally mauled by the other panellists, the audience and reviewers. Support for the party evaporated, and by 2012 Griffin was its last surviving MEP. By the year of the Brexit referendum, the BNP was de-registered as a political party, having failed to pay its annual fee of £25.

Yet those 16 per cent of voters, who had been perfectly happy to embrace a party born out of racism and fascism, did not go away. Their opinions did not moderate.

Nobody would – or at any rate, should – claim that every UKIP supporter is a racist, but you can be damn sure every racist approves of UKIP. The fall in the BNP vote corresponded remarkably closely to the rise of the Faragist vote, so it's a fair bet that the kernel of UKIP's support in 2013 had been sympathetic to fascists only a few years before.

Those sympathies go back still further. In the 1970s, the National Front had printed a poster listing their core policies. It read: 'STOP immigration. REJECT Common Market. RESTORE capital punishment. MAKE Britain great again. SCRAP overseas aid. REBUILD armed forces.'[70]

Those had become British National Party policies, and after its electoral collapse became UKIP policies too. There was, as the BNP's neo-Nazi founder Tyndall had put it, 'scarcely any difference in ideology or policy'.

The Tories had been assiduous in their attacks on the BNP, yet rolled over in a heartbeat for UKIP, a party that shared all the same obsessions and prejudices. Those could be characterised as: only people of British blood should live here, and being raised on British territories makes us superior.

Our blood is best. Our soil is best. Blood and soil.

This explanation is ugly. Nobody is denying that. It says ugly things about the nature of many of our fellow citizens, and it expresses ugly ideas about the nature of the ascendent political dogma of the last decade. But there's another, simultaneous explanation for the rise of UKIP, and one that's built on profound cynicism.

The audience for Nick Griffin's appearance on *Question Time* was 8 million people, unprecedented viewing figures for the programme.[71] Most tuned in for the bear-baiting, not to support BNP policies, but the controversy, to put it bluntly, put bums on seats, and *Question Time* wanted more of it, please.

The BBC is supposed to provide fair and balanced representation of a range of political views. Yet in the five years leading up to the 2013 local elections, Nigel Farage appeared on *Question Time* 25 times, compared to 11 appearances by every representative from the Green Party *combined*.[72] Farage has appeared on the programme more than anybody else this century.[73]

The Beeb wasn't alone in embracing this controversy-magnet: in the whole of 2003, Nigel Farage was mentioned just 36 times in national media. By 2012, it had risen to 23,000.[74]

The result of wall-to-wall promotion was, unsurprisingly, a rise in popularity; how could it not be, when Farage is, above all else, a self-aggrandising populist, to whom the media had granted countless hours of free publicity?

By the time we reached the 2013 local elections, UKIP were just 2 per cent behind the Tories. Farage had hoovered up the votes from the violent British National Party and was now hoovering up huge numbers of Tory voters, who, it turns out, held exactly the same views as the BNP on everything except for stabbing.

There was, after all, scarcely any difference in ideology or policy.

There were plenty of senior Tories who were well aware of this tendency within their base: Steve Hilton had talked about how the party should 'replace the membership' to oust those who rejected modernity.[75] Cameron contemplated Tory activists' obsessions with immigration and Europe, and called them 'mad, swivel-eyed loons',[76] while his former party chairman was reported as saying the grassroots membership was driving Tory MPs towards 'obsessive and destructive behaviour'.[77]

UKIP was a magnet for the swivel-eyed contingent. It didn't seem to matter when high-profile UKIP politicians like Godfrey Bloom referred to recipients of foreign aid as living in 'bongo-bongo land'. Or that, as he first took his seat in the EU Parliament, he said he wanted to 'deal with women's issues because I just don't think they clean behind the fridge enough'. When women at a later conference remonstrated about this remark, he said the room was 'full of sluts', and then hit a journalist round the head with a brochure.[78]

There was clearly a large segment of the Tory grassroots that lapped this up, and UKIP seemed like the ideal place for them to be. Cameron, who in early 2010 had been blithely certain he'd get an outright win at a general election, now lived in fear of failing for a second time. He needed a strategy to regain those haemorrhaging votes; and so, a fortnight after the May elections, he promised a referendum on leaving the EU, just as UKIP had demanded.[79]

It was a transparent act of placing personal ambition above any benefits to his party, and of placing benefits to his party above the good of the country. With a single, lazy, backwards step, Cameron had turned the Conservative Party into UKIP, a party that had, in turn, absorbed the BNP and National Front.

Remember those six policies on the National Front poster? End immigration, leave the European project, scrap overseas aid, boost our military might, make Britain great again, and restore the death penalty.

Five of these are now official Tory policy. There are Tory MPs agitating for the last one, including Home Secretary and part-time Dementor Priti Patel, and regular contributor Christopher Chope, who in June 2013 was one of four MPs to camp outside Parliament, demanding the right to deliver their own 'Alternative Queen's Speech'. Its policies included, naturally, the reintroduction of capital punishment.[80]

The change had been gradual, like boiling a frog. If you've always voted Tory, you now vote for the National Front, and probably didn't notice.

There is scarcely any difference in ideology or policy.

—

Largely overlooked due to the referendum announcement, in May Patrick Mercer resigned as an MP, following yet another revelation that yet another Tory had been happy to take yet more cash to influence his parliamentary activities.[81] He was filmed agreeing to accept £4,000 from undercover reporters.[82]

It was the end of a distinguished political career, during which he had advocated the use of water cannon on Britain's streets,[83] campaigned for creationism to be taught in schools,[84] said to an Israeli conscript, 'You don't look like a soldier to me, you look like a bloody Jew,'[85] referred to ethnic minority soldiers as 'idle and useless', and said it was to be expected that people from ethnic minorities should be referred to as 'black bastard' or 'ni--er'.[86]

He truly was a great loss to the Mother of Parliaments.

The Standards Committee report on Mercer's rent-an-MP activities said they were 'not aware of a case relating to a sitting MP which has involved such a sustained and pervasive breach of the house's rules,'[87] but then again, Boris Johnson wasn't an MP at the time.

It's easy to judge Mercer, but let's remember he also said David Cameron was 'a most despicable creature without any redeeming features',[88] reportedly called him an 'arse', and stated he was 'the worst politician in British history',[89] proving that even a broken cock is right twice a day.

Sorry, did I say cock? I meant cock.

—

In June, Britain celebrated the 65th anniversary of the NHS with the revelation that the health service, which the coalition boasted was officially protected from cuts, had suffered 0.9 per cent cuts in its budget for the most recent financial year.[90] Lansley was gone, kicking his heels until it was time for him to ponce around in ermine with his sponsors,[91] and we were left with a new health minister, Jeremy Hunt, whose expression projected the giddy, uncomprehending optimism of a spaniel chasing a ball into the Large Hadron Collider. Hunt had once explained bogus expenses claims by saying he'd forgotten about seven houses he half owned – and who among us can honestly say we haven't occasionally forgotten about our ownership of seven houses?[92]

Hunt responded to accusations of cutting health spending by telling Parliament that 'real-terms spending on the NHS has increased across the country',[93] which was followed by an abrupt correction by the chair of the UK Statistics Authority, Andrew Dilnot, who gave the correct figure: 'expenditure on the NHS in real terms was lower in 2011–12 than it was in 2009–10'.[94]

Meanwhile, George Osborne continued to hack maniacally at the nation's finances in his annual spending review, which promised an additional 2.8 per cent cuts across Whitehall, due to our lingering fiscal deficit and the eternal failure of his own policies.

But Osborne had absolutely no other ideas. He wasn't alone in his squeamish aversion to original thought, as we shall see by welcoming back to these pages the delightful Owen Paterson, excitedly flinging himself once more into his favourite pastime: the mass slaughter of badgers.

Practicality and effectiveness meant little to Paterson, a man of unwavering conviction in the face of overwhelming evidence that he's wrong. The Berne Convention, of which the UK is a signatory, said culling must only happen if there is no satisfactory alternative method of disease control, yet vaccination was working perfectly well in both Wales and Northern Ireland.[95]

The chair of the Independent Scientific Group produced research showing that while it is technically possible for cattle to catch tuberculosis from a badger, the real problem is the other way around: the cattle were infecting the badgers with the disease.

Scientists from a coalition including the RSPCA, Wildlife Trust and RSPB produced a report showing a badger cull could kill off an entire local population but would still not in any way solve the problem of bovine tuberculosis.

But Paterson was determined to go ahead with a cull in England, ideally in a way he had already proven to be dizzyingly ineffective.

And so, once again, marksmen were sent out to clatter around in the nocturnal undergrowth, hoping they'd somehow manage to stumble upon more than 5,000 notoriously elusive subterranean animals, and then accurately shoot them in pitch darkness.

The cost of this farce was £7 million, and our crack-shots failed to hit 70 per cent of their targets. Of those animals that did manage to get themselves killed, testing found six out of seven didn't even carry bovine TB.

Unsurprisingly, after two years of culling in Dorset, research found there was absolutely no change to the prevalence of tuberculosis in cattle.

—

More livestock news in September, as the sky darkened with the wings of chickens coming home to roost. Nigel Evans resigned as Deputy Speaker, having been arrested and charged with the sexual assault and rape of seven men.[96] He was acquitted of all charges.

Yet only months before, he had been one of the 241 Tory MPs to vote for LASPO,[97] the Conservative bill that demolished the right to legal aid.[98] And now, overnight, he realised that he needed it.

The charges led to Nigel Evans losing his life savings, and by the time the trial was over, he was telling newspapers, 'It's wrong, completely wrong, to remove people's right to have expert legal representation,' which was literally what he had just done to us all. 'We're definitely talking about justice being denied as a result of LASPO,' said the man who had voted to deny justice as a result of LASPO.[99]

'There is joy in heaven over one lost sinner who repents,' sayeth the Bible, but it sayeth utter crap in the case of Nigel Evans, because he learned bugger all from his experience. For the next half-decade or more, he relentlessly voted for cuts to other people's benefits,[100] including confirmation that the bedroom tax was here to stay.[101]

When Raquel Rolnik, the UN Special Rapporteur on housing, started looking into the bedroom tax later that same month, the Tories leaped like a scalded cat. She said she was 'very shocked' by the living conditions she saw in Britain, and that those most affected by the policy were 'the most vulnerable, the most fragile, the people who are on the fringes'. She concluded: 'My immediate recommendation is that the bedroom tax is abolished.'[102]

Grant Shapps put on his best indignant voice and stomped into the BBC to assert it was an 'absolute disgrace' that the UN had got involved in British politics: clearly it should focus on problems in developing countries where people were being killed by poverty, rather than the UK, where people were being killed by poverty.[103]

(The previous winter, excess deaths rose by one-third – that's an extra 10,000 deaths[104] – as 2.3 million households now earned too little to heat their homes.[105])

It's a question of whether you could trust the United Nations, or Grant Shapps. When, in 2005, the media had started to investigate the weirdness about his secret identity as Michael Green, a get-rich-quick salesman, Shapps, dogmatically tied to tradition, put on his best indignant voice, and stomped into talk radio station LBC to assert, 'Let me get this absolutely clear. I don't have a second job. And I have never had a second job while being an MP. End of story.'[106]

It wasn't the end of the story. Shapps had a second job when he was an MP and was definitely pretending to be Michael Green.[107] He had more identities than Jason Bourne, somebody else who people would travel halfway around the world to punch.

—

All in all, not a great time to be a Tory MP.

But a great time to be a Tory MP's relative, as Matt Hancock's brother was about to find out. As Minister of State for Skills and Enterprise, Hancock had been responsible for setting up the regulations relating to crowdfunding and peer-to-peer finance, a role in which he should have been entirely independent of influence. It was in this guise that he told the House of Commons in December 2013, 'We are supporting crowdfunding.'[108]

This was very fortunate news for Matt's brother Christopher, who, a few months earlier in April 2013, had started a crowdfunding business called Crowd2Fund. After it had been running a few months, in October 2013 Matt Hancock, who was independently overseeing that very sector, urged fellow MPs to become involved in – wouldn't you know it – crowdfunding and peer-to-peer financing.[109]

—

The Tories next turned their attention to the Royal Mail, which went on sale in October for approximately half what it was worth.[110]

It mattered not a jot that the privatisation of rail had been an unmitigated calamity. Who cared if the privatised energy providers had raised prices 10 per cent at a time when millions of us couldn't afford to heat our homes, and that even the former Tory leader John Major was calling for taxes on the excess profit of privatised utility companies?[111] It didn't matter a tuppenny fuck that two-thirds of the public opposed the sale of the postal service: 70 per cent of it was to be sold off, because that's what Tories do.[112] They'd done it ever since

Thatcher, who despite her prodigious flaws, had explicitly refused to sell off Her Majesty's mail service to a collection of spivs and chancers in the City of London.[113]

Michael Fallon, the business minister, said the sale was not ideologically driven, but was a 'practical, logical, commercial decision'.[114]

Let's examine the practicality, logic and commerce of the sale.

The prelude to privatisation was the taxpayer taking on the Royal Mail's pension liabilities. This landed the state with around £40 billion more debts that somehow had to be paid for, but it made the Royal Mail a much more valuable investment opportunity.[115]

Having nationalised the debts, the government then privatised the profits. They commissioned half a dozen banks to tell them the price of the Royal Mail, and those banks, including Goldman Sachs, charged the taxpayer a fee of £12.7 million to advise that the share price should be 330p.[116]

Within 24 hours of the sale of Royal Mail, the share price was 455p, an instant profit of 38 per cent. Within weeks, Goldman Sachs was advising its customers that the price would reach 610p, almost double what we had sold it for on their specific advice.[117] At the time of writing, it is still 595p.[118]

The government bragged that the sale had made £3.3 billion for the nation. According to the share price straight after the privatisation happened, we should have made £5.5 billion.[119] And, of course, the public purse had assumed liabilities of £40 billion, so the purpose of the sale – which was to raise money to repay our debts – had in fact created a £36.7 billion loss. That's £1 per second for 1,163 years, or £3,600 per hour, every hour since the Vikings raided Lindisfarne.[120] Somebody made a lot of money in the trading of those stocks, and it wasn't you and me.

The careful husbandry of our nation's finances continued a month later, as the government flogged off £890 million of student debts to a private company for £160 million, a loss of a further £730 million.[121]

The year ended, much as it had begun, with the inexorably execrable Christopher Chope attempting to block an official apology to Alan Turing, the Second World War codebreaking hero and father of modern computing, who was chemically castrated by the state for his homosexuality, and eventually driven to suicide.[122]

It had been another stunning year for the modernising, debt-paying, economy-balancing Tory party.

2014
Lagoons of Urine

In January David Cameron appeared before the Joint Committee on the National Security Strategy, and told them, 'I love watching crime dramas on the television. There is hardly any crime drama where a crime is solved without using the data of a mobile communications device.'[1]

By his own admission, the source of his ingenious plan for a so-called Snoopers' Charter, which allows the state to essentially listen to everything you say and do, was his endless consumption of cheap TV. He'd learned all about it while chillaxing in front of what he told us was his current favourite: *Elementary*. One hundred and forty-one hour-long episodes of it.

But at least Cameron was consistent about his commitment to his BarcaLounger. He seemed a tad more flexible about that pesky, inconvenient pledge to rein in his party's sponsors from the banking sector. When he became prime minister, Cameron had promised a £2,000 per person limit on cash bonuses for employees of banks that had received state bailouts, and he refused to allow those banks' overall pay bills to rise. Now he had to put our money where his mouth was, and it was such a bore.

Thankfully he'd avoided mentioning limits on bonuses paid in the form of shares, and this careful omission gave him wriggle room when challenged on whether he would veto huge pay-outs.[2] Naturally, he obfuscated and somehow ended up blaming it all on Ed Miliband, who, Cameron claimed, had 'all the moral authority' of Paul Flowers, the Co-op banking chief who had resigned in a flurry of reports about paying male sex workers and using drugs.[3]

Paul Flowers didn't seem an apt subject for discussion when it was reported that Tory MP Mark Menzies had hired a male Brazilian sex worker, taken him on a tour of the Palace of Westminster, and asked him to procure a big bag of amphetamines.[4] Menzies resigned from his position at the Department for International Development, saying, 'A number of these allegations are not true, and I look forward to setting the record straight in due course.'[5] I don't know how long 'due course' is, but it's eight years later, and we're still waiting.

But we didn't have to wait long for the revelation that directors of Royal Bank of Scotland had, yep, agreed to pay themselves £23 million in share options, just as predicted, skipping easily around Cameron's empty rhetoric. The bonuses were despite the RBS recording losses of £8.2 billion.[6]

Imagine the problems we could have avoided if the BBC had commissioned a middle-brow drama about a TV detective who went around revealing the machinations of international banking.

—

If you were to believe UKIP's David Silvester, the floods in February 2014 were entirely caused by gay marriage,[7] but scientists who had looked into the matter with a little more rigour had come to a different conclusion. As long ago as 1897, the Swedish chemist Svante Arrhenius had described the greenhouse effect on our environment.[8] The facts have been available for a quite a while, so unless you're a UKIP councillor, little of this will be new to you: heating the atmosphere by releasing large quantities of CO_2 increases the likelihood of extreme weather, including heatwaves and flooding. Climate change has been proven beyond the doubt of anybody sane, and although it remains impossible to predict exactly *what* extreme weather will occur, it's absolutely certain that it *will* occur.

This had been explained to the government, at least those who bothered to attend the briefings; they had been told in 2010 that for every £1 spent on flood defences, £9 is saved in property damage.[9] Yet they mindlessly cut the budget for flood defences by 15 per cent,[10] and now, as Britain experienced the wettest winter since 1766,[11] Cameron was shoved in front of cameras to insist that 'money is no object'[12] in trying to ameliorate a largely preventable problem that he'd deliberately avoided preventing.

Over 10,000 homes were damaged. The cost was estimated at £1.3 billion,[13] yet the amount saved by the cuts to flood defences had been just £40 million.[14] Total lost: £1.26 billion. Or if you prefer, we wasted the equivalent of £3,600 per hour, every hour for 40 years.

There were 913,138 people reliant on food banks in 2014.[15] That's an annual increase of 163 per cent.

—

Speaking of which, Esther McVey claimed there was 'no robust evidence linking food bank usage to welfare reform'.

'All the empirical evidence and research shows that welfare reform is the main force driving increasing demand for food banks,' said the UK's largest food bank charity. 'In 2012–13 the Trussell Trust supported 14,318 people. In the past financial year, we supported 71,428.'

McVey then refused to attend a meeting of the Scottish Parliament's Welfare Reform Committee to answer questions on the matter.[16]

—

If all of this seems a little bit disconnected from logic, wait until you hear about clause 119 of the Care Act.

Much of the Care Act was standard-issue fannying around, trying to keep the wheels on the NHS as it battled to recover from Andrew Lansley's reforms and the ongoing real-term cuts in spending. But clause 119 was an absolute corker.

Since Lansley, hospitals had been forced to fight one another for the shrinking pool of funding. This meant that if Hospital A had a thriving maternity ward, but the nearby Hospital B did not, Hospital

B would have a funding shortfall. The Tory solution was to close the highly successful Hospital A, forcing patients to the less successful Hospital B, thus saving it from money troubles.

This is not a joke. This was an actual policy sent to the House of Commons.

The idea – and I use the word 'idea' in the loosest possible sense – had arisen out of Jeremy Hunt's embarrassment when, in October 2013, the High Court had ruled he acted unlawfully in cutting back maternity cover at Lewisham Hospital to save nearby Queen Elizabeth Hospital from going bust.[17] The conclusion Hunt drew from this was: if it is unlawful to do something stupid, the law must be changed. Stands to reason.

And to avoid inconvenient questions from anybody equipped with more than a mealworm's grasp of common sense, the Care Act stipulated that in future such decisions would not require consultation with the public, NHS commissioners or hospital staff.

In March, the Care Act, including clause 119, squeaked through the House of Commons with a small majority; but the House of Lords wasn't going to be railroaded into madness, and amended the bill to remove the clause. Thankfully, the government backed down, and it never made it into law.[18]

———

By now, it had been almost a month since an embarrassing ministerial resignation, so Maria Miller stepped up. You might think it's a bit of a disgrace that she claimed £90,000 for a second home in Wimbledon in which she and her parents lived, but the Parliamentary Standards Committee found it was mostly within the rules – they asked her to repay a paltry £5,800.[19]

But the main problem they had was her attitude throughout the year-long investigation into her conduct. She was described as having deliberately caused 'delay and difficulty'; to have made a point of providing the committee with incomplete information or with 'the minimum necessary'; and of responding to civil questions in a way that was described as 'legalistic'.[20] In layman's terms, she was a bit of an arse about the whole thing and was told to go to the House of Commons and make a statement, apologising for her curt attitude.

Her apologetic statement lasted a curt 31 seconds, which was exactly the sort of 'minimum necessary' crap the committee had warned her about.[21]

It's not often Esther McVey manages to have the moral high ground, but she said it was 'not how I would have apologised'. Norman Tebbit was dragged from whichever corpse he was feasting on to assert Maria Miller had 'by the arrogance of her response, poured petrol on the fire'. Thankfully, Boris Johnson was available to demonstrate the mastery of superpredicting that would become a hallmark of his premiership: he went on Radio 4 to assert 'she is staying'.[22]

She quit the next day, the third resignation in 2014.

Weirdly, dying palm tree Michael Fabricant also managed to get himself sacked from his position of party vice-chairman for tweeting 'about time' when he heard the news.[23]

But no resignations arose from the revelation that same month that computers on a secure network, all with IP addresses based in government offices in Whitehall, had been used to amend the Wikipedia entry for the Hillsborough disaster. The lyrics to the Liverpool anthem 'You'll Never Walk Alone' had been amended to 'you'll never walk again,' and the phrase 'Blame Liverpool Fans' had been added to the page.[24] Aren't they a delight?

—

Let us change the mood with a rare opportunity to celebrate good news. George Osborne announced an above-inflation increase to the minimum wage.

'The economy can now afford it,' declared the Torquemada of the Treasury.[25] So: glad tidings for the 1 million workers earning the minimum wage. The rate for adults increased by 19 entire pence, to £6.50. Meanwhile 18- to 20-year-olds got an additional 10p per hour, bringing them up to a positively exorbitant £5.13. And apprentices gained an extra 5p, so could now pocket £2.73 per hour, the lucky bastards.[26]

And more good news for apprentices, as Michael Gove finally got around to applying his very particular genius to the National Apprenticeship Service, which he saw as being excessively cumbersome and bureaucratic.

The service had been launched in 1994,[27] and was built around a framework containing 216 different apprenticeships, each designed in collaboration with employers, and mapped to the National Qualifications Framework.[28]

But the Tories thought 216 courses was excessive: the entire system was complicated and messy, so Gove set about tearing it up, and replaced it with a new streamlined and efficient set of Apprenticeship Standards,[29] which now contained a trimmed-down list of 751 apprenticeships, which maths fans will instantly realise is three times as many.[30]

This 300 per cent increase in courses didn't end Gove's 'simplification'. Apprenticeships were no longer mapped to national qualifications, rendering them less useful than the old courses had been. And each one now contained a subset of 'standards' – typically 30 to 40 skills or behaviours – each of which needed to be individually signed off by a college tutor before being sent for further assessment by one of a plethora of newly formed companies that emerged simply to handle this task.[31] Those end-point assessors each earn around £58,000 per year,[32] which is more than double the starting salary of a teacher.[33]

When you hear Tories speak of investing in education, remember this absurd profligacy still counts as investment. And it didn't stop there.

The apprenticeship for digital and technology solutions, for example, attracts funding of £25,000 for 24 weeks of tuition. A grand a week is pretty much what you'd pay at a top private school and compares with just £131 per week spent on secondary-school students.[34] Money was never hard to find when one of Gove's brilliant ideas needed to survive contact with reality.

Unfortunately, reality fought back: for all the money poured into the new service, apprentices still got a minimum wage of £2.73 per hour, which is 2 per cent of that £25,000 funding. Private businesses and assessors scooped up the rest, and the number of people doing an apprenticeship fell from 457,000 to 323,000, a drop of nearly a third.[35]

—

Britain, we are often told, is essentially a Conservative nation. As a stirring illustration of this theory, in June 2014 the Tories won their first by-election while in government for 25 years.[36]

They enjoyed the benefit of the interminable backing of 92 per cent of national print media. Most of the BBC's political output was directed and presented by a raft of Conservatives. The electoral system required Tory politicians to get fewer votes per MP than any other party; their opponents were divided; and Tories receive twice as much income in donations as every other party *combined*.[37]

And it was still a quarter of a century since they had won a by-election.

'By-elections are notoriously tricky,' said David Cameron, laying out his stall for Nobel Prize in Bathetic Understatement.[38] But at least he had some good news to celebrate, which hadn't been the case the previous month, when UKIP once again exploited groundless terror over immigration – thanks, Mark Harper – to sweep to victory in the European elections. They gained 26 per cent of the vote, the first time anybody except for Labour or Tories had led in a national election since 1906.[39]

Their win was unsurprising when you consider the Tories had essentially run UKIP's campaign for them. In 2014, restrictions had been lifted on people from Bulgaria and Romania coming to work in the UK, and you might as well have informed the Tory grassroots that you planned to flambé their dog.

Philippa Roe, a Tory councillor in Westminster, suggested Roma from Eastern Europe were queuing up to exploit their new right to work in the UK by, erm, not working in the UK. They were coming, she claimed, to 'pickpocket and aggressively beg' in London, causing 'a massive amount of disruption and low-level crime' including, but not limited to, 'defecating in doorways'.[40]

They do have toilets in Europe. They have had for quite a while. They're pretty much all house-trained over there. But for months, the rhetoric of the Tory party had told of a thousand, ten thousand, a million Transylvanians surging past Luton Airport's passport controls like a swarm of doorstep-shitting zombies.

With this apocalypse imminent, the innately doltish potato of hatred Mark Reckless rounded up the media and charged off to meet the rampaging horde about to sweep in from Bucharest.[41]

'I'm here this morning because my party, the Conservatives, made a promise we would cut immigration from hundreds of thousands to tens of thousands a year,' Reckless told the press. The plane landed. The doors opened. Breath was bated and cameras were set to 'wide angle' to accommodate the baying multitude about to disembark – and from the aircraft stepped just two new Romanian workers. One of them, Victor Spirescu, was 30 years old, and very much not the living dead; simply here to earn a bit of money washing cars, so he could afford to go home again and fix up his house.

'Have you come here to exploit the NHS?' asked the assembled media.

'What is that?' asked a perplexed Mr Spirescu.[42]

There was no invasion. There were no zombies. The entrances of homes across the Bedfordshire area remained blissfully free of excrement. The only shit being created was that emerging from the mouth of Mark Reckless.

More setbacks for xenophobia in June, as the Supreme Court ruled that Theresa May's 'deport first, appeal later' policy was unlawful.[43] Thankfully, David Cameron, the leader of the 'party of law and order', had complete respect for the highest court in the land, which is why he subsequently made a speech in which he announced, 'We will extend our new policy of "deport first, appeal later" to cover all immigration appeals,' if Tories won an election in 2015.[44]

They needed all the help they could get at that election, and this probably explains the decision of Tories to begin taking very large donations from a collection of squillionaire Russians.

Nobody is claiming there was anything illegal in the receipt of a donation of £160,000 to play a tennis match with David Cameron and Boris Johnson. Perverse, yes. Unfathomable, certainly. But not illegal. And we can trust the motives and morals of Cameron, who assured us he would not accept money from a 'Putin crony', but that Lubov Chernukhin 'certainly wasn't that' before accepting £160,000 from Chernukhin's wife.[45] Chernukhin is Putin's former finance minister.

There was also nothing untoward about Alexander Temerko, a Ukrainian energy magnate, head of a Russian state arms company and self-declared fan of Russia's FSB security services,[46] who paid £90,000 for a bronze bust of Cameron.[47] I would merely point out that you can get a C-3PO bobble-head on Amazon for £24.95, so Mr Temerko's shareholders might want to question his eye for a good deal.

Similarly hard stares should be directed at whoever decided to part with a £15,000 donation in return for a jar of honey produced by Foreign Office minister Hugo Swire.[48] It's to be assumed bees were involved somewhere in the process, rather than Mr Swire being a bit Brundlefly, but by this stage things were so weird that we should rule nothing out.

Having dedicated sufficient time to playing tennis, producing honey and posing for bronze sculptures, our leaders then began serious preparation for the following year's elections. Cameron launched a major Cabinet reshuffle in July, with a modernising determination to increase the number of women in Cabinet to more closely represent the 50-50 gender split in our population. Which is how he ended up with five of his seventeen Cabinet ministers being women, up from four.[49] Well done, Dave.

But that was too much for some Tories. 'If you're white and male, you've got no chance of promotion,'[50] said one anonymous MP, speaking up once more for the oppressed group that represented 70 per cent of the people in top government jobs. Former MP and current bad mathematician Jerry Hayes tweeted, 'Bad weekend for any ambitious Tory MP with a penis.'[51]

All Tories have a penis, and that penis is Jerry Hayes.

Cameron threw a handful of knighthoods at recently demoted Tories, and 'consolation prize' is exactly why the honours system exists. This most modern of Conservatives ended up having sacked and then knighted more men than he had appointed women to his Cabinet.[52]

There were, however, some bright spots in this mire: somebody finally spotted how bereft of clues Owen Paterson was, so he lost his job, and had a right old hissy fit about it too, claiming it was 'a kick in the teeth to 12 million countryside voters'.[53] No Owen, it was a kick in the teeth for you.

We lost relatively sane, intelligent, rational ministers, such as Dominic Grieve and Kenneth Clarke, but on the positive side, Michael Gove, having committed as many shocking violations upon our education system as a man could reasonably be expected to do in a lifetime, was demoted sideways to become Chief Whip. 'It's not a demotion,' said the prime minister,[54] in much the same tone of voice you would use to tell a wailing four-year-old at a nativity play that 'Third Camel' is just as big a role as Mary.

Robert Buckland became our new Solicitor General, despite having recently been found guilty of professional misconduct by the Bar Standards Board, which wasn't a terrific start.[55] But at least we had a new environment minister, Liz Truss, a sort of Margaret Thatcher you'd expect to buy at Elizabeth Duke. She at least believed in climate science, and recognised that bees have an important role to play, not least in the funding of the Conservative Party.

Truss immediately launched an urgent 10-year pollinator strategy to reverse the widespread collapse of bee populations,[56] which lasted almost nine months, at which point she lifted the EU ban on the neonicotinoid pesticides that scientists largely blame for bee extinctions.[57] But for those nine months, she was temporarily more scientifically literate than Paterson had ever managed, and the Cabinet missed his profound unsuitability for the role.

Fortunately, it was quickly filled by the appointment of Greg Clark as science minister, despite his history of campaigning for the provision of homeopathic treatment on the NHS. Yep: our science minister backed the idea that drops of water have a memory, and that a red onion cures allergies because they are both things that make your eyes water.[58]

—

In August, London Mayor Boris Johnson announced that he was trying to find a safe seat, so he could return to Westminster.[59] He was immediately parachuted into Uxbridge and South Ruislip as the candidate for the forthcoming election, despite his promise to London voters that he would not return to the Commons while remaining mayor; he was still contracted to be London Mayor for another two years.[60] But for once, Johnson appeared to have told an untruth, and betrayed the trust that was placed in him for personal gain. It was so uncharacteristic.

Let us consider for a moment Boris Johnson, a moral man, and a fine politician: I'd love to talk about all three of them, but I only have space for Boris.

Johnson may well be second only to Donald Trump as the biggest, most relentless elected liar in recent history, and has a decades-long record of racism, sexism, homophobia, Islamophobia, xenophobia, amorality, ineptitude, deception and betrayal. He owes his success almost entirely to being able to persuade the gullible that he's a fun, clever and jovial scholar, hiding inside the bloated corpse of Billy Bunter, but he's actually a nasty, inept, narcissistic, bullshitting nincompoop who went on *Have I Got News for You* and was unable to correctly answer the question, 'What is your name?'[61]

He was sacked from his first job as a *Times* reporter for inventing a quote, then lying about having invented it.[62] He doesn't appear to have been much of a loss, with colleagues reporting that he was disorganised and lacked basic skills.[63] But, by pulling on family strings (his father had been an EU diplomat), he soon landed a job as the Brussels correspondent of the *Telegraph*, and almost immediately started to fuck up an entire continent.

Diligently reporting the mundane-but-necessary reality of EU politics bored Johnson, so he stopped attending briefings, and began to flagrantly concoct absurd stories about perfidious foreigners from the comfort of his hotel room. Not content with directing this serpentine stream of bum-slurry towards his *Telegraph* handlers, he even boasted of his lies in an article for that paper. 'Some of my most joyous hours have been spent in a state of semi-incoherence, composing foam-flecked hymns of hate,' he admitted in 2002.[64]

'Snails are to be designated as fish'[65] was one example of him plucking sheer gibberish from the fecund gap between his ears, and the *Telegraph*'s editors and owners would believe this crap. Or viewed more cynically, they wouldn't believe him at all, but they'd see the commercial value in feeding xenophobia to their readership.

Many of his headlines sounded like they were ripped straight from *The Onion*, and you'd certainly giggle if this stuff appeared in a satirical magazine. 'Brussels recruits sniffers to ensure that Euro-manure smells the same,' he claimed, which is so ludicrous you wonder how anybody ever bought it. Johnson himself certainly found it entertaining, saying he was 'sort of chucking these rocks over the garden wall and I listened to this amazing crash from the greenhouse next door over in England as everything I wrote from Brussels was having this amazing, explosive effect on the Tory party – and it really gave me this, I suppose, rather weird sense of power'.[66]

There were three problems with this. Or four if you include basic morality, but we're talking about Johnson, so forget about that.

First of the three problems: he became addicted to that 'weird sense of power', and the only way to keep getting his daily hit was with more falsehood. Nobody at the *Telegraph* stopped him because he was a star and made them money. Nobody in the Tory party stopped him because their credulous voters believed every word, and consequently roared demands for change so loudly that few of their MPs had sufficient spine to stand up to it. And he certainly wasn't going to stop himself, because he has absolutely no self-control or sense of shame.

The second problem was: like any big success story, he inspired copycats. He was a headline act at the *Telegraph*, a media sensation for his buffoonish persona on chat shows and late-night comedies, and he caused the kind of outrage among liberals that the *Daily Mail* could only dream of. If the *Telegraph* could print, in the judiciously chosen words of EU spokesman Willy Hélin, 'a load of bullshit', the other papers saw no reason not to join in.[67]

A certain strain of British newspaper had always acted like a malfunctioning vacuum cleaner: an unmoderated, monotonous background whine, hurling scattergun gobbets of garbage across the nation's living rooms, secure in the knowledge that grown-ups in government would come along and tidy up. Boris Johnson the columnist was currently chief shit-slinger, but also – and this is the third major problem – had ambitions to replace those grown-ups, and to turn into Boris Johnson the politician.

He wanted to be prime minister. That's as deeply as he'd thought about it. Some people want power because they long to *do* things, and others because they long to *be* things. Johnson was in the latter category; in fact, he practically defined that category. He never had a clue what he wanted to actually *achieve* as PM, and a year into the job he appeared to yearn for the end of his sentence, so he could quit and make a shedload of money by exploiting his contacts.

But he always wanted to have *been* prime minister at some point in his life. In fact, as a child, he had declared a wish to be 'World King',[68] so I suppose we should celebrate a rare example of Johnsonian moderation, but lacking the temperament, skills, intellect or diligence the job requires, he decided bullshit was his route to power. Play to your strengths, I guess.

It's important to note that Johnson is a bullshitter, not a liar. There's a difference. A liar cares what the truth is and is attempting to conceal it; a bullshitter simply doesn't care what the truth is. The truth, for him, is whatever he can persuade the gullible to believe.

We've all met one: the guy in your office who claims his next-door neighbour owns a Harley-Davidson that once belonged to both Elvis *and* James Dean; or that he's leaving his job to assume a high-powered management role in a major Strasbourg technology company, and then a month later you find him working as a traffic warden in Stockport. They do it for effect and attention, and they don't seem to have any shame. They are weak, insecure men, finding power and validation in bullshit.

Boris Johnson understood this. He weaponised it. It became his superpower. Boris Johnson is a real-life IBM: the Incredible Bullshitting Man. And the newspapers are all IBM-compatible.

He bullshat about an EU law demanding straight bananas.[69] It never happened. Made up. Total crap.

He spread the bullshit about the EU banning prawn-cocktail crisps.[70] He bullshitted that the EU was introducing mandatory smaller coffins, and blocking plans to make lorries safe.[71]

He bullshitted about the EU demanding plastic wrapping around individual kippers,[72] and that 80 million people from Turkey would come to the UK if we didn't leave the EU,[73] and then he lied about bullshitting about Turkey.[74]

He was sacked from his first job as a frontbencher for having an affair, then lying about having an affair.[75] He was castigated by the UK Statistics Authority for bullshitting about the NHS,[76] then blithely repeated the lie in the *Telegraph* a year later.[77] The actions of Boris Johnson since 2016 should be no surprise to anybody, because bullshit is his chief weapon.

He could deploy it so lavishly because there were never any consequences for him. His ardent believers didn't want to hear that it was all fairy tales, and they didn't care anyway: 'Oh, that's just Boris,' they would say until eventually 'Just Boris' became baked into his persona, and he could get away with absolutely anything.

The grown-ups who once cleaned up the mess were boring, and Boris was on the route to power. Bullshit was the new normal.

—

The same month that Johnson announced his intention to return as a Tory MP, Douglas Carswell announced his intention to stop being one, and become a UKIP MP instead. He was quickly followed by Mark Reckless.[78]

Carswell, one of the Conservative Party's deepest thinkers (also voted the least trustworthy MP in Britain in 2016),[79] said the problem with the Tories was that they were part of a 'cosy little clique called Westminster',[80] and his solution was to, erm, give more power to Westminster by leaving the EU. He dazzled us yet further with his analysis that Tories had reneged on promises to clean up politics. Perhaps a different Douglas Carswell was among the group of MPs ordered to repay £1 million in expenses,[81] including £655 for a love seat in the 'second home' he flipped.[82]

Taking the piss had become quite a lucrative side-line for MPs, but his fellow Eurosceptic Andrew Bridgen was more focused on creating piss: AB Produce, the vegetable processing business of which he is a director, was warned by the Environment Agency that it would lose its licence if it didn't finally – after years of complaints – get around to cleaning up the 'urine-like' stench emerging from 'lagoons' of putrid vegetable matter on its site.[83]

Its website boasts that AB Produce is 'managing waste creatively',[84] and I think we can all agree that creating rancid lagoons that reek of urine is pretty creative, but following the warning from the Environment Agency AB Produce went down the more traditional route of paying for equipment to remove the stench.

Unlike Andrew Bridgen, Mark Simmonds, Parliamentary Under Secretary at the Foreign Office, didn't have recourse to a second career, and the poor lamb had been forced to do the only job we were paying him to do. But wait: suddenly, in August, he resigned from his post, claiming it was impossible to live in London on his salary of almost £90,000 (plus inconsequential expenses reported to exceed £500,000 since 2001).[85]

Following the 2009 expenses scandal, the government had stopped MPs from claiming mortgage relief, and this had pushed Simmonds into the absolute penury of having to cope on an average annual income of a mere £117,435.[86]

He was only rescued from the inevitability of the workhouse by the sale of his lowly hovel – for which much of the mortgage and bills for the previous 13 years had been paid by the taxpayer[87] – for a barely-worth-mentioning profit of £537,000, which is more than double the amount an average Briton earns in a lifetime, after which he bought an abbey to live in.[88] Yes, an abbey. Simmonds pointed out all of this was cleared by an internal Conservative Party investigation, and regretted that the new limits on expenses 'can only be a deterrent to people wanting to come into Parliament'.[89]

He was replaced by James Duddridge, who took a markedly different stance towards what he thought he was due from the public trough: in September, having been in the role just a month, he claimed £11,348 in expenses accrued while staying in London hotels, despite already owning two homes in the city. Duddridge said he had used hotels because he was 'working late in London', but had now changed his practices, and was renting a studio flat instead.[90]

There were a few calm days during which nobody had resigned from government, so Foreign Office minister Sayeeda Warsi stepped up by stepping down. This time, the resignation was in protest at Tory policy on Gaza, which she called 'morally indefensible'.[91]

The relentless churn of resignations seemed to just wash over the glazed, slovenly pebble that occupied Downing Street's TV room, but even he wasn't keen on the idea of losing a whole country. So he sat up and noticed in September, when the referendum on Scottish independence was held, and Scotland came vertiginously close to leaving the union.

Exit polls found the stench of Westminster politics was 'the deciding factor' for the 45 per cent of pro-independence Scots. The deciding factor for those who chose to remain part of the union was 'the retention of the pound sterling', which just goes to show having the Queen's head on things *really* mattered a lot to the very people who were content to ignore the Tories selling off the Queen's head as part of Post Office privatisation.[92]

To many Scots, the referendum had been a great disappointment, but they didn't seem to consider it the end of the matter. Membership of the SNP trebled in the two weeks following the referendum,[93] and the Labour Party, which had been the traditional home for Scots who wanted nothing to do with the Tories, now vanished as a political force north of the border; many in Labour had campaigned alongside the Conservatives to reject independence, and that had been the final straw.

Having barely avoided the loss of Scotland, the Tories returned to the loss of ministers. Brooks Newmark, minister for civil society, jumped ship the day before the Tory Party Conference began, after newspapers revealed he'd been exchanging sexually explicit messages with a '20-year-old blonde female party activist'.[94] Brooks had donned paisley pyjamas for their romantic encounter, lending the entire thing a Noël Cowardesque aura of old-world charm, which he then ruined completely by whipping out his tallywacker, taking a photo of it, and sending it off to the poor girl.[95] Except the poor girl wasn't a poor girl at all, but a male undercover reporter from the *Daily Mirror*, who had deliberately targeted him.

In an indication of just how far our nation had fallen, this ungainly carnal collision between a squirrelly tabloid hack and a gullible middle-aged masturbator led Marks & Spencer to sell out of paisley pyjamas.[96] For shame, Britain. For shame.

Newmark became no-mark when he resigned as a minister in September, and then bewilderingly managed to resign a second time in October, this time quitting politics completely: he decided to step down from Parliament when it was revealed he'd also been sending photos of his gigglestick to a second woman.[97] Having been twice outwitted by his own penis, he decided enough was enough. He was, he admitted, 'a complete fool',[98] which at least suggests some degree of self-awareness.

—

Cameron certainly must have been glad the end of a godawful year approached, but as tradition dictates, we must turn once more to Christopher Chope and Eric Pickles for a big finish.

Pickles, who hails from the modern, 'Cameroon' wing of the party, announced that people who leave their dustbins in the road 'should be flogged, flogging is too good for them'.[99] Whereas the more traditionalist Christopher Chope was one of seven white, male Tory MPs to vote against a new policy requiring big companies to reveal the gap in pay between male and female employees. Among the others was cuddly old Aidan Burley,[100] famed for despising the Olympic opening ceremony, and for his attendance to a Nazi-themed stag do. In his defence, an investigation by the Tory party did conclude he had 'not been present during any Nazi chanting'.[101]

And which of us realistically expects more than that from their MP?

2015
A Statesman or a Twat?

I know it's boring. I know it is. But the purpose of politics is not to build Millennium Domes, or to hand money to your pals, and it's not to have bendy buses named after yourself, or screw over the opposition.

The purpose of politics is to do things that improve people's lives.

So let us take a rare – possibly even unique – moment to thank Tory MP Steve Baker, who started 2015 displaying admirable dedication to the theory that politics should make people feel better, by visiting a bit of spare ground by the bins and asking a burly man with a buzzcut and army trousers to kick the shit out of him.[1] Twice.[2]

Baker, who has the ever-so-pleased air of someone desperately longing to be asked if he's solved his Rubik's Cube yet, released videos of the voluntary assaults on YouTube, and they remain the single best thing the Conservative Party achieved in an entire decade.

Perhaps feeling left out of this unexpected orgy of political violence, Nick Clegg went on live TV to announce he had wanted to slap David Cameron at least 20 times, thus putting 19 more of us out of jobs. When asked on a Channel 4 comedy show whether Boris Johnson was a statesman or a twat, Clegg replied: a twat,[3] but apparently the people of Britain still preferred to find that out the hard way.

The motivating impulse behind this sudden flurry of nincompoops, failures and complacent cyborgs experimenting with what it must feel like to have a personality was – of course – the forthcoming general election.

Downing Street feared justifiable criticism during a pre-election debate between the party leaders. Cameron didn't chicken out completely, he simply refused any debate that didn't include all the people he had spent the previous five years telling us were irrelevant nonentities. The more candidates appearing on stage with him, the fewer questions he would have to face. If he could get the numbers up to a good half-dozen, he might only need to answer three questions in the hour. So Cameron declined to appear in any debate unless it included representatives from absolutely everywhere.[4]

'You can't have some minor parties in and not other parties in,' said Downing Street, while drafting invitations to the Monster Raving Loony Party, David Icke, Hornchurch Residents' Association, the Urmston Women's Knitting Circle, and a quick round-up of opinionated indigent boozehounds outside Arnos Grove tube station. Anything to wriggle out of debating Ed Miliband, despite Cameron telling the nation Miliband was too weak to be PM.

Even his own coalition partners couldn't defend the PM. Former Lib Dem leader Paddy Ashdown pointed out that Cameron was not merely proposing a 'ludicrous, seven-sided, bite-sized squabble-fest',[5] but that the Tories wanted to have the debate before their manifesto was even published, so nobody could ask difficult questions about it.

By the time Cameron had managed to increase the guest list to seven, the threat of anybody focusing on his answerability had reduced, so he agreed to a solitary debate, even though the broadcasters planned three of the things.[6]

—

Cameron was too busy running away from scrutiny to tackle much else, least of all housing. The causes of Britain's housing crisis hadn't happened overnight, and they weren't caused by Bulgarians: they were the inevitable outcome of humans having the capacity to reproduce, while houses stubbornly refuse to even try.

In the 1960s, the UK built one new home for every 14 people, recognising that it was very likely some of those people would have children, and that those children would one day need a place to live.[7]

Under the Cameron-led government, that had fallen to one home for every 43 people, and yet sexual intercourse continued to be quite a popular pastime. Each household produces on average 0.6 children, so 43 households would inevitably create around 25 additional people, and in time they'd all want a roof over their heads.

But now those roofs weren't being created.

For a party that claims a unique capacity to understand market forces, the Tories seemed incapable of spotting what would happen if you had a vast demand for a limited supply. By 2015, London house prices were 16 times the average salary, making it all but impossible for practically anybody to buy a home.[8] This shouldn't have come as a shock: a decade earlier the government-backed National Housing and Planning Advice Unit had warned that prices would rise 'inexorably' if we didn't build homes – and lots of them.[9]

The report found we needed 223,000 new homes per year for the next 20 years: the 2015 Conservative Manifesto promised to build 200,000 starter homes, spread over five years – less than 20 per cent of the minimum needed simply to stand still. By 2019 the National Audit Office found they had built absolutely none of those promised homes.[10]

In fact, rather than building, the government *reduced* the availability of homes: in London alone, the stock of social housing had fallen 43,000 since the previous year.[11] Those homes were sold off in the ideological pursuit of the one policy that made Thatcher popular: giving away national assets for a fraction of their value.

All this relentless mismanagement of a basic human need resulted in a 32 per cent fall in the number of people who could afford to buy the home they lived in.[12] The government responded by partially abolishing stamp duty, despite its own Office for Budget Responsibility telling them this would push up house prices yet further, which it did.[13]

Soaring house prices delighted older Tory voters who saw their cheap 1970s mortgages turning into vast piles of unearned wealth that was simultaneously very satisfying and utterly useless, since they could only spend it if they made themselves homeless. But those spiralling prices also pushed increasing numbers of their kids and grandkids into rented accommodation.

Families with children living in privately rented housing tripled by 2015,[14] which in turn pushed the cost of rents higher: the same pressure for limited resources applied to rented properties too. Rents were climbing 8 per cent per year.[15]

As a result of the unremitting unaffordability stoked by Tory housing policies, 20 per cent of those renters relied on housing benefit,[16] which by 2015 was costing the taxpayer an absurd £24.3 billion per year.[17] That's the equivalent of £3,600 per hour, every hour since Magna Carta was signed, and we were handing that out every year, not to the poor, but to landlords. The state gave landlords £2,770,000 every hour. Each year that was enough to build 182,000 average-priced homes, which isn't far short of all the homes we needed.[18]

But if you own an asset, escalating demand means you can charge whatever you want. So if you were a homebuilder or landlord, the last thing you wanted was an additional 182,000 houses per year, because this would reduce your profit margins. It's a coincidence, I'm sure, but property developers had donated at least £3.3 million to Tories before the election[19] and a further £11 million since.[20] And by pure happenstance, they made sizeable profits from the Tory policy of doing all the wrong things to resolve the housing crisis.

The £24 billion per year stream of housing benefit pouring from the public purse was a pretty good deal for landlords, too. And wouldn't you know it? A quarter of Tory MPs turned out to be private landlords, including nine Cabinet ministers.[21]

And then politicians blamed immigrants for taking all the houses.

—

February was a rare month for the Tories, filled as it was with scandal, ineptitude, unfairness, hypocrisy, corruption and lies.

To start with, Caroline Dinenage was made minister for equalities, despite her voting against equal marriage.[22]

Tobias Ellwood backed a move to increase his salary by 10 per cent, while voting to restrict public-sector pay increases to 1 per cent. He excused this by promising to 'watch the pennies',[23] and then the Independent Parliamentary Standards Authority named him as one of a group of MPs who still hadn't repaid overclaimed expenses from the previous year. Ellwood quickly coughed up.[24]

Richard Graham MP was accused of quoting Joseph Goebbels when he defended a surveillance bill with the words 'if you have nothing to hide you have nothing to fear'. Graham, ever capable of grasping the point, said this was 'clearly absurd', because Goebbels would have spoken German.[25]

New MP Lucy Frazer brought her fierce intellect to the West Lothian question during her maiden speech in the House of Commons. This is the constitutional conundrum by which Scottish MPs can vote on matters that affect England, but English MPs cannot vote on matters affecting Scotland. Frazer posited a bold solution. The answer to the West Lothian question, she told the House, was selling Scots into slavery.[26]

Transport Minister Stephen Hammond was one of multiple Tory MPs whose Wikipedia pages were allegedly doctored by computers within the Houses of Parliament,[27] in his case to remove embarrassing information about his frequent use of chauffeur-driven cars: 138 journeys, of which 19 had no human passengers – they were to carry his ministerial red box alone.[28]

As Stephen Hammond's briefcase luxuriated in a publicly funded chauffeur-driven car, we reached 1 million people depending on food banks.[29]

—

The rigorous application of the government's fairness agenda continued to roll out across the nation, as indeed did Eric Pickles.

He announced a cut in central government funding to local councils, which he described as 'fair to all parts of the country'. The cuts, he said, would be an average of 1.8 per cent, which Pickles presented as modest, practically painless, and eminently even-handed.[30]

Analysis by the Chartered Institute of Public Finance and Accountancy (CIPFA) revealed a different picture. The average wasn't 1.8 per cent, but 6 per cent. What was even more telling than the whopping exaggeration – or stupefying arithmetical error – was the distribution of those cuts: poorer, Labour-voting councils in London and the North saw cuts of up to 8 per cent, while 17 wealthy, Tory-led councils in the Home Counties had budget *increases* of between 2 and 3.2 per cent.[31]

When he was an opposition MP, Eric Pickles had argued in favour of an independent body to allocate local authority funding, but ever since he'd had the opportunity to give his own side 10 per cent more money in an election year, he had become curiously reticent on the topic. Even after CIPFA had publicly called his spin 'disingenuous'[32] (posh accountancy-speak for 'bollocks'), there was little contrition from Pickles about his struggle with basic mathematics, or his facility with blatant pork-barrel politics. After all, there was a vote coming, and the last thing we needed was a scandal.

And yet one arrived a few days later, when Sir Malcolm Rifkind, chair of the Intelligence Committee, was discovered to be too stupid to remember he got paid for his job. He became yet another Tory MP captured on film allegedly offering access to power in exchange for bungs of iffy money.

'I'm self-employed. Nobody pays me a salary,' Rifkind said,[33] which will have come as a surprise to the taxpayers who funded his MP's salary of £67,000.

Sir Malcolm, who was also the former chairman of the Standards and Privileges Committee,[34] went on to boast that in exchange for at least £5,000 per day and no questions asked,[35] he could arrange contact with any ambassador worldwide, reassuring his generous benefactor that he had plenty of time to dedicate to such activities because 'you'd be surprised how much free time I have'.[36]

He had even more free time after the footage was broadcast and he was suspended from the Conservative Party.[37]

There was a realistic chance that the stench of endemic sleaze would overwhelm Cameron's election chances, but fortunately independent health experts The King's Fund distracted the public's gaze with a report that called Tory NHS changes 'disastrous'.

The reforms had created a system that was 'designed to streamline and simplify the organisation of the NHS [yet] ended up having the opposite effect'. It was 'bewildering in its complexity' and left the NHS with a 'strategic vacuum'. The report concluded the Tories had wasted three years, caused huge financial distress, and failed patients.[38]

—

Given all of this, you can hardly blame Cameron for wanting to give it all up and spend more time with his box sets; in March he announced that he wouldn't serve a third term in office if he won the election.[39] Little did he know he'd barely serve a second term.

As if things weren't going badly enough for the PM, Oxford University published a report in March that conclusively proved a statistical link between political donations and nominations for peerages.[40] It said that while it could find no cast-iron proof that any *specific* peerage had been sold, there was a significant relationship between donations given and honours received.

This book will now pause while you have a lie down to recover from the shock.

The research ignored people who could normally be expected to become peers – high-ranking officials, former parliamentarians, and 'people's peers' nominated by the public. The remaining 92 life peers had donated 98.9 per cent of all the donations coming from the Lords.

A donation is not the same as a bribe. They are very different things; although just occasionally, by mere chance, they can produce similar results.

The Tory peerages included Lords Farmer, Fink and Bamford, each of whom parted with seven-figure donations,[41] while lucky Lord Edmiston handed over a mere £377,000.[42] Perhaps the Tories were running a Black Friday.

Awkward questions about money simply would not go away. It suddenly became increasingly difficult to defend the speed and savagery of austerity, as Britain finally finished repaying its debts from the First World War.[43] Massive debt, including that from both the First and Second World Wars, had not prevented us from building the NHS, welfare state, road infrastructure, and at least 4.4 million social houses.[44]

It's perfectly legitimate to ask why slashing public debt in just five years was suddenly so essential. Was it economics? Or merely a spasm of cruel political opportunism that made it possible to ideologically shrink the state while placing the blame for all the pain on Labour?

If you think the answer was 'economics', allow me to draw your attention to two small facts.

One: you're wrong.

Two: the economics wasn't working anyway. In April economic growth halved again,[45] which honest George Osborne met with the words, 'It's good news that the economy has continued to grow,' despite the fact that average wages had fallen almost 10 per cent on his watch,[46] and had dropped by more in the UK than in almost any other developed nation.[47] Of 26 large economies measured by the London School of Economics (LSE), only three had wages that had dropped further than ours. Twenty of those countries saw wages grow by up to 13 per cent.[48]

'Today is a reminder that you can't take the recovery for granted,' said Osborne. 'The future of our economy is on the ballot paper at this election.'[49]

Yes, George, but not in the way you mean.

Three issues were most important to voters heading into the election: the economy, health and immigration.[50] Economically, the government was performing shockingly badly – the worst recovery from a recession since records began, and three times slower than the recovery from the Wall Street Crash of 1929.[51] And now more terrible news arrived about health, as the NHS Support Federation produced analysis showing NHS privatisation had grown by 500 per cent in the last year alone, when only 7 per cent of the public wanted that to happen.[52] Even among Tory voters, only 13 per cent wanted it.[53]

Having failed miserably on two of the three highest priorities for the public, the Tories latched on to immigration as an area where they could campaign without shame; and they were certainly shameless in their relentless hammering home of UKIP's message, despite the number of people migrating into the UK falling.

But battling problems that don't exist is a great way to distract from problems that do. Here's a fine example: in the 1979 Winter of Discontent, the UK lost 29 million days to strike action,[54] but by 2015 that was down to 169,000, a fall of 99.5 per cent.[55] Tories were desperate for us to believe there was a strike crisis as we lost – brace yourself for a terrifying figure – 0.002 per cent of the nation's total working hours in 2015, which, if you do the maths, equates to everybody turning up to work 30 seconds late on a single day. It was clearly crippling us.

So obviously, it was suddenly essential to make it almost impossible to strike at all. Cameron announced that in future, a strike would be illegal unless it was supported by 40 per cent of people who were eligible to vote for industrial action.[56] He could propose this law because he was prime minister, having received the support of 23 per cent[57] of people eligible to vote.[58]

While many Tories cheered his pointless promise to end strikes that never happened anyway, Michael Gove kept his head down, probably to avoid questions about the time he joined the picket lines in support of a strike by the National Union of Journalists.[59]

—

The election campaign reached its crescendo as David Cameron visited Croydon and forgot which football team he was supposed to be a fan of. 'I'd rather you supported West Ham,' he told an invited audience,[60] despite having previously claimed to be a big fan of Aston Villa.

I miss the days when this was considered a fuck-up by a prime minister.

Cameron then provided the tweet that sums up his premiership in the minds of the public: 'Britain faces a simple and inescapable choice – stability and strong Government with me, or chaos with Ed Miliband.'[61]

Can we rewind and pick chaos, please?

By April, it already looked like Labour was going to lose the election, despite the scrupulous fairness of the coverage they received. Unlike 2010, when out of 23 major newspapers only two backed Labour, this time there was a fastidious focus on balance: four now backed Labour, and the others were rigorous in their appraisals of the last five years.

On one side, you had the Tories, who had vandalised the NHS, wrecked the economy, inflated our debts, sabotaged countless public services, incapacitated the legal system, buggered up schools and universities, sold off democracy, lied, cheated, abandoned thousands to flooding, increased inequality, doubled homelessness, impoverished the sick, women and minorities, squandered untold billions, and pursued a policy of austerity that led directly to the deaths of at least 120,000 people.[62]

But on the other side you had Ed Miliband, who looked a bit funny eating a sandwich. It was a tough choice.

But before we went to the polls, there was just time for one more appearance by Mark Menzies, Tory MP for Fylde, in a spot of bother again barely a year after hiring a Brazilian sex worker, showing him around the House of Commons, and then asking him to supply crystal meth.[63]

Troubles seemed to haunt Mr Menzies, who now found himself questioned by police after being accused of going round to a friend's house, then locking himself inside and feeding alcohol to his mate's dog, until the two men got into a shitfaced brawl, which spilled out onto the streets.[64]

Police didn't charge Menzies, who, thankfully, was able to provide evidence that he hadn't poured alcohol into a dog: he had simply stood around taking photos while his friend poured alcohol into a dog, and that's exactly the behaviour you would expect from the person you have elected to represent you in Parliament. The dog lived, with a vet's bill of £500, but God alone knows what it would cost to remedy whatever the hell it is that afflicts Mark Menzies.

Menzies was re-elected that same month, with 49 per cent of the vote.[65] People of Fylde: take a long, hard look at yourselves.

In fact, people of Britain: likewise. Despite five years of relentless misery, cruelty, ineptitude, failure, corruption, and craven, grasping self-interest, in May 2015 we elected a Conservative government. The Lib Dems were gone. It was the first time a Tory had won a general election for 22 years.

—

Miliband resigned as Labour leader. Clegg resigned too, although it didn't affect British politics very much, since his acquiescence to the previous five years of broiling catastrophe had reduced the Lib Dems to a paltry eight MPs. You can fit 12 in a phone box.[66]

Nigel Farage also resigned as leader of UKIP. He claimed he had 'never felt happier' about failing to become an MP, which is difficult to square with his two-decade battle to be elected to Parliament, involving seven attempts in five constituencies, and not a single success.[67] But logic and Nigel were never comfortable bedfellows, and he was barely on nodding terms with bashful reserve. Having resigned as leader (again), he suddenly realised the cameras no longer pointed his way, so he immediately unresigned as leader (again).[68]

Farage was proof that despite the election, all the fucking horrible problems that cursed our nation still existed, not least of which was housing. Despite throwing £2,770,000 of housing benefit every hour at private landlords, they were now evicting tenants at double the rate they had when the coalition entered power.[69]

Fortunately, Osborne the Cruel suddenly turned into Osborne the Beneficent: his post-victory Budget offered to cut social rents by a wildly generous 1 per cent, as part of a package that also – probably best skim over this bit – prevented 27,000 new homes being built, which obviously had the effect of increasing prices by more than 1 per cent.[70] Meanwhile benefits were frozen for another four years, during which inflation would also wipe out that 1 per cent rent cut. Oh, and housing benefit was abolished completely for people under 21.[71]

So: the poorest people in our society got practically nothing, which the government then took back, and Osborne engineered the housing market to make it even more expensive.

But what about wealthy people who owned massively expensive homes? How did they come out of the Budget? Prepare yourself for a shock: they did rather well. Corporation tax, already one of the lowest in the world,[72] urgently needed cutting again so Britain could compete with *absolutely nobody*, because we were already one of the lowest in the world. From a rate of 28 per cent a decade earlier,[73] Osborne now planned to drop it to a mere 18 per cent,[74] meaning Shell, the oil and gas giant, would pay half the tax rate a doctor does. That's assuming big corporations paid tax at all: the Tories also announced the closure of 137 tax offices and loss of 11,000 staff from HMRC, which is exactly what you'd do if you were attempting to tackle tax avoidance.[75]

And while giant corporations benefited from that corporation tax giveaway, their shareholders were relishing changes to inheritance tax: the threshold was increased to £1 million,[76] which Tories pretended was a great advance for common people, even though it only affected the richest one out of every 20 people, and one out of every one of them would be dead.[77]

However, things were still very much alive – briskly so – outside the House of Commons, as 150,000 people marched in the People's Assembly Against Austerity. It made Tory MPs feel very cross, and made everybody participating feel very cross, and it achieved absolutely nothing. A bit like this book. The Tories had won the election; they didn't need to even pretend to listen to voters for another five years.[78] The protests affected government thinking so much that they had barely ended before Osborne ordered Whitehall to draw up plans for Austerity 2.0, and another 40 per cent cut in public spending.[79]

The Institute of Fiscal Studies found that by 2015, GDP per adult was 18 per cent lower than it would have been if growth had continued at the rate when Labour left office and austerity began; but that didn't matter any more.[80] Osborne's previous debt-reducing Budget cuts had pushed our debt from 62 per cent of GDP to 80 per cent, but that didn't matter either.[81]

All that mattered was dementedly cutting things, oblivious to the mountain of evidence that if you starved the economy of most of the money and all of the hope, you'd end up with a hopeless economy and no money. But Osborne's solution was: more of the same. He was operating on the rationale that if you hang a man and he dies, the best thing to do is to keep on hanging him until he gets used to it.

—

In July, Michael Gove's then wife, Sarah Vine, used her *Daily Mail* column to deliver heart-rending news to a rapt nation: the beloved Michael had broken his foot, and lo, the people did weep.[82]

Rumours that he'd gone out tramp-kicking and had accidentally booted one that was frozen were swiftly dispelled: he had, in fact, tripped over a toy in the middle of the night.

Nicely played, Buzz Lightyear. Nicely played.

Vine claimed she had taken Gove to a minor injuries unit, where she was told they didn't do X-rays at weekends, and he'd have to go home in excruciating pain, and simply suffer until the radiologist could be bothered to do his bloody job.[83] And lo, the people did weep, and wipe their eyes, and say, 'Oh my aching sides.'

Fortuitously, this incident coincided with the government's push to force junior doctors to work seven days a week for no extra money, and Vine used her column as evidence that the policy must be introduced immediately.

Less fortuitously, a slight problem undermined her argument, and it was this: the entire thing was complete bullshit.[84] Not the 'Buzz Lightyear Broke Michael Gove's Foot' bit, I'm happy to say, but the 'No X-rays at Weekends' bit. It was bollocks. There wasn't a radiology department at the unit they attended, so there was no way she could have been told it was closed at weekends; the Independent Press Standards Organisation called the claims 'significantly misleading'.

The doctored attempt to discredit doctors was discredited, so the government sought other ways to try to force dangerously overworked medics to work even longer hours and the NHS continued to move towards unprecedented strike action.

Talks broke down in acrimony as junior doctors earning £28,800[85] – half the salary of a store manager at Aldi[86] – were told they'd lose almost any chance of earning the overtime that made their lives financially viable. The British Medical Association found the strikes had the backing of 98 per cent of staff, and 20,000 doctors attended a protest rally in London. It was to be the first NHS strike action for 40 years.[87]

Joining Vine and Gove in peddling inaccuracy was Iain Duncan Smith's department, which admitted inventing quotes in one of their advice leaflets that appeared to show how delighted people were to get lower benefits.[88] The story of 'Sarah' revealed how she was 'really pleased' to get less money than it takes to survive, because it motivated her to update her CV. 'It's going to help me when I'm ready to go back to work,' wrote 'Sarah', revelling in the comfort that IDS's reforms couldn't kill her because she didn't even exist.

People who did exist were dying all over the place, but this didn't change Duncan Smith's mind, because that also didn't exist. IDS's own department's figures showed 2,380 people had died shortly after his work capability assessments had declared them fit to work.[89] He followed up this cheery bit of news with the announcement that he was about to make a further £12 billion in welfare cuts. The government's own child poverty advisers said the cuts were 'highly likely to raise child poverty', and so IDS announced he was also scrapping legally binding child poverty targets.[90]

'I believe that the best route out of poverty is work,' said Duncan Smith, either failing to grasp that children no longer go down mines and up chimneys, or suggesting that they should.[91]

Meanwhile, at the other end of the financial spectrum, the government produced a list of all the new life peers they were creating: 26 lovely new Tory votes in the House of Lords, including James Lupton (who donated £3 million)[92] and Stuart Polak (£377,994).[93]

—

The hatred of immigrants in our newspapers continued unabated. 'Mass immigration will DESTROY Britain' screamed the *Express*.[94] 'Britain is a magnet for migrants' howled the *Daily Mail*.[95] 'UK's migrant invasion is OUT OF CONTROL'[96] and 'End This Migrant Madness'[97] they bellowed. The camp used by a group of 6,000 migrants outside Calais had become known as 'the Jungle', as if its residents were animals.[98] When around 2,000 of them attempted to cross into the UK, newspapers reported it as if it were a literal annexation of our sacred soil.[99]

Calmer voices struggled to be heard. Even if the UK had accepted every one of those 6,000 people, it's extremely unlikely we would notice. There are 66 million people in the UK, distributed among 48,000 cities, towns and villages. Six thousand extra people is one individual for every eight towns. The chances of you ever meeting one of those immigrants is tiny. The chance of your life being materially affected by their presence in the country is ludicrously miniscule.

But to tackle a problem that would have zero effect on you, the government introduced ever more drastic immigration restrictions, preventing the valid – indeed essential – immigration upon which much of our infrastructure depended. By 2015, these policies had already led to a 24,000 shortfall in nursing numbers.[100] The Royal College of Nursing predicted that by 2020, the recruiting fees for finding nurses to replace those driven out of the NHS by the government's immigration policy would exceed £178 million.[101] That's not the nurses' wages: that's just the cost of recruitment.

But regardless of how irrational the fear of migrants had become, and the harm being caused by policies that simultaneously responded to and exacerbated that fear, the horror of Johnny Foreigner just kept on mounting and mounting.

And then, on 2 September, a single photograph seemed to change everything.[102]

On front pages across the world, there appeared the serene image of three-year-old Alan Kurdi, his feet neatly collected together, his arms calm by his side, looking for all the world like he'd nodded off after playtime. The heart-rending truth was that he was not peacefully resting. He was dead. Drowned while attempting to flee the Syrian conflict, lost in what must have been unimaginable terror beneath the Mediterranean waves, and now washed up by the seas, dumped cold and lifeless in the gentle surf of a Turkish seaside resort.

Except, of course, the photo changed nothing. It paused tabloid ravings for a while, and for a few short days in late summer the visceral voices of Britain's anti-immigrant right were silenced. But the right had breezily ignored the other 3,771 migrants who drowned in the Mediterranean in 2015,[103] 10 people per day experiencing the same terminal terror that overwhelmed Alan Kurdi, and it was a pretty safe bet they'd ignore the 5,143 who went on to drown in 2016 too.[104]

They had form: only three months before the photo of Alan Kurdi appeared, the government had said 'the UK has a proud history of offering asylum to those who need it most',[105] yet we had offered asylum to only 174 (not a typo)[106] of the 6 million refugees fleeing the Syrian conflict.[107] And then Home Secretary Theresa May refused[108] to take part in the emergency resettlement plan hammered out by the international community.[109]

Following Alan Kurdi's death, David Cameron sombrely announced Britain would now welcome 20,000 Syrian refugees,[110] but one-third of local councils refused to take any of them: not because of xenophobia, but because Cameron's cuts left them incapable of caring for displaced persons.[111] The resettlement handouts the government provided covered only 70 per cent of the costs. Local government had already been bled to the bone and, as a result, 60 per cent of the refugees we promised to rescue could not be homed here.[112]

—

In September Labour elected Jeremy Corbyn as the next person it wanted to lose a general election. Once he'd finished giggling about what Labour had decided to do to itself, David Cameron tweeted: 'The Labour Party is now a threat to our national security, our economic security and your family's security.'[113] The same David Cameron introduced the biggest defence cuts since the 1980s,[114] mislaid 18 per cent of our economic performance,[115] and pushed 143,500 households into homelessness.[116] There was ample opportunity for a fast, witty and agile opposition to turn Cameron's attack back on himself, but this didn't happen, for two reasons.

Firstly, we didn't have a fast, witty or agile opposition.

And secondly, overnight, nobody cared any more, because the greatest news story in history had just landed. David Cameron, as part of an initiation ceremony into an exclusive university dining society, had inserted his penis into a dead pig.[117]

It's almost impossible to follow that sentence with any kind of sensible analysis, but let's try anyway.

Lord Ashcroft, the billionaire former chairman of the Tory party, had for a long time been its biggest donor. Over the years he had given something like £10 million to the party. But in 2013, his generosity suddenly ended when he fell out with Cameron over the PM's refusal to give him a senior role in government. This isn't a supposition based on the traditional relationship between donations and jobs: in the foreword to *Call Me Dave*, the book that contained the piggy allegation, Ashcroft flatly states his sense of betrayal over not getting the job he felt he, and maybe his donations, deserved.[118]

A donation is not the same as a bribe, so let's be perfectly clear about that. They are very different things, although just occasionally they can produce similar results.

But not this time.

So Ashcroft decided to fund a book about the PM, and include all the salacious stories he could find, including Cameron smoking weed, cocaine 'circulating' at dinner parties at Cameron's home, and what in other circumstances might be the most nauseating and scandalous exposé of all: Cameron's love of defunct prog-rockers Supertramp.[119]

While Ashcroft was researching the book in 2014, an MP and 'distinguished Oxford contemporary' of Cameron's happened to tell a story at a business dinner they were both attending; he explained how, in order to join the prestigious Piers Gaveston Society, Cameron had been obliged – how can I put this delicately? – to whap his dingus into the mouth of a pig carcass, in full view of everybody at the dinner table. At first, Ashcroft and his co-author Isabel Oakeshott dismissed it as a blue joke or wild exaggeration. But a few weeks later, the same MP repeated the allegation, and then did so a third time, with even richer detail, a few months on.

The source was widely assumed to be either Mark Field, the party vice-chairman, or Ed Vaizey, the culture minister, or Boris Johnson, the amoral tuft of regurgitated cud, cursed into life by a passing necromancer. Each of them fitted Ashcroft's vague description of the person who told the tale, and all three denied it, although one of them is not renowned for his adherence to honesty.

Social media went absolutely insane: so much of Britain's time was spent exchanging pig jokes on Twitter that there were official concerns it could affect UK productivity figures.[120]

Cameron denied everything about the story, of course, but can you imagine any circumstances under which somebody would admit to it? Regardless of whether it was true or not (and it probably wasn't), the public was inclined to believe it because it was hilarious, and because it fitted neatly into our assumptions about Cameron's character.

He (along with Boris Johnson) had been a member of the infamous Bullingdon Club, which as part of its initiation requires candidates to burn a £50 note in front of a homeless person.[121] It engages in ostentatious awfulness, flamboyant shittiness, superhuman wankery, and the boisterous vandalism of restaurants, followed up by on-the-spot cash payment for any damage done, simply to show how little money matters to you. Its behaviour is so bad that the club has been banned from meeting anywhere closer than 15 miles from Oxford University.[122] The original exclusion zone around Chernobyl was only 18 miles.[123]

Cameron could have put the matter to bed, of course. He could have sued Ashcroft, and he would almost certainly have won any libel case, but instead, he said he was 'too busy running the country',[124] having just returned from his 15th holiday since becoming prime minister.[125]

And so the story remains denied, but not disproven; and unless lawyers advise otherwise, it might still be legal to go on social media and joke that David Cameron is guilty of cruelty, necrophilia and bestiality.

But that's just flogging a dead horse.

—

Four months earlier, in June, Philip Davies had posed with carers and Macmillan Cancer nurses for a photograph, which shows him smiling and holding a plaque that reads 'I pledge to speak up for carers in Parliament'.[126]

He wasn't wrong about speaking: in October, along with regular contributor Christopher Chope, Davies filibustered a proposal to limit car-parking charges paid by carers at NHS hospitals.[127] There was a time limit on the debate, and if it ran out of time, the legislation would inevitably fail: Davies slowly spoke for 93 insufferable minutes, the clock ticked down, and carers still pay an average of £53 per week to park at hospitals.[128]

On 10 January 2015, Philip Davies claimed expenses of £4.17 for car parking.[129]

He repeated his little act of sabotage in November, this time speaking for 52 minutes to prevent legislation ensuring children are taught first aid in schools.[130] The proposal was backed by St John Ambulance, the British Red Cross and the British Heart Foundation, but that didn't seem to matter to Davies.[131] The debate ran out of time, and he went home presumably feeling he'd really helped the nation.

Much darker news emerged that same month, with the suicide of Tory youth activist Elliott Johnson, at the age of just 21.[132] He left behind a note blaming Conservative parliamentary candidate Mark Clarke for bullying him; in the wake of Johnson's death, an increasing number of stories emerged about Clarke, widely reported by reputable newspapers.

Mark Clarke issued denials, but not lawsuits.

Clarke seemed woven into the fabric of young Tory grassroots. He had been chairman of Conservative Future, a grouping for Tories under 30, which is now defunct, maybe because of the allegations about Clarke's behaviour, and partly because there are vanishingly few Tories under 30. He had also been chairman of the Young Britons' Foundation, a thinktank and pressure group which its own chief executive described as 'a Conservative madrasa' that 'radicalises young Tories', and which backed the use of waterboarding, and arranged day trips to meet fellow Conservatives and fire submachine guns with them.[133]

Clarke founded the RoadTrip campaign, bussing young Tories into marginal constituencies ahead of the 2015 election.[134] RoadTrip was personally endorsed by Grant Shapps and had the backing of Conservative campaign HQ, although it seemed less popular with the local associations they would roll up to help.

'They were utterly useless,' reported one local member. 'They were more interested in ensuring they could develop their career opportunities.'[135] Well, yeah: what else would you expect from a parcel of young Conservatives? The group was described as drunk and chaotic, and when sent out canvassing, one member spent two hours attempting to take a perfect photo for his Twitter account and delivered just two leaflets in a day. Frankly, we need more of this sort of thing from the Conservatives.

But it wasn't all fun. Clarke ended up facing accusations of bullying, harassing and threatening the young activists in his care. There were claims of sexual harassment and even sexual assault, and suggestions that Clarke had filmed people – including MPs – engaging in sexual activity, with the goal of using the material for blackmail.[136]

Tory MP Robert Halfon admitted to an affair with the chair of Conservative Future apparently after he became convinced Clarke was about to blackmail him.[137] Ben Howlett, another MP, told the BBC that he had 'warned the party leadership about Clarke's behaviour and felt personally bullied in a way that affected my health'.[138]

The chief of staff to the Tory party's chairman had raised concerns about Clarke's behaviour a year before Elliott Johnson's suicide. 'I made several formal complaints to the party about his behaviour,' he said, 'along with other young people who [Clarke] has tried to blackmail or threaten. He is an appalling man and I wish I had never met him.'[139]

That was in 2014. In July 2015, the National Conservative Convention confirmed its intention that Clarke's RoadTrip campaign would continue until 2020.[140]

Following the tragic death of Elliott Johnson, all those threads tying Clarke to the future of Conservatism came undone. Grant Shapps, who had been chairman when all of this was going on and was now international development minister, resigned from his post, the blow softened by his decision to take an entirely optional £8,000 'golden goodbye' from the taxpayer, cos disgrace doesn't mean you need to take whatever money is available.[141] He denied knowledge of Clarke's behaviour,[142] although his predecessor, Baroness Warsi, produced a letter she had written to Shapps, telling him about the bullying, blackmail and sexual abuse allegations, and asking him to take action.[143]

It's amazing just how much the Tories had been prepared to overlook. It was alleged that as early as 2010 a 20-page dossier of evidence against Mark Clarke had been passed to Lord Feldman, who was then Tory chairman; no action was taken, and Feldman maintains he hadn't been aware of the allegations.[144]

In the end, even after Elliott Johnson's death, Clarke faced no charges: the Crown Prosecution Service said there was insufficient evidence.[145] But he was thrown out of the party for life because Tories simply will not put up with lying and bullying.[146]

The following week, Tory MP Lucy Allan was accused by several members of her staff of bullying,[147] and then posted an email on Facebook that she had doctored to make it look like a death threat. The email had come from a constituent, and Allan had added the words 'unless you die' at the end.[148]

Allan claimed the addition was done by accident, and who among us hasn't 'accidentally' copied words from one email, pasted them at the end of another, added the correct punctuation, composed our own introduction, and posted it on Facebook?

2016
Nonsense on Stilts

On 11 March 1702 – 80 years after the Germans did it – Britain gained its first daily newspaper, the *Daily Courant*.[1] It shouldn't be remarkable, but this is the world we live in, so it is: the first editor was a woman, Elizabeth Mallet. She set up a premises next door to a tavern on Fleet Street, London, and over three centuries later journalism is still inseparably associated with that location. And with taverns.

The *Daily Courant* stated its aims with admirable rectitude and probity: Mallet announced she would not add any comments of her own to the news she reported, on the basis that she imagined readers would have 'sense enough to make reflections for themselves'. A lovely idea, which lasted a surprisingly long time: 40 days, after which the newspaper was bought out by the future publisher of the *Spectator*, who relocated it to a place called Little Britain.

You may laugh darkly now.

Fast-forward to December 2015, when Ipsos MORI found only 1 per cent of Britons considered the EU and Europe to be the most important issue facing Britain.[2] And that's where opinion should have stayed, were it not for the obsessions of a small group of utter bastards who had taken Elizabeth Mallet's dream of unbiased reporting and turned it into Britain's deranged tabloid industry.

Chief among these were Rupert Murdoch, the Barclay Brothers (who own the *Telegraph*) and Viscount Rothermere (largest shareholder of the *Daily Mail* group of newspapers).[3] Between them, these four fiercely right-wing libertarian men – each of them tax exiles[4] – owned 68 per cent of Britain's print media, and set the tone for the rest.

Mainstream Tory hostility towards Europe had been kickstarted by Thatcher's opposition to the EU's moves towards closer integration,[5] which – amongst other things – implied the UK would have to match European standards and workers' rights, things she had just spent 10 wild-eyed years brutally dismantling in Britain. Her response was a famous 1988 anti-EU rant, which has been elevated to the status of holy writ by the Tory press, partly because it showcased the stentorian Maggie they loved – haranguing the nation, and stridently shouting 'no, no, no!' at Johnny Foreigner – and partly because it reflected their own narrow interests in preventing the EU from re-establishing the workers' rights they preferred to avoid.

But mainly because shouting about the EU sold a lot of papers, and you didn't even need to print things that were vaguely honest, as ace hotshot-slash-bullshit reporter Boris Johnson had proven.

The issue of Europe had precipitated the end of Thatcher,[6] made life an unholy nightmare for John Major, and wreaked havoc throughout the leaderships of Michael Howard, Iain Duncan Smith and William Hague. Throughout that 30-year period, Labour, the Lib Dems, the SNP and every other party in these islands had been almost entirely unaffected by the debates about the EU, because it had nothing to do with them, with this country, or indeed with Europe: it was an internal party war that was best left to those nutters in the blue rosettes.

Cameron was determined to put an end to the squabbling by tearing the entire country apart instead, so the battles inside his party would finally seem comparatively normal.

But first, he kicked off a hectic and vitally important 2016 by informing the *Spectator* that he was spending his hours watching his new favourite show, *The Last Panthers*. The news of his incomparable torpor barely raised an eyebrow, until the next episode of the crime drama, which described him as 'a cunt'.[7]

It had been filmed months before, but clearly his reputation had preceded him, rather than this being an entirely natural response to

January's parliamentary vote on making rented homes fit for human habitation. As an indication of exactly how much the Conservatives cared about the population, every one of the 309 Tory MPs voted against the motion.[8]

Philip Davies protested that making the properties he rented out fit for humans to live in would be a 'huge burden'.[9] He was only one of 72 Tory MPs who are also landlords and voted the bill down, including Chris Grayling, Jacob Rees-Mogg, David Cameron, Thérèse Coffey and Geoffrey Cox.[10]

Cox presumably felt he could justify voting to keep his tenants in subhuman conditions because he was having to cope on such a miserly income: in addition to his MP's salary of £74,000, he had found the time to do £820,000 of legal work, because helping to run a country and representing his constituents wasn't keeping him busy.[11] If he's your MP, perhaps you should consider whether he's required at all?

Cox also sat on the Committee on Standards and Privileges for a while, but had to resign in 2016 after it was found he missed out on registering another £400,000 of freelance work. Though he did find time to enter an expense claim for a 49p bottle of milk.[12]

The money claimed by MPs was always a bit of a challenge for Cameron: the expenses scandal had emerged in 2009, before the Tories took office, and as an opposition leader, David Cameron had loudly proclaimed his disgust, and his desire to solve the problem. 'I don't care if they were within the rules, they were wrong,'[13] he said about the wildly disproportionate claims being brought to light, including the £1,000 a month he had personally claimed for a second home.[14] He didn't know this was 'wrong' until he was found out.

He proposed fundamental changes, which he described as a 'radical redistribution of power', and you can probably already predict what happened next: in the five years following Cameron's entrance to 10 Downing Street, expenses claimed by MPs increased by 43 per cent.[15]

Ben Bradley, that fan of police brutality and the involuntary sterilisation of the poor, was merely a Tory councillor at this point, but that didn't prevent him from being yet another arch-opponent of money wasting. As we entered February, he kept himself busy hunting down anybody guilty of profligacy with the public purse.

'I have just discovered that our wonderful Ashfield District Council,' he wrote, 'has spent £17,000 this month on paying an Indian company to call 1,000 residents in Ashfield from a call centre in Mumbai to ask what you think of council services.'

It turned out to be a complete fabrication. 'I admit the post about using an Indian call centre was untrue,' Bradley confessed. 'I was just emphasising the point that the council was wasting money.'[16]

In 2017 he became an MP and claimed £151,000 in expenses.[17]

—

The response of the government was essentially: ignore all that, and let's have a Brexit. Cameron announced the promised referendum would go ahead in 2016, and normal politics pretty much stopped dead. Over the coming weeks, the two armies arranged themselves.

Cameron was for Remain, as was every living former prime minister. Remain had the backing of 479 MPs, compared with Leave's 158. As an indication of how much this was a purely Conservative issue, only 10 Labour MPs backed Leave. Other than the Democratic Unionist Party (DUP) and the two former Tories who had defected to UKIP, no MP from any other party wanted us to leave the EU.[18]

It was clear to even the most profound dunderhead that having Cameron at the Remain helm would crash the ship: a third of the nation hated him, a third of the nation voted for him despite disagreeing with him about Europe, and the remaining third found it hard to distinguish between him and a tin of Spam that had been upended onto a TV chair. And since the referendum would end up being largely a protest vote against the government – because referendums always are – if Remain were going to win, they needed to be distinguished from Cameron's Tories as much as possible.

So instead of being directed by a capable MP or widely popular figurehead, the official Remain campaign, named Britain Stronger in Europe, was led by people you have literally forgotten existed, or would be shocked to learn existed at all.

Remain's main guy was Stuart Rose.[19] What do you mean, you've never heard of Stuart Rose? He was famous – if that's the word – as the CEO of Argos two decades earlier, and then as a non-executive director of Woolworths in South Africa, where presumably pick 'n' mix is still a thing.[20] His biggest impact on British headlines had been the time he was chairman of Marks & Spencer during the period it lost 40 per cent of its value.[21]

Rose was unconstrained by campaigning experience, political nous, or any recognisability factor whatsoever. He was, to the general public, nothing and nobody. Yet this was the man Remain put up against Boris Johnson, that mendacious, scheming supernova of charisma, if not integrity, who was famed throughout the land for his bikes, his bridges, his positively barnyard breeding habits,[22] and for battering a 10-year-old boy to the ground in an ad hoc game of rugby.[23]

In one of his first acts as chairman, Stuart Rose did a piece to camera in which he made five consecutive failed attempts at remembering the name of the campaign he was leading.

'I'm chairman of Ocado. Sorry, I'm chairman of, sorry, of Stay in Britain, Better in Britain campaign. Right, start again! I'm Stuart Rose and I'm the chairman of the Better in Britain campaign, Better Stay in Britain campaign.'[24]

Well done, Stuart. Just spiffing.

Fortunately, he could still fix everything by going in front of a parliamentary committee, as long as he avoided doing anything stupid, such as telling them everybody's wages would rise if we leave the EU.

He went in front of a parliamentary committee and told them that everyone's wages would rise if we left the EU.

Despite insisting he was misquoted, Rose was sidelined, and the leader of the Remain campaign effectively vanished from public view.[25]

As luck would have it, Remain had a spare failed nonentity in case of such an eventuality. He appeared in the irregular, mildly undulating shape of Danny Alexander; you've just googled Danny Alexander, because you vaguely recognise the name, but can't place him. Don't deny it.

You will have discovered he looked like a preternaturally large, orange child, and until you read this page, you'd forgotten he even existed. That's even true if this sentence is being read by Danny Alexander's immediate family. He was, is, and always will be an uninspiring, redundant Lib Dem whose greatest achievement in life was agreeing to have a beer named in his honour: it's called 'Ginger Rodent', and he's absolutely fine with that.[26]

Filling out the front row of the Remain campaign was Damian Green, a government minister mainly associated with the quite bewildering quantities of pornography discovered on his computer.[27] This triumvirate was the Remain movement's plan to disassociate themselves from the Tories in the forthcoming referendum: two of them were Tories, and the other was a former member of a Tory-led coalition.

But rather than risk being comprised entirely of personality vacuums and creepy rejects from the recently dismantled coalition government, they invited along Peter Mandelson, an eerie four-legged arachnid looming from the darkness like an apparition from your most harrowing nightmare. And to further entertain the electorate, Remain included June Sarpong, presenter of a TV show in which she and Derek Acorah went searching for the ghost of Michael Jackson. They didn't have much luck with that, or, indeed, with the referendum campaign.

Opposing them were two pro-Brexit teams: the official group was called Vote Leave and had been established by Dominic Cummings and Matthew Elliott, who is founder of both the TaxPayers' Alliance and Conservative Friends of Russia, a fact that should really set your mind at ease. With just two exceptions, every member of the Vote Leave campaign committee was a Tory MP or MEP.[28]

The campaign was led by viciously polite ventriloquist's doll Michael Gove, and he packed his team with talent. There was Steve Baker, last seen urging a brawny man to beat him senseless by the bins, but now upright again, and resuming his original role as a complacent cyborg assembled in an underground laboratory from bits of discarded sociopath.

Iain Duncan Smith wanted to join in the fun, so he managed to pry himself away from his (presumed) hobby of biting the faces off live puppies and began dragging his sepulchral corpse from studio to studio, whispering nothing sweet into the ears of the nation.

Priti Patel was there, like a smirking, razor-faced angel of death. They had bellowing Oompa-Loompa Mark Francois and disgraced former minister Liam Fox. They were joined by the bellend's bellend, Chris Grayling, and former Chancellor Nigel Lawson, a wheezing antique chamois leather who was campaigning against our right to live in the EU from his home in France.[29]

And finally: Andrea Leadsom, who in a crowded field was reported to be described by civil servants who worked with her as 'the worst minister ever'.[30]

This, I should remind you, was the 'sane' version of the Leave campaign.

And they had money too: Peter Cruddas, last seen offering access to the prime minister, now donated a million quid to the Vote Leave campaign.[31] Billionaire Tory donors Michael Hintze, Crispin Odey[32] and Peter Hargreaves[33] also offered huge financial support.

Hintze and Odey run hedge funds, which get rich on financial failure via a process known as 'shorting the market'. They make money by betting that the value of a traded stock or currency will drop. They don't even have to own the stock they bet with, but simply borrow it from whoever owns it and sell it at the current price, betting that the value will soon fall. When it drops, they buy it back at a lower price, and then return it to the people they borrowed it from.[34] The difference is their profits. It benefits them if a company – or for that matter, an entire country – makes a stupid decision that sinks its value.

When the whole of Britain became 8 per cent poorer the day after the referendum result,[35] Crispin Odey personally made £220 million by shorting the market on the UK.[36] Not a bad return on his investment in the Brexit campaign. By 2019, Odey, that avid fan of Brexit, was simultaneously betting £300 million on more financial catastrophe as the nation finally left the EU[37] and predicting Britain would re-join the EU, so he could bet on financial turmoil once again.[38]

The leaders of the Leave movement definitely had your best interests at heart.

Meanwhile a rival group of Leavers sprang up, even less glued to sobriety, morality or normal vertical-hold settings than Gove, Odey or Mark Francois. A Cabinet minister described them as 'an angry, unintelligent, divided mob which sensible Eurosceptics want nothing to do with',[39] and this is the cluster of turds most closely associated with the success of the Brexit campaign.

Arron Banks and Richard Tice had founded the group and named it Leave.EU, like the domain name for a website that wants you to fuck off. It may have had other members, but who knows, because the limelight belonged entirely to Nigel Farage.

The main problem with Farage was not his easy comfort with palpable lies, his remarkable hypocrisy, or his cynical racist dog-whistling. It wasn't even his history of singing Nazi songs about gassing Jews,[40] or that as far back as his schooldays his teachers were troubled by his 'fascist' views.[41]

No: the biggest problem with Nigel is that he is, regardless of what you think of the man or his opinions, an extremely capable exploiter of political fear, far more so than anybody on the Remain team. And as a result, he was able to do more for the hard right than any British politician since Oswald Mosley.

It helped that he was embedded in Leave.EU, the messy, uninhibited sibling who got to say all the horrible things Vote Leave was too refined to mention in public, but from which it must have been delighted to slyly benefit.

—

Having just voted to allow tenants to be kept in inhuman conditions, the Tories now hurled themselves into a plan to finally solve the problem of slum housing. Hey, don't ask me to explain their reasoning; I'm just keeping the receipts.

Cameron announced a revolutionary scheme to bulldoze what he called 'sink estates' where 'poverty has become entrenched'.[42] The brutalist towers would be razed to the ground, and replaced with – well, he didn't really get that far, but the horrible places where poor people lived would be gone, and This Would Be Good. To ensure the job got done – whatever that job might have been – he promised George Osborne would commit £140 million in the Autumn Statement, and then the PM told us it was now easy to buy your own home. All you had to do was 'work hard enough'.[43]

Osborne never made another Autumn Statement, but the bigger problem was that by 2016, people earning the Tories' 'living wage' couldn't afford a typical starter home in 98 per cent of Britain's local authority areas.[44] How hard they worked didn't make a lot of difference if their hourly rate was too parsimonious to feed them, let alone buy them a house.

In London, the Conservative interpretation of 'affordable housing' now meant affordable homes were only affordable to people earning at least £77,000.[45] Nationally, the standard deposit required for a new home reached £78,000, in a country where an average household could save just £2,160 a year.[46] It would take you 36 years to save a deposit, after which you'd still face a 25-year mortgage. If you started saving at 18, you'd be working to pay for your home until you were 79; Cameron's promise of £140 million to knock down ugly houses wasn't going to help very much.

As Brexit approached, the Leave campaign, populated almost entirely by the people whose policies had exacerbated this crisis, assured us that quitting the EU would reduce immigration, and therefore help young people to get on the housing ladder.[47] Complete bollocks, of course. Immigrants weren't the cause of the housing crisis.

But the Tories simply could not resist blaming foreigners, which all played into the Brexit paranoia. In January, Baroness Warsi, the

Tory who had become Britain's first Muslim woman Cabinet minister, had to tackle Cameron after he appeared on the radio and began blaming people not speaking English for Middle Eastern extremism.

'If you're not able to speak English,' he said, 'you could be more susceptible to the extremist message from Daesh [Islamic State].'[48] Insinuating that Muslims are somehow incapable of thinking until they're taught English was his attempt at launching an 'integrated approach to community cohesion'.

Warsi politely called his statement 'lazy and misguided', but I think 'befuddled xenophobia' might be closer to the mark.

—

In February, David Cameron was shocked to discover the cuts he had imposed on everybody's local government had somehow included *his own* local government: a leaked letter showed him protesting to Oxfordshire County Council over what he termed their 'disappointing' cutbacks, and claiming they were unnecessary because their funding had been increased.[49]

The council leader pointed out some reality: their grant funding had been 'increased' from £122 million down to £62 million on Cameron's watch. Now, to the embarrassment of Tories and the delight of everybody else, David Cameron's own mum signed a protest letter opposing the cuts.[50]

Your own mum, Dave. Your own mum.

That same mum probably wasn't overjoyed to learn that the same week, her son referred to being on benefits as a 'lifestyle choice' in a speech defending the blunderbuss of cuts his government continued to fire into the nation's face.

You know you've crossed over to the Dark Side when Tim Montgomerie, co-founder of the ConservativeHome grassroots website, quits the party in protest at your failure to build a socially just society. 'I'm just glad that Mrs Thatcher cannot see what her party has become,'[51] said Montgomerie.

As the awful news for local councils continued, the shrieks of pain finally reached government backbenchers: Cameron faced a rebellion against yet more cuts to local funding, but suddenly discovered £300 million of 'transitional relief' to ease the pain. You won't be shocked to learn 83 per cent of this money went to Conservative councils. Labour areas in the North, which experienced the highest levels of deprivation, got just 5 per cent.[52]

'Whatever happened to the one-nation Tories?' asked the shadow local government minister. 'If the word gerrymander didn't already exist, we'd have to invent it to describe a fix like this. What about the Northern Powerhouse?'[53]

Well yes, quite: what about the Northern Powerhouse?

—

The Northern Powerhouse had been announced in 2014 as a proposal to boost growth in the North of England. Instead of the government in Westminster focusing on London and the South-East, there would now be more money and devolved powers for the major cities and regions of the North, investment in transport links, and a specific department based in Sheffield dedicated to levelling up the inequalities that blight our nation.

In 2016, without any consultation whatsoever, the Northern Powerhouse Department was moved from Sheffield to – hold on, let me check my notes – ah, yes: London.[54]

The reasons given were, as always, cost savings. But the government refused three requests to publish the business case for the relocation; instead, they paid McKinsey management consultants – home of multiple Tory MPs, including William Hague,[55] Archie Norman,[56] Chris Philp[57] and Helen Whately[58] – £200,000 to draw up the plans.[59] Internal documents say the decision was based less on saving money than what it describes as the intangible benefits of 'London water-cooler conversations'.

They have water coolers in Sheffield. Phones exist north of Watford.

You may wonder: what was the cost of setting up a government department in Sheffield, and then two years later closing it down and setting up an identical department in London, where office prices are the highest in Europe?[60] It's hard to say: the figures haven't been released. But the government's disjointed and irrational attempts at cost-saving continued to cost more than they saved.

Osborne next suggested he would swing his axe against bursaries for trainee doctors.[61] The previous year, the Tories had cut bursaries for student nurses[62] and, as a direct consequence, applications to train as a nurse fell by a third.[63]

The cuts saved £800 million,[64] but by 2016, the NHS was already wasting £1 billion *every year* on 'bed blocking'[65] – being unable to discharge patients from hospital because there weren't enough social-care nurses to ease them back to their homes – which in turn delayed access to the next lot of patients awaiting stays in hospital. And following the bursary cut, by 2019 the NHS in England was unable to fill another 43,000 nursing vacancies.[66]

Cutting the training budget for more nurses had been a dazzling success for the fourth and final Horseman of the Apocalypse, which is why an emboldened Osborne decided to move on to slashing support for trainee doctors too. Osborne did this, remember. Not Muslims or the family speaking Polish in your local Tesco Metro.

—

But we must wrap up February with the launch of Clean for the Queen, a beltingly misguided campaign in which posh people told oiks to tidy up their patch of Britain in time for the Queen's birthday, as if she was likely to visit. No offence to the Queen, or indeed to your own town's collected heaps of discarded bottles, used condoms and terrifying needles, but we used to employ people to do this work, and provided them with safe equipment with which to carry it out. Their homes and food and kids' shoes depended on the work, and it might not have been especially dignified, but it beat the hell out of starving.

Now, the people who had sacked *real* cleaners decided to dress up as a Disney version and urge you and me to do the work instead. For free. With our bare hands. In amongst all the needles and condoms and whatnot.

Clean for the Queen outfits had been provided for MPs to pose in, although they only appeared to have been made in one size. And it isn't until they're asked to don a one-size-fits-all t-shirt that you realise how very few Tory MPs are a normal shape.

At one end of the spectrum, we had Rory Stewart looking like Q from James Bond had been sent undercover as a street sweeper and was feeling quite emotional about it. He looked like a stiff breeze might knock him over. It was positively Dickensian.

Michael Gove took dressing-up day one step further, donning a reflective street-sweeper's tabard that went beautifully with his gold cufflinks, and wearing an expression like somebody who has had smiling described to them but never actually seen it.

Boris Johnson, meanwhile, clutched his bin bag like he didn't want anybody to find out it contained his collection of human hands. His purple t-shirt was so tight, he looked like he was auditioning for the part of 'Sexually Deviant Blueberry' in a terrifying fruit-themed circus for people with head injuries. It was a remarkable tableau.

—

David Cameron headed off to engage in the renegotiation of EU treaties absolutely nobody cared about any more. He had announced he would return in triumph, rendering it pointless to leave Europe, because he'd already forced those bloody French to give us everything we could dream of. It didn't work out that way.

Tories who were determined to leave the EU dismissed his efforts as a failure, but they would have done so even if he'd negotiated a free solid-gold hovercraft for everybody, and ceremonially presented Jacob Rees-Mogg with the severed head of EU president Donald Tusk.

Proliferating groupuscules of bloody-minded Tory Eurosceptics declared the negotiations a disaster, and claimed adjustments to dozens of EU policies were 'not attempted' or 'only partially achieved',[67] which, having read the previous chapters, you would have thought was right in the Tory sweet spot. But their griping prepared the ground for the big non-shock of the early campaign: Boris Johnson officially coming out in favour of Brexit.

Johnson drafted two newspaper columns: one arguing that we should remain in the EU, and one arguing we should leave. The 'Remain' column was leaked into the public realm eventually, and it makes for astonishing reading.[68] He argues that it is 'surely a boon for the world and for Europe that Britain should be intimately engaged in the EU'. He warns of 'economic shock' if we left.

He points out that as members, we gain from the single market, jobs and security, and we become a more attractive investment location by having 446 million customers available to us with no barriers. Membership fees, he says, are a 'rather small price to pay for all that access'.

He urges readers to: 'Think of Britain. Think of the future. Think of the desire of your children and your grandchildren to live and work in other European countries; to sell things there, to make friends and perhaps to find partners there.'

Every word he wrote is now a heretical thought-crime within Tory ranks.

—

Johnson didn't hate Europe. He didn't love Europe either. He didn't care at all, quite frankly, because he doesn't care about anything except for Boris Johnson. His Remainer articles are easy to find: the one with the headline 'Quitting the EU won't solve our problems'[69] is particularly fun to read, especially the bit where he says, 'If we left the EU, we would end this sterile debate, and we would have to recognise that most of our problems are not caused by "Bwussels" [sic], but by chronic British short-termism, inadequate management, sloth, low skills, a culture of easy gratification and under-investment in both human and physical capital and infrastructure.'

If he believed that, why did he back Leave? Simple naked

self-interest: if he campaigned for Britain to stay in the EU and won, there would be no personal benefit for Boris Johnson. His Etonian rival David Cameron would claim the victory and persist as a permanent feature of the 10 Downing Street TV lounge.

Whereas if Johnson backed Brexit, he couldn't lose. If Leave won the referendum – a quite unlikely prospect at this early stage of the campaign – Johnson, as the most visible face of Brexit, would most likely end up prime minister.

And it would be even better for Johnson's career if Leave lost the referendum: for one thing, he's far too much of a living embodiment of all those things he listed – short-termism, sloth, low skills and easy gratification – to tackle something as complicated as untangling 100,000 legislative acts in two years.[70]

In losing, he'd gain all the advantages of being perceived as on the side of something his members wanted, but none of the disadvantages of having to be responsible for delivering it. He'd also retain that permanent whipping boy just over the Channel, which has traditionally been such a handy way for British governments to pass the blame for their own fuckups.

As King Over the Water for the defeated Eurosceptic movement, he could take the crown when the PM stood down before the following Parliament – as Cameron had already promised to do.

Yet reviews from associates didn't exactly provide a sense of reassurance about a potential Johnson government. Simon Heffer is, I think it's fair to say, somewhat right of centre. He's a columnist for the *Telegraph* and *Daily Mail*, backs congenitally wrong Tory nincompoop John Redwood, and as an uncompromising Brexit supporter would go on to become the political adviser to Leave Means Leave.

'He is lazy and dishonest,' Heffer wrote about Boris Johnson, 'traits that few former colleagues in journalism or politics would dispute.'[71] He described Johnson as 'the most rampantly ambitious person [he had] ever met' and said the future PM 'believed in nothing apart from himself'.

He reported that few Tory MPs liked, trusted or were remotely impressed by Johnson as Foreign Secretary, with the exception of 'three or four mediocrities on the back benches', who were 'people whose only hope of office is if Johnson ever leads their party'.

Priti Patel, Liz Truss, Gavin Williamson and Matt Hancock held office under Johnson. I'm just saying.

Heffer's conclusion is one that seems ever more prophetic in the midst of the chaotic, dismal, and grimly hilarious Boris years.

'Johnson is so self-serving that he cannot be relied on to put any other consideration first,' he wrote. 'He is not up to it, he is not straight or reliable, and [parliamentary colleagues] dread Tory activists handing him the keys of Downing Street.'

—

That same week, the three most significant people in the Brexit campaign made suggestions for resolving the problems inherent in their project. Every single bit of this will make you scream.

Dominic Cummings recommended that in the event of a vote for Brexit, Britain should not invoke Article 50 to trigger a two-year countdown to final divorce from Europe; instead, we should use the referendum mandate to demand better terms from Brussels, and ultimately stay in the EU.[72]

At the time, Cummings was special adviser to Michael Gove, the head of the official Leave campaign, and both Gove and Johnson backed Dom's proposal and suggested it to the PM.[73] Sadly, Cameron, that futile, complacent, glistening human butterbean, rejected the plan, dooming us to five extraordinarily costly years of confusion, turmoil and deceit. In the end, the proposal to remain and get better terms joined the ever-increasing ranks of Things Leavers Deny Ever Happened.

—

In the last days of February, all the venom that would pollute and fragment our nation for the next half-decade (and more) was casually released into the public realm.

First, Cameron confirmed the referendum would finally take

place on 23 June. The legislation allowing for the referendum had been idly waved through Parliament without any significant thought in 2015, with consequences that spiralled throughout the coming years.

It had been decided the vote would be purely advisory, opening the result up to endless challenges (whoever won). The advisory nature of the vote also meant our (relatively) strict rules on electoral spending didn't apply; nor did our hopelessly feeble rules about campaign accuracy and honesty, which even at their best demand higher standards of truth from adverts about washing-up liquid than they do about political promises. In an advisory campaign, no standards applied. The anarchist wing of the Brexit movement could do and say whatever they liked.

Unlike almost any vote for major constitutional change worldwide, there was no stipulation that we needed a super-majority, or for that matter, no stipulation that the meaning of Brexit should even be defined before we decided whether we wanted to do it. When Cameron promised a referendum, he was simply focused on appeasing his Eurosceptic membership and neutralising the electoral threat from UKIP; nothing more.

Compare and contrast: in the referendum that followed the Good Friday Agreement – the peace treaty that ended the Troubles in Northern Ireland – the full details of the agreement were sent to every person on the island of Ireland, north or south of the border, so the full consequences could be understood before anybody voted.[74] Even Jacob Rees-Mogg advanced the idea of a second EU referendum on the details of the agreement: 'We could have two referendums,' he said. 'As it happens, it might make more sense to have the second referendum after the renegotiation is completed.'[75]

But Cameron decided to leave everything as vague as possible, so the next half-decade was a relentless battle over the meaning of what the hell we were doing.

This shroomed-up experiment with democratic norms got even better: having given the vote to 16- and 17-year-olds in the

2014 Scottish referendum, the Tories now took it away again.[76] And seemingly, nobody remembered about the 3.3 million EU nationals living in the UK. Those people lived here, paid tax here, and were allowed to vote in our 2016 local elections; but they were *not* allowed to vote in the 2016 referendum. Not only does this make no sense, it's also contrary to the UN Declaration of Human Rights.[77]

However, for reasons that banjaxed even the most expansive of minds, people living in the UK who were citizens of Australia, Canada, New Zealand, Pakistan, India, Bangladesh, Malta and Cyprus *were* allowed to vote in the referendum. If this makes any sense to you, please write in to explain.

Our minds suitably boggled, we set about our business: Boris Johnson headed off to Northern Ireland, where he would squat and extrude the first of countless miles of thick, lustrous bullshit about the Irish border: nothing would change, he said, except that 'in many ways, farmers will be better off'.[78]

Immediately, the pound collapsed to its lowest level since 2009[79] and the international credit rating agency Moody's warned the UK's creditworthiness would be worth shit-all if we left the EU.[80]

As a preview of the rancorous splits that would go on to shatter families across the nation, Boris Johnson's father Stanley announced he would be voting to Remain.[81]

And finally, an unnamed government minister told *Channel 4 News*, 'Boris and Michael don't buy the economic arguments that we'd be freer to trade outside the EU. They don't buy the immigration arguments' – that's two of the most important arguments for Brexit privately disowned by its own chief proponents. Instead, the minister said, they had both opted to campaign on 'sovereignty, which literally means nothing to anybody'.[82]

—

It's been a while since we heard from two-legged clown-car Owen Paterson, and I don't know about you, but I've been missing his special brand of farcical sixth-form performance art. So thank God for the

March publication of the memoirs of a former Cabinet colleague, which described how Paterson, when still environment minister, had pitched his formidable intellect against the intractable problem of what would happen when all those horrible Europeans stopped coming over here to farm, prepare and deliver the food that we eat.[83]

'Oh, but I've thought of that,' Paterson told a startled Cabinet, who hadn't, until that very moment, known he was capable of such feats. 'We'll get more British pensioners picking fruit and vegetables in the fields instead.'

Indomitable in the face of the Cabinet's combination of flat, silent stares and stifled giggles, he pressed on with his thesis.

'Of course,' he continued, 'getting pensioners to do this work could lead to an increase in farmers' costs. After all, they may be a bit slower doing the work. I've thought of that too!'

He'd thought of that too, ladies and gents. We're saved.

'We might arrange to exempt British pensioners from the minimum-wage laws, to allow them to do this work.'

Try running that one past your great-auntie Gladys, with her lopsided hip and corkscrew fingers: eight hours a day picking sprouts in the rain for less than the minimum wage.

We were still only four days into March, and the few remaining self-aware souls in the Tory party had clearly started to realise how acutely ludicrous all of this looked; their solution – and I'm not making this up – was to send Chris fucking Grayling to the House of Commons to inform MPs that the ridiculing of Parliament should, in future, be banned.

'I think it's very important that we make sure the coverage of this House is used in an appropriate way,' said Grayling. 'I am not in favour of it being used for satire.'[84]

———

March was Budget time again, and although he didn't know it yet, it was Osborne's final chance to rescue his reputation. He didn't.

Personal Independence Payment (PIP) is a benefit that assigns 'points' to disabled people, based on the extent to which their disability affects their life. A person with more points receives more money to cover the costs associated with their disability. It is targeted at each individual's requirements, and nobody is getting cash they don't need.[85]

So Osborne cut their cash by £4.4 billion,[86] which would mean 370,000 disabled people losing an average of £3,500 per year.[87]

A stickler for tradition, if not decency or sense, Osborne chose this moment to raise the threshold at which the richest people in the country would pay their 40p top rate of tax. This once again cut the tax bills for the people who earned a fortune.[88] He cut capital gains tax – predominantly paid by the rich – by a further 8 per cent,[89] and announced corporation tax, already among the lowest in the world, would drop to just 18 per cent.[90] It was 30 per cent when Thatcher left office, and I seem to remember her telling us business was booming.[91]

And the 'greenest government ever' then cut taxes on oil companies by 50 per cent.[92] To be fair, it was reported Cameron had wandered around Downing Street insisting: 'We have to get rid of all this green crap', so at least he was consistent in his inconsistency. [93]

Our growth forecast was cut again, because of course it was.[94] Meanwhile, the nation's debt rose to 82.5 per cent of GDP,[95] one-third higher than the figure Labour had left behind. Five years in, and Osborne still hadn't learned that austerity wasn't working.

The PIP cuts caused outrage: Kit Malthouse, James Cleverly and London mayoral candidate Zac Goldsmith voted for the cuts, and as a result were asked to stand down as patrons of disability charities.[96] A leading Tory disability campaigner – yes, one existed – who had voted Conservative for 40 years, quit the party, and as a parting gift sabotaged his own party's website, replacing the homepage with the message 'This website is temporarily closed owing to Disability Cuts'.[97]

For a short while, Iain Duncan Smith defended the cuts to his department, but it didn't last. He suddenly resigned in a tornado of recrimination and abuse. It began on *The Andrew Marr Show*, with a lovely bit of subtle evasion.

Andrew Marr: 'Do you think George Osborne would make a good prime minister?'

IDS: [Cough.] 'I'm sorry, I missed that question.'[98]

David Cameron was a touch less shy about expressing his views, reportedly phoning IDS up to call him a 'dishonourable shit'. Cameron denied using the word 'shit', which I think qualifies as damning Smith with faint praise.[99]

IDS didn't appear to be much of a loss from Cabinet. 'I found him exceptionally difficult to work for,' revealed pensions minister Ros Altmann. She said he 'has often been obstructive to my efforts to resolve important pension policy issues.'[100]

Nadine Dorries – a beef-witted, one-woman riot of idiocy – was equally unhappy, while being too dense to avoid revealing that her opinions were available for hire. 'I am angry that he made me vote for something I did not want to vote for, bribing me with a promise,' she confessed, 'and now *he* resigns.'[101]

Every Tory seemed to hold an opinion about Osborne, except for Peter Lilley, who held two at the same time: 'He's an extremely able person and in many ways,' he floundered, 'well, I was going to say a safe pair of hands, but not in this case. But generally, a safe pair of hands. And so not necessarily therefore the best person.'[102]

In the inspiring words of our greatest political thinker, Vicky Pollard: Yeah, but no, but yeah, but no.

Inevitably, it all fell apart. Stephen Crabb, who had been swiftly shoved into the demon-shaped hole left by IDS, had to crawl to the House of Commons and declare, 'We have no further plans to make welfare savings.'[103]

—

As March started, Andrew RT Davies, the leader of the Welsh Conservatives and an ardent, vociferous backer of Brexit, was revealed to have raked in £96,000 from the EU's Common Agricultural Policy for his own farming business – and that's just in 12 months up to October 2015.[104] A spokesman for Welsh Tories said this simply proved Davies was 'against the European gravy train'.[105] Davies was sadly incapable of making the statement himself. He was too busy drinking £96,000 of gravy.

Meanwhile Boris Johnson, who had been out of the papers for almost two consecutive hours and was clearly feeling the strain, once again floated the idea of a floating airport in the Thames Estuary. This may or may not have been related to the fact that people were starting to nickname it Boris Island. In the words of Mr Johnson, it was 'the only credible solution'. In the words of the expert commission that had already rejected the plan in 2014, it was 'financially, geographically and environmentally wrong'.[106]

Things like that didn't bother Johnson: back when he was merely Witless Dickington, the shambolic Mayor of London, he spent £60 million on a commuter cable car across the Thames which, by the October after it opened, had just four daily commuters a week.[107]

But such endless self-promotion had pushed Johnson into prime position to replace Cameron. Astonishingly, even then, many of us appeared happy to place our futures in the hands of an amoral, priapic, quasi-autonomous haystack who former Tory MP Matthew Parris denounced for 'dishonesty, vacuity, sexual impropriety and veiled homophobia'.[108]

People assumed Boris was a laugh, wrote Parris, but: 'Incompetence is not funny. Policy vacuum is not funny. A careless disregard for the truth is not funny. Advising old mates planning to beat someone up is not funny. Abortions and gagging orders are not funny. Creeping ambition in a jester's cap is not funny. Vacuity posing as merriment, cynicism posing as savviness, a wink and a smile covering for betrayal … these things are not funny'.[109]

The members of the Treasury Select Committee tended to agree. Johnson appeared before them in March, and under questioning from Conservative MP Andrew Tyrie, he proclaimed, 'I've got this new piece of research hot off the press, published today by the House of Commons Library, saying that 59 per cent of British legislation is imposed by the EU.'

Tyrie corrected him: the research was not 'published today', but two years earlier, and it showed the true figures were not as high as 59 per cent, but as low as 15 per cent.[110] And as for these laws being 'imposed': we, as members of the EU, had helped to draft all that legislation, and voted for it too.

Never one to be daunted by the truth, Johnson poured out a bewildering stream of lunatic claims: insatiable Brussels bureaucracy was preventing children from blowing up balloons, claimed Boris; it was thwarting our God-given right to recycle tea; it was obliging our mighty, bloated British corpses to be forced into tiny coffins designed for measly foreigners. Worst of all, he claimed, it was requiring French lorry manufacturers to literally murder cyclists.

'This is all very interesting, Boris,' said Andrew Tyrie, 'except none of it is really true, is it?'

—

The Easter break was upon us, and at 5pm on the evening Parliament broke up, the Tories announced plans to sell off Her Majesty's Land Registry, the body that holds the details of all land ownership in England and Wales.[111]

The previous year, privatisation plans had been dropped after 70 per cent of the public opposed it, and the Conservative's Lib Dem partners challenged it;[112] it was also opposed by the Competition and Markets Authority. Not only that, but the agency brought in £100 million to the Treasury every year,[113] whereas every single potential buyer was linked to tax havens, which pretty much guaranteed any future profits they made would produce zero for the Treasury.[114]

And so, just as everybody was leaving for their Easter break, and all the opponents of privatisation were focused on Brexit, Osborne said it was going ahead anyway.

—

More great news for Mr and Mrs John Q. Taxpayer, as Peter Bone, a 63-year-old Tory MP, decided to piggyback on the government's new Help to Buy scheme for what you'd imagine were predominantly young first-time buyers.[115] Under this policy, the government would loan up to 20 per cent of the purchase price to people struggling to save for a deposit, as long as the property was a new build.

Bone might well have been struggling to get a deposit, as he was only earning £75,000 as an MP, plus the £177,000 he claimed in expenses that year alone. In addition to this, AJWB Travel,[116] one of the two companies he owned,[117] had been registered at the (apparently new build) property since the previous January.

However, the Help to Buy loan had been given to his wife, not to Peter Bone; it was merely a coincidence that he lived with her.

'As Mrs Bone is a private citizen, I do not comment upon her financial arrangements,' Bone said, also overlooking the fact that Mrs Bone also took home a £45,000 public salary as his executive secretary.[118]

It must have been distressing for Mrs Bone to realise all her executive secretarial duties were less valuable to the nation than the person who picked out Samantha Cameron's frocks for her. Rosie Lyburn, who was (naturally) the wife of a Tory candidate and granddaughter of a Tory politician, was paid £53,000 of taxpayers' money to help the prime minister's wife with her social diary and clothing choices.[119]

Three hundred and seventy thousand disabled people had just faced cuts of £3,500 and 1.2 million people relied on food banks in 2016, up from 40,000 when Mr Cameron entered office. That's a 2,800 per cent increase.[120]

Nice frock, though, Mrs Cameron.

—

In April, there was a brief hiatus from the increasingly rancorous and dishonest campaign for Brexit to make room for a rancorous and dishonest campaign to become London Mayor. The competition was between Labour's Sadiq Khan and the Conservative Zac Goldsmith.

Goldsmith had it all: tall, lean, handsome, charming and vastly rich. He was the son of a billionaire, and grandson of two Conservative

MPs; an avowedly cool environmentalist, rarely seen away from a bicycle or a Gerald Durrell book. He was edgy enough to have been kicked out of Eton for smoking pot, but a scrupulously respectable scion of Anglo-Irish aristocracy; thoroughly British, proudly Jewish, and internationalist enough to have boasted the prime minister of Pakistan as his brother-in-law.[121] Chances are, he could have romped home as party leader one day, and eventually beguiled his way into Downing Street.

It could only go wrong for him if – oh I don't know – his mayoral campaign turned out to be massively Islamophobic or something.

The Goldsmith campaign was shocking, not for the fact of its dog-whistle politics, but for the clodhopping ineptitude with which that dog-whistle was blown.

He targeted voters based on their ethnicity, and in deliriously clumsy ways. White British voters were sent leaflets that not-so-subtly pointed out that Sadiq Khan was a Muslim, called him 'radical', and linked him to 'extremist views'.[122] Goldsmith even criticised Khan alongside a photograph of a bus destroyed in the 7/7 terror attacks, and said a win by his opponent would see London controlled by a party that 'thinks terrorists are its friends'.[123]

People from Indian backgrounds, meanwhile, were warned that Sadiq Khan would tax their jewellery, which somehow managed to be racist to everybody at once: Indian-heritage voters described the leaflets as 'reductive and patronising'.[124]

Former Conservative minister Sayeeda Warsi, herself a Muslim, said 'the right needs to weed out its Islamophobes. Dog-whistle nasty politics is damaging the UK', and she suggested the campaign was like a reality-TV show called *Britain's Biggest Bigot*.[125]

Other Tories defended Goldsmith, saying it was utterly predictable that Labour would accuse them of Islamophobia, and that they'd also accused their previous squeaky-clean mayor, Boris Johnson, of employing racist rhetoric.[126]

Well… yes, but there might have been a reason for that.

Johnson had referred to Commonwealth citizens as 'picaninnies'. He said Black people had 'watermelon smiles'. [127] He was forced by the *Telegraph* to apologise after calling the people of Papua New Guinea 'cannibals'. [128] He said 'black people have lower IQs' and were 'multiplying like flies'. [129]

He wrote that 'Islamophobia – fear of Islam – seems a natural reaction', and that Islamic holy texts are intended to provoke terror;[130] therefore, he reasoned, the UK must accept that 'Islam is the problem'. [131]

He informed stunned attendees at the World Islamic Economic Forum that Muslim women 'only went to university to find husbands',[132] which is both racist and sexist; and since we've moved onto sexism, what about the time he asserted: 'Voting Tory will cause your wife to have bigger breasts.'[133] Or the time he reviewed delegates to the Labour Party Conference based on their 'hotness', using what he referred to as his 'tottymeter'. [134]

And having covered racism and sexism, it seems churlish to leave out homophobia. 'I am a liberal cosmopolitan,' asserted Boris Johnson in a Brexit campaign speech in May 2016,[135] but I can't think of any other liberal cosmopolitans who go around calling gay men 'tank-topped bumboys', [136] or claim gay marriage would lead to consecration between 'three men and a dog'.[137]

All this damaging background could have been used by Cameron to de-fang Johnson in the Brexit referendum, but Cameron was suddenly focused on new problems.

—

In 2014 and 2015, documents from a Panamanian law firm, Mossack Fonseca, were leaked by an anonymous whistle-blower to a German investigative journalist.

The files described the simply enormous scale of exploitative offshore tax regimes, and revealed the multibillion-dollar network of political and business figures embroiled in the scandal. The scale of the leak was also extraordinary – over 11 million documents, detailing the activities of at least 200,000 offshore entities, covering a timescale of over 40 years.

More than 100 journalists in 80 countries worked to unpick the global scandal, and in April 2016, details of the Panama Papers finally reached the public, whereupon David Cameron shat himself inside out.

Three former Tory MPs and six Tory peers were named in the Panama Papers, as were several very substantial Tory benefactors.[138] These included: David Rowland, tax-exile donor of at least £5 million to Tory coffers; Tony Buckingham, who had coughed up £100,000; Anthony Bamford, heir to the JCB fortune, and source of more than £4 million in donations – and who, in yet another of those extraordinary coincidences, had been ennobled Lord Bamford by Cameron.

Large-scale donor Howard Flight – also made a life peer in 2011 – was named. And that lovely patriot Arron Banks was busy avoiding paying tax here, although, to be fair, he was a £1 million donor to UKIP, and had only given £25,000 to the Tories.

The scandal started to edge closer to Cameron when it was revealed the Fleming family, who had directly bankrolled his leadership bid, had held at least 18 Panamanian accounts.

But the sleaze didn't stop there. Cameron's own father had run an offshore fund that avoided having to pay any tax – ever – in the UK. It did this by hiring a small army of offshore residents including, bizarrely, a part-time bishop to sign all its paperwork so it could be said to be operating overseas.[139]

In September 2015 – just eight months earlier – Cameron had made a speech imploring action to stop this sort of thing.

'If we're to beat corruption,' he said, 'we need transparency. I've taken the lead by pledging much more transparency... so that terrorists, tax-avoiders, money launderers and criminals have nowhere to hide their ill-gotten gains. I say to them all today... if we want to break the business model of stealing money and hiding it in places where it can't be seen: transparency is the answer.'[140]

When news broke that Cameron's own father was embroiled in tax avoidance, the office of the prime minister said, 'That is a private matter.'[141] But they said it in a transparent way.

The public may have been bewildered by the blizzard of company names, complicated tax arrangements and obscure financial instruments being contorted by clever lawyers, but we all knew it stank: our prime minister, his financiers and multiple members of his party were entangled in a tax avoidance scheme with a bunch of lawyers allegedly associated with dodgy South American drug and mafia clients,[142] and it reeked to high heaven.

A month later, our lacquered, indolent, entitled prime minister, who had just been revealed as a beneficiary of tax avoidance,[143] was chairing (of all things) the long-planned Anti-Corruption Summit 2016. 'The evil of corruption reaches into every corner of the world,' he told them. 'A global problem needs a truly global solution.'[144]

In 2013, David Cameron had personally stepped in to shield offshore trusts from being investigated by the EU as part of a global crackdown on tax avoidance.[145] He really was a one-nation Conservative, and that nation was the Cayman Islands.

In a bid to clear the air, Cameron – who had been promising to release his tax records for the previous four years[146] but was too busy watching (ironically) *Shameless*[147] to get around to it – suddenly found time to make it all public. It just made things worse. Records showed his mother had put two separate payments of £100,000 into Cameron's bank account, potentially allowing him to avoid £80,000 of inheritance tax.[148]

His wilier Cabinet weren't about to have their laundry washed in public: George Osborne and Sajid Javid flatly refused to reveal their financial interests, while Amber Rudd said she didn't think transparency was a good idea: it might put rich people off entering politics.[149]

And what a terrible shame that would be.

Alan Duncan agreed with Rudd: 'We risk seeing a Commons which is stuffed full of low-achievers who hate enterprise,' he said, 'and hate people who look after their own family.'[150] There's an Italian word for an organised group of people who will do whatever it takes to look after the Family, but I can't bring it to mind right now.

The pressure continued, and so eventually Osborne relented: his accounts revealed he'd somehow contrived to receive a £44,000 dividend on profits from the company his father founded, despite the company paying no UK tax since 2008 because it claimed its profits were eaten up by losses.[151] Nothing to see here. All normal.

Meanwhile, the all-new David Cameron, with his fresh determination to tackle tax avoidance, had yet to address the problems left by the old David Cameron from a couple of weeks before, not helped by the Tory policy of having 3,250 Department for Work and Pensions staff investigating benefit fraud, while only 300 investigated tax evasion.[152]

Since 2010, there had been only 11 – yes, 11 – prosecutions for offshore tax evasion.[153] A reminder: 200,000 offshore entities were revealed by the Panama Papers.

Figures from HMRC demonstrated the value of hunting down missing tax: every £1 spent on investigation yielded £97 of revenue.[154] HMRC said in 2016 alone, at least £34 billion was lost to tax avoidance and evasion.[155] Independent research showed it may have been as high as £119 billion.[156] That's £1 per second for 3,773 years. Or, if you prefer, £3,600 per hour, every hour since the woolly mammoth went extinct.

Meanwhile, benefit fraud was a comparatively tiny £1.1 billion.[157] Yet the Tories, as part of their sudden desire to persuade the public how much they hated corruption and swindling, committed 10 times as many people to resolving something that cost us 1 per cent as much.

—

Cameron decided to cheer the party up with an awayday in Chipping Norton. It was hoped this would instil a sense of unity and recreate the jolly atmosphere of their 2014 shindig, when free wine was served until 3 a.m., Alan Duncan unveiled a painting of George Osborne posing naked with a carrot, and Michael Gove had to 'insist MPs do not sleep with one another tonight'.[158]

Boak.

April 2016's day out didn't get off to the most dazzling start, as one MP said he objected to being taken away to be 'reprogrammed', and another was reported to have said, 'The last thing I want to do is spend my spare time with these people.'[159]

You and me both, mate. You and me both.

—

The whiff of sleaze hung in the air, as it pretty much always did: Culture Secretary John Whittingdale endorsed the Electric Jukebox music streaming service as 'a very exciting idea for consumers',[160] even though reviews for it read: 'it looks like the most ridiculous digital music launch in history', 'it isn't a joke, but it probably should be', and, 'Electric Jukebox is definitely enough to get any sane person streaming – right out of their tear ducts.' The hardware-software hybrid cost £179 for the box, followed by annual costs that were five times what the average Briton spent on Spotify. In total, 149 people followed Electric Jukebox on Twitter.[161]

Electric Jukebox had donated £5,000 to John Whittingdale just before he completely independently decided to endorse a barely known, soon-to-fail business. No rules were broken, but the former sleaze parliamentary watchdog described Whittingdale as 'unwise', something many of us can get on board with.[162]

It was a busy week for Whittingdale. Not only was there this unexpected serendipity between the money he received and the recommendations he made, but he was also asked to withdraw from decisions relating to press regulation, on the grounds that he was vulnerable to pressure from the press.

Whittingdale had, for a period until 2014, been in a relationship with a sex worker, and the information was known by at least four newspapers. He insisted he had not known of her occupation, and the potential for newspapers to blackmail him had not affected his decisions.[163] It's easy to be cynical about these things, but c'mon – how likely is it that anybody would know what their partner's job is? Even asking is a monstrous intrusion. Whittingdale's ignorance strikes me as being completely above board.

It was probably equally above board when, within a couple of days, it was reported Whittingdale had accepted hospitality from the Lap Dancing Association and failed to declare it in the Register of Members' Financial Interests. He also failed to mention it when he objected in Parliament to new rules limiting lap-dancing clubs from opening.[164]

All above board. Above board is what that is.

Meanwhile, another regular feature: the Tories admitted failing to declare thousands of pounds in expenditure at the 2015 election. The Electoral Commission had powers to investigate national spending but not local – and the Tories wriggled free by claiming their excess spending was a local matter.

Local. But it happened simultaneously in 29 different constituencies.[165]

The payments were signed off by key aides to David Cameron, including Lord Feldman, and even the *Daily Mail* was disturbed by this latest bout of apparent cheating. *Mail* columnist Peter Oborne reported, 'Cameron and his crony Feldman stand open to the charge, therefore, that they "bought" their 2015 general election victory using money the Tories had received from rich donors.'

It went on to say, 'The Tories cheated, which means that in some key marginal constituencies, last year's general election was not fought fair and square', and it concluded that a 'culture of dishonesty is eating away the soul of the Tory party'.[166]

Firstly: what soul? And secondly, you ain't seen nothing yet, buddy.

Which brings us back to Boris Johnson, outgoing Mayor of London, who took Zac Goldsmith to pose with some beer at a start-up brewery in the city. There can be few doubts Johnson knew his way around a pint, and photographs show him guzzling it down. Meanwhile, Goldsmith simply sniffed the stuff.

'Wonderful,' he said, 'marvellous smell,' and then held the glass in two hands like it was a clarinet, and delicately pressed it against his upper lip. In the most literal sense possible, they couldn't organise a piss-up in a brewery.[167]

Before we move on to May, let's return to the referendum campaign for a speedy catch-up of the latest developments.

—

Treasury analysis predicted UK economic investment would shrink by 6 per cent, costing the average household the equivalent of £4,300 per year.[168] 'Rubbish,' shouted the Leave campaign. 'We will, in fact, be richer.'

In 2018, Stamford University found UK economic investment had fallen by 6 per cent.[169]

—

The BBC continued their perfect record of granting absolutely equal amounts of coverage to both Leave and Remain groups. A study of appearances on *Question Time* between 2010 and 2019 found zero – none, absolutely not one – MEP had appeared from Labour, Lib Dem, SNP, the Green Party or Plaid Cymru.[170]

Meanwhile three Conservative MEPs had appeared. The rest – 45 appearances – had come from UKIP. As a result, every single MEP appearing on *Question Time* for an entire decade was anti-EU.

—

Boris Johnson promised leaving the EU would slash our gas bills, and domestic heating would become much cheaper.[171] Energy bills actually rose by the maximum amount permitted by the regulator, driving millions into fuel poverty.[172]

—

Patrick Minford, the Brexit-supporting economist who was – let's be charitable – something of an outlier in terms of his predictions of economic success after we left the EU, let his mask slip when he admitted voting Leave would 'mostly eliminate manufacturing'.[173] His opinion was echoed by Japan's prime minister, Shinzo Abe, who said Brexit could lead to withdrawal of Japanese companies from the UK, as they often see the UK as a gateway to European markets.[174]

Most of Sunderland neither listened nor cared.

—

It was in a spirit of harmless fun that in May Boris Johnson compared the EU to the Nazis, and not in a 'hey, they're loads better than the Nazis' sense.[175] He likened the alleged attempts at unifying the 28 member states into a single integrated superstate to Adolf Hitler's conquests of continental Europe.

I say 'alleged attempts' because the European Union – and before that the European Economic Community (EEC) – has existed for over 60 years, and the terrifying spectre of unification, which the anti-EU campaigners have continuously warned were imminent, still hasn't happened. It's never come close. There is no EU army. National politicians are still elected. There are no suggestions we dissolve Denmark or suspend Sweden. The integrity of Italy is inviolate, as is the permanence of Poland, and the sovereignty of Slovakia.

Still, regardless of how patently false a claim you make, it's ludicrous – and as we shall soon see, quite dangerous – to rhetorically paint your political opponents as a totalitarian, mass-murdering military regime bent on the dictatorial suppression of a continent, when all they really wanted to do was set minimum standards for the efficiency of lightbulbs.

Tory MP Sir Nicholas Soames, Winston Churchill's grandson, said Johnson had 'gone too far',[176] and described him as 'unchallenged master of the self-inflicted wound'.[177]

He was having a bit of a week, Soames. According to former Tory MP Jerry Hayes, when faced with the prospect of having to speak to Brexit-supporting misnomer James Cleverly in the Westminster dining hall, Sir Nicholas told Cleverly to 'fuck off, you cunt'.[178] Is it possible to knight Soames a second time?

Meanwhile, Andrew Dilnot, the chair of the UK Statistics Authority, had been looking into Boris Johnson's famous claim that we sent £350 million a week to the EU and should be spending it on the NHS instead. Dilnot had already privately written to Vote Leave, telling them the claim was misleading, which was traditionally all that had been required for a false statement to be withdrawn.[179] But we were dealing with Johnson now, and he operated under a regime of uniquely different morals, by which I mean none. Johnson was aware that verifiable truths existed, and realised he would probably have to bump into them occasionally, but on the whole he only used them for publicity purposes, and the rest of the time he didn't lose a wink of sleep about totally ignoring them. And in that respect, they're very much like his children.

Dilnot was forced to issue a rare public rebuke to Vote Leave, saying he was 'disappointed to note that there continue to be suggestions that the UK contributes £350 million to the EU each week', and that the claim was 'misleading and undermines trust in official statistics'.[180]

That's kind of the point, Dilnot. As Churchill said, a lie gets halfway around the world before the truth has a chance to get its pants on. Johnson's entire modus operandi was to fib relentlessly, sure in the knowledge that it would take boring old fact-checkers days to explain the dreary reality, by which time he was already ahead of them by 10 fresh, exciting new lies.

The £350 million bullshit wasn't going to be killed by Johnson, and it wasn't about to die of loneliness either. If we're feeling charitable, we could say the entire Tory party was stupid, and totally unaware that what they were telling us was bollocks. But I'm not feeling especially charitable, so let's take a quick tour of the major lies of the campaign.

First: the scare stories. There were Vote Leave leaflets claiming: 'Turkey (population 76 million) is joining the EU'.[181] False. And that therefore: 'Britain's new border is with Syria and Iraq'.[182] False.

There was the Vote Leave leaflet claiming that the EU controlled our borders.[183] False: we controlled our borders, which is why you go through passport control every time you enter Britain. If we did it badly, it was because of Tory cuts to the Border Force, and Theresa May's mismanagement and demolition of the nascent ID-card system, which would have allowed us to track people entering the country.

Vote Leave claimed that because we were in the EU, Britain was not allowed to make trade deals of its own. False. We had just signed a £14 billion bilateral trade deal with China in 2014, for example.[184]

They claimed the EU controlled our public services. False. They claimed the EU determined whether our prisoners could vote. False.[185]

They claimed that quarter of a million EU citizens came to the UK in 12 months: this one is technically true, but it doesn't mention that almost half of them also left within the same 12 months, or that 1.2 million British-born people lived – not just visited for a few months, but lived – in other EU countries.[186]

So much for the scare stories. Now let's move onto the reassuring dismissal of every negative prediction.

'People in this country have had enough of experts,' said Gove.[187] Perhaps he meant exports, in which case, spot on.

He also told us, 'If we vote to leave then I think the union will be stronger. I think when we vote to leave it will be clear that having voted to leave one union, the last thing people in Scotland wanted to do is to break up another.'[188]

Oh, as Billy Connolly would say, do you think sooooo? In 2017 the Scottish Parliament voted to hold a second independence referendum.

Brexiter Lord Digby Jones assured us 'not a single job' would be lost because of Brexit.[189] By January 2020, before we had even left the EU, at least 436,296 jobs had been lost as a *direct* result of Brexit, costing the Treasury £3.7 billion in income tax.[190]

Hapless, helpless, hopeless Chris Grayling assured us, 'We will maintain a free-flowing border at Dover. We will not impose checks in the port.'[191] By 2021 the government was still struggling to complete the 66-acre lorry park at Dover that was needed to cope with extended border checks[192] and had bought space to perform yet more border checks just down the road.[193]

David Davis (so good they named him once) was confident that, 'Our trade will almost certainly continue with the EU on similar-to-current circumstances. The reality is that the hard-headed, pragmatic businessmen on the continent will do everything to ensure that trade with Britain continues uninterrupted.'[194] Didn't happen.

Dan Hannan reassured us that 'absolutely nobody is talking about threatening our place in the single market',[195] which, of course, we went ahead and left.

Hannan also claimed, 'Without our EU budget contributions, we could give everyone a 60 per cent council tax cut.'[196] I can't wait for mine! And it gets better: a Vote Leave press release promised 'lower taxes as a result of no longer having to pay into the EU budget'.[197]

Boris Johnson assured the people of Northern Ireland that the border would be 'absolutely unchanged',[198] and Theresa Villiers joined in: 'There is no reason why the UK's only land border should be any less open after Brexit than it is today.'[199]

And Vote Leave sent a leaflet to millions of households with the following reassurance: 'There is a free trade zone from Iceland to Turkey and the Russian border and we will be part of it.' It went on, 'Taking back control is a careful change, not a sudden stop – we will negotiate the terms of a new deal before we start any legal process to leave.'[200]

You have to feel sorry for those fact-checkers. Try as they might, they were still putting their boots on.

—

Legendary chess grandmaster Garry Kasparov said, 'The point of modern propaganda isn't only to misinform or push an agenda. It is to exhaust your critical thinking, to annihilate truth.'[201]

But you didn't need much propaganda if barely anybody in print or broadcast media gave a damn about reporting the important things.

A study found just one in every ten contributors to the public debate over Brexit were women. And, as is befitting of what was essentially a battle within the Conservative Party, the entire campaign was presented as little more than a conflict between Tory big beasts.[202]

Of the top 10 people who appeared most frequently in Brexit reporting, only two were from Labour, and they both got less than 2 per cent of the total coverage. The research found the SNP and other parties to be 'virtually invisible', and even Nigel Farage had been 'comparatively marginalised' in favour of reporting the clash of personalities between Cameron, Osborne and Johnson.

A breakdown of the most-reported 12 issues was similarly disheartening. The biggest share of the coverage (a whopping 33 per cent) was not about the issues raised by Brexit, but about the conduct of the campaign – schoolyard squabbles between mewling Tories about who had the best invisible friend. By comparison, immigration stories, which you'd probably assume was the biggest issue for most people, accounted for just 10 per cent of coverage.

Only 6 per cent of the discussion was about constitutional issues – what happens with the Irish border, for example. Or what becomes of the United Kingdom if an independence-favouring Scotland votes to stay and yet is forced to leave the EU. These things were scarcely mentioned by the press, so it's unsurprising that few of us were prepared for the outcome.

What the EU actually does – as opposed to what that abandoned candyfloss Boris Johnson claimed it did – was limited to just 1.3 per cent of the entire debate. On TV, the environmental issues involved in leaving the EU (such as – to pick a wildly improbable thing that probably won't ever happen – the UK making a trade deal with Australia that means we will fly food halfway around the world rather than buying it from the farm next door) got statistically zero coverage. So little, it failed to register. Effectively: nothing.

Thankfully, the government was all over the important issues facing our country. That week it announced plans for a spaceport in Cornwall,[203] which, in keeping with this government's sterling commitment to unremitting ineptitude, was described as 'not the ideal location' by the Royal Astronomical Society.[204]

Let's quickly dash to the end of May before our will to live goes missing.

—

We will begin with Penny Mordaunt, the former magician's assistant who somehow ended up director of a diabetes charity while believing in the curative benefits of homeopathy; or, as doctors call it, 'a cup of water'.[205] Mordaunt went on TV to argue that Turkey was about to join the EU, and the UK could do nothing to stop the madness.

'Except the British government does have a veto on Turkey joining,' corrected Andrew Marr.

'No, it doesn't,' incorrected Mordaunt. 'We would be unable to stop Turkey joining.'[206]

Long story short: we could always stop Turkey joining. Every EU member, including Britain, had a veto on other nations joining. Mordaunt was either nakedly lying or fiercely ignorant.

She believes in homeopathy, and I believe that answers the question.

—

An unnamed Tory MP had clearly grown weary of David Cameron. When asked if he was ready to stab the prime minister in the back, he told the *Sunday Times* he would prefer to 'stab him in the front so I can see the expression on his face. You'd have to twist the knife, though, because we want it back for Osborne.'[207]

He added, 'All we have to do is catch the prime minister with a live boy or a dead girl and we are away.'[208] Apparently, dead pigs don't count.

—

June began with Boris Johnson and his emotional support turbot, Michael Gove, audaciously claiming a vote for Brexit would deliver 'one nation politics', and telling a startled world that they were both 'liberal internationalists'.[209]

Johnson, rarely short of chutzpah, continued, 'The impact of EU-enforced uncontrolled immigration to the UK has been to depress the wages of the low-paid, while fat-cat FTSE-100 chiefs have seen their pay packets soar to 150 times the average pay of their workforce.'

He was a Cabinet minister in a party that had undermined low-income wages by forcing the unemployed to take low-skilled jobs at one-sixth the amount workers were being paid.[210] But clearly the major problem was people in Brussels.

It's just possible Johnson and Gove's chary relationship with the truth was mere light-headedness, brought about by the latest polling developments. Probably as a result of Cameron's reputation being yet further besmirched by the whole pig-fucking/Panama Papers combo, the Leave campaign was finally ahead of Remain.

Yet, despite the paucity of coverage about the impact of Brexit, a few people were starting to see the truth. Sarah Wollaston, the former GP who had become a Tory MP and chair of the Commons Health Committee, abandoned the Leave campaign, and began pleading for a Remain vote.

'The consensus now is there would be a huge economic shock if we voted to leave,' she said. 'Undoubtedly, the thing that's most going to influence the financial health of the NHS is the background economy.'[211]

John Major tended to agree. He warned that under Johnson and Gove, the NHS was 'about as safe as a pet hamster in the presence of a hungry python', and said the nation was being 'misled' by Johnson, who was leading a Brexit campaign built around deceitful 'nonsense on stilts'.[212]

We all know this about Johnson. It's hard to find new revelations about his dishonesty that genuinely surprise. Yet he still managed it when, on 12 June, he told the *Sunday Times* that he dyes his hair blond.[213] He later denied it, but 'later denying things' is par for the course with Johnson. Just ask his kids.

Among the things he later denied was the claim aeons before – by which I mean two weeks previously – that the EU was like the Nazis. He never said that, protested Johnson: 'I don't write the headlines.'

The Nazi claim didn't appear in the headlines: it appeared in the stuff he did write.

This sort of endless misinformation from our future prime minister had led to an electorate that had a shockingly poor grasp of the realities. Research showed we overestimated the number of EU immigrants in the country by 300 per cent; among people planning to vote Leave, the estimates were even worse, with Leavers believing that a perfectly ludicrous one-fifth of people living in Britain was an immigrant from the Eurozone.

Eighty-four per cent of us thought Britain was the top contributor to the EU budget. In fact, we were fourth,[214] which seems more than fair, since we had the second-highest GDP.[215]

We misjudged the economic importance of the EU profoundly, believing 30 per cent of the UK's foreign investment came from EU countries, and a similar amount from China. The reality: half our trade was with the EU, and just 1 per cent with China. We would need to increase our China trade by 4,900 per cent to replace what we risked losing from the EU.[216]

Perceptions of EU immigrants were largely driven by fears of how much they were costing the country. For all the cries of racism – which was certainly a factor, and it would be foolish to deny it – the major concern was much more about 'the economy, stupid'. But here, the operative word is 'stupid'.

Britons assumed EU citizens took about 30 per cent of the child benefit Britain paid out, rather than the true figure of 0.3 per cent.[217]

But even that paltry figure is only half the story, because it doesn't touch on how much migrants contributed to our economy. On average, EU migrants living in the UK contributed £2,300 more to the public purse every year than the average British-born adult. Total contribution: over £8.5 billion a year.[218]

One in seven of us believed at least one of the myths about Europe (which had so often dripped from the creative pen of Boris Johnson). For example, we might not have been aware the EU was responsible for giving us statutory holiday pay, but we were perfectly happy to buy the nonsense that Brussels had banned barmaids from showing cleavage or was demanding we call sausages 'emulsified high fat offal tubes'.[219]

But still the tsunami of bullshit swept over the land. In a joint statement, Johnson, Gove and Priti Patel (the answer to the question 'What did Frau Blücher do next?') outlined their vision of an Australian-style points-based system for immigration, leaving us all with the impression this would cut the number of migrants.[220] But research showed an Australian-style system would actually double the number of immigrants.[221]

—

And then there's fishing. The fate of Britain's fisheries became talismanic for the Brexit campaign, with leading campaigners visiting every port they could find on a map to pose alongside proud Britons who had plucked British fish out of British waters for a hundred generations but were now stymied by Brussels. Once we left the EU, there would be no end to the fish we could catch, and nothing to stop us.

It wasn't quite that simple. Across the world, and for generations, fish stocks had been exploited to an insane and unsustainable extent. Standard practice led to fish being caught before they were able to reproduce, and those escaping the trawlers would lay eggs on a sea floor regularly scraped clean by the gigantic, weighted nets the ships hauled in their wake.

The effects on the ecosystem and the species it supports are almost too big to comprehend, so let's focus on just one species: cod.

A cod lives around 25 years, and becomes increasingly fertile as it ages, so the older fish are the ones on which the survival of the species depends. In 2011, a study in North Sea fisheries found only 600 cod over the age of 13, and 200 of those were subsequently caught in a single year.

In 2012 there were only around 100 fully grown cod left in the North Sea.[222]

Experts started to describe the species as 'economically extinct' – not wiped out, exactly, but very vulnerable, and there were so few that it made no economic sense to go and fish them. Yet we still did.

Environmentalists presented governments around the world – including the EU – with a simple choice. Keep going as you have, and you will wipe out cod, and hundreds of other species as well. If you have no fish, you have no fishing industry.

Alternatively, voluntarily reduce fishing, knowing it will reduce the size of your fishing fleets, but that you'll give the species time to recover, and will at least maintain some of your industry.

Every nation chose the second option. Naturally, this hurt fishing communities, but it definitely hurt them less than the alternative, which was the near total extinction of the fish we eat, and therefore the total, permanent collapse of their industry.

Vote Leave said bollocks to that and promised the restrictions would end.

It had been admitted that Brexit would 'mostly eliminate manufacturing'.[223] Most of our allies said it would weaken our international standing. Research showed a 20 per cent increase in hate crimes.[224] The government was planning for widespread food shortages and damage to the NHS, and almost every economist worldwide predicted huge, near permanent damage to our trade and economy.

And it was all being done so we could catch a fish that didn't exist.

Ah, said the Brexiters, all that environmental fish-counting stuff might explain why cod have vanished, but it doesn't explain why Spanish trawlers are in our British waters.

The explanation for that is much simpler: Britain had privatised the ownership of our quotas. Those fishing rights were flogged off to private businesses at a knockdown price, and they immediately flipped them for a quick profit. It was exactly what happened to the Post Office and countless other privatised national assets.

Each of these privatisations had been advertised as a way to turn ordinary citizens into active and happy shareholders in a mighty endeavour, but in reality just further enriched a tiny group of already intensely wealthy people, while making the rest of us worse off.

By the time Brexit happened, just five families, all of them on the *Sunday Times* Rich List, controlled 29 per cent of our fishing quota. Half of the remaining quotas had been sold off to overseas businesses. In total, 80 per cent were owned by overseas businesses or a handful of multimillionaires. [225]

The small, inshore vessels that make up 79 per cent of the UK fishing fleet ended up fishing from just 2 per cent of the quota. Brexit wouldn't change this, because it had nothing to do with the EU: it was British privatisation policy, run from Westminster.

In fact, the EU tried to help us, but we refused. As far back as the late 1980s, EU grants were made available for fishing communities to upgrade and modernise their boats, nets and equipment. But these grants had to be match-funded by the national government. The 1980s version of the Tories decided not to provide funds to those squalid working-class people in Grimsby, so our industry languished while that of Europe surged ahead.[226]

The result: by 2016, the Tories had deprived the fisheries of investment, sold off their quotas to some of the wealthiest people in the country, and condemned ordinary fishermen to fighting over the last 2 per cent; and then blamed Johnny Foreigner for it all.

—

As we entered the final 10 days of the campaign, Osborne mocked up an emergency plan for preventing economic crisis if we voted to exit the EU, which Vote Leave immediately named a 'punishment budget'.

To be fair, the Budget was mostly nonsense. Nothing new about that, you might say, and you'd be right: Osborne had spent five years proving himself to be a lousy Chancellor with a dismal, one-size-fits-none solution to economics – namely, hope the economy responds to being hacked to bits with a machete by jumping up and becoming massively productive.

Osborne's plan for the worst might have been stupid, but imagine the levels of idiocy required to equate 'planning for the worst' with 'punishment'. At least 58 Tory backbenchers from the party of fiscal responsibility vowed to block any such preparations.[227] Plans were for wimps, and Britain was about to become mighty again.

Boris Johnson shrugged off all predictions of disaster, which were being made practically hourly by pretty much every major financial and economic expert body in the world; he said he would go on TV and apologise if Brexit caused economic damage.[228]

Fast-forward to 100 days after we finally left the EU in 2020, and the Office for Budget Responsibility said following Brexit our GDP was, and would remain, 4 per cent lower than if we had remained in the EU.[229] No TV apology.

And then into the fray jumped Nigel Farage, with his rational argument that the EU had ruined this country so much that everybody wanted to come and live here.

Nobody could claim Farage alone had raised social tensions, or that he was the only person to be dog-whistling racism, but he took things to a new level of vast irresponsibility when, on 15 June, he revealed the notorious 'Breaking Point' poster.[230] The poster depicted a vast queue of exhausted refugees, many of them from war-torn Syria, being escorted across fields to a new refugee camp in Slovenia. That was the reality. But Farage presented it as if these people were about to invade Britain.

'Every one of these can get to Calais,' he said. 'We know how bad our government is at defending our borders, and within a few years all of these people will have EU passports.'[231]

It was quickly noted how visually and thematically similar this poster was to images used by the Nazis, including a near-identical image that described 1940s refugees as 'parasites, undermining their host countries'.[232] Farage had also used that word, attacking 'parasites' and saying it was UKIP's role to 'sweep them all away'.[233]

There is an unending list of problems with this sort of rhetoric, but let's just focus on the one that was about to become shockingly important: not everybody who hears this bombastic hatred is rational or unarmed.

The day after Farage unveiled the 'Breaking Point' poster, Jo Cox, a 41-year-old Labour MP, spent the morning meeting constituents in a local library. As she left the building, she was approached by Thomas Mair, who shouted, 'Britain First,' and shot her twice in the head. He then stabbed her 15 times and shot her again.

After brandishing a knife at people rushing to Jo Cox's aid and stabbing a 77-year-old retired miner who was courageous enough to tackle him, Mair fled. He was arrested soon after and will spend the rest of his life behind bars.[234]

Jo Cox died within an hour.

—

An appeal was set up for Jo Cox's family. As news was announced that the public had already donated £1 million, Conservative councillor Dominic Peacock posted on Facebook, 'I've just donated the steam off my piss.'[235]

I don't know how much lower you can get than that.

—

In the wake of Jo Cox's murder, the Brexit campaign was paused for as long as Boris Johnson could maintain his sad face, which it turned out was 96 hours, a full 95 hours longer than any of us could have predicted. Four days after the shooting he was reported to have 'caused chaos' at the graduation of his eldest acknowledged child by unveiling a campaign poster in the middle of the ceremony.[236] Not much gets in the way of Boris's ambition; certainly not the recent murder of a Member of Parliament, or the happiness of a minor franchise branch from his own incomprehensibly fruitful loins.

Not that it mattered. The campaign was over, the damage was done – well, actually, the damage had barely started, but this particular episode was ending, as was the premiership of David Cameron. Leave won, with 51.9 per cent of the vote to Remain's 48.1 per cent.[237]

The following morning, Cameron pootled out of Downing Street, wandered into the middle of a road that was sadly bereft of traffic, and read out his resignation speech.

'We should be proud of the fact that in these islands we trust the people for these big decisions,' he said, although if they'd trusted us, perhaps they wouldn't have had to tell us so many lies. He then went on to list the accomplishments of his time in office. It didn't take long: there were just five items, which are examined below.

'More people in work than ever before in our history,' said Cameron.

Technically true, although largely because the jobs were spread thinner – unemployment was down from Cameron's high of 8.5 per cent,[238] but *under*employment had soared to an even greater 9.9 per cent.[239] Two out of every five jobs created were part time.[240] People might be working, but not enough hours to pay their way. UK salaries were now lower than they had been 12 years earlier.[241]

Accomplishment two: 'Reforms to welfare and education.'

Welfare had been cut by at least £18 billion per year since Cameron entered office,[242] with a further £17 billion planned,[243] a total of £35 billion – or if you prefer, £3,600 per hour, every single hour since the Battle of Hastings. Meanwhile, food bank users had swelled from 40,000 to well over a million.[244]

And as for education: £7 billion of cuts,[245] university budgets slashed by 40 per cent,[246] over £4 billion wasted on free schools. Students were leaving university facing a lifetime of debt, and the abolition of the bursary for nurses had caused the number of healthcare trainees to plummet.

Accomplishment three: 'Keeping our promises to the poorest people in the world.'

This one he did do. Fair play. We kept our promise to pay 0.7 per cent of our GDP in foreign aid – that is until 2021, when the Tories broke that promise too.[247]

Accomplishment four: 'Enabling those who love each other to get married whatever their sexuality.'

True, although it's not a great idea to boast about your party's modernism when more of you voted against it than for.[248] If anything, this was brought about *despite* the best efforts of the Conservative Party.

And last on his extremely short list of achievements, David Cameron named 'above all, restoring Britain's economic strength'. We had lost our AAA credit rating, our national debt had grown by a third, and we had been overtaken in the global economic rankings by Brazil.

And with that, for one last time, David Cameron put on his tense face and walked away from the cameras.

As he wandered back towards the doors of Downing Street, turning his back on all responsibility, contemplating a future of lounging around in a preposterous shed, fabricating memoirs and lobbying one group of Etonian schoolfriends on behalf of another group of Etonian schoolfriends,[249] he was heard to hum a chirpy little tune to himself.[250]

It was a bit like an arsonist being led from the dock and pausing to give us a quick chorus of 'Ob-La-Di, Ob-La-Da'.

Part 2
The Bewilderness Years

2016
It's an Utter Fiasco

The shit hit the fan.

This came as a surprise, because with the exception of the millions of people who had predicted the shit would hit the fan, nobody had predicted the shit would hit the fan. But it did.

The referendum was held on a Thursday. On Friday, the pound fell to a level not seen since 1985. Shares in British banks dropped 30 per cent.[1] The Bank of England had to stump up £250 billion to stabilise the markets,[2] which, even compared to all the large amounts of wasted money previously mentioned, still manages to stand out as a really quite gigantic amount of money: £1 per second for 7,927 years, or £3,600 per hour, every single hour since the earliest known human civilisation arose in ancient Mesopotamia.[3]

By Monday, total stock-market losses were £2.17 trillion,[4] which would have paid for the UK's membership of the EU for the next 241 years.[5]

Within 12 hours of the United Kingdom voting to 'take back control', ministers in the Scottish government proposed a new referendum to end the United Kingdom.[6]

The only global credit ratings agency to have thus far maintained a AAA rating for the UK dumped us down to AA. The other credit agencies, who already had us at AA because we were a nation heading in the wrong direction, now downgraded us yet further.[7]

This might sound like an abstract thing, but it meant the repayments on all this new borrowing were suddenly higher, which meant the government suddenly had even less money for the NHS or public services.

Shit: meet fan.

But it wasn't all fun with money: we also experienced a five-fold increase in racist hate crimes in the week following the referendum, which police said was just the tip of the iceberg, because such attacks were 'significantly under-reported'.[8]

Nonsense, it's just a blip, claimed Brexit apologists, speculating wildly in the total absence of any evidence. The evidence came in 2020, when research found the long-term effects were a 15 to 20 per cent increase in racial and religious hate crime in Britain, starting immediately after the referendum.[9]

But we're getting ahead of ourselves: we still had four years of divisive, delusional chaos before that report came out. So let's rewind to the morning after the vote.

As he trundled in to make his triumphal address, Boris Johnson emanated the sweaty terror of somebody from the HR department suddenly called upon to make good on their boast that they knew how to defuse a bomb. Johnson and Gove had convened a celebratory press conference, which with the sound off you could have easily mistaken for an official response to a school shooting. The body language screamed 'oh giddy Jesus, this is awful' as the pair of them gazed unblinking at the floor, pale and shellshocked. They looked like a pair of gormless game-show contestants who by a series of miraculous flukes had accidentally won a speedboat, and only now did it dawn on them how much it would cost to run it.

Johnson began by praising David Cameron, calling him 'one of the most extraordinary politicians of our age',[10] in much the same way people called Katrina one of the most extraordinary hurricanes to ever hit New Orleans. He went on to mourn Cameron's resignation. 'I know I speak for Michael in saying how sad I am,' said Johnson, unable to get through a single sentence without shifting responsibility.[11]

Europe's leaders, keen to get out of this mess before any more damage was done, implored the UK to implement Brexit as quickly as possible. But Johnson, having spent months telling us how important it was that we leave the EU immediately, now told us there was 'no need for haste'.[12]

Word spread that Johnson hadn't meant Brexit. It was a joke. Just shits and giggles, lads. He, like most of Westminster, had always imagined we'd be sensible enough to begrudgingly choose to remain in Europe, but in the wake of losing the referendum he would personally benefit from 'being seen as having stood up for a principle', in the words of one Cabinet minister.[13]

'People talk about reluctant Remainers,' continued Johnson's colleague, 'but I think there have been a lot of reluctant Brexiters around, people who voted Leave thinking it wouldn't happen, but they'd be able to vent and to tell all their friends at dinner parties they'd done it.'[14]

—

Done what, though? It was amazing how few people knew. Around 17 million people had voted for Brexit, and there seemed to be 17 million opinions about what it meant. The leading two Google searches the day after polling were: 'What is the EU?' and 'What does it mean to leave the EU?'[15]

To summarise: we didn't know what we had, and we were a bit hazy about why we'd given it up.

Less than 24 hours after polling stations closed, leading members of the official Brexit campaign started walking back on all their false promises. Iain Duncan Smith denied he had ever been associated with the pledge of £350 million for the NHS, telling Andrew Marr, 'I never said that during the course of the election,' even though there were numerous photos of him posing in front of the infamous bus emblazoned with the NHS lie.[16]

Nigel Farage expressed similar sudden reservations. 'I would never have made that claim,' he said, and noted that anybody who voted to leave the EU based on getting money for the health service had 'made a mistake'.[17]

Well yeah, clearly. And yet more than two years later, 42 per cent of the British public still believed the NHS was about to get £350 million a week.[18] I almost hate to ruin it for them. Yet there was a perfectly honourable reason for all those Tory Brexiters denying the lies that had been told the day before: they wanted to look ahead to all the lovely new lies they could tell as part of the forthcoming leadership campaign.

Britain is a modern, functioning, inclusive democracy, and that's why our new prime minister was going to be selected by the 0.4 per cent of the public who had paid money to become a member of the Tory party.[19] It was obvious to everybody that the next leader would be one of the big players in the Leave campaign, yet even so, Theresa May, a preposterous, tottering Meccano giraffe, threw her hat into the ring and surprised everybody by opening a tiny lead over bookies' favourite Boris Johnson.

May's offering to the public – or at least, to the one in 250 of the public who would get to have a say in who became prime minister – was that she was a 'serious person for a serious time'; in short, she assured us she knew what she was doing.[20]

There will now be a 10-minute pause for bleak laughter.

Johnson, meanwhile, demonstrated his suitability for the job by knobbing off to play cricket with some aristo pals[21] and then holding a massive piss-up at his farmhouse.[22] When he did deign to return to work, it wasn't as a prospective prime minister, but in his moonlighting job as a *Telegraph* columnist, and it was an absolute dog's dinner. While the markets crashed, and to prevent catastrophe the Bank of England had to spend 12 per cent of our entire national annual income *in a single day*, Johnson got squiffy and floundered through a series of confused statements that clearly demonstrated he hadn't got the foggiest notion what to do next.

'We who are part of this narrow majority must do everything we can to reassure the Remainers,' he wrote. Is it time for another bleak-laughter break already?

His article continued: 'We had one Scotland referendum in 2014, and I do not detect any real appetite to have another,' to which Scotland collectively said, 'Oh is that right, pal?' and hung up another Saltire.[23]

'British people will still be able to go and work in the EU; to live; to travel; to study; to buy homes and to settle down,' Johnson assured us, while simultaneously insisting we would be able to prevent European immigrants having those same rights to live, work and study in the UK.[24] We would, he explained, remain members of the lucrative single market, but also free ourselves from every bit of legislation that makes a single market into a single market.[25]

'There is no need to invoke Article 50,'[26] he wrote, and declared that Leave voters were not remotely anxious about immigration.[27]

Leavers, who until now had been left to themselves to work out what Brexit meant, now found that Boris Johnson's vision was not their own. What do you mean: we're not leaving the single market? What do you mean: we're not changing immigration? What do you mean: we're not invoking Article 50?

The Johnson camp said he was 'tired', and that *of course* we would leave the single market, which is why they'd guaranteed we *wouldn't* leave it during the campaign.[28] And then promised we *would*. And then not. And now it was back again, but only because Johnson was knackered or suffering from wine-flu.

Johnson had performed so many juddering, crashing reversals in the last week that by this time he was basically corrugated. While Britain was right in the middle of the biggest constitutional crisis we had seen since the Second World War, it was becoming clear that the leader of the revolution hadn't got a scooby doo, and was making up policy on the hoof, often while inebriated.

On the Wednesday after the referendum result – because all of this had happened in just five days – Gove and Johnson attended the Conservative Summer Party, putting on a show of smiles and bonhomie while the two of them negotiated their joint pitch for leadership: Johnson would be the PM, and Gove would be Chancellor.[29]

Gove isn't naïve. He's an absolute clattering fanny – I'll grant you that – but he's not a naïve one. He knew how little he should trust Johnson's promises, and just in case he didn't, Gove's (then) wife, the *Daily Mail* journalist Sarah Vine, reminded him in a leaked letter, weirdly written in the same erratically shouty style that defines her own headlines: 'You MUST have SPECIFIC assurances from Boris OTHERWISE you cannot guarantee your support.' She went on to say that such reassurances were needed for the benefit of *Daily Mail* editor Paul Dacre and Rupert Murdoch, the pair of whom 'instinctively dislike Boris'.[30]

Gove got cold feet, which is unsurprising, given that he's a lizard. Johnson might be a lazy, mendacious, inept, floundering one-man game of shag-marry-avoid who had led the nation off a cliff for a laugh, but if he lacked the backing of Murdoch and the *Mail*, the Tories would be in *real* trouble.

'I have repeatedly said that I do not want to be prime minister,' said Gove, announcing that he wanted to be prime minister.[31] His reasons? 'I have come, reluctantly, to the conclusion that Boris cannot provide the leadership or build the team for the task ahead.'[32]

Johnson learned that his sentient comfort blanket, Michael Gove, had decided to smother his career at the same time the rest of us did: just before taking to the stage for the launch of Boris For PM.[33] He began his speech as planned, outlining whatever version of our future had emerged from that morning's spin of the Brexit Randomiser Wheel, and depicting a simply *smashing* future under a bold new shaggy-haired leader. But then, to the palpable shock of supporters who had packed the room, pockets full of bunting and eager to ride his coattails into power, he finished by saying, 'Having consulted colleagues and in view of the circumstances in Parliament, I have concluded that person cannot be me.'[34]

For once, the laughter wasn't bleak.

—

A shifting cloud bank of temporary allegiances immediately began drifting across Westminster, haunted by fugacious, self-serving Tory goons desperately trying to work out who now offered them the best career opportunities.

Perhaps it would be Theresa May, who had just campaigned against everything the Tories were now committed to doing, and made up for it by lurching around uttering inane platitudes in a strange, inhuman croak.

Or Michael Gove, whose combination of unthinking cruelty and impeccable manners would make him a perfect British Hollywood villain, if only he didn't bear a queasy resemblance to a beached mudskipper who has been dressed in boy clothes and forced to work in accounts.

Disgraced former minister Liam Fox also decided to stand, amazingly without the assistance of Adam Werritty. Fox was determined to make Britain a strong, independent nation, which is why as defence secretary he had let his mates bypass security and conduct secret meetings with Israeli intelligence agents,[35] and oversaw the loss of 7,000 soldiers, 5,000 airmen, 5,000 from the navy, and 25,000 civilian defence jobs.[36]

Something called Stephen Crabb wanted to be prime minister too, although it's difficult to see why: pollsters found he was only the 93rd most popular Tory MP, which is a bit like being the 93rd most popular house fire.[37]

And bringing up the rear, in a field comprised entirely of absolute rears, there was Andrea Leadsom, who had really made an impression on officials in her department. Her period as City minister was described by one as 'a disaster'.

'The worst minister we ever had,' one official told the *FT*. Another said: 'She found it difficult to understand issues or take decisions. She was monomaniacal, seeing the EU as the source of every problem.'[38]

In fairness, she sounded like exactly the right person for that moment in our nation's history.

—

Let's pause for a moment to enjoy a lovely bit of dialogue. Ken Clarke and Malcolm Rifkind were caught on camera having a private discussion about the candidates – and it's best if you read this in the voices of Statler and Waldorf from *The Muppet Show*.

Clarke: 'It's an utter fiasco.'

Rifkind: 'I don't mind who wins, as long as Gove comes third. As long as Gove doesn't come in the final two, I don't mind what happens.'

Clarke: 'I think with Michael as prime minister we'd go to war with at least three countries at once. He did us all a favour by getting rid of Boris. The idea of Boris as prime minister is ridiculous.'

Rifkind: 'That could have happened!'

Clarke: 'I don't think either Andrea Leadsom or Boris Johnson actually are in favour of leaving the European Union.'

Rifkind: 'Well, I don't think they cared very much either way.'

Clarke: 'She is not one of the tiny band of lunatics who think we can have a sort of glorious economic future outside the single market. So long as she understands that she's not to deliver on some of the extremely stupid things she's been saying. Theresa is a bloody difficult woman. She doesn't know much about foreign affairs.'

Rifkind was later asked about this conversation. He said, 'My comments speak for themselves, and they appear to be shared by quite a high proportion of the human race.'[39]

Beautiful.

—

Tory members voted for their favourite inept dingleberry in a series of ballots. Crabb and Fox were eliminated immediately, and Gove went out in the second round, leaving just Andrea Leadsom and Theresa May to battle it out; thank God those awful Tory men had all gone, and we could finally have a dignified campaign based around the issues.

Which doesn't quite explain why 53-year-old Andrea Leadsom's pitch boiled down to: vote for me, I'm fertile.

She subtly acknowledged that her rival had been unable to start a family in an interview in *The Times*: 'I don't want this to be "Andrea has children, Theresa hasn't" because I think that would be really horrible,' (which it was, but she didn't let that prevent her from saying it). '[May] possibly has nieces, nephews, lots of people,' she went on, 'but I have children who are going to have children who will directly be a part of what happens next.'[40]

After a flange of Tory backbenchers howled their outrage, Leadsom defended herself by blaming misreporting from *The Times*. 'Truly appalling and exact opposite of what I said,' she tweeted. 'This is despicable and hateful reporting. You must now provide the transcript.'

The Times provided the transcript, and an audio recording too. It was exactly as reported.[41]

Leadsom denied she had tried to exploit the fact of her motherhood in a campaign, but her campaign was wrecked, and Theresa May was the last candidate standing. Every significant policy the nation had voted for the year before could now be abandoned and replaced with something different. The leader of the party of Brexit ended up being a confirmed Remainer, and our national experiment with just how far you can bend a democracy reached Pretzel Level Nine.

—

In early July, right on schedule, Nigel Farage resigned again as leader of UKIP. He had resigned as leader of UKIP in 2009, and a second time in 2015, but this time he was serious.

'During the referendum I said I wanted my country back... now I want my life back,' he told a press conference, adding that when it came to withdrawing from public life, 'I won't be changing my mind again, I can promise you.' And he was never heard from again.[42]

If only the same were true of the Tory MPs who unironically referred to their new leader as 'Mummy' when speaking to journalists.[43] After you've wiped away the bit of sick that just slid onto your chin, consider this empathetic interpretation of their behaviour: perhaps they simply needed a bit of tender loving care, although I'm not sure it was wise to expect it from Theresa May, a cross between a tin heron and a low-budget Albanian supervillain, who gave the impression she'd cut your nose off with a pair of pinking shears if you said 'less' instead of 'fewer'.

If only she'd been anywhere near that exacting about what Brexit meant. When asked to explain her plan for leaving the EU, she responded, 'Brexit means Brexit,'[44] an approach to definitions that would have made Samuel Johnson's life a lot easier. It marked the beginning of an epic five-year quest for the meaning of exactly what it was we had just decided we would do.

May headed off to Ireland to tell them there would be no border, which was confusing because two days before the referendum she had said it would be 'inconceivable' that we could avoid a border.[45]

Then she went to Rome to perplex European leaders with self-evidently demented reassurances about EU citizens living in the UK: 'I want to be able to guarantee their rights in the UK, I expect to be able to do that, I intend to be able to do that, to guarantee their rights,' she said, and then insisted we would end their right to freedom of movement.[46]

Fortunately, we could turn to John Redwood for one of his always reliable predictions: 'Getting out of the EU can be quick and easy,' he wrote, 'the UK holds most of the cards in any negotiation.'[47] At the time of writing, the evidence of this still hasn't revealed itself, unless those cards are all jokers and knaves, and we're playing solitaire.

—

New prime minister, new Cabinet.

Out went George Osborne and in came Philip Hammond, with a totally new attitude to the banks. No, hold on, let me correct that: *exactly the same* attitude to the banks.

Bankers were not responsible for the financial crisis, he said (although in Iceland alone they had jailed 36 senior bankers for their part in the global collapse).[48] But according to Hammond, such gigantic corporate misbehaviour was *your* fault, plebs, because bankers 'had to lend to someone,'[49] and then he got on with the job of cutting the banks' corporation tax to 17 per cent.[50]

Meanwhile, over at the Foreign Office, Hammond's previous job was filled by honest broker and expert diplomat Boris Johnson, to whom global leaders gave a suitable welcome. US State Department Deputy Spokesman Mark Toner had to stifle a laugh when he was told the news on live TV.[51] At a diplomatic meet-and-greet reception at the French Embassy the day after becoming Foreign Secretary, Johnson was booed.[52] The French foreign minister bluntly called him a liar over his unachievable promises for Brexit, and an EU source told the BBC, 'Everyone in the European Parliament thinks it's a bad joke and that the Brits have lost it.'

Members of the German Parliament continued the theme, saying it wasn't a good omen for future relations if Johnson 'inflicted his capricious and monstrous approach' on his neighbours, while *Der Spiegel*, the bestselling news magazine in Europe, wrote, 'Haha! Boris Johnson as foreign minister. I can't stop laughing. The Brits are crazy.'

The former prime minister of Sweden tweeted, 'I wish it was a joke, but I fear it isn't,' while the *Sydney Morning Herald* opined that Johnson should be 'removed from Conservative Party plotting at Westminster and allowed to get on with being a travelling circus'.[53]

The most immediate problem facing Johnson was fixing our relations with Turkey, which had crumbled to a terrible low the previous September, when some shambolic, thermonuclear tribunal-magnet had felt moved to write and publish a poem calling the President of Turkey a wanker and accusing him of having sexual congress with a goat.[54]

That thermonuclear tribunal-magnet was now Foreign Secretary and was due to meet the Turkish leader face to face within weeks. In an effort to mend fences, Johnson issued a bizarre apology to the government in Ankara, which took the form of him praising the quality of his 'very well-functioning Turkish washing machine'.

—

By comparison, the rest of the Cabinet seemed almost sane. David Davis held a newly created Cabinet post at the Department for Exiting the European Union (DExEU). His job was leading the negotiations for our divorce from Europe, and our new trading relationship with the EU, but really he should have focused on inventing a time machine so he could scrub out all his previous utterances that he now disagreed with, not least of which was this little pearl from 2002.

'There is a proper role for referendums in constitutional change, but only if done properly. If it is not done properly, it can be a dangerous tool,' he told Parliament, being something of an expert in dangerous tools. 'What is certain is that pre-legislative referendums are the worst type of all.

'Referendums should be held when the electorate are in the best possible position to make a judgement. They should be held when people can view all the arguments for and against and when those arguments have been rigorously tested. In short, referendums should be held when people know exactly what they are getting. So legislation should be debated by Members of Parliament on the Floor of the House, and then put to the electorate for the voters to judge.'[55]

But it was now 2016 in Brexitania, so sod all that. Davis set about his task with the swaggering confidence of a virtuoso dingbat, boasting: 'Be under no doubt we can do deals with our trading partners, and we can do them quickly.'[56]

German industry would rescue us, he breezily declared, because 'within minutes of a vote for Brexit, CEOs would be knocking down Chancellor Merkel's door, demanding access to the British market'.[57]

The negotiations would be easy, he airily explained, and not only would they be completed 'within between 12 and 24 months', but they would also result in the UK joining a free trade area 'massively larger than the EU', including Hong Kong, Canada, Australia, India, Japan, the UAE, Indonesia, and many others.[58]

It's hard to know whether he believed any of that, or knew it was crap and was simply lying to us: one possibility makes him a fool, and the other makes him a scoundrel. Of course, it's always possible he's both.

I don't know why, but that reminds me of Liam Fox, back in Cabinet as international trade secretary, where he immediately told the entire world British business was 'too lazy and too fat'. Was it too soon to suggest a different sales strategy if we wanted to get people to trade with us?[59]

There was also a big promotion to Chief Whip for Gavin Williamson, a supernaturally incompetent lurching tower of wrong wearing the teeth of a starved horse. A colleague summed him up: 'He looked a bit goofy. He wasn't a good speaker. I looked him up, and he'd had an undistinguished North Country career,'[60] and I think we can all agree he's lived down to everybody's expectations.

Williamson's primary talent appeared to be chasing headlines, which he did from the moment he got the job by breaking the Palace of Westminster's no-animals rule: he parked his pet tarantula on his desk and absolutely refused to shift it. 'I've had Cronus since he was a spiderling, so I have a very paternal sort of approach,' said Williamson. 'It's very much the same sort of love and care that I give to my spider as I give to all MPs. Cronus is a perfect example of an incredibly clean, ruthless killer – absolutely fascinating to rear.'[61]

Trundling Horcrux Priti Patel had called for the Department of International Development to be dismantled, so obviously she was now put in charge of that very department.[62] It was a brilliant day for the advancement of hypocrisy as the formal basis of our national character.

Theresa May sacked crepuscular backstabbing vowel-strangler Michael Gove, who took it well ('If I'd been in her shoes, I would have sacked me too').[63] With him gone, Liz Truss, ITV4 made flesh, became the nation's most senior law officer, and the third successive Lord Chancellor to have no knowledge whatsoever of the law. She was considered so much worse than Gove – yes, even than him – that the Tory justice minister immediately quit in protest, saying of Truss's appointment: 'I fear this could be damaging to the justice system.'[64]

But we were just getting started with incomprehensible decisions: in July, a government report warned 'Britain must urgently prepare for flooding, heatwaves and food shortages,'[65] so two days later Theresa

May abolished the Department for Climate Change, a decision that was denounced as 'deeply worrying', 'terrible', and 'plain stupid'. This came as news broke that the first question asked by newly appointed Environment Secretary Andrea Leadsom on entering her department was: 'Is climate change real?'[66]

May then abolished the minister responsible for resettling Syrian refugees.[67] Britain had committed to help people fleeing the war the previous September, after the photo of little three-year-old Alan Kurdi's body lying dead on a beach briefly made us remember migrants were human beings. But we'd forgotten again by July 2016, allowing the Tories to forget their pledge too. The previous year we had committed to take 20,000. In reality, we had taken 2,800.[68]

Good news, though. May said it was now her mission to rid the world of modern slavery: poor people tricked into making life-harming choices by shadowy, merciless figures, and then exploited, forced into jobs they don't want to do and can't escape, for so little reward that they can't even afford to feed themselves.[69]

Iain Duncan Smith took the news hard, because that had literally been his welfare policy.

—

You'd only just learned Stephen Crabb's name, and now you had to unlearn it because he sent a message to a 19-year-old woman he had interviewed for a job in his office, informing her he wanted to have sex with her: and bingo! – he was gone from his job as work and pensions secretary after only three months in the job, one of which he spent miserably failing to become prime minister.[70]

All things considered, it's fortunate he didn't get that promotion: imagine the scandal if the replacement for David Cameron and forerunner of Boris Johnson had shamed the party by being led into an uncompromising position by his irrepressible penis.

And speaking of Dave: he had one more task to perform before he vanished from public life to spend less time with his box sets – his resignation honours list, which, true to form, was packed with people who had coincidentally handed vast sums of money to the Conservative Party.

Cameron attempted to be mildly sneaky this time, listing one new peer as Andrew Fraser: his real name was Alexander Fraser, and it was under this name that he'd given £2.5 million to the Tories. This made Fraser the fifth biggest donor since 2010; the biggest two, James Lupton and Michael Farmer, had already been made peers by Cameron. The fourth biggest, Michael Hintze, was given a knighthood.[71]

Andrew Cook also got a knighthood by the departing Cameron, for 'political service' and not – definitely *not* – because he had shoved £1 million into Conservative Party pockets.[72] Sadly, Michael Spencer, who had stumped up £4 million, had his nomination for a peerage refused by the Honours Committee[73] – his business had become (entirely innocently) embroiled in a financial scandal, and some speculated that this was the cause of the refusal.[74] The delay didn't last long: by 2020 he was a member of the House of Lords, by which time Cameron had proposed him for the job three times.[75]

And what did all these new appointees do once they got to the mother of parliaments? Not a whole lot. Half of the new members of the Lords created by Cameron had spoken fewer than five times by the time he was replaced by Theresa May. Eighteen of them had not asked a single question. Peers aren't paid a salary, but can claim an attendance allowance: Baroness Mone, for example, claimed £7,500, yet had managed to speak just once. Lord Arbuthnot had exerted himself a bit more and had managed to speak twice in a single year, although he did claim £2,700 every month for the effort.[76]

Cameron had now created 13 more peers. In fact, by the time he left office, he'd expanded the House of Lords to 859 unelected members.[77] The elected House of Commons, meanwhile, has only 650.[78]

And it was in that same spirit of returning democratic powers to Parliament that Theresa May now planned to deny MPs the right to a vote on triggering Article 50 and begin the Brexit process.[79] It was just the start of a long-running battle about whether Parliament had any role to play in our lovely new post-Brexit democracy.

—

In September Diane James was elected leader of UKIP.[80] Just 18 days later she resigned, saying, 'I wish the party well for the future under new leadership,' which turned out to be old leadership: shy, retiring Nigel Farage was back again.[81] It was another one of those things that nobody (except for absolutely everybody) could see coming. And this leads us with grinding inevitability to the dismal but unsurprising failure of Big Trade Deal Day.

A few months before, David Davis had asserted, 'I would expect the new prime minister on September ninth to immediately trigger a large round of global trade deals with all our most favoured trade partners,' and in anticipation of this event he had organised a summit on 13 September, at which hordes of political and business leaders from favoured trade partners would meet, pens poised, ready to sign all those lucrative contracts.[82]

I regret to inform you that wasn't how things panned out. Big Trade Deal Day ended up held behind closed doors, possibly to disguise the fact it attracted fewer than 50 people, including those giving speeches. No attendees whatsoever were from outside of the UK. The summit agreed no deals, and instead was described as an exercise in 'scratching around for ideas'.

Perhaps this was a bit of a wake-up call for Davis. Just before he was handed the job of Brexit secretary, he had claimed Britain could easily secure tariff-free access to the single market, but now, mere days into the job, he was saying, 'This is likely to be the most complicated negotiation in modern times.'[83]

He still hadn't recognised the problem of the Northern Irish border, however. He persisted in telling people, 'We had a common travel area between the UK and the Republic of Ireland many years before either country was a member of the European Union.'[84] And that's technically true, while also being entirely wrong: customs controls were introduced in 1923,[85] only one year after the foundation of the Irish Free State.

—

This might be a good moment to provide an explanation of the Irish border conundrum that David Davis was currently saying he couldn't see, along with Theresa May, Boris Johnson, and all the major figures who'd staked their careers on delivering Brexit.

When Britain was still inside the EU, we belonged to a collection of nations that had agreed on shared standards, free trade and no tariffs. Widgets, doobries and thingamabobs produced in any of these nations could be sold to any other of them without any checks being made at national borders: the convergence of our regulations meant everybody could be sure our products all met agreed minimum standards.

We called this the single market.

During the Brexit campaign, almost every major Leave activist had at some point assured us we would remain in the single market. To be fair, many of them had also said we would abandon the single market – sometimes they'd say both things, often in the same speech. But since the referendum it had become increasingly clear we were definitely going to leave the single market. Theresa May had drawn red lines, and you can't rub out red. It's one of the rules.

This raised a major concern, since leaving the single market risked making our economy hugely uncompetitive. Without a trade deal with the EU, Britain would have to trade with Europe on World Trade Organization (WTO) rules, and those rules included tariffs.

Tariffs are basically just a tax, usually between around 10 per cent and 90 per cent of the value of the thing being traded. They make money for the government, and act as a kind of crude protectionism: if you charge an extra 25 per cent on a widget made abroad, it makes it more likely that your population will buy widgets made in your own nation. While that sounds great on the face of it, tariffs go both ways: if we have them, so do the people we sell to. This means people overseas won't buy our stuff, which is a significant problem for the 6.5 million British jobs reliant on exports.[86]

Tariff values are set by the WTO, and they're set pretty high as an encouragement for nations to agree trade deals that offer better terms. That's why almost every country in the world has joined a trade bloc with its neighbours. The list of seven – yep, just seven – countries we were about to join in trading isolation isn't one that fills the mind with images of prosperity or stability: Somalia, Turkmenistan, South Sudan, Iran, Mauritania, Western Sahara and Mongolia.

And that's it. Every other country worldwide is part of a free-trade bloc with neighbouring countries, except for those seven.

And now us.[87]

The problem Britain faced was vast: we imported huge amounts of goods, services, fuel and something like 80 per cent of our food.[88] It changed seasonally, but typically the EU alone provided around 45 per cent of our vegetables and 80 per cent of our fruit.[89] If we adopted WTO terms, all of those things would attract additional import fees.

And export fees too. A typical car has about 30,000 parts, made in complex supply chains stretching across the world. Even if Britain boasted of having a car factory in Sunderland, it was likely that thousands of pieces of each car (and almost all their raw materials) would have been sourced overseas and shipped into Britain. Under WTO terms, each time we shipped in a part it might attract a tariff of 10 or 20 per cent. We would then assemble the parts and ship the finished car back to mainland Europe to be sold – but exporting it would attract another 10 or 20 per cent.

Under WTO terms, by the time a British-assembled car hit a showroom in, for example, Denmark, it might end up costing 10, 20 or even 40 per cent more than if the same car had been assembled in another EU member state.

That didn't mean a manufacturer would instantly shut their car plant in the UK. Over decades, they had sunk billions into their factories, and wouldn't want to simply write off that investment. But the next time a car company was assessing where to assemble a new model or invest in a new factory, Britain might start out with a 10, 20 or even 40 per cent price disadvantage. Consequently, there was a much higher risk that manufacturing jobs – and the associated tax income the Treasury needed to pay off our national debt – would gradually shift overseas.

This is a key characteristic of Brexit. Yes, there was an immediate risk of sudden chaos as we left the EU, but the biggest economic problem we faced was a long, slow puncture of protracted decline.

Any sane government (and some insane ones too) would battle to save big household-name manufacturers like Nissan or Ford. So those car giants would most likely get government guarantees and grants to keep them open, shifting the additional cost onto the taxpayer. But the same tariff issue would apply to tens of thousands of smaller businesses, lacking the clout required to pressure Downing Street into giving financial backing. They'd inevitably get squeezed out of selling to overseas markets, while finding any materials they imported were suddenly more expensive too.

Fortunately, a simple solution existed: Britain could agree a trade deal with the EU. Both sides would benefit from such a deal, and both sides really wanted one. It should have been very straightforward.

Unfortunately for Britain, there was an added complication: the Irish border.

The Good Friday Agreement (GFA), signed in 1997, was a neat bit of trickery under which – to massively simplify the issue – governance of Northern Ireland was shared between both communities, and the border was effectively magicked away. Overnight, there was no appreciable, street-level difference between north and south. This meant Catholics in Belfast felt they were walking around in a country called Ireland, while the Protestants felt they were still walking around a part of Britain. In a sense, they were both correct.

The killings stopped, and an era of peace began.

But the GFA had only been possible because both Britain and Ireland were inside the EU, the single market and the customs union.

The agreement explicitly mentions this. Ireland and Britain shared those regulatory standards, which meant nobody needed to check goods crossing the Irish border. Therefore, it was easy to pretend the border wasn't there, and everybody could be happy.

In 2016, however, the UK decided it wanted to leave both the EU and the single market. We might deviate from those EU standards in future, which meant there would need to be some sort of border where goods could be checked.

There were only two places a hard border could be added. We could reinstitute a border between Northern Ireland and the Irish Republic, which the GFA had magicked away, but this would infuriate the Catholics. Now, once again, they'd be separated from part of what they considered to be their own country by a land border necessitated by those hated Brits.

Alternatively, we could introduce a border somewhere between Northern Ireland and the rest of the UK. But this would enrage the Protestant community, which felt fearsomely British.

It would also technically split up the United Kingdom by putting a physical, legislative and trading border between one bit and another. And if your party's official name is the Conservative and Unionist Party, you don't want to implement a policy that is the literal opposite of conserving the union.

That conundrum is bad enough – but it gets worse. The GFA was only signed because various nations and bodies had agreed to be guarantors of it, offering to step in to prevent anybody from breaching the terms. Among those terms was: no border checkpoints.

These guarantors included the USA, which has a large and powerful Irish lobby, a great many of whom were now telling Britain that America would not sign any future trade deal with the UK if we broke the GFA.

Meanwhile the EU, another guarantor, was legally bound not to sign any deal that broke the GFA. These two markets are vastly important to the UK: the EU accounted for 50 per cent of our entire export trade[90] and the USA was a further 19 per cent.[91] Yet now our

Brexit position risked making it impossible to trade with either of them – at least not without adding huge WTO tariff costs that would make us uncompetitive.

The consequence of all of this was that the second Britain voted for Brexit, we found ourselves facing three unpalatable options.

Option 1: We could place a border between Northern Ireland and the Irish Republic.

Option 2: We could place a border between Northern Ireland and the rest of the UK.

Option 3: We could have no border at all, and the entire UK would continue to accept EU rules on goods and services that came with remaining in the single market, but we'd have no say in defining those rules because we had left the EU.

Unfortunately, the first option breaks the GFA; the second option breaks up the UK; and the third option is the opposite of the Brexit we had just been promised.

All these issues had been patiently explained to the advocates of Brexit well in advance of the referendum; they were dismissed as Project Fear, and most of the major players in the winning Leave campaign – not least Boris Johnson – had airily waved aside any concerns, calling the warnings 'totally and utterly absurd' and the ravings of 'pessimists and merchants of doom'.[92]

—

In October, Theresa May attended her first Tory conference as leader, and before we get stuck into the meat of the gathering, let's do a quick summary of observations by minor attendees, beginning with the opinions of John Redwood: 'People are the only way of keeping governments honest and sensible,' he gabbled, not realising he'd just confessed the government would be corrupt imbeciles if we don't watch them like a fucking hawk.[93]

And also if we do.

Deranged baby factory Andrea Leadsom made one of the more surprising claims of the conference: 'Tourists are buying bottled

English countryside air for up to £80 a go,' she howled, wriggling free from the man with the big net.[94]

Our new Home Secretary Amber Rudd was having a difficult time of it. She was now the minister with official responsibility for hating foreigners, which wasn't helped by the indefatigable falsity of her fellow MPs. A journalist surprised her by asking about suggestions the government was planning to increase immigration from Australia.

'There are no plans to increase immigration from Australia,' she reassured him. 'Did somebody promise to increase migration from Australia? Who was that?'

The journalist told her who.

'Oh,' she sighed, 'Mr Johnson again.'[95]

Meanwhile, on the big stage, Theresa May laid out plans for a Great Repeal Bill, in which over 100,000 pieces of legislation, carefully knitted into our international relationships over a four-decade period, would be abruptly crowbarred into UK law overnight, without any parliamentary scrutiny whatsoever.[96]

What's more, now we had restored parliamentary sovereignty, the prime minister was suggesting using a legislative tool called the royal prerogative to allow her to make decisions without reference to Parliament whatsoever. 'It doesn't feel very democratic to me,' said one Tory peer, 'to have one individual, using the royal prerogative, deciding exactly when we're going to commit to that momentous path.'[97]

As the conference kicked off, the competitive hardening of Tory attitudes about Brexit was putting the willies up the financial markets. The pound slumped again towards 31-year lows, making life harder than ever for Chancellor Philip Hammond.[98] His speech unceremoniously dumped Osborne's timetable for balancing the Budget[99] because suddenly, after 120,000 people had died in pursuit of that fiscal dream,[100] it had stopped being important: the only thing that mattered today was Brexit, and he was going to have to spend like there was no tomorrow if we were going to avoid feeling the consequences.

'We are leaving the European Union,' he told delegates. 'But it is equally clear to me that the British people did not vote on 23 June to become poorer or less secure.'[101]

You aren't paying attention, Hammond. That's precisely what we did.

Elsewhere at the conference, Gavin Barwell was explaining his novel suggestion for solving our housing crisis: build homes with smaller rooms.[102] Britain already built the smallest homes in Europe, and they were already the second most expensive – beaten only by Monaco,[103] where the average wealth per person is $2.1 million.[104]

So obviously what Britain needed was even tinier, even more ludicrously expensive housing. The Tories had already done a secret test run of this idea. In 2015 Tony Gallagher, a Cambridgeshire housebuilder, had asked permission from the government to avoid meeting our already pitiful minimum room dimensions, presumably allowing him to make higher profits by selling more houses per square foot. The government waived aside the regulations and allowed it. Also, he got handed a £30 million public subsidy to do the job.

Good guess: Tony Gallagher *is* a Tory donor.[105]

But now Barwell was singing the praises of a company that sold apartments that were a further 20 per cent smaller than the minimum one-bedroom flat: smaller, in fact, than a two-car garage, and all yours for a mere £250,000.[106] The argument was that we were running out of room, although Germany has a population density only 5 per cent lower than ours[107] yet somehow builds houses 50 per cent bigger and sells them cheaper.[108]

Barwell moved on to rubbishing Labour's plan to build half a million new council homes, saying social housing was 'the denial of people's ambitions and dreams', an announcement predicated on the curious notion that people dream of sleeping in bus shelters, yet have nightmares about kind and empathetic governments.[109]

Meanwhile, at the same conference, Communities Secretary Sajid Javid promised twice as many new homes as Barwell had just derided as being completely unachievable.

Javid claimed there had been 'massive progress' on housebuilding under Cameron's manifesto pledge.[110] The National Audit Office found no evidence that any homes whatsoever had been built under the programme.[111] But let's not get bogged down in finickity details.

Various fringe debates were dogged by an unexpected fightback by ironical whimsy. The Taxpayers' Alliance held a talk by Priti Patel, as warm a presence as Dolores Umbridge with rabies, who had to pretend not to notice the revelation that one of her host's directors lived in France, and so had paid no tax in Britain for several years.[112] The Northern Powerhouse stand might well have been great, but with effortless symbolism, they hadn't finished building it by the time the conference started. And the event named 'From Poverty to Prosperity' was cancelled.

The 'Solving Poverty the Conservative Way' debate did go ahead, though. A gin and tonic at the event cost £7, which was just 20p less than the minimum wage paid to the people serving the gin and tonic. So of course, one speaker at the event called for the abolition of the minimum wage, and another called for a two-child limit for people on benefits.[113] Poverty solved!

Or not quite, because just as the conference was ending, a report showed the number of children living in poverty had increased by 250,000 under the Conservatives.[114] It was now one child in four. So, the next month, the government announced it was abolishing the Child Poverty Unit.[115]

Now *that's* how to solve poverty the Conservative way!

—

Back in July Theresa May had gone to Europe to guarantee the rights of EU nationals living in the UK.[116] It was October now, so Liam Fox announced that EU nationals would be treated as 'one of our main cards in the negotiations'.[117]

Seasoned commentators suggested that there might be some retaliation from the EU for the calculated treatment of its citizens as expendable bargaining chips, but David Davis brushed aside concerns: 'There will be no downside to Brexit, only a considerable upside.'[118]

There was certainly an upside for Michael Gove, who had no sooner been sacked than he was back again, proof that it's not only a good man that you can't keep down. This time he was on the Brexit Select Committee. All that backstabbing business was, Gove said, 'water under the bridge', regardless of October's report in the *Sunday Times* that Boris Johnson wanted to punch him, which marks the first and last time I have agreed with Johnson about anything.[119]

Eight of the ten Tories joining Gove on the committee scrutinising Brexit had voted to leave the EU,[120] a sure indicator that the party wanted no heretics to stand in the way of their mission to do whatever the hell it was they were going to eventually decide to do. At this stage, it could have been anything. The guesswork was half the fun.

But the hazy nature of things was really starting to worry major manufacturers, and as October ended, Tories did what they had spent the last 40 years telling us was nascent socialism and the dead hand of government interfering with the perfect, invisible workings of the divine market: they wrote a blank cheque to Nissan, so the carmaker wouldn't bugger off to a less palpably weird location, such as Discworld.[121]

The Tories had previously told everybody that this sort of state aid was forbidden by the evil EU – one of the main reasons for the urgent need to leave Europe was to free our government to save our industry. But now the referendum was won, the government admitted the reality: state aid was prevented by World Trade Organization rules, and not by the Europeans.[122] Still, with a bit of cheating they could bypass those restrictions – and creative accountancy was right in the Conservative Party's sweet spot.

Within a couple of weeks, Nissan boss and future international fugitive[123] Carlos Ghosn held a meeting with Theresa May, after which the Tories handed them what was called 'unconditional investment aid' – and if the word 'unconditional' wasn't expansive enough, we went on to promise 'further relief if the terms of Britain's European Union exit ended up harming the plant's performance'.[124]

Remember Cameron's transparency agenda? Neither did the Tories. The details of the Nissan deal were kept from the public, leading one state-aid lawyer to comment that the opacity was worrying. 'Perhaps as part of the Brexit fever they've just decided they won't follow the rule book,' he said. 'That would be unwise. The EU won't engage with us if we're subsidising our businesses.'[125]

Meanwhile we saw the first signs of the endless parliamentary Brexit revolts that would plague the coming years. Ministers announced they would refuse to share details of their negotiating position with MPs, and May said she would trigger Article 50 without the permission of the House of Commons – neither of which is particularly emblematic of a parliamentary democracy.

Former Tory health minister Anna Soubry accused Theresa May of using Brexit as a cover to achieve a wide range of policy objectives that hadn't been part of the referendum. 'It is wrong to assume that there is a whole series of mandates that flow from that one simple and very straightforward question,' said Soubry.[126]

The matter went to the High Court, which ruled that Parliament is sovereign, and must have a say over Brexit;[127] it was a huge setback for Theresa May's plans, which were already phenomenally complicated. From now on, she had to persuade a majority of MPs to agree to each subsequent act of national self-harm.

But even though the government attempted to keep everything secret, information still leaked out. As we got to November, a government report quite worryingly revealed at least 500 of the Brexit-related tasks being undertaken were 'beyond the capacity and capability' of the government, and that we would need to employ an *additional* 30,000 civil servants to get through this chaos.[128]

The giant, bureaucratic hellscape that is the European Commission only employed 33,000 staff, and that was to cover 28 member states.[129]

More worryingly still, the leaked report concluded that there was still no plan for how to achieve Brexit.[130] The inappropriately named European Research Group (ERG) of Eurosceptic Tory MPs had apparently formed to carry out Brexit planning, with members claiming almost a quarter of a million pounds in expenses to carry out their 'research'.[131] In that time, did the ERG produce a workable plan for Brexit? It did not. Money well spent for chairing an ineffectual talking shop. Well, bellowing shop.

In November, the ERG's Andrew Rosindell decided to lay aside the vast crisis washing over our entire nation and focus instead on the really important stuff: 'I am calling for BBC One to play our national anthem at the end of each day!' he tweeted.[132] The BBC kindly obliged, and the next evening's broadcast of *Newsnight* ended with 'God Save the Queen', performed by the Sex Pistols.[133]

But finally, thank the Lord in heaven above, a thorough and realistic Brexit plan emerged. As an official carried a document to a Brexit planning meeting with David Davis and Theresa May, a handwritten note could be made out: 'What's the model? Have your cake and eat it.'[134]

—

Having already blown £250 billion propping up the markets on the day the referendum result came in, Philip Hammond now admitted Brexit would add an additional £122 billion to government debt.[135] So far in 2016, that made it £372 billion: equal to £3,600 per hour, every hour since the Palaeolithic era, when humans first domesticated the goat, and the giant ground sloth still walked the earth.[136]

Need cheering up? The Office of Budget Responsibility added another little gem for us, predicting a further £58 billion of borrowing in the next five years 'related to the referendum result and exiting the EU'.[137] That would be an extra £226 million per week of costs relating to a Brexit that – after quarter of a century of agitating – nobody could yet define, and which was stymied by an Irish border problem that nobody had an answer to.

It was gobbling up not just money, but the capacity of the entire government. Not much else was getting done, and the problems that affected the nation kept on mounting.

There were 1.2 million people reliant on food banks in 2016, up from 40,000 when Tories entered office.[138] By 2016, wages were no higher than they had been 13 years earlier. The Tories had not only borrowed more than Labour planned to in 2010,[139] but had borrowed more than every single Labour government since 1945 *combined*.[140]

In Labour's last year in office, national debt was 62 per cent of GDP.[141] It was now predicted to exceed 90 per cent, and the Chancellor admitted they wouldn't return to the levels Labour had achieved until at least 2045.[142]

Shall we quickly whizz through the last month of 2016, and then go for a pint or two of absinthe?

—

Michael Fallon, the defence secretary, decided to close a 'super-barracks' for a garrison in Scotland, which we'd only just refurbished at a cost of £60 million; and then he omitted to tell Parliament what he was doing.[143]

It was found that the Tory pledge to plant 11 million trees to 'safeguard the green belt' had slightly underperformed: they'd managed to plant barely 10 per cent of that.[144]

Every single former health secretary since 1988 signed a letter condemning the Tories for failing the mentally ill, as figures showed people with mental health problems were 370 per cent more likely to die early – and that the figure had grown every year since Tories took office in 2010.[145]

The Department for International Trade, headed up by the ever-assiduous Liam Fox, appointed executive directors responsible for 'independent scrutiny of the department'. There were complaints when those independent scrutineers included people who had supported his leadership bid, and this topped off a typically bad week for Fox, which included news that only 30 per cent of staff in his department were satisfied with his leadership.[146]

David Davis confirmed for the nation what we had all begun to suspect. 'What's the requirement of my job? I don't have to be very clever, I don't have to know that much,' he confessed, which was fortunate, all things considered. 'I just have to be calm.'[147]

Well, to be honest, David, I think a bit of panic was appropriate by December 2016.

Theresa May had finally managed to express what we had actually voted for using – it seemed – a Dulux colour chart. 'Black Brexit, white Brexit, grey Brexit – actually what we should be looking for is a red, white and blue Brexit.'

Oh well, that's cleared that up, then.[148]

The outgoing director general of the prison service said the three consecutive Lord Chancellors should be blamed for 'bringing the custodial system to the brink of collapse' with their 'operational disaster' that would 'take years to put right.'[149] Fortunately, the Lord Chancellor at the time, Liz Truss, had some positive news: prison officers, she claimed, were able to scare off drones with barking dogs.[150]

I knew Labradors were clever, and I knew Truss wasn't, but until that moment I hadn't grasped the full extent.

Philip Davies was back, this time elected by fellow Tory MPs to sit on the Equalities Committee. Davies was the chairman of the Campaign Against Political Correctness,[151] had voted against same-sex marriage, and appeared alongside anti-feminist bloggers who called single mothers 'bona fide idiots'.[152] Only months before his appointment to the committee, he had said, 'I don't believe there's an issue between men and women. The problem is being stirred up by those who can be described as militant feminists and the politically correct males who pander to this nonsense.'[153]

Women earn 18 per cent less than men for doing the same jobs.[154] Even militant feminist ones.

And then three days after joining the committee, Davies tried to use his usual tactic of filibustering – talking without purpose until the time for legislation runs out – to block a bill tackling domestic violence.[155]

Labour MP Jess Phillips responded to his appointment, 'I have every faith that the intelligence and skills of those on the committee will mean he will have little effect, much like in the rest of his career.'[156]

Spindly, posturing mantis Jacob Rees-Mogg, who was beaten with a Latin phrasebook at an impressionable age (but in my opinion, nowhere near hard enough), told a select committee that the UK should slash environmental and safety regulations. Regulations that were good enough for India were good enough for us, he said.[157]

Workplace deaths per year in the UK: 111.[158]

Workplace deaths per year in India: 48,000.[159]

Stop me if you've heard this one before, but David Ord turned up in the New Year's Honours List. He was a member of the Conservative Leaders' Group, a dining club of invited business leaders who got exclusive access to Cabinet ministers. He had, entirely coincidentally, given the Tories £930,000, and now was being knighted.[160]

And to end the year, the government decided to take time off from the most important and complicated constitutional challenge the nation had faced since the outbreak of the Second World War, and instead engage in a schoolyard squabble about Theresa May's pants.

Nicky Morgan, who Theresa May had recently removed from her role as education secretary, took issue with the £995 leather trousers the prime minister wore for a photo shoot, saying, 'I don't think I've ever spent that much on anything apart from my wedding dress.'

In retaliation for mocking her clothes, the *actual prime minister* barred Nicky Morgan from coming to Downing Street.[161] The *actual prime minister* did this. I've checked, and she really had left primary school half a century earlier.

2017
Perpetually Intoxicated and Inappropriate With Women

In the first week of January, there was finally a financial crisis that the government cared about: Conservative donors began threatening to stop handing over money as the consequences of what Tory Brexiteers had sold to the nation became increasingly clear. Sir Andrew Cook – who the departing Cameron had only just knighted for something probably completely unrelated to Cook handing over £1.2 million[1] – warned May he would end future donations if she pulled Britain out of the single market.

Charlie Mullins, founder of Pimlico Plumbers, who had given £60,000 to help the Tories win the election,[2] now found himself giving £80,000 to fund a legal challenge to prevent Tories from doing what they promised to do if they won an election.[3] It doesn't sound like his marbles are all accounted for, but he had moments of clarity too: he predicted Theresa May would be gone within two years, saying, 'When she goes, the damage will have been done and it's going to take a long, long time to get back to where we are today. People in business just cannot believe that she is cutting us off from a market of 500 million people.'

So a bad time for the important business of government – fundraising – and now back to politics.

Gavin Barwell, who has never been seen in the same room as Karl Pilkington, suddenly announced plans to build 17 wonderful new towns and villages, spread widely across the land. These would not be cramped estates full of soulless boxes, but 'garden communities', and they would contain 200,000 new homes.[4]

The 200,000 announced (but not built) homes from two years earlier had been cancelled, or got lost, or were tired and had gone for a sleep or something.[5] Forget about them, they're not important: Barwell was talking about entirely new homes. And to ensure they got built this time, the government was spending an impressive £7.4 million, which sounds spiffing until you get out your calculator and see that £7.4 million is £370 per house.[6]

Having observed Barwell's great success in regurgitating a semi-digested policy on the assumption a hungry public would scoff it down, a few days later Theresa May pledged a spangly new 'Shared Society', which would respect the 'bonds of family, community, citizenship and strong institutions', and emphasise 'the obligations that make our society work'. All of this is nothing at all like Cameron's Big Society, so stop laughing.[7]

But wait, there's more! In 2016 Tories had promised £1 billion over five years to power a 'mental health revolution'. Cameron made a speech proclaiming that the stigma around mental illness should be reduced, and said, 'I want us to be able to say to anyone who is struggling, "Talk to someone, ask your doctor for help and we will always be there to support you."'[8]

Theresa May now re-announced the same policy, but without the bit involving money. In future, anybody suffering with mental illness would get cured by people with no expertise, who didn't know them and had never cared about them in the past, but who – thanks to the Shared Society – would now be responsible for treating mental health issues. For no wages. Huzzah!

May's policy chief, George Freeman, had the measure of what all of this meant for those suffering with mental health conditions: fuck all. He condemned treatment given to people 'who are taking pills at home, who suffer from anxiety', and said, 'We want to make sure we get the money to the *really* disabled people.'

He apologised for saying what he thought, but not for thinking what he said. 'I totally understand anxiety and so does the prime minister. We've set out in the mental health strategy how seriously we take it.'[9]

So seriously that they were going to spend absolutely no money on it. May said, 'It is always wrong for people to assume that the only answer to these issues is about funding.'[10] Yeah, and it's also always wrong to assume it isn't. NHS Clinical Commissioning Groups said they were under such financial pressure that 57 per cent of them would have to reduce spending on mental health in the next year.[11] Shortages already meant a fifth of children referred to mental health units – including those with problems arising out of abuse – got no help.[12]

Brexit had already cost £372 billion, which would have funded Cameron's mental health revolution for 1,860 years, and May's for infinity, because May's promised no money.

While we, the people of Britain, tried to work out for ourselves how to magically strengthen the bonds of our institutions, May's policies were busy pulling those very bonds apart. The Red Cross described the state of the NHS as a 'humanitarian crisis' and had to intervene to assist 20 desperately overstretched accident and emergency units across the country.[13]

The number of hospitals turning away ambulances because they could not cope with a single additional patient had doubled in a year. At least 140 A&E units had to refuse any new patients, so patients clogged up ambulances in car parks instead. This took ambulances out of service, so health workers had to beg car manufacturers for the loan of vehicles to help ferry sick people all over the country on a forlorn quest to find the last remaining hospital bed.[14]

Obviously, the problem was blamed on immigrants rather than seven successive years of dysfunctional austerity and serial mismanagement. But after a Freedom of Information request by the BBC, the government released figures that undermined the 'health tourism' rhetoric that had propelled so much of the Brexit debate. The statistics showed Britons in EU countries put 3.5 times more demand on Europe's health services than EU immigrants put on Britain's. Seventy thousand Britons used Spain's health system, while a mere 81 Spaniards used the NHS.[15]

Stop me if this sounds like wild exaggeration, but it was beginning to look as though the arguments that drove Brexit hadn't been entirely based on reality.

For example, we were told we were returning sovereignty to Parliament, but it was hard to reconcile that claim with the events unfolding in Westminster. Theresa May rejected calls for the government to consult Parliament over the deal being negotiated with the EU. Instead, she said, she would offer a 'meaningful vote' on the final deal, but without granting Parliament the chance to make or suggest any amendments.[16] Take it or leave it.

Leave it, in the case of Sir Ivan Rogers, the UK's Ambassador to the EU. He had been a key figure in the negotiations to date, but quit without warning in early January, after a leak showed he thought agreeing a new permanent trade deal could take a decade, and still fail.[17]

In his resignation letter, Rogers outlined the fundamental problems behind Brexit. 'We do not yet know what the Government will set as negotiating objectives,' he wrote,[18] which couldn't have come as a shock: it was now 24 years since the campaign to leave the EU had begun, and the prime minister was still describing what it meant by listing the colours in our national flag.

The next major problem we faced, said Sir Ivan, was that 'serious multilateral negotiating experience is in short supply in Whitehall, and that is not the case in the [EU] Commission'. In short, in the forthcoming negotiations we were Torquay United going up against the 1970 Brazil squad, and now our top player had quit. This would be bad enough, but the entire plan for our future outside the EU revolved around this inexperienced metaphorical Torquay United charging off to strike new deals all over the world. How would we cope when we came up against the USA or China?

Ivan Rogers implored civil servants to 'continue to challenge ill-founded arguments and muddled thinking' that swirled around Brexit, but muddled thinking was the founding principle of Brexit. The moment you attempted to apply clarity to the situation, it began to look like madness.

Our chief madness clarifier, Theresa May, gave a milestone speech at Lancaster House in January. The ambiguity was over, and we were definitely leaving the single market.[19] She described her 'red lines', which were predominantly gibberish, and which encouraged her most ardent Eurosceptics to believe they'd get all their earthly desires with no compromises. This was a vast tactical error on May's part, because any subsequent compromise was treated as an unacceptable betrayal. But we'll get to that.

First, we had to hear May tell us that 'we do not seek to adopt a model already enjoyed by other countries', rightly recognising that people in Britain do not want to enjoy anything.

She promised she would fight for 'the greatest possible access' to the single market and would gain privileged trading arrangements for key industries such as financial services.[20] She would negotiate frictionless trade, exemption from the jurisdiction that governs EU commerce, and keep the right to everything we gained as members of the single market but without being members of it.

All the rights but none of the responsibilities is what you'd expect a five-year-old to demand.

Once free from the bonds of adult behaviour, May promised 'competitive tax rates'[21] would boost the economy. George Osborne used competitive tax rates to boost the economy for half a decade, and it had been such a success that he'd announced cuts in the UK's growth forecast every single year from 2010 to 2016, at which point he gave up.

May's speech featured the barmy assertion that 'no deal is better than a bad deal', which radiated the same energy you get from somebody insisting they'll walk out of their own home and never pay a mortgage again. Sure, they'd feel empowered for a day, but they'd spend every subsequent night freezing in a puddle under a bush. And the EU knew it.

For all her assertions about what she'd get from a trade deal, the truth was that she'd only get what the other side was prepared to concede. May's threat of No Deal wasn't better for Britain; it was just a performative exercise in pretending to have some control over the chaotic maelstrom erupting on all sides.

—

Theresa May's fundamental problem arose from the fact she'd been the longest-serving Home Secretary for 60 years.[22] In a nation essentially governed by unthinking, howling, one-dimensional tabloid headlines, the purpose of a Tory Home Secretary was to be as callous and obdurate as humanly possible, and May did this remarkably well, and for longer than anybody could have imagined. By the time she got into Downing Street, she'd come to believe that deliberately making it easier for refugees to drown wasn't an unforgivable moral failing but a career highlight.

You don't need much imagination to understand why she assumed the intransigence and cruelty that played so well at the Home Office would be powerful weapons in Downing Street too. Inevitably, given her past, any suggestion that we should keep open a door to the rest of the world was rejected out of hand. The Brexit she ended up describing sacrificed every national interest to the false gods of stopping harmless Bulgarians arriving at Luton Airport.

She was astonishingly blinkered about this, but not entirely stupid. She knew how fraught the coming negotiations would be, so used her Lancaster House speech to implore restraint from her British colleagues, warning that 'any stray word' could make securing a good deal much harder.[23] It was less than 24 hours before Boris Johnson caused a diplomatic incident by accusing the French of trying to 'administer punishment beatings to anybody who seeks to escape',[24] which the EU's lead Brexit negotiator called 'abhorrent and deeply unhelpful'.[25]

But Johnson was just warming up: the day after the prime minister had promised to negotiate tariff-free trade, Johnson said Britain should 'put a 10 per cent tariff on 820,000 cars, Mercs. That's a lot of money for the exchequer.'[26]

—

Let's visit one of January's smaller events.

Jacob Rees-Mogg, the precise physical intersection of a cursed oboe and the concept of gout, decided to denounce a plan to stop the ancient custom of House of Commons clerks having to wear horsehair wigs.[27] Their wigs and gowns cost £4,000 each,[28] and most of us stopped wearing such things when the British put a tax on imported wig powder in 1775,[29] but for Rees-Mogg, 220 years was unseemly haste, and money for pointless symbolism was never in short supply. The plan to stop wasting a fortune maintaining the fashions of King George III was, Rees-Mogg claimed, a 'covert modernising agenda'. When informed that the wigs were uncomfortable and itchy, he said, 'That's feeble. They must have been itchy for centuries.'[30]

Plagues have also existed for centuries, Jacob, but sane governments do things to stop them... hold on, that's a bad example.

—

Back to Brexit.

Before the referendum, David Davis regularly encouraged us to believe Britain's sovereignty had been stolen away by the EU. 'It is time for Britain to take control of its own destiny,'[31] he had said, accusing the EU of 'taking away vast sovereign powers from member states,'[32] and claiming, 'We need a new deal with Europe [which] keeps law-making powers in Westminster, not Brussels.'

In the first days of February, he introduced the White Paper setting out Britain's plans for Brexit. It read: 'While Parliament has remained sovereign throughout our membership of the EU, it has not always felt like that.'[33]

Yes, you did read that correctly.

Tory MPs had already admitted they didn't believe in either the economic, trade or immigration arguments for Brexit, and had declared the reason we must leave the EU was 'sovereignty'.[34] And suddenly they admitted the sovereignty issue was all in their demented imaginations.

That was just the first of a swarm of monumentally wrong assertions contained in the bill. Davis assured us that by the end of the two-year transition period that would begin when we triggered Article 50, Britain would have a new free-trade deal with the EU; agreement to secure the rights of EU citizens in the UK; devolution to Scotland, Wales and Northern Ireland; and a new system of immigration that would be 'phased in slowly to give businesses time to prepare'.[35]

Those of you who have been paying attention will be aware none of that happened.

On the Irish border, the levels of deception in the White Paper are simply staggering: Brexit would magically retain 'as seamless and frictionless a border as possible between Northern Ireland and Ireland', while guaranteeing that Irish and UK citizens would continue to move freely across the border; but it would also 'protect the integrity of the UK's immigration system'.

Davis couldn't explain how the border would be simultaneously airtight, porous and non-existent.[36]

What's more, the government intended to keep the entire thing secret from public, Parliament, press, and anybody else who might wish to hold power to account. The White Paper said Tories would 'keep our positions closely held'[37] for the next two years, because the last thing you need while returning power to Parliament is Parliament is having any power.

Meanwhile, to add to the £372 billion that Brexit had already cost, the previously unexplored issue of the so-called 'divorce bill' raised its ugly head.[38] Britain had committed to help fund multiple large-scale pan-European projects, and we were obliged to clear our liabilities before we left.

You can't put a price on sovereignty, especially not the kind of sovereignty that you already have, even if your wall-eyed xenophobic paranoia makes you imagine you don't. But if you could put a price on it, that price would be eye-watering. By 2020 a figure of £37.3 billion was agreed on for the divorce settlement, bringing the cost to the taxpayer of 'reclaiming' the sovereignty that we already possessed to £410 billion.[39]

That would form a tower of £10 notes 2,700 miles high.[40] Which is 10 times higher than the orbit of the International Space Station.[41]

—

Tempers were beginning to fray.

Inside Westminster, David Davis approached Labour's Diane Abbott in a bar and attempted – uninvited – to kiss her. She told him to 'fuck off', and he wandered away laughing.[42]

Outside Westminster, 250,000 people attended a protest march against the latest cuts to the NHS.[43] Hospital services in almost two-thirds of England were, once again, about to be cut or scaled back, ranging from mothballing units for stroke care and A&E to the closing of entire hospitals, while we blew £410 billion on making ourselves feel better about flags.[44]

The government claimed they would solve the NHS problems with 'efficiency savings', but the King's Fund held a different view. It said that without very substantial investment of new funds, the efficiency savings simply would not work. Who to believe, though: an internationally respected thinktank of healthcare experts or the guys who believe in enchanted borders?

Parliament was heading towards recess, but there was just time to cram in a couple of bits of fucking awfulness.

The SNP's Eilidh Whiteford introduced a Private Member's Bill aimed at forcing the government to sign up to an international law that tackles sexual violence and domestic abuse.[45] As with all Private Member's Bills, there was little time allocated for the debate, but thankfully this bill had the backing of most of the House of Commons, and would therefore sweep into law unopposed, provided there wasn't a monstrous, amoral, flapping subhuman gash on the backbenches who would decide to filibuster until time ran out.

Philip Davies spoke for 91 minutes. Thankfully, this time his attempt at scuppering basic decency failed, and he was the only Member of Parliament to vote against it.

We weren't so lucky a few days later. David Cameron's grudging promise to take 20,000 Syrian refugees was already failing, with the UK having taken just 2,800.[46] In response, Lord Alf Dubs – himself a child refugee from Nazi-occupied Czechoslovakia – had introduced an amendment to legislation, which granted UK support and asylum for unaccompanied children fleeing the war in Syria.

On the evening before parliamentary recess, the Tories scrapped it.[47] Then they went on holiday.

—

As we entered March, the Electoral Commission handed down a record fine to the Conservative Party for a string of breaches of election rules – they had spent hundreds of thousands of pounds more than the regulation spending limits, and thus gained an illegal electoral advantage in multiple constituencies.[48] Again.

'We have complied fully with the Electoral Commission throughout their investigation,' said Theresa May, yet the Electoral Commission cited 'lack of co-operation by the Party during the investigation' as one of the reasons for the record size of the fine.[49]

This is the party that can be trusted with money, as any fool knows, so it's unreasonable to expect them to keep legal accounts. And as David Davis was about to demonstrate, it was also unreasonable to expect them to do the bare minimum of planning or research. He'd rubbished the Treasury's forecasts of economic harm if we left the EU without a trade deal, but in March, when the Brexit Select Committee asked him for his own impact assessment, he said he hadn't done one.

'You don't need a piece of paper with numbers on it to have an economic assessment,' he said.

When asked if holidaying Britons would lose access to healthcare across the EU, he replied, 'I haven't looked at that one.'

When asked about the implications on personal data sharing, he said he 'did not know'.

When asked if the services sector – which is 79 per cent of Britain's GDP – would lose rights to trade in the EU after Brexit, he said, 'That's an area of uncertainty.'

When asked what the WTO tariff rate for dairy and meat products were, he ambiguously said he wasn't certain, but that 'the numbers are high'.

And when reminded he had declared there would be 'no downside to Brexit, only a considerable upside', David suddenly appeared to lack his earlier confidence, telling the committee, 'I was expressing an ambition.'[50]

Dominic Cummings described Davis as 'the perfect stooge... thick as mince, lazy as a toad, and vain as Narcissus'.[51]

—

Yet despite the vast, almost surreal expense; despite the entire rationale being denied in writing by the very people demanding we do it; despite the patent lack of understanding, planning, strategy or capability; despite over 100 pages of amendments waiting to be debated,[52] each one of which tore apart the gobbledygook contained in the Brexit White Paper – despite all of this, on 29 March we triggered Article 50 of the Lisbon Treaty, and began a two-year countdown to leaving the EU.[53]

Millions wanted none of it, but for a lucky few there was a way out. Geography and history gave Scotland a chance to escape Brexitania, so just before Article 50 was triggered, the SNP's call for another referendum on independence was formally backed by the Holyrood Parliament, and it was hard to see how a Tory government so obsessed with the will of the people and the breaking up of unions could deny the Scots' wishes.[54]

They denied the Scots' wishes.

'Now is not the time,' said Theresa May. 'It would be unfair to the people of Scotland that they would be being asked to make a crucial decision without the information they need to make that decision.'[55] At this point, I'm not even writing. I'm just emitting exasperated howls.

Exiting the EU was causing almighty political headaches, and it wasn't simply due to the number of times per day everybody observing the process was slapping their own forehead. Every decision became a battle and – not without justification – people continuously pointed out that May had no mandate for most of this stuff.

The promises of the Leave campaign – that we would remain in the single market, that we would gain £350 million a week for the NHS, that it would be simple and painless – rarely matched what was now being proposed. Predicted outcomes the Brexiteers had breezily dismissed as Project Fear became Project Truth with sickening regularity. There was a sense of barely contained panic and chaos, and the only moments of relief were the regular occasions when the panic was replaced by exasperation at the delusions of those who still hadn't grasped what was happening.

Remainers agitated constantly for a second referendum, and polling suggested widespread regret over the decision we'd made: less than a year after voting to leave, 60 per cent of Britons now wanted to keep their EU citizenship.[56] May's backbenchers rebelled constantly, and from both directions. The moderates wanted her to think again before too much damage was done, while the right of the party didn't care if she burned the nation to the ground, as long as the ERG got to be in charge of the ashes.

Rumours began to swirl that an election would be called, with a view to Theresa May gaining a stronger mandate for shooting the nation in both feet. From the Conservatives' point of view, it seemed like a wise choice, since opinion polls often gave them at least a 20 per cent lead over a Labour Party riven with conflict and rancour, and headed up by a hugely divisive leader.[57] After months rejecting the very concept of an election, Theresa May went on a walking holiday and came back with an announcement.

'We need a general election, and we need one now,' she said. 'The country is coming together but Westminster is not.'[58] But in truth, the country had rarely been more divided. If anything, the acrimony in Westminster represented us better than at any time for decades.

Yet the prospect of Theresa May with a greater mandate shook those who had to work with her. Two of her most senior advisers quit in the week of the election announcement, frustrated at May's style of leadership, and concerned about what the future may hold.

Leadership, especially in a democratic body, is about bringing together as many people as possible, creating compromise solutions that build trust and cohesion, and having a definite sense of direction. But Theresa May was all over the place, and preferred to make decisions in secret, in the company of just two of her closest aides, Nick Timothy and Fiona Hill. With everything to gain from the forthcoming electoral shoo-in, it almost looked as if the resignations within May's team were because nobody could stand working with those two, but that couldn't possibly be true.

'It's exactly what it looks like,' said a senior Tory. 'No one can stand working with [them].'[59]

Meanwhile Deloitte, the management-consultancy giant responsible for assisting the government with much of the analysis for Brexit, opted to stop accepting government contracts worth tens of millions[60] after an internal memo was leaked saying May's habit of not consulting with colleagues was 'unlikely to be sustainable'.[61]

Westminster was not coming together, and was getting no help from May's frigid, isolated management style. She just didn't play well with other kids.

—

Unsurprisingly, after years of reflexively lurching further and further to the right, research showed Tory members now believed the Conservatives were more right-wing than UKIP, a party that had all the same policy objectives as the National Front.[62] Yet despite stiff competition from the tub-thumping libertarian wingnuts that populated her backbenches, the stiffest thing in the election campaign was still Theresa May. She tottered mechanically from photo-op to photo-op, cawing out a single catchphrase with brain-mangling regularity.

'Strong and stable leadership,' she would proclaim in Pontefract.

'Strong and stable leadership,' she would blare in Bradford.

'Strong and stable leadership,' she would clang in Clacton.

It was like being Rick-rolled by a bewitched Anglepoise lamp. Message discipline around the repetition of a short, memorable catchphrase is a vital tool in the shallow end of our political gene pool: Thatcher had told us 'There is no alternative'; Cameron had promised us a 'Long Term Economic Plan'; Johnson urged us to 'Take Back Control'.

But in each case, those campaigns worked for two reasons: the message reflected a perceived truth the target audience sincerely felt, whether it was accurate or not. Thatcher's Britain *did* feel like we were out of options; after short-termism caused a global crash, it *did* feel like we needed a long-term plan; Leave voters *did* feel they lacked control over their lives.

The second reason message discipline worked: those earlier slogans were all delivered in a polished presentational style by somebody who could at least summon the pretence of a recognisably human personality.

Neither of those factors was conspicuous in Theresa May. While Thatcher radiated determination and Johnson radiated bonhomie, May simply radiated crippling discomfort. She appeared to be constructed entirely out of a nana's elbows.

As for strong or stable leadership: her time in office had been characterised by a series of failed battles with the heretic-hunting absolutist maniacs that now dominated her party. Even as the campaign tried to carpet-bomb voters with the notion of firm, dependable governance, her team of wayward racists, conmen and homophobes was busy reminding the country how awful they all were in a seemingly eternal gobshite jamboree. I present some prime examples from during the campaign.

Andrew Turner, the Tory MP for the Isle of Wight, announced his decision not to stand for re-election. His resignation letter didn't mention anything about his recent decision to tell a room full of schoolchildren that 'homosexuality is wrong' and a 'danger to society',[63] or that he had already been called upon to resign two years earlier by four former party chairmen during a 'toxic' row over his personal life, resulting in Turner being labeled the laughing stock of the island.[64]

So there was now a vacancy for a laughing stock in the Tory ranks. Fortunately, GMTV presenter Esther McVey was parachuted into George Osborne's super-safe seat of Tatton. Breakfast television's loss was about to become everybody else's loss too.

Osborne, meanwhile, was handed the job of deciding what appeared in the *Evening Standard*. Tory supporters already owned 68 per cent of the UK's print media, and now former Tory ministers would be editing them too.[65] If this feels suspiciously like the way *Pravda* got published, there may be a reason: the *Evening Standard* was owned by Boris Johnson's friend Evgeny Lebedev and his father, the former KGB agent Alexander Lebedev.[66] It's barely worth mentioning, but (according to *Byline Times*) MI6 officers and the UK's Special Branch – responsible for national security and intelligence – had described Evgeny Lebedev as 'a potential security risk',[67] an accusation Lebedev denies, telling the BBC, 'I am not some agent of Russia'.[68]

Regardless, instead of newspapers holding power to account, they were now paying the powerful to decide what news Londoners got to read about.

Across town from Osborne's new job, the principled environmentalist and serially whoops-a-daisy Islamophobe Zac Goldsmith, who had stepped down as an MP six months earlier in protest at what he called the 'catastrophic' planned expansion of Heathrow Airport, now chose to stand as a Tory candidate in the same constituency, on a platform of – yep – supporting the expansion of Heathrow Airport.[69]

Meanwhile, moral midget Dominic Raab, the former minister for human rights – one of which is eating – reckoned the massive increase in poverty was unrelated to the massive increase in demand at food banks. Instead, he claimed, 'the typical user of food banks is not someone that is languishing in poverty, it is someone who has a cash flow problem episodically'.[70]

Yet isn't it strange how such 'cash-flow problems' had grown 3,211 per cent as soon as the Tories started austerity?[71]

—

The only bright spot for May was the decision of Gerald Howarth to stand down as MP for Aldershot at the election. In a party not short of horrible reactionary bigots, Howarth had still garnered quite a record for being simply appalling.

He rejected the idea that Stephen Lawrence died as a result of prejudice and said the findings that the Metropolitan Police was institutionally racist were a grotesque overreaction.[72] He said of Muslims living in Britain: 'There is a simple remedy: go to another country, get out.'[73]

In case you think this is a mere slip of the tongue, he clarified matters in an email to a constituent in which he declared Enoch Powell was right in his 'rivers of blood' speech.[74]

He said gay people were less deserving of British citizenship than others and described homosexuals serving in the military as 'appalling'. But hold on – it's not all bad. He at least recognised these views belong in a different century: he justified his violent opposition to gay people who were prepared to fight for their nation by claiming people joined the service 'precisely because they wished to turn their backs on the values of modern society'.[75]

—

Yet despite the imminent departure of the grotesque Howarth, the election campaign wasn't going at all well for the Tories, and it was about to get much, much worse when they published their manifesto.

They pledged to 'build a new generation of fixed-term, high quality council homes', but weren't prepared to be pinned down on how many homes that meant. Was it a thousand? Was it a quintillion? Was it nine? In truth, the number was supremely unimportant, because none of it was going to happen anyway. Any homes provided under this scheme would have to be built for free, because the Tories admitted they were providing no money.[76]

Cash was finally promised for the NHS, though: £8 billion of it, which came nowhere near close to making up the previous seven years of the most miserly NHS funding awards in its history.[77] NHS England had told the government they faced a £30 billion funding gap. The government had responded by telling them to find £22 billion of 'efficiency savings' from what was already the most efficient health service on earth. Experts at healthcare thinktanks said that even if the £22 billion was miraculously found – and they said doing so would be 'unprecedented' – it would still leave a multibillion-pound shortfall, because the small print showed that the headline-grabbing manifesto figure of £8 billion was to be spread across five years.[78]

Funding for schools would be increased by £4 billion.[79] This is less than the amount they had already wasted on free schools the National Audit Office said were 'not needed'.[80] But even the promise of new funding for regular schools was a lie: the money wasn't new; it was created by scrapping free lunches for the first three years of primary school. Instead, children would now be offered a 'free school breakfast'.[81]

The budget for kids' breakfast was set at 7p per meal. Iain Duncan Smith claimed £39 in expenses for his breakfast, which according to him was enough to feed 557 children.[82]

Finally, May confirmed a vote on repealing the ban on fox hunting,[83] which really caught the mood of the public: over 80 per cent of us wanted it to remain illegal.[84] Regardless, May promised her tiny minority of tweedy sociopaths the chance to murder animals again, a decision that must have required Owen Paterson to be bathed in bromide six times a day, for decency's sake.

Everything about the manifesto was terrible – a few ineffectual sticking plasters to try to disguise the worst effects of austerity, a bit of light starvation for somebody else's kids, and empty promises of an unspecified number of magical houses. But the real kick in the balls came with the pledge on social care for the elderly.

Under the existing system, if you were an older person with assets of at least £23,250, you had to part-fund any care you received if you went into a care home.[85] If you were provided with care in your own home, you didn't need to contribute towards the costs.

May scrapped all of that. She made charges apply to everybody, so in future, if you were a little old lady and your husband had developed dementia, you might need to sell your home because a nurse came round to help him into the bath.

To core Tory voters, who had spent decades being relentlessly terrified by warnings in the *Telegraph* that Labour wouldn't let them access all their money after they were dead, this was a massive betrayal.

Research shows 67 per cent of people don't read manifestos, and 10 per cent of us don't even know what a manifesto is,[86] but the phrase 'dementia tax' broke through the fog of ignorance, and the rush to read about it panicked the Tories. They spent thousands buying Google Ads associated with the search term 'dementia tax', so anybody researching it would be redirected to propaganda on the Conservative campaign website, rather than finding out what was actually going on.[87]

The headlines were lousy, so inevitably May performed a U-turn[88] and then immediately resumed her habit of reflexively barking 'strong and stable' at 20-second intervals. But her message discipline, which was already annoying the public, had now been rendered ludicrous in the mouth of a woman who was demonstrably weak and floppy. 'Nothing has changed, nothing has changed,' she shrieked to the assembled press in a high, panicky voice, the repetition presumably being some sort of ironical comedy.[89]

Her campaign masterminds decided it was time to shift the conversation and to demonstrate to the proles that the prime minister wasn't merely a soulless, tottering, avian monstrosity, but had a real personality. Time to reveal the fun side of Theresa May.

'What's the naughtiest thing you ever did?' she was asked.

'Run through the fields of wheat.'[90]

Okay, we have proven conclusively that May doesn't, in fact, have a personality, so her campaign masterminds decided to return to the original plan of being exuberantly cruel and inept, but hiding it behind a façade of being 'honest with the public'. During an election special of *Question Time*, a nurse asked why her wages hadn't increased for eight years. Another nurse pointed out that the 1 per cent cap on public-sector pay meant his pay had decreased 14 per cent in real terms due to inflation since the Tories came into office.

'There isn't a magic money tree,' mouthed a forlorn, dead-eyed Theresa May.[91]

There isn't a magic money tree. There isn't a magic nurse tree either. Or a magic teacher tree, or a magic police officer tree. None of those people can survive on a diet of praise for their sense of duty. They need money, something the government could quite easily get its hands on by, for example, cancelling their manifesto pledge to cut corporation tax for the umpteenth time.

But in that respect, May was right. Nothing had changed.

—

When she launched the election campaign, Theresa May was more popular than either Thatcher or Tony Blair had ever been, even at their peak.[92] Her party was 25 per cent ahead of her rivals in opinion polls, and she was all but guaranteed a landslide victory, leading to a massive triple-figure majority in the House of Commons.[93]

After a 51-day campaign, the Tories lost their majority.

—

Tory former minister Anna Soubry said the prime minister had run 'a dreadful campaign', which was a fair comment.[94] George Osborne called May 'a dead woman walking',[95] which wasn't fair at all: are robots technically alive in the first place?

May said she wouldn't stand down because, 'At this time more than anything else, this country needs a period of stability.'[96] Since 2010, the Tories had given us a coalition nobody voted for; a referendum they called and then opposed; another one they lost; a new prime minister selected by just one in 250 voters; a parliament they couldn't control; a general election we didn't need; and now yet another hung parliament. I'm not convinced 'more of the same' was the right way to bring stability.

May admitted she wept when she heard the results.[97] But then she brightened up a bit and wandered into the Downing Street garden to find a magic money tree, from which she plucked £1 billion, and handed it to the Democratic Unionist Party.[98]

May had once warned Tories that they were 'the Nasty Party', perceived as being anti-gay, anti-minorities, blinkered, regressive and cruel. She now got into bed with the DUP, a party of homophobic, sectarian, climate-change deniers[99] with close historic associations to the terrorist Ulster Volunteer Force (UVF).[100]

This time it wasn't an official coalition, but rather a 'confidence and supply' agreement, under which the DUP would stay outside of government, but support the Tories on major issues.[101] This would keep Theresa May in Downing Street, and prevent Gavin Williamson and Chris Grayling from being released upon an unsuspecting job market. In return for the support of the DUP, the Tories would blindly hand over £1 billion, a bribe big enough to form a stack of £10 notes over six miles high.[102]

There were 1.3 million people reliant on food banks.[103]

The editor of the grassroots ConservativeHome website called it a 'farcical failing',[104] and the official Twitter account of Britain's police officers, who had been asked to stretch budgets for years, spoke for the nation when it tweeted, 'Dear Theresa, it's not the number of MPs that counts, it's how you use them. You have to do more with less.'[105]

The potential for mischief and power politics wasn't lost on May's new partners either: the former DUP mayor of Ballymoney posted an edited photograph on Twitter, depicting the flag of their UVF paramilitary wing flying outside Downing Street.[106]

Thus began our period of stability.

—

The election failure came just nine days before withdrawal negotiations were due to begin with the EU,[107] and the European foreign policy chief was quoted as saying, 'We still don't know the British position in the negotiations on Brexit and it seems difficult to predict when we will.'[108]

It didn't help that May's team was disintegrating at the exact moment she had assumed she'd have the power to assert authority. Her chief strategist and speechwriter walked away from his job. Her policy chiefs resigned.[109] Nick Timothy and Fiona Hill, the much-hated advisers with whom she had made practically every decision, both quit. They'd been in Downing Street less than a year, and each got a £35,000 golden goodbye[110] for executing the worst political operation in British history.[111] Yet without them, remarkably, Theresa May's performance became even shitter. Things had been bad before, but now, 'It is more chaotic, no doubt about it,' according to one official.[112]

The sense of a government inexorably disintegrating was re-enforced when the Under Secretary for the Northern Powerhouse and Local Growth resigned.[113] The Under Secretary at DExEU quit two days later,[114] and was replaced by Steve Baker, whose career highlights to date had been: getting filmed while a burly man slapped him about; helping to author a report that claimed repeated acts of torture in Equatorial Guinea were 'trivial';[115] and being chief architect of global finance at noted success story Lehman Brothers.[116]

Meanwhile, off to Brussels went David Davis, to begin the hard work of hammering out the details of our future trading relationship. Davis said the talks got off to a 'promising start', although it's hard to comprehend how he could possibly know.[117] An official photograph was taken at the first meeting: on one side of the table sat the three lead negotiators from the EU, serious, focused and professional, with stacks of documentation before each of them. On the other side sat

Davis, gurning at the camera, with not a scrap of paper. Not a plan. Not a pen. Not a notepad. Nothing. Just swaggering confidence and monumental ignorance.[118]

He returned to the UK after less than half a day.[119]

—

Two notable things happened on 14 June 2017.

The first was a meeting of the Red Tape Initiative, chaired by Tory MP Sir Oliver Letwin, to agree further reductions in fire-safety regulations for residential buildings.[120] It was the latest in a series of policies that David Cameron had kicked off in 2011, with a promise that he would 'kill off the health and safety culture for good'.[121] In 2012 Eric Pickles had repealed laws requiring extra safety measures in multistorey construction.[122] By 2014, housing minister Brandon Lewis was rejecting demands from MPs that sprinklers be made mandatory in tall buildings.[123] Cameron insisted that no new safety law could be introduced unless two existing safety measures were simultaneously abolished, and then he updated this policy to require *three* safety measures removed for every new one created. He described standards that kept us safe in our workplaces, shopping malls and homes – but ate into the profit margins of the multiple construction companies that bankrolled his party – as 'red tape folly', and it all had to go.[124]

Just as the Red Tape Initiative sat down to meet, the other important thing to happen on 14 June was unfolding: a small fire had broken out on the fourth floor of a block of flats in west London. It quickly ignited the building's external cladding, and swept up each of the remaining floors, engulfing the whole of Grenfell Tower in flame. Seventy-two people died. It was the worst residential fire in the UK since the Second World War.[125]

The Conservative Party did not start the fire in Grenfell Tower. Let's be absolutely clear about that. Sure, they'd abolished vital safety measures that could have prevented it, and austerity imposed from central government had reduced the local council's funding by 20 per cent, but the Tories didn't decide where those cuts fell: the council did.[126] Local government was forced to choose between providing social care and building safe homes, and social care won out. The council's housing budget was slashed by 76 per cent[127] and as a result they chose the cheaper, less safe cladding for Grenfell Tower: it saved them £5,000.[128]

Firefighters attending the disaster had advised residents to stay in their flats, which was standard practice: keep people out of smoke-filled stairwells where the fire would normally be expected to spread, and allow space for emergency services to ascend the tower and tackle the blaze. The fire service hadn't known reduced safety guidelines meant the cladding would accelerate the fire up the *outside* of the building, killing most of those trapped inside.[129]

Widespread opinion held that people died because work was done on the cheap by a system that didn't care enough about residents' safety or listen to their concerns. Jacob Rees-Mogg took a different view. He said people died because they lacked 'common sense'.[130]

He's a Christian, don't you know?

To repeat: the Conservative Party did not start the fire at Grenfell Tower. That's incontrovertible. But they were incontrovertibly to blame for the response to it. Theresa May refused to meet survivors.[131] Gavin Barwell, the latest moral void at the heart of housing policy, was reported to have resisted publication of a review into the Lakanal House tower-block fire in 2009, which highlighted the risk posed by cladding that lacked fire resistance and 'strongly recommended' installing fire suppression in 4,000 tower blocks nationally.[132] The inquest was completed in 2013.[133] Barwell had sat on the report for a year.[134]

On the other side of the world, three weeks after the disaster at Grenfell, the government in Canberra set up the NSW Cladding Taskforce, which committed to removing all such fire hazards nationally, with a central government fund.[135]

In Britain, the Tories were still discussing potential solutions four years later – that's eleven years since Lakanal. They didn't go down the Australian model of just bloody fixing it. Instead, they identified half the number of buildings recommended in the Lakanal report – 2,000 high-rise residential buildings – and promised a small amount of funding for some renovations, but the money was only for a narrow range of safety improvements, and only for buildings higher than six floors. If your terrifying death-trap was only five storeys high, you were on your own, mate.[136]

The House of Lords tried to prevent owners and landlords of blocks of flats from passing the costs of legally mandated fire safety on to their residents. The Tories, a quarter of whom were landlords, rejected this move, leaving each leaseholder to find the money to fix the problem themselves.[137] To help out, the Tories told those residents they could 'access a loan to help pay for cladding removal', and said the costs would be limited to a maximum of £9,000 per leaseholder.[138]

You'll be amazed – simply amazed – to discover that reassurance wasn't all it was cracked up to be. Sixty-two per cent of leaseholders faced bills of over £30,000, and for 15 per cent the costs exceeded £100,000. They couldn't sell their fire-hazard homes, and few of them could afford to make them safe. One in six were 'exploring bankruptcy'.[139]

The Conservative Party did not start the fire at Grenfell Tower. I can't make that clear enough. It's unequivocal.

But in the same year they found £1.2 million to replace the doors to the orangery at Windsor Castle and allocated a further £369 million to refurbish Buckingham Palace.[140]

—

To be fair, the monarchy probably needed somewhere nice to chill out for the next couple of years, because Tories also announced they were cancelling the Queen's Speech, at which the government traditionally lays out its agenda for the coming year. No point announcing an agenda where there wasn't going to be an agenda. There was now only Brexit. The entire business of government would grind to a halt.[141]

It wasn't as though it could afford to: polling by the British Medical Association (BMA) showed 82 per cent of us were worried about the future of the NHS. The BMA chairman said, 'It doesn't have to be this way. It is the result of an explicit political choice. We don't have to spend less of our GDP than the other leading European economies on health. Our government has chosen to do this. If we spent the average – the average, not the most – then patients would see £15 billion extra investment in the English NHS within five years. We're not asking for the world. We're asking for the average.'[142]

Meanwhile one of the Conservative's other great successes, the justice system, also reported an entirely predictable, policy-generated crisis: incidents of self-harm in prisons had increased 73 per cent in the five years since the justice budget had been cut by a fifth.[143] The government admitted it had no idea how many people in prison had mental health issues, and even more worryingly, couldn't even tell us how much money it spent on mental health. In 2016 alone, half of all prisoners self-harmed, or in many cases committed suicide. But the government had elected to stop collecting the data.

—

Theresa May celebrated the first anniversary of her entrance to Number 10 by being voted 'Worst Prime Minister in History'.[144] Let's see if things can get any worse for her in July.

Yes, they can.

She had to suspend Devon MP Anne Marie Morris for using the N-word in a speech at a public event, only a couple of months after Morris herself had been forced to apologise for her own partner's prejudice in a speech at a public event. He'd told an election rally that 'the crisis in education is due entirely to non-British-born immigrants'.[145] A visit to Devon's Conservative associations sounds like a game of racist whack-a-mole. Bring mallets.

—

The xenophobia festival down in Devon was eclipsed by the arrival of another blessing from the bewilderingly fecund loins of Jacob

Rees-Mogg. This was the sixth demonstrable time he had committed intercourse, and as a result he named the poor child Sixtus, so that for the rest of the boy's life people would pay attention to the thing Jacob loved most in the world: his own persona.[146]

Just in case there were still people who hadn't noticed his ludicrous posturing, he then announced to an indifferent public that he had never changed a nappy: 'I don't think nanny would approve, because I'm sure she'd think I wouldn't do it properly,' he said. He wasn't talking about his child's nanny, you understand; he was talking about his own.[147]

Jacob Rees-Mogg was 47 years old.

—

Transport Secretary Chris Grayling was dragged to the House of Commons at 10 p.m. on a Monday night to defend his handling of the HS2 high-speed rail-link project.[148] In 2012 the budget for HS2 had been £32 billion. By 2017 it had risen to £55 billion,[149] and in July Grayling was found to have started issuing billions of pounds of contracts without telling Parliament. MPs wanted answers, and Grayling had to abandon his Duplo for the evening and rush back to the chamber. He attributed his lapse to 'cockup, not conspiracy', and for once I think we can all agree this sounds exceedingly likely.

'HS2 will be the new backbone of the UK rail network,' boasted Grayling, proud of his ambitious project to modernise rail services between London, Manchester and Leeds. 'It will transform the UK rail network from one built for the 19th century into one designed for the 21st century.'[150]

Three days later he cancelled rail improvements between Manchester and Leeds on the grounds that, 'There are places that are built in Victorian times where it is very difficult to put up electric cables.' The North was staying in the 19th century,[151] although it seems Grayling neglected to tell whoever wrote the cheques: by 2021 the budget for HS2 had risen 243 per cent, to £107 billion.[152]

—

At the start of her premiership, Theresa May had addressed the issue of EU citizens who lived in Britain. 'I want to be able to guarantee their rights in the UK,' she had told EU negotiators. 'I expect to be able to do that; I intend to be able to do that, to guarantee their rights.'[153]

In July she stopped guaranteeing their rights.

Instead, she now told Europeans living in Britain they'd be able to apply for – but not necessarily be granted – the status of 'third country nationals', but she also demanded the EU continue to grant the existing residency status of Britons living on the continent.[154]

She followed up by quietly abandoning the policy of giving a free breakfast to primary school pupils, which she had campaigned for at the election just six weeks earlier, and for which you might remember she had allocated a mighty seven pence per meal budget. She didn't announce to Parliament that the policy had been dropped; instead, she courageously let the news slip out in a written answer while MPs were on holiday.[155]

She also scrapped her own weeks-old guarantee that she would reform social care, curb price increases on energy bills and introduce fairer pension funding.[156] All those policies that the electorate had voted for were now unobtrusively abandoned, because apparently that's what voting for a policy means in Britain's sparkling new democracy.

—

Christopher Chope had spent much of the previous seven years in a constant battle to prevent anybody from making any improvements to anything. He would simply filibuster for hours, until the time for debate ran out and it was too late to vote on the bill.

But sabotaging ongoing debates was no longer giving Chope the tingle he needed. His dark urges were growing, and he decided to escalate his wild-eyed opposition to the workings of democracy: from now on, he would prevent debates from even beginning.

In July he slept in the House of Commons for three days so he would be first in the queue to submit new bills for debate, and then he and fellow wingnut Peter Bone submitted 73 of them in a deliberate effort to stop any other backbenchers' ideas from even being discussed.[157]

Perhaps he thinks other MPs are idiots. Who can blame him? In July Andrea Leadsom told the House of Commons Jane Austen was 'one of our greatest living authors'.[158]

—

Philip Hammond, the second-richest Member of Parliament, was worth an estimated £9 million and took home a public salary of £134,565.[159] As Chancellor, he had use of a taxpayer-funded flat in central London and a taxpayer-funded country house in Buckinghamshire.[160] This left him free to rent out his own Belgravia townhouse for a modest £2,500 a week,[161] and before he decided to put it on the rental market, he had claimed an even more modest £24,000 per year from the taxpayer in mortgage interest payments on that property. In short, he had a bob or two.

Meanwhile, the typical salary for a nurse in 2017 was £23,000.[162] So you can understand why nurses got cross when in July Hammond said, 'Public-sector workers are overpaid.'[163]

Over 5 million public-sector workers hadn't seen a pay increase for seven years, and inflation had turned the 1 per cent cap on public-sector pay rises into a 14 per cent real-terms pay cut for NHS workers.[164]

But Hammond wasn't finished yet: he focused his commitment to equality and humanitarianism in the direction of train drivers, who he said were not just overpaid, but 'ludicrously overpaid'[165] because, in his words, 'even a woman' could drive a train.[166]

And he was one of the moderates.

—

Given the team she was leading, it is perhaps unsurprising that as August began, insiders described Theresa May as being 'too depressed to function properly'.[167] She wasn't alone: Bernard Jenkin, a senior Tory backbencher, described the Conservative Party as a 'failing organisation, which is beset by an atmosphere of crisis'.

'It can be very difficult to talk truthfully about why things have gone wrong,'[168] said Jenkin, to which I can only reply: 'This volume is available in all good bookshops, and some terrible ones too.'

Rumours began that David Davis was plotting to oust May. Davis himself said it was baseless gossip, but it was hard to entirely believe his protestations of innocence when his friend and confidant Andrew Mitchell was haunting the assorted tearooms and bars of Westminster, apparently telling one dinner that Theresa May was 'dead in the water'.[169]

But while Davis was busy undermining May, a separate group of Tories was equally busy undermining him. We didn't have a government; we had a set of babushka dolls made entirely out of squabbling wangs.

James Chapman, the former political editor of the *Daily Mail*, had been the senior aide to David Davis until the election. He now tweeted an extraordinary series of revelations about his time working alongside Davis, describing him as a 'bone idle' man who had 'been working three days a week since day one'. Chapman even tweeted an apology to the prime minister of Slovakia for the brevity of the meeting between him and Davis, explaining it was 'only one hour as [David Davis] wanted to go home'.[170]

Davis, according to Chapman, was a drunk, a bully, a misogynist, and sexually inappropriate. Inept too, having put in a call to 'a far-right friend', only to discover he'd accidentally been speaking to EU negotiator Michel Barnier.[171]

He said May and Davis 'don't have the first idea what they are doing', called Davis a liar – although was kind enough to offer an alternative explanation, suggesting that Davis didn't read his ministerial briefings – and said his former colleagues in the DExEU should resign rather than 'facilitate misconduct in public office'.[172]

The House of Lords tended to agree. In August they censured Davis because he couldn't be arsed to turn up and give evidence to them, possibly because he was too busy orchestrating a secret leadership bid. The independent peer Lord Macpherson said, 'All too frequently in the last year the national interest has been subordinated to party interest.'

Reports from inside Downing Street claimed civil servants were 'shielding' a fragile Theresa May from difficult news, and that the EU was 'significantly ahead of us' in planning and organisation for Brexit. Due to her dreadful leadership, civil servants said the UK wasn't merely 'starting from scratch: it's worse than that'.[173]

—

The governing party was supposed to be focused on the nation's future, but instead it was worrying about its own. In August, the Tories launched Activate, a grassroots movement to 'engage young people with Conservatism'. Activate clearly had its finger on the pulse of young people's financially difficult lives, since it offered membership for £500.

The movement's website asserted that 'Conservatism is a broad church made up of many different strands', yet every single photograph of its organising committee showed a besuited white male; at least for a couple of hours, after which the evidence was removed.

That wasn't fast enough for some. Recently ousted Tory MP Ben Howlett said of Activate: 'I would say it needs to be rebranded, and it's only been in existence for about an hour.'

Activate's efforts to raise £10,000 to 'help Conservatives campaign' had attracted just £39. Two of the top donors gave their names as 'Harold Shipman' and 'Theresa May is wildly incompetent'.[174]

That was in public. In private, things were even worse. A leak from the group's WhatsApp chat included people discussing 'gassing chavs' and 'shooting peasants'. [175] 'We could use them as substitutes for animals when testing,' suggested one lovely member.[176]

The campaign was shut down after two months.[177]

Keen to build on this triumph, the Tories next announced a 'Conservative Glastonbury' to counter the mass cheering and singing that had accompanied the appearance of Jeremy Corbyn at the real – and emphatically *not* Conservative – Glastonbury earlier that year. The intention of the Conservative Ideas Festival was to engage with the new generation and build the long-term future of British Conservatism.[178]

Glastonbury attracts 200,000 people. The Conservative Ideas Festival attracted 200.[179]

—

It was suddenly fashionable to spend August abandoning the future: Boris Johnson's planned Garden Bridge across the Thames was finally cancelled.

It had originally been intended that the entire thing would be funded by philanthropists; however, due to unforeseeable circumstances, philanthropists prepared to cough up £200 million to realise Boris Johnson's dream of a gibberish aquatic patio were a bit thin on the ground. Rather than disappoint Boris, the Tories – sadly incapable of finding money for the NHS – suddenly found £60 million for a long, thin park on a non-existent bridge across a river that already had 35 *real* bridges, in a city that already boasted over 2,000 hectares of Royal Parks.

They had been reassured by the relentlessly honest Mr Johnson that private backers would definitely, definitely hand over the rest.

By 2017 they had burned through £46 million of taxpayers' money without a single brick being laid.[180] The bridge was cancelled. The money simply evaporated.

The people of Britain seemed to assume Johnson was an innocuous comedy character, a bit of a good laugh, and mostly harmless – but this wasn't a widely held view. It's pretty remarkable, considering the ineptitude, corruption and farce unleashed by the orange maniac on the other side of the Atlantic, but officials in Donald Trump's White House were already telling people they 'don't want to go anywhere near Boris because they think he's a joke'.

An unnamed minister in the UK government said, 'It's worse in Europe. There is not a single foreign minister there who takes him seriously. They think he's a clown.'[181]

He wasn't doing a lot to disprove the impression: in August he congratulated Uhuru Kenyatta on his re-election as President of Kenya, commending his 'commitment to democracy'. Kenyatta's election had been dissolved the day before, when Kenya's Supreme Court ruled his campaign – a bloody affair that left 28 people dead – had been vastly corrupt. They pronounced the result invalid.[182]

There were those who assumed Johnson was an astute and intelligent man masquerading as an ignoramus. After a few months in the Foreign Office, it seemed more likely he was, in fact, a genuine ignoramus masquerading as an astute and intelligent man, masquerading as an ignoramus. The only surprise about this was that he had such depths.

—

In September, a National Trust property that had once been the home of 17th-century explorer and Tory MP William John Bankes unveiled a memorial to the 51 gay British men hanged for their sexuality during Bankes's lifetime. Bankes himself had been gay and was forced to flee the country to escape prosecution.

Keen moralist Andrew Bridgen described the memorial as, 'Totally inappropriate. It's not what people visit the National Trust for. If I want moral guidance I go to church – not the National Trust.'[183]

Bridgen had voted to stop gay people being allowed to marry in church.[184]

Further ethical leadership emerged from Jacob Rees-Mogg that month, when he said he opposed abortion, even in cases of rape. This didn't prevent his investment business from profiting from its £5 million share in a company that makes pills used during abortions.[185] 'It would be wrong to pretend that I like it, but the world is not always what you want it to be,' said Jacob.

Thankfully, he held raped women to stricter standards. He's a Christian, don't you know?[186]

—

The UK's credit rating was downgraded yet again in September.

Britain had maintained the top-rated AAA score for 35 years before the Cameron government took over, even through the Winter of Discontent and the 1976 bailout by the International Monetary Fund, events that have provided ammunition for the Conservatives' 'You can't trust Labour with money' propaganda for almost half a century.[187] But now the global ratings agencies downgraded us once more, saying Britain faced 'immediately apparent challenges' in the aftermath of the referendum, and the catastrophic leadership of the Tory government.

Not that any of this affected Boris Johnson's ambitions to make things worse.

Since his withdrawal from the race to succeed Cameron, he had become something of a marginalised figure; his cheerleaders reckoned he'd bottled it, and in the first few months of her premiership, Theresa May's vast polling lead had made it seem impossible that she could be swiftly dislodged.

And then came the shambolic election, and everything changed. Johnson was on her like a fucking puma.

May had just headed off Canada to begin laying the groundwork for a possible future trade deal. She probably looked forward to a break from domestic politics after an astonishingly acrimonious summer, during which the pack of slow-witted, fast-tempered feral maniacs in her Cabinet had painfully hammered out an agreed position on Brexit. She'd been in the air about three minutes before Boris Johnson bypassed both her and the fundamental Cabinet principle of collective responsibility. His fan-club newsletter, the *Telegraph*, published Johnson's latest clammy lunge into the Brexit Policy Tombola, which he laid out in a 4,000-word manifesto containing a whole new set of demands.

While the grown-ups were desperately trying to persuade vital trading partners that Britain wasn't ruled by a demented flock of irrepressible rogues, liars and vandals, our Foreign Secretary repeated all of his disproven lies about £350 million for the NHS and boasted of how Britain had made a 'gallant attempt [to] strangle at birth' the agreed financial plans of an entire continent.[188]

He then invited the *Sun* into his office for a hagiographic interview-cum-job-application. When it came to Brexit, he told them, 'Most people can't understand what this conversation is all about,' which is hardly surprising: very few Brexiteers could begin to define exactly what they wanted, and yet the wretched, hapless Theresa May had guaranteed she would deliver it, whatever it was.[189]

Johnson conjured up whole new strands of policy before the *Sun*'s very eyes: the Tories were going to 'act now' on student debt, he said. They were about to crack down on tax-avoiding tech giants. The minimum wage wasn't high enough, and an increase in public-sector pay should be funded by sacking people in the public sector.[190]

No part of this was official policy, but he announced it anyway. Five years later, reading back Johnson's promises from that interview, it's hard to believe it was said by the same man. Any delays to Brexit beyond the two-year agreed transition period would be a 'betrayal', he told us, and yet four years later, in July of 2021, he was asking the EU to extend their 'grace period' yet further.[191] The UK must never agree to shadow EU regulations,[192] he said, and yet his solution – if you could call it that – for the Irish border question relied explicitly on parts of Britain keeping those standards aligned.[193]

And it goes without saying that at the time of writing, the student debt crisis has not been acted upon, tech giants still avoid colossal amounts of tax, and public-sector pay remains abysmal.

Possibly worried that he hadn't made the front page of the *Telegraph* for an entire day, Johnson followed up this geyser of unplanned policy diarrhoea with a threat to resign before the weekend if Theresa May didn't agree to it all.[194] The resignation threat was about as true as the policy promises.

But only days later, Johnson faced calls for him to be sacked – not for massively undermining the government's agenda, but for having breached the Ministerial Code in at least four different ways.

It's against the rules for ministers to use official government resources for partisan purposes, but Johnson did it anyway: he chose a location that is only supposed to be used for official duties, and that's where he hosted a 'hard Brexit' launch event for yet another Eurosceptic thinktank, this time headed up by Daniel Hannan.

That's the same Daniel Hannan who had promised we weren't going to leave the single market, called the NHS a 'mistake' and said the minimum wage should be scrapped.[195] His movement was being promoted by Boris Johnson, who had just demanded we leave the single market so we could fund the NHS and increase the minimum wage.

They claimed to share the same policy objectives. Is it any wonder Theresa May couldn't please these people?

—

It had been a hectic September, but the Tories had got through it, and could now head off for a bit of relaxation in a place they knew things couldn't possibly go wrong: the hermetically sealed right-wing playpen of the Conservative Party Conference.

Graham Brady, the chairman of the 1922 Committee, which represents all backbench Tory MPs, set the tone for the event with his assertion that, 'There are two alternatives at this conference. One is to bugger about and make things worse; the other is not to.'[196]

They went with Option A.

Boris Johnson kicked things off, continuing his matchless record as our nation's top diplomat by suggesting the war-ravaged Libyan city of Sirte could easily become the new Dubai. 'All they have to do is clear the dead bodies away,' he said.[197] At least 7,000 people had died in battles in the city during the previous 12 months.[198] Johnson refused to apologise.[199]

Party chairman Eric Pickles launched a workshop to boost the numbers of young Tory voters who might be attracted by such opinions. It was a valiant effort, but doomed: just 70 people turned up to PicklesFest, and their average age was 50.[200] Within a couple of hours, the conference's Youth Zone was found to be completely empty.[201]

The future of the Conservative movement thus assured, the MPs assembled for their annual self-congratulatory shindig, oblivious to the words of one ministerial aide: 'the clever ones stay away'.[202]

The health secretary, Jeremy Hunt, hadn't stayed away, and used the conference to claim Labour, under their health minister Nye Bevan, had not founded the NHS. 'That wasn't him or indeed any Labour minister,' he claimed: it had all been thought up by the Tories. In reality, the Conservative Party had voted against the health service's creation 22 times.[203]

While the assembled journalists were still busy picking their jaws off the floor, Hunt announced that Britain 'has to do a lot more' to tackle obesity, while wearing a lanyard emblazoned with the logo of the event's sponsor, Tate & Lyle Sugars.[204]

The bar had been ratcheted down to record-breaking lowness in advance of Theresa May's speech, but she still managed to limbo under it in an appearance that has become legendary.[205] History's great orators take to the stage in confidence, reach out to their audience, and express profound ideas in rich, mellifluous tones. May lurched onto the stage with no new ideas at all, displayed the graceful poise of a bewitched trellis, and launched into her speech in a weird, discordant croak, like a spindly seabird that's swallowed a kazoo.

Thankfully, the noise was short-lived: her voice soon gave out completely and was replaced by a seemingly unending series of coughing fits. It was mesmerising to watch. Spectators cringed so hard, they bent time. And that was before we'd even got to the bit where a prankster wandered up to the platform and passed her a P45.

Astonishingly, she took it.

We were just minutes into the speech, and it was already the worst political experience near a stage since Abraham Lincoln. The few still able to focus on the words she was saying were surprised how much of it was directly plagiarised from a speech by the fictional president in

The West Wing,[206] but to be honest she could have read out the lyrics to 'Agadoo' and nobody would have noticed.

In the forlorn hope that it might make the horror end, Philip Hammond took it upon himself to crunch into a small ball, perhaps believing this made him invisible, and crawl to the platform to hand her a cough sweet. It had no effect whatsoever, so in a brief hiatus from literally dying on stage, the prime minister complained to the audience that the Chancellor's medicine didn't work, which was not a shock to anybody observing the economy for the previous seven years.

Even the sign behind her lost the will to live. It had begun the day reading 'Building a country that works for everyone', but just as May was boasting of Britain's 'strength that is shared around the globe', bits of the tagline began detaching themselves from the wall and leaping to their death. It ended up looking like a slogan designed by Norman Collier. For a brief moment, every satirist on the planet contemplated having to give up and get a proper job.

And just when you thought the torture was over, and the legally mandated period of standing ovation was about to begin, TV cameras caught Home Secretary Amber Rudd having to remind a distracted Boris Johnson that he should stand up and clap.

Weirdly, the disaster probably saved Theresa May. Before the speech, Sajid Javid, the communities secretary, had made a point of not backing her,[207] Grant Shapps was revealed as the ringleader of a group of MPs trying to oust her, and it was patently obvious Johnson wanted her job more than he wanted his own wife.[208] Or anybody else's wife, for that matter. He's not picky.

But after the speech, not a soul could bear to stick the knife into May because, in the words of one rebellious MP, 'people feel sorry for her'.[209]

—

Little noticed in all this chaos, the Office for National Statistics announced a minor adjustment to their estimate of Britain's wealth.

We were suddenly £490 billion poorer. Very nearly half a trillion pounds. Equivalent to 25 per cent of the nation's GDP.

There were two main causes. The first was that our stock of domestic wealth had fallen from a £469 billion surplus to a deficit of £22 billion as we poured cash into averting financial disaster after the referendum result. This was accompanied by the second reason: a monumental collapse in overseas investment.

In the first half of 2016, investment in the UK from overseas had added £120 billion to our nation's value. Since the referendum, investors pulling out had turned that into a deficit of £25 billion. The Bank of New York made it pretty clear what had happened: 'The big buyers are disappearing.'[210]

To get a sense of how big those lost big buyers are, £490 billion is £1 per second for 15,000 years. Or, if you prefer, £3,600 per hour, every single hour since the prehistoric era when ancient humans domesticated the dog.[211]

—

Tory sex scandals are like buses. You wait ages, and then three come along at once. Hold on, let me correct that: not three. Thirty-six.

In October a spreadsheet, thought to have been assembled by Conservative staffers, was leaked to the press. It listed warnings about inappropriate behaviour towards colleagues allegedly perpetrated by three dozen serving Tory MPs,[212] including 18 current ministers also accused of various forms of inappropriate sexual behaviour.[213]

Theresa May said she would sack any MPs named, but when it became clear this appeared to mean several members of the Cabinet and slightly more than 12 per cent of her entire parliamentary party, that pledge miraculously vanished.[214]

Some of the entries failed to identify the MP in question, simply stated their rank: a current Cabinet minister had put his hand on the thigh of a female journalist and told her, 'God, I love those tits.' Another charming minister asked his secretary to 'come and feel the length of my cock'. There were warnings that a minister was 'handsy with women at parties', while another was described as being 'perpetually intoxicated and very inappropriate with women'.

A few of the stories of sexual misconduct had already become public, such as the accusation that Mark Menzies paid a Brazilian male escort for sex and asked him to precure drugs, or the time Stephen Crabb messaged a 19-year-old he had just interviewed for a job, and invited her to meet him for sex.

Mark Garnier said he 'wasn't going to deny it' when it was revealed he referred to his secretary as 'sugar-tits' and would instruct her to go shopping for sex toys on his behalf.[215]

Daniel Kawczynski admitted urging a young researcher to go on a date with a wealthy businessman 'older than her father'.[216] Kawczynski made the approach apparently aware she had already rejected the man's advances several times.[217] Sources close to the woman called the incident 'sleazy in the extreme',[218] and Kawczynski admitted it had happened – yet he was cleared of wrongdoing by the party.

Chris Pincher stood down and referred himself to the police after being accused of sexual assault by a male Labour MP, and of making unwanted sexual advances to a British Olympic rower. He was also cleared of breaching party rules.[219]

Meanwhile the First Secretary of State (and de facto deputy prime minister) Damian Green was back again: a report said it was 'plausible' that he'd been a bit hands-on with a young activist, Kate Maltby, and concluded he had misled colleagues over the enormous quantities of porn found on his office computer a few years earlier.[220]

The whole thing was deeply unpleasant, but that didn't mean it couldn't be made worse: no sooner had Damian Green resigned and issued an apology to Kate Maltby than messages between the two of them were leaked to the press.[221] They seemed to show she had sent flirtatious texts to Green, but the messages were fake: no such conversation had happened. Somebody had mocked them up and shared them with the *Mail on Sunday*.

Some Tory MPs were appalled: one said, 'It appears that Green's allies barely paused for breath after he apologised for the distress caused to Kate Maltby before launching an attack. It smacks of a dirty tricks campaign.'[222]

But other Tories simply seemed to feel they were missing out: Andrew Bridgen informed *The Times* that his Tory colleague Dan Poulter had sexually assaulted three women. *The Times* foolishly assumed Bridgen was capable of accuracy, published the accusations, and ended up having to pay the entirely innocent Poulter substantial damages.[223] I wonder if Bridgen and Poulter still exchange birthday cards?

There was, in the eyes of some Tories, a perfectly valid defence for all this brouhaha. Sir Roger Gale expressed it when he said female journalists who had been subjected to sexual assaults by his colleagues were merely 'wilting flowers'. He went on to say, 'I'm afraid you [the media] are responsible… well, mainly female journalists are responsible.'[224]

It was a witch hunt, he declared, a view shared by Michael Fabricant, who seems to be so thick you could stand a spoon up in him, and chose to prove it by admitting the behaviour was 'wrong' and 'unprofessional', but also claiming the accusations were unfair because, 'at the time everyone was sloshed'.[225]

The sloshed people he was describing were the MPs who were supposed to be running the country, and most of the allegations referred to incidents in their workplace.

I have no idea how sloshed Dover MP Charlie Elphicke was, but it didn't appear to be a valid defence anyway. He was suspended from the party while he faced accusations of sexual offences against two members of his own staff. Theresa May, who was at one point going to sack anyone involved, reinstated him within a year, and then had to suspend him again when police charged him with three counts of sexual assault.

'I am completely confident I will be able to prove my innocence,' said Elphicke. He was found completely guilty and was sentenced to two years.[226]

—

Among those whose career had just been derailed by their wayward libido was Defence Secretary Michael Fallon, who was unable to deny embarking on an uninvited romantic approach to journalist Jane Merrick, which was described as a 'lunge'.[227] So now we needed a new defence secretary, and that man would be Gavin Williamson.

In the real world, Williamson would be the kind of employee you could trust with money up to the value of £5 – but not with mops – at your local hand car wash. But in the politics of 2017, different standards applied. Skills, competence, brains or effectiveness did not factor into the equation if you had one other, vitally important attribute, and Williamson had it in spades. He emitted such a powerful stench of raw ambition that it could bring down light aircraft.

As Chief Whip, Williamson had two responsibilities: knowing where the bodies were buried and consulting with the PM about all appointments. Some speculated that he'd had at least something to do with the leak of the spreadsheet that had ended the careers of his rivals for Cabinet posts, and had then advised the malleable and enfeebled Theresa May to give him the job he wanted.

A senior Tory MP sent a text message to the editor of *Newsnight* saying as much. 'Knifed Fallon and pinched his job. It's way above his ability'.[228] A minister told the BBC this showed Theresa May was 'so weak she has let Williamson appoint himself – this is appalling'.[229]

The quotes from Williamson's admiring colleagues just kept on coming.

'Unbelievable. Ludicrous. Astonishing'.[230]

'An appalling appointment. He's never stepped foot in a department and now he's running one of the most important.'

'[Theresa May] has gone mad. It's real "end of days" stuff. He's a real slimeball, with his own leadership team in place'.[231]

'She's just blown it and exposed herself as weaker than any of us thought. She's being controlled by young men in suits. I now despair'.[232]

You and me both, mate. But the truth is, there is a limited bench of talent in any political party. After a few years in office – especially if the party suffers widespread resignations – the government inevitably runs out of even moderately competent people to put in ministerial jobs. After five years of minority government, the Tories had lost a further thirteen seats in a general election, and in the subsequent two years had followed up with a raft of resignations. They were not going to suddenly discover a backbench Michael Heseltine or Ken Clarke that nobody had spotted before. From this point on, every minister would be – perforce – scraped from the very bottom of a very shallow, increasingly right-wing barrel.

It was bad news for Cronus too. Williamson's pet tarantula, named after the Greek god who castrated his father and ate his own children to prevent them from stymieing his ambitions, was not allowed to move into Williamson's new MoD office; our soldiers were scared of spiders.[233]

—

October had brought three dozen accusations of sexual misbehaviour, a slack handful of resignations, an arrest, and a homeless Greek tarantula; and we weren't even out of the first week. Surely it couldn't get worse.

Meet Priti Patel, who had somehow ended up as Secretary of State for International Development, despite professing she wanted to scrap her own department.[234]

In October, the BBC reported that Patel, the Shetland Pony of the Apocalypse, had visited Israel back in August on what she described as a 'private holiday', although she appeared to spend a surprising amount of her time attending meetings in the company of Lord Polak.[235] He's the president of Conservative Friends of Israel, a group that has funded dozens of such trips by Tory MPs – and who among us hasn't spent big chunks of our private family vacation with the president of a major lobbying group?

While on her private holiday, she held around a dozen meetings with Israeli politicians, including prime minister Benjamin Netanyahu.

Totally normal vacation stuff. Drink ouzo from a kettle. Get a regrettable henna tattoo. Pick up an infection at a water park. Attend a secret meeting with the prime minister.

It has been claimed that at least one of these meetings had been arranged on the specific suggestion of the Israeli Ambassador to London, while British diplomats knew nothing about it.

Following the surprisingly work-related holiday, she returned to her department and apparently made suggestions that Britain's international aid should, in future, be redirected to support the Israeli army's humanitarian facilities in the Golan Heights,[236] an occupied region which Britain – along with the EU, the USA and the security council of the United Nations – did not recognise as Israeli territory.[237]

Patel's story of What I Did On My Holidays didn't go down well.

'Boris knew about the visit,' Patel told the *Guardian*. 'The point is that the Foreign Office did know about this, Boris knew about it. And there is nothing else to this. It is quite extraordinary. It is for the Foreign Office to go away and explain themselves. The stuff that is out there is *it*, as far as I am concerned. I went on holiday and met with people and organisations. As far as I am concerned, the Foreign Office have known about this.'[238]

Pretty unambiguous. There was nothing else to emerge. The Foreign Office knew. Boris Johnson knew. She said it four times.

Shortly afterwards, she released a statement apologising for accidentally giving the false impression the Foreign Secretary knew about the trip.[239] Three days after that, it emerged that Patel had held other secret meetings with Israeli officials, this time not on her private holiday, but in New York in September.[240] This news broke when Priti Patel was on an official visit to Uganda, which was cut short so she could fly home to be sacked, and it became something of a public spectacle: 22,000 people logged onto Kenya Airline's live flight tracker to follow the descent of Priti Patel's flight and career.[241] That's more than the capacity of Millwall Football Club.

After what must have been an incredibly entertaining six-minute meeting with Theresa May, Patel stepped down.[242] The government faced its second reshuffle in a week.

—

Fortunately, we could still rely on the professionalism, integrity and diplomatic skills of the Foreign Office, here represented by its most senior figure, Boris Johnson. In a statement to a parliamentary committee, he falsely claimed the British charity worker Nazanin Zaghari-Ratcliffe was 'teaching journalists' in Iran, when in fact she was there on a family holiday.

Teaching journalists wasn't something the Iranian authorities looked kindly on, and as a result of Johnson's false statement she now faced espionage charges in Tehran, which would lead to at least five years in an Iranian prison.

'It is simply untrue,' Johnson told the House of Commons, 'that there is any connection whatever between my remarks last week and the legal proceedings under way against Nazanin Zaghari-Ratcliffe.'[243]

Oh really? Let's ask the Iranian prosecutors. They cited Johnson's words in their evidence against her: 'His [Mr Johnson's] statement shows that Nazanin had visited the country for anything but a holiday.' Had Johnson apologised and corrected the statement, the case may well have collapsed. But he refused, because narcissists can never admit they have made a mistake. As a result, Zaghari-Ratcliffe remained a prisoner in Iran for six years, until her release in March 2022.[244]

—

In project management there is a law known as the Iron Triangle, which states that in delivering any project, there are three points on a metaphorical triangle: deadline, budget and scope. In other words: how fast it can be done; how cheaply; and the features and quality of the thing being delivered. Every project manager knows that there is always a trade-off: you can deliver two of these things, but never all three.

For example, imagine your project is to get a garden shed built. You can have the shed cheaply and quickly, but it'll be rubbish. You've sacrificed quality.

Or you can build the shed quickly and deliver exceptional quality, but you'll need a team of joiners working 24/7, and that means it'll be very expensive. You've sacrificed price.

Or you can build it to a great quality and keep it cheap, but that means you have to do all the work yourself, learn the skills, prepare the timber, and so on. You've sacrificed speed.

The Iron Triangle applies to everything. It doesn't matter if your project is a garden shed, a rocket to Mars, or a massive change to the constitutional and trading arrangements of a nation: it's simply not possible to do the job quickly, cheaply and well. The Iron Triangle forbids it.

By this point, the government had made all kinds of promises about Brexit, but the main pledges were that it would be cheap and brilliant. This meant the only variable that could be changed was the speed at which the project was delivered. Delaying for a few years would allow the nation to prepare, to build new trading arrangements, to ensure we had enough doctors, enough drivers, enough food and energy supplies, enough administrators. Only an idiot would insist on it all being done in record time, and before we had an opportunity to properly plan and prepare.

In October, the government decided to enshrine the two-year deadline for Brexit in law.

More than a dozen of their own backbenchers opposed the move: not to stop Brexit (although plenty of MPs still wanted to do that), but to make it achievable without wrecking the joint.[245] The Tory press went apeshit.

'Mutiny!' shouted the *Telegraph*. 'Proud of yourselves?' asked a *Daily Mail* headline, the article accusing Ken Clarke, who had spent a decade as a member of Margaret Thatcher's Cabinet, of working to put a Marxist in Number 10.[246]

It was hard to avoid the conclusion that the country was losing its mind, which explains why the European Banking Authority and European Medicines Agency announced they were getting out of

London and relocating to Amsterdam, where people didn't act like they were off their tits on drugs all day.[247]

Prime example: leading Brexiteer John Redwood, who was paid £180,000 a year in his side-line as an adviser to a global investment group, and who had insisted to voters that Brexit would make Britain a great trading nation, now told his clients to withdraw their money out of the UK and invest in the EU instead.[248]

Meanwhile our growth as an independent power was in the hands of Boris Johnson, who took a break from lumbering around looking like his evening job was welcoming guests to Castle Frankenstein, and instead spent his November failing to keep a British member on the International Court of Justice. It was the first time we had not been represented in the body since we'd helped create it 71 years earlier, and in the words of Tory MP Robert Jenrick, it represented 'a major failure for British diplomacy'.[249]

—

At the end of November, David Davis finally acceded to demands that he hand over his department's impact reports, which outlined the effect of Brexit on the British economy. It had been a long journey.

In October 2016, Davis had been asked about governmental analysis of the impact of Brexit: 'We currently have in place an assessment of 51 sectors of the economy. We are looking at those one by one, but the aim at the end is that this will inform the negotiating approach so that no one gets hurt.'[250]

Two months later he repeated this, with a minor adjustment to the figures: 'We are in the midst of carrying out about 57 sets of analyses, each of which has implications for individual parts of 85 per cent of the economy.'

Yet curiously, three months after that, in March 2017, he told a parliamentary committee the government had done no economic assessments, nor were they necessary.[251]

In June 2017, assessments had once again popped into existence. Davis told Andrew Marr the impact assessments had been prepared in 'excruciating detail'.[252] Around 50 or 60 had been completed, he said, and work was proceeding on another few dozen. There would end up being '127, all told'.[253]

But he still refused to publish the reports, meaning MPs still had no idea of the predicted impact of the things they were voting on. So in October, a year after this debacle began, Parliament passed a motion that the assessments (now back down to 58 again) must be released.[254] The government agreed to honour the will of Parliament. All the reports were going to be published.

The following month, Downing Street issued a statement: 'We have been clear that the impact assessments don't exist.'[255]

Six days after this, having been threatened with contempt of Parliament, David Davis released those non-existent assessments to MPs, in a single 850-page document. It was so heavily redacted as to be meaningless.[256]

After being threatened with contempt a second time, Davis appeared before the select committee and told them the government had not carried out impact assessments, even though the 850 heavily censored pages of those very reports sat on the committee table in front of them all. Davis claimed the usefulness of any reports would be 'near zero', because what Brexit meant was changing so often and so radically.

Let's consider the logic of this: the people voted for Brexit, so Davis did an analysis of what that implied. But that analysis was useless because Brexit was radically different from what people voted for.

Yet he still claimed to have a mandate for doing it.

He then told the committee he had read just two of the 85 chapters of analysis, upon which the nation's entire negotiating position was to be based. And he was our lead negotiator.

Despite this remarkable, demonstrable, documented ineptitude and inconsistency, the endlessly patient EU ploughed on with talks, and in December ended up with a draft agreement on the Irish border. The Tories had resolved the matter by simply agreeing to do what they had absolutely guaranteed they would never do: leave Northern Ireland aligned to EU regulations, essentially putting a border between two parts of the UK and breaking up the nation.

May hadn't bothered to alert her fiercely pro-union DUP partners to her plans for smashing up the union before she agreed the plan with the EU, and naturally the entire agreement immediately fell apart, as it was always going to. A leading Eurosceptic Tory MP was quoted as saying: 'I find the whole thing quite inexplicable, that you would go to Brussels ready to table a proposal that you haven't squared with your confidence-and-supply partner.'[257]

Yet the double-talk continued. On 9 December Michael Gove wrote in the *Telegraph* that if UK voters disliked the final deal, we could change it. He claimed that 'any new treaty with the EU will cease to have primacy or direct effect in UK law', so we could simply vote to 'diverge' from our agreements.[258] Here was a government minister in a national newspaper informing everybody that Britain fully intended to lie to the EU and break any treaty we agreed, and that he wanted Britain to go out and agree new treaties with partners around the world.

Fine, but who on earth would possibly trust us?

In the increasingly unlikely event that the government stuck to their proclamations about the Irish border, the only options remaining were to leave the entire UK inside the single market, or to hope the whole of the EU would suddenly abandon its central credo simply because the British government was having a bit of a breakdown.

May rushed home, triumphantly clutching her crumbling, esoteric, quantum Withdrawal Agreement, and it had no sooner twinkled back into existence than she suffered a fresh disaster: she lost another vote in the House of Commons. She had argued that giving MPs a democratic vote on any agreement was inconsistent with Britain getting back its democracy, but MPs, and sane people who knew the definition of 'logic', disagreed: eleven of her own backbenchers voted against the government, including eight former ministers.

As a result, there was now a legal guarantee that Parliament would get a vote on both the Withdrawal Agreement, and on the final deal.[259]

—

Shakespeare wrote, 'When sorrows come, they come not single spies, but in battalions.' The sorrows that came in December were bigger than the Chinese People's Liberation Army. It was an absolute blizzard of shit.

Former Tory MP Bob Spink was convicted of four counts of election fraud and got six months.[260]

The next day Chancellor Philip Hammond blamed Britain's seven consecutive years of abysmal economic performance on disabled workers not pulling their weight.[261] If you think that's shocking – and you should, cos it is – spare a thought for the trauma felt by poor old Owen Paterson. He once more had to suffer thwarted ambitions and the loss of his seeming lifelong dream of a harrowing bloodbath among Britain's beloved wildlife: Theresa May abandoned yet another manifesto pledge, this time on bringing back fox hunting.[262]

Morecambe MP David Morris got into a row with public services in his Lancashire constituency: local teachers were having to wash pupils' uniforms and buy them shoes and coats because their parents couldn't afford to pay their electricity bills or clothe their kids. Meanwhile a nearby GP practice reported seeing incidences of the Victorian-era disease rickets among local children, a condition that in the 21st century was usually only found in developing countries.[263] It is caused by the vitamin deficiencies associated with extreme, prolonged hunger.[264] David Morris could have demanded a government response, as the elected representative of these people. Instead, he falsely accused the schools and doctors of being connected to Momentum, the grassroots Labour movement.

In Morecambe, 5,087 children– not far short of one in every four – lived in poverty.[265] In 2013, David Morris reportedly had the second-highest expenses claims in the country.[266]

These levels of poverty were not isolated incidents. On Christmas Day 2017, 128,000 children would be homeless, up two-thirds since

2011. Compared to four years earlier, an additional 400,000 children and 300,000 pensioners were living in poverty.[267] If that's too much to handle, just think about one child. One child being homeless and hungry on Christmas Day. One child without shoes or wearing unwashed clothing. You would immediately put your hand in your pocket. We all would. We wouldn't think twice.

Now multiply that by 128,000, and vote for a tax cut for rich people. Congratulations: you're a Tory!

The government's entire Social Mobility Commission quit overnight – not just the commission's leader, or one narky official: the entire body.[268] They were followed days later by the chair of the National Infrastructure Commission, who said the Tories were engaging in 'a dangerous populist and nationalist spasm worthy of Donald Trump'.[269]

In the same week, it was revealed that Brexit would rob UK charities of at least £258 million of funding. Charities hadn't even been among the sectoral analysis that David Davis had simultaneously written and not written (but definitely hadn't read). It turns out many of our charities – including the Prince's Trust, Save the Children and various royal wildlife charities – were hugely reliant on endowments from the EU, many of which had always been discreetly distributed as part of the UK's Lottery Fund, so as not to confuse the natives with positive stories about Europe.[270]

Only days after blaming the government's disastrous economic performance on the disabled, Philip Hammond was back, this time telling the BBC, 'There are no unemployed people,' at a time when 1.4 million were unemployed.[271] He went on to say he was just about to set out plans for 300,000 new homes per year – a bit of variety from the non-existent 200,000 homes previously promised in 2015, 2016 and twice in 2017. But some things never change: he still said the government would provide no money.[272] Magical homes!

It had been, even by the standards we had come to expect since 2010, an unutterably terrible year; but at least Theresa May ended it by making good on her promises to stop the cronyism that had plagued David Cameron's time in office. He'd become notorious for handing out honours and knighthoods to his friends and supporters, and May was not going to get caught doing the same thing.

She handed out honours to 17 friends from her days at the Foreign Office, and a knighthood to Graham Brady, indefatigable May loyalist and chairman of the backbench 1922 Committee, who had seen off calls to oust her following the election debacle.[273]

Oh yeah, and Christopher Chope also got a knighthood. Truly, they are the best of us.

2018
An Aggressive and Fruity Meltdown

Let's rewind 1,000 years and travel to Bernburg, Germany, where one Christmas Eve in the year 1020, an otherwise unremarkable church service was interrupted when a dozen of the worshippers suddenly began to maniacally and involuntarily dance. They didn't know why. Nobody knew why. They checked the Bible, but God had no answers. The dancers couldn't make themselves stop, and it lasted for hours.

Two hundred years later and a few hundred miles away, another incident: a large group of children started to unwillingly dance, boogying out of town and 12 miles down the road, almost certainly starting the Pied Piper myth in the process.

Half a century on, a group of around 200 uncontrollable dancers were so vigorous they caused a bridge to collapse. In 1518, over 400 people spontaneously gyrated for several days, and didn't even stop when 15 of them danced themselves to death.

You could write all this off as the wild exaggerations of overimaginative medieval storytellers, were it not for more recent examples of baffling group behaviour.

In the 1960s, ambulances rushed to a school in Blackburn after dozens of girls began compulsively moaning, and then 85 of them fainted. Medics found nothing physically wrong with them. In Singapore in the 1970s, a group of factory workers began screaming one morning, and could not stop themselves. Emergency services were called and did what they could, but not even hospital-grade tranquillisers worked. The outbreak lasted a week.

This sort of phenomena is called *mass sociogenic illness*: the compulsive, inexplicable and harmful behaviour of a large group, which has no corresponding cause; and I mention these events in the hope that researchers might investigate the population of Epsom and Ewell, which since June 2001 has compulsively, inexplicably and harmfully elected Chris Grayling to be their MP.

Most politicians believe themselves to be intrepid and invincible, but not Grayling. He is unfailingly vincible, and steadfastly trepid. He's an artless agent of pure chaos, and try as I might, I can find no record of him ever being hapful, reckful, gormful or ept.

When they put him in charge of getting people into employment, he made 10,000 of his own Jobcentre workers redundant.[1]

When they put him in charge of crime, serious offences rose by 21 per cent.[2]

When they put him in charge of the probation service, his tenure was described as an 'unmitigated disaster' by the British Sociological Association.[3]

When they put him in charge of prisons, he relieved jails of a quarter of their staff.

And when they put him in charge of transport, he somehow contrived to get entangled in his own car door, which knocked over and injured a passing cyclist; and then he reportedly left the scene without providing his formal details.[4]

The Home Bargains Pennywise entered 2018 trailing a record of calamities that you could wrap twice around the world, and he hadn't even broken a sweat. The year began with Grayling being made party chairman for as long as the Tories could trust him not to screw up, which turned out to be 27 seconds. His appointment was announced on Twitter at 1.43 a.m., not an hour that screams: we're proud of this. The tweet was deleted less than half a minute later, which, as we all know, is more than enough time for Grayling to fall down the stairs, accidentally glue his own head to a toaster, and set fire to the Queen.[5]

After his incredibly brief tenure as chairman, Grayling went back to being transport secretary, and was almost immediately castigated by a select committee for cancelling multiple promised rail electrification schemes in the North of England, on the grounds that there was 'no obvious benefit' to spending money in the North.[6]

Under the Tories, public spending on transport in London is £903 per head. In the North, it's £276.[7] Hey everybody, gather round: I've found an obvious benefit!

To avoid levelling up the country (which is, apparently, a major Tory policy), Grayling decided to stick with diesel-electric trains for the North. These require twice as many engines and a huge fuel tank. As a result, they're so much heavier than the electric alternative that they damage tracks, and therefore cost twice as much to maintain. The operational costs on a single line are £63,000 a day.[8]

The National Audit Office discovered Grayling made this cloth-brained decision before the 2017 general election, but he'd suppressed its release because somewhere in the back of what I suppose we must call 'his mind', he realised it wouldn't play very well with voters.[9]

It was literally weeks before his next fiasco came to light. Britain's rail network announced the largest change to timetables in living memory, and under Grayling's watchful eye managed to make the biggest cockup in living memory too. Over 10,000 trains were cancelled or severely delayed. During peak travel times in two of the busiest locations in Britain – Greater Manchester and the Thameslink area – two out of every three trains were cancelled.[10] Millions of passengers were affected.

There were multiple causes of this mess, all of them eminently foreseeable by a competent minister. For example: even for a normal, minor change to a route or timetable, it's recommended rail services allocate around 16 months to training, so drivers can be sent to do training without too much disruption to the network. To prepare

20,000 drivers for the biggest change anybody could remember, the government allocated barely a month.

And just as the timetable changes were due to take place, dozens of track upgrades were being undertaken by the giant contractor Carillion. But Carillion had collapsed in January with the loss of 2,400 jobs after the Tories refused to give them financial assistance.[11] Work ground to a halt, leaving disruption across the network.

As a result, we were faced with the largest upheaval in a generation coinciding with unfinished work along hundreds of routes, along which 20,000 untutored drivers would be steering trains they'd never been on before.

The warning signs were written in 60-foot letters of fire, so the quango Grayling was responsible for made an executive decision: we've got no tracks, no preparation, and no drivers. Let's do it anyway!

Full figures are hard to come by, due to the fragmentary nature of the privatised rail system, but during the most badly affected week, business losses exceeded £38 million in the Manchester area alone.[12] If you think that's an isolated case, think again: the chaos lasted for weeks and affected the entire country. The government's own Northern Powerhouse Partnership found Grayling's screw-up caused 945,000 hours of lost work just in their region.[13] Meanwhile in London, the crisis caused one company to turn a £130 million profit into a £5 million loss.[14]

The editor of trade magazine *Rail* called it 'the most chaotic, fundamental and humiliating failure it has been my misfortune to witness in 40 years as a rail journalist'. Sir Michael Holden, retired head of East Coast rail, said, 'Never in my worst nightmares did I imagine it could conceivably be anything like as bad as it is.'[15]

Your worst nightmares clearly weren't haunted by Chris Grayling. I envy you.

A report by the Office of Rail and Road found the problem was caused because 'no one took charge', and that there was a 'lack of responsibility and accountability'.[16] So the Tories held Grayling responsible and accountable by supporting him against a vote of no confidence and leaving him in charge.

Let's now move on to August, where we find Grayling's previous existence as Minister for Fucking Up Prisons had suddenly come back to bite him on the elbow. Or do I mean arse? It doesn't matter: he can't tell the difference anyway.

Grayling's tenure as prisons minister is best encapsulated by his realisation that even proven national embarrassment G4S were better than he was, which is why he handed over control of so many prisons to that company. It went about as well as could be expected.

In August 2018, when the Chief Inspector of Prisons, Peter Clarke, visited the G4S-run jail in Birmingham, he found it to be 'the worst prison I have ever been to'. There had been 1,147 assaults during a single year, which was not only the highest in the country, but it was also the highest incidence of violence ever recorded in any jail in England and Wales. Ever. It was a fivefold increase since the day G4S took over.

'Surely somebody must have been asleep at the wheel,' said Mr Clarke.[17]

'Wheels,' said Chris Grayling, startled from a power-nap. 'Hey, I'm transport minister, I know all about wheels.'

(He didn't say that. I made that bit up. Of course he doesn't know about wheels.)

By October, Grayling had redirected his special genius to the roads of Kent, where Tory MP Tom Tugendhat awoke one morning to discover that overnight, and without any warning, the transport secretary had turned big chunks of his nearest motorway into a lorry park.

'I wrote to [Grayling] in April asking whether or not this would happen,' a stupefied Tugendhat told Parliament. 'I was assured that works were not planned. Yet only yesterday was it confirmed to me that that is *exactly* what was planned, despite having told me the reverse over a week earlier.'[18]

Trains: tick.

Roads: tick.

Where next? Oh yes, the skies.

In November 2018, Gatwick Airport had to close for several days after a drone repeatedly entered its airspace. More than 140,000 passengers had flights disrupted, the army had to be called in, and at one point a drone came within 20 feet of an aircraft carrying 180 passengers.

You might think: nobody can blame Grayling for drones. But then you discover he'd ignored numerous warnings about the vulnerability of airports to drones, and only a few months earlier had deliberately cancelled legislation designed to prevent it.[19]

The disruption cost just one of the affected airlines more than £15 million.[20]

Some are born hapless, some achieve haplessness, and others have haplessness thrust upon them. Uniquely, for Chris Grayling, it's all three. Sadly, such consummate ineptitude does not come cheap. During his time in office, a Labour Party study using National Audit Office figures claimed that his personal cockups have cost the taxpayer more than £2.7 billion.[21] That's the same as a stack of £10 notes over 18 miles high. It's the yearly salary of 80,000 nurses.[22]

And he's just one man.

I beseech you, by the Sacred Toboggan of Imhotep, not to let him breed.

—

It's not as if Chris Grayling was operating in a vacuum. Would that he were! But while his exotic experiments with the acceptable bounds of normal management theory were going on, the other Tories had been far from idle. So let's rewind again to the start of 2018, and see what Grayling's playmates were up to.

On 8 January, Theresa May announced yet another reshuffle. It would be her third in two months, and this time she promised it was going to be a whopper.

The party was in a moribund state, her ministers were flailing, failing and Chris Grayling, and things needed shaking up.[23] So she briefed the press that a quarter of the Cabinet was going to go, and that there would be changes so massive you could see them from space.[24] In the event, you'd have been hard-pressed to notice the reshuffle if you were trapped in a phone booth with it. Only three ministers left the Cabinet, and two of those were voluntary resignations. Twenty of the 25 ministerial posts remained unchanged.

Tory grandee Nicholas Soames tweeted, 'Is that it?', which was a fair question.[25] When you consider how many ministers had demonstrated their natural flair at being dipsomaniac fraudsters, venal, moneygrubbing failures, erotically ungovernable masturbators, or grubby, self-seeking, venomous bags of pustulant bigotry, it's surprising she could only find three people she didn't fancy sitting next to at the Cabinet table.[26]

Whatever was afflicting Grayling seemed to be contagious. Tories managed to announce Baroness Mobarik was leaving the government, even though she'd actually left the government the previous April. Baroness Chisholm was named as the new appointee to a post that she'd actually left back in 2016. And both John Glen and Tracey Crouch were simultaneously announced as the new minister for civil society and ended up fighting it out.[27] Tracey Crouch lost and had to be the minister.

Jeremy Hunt flatly refused to be prised out of the health secretary job, and Justine Greening was either sacked or quit (depending on who you ask) after she declined to be reshuffled away from the education brief.

In the modernising, equal-opportunities Tory party, by the end of the day five government departments employed no female MPs, and Maria Caulfield was appointed Vice Chair for Women, despite having voted to oppose the removal of the tampon tax.[28]

George Osborne wrote, 'Theresa May's Cabinet reshuffle is the worst in modern history.'[29] And he knows a thing or two about shit governance, so listen to the man.

—

As was by now traditional in a Tory January, the health service was on its knees. NHS England recorded its worst ever waiting-time performance,[30] and over a single 24-hour period one in every 10 NHS trusts declared a major incident: not because of a train crash or a terrorist atrocity, but because they were stretched so thin they could no longer cope with an unremarkable Wednesday.[31] Eight solid years of underfunding will do that.

The PM denied the NHS was in crisis on the very same day her health minister apologised for the crisis in the NHS. May said, 'The NHS has been better prepared for this winter than ever before,' while in the background the health service abandoned all those preparations: every non-urgent treatment was cancelled for the entire month.

Meanwhile, rough sleeping in England rose for the seventh successive year, which was also the seventh successive year since Tory austerity began. The number of people sleeping on the streets had doubled since Cameron was elected.[32]

Faced with such an urgent crisis in health and social care, Boris Johnson suggested what I'm sure we can all agree is the only sensible solution: build a 22-mile bridge to France, pronto.[33] And ideally call it something that rhymes with the Smoris Smidge.

The cost would be a piddling £120 billion,[34] as estimated by the party who told us the £107 billion HS2 would cost one-third as much.[35] Even assuming their guess about the bridge was right – and let's face it, their guess was wrong – it's still a stack of £10 notes over 800 miles high.[36] If your mind is still insufficiently boggled by this, allow me to remind you that the bridge to France scheme was conjured up by the guy who had just led the campaign to stop people moving between Europe and the UK.

Which drags us inexorably back to Brexit. I'm so sorry.

At the end of January, government analysis of the impact of leaving the EU was leaked: it examined each of the possible scenarios for the future and concluded that the UK would be worse off in every case, and across every region. Nobody would escape the harm. Even the best-case scenario left us 5 per cent worse off over the next 15 years; at worst, 10 per cent.[37] And all delivered by a party that bewails the imminent death of the economy if you suggest a 1 per cent tax increase for the richest 1 per cent of people. Even at its worst point, the history-defining, catastrophic financial crisis of 2007 only reduced Britain's GDP by 2.6 per cent.[38]

But surely there would be benefits to Brexit? Yes, says the report: if we got all the trade deals we wanted, it would add an absolute maximum of 0.4 per cent to our GDP, which the statisticians among you will spot is slightly less than the 5 to 10 per cent we would simultaneously lose.[39]

The government refused to answer any questions, using the excuse that it never comments on leaked reports. So the media asked them to release the real report. They refused to do that too. When asked why the analysis wasn't being made public, a Brexity official from the Brexit department admitted, 'Because it's embarrassing.'[40]

Remainers hated the report because it was true. By contrast, Leavers hated the report because it was true. Their solution was to surround the truth with lies and hope it just blended in.

Enter Jacob Rees-Mogg, who had the aura of Nosferatu trying to fit in at a Bible study meeting, and claimed he'd heard Charles Grant, an expert on EU negotiations, tell Steve Baker that the Treasury was inventing fake predictions just to make Brexit look bad. Rees-Mogg asked Baker to confirm this to the House of Commons. As Baker stood to answer, his boss, David Davis, loudly whispered instructions to deny the story. Baker nodded, stood up, and told Parliament it was 'essentially correct'.

Only two parts of that answer were wrong. The word *essentially*, and the word *correct*.

Several people had witnessed the original conversation between Baker and Grant, and there was even a recording of it, proving no such thing had been said.[41] Rees-Mogg had apparently made the whole thing up, and Steve Baker, one of the many vainglorious bionic wazzocks working to deliver something they vaguely hoped might answer the description of 'Brexit', willingly went along with it.

'I will apologise to Charles Grant, who is an honest and trustworthy man', tweeted Baker after audio emerged. He said the entire thing was based on an 'honest recollection of the conversation', and went on to write: 'As I have put on record many times, I have the highest regard for our hard-working civil servants. I will clarify my remarks to the House.'[42]

Fine, but could you perhaps refrain from talking bollocks in the first place? No, of course not; silly of me to ask.

We weren't even out of February when Tory Twitter brought another embarrassing episode: Ben Bradley accused Jeremy Corbyn of having 'sold British secrets to communist spies' back in the 1980s. After being issued with a threat of a libel action, Bradley deleted the tweet and offered a £15,000 donation to a charity of Corbyn's choosing. The apologetic email from Bradley was the most-shared tweet ever made by a Conservative MP.

Bradley was in such a sharing mood that he then allowed Tory donors to share the joy of paying £15,000 towards his costs, thus neatly sidestepping the inconvenience of facing responsibility for his own actions. He'll do well in the Conservative Party, that boy.[43]

—

Theresa May's latest solution to the unfixable conundrum of the Irish border was yet another complicated bit of political fabulism. Tory responses to this problem have had various names, each intended to persuade a jaundiced public that all the old absurdities have been quietly resolved, and now we're talking about a brand-new helping of bewildering gibberish. But it's always described the same problem, whether you call it Theresa May's Brexit backstop or Boris Johnson's Northern Ireland protocol.

May's idea was both gloriously simple and magnificently stupid. Essentially: photocopy the single market, give the duplicate a new name that won't frighten Jacob Rees-Mogg, and run both systems simultaneously across the entire continent.

She called this replica of the single market 'mutual recognition of standards'. The benefit to the UK was that it would provide all the advantages of free trade and seamless borders with the 450 million customers next door, but we would never have to tell the people of Bolsover that Brexit was an impossible dream.

But for the EU, 'mutual recognition' meant creating an entirely new, vastly complicated trading entity, which pointlessly duplicated all the existing administration, legislation, bureaucracy and political headaches from the single market. And then they'd have to run both systems side by side.

The idea was flatly rejected, and the next proposal came from the EU: they suggested we leave Northern Ireland inside the EU's single market and customs union, and let the British worry about problems of border checks between NI and the UK. But the practical consequence was a de facto chopping-up of the union, and Theresa May said 'no UK prime minister could ever agree' to this happening.[44]

May continued to tell Britain she would find a solution to all of this, a deal that would allow seamless trade, less bureaucracy, and more freedom. But all her solutions were built around using the copy/paste function. It was stark madness, and the basic premise of duplicating everything was a non-starter for the EU.

Donald Tusk, the president of the European Council and frustrated therapist to David Davis, made it as clear as he could. 'There is no possibility to have some sort of exclusive form of single market for some part of our economies,' he said. 'Our Free Trade Agreement will not make trade between the UK and EU frictionless or smoother. This is the essence of Brexit.'[45]

Inevitably, Theresa May signed the terms of the Withdrawal Agreement. A transitional period would last until 31 December 2020, and then we were on our own. And Northern Ireland would remain part of the single market if we didn't think of anything better in the meantime.[46]

May had just agreed to something she'd told us no UK prime minister could ever agree to.

Meanwhile, the Bank of England revealed Brexit was already costing us £800 million a week, which tots up to a chunky £40 billion a year.[47] If that feels like a small price to pay, think of it like this: it's a stack of £10 notes over 260 miles high for a worse trade deal, at a time when there were 1.6 million people reliant on food banks.[48] That's an annual increase of 18 per cent.

—

Wanking news: and the Tories became the first government in the world to announce it would introduce compulsory age verification for porn sites.

In the minds of the Conservatives, the process would be simple: all you'd have to do is provide your proof of ID (of the kind Theresa May had abolished in 2011), and then all your personal data could be held by pornographers (which broke data-protection regulations).

When reality proved more complicated than the simple headlines – and isn't that becoming a theme? – the government suggested a new solution: 'gift-card-style vouchers', which would be purchased from local retailers. In future, prospective masturbators would have to pop to the corner shop and ask the 16-year-old behind the counter for permission to paddle the pink canoe.

'I'm sorry, Gordon, I'm not old enough to serve you a wanking pass, I'll have to fetch Mrs Arbuthnot.'

While the Tories were busy protecting kids from the porn that seemingly half the Cabinet was whapping away to day and night, a generation of infinitely more tech-savvy kids spent 10 seconds installing free VPN software, which instantly circumvented the entire thing.

The policy was delayed, reviewed, 'placed in a holding pattern', and then quietly abandoned. But not before a group of age-verification-software companies – which had upscaled to handle this fiasco – began legal action against the government, seeking £3 million in damages.[49]

—

At the end of March, at long last, the government caved in to pressure, and increased the minimum wage. Don't start celebrating just yet.

If you were working full time, the increase still left the average recipient £1,800 short of the 'living wage' – the absolute minimum income required to afford basic housing, transport, food and childcare. To survive on the new minimum wage, a person would need to work 58 weeks per year.[50]

Dominic Raab had said, 'The British are among the worst idlers in the world.'[51]

—

Defence minister and top fireplace salesman Gavin Williamson took a strong line with Russia following the Salisbury chemical attack in March, in which two Russian intelligence operatives were strongly suspected of using a nerve agent to poison Russian nationals living in the UK.[52]

Russia should 'shut up and go away', he said.[53]

Gavin Williamson is not 11 years old. But honestly, I had to check.

His pugnacious tone might have had more impact in Moscow if he didn't represent a government that had cut defence spending by a quarter since 2010.[54] But by now, ineffectually shouting at foreigners was basically all that was left of our national identity, and Gavin Williamson would be damned if he was going to let the side down.

—

In April, Amber Rudd, the Home Secretary, denied that her party cutting 21,000 police over seven years had contributed to the rise in violent crime. 'The evidence does not bear out claims that resources are to blame for rising violence,'[55] she assured us, and then almost immediately afterwards a Home Office report that she had commissioned was leaked to the press. It stated cuts had 'encouraged' violent offenders and had most likely contributed to the rise in serious and violent crime.[56]

There had been a 15 per cent-plus cut in police numbers, which corresponded nicely with a 15 per cent-plus increase in gun, knife and serious violence offences.[57] Junior Home Office minister Victoria Atkins was shoved onto the airwaves to insist the government knew what it was doing and was fully abreast of all the facts and figures.

'How many police officers do we have?' the interviewer asked.

'It's, er, er, you're testing me,' she replied. 'It's, um, um, I'm not going to hazard a guess, I'm just going to front up and say I'm so sorry.'[58]

—

Let's take a welcome break from the catastrophes of the Conservative Party to discuss the catastrophes of their suppliers, with a brief introduction to Capita, the professional services and outsourcing giant.

Their name is not widely known across the land, but it should be, because they run almost as much of the land as government does. And just like the government, they have an impressive record of dismal and repeated failure.

A few recent examples.

Capita were handed the HR contracts for multiple NHS trusts and made such a pig's ear of it that staff were repeatedly underpaid, and some of the trusts exited the contract just 18 months into a seven-year term.[59]

They ran the system of Personal Independence Payments introduced by Iain Duncan Smith, which was described as 'nothing short of a fiasco' by the chair of the Public Accounts Committee.[60]

They were fined £2 million for failing to properly undertake Disclosure and Barring Service checks on teachers, which for some reason was now the job of a private company, rather than the police or government.[61]

Their finance division was fined after some of its staff helped to defraud multiple customers of hundreds of thousands of pounds.[62]

They were handed a contract to recruit temporary and locum nursing staff for the NHS, and then creamed off 49 per cent of the salary as a fee,[63] and by this point even Jeremy Hunt was criticising the fees charged by 'rip-off agencies'.[64]

They ran a £290 million scheme for adult learners that was scrapped after one year, in the wake of widespread and massive fraud.[65]

They replaced regional health services across the country, then ended up neglecting to pay hundreds of GPs, and failing to handle 85 per cent of records.

Throughout 2016, around 1,000 doctors, dentists and opticians were left unable to work for months – in the middle of unprecedented pressure on the NHS – because Capita had failed to process their paperwork. And Capita created a backlog of 500,000 healthcare-related letters, causing failures to order medical supplies, and lost or delayed patient records.

Almost the entirety of Barnet Council's local services was handed to Capita, a supposedly cost-saving decision which ended up costing £217 million more than the original value of the contract.[66]

As part of a £250 million scheme to train all our civil servants, Capita faced an investigation into allegations it 'exploited its dominant position at the expense of the small suppliers it works with', causing some of them to go out of business, while Capita took a minimum 20 per cent administration fee. This was described as a model of how to 'provide better value for the taxpayer'.[67]

And finally, they inherited a £1.3 billion contract to deliver recruitment for the British Army. They missed enlistment targets by between 21 per cent and 45 per cent every single year for a decade, delivered the core recruitment website four years late, and made more than £100 million in just two years.[68]

Naturally, they were then handed another two-year contract.

If this doesn't worry you, could I please have some of whatever it is you're smoking?

Capita is a private business, unaccountable to voters, and heavily responsible for the delivery of huge swathes of the UK's health services, social care, education, criminal-record checks and military recruitment. They run entire local councils, and the training and support for the whole of the British civil service. You cannot, under any circumstances, vote them out of power. And a lot of it appears to be utter dogshit.

Why am I telling you this? Because in 2012, when the then Home Secretary Theresa May implemented her hostile environment policy, there was a sharp increase in income off the back of fees paid for applications to remain in the UK. Profits had reached £800 million by 2017.

Terrifying immigrants turned out to be a pretty decent money-making scheme, not least for Capita, to whom May had handed the lucrative contract to order people to get out of the country. Unsurprisingly, given the people involved, we were only one year into that contract when reports started to emerge that it was all going a bit Chris Grayling.

Caseworkers handling immigration applications found approximately half of the people being politely asked to fuck off back where they came from were here legally. Yet some of them had already lost their jobs as a result of their status even being questioned. In the hostile environment, companies faced fines of £10,000 for employing illegal immigrants, and businesses just didn't want to take the risk.[69]

Those affected weren't just workers: often, they were elderly people who had been born in the Caribbean up to 70 years earlier and had migrated legally to the UK when they were young children. Their arrival – and that of their parents – was a response to Britain's desperate need for labour after the Second World War. We urged people to come here and offered settlement rights to anybody born in a British colony. Hundreds of thousands came. They were given no official documentation because none was needed. They were British. End of story.

They became known as the Windrush Generation, after the *Empire Windrush*, the ship that brought the first arrivals from the West Indies.

Many had been British residents since 1948 yet were now threatened with immediate deportation to a land they hadn't lived in since they were a baby, simply because they couldn't meet Theresa May's ludicrously high threshold for evidence. May stipulated they must each provide four pieces of documentation for every year they'd lived in the UK, which in some cases went back almost 70 years.[70] If somebody missed a single document from a single year, they could be thrown out of the country. Yet because during those years no documentation had been provided – or even legally required – it was literally impossible to comply with May's new rules.

Even their children, who had been born in the UK and were British citizens, now found themselves targeted. Unable to provide evidence of their parents' right to live here, they suddenly found themselves accused of not being British, and faced immediate deportation to a land they might never have even visited, and in which they had no legal status.

It's barely worth mentioning, but Boris Johnson was also born outside of the UK. He wasn't even born in a British colony, unless we're still counting Manhattan as 'one of ours'. Yet he wasn't threatened with deportation. I can't for the life of me think what is different about posh white Boris Johnson.

At least 83 poor Black people were wrongly deported. Others were locked up in detention centres often for months, awaiting deportation. Countless numbers – literally countless, because the government neglected to keep count – had their passports confiscated, lost their jobs, their homes, the benefits to which they were entitled, and in some cases, feared they would lose their lives.

Albert Thompson, who had lived legally in the UK for 44 years, suddenly faced a £54,000 bill for healthcare because the Home Office reckoned he was here illegally, and therefore not entitled to NHS care.[71] Unable to pay, he had to stop his cancer treatment. Lacking the required 176 pieces of non-existent official documentation dating back almost half a century, he was evicted from his council home, and ended up sleeping on the streets.

He was far from the only one: Oxford University estimated 57,000 people living legally in the UK had been affected by the Windrush scandal.

News of this spiralling crisis reached the government's ears long before it reached the newspapers, and they had ample time to address it. They simply chose not to. As far back as 2013, Caribbean governments approached Philip Hammond at an international conference and raised their concerns. Twelve Caribbean countries made a formal request to meet Theresa May to discuss the issue, and all 12 were refused.

When the story broke, Amber Rudd, by now the Home Secretary, was hauled in front of the Home Affairs Select Committee and asked whether people had been wrongly deported simply to meet targets. She said, 'That's not how we operate,' and denied there were any targets for deportation numbers.

Two days later, a memo from her department was leaked to the press. It stated there was 'a target of achieving 12,800 enforced returns in 2017–18'.

Rudd claimed she had never seen the memo and insisted again that there were no targets. Another two days later, a letter from Rudd to Theresa May was published, in which the Home Secretary discussed her 'ambitious but deliverable' targets for removal.[72]

Rudd resigned, which was the least she could do. By which I mean, if she could have done less, no doubt she would have.

But what about Theresa May? She'd initiated the policy, boasted of the policy, and driven its implementation and delivery for the first six of its seven years (including five years when the international community was begging her to stop). Surely, she couldn't remain in office.

She remained in office.

The Windrush Generation had been expected to provide four documents for every year of their life in Britain. The Home Office couldn't even provide one document showing how many people had been affected. They knew they'd spent £52 million on plane tickets to fly legally resident Black people out of the country, but hadn't bothered to keep a record of how many had actually left. And for 2018, not even financial records existed.

The select committee demanded a compensation scheme for the victims. By August 2018, it still hadn't been implemented, and those affected were often still legally prevented from having any form of income whatsoever. A former nurse entangled in this mess told her caseworker, 'I am not allowed to work, I have no benefits, and I have a 12-year-old child.'[73]

When it did finally arrive, the compensation scheme allocated a range of payments that could be as high as £120,000, but also as low as £1.

One pound. One.

By February 2020 – over three years after the story broke – only 36 compensation claims had been settled, out of at least 15,000. Nine people living in the UK had died without receiving their compensation. A further 24, who had been wrongly deported to Caribbean countries, had also died of old age before getting a penny. The Home Office refused to even attempt to trace victims sent to non-Caribbean countries, so God alone knows what happened to them, but the government wasn't going to lift a finger to find out.

Meanwhile, 23 per cent of immigration enforcement officers who had worked towards deporting victims were given bonus payments 'linked to targets to achieve enforced removals'. Those would be the targets that didn't exist.

Rudd's replacement as Home Secretary was Sajid Javid, a child's drawing of pure greed superimposed onto a competitively evil gonad. He announced 'major changes' to the hostile environment policy, which turned out to be replacing the word *hostile* with the word *compliant*.[74] A report from the Home Affairs Select Committee said, 'Simply rebranding it the compliant environment is meaningless,' and demanded a change of culture at the Home Office.[75]

So how did that change of culture work out? Well, deportations were stopped after public outcry in 2018, and then in February 2019, deportations started again.[76]

—

Off we go, then, to Palazzo Terranova, the luxuriously restored 17th-century Italian castle belonging to Evgeny Lebedev, billionaire son of a billionaire former KGB officer, and owner of the *Evening Standard* and *Independent* newspapers.[77]

Lebedev doesn't live there full time, of course. He is – to coin a phrase – a London-based Russian oligarch.

As Mayor of London, man-of-the-people Boris Johnson had borrowed a friend's private jet to fly out to Lebedev's play-palace on four occasions. One fellow guest described the delights awaiting those fortunate enough to be invited: 'Nothing is off the menu from the moment you are greeted to the moment you leave. A quiet English country house retreat it is not.'[78]

But by April 2018, Boris Johnson was no longer the mayor: he was Foreign Secretary, and thus expected to display at least a smidgeon of decorum. So, for his latest trip to the party mansion of a Russian billionaire with (as journalist Robert Peston puts it) 'opaque' connections to Putin's regime, Johnson eschewed the private plane, and got on board an EasyJet to Pisa.[79]

A few days later, his weekend revels complete, he boarded the return EasyJet home, and was recognised by fellow passengers. They described him as 'looking like he had slept in his clothes', and incapable of walking in a straight line. 'I thought he was going to be sick on the tarmac,' said one witness.

If Johnson had travelled to Italy with luggage, he had mislaid it along the way, cos he got on the plane bagless as well as legless. He had also managed to mislay the close-protection officers who travel with every Foreign Secretary 24/7. Fellow passengers confirmed he was travelling alone.

So there were no witnesses to what happened to the famously impulsive and erotically unbridled Foreign Secretary during his weekend at an Italian pleasure palace, where 'nothing is off the menu'.[80]

Birds of a feather: Johnson was described as 'a security threat' by a senior Cabinet colleague,[81] and it was alleged that almost as soon as he was appointed Foreign Secretary, responsibility for MI6 was 'quietly shifted from Boris Johnson to the prime minister and the National Security Council'.[82]

There is no evidence that anything compromising happened to Boris Johnson in Italy. Maybe he just played Connect 4 and had an early night. Perhaps he got his paints out and worked his way through the discarded boxes in Lebedev's wine cellar. But he refused to provide details of the trip, and neither he nor the government would comment on speculation he'd deliberately given his security detail the slip.[83]

Still, let's take Boris Johnson at his word. It's not his fault that his personal protection team couldn't keep up with his renowned physical grace and agility.

We must also dampen down our curiosity about the pressures and influences behind events in 2019, when the government, by then led by Johnson, was preparing its report into Russian interference in the operations of Britain's democracy. A source connected to the Intelligence and Security Committee was reported as saying that Johnson had acted 'beyond the conventions of his authority' in demanding that the names of – to coin a phrase – 'London-based Russian oligarchs' be purged from the report.[84]

—

Speaking of blackmail targets, later that same April, Dominic Raab's diary secretary hit the news, as it was discovered she was selling sex online through a 'sugar daddy' website, and had boasted how she'd 'love to get sacked' for shagging a customer on Raab's desk.

She told an undercover journalist posing as a client, 'I know everything about [Raab]. I know his every move,' and went on to deliver this exquisite thumbnail portrait of her boss.

'He thinks he's the prime minister,' she said, but 'when things go out of line, he panics.'[85]

Pretty sure that won't matter during any – oh, I dunno – future negotiations over our nation's trading relations, coping with a pandemic, or abandoning a central Asian country to a group of terrorist brigands.

—

In early May, local elections were held across the country, and it was yet another disaster for the once wildly popular Theresa May. Tory vote share fell a further 2 per cent.[86] You might assume UKIP had taken their vote, but in fact UKIP had all but vanished. They had held 126 council seats the day before the elections, and just three the day after. Their job, it seemed, was done.

And what a job it was.

A UN special rapporteur on racism found 'extreme views' had gained ground in Britain, and there had been a 'Brexit-related' increase in racism and intolerance.

'The environment leading up to the referendum, the environment during the referendum, and the environment after the referendum has made racial and ethnic minorities more vulnerable to racial discrimination and intolerance,' the rapporteur said.[87] To be fair, Leavers had promised us Brexit would be good for growth. They hadn't specified growth of what.

It certainly wasn't wealth: a Channel 4 documentary went behind the scenes at the US Embassy in London and filmed American diplomatic staff discussing what Brexit was going to do to Britain.

'People haven't yet internalised "the economy is going to tank",' said one diplomat. 'But the British government isn't interested in telling people, "This thing 52 per cent of you said you wanted – well, here are the range of options. There's less good, and then there's very, very bad."'

They concluded we would suffer 'the worst kind of inflation', that Brexit would 'not end up helping people economically', and that the political leaders of the Leave movement were now 'absolutely terrified'.[88]

Naturally, many who had backed Brexit denied the gloomy predictions, but it was harder to deny things that had already happened: the Bank of England reported the economic contraction following the referendum result had already cost each UK household £900. This was despite the global economy – and the Eurozone economy – growing faster than had been predicted.[89]

Jeremy Hosking, a long-time Tory donor who had donated £1.7 million to Vote Leave,[90] spoke in an incredulous tone of the consequences of what he'd voted for. 'Somebody's got to say it – it ain't working.'[91]

'A lot of the parliamentary Conservative Party, they think it's going very well. And I'm talking about some of the Brexiteers,' he said. 'It's like the man who jumps out of a 50th-storey window. By the 20th storey, it's all going very well, but it's not gonna have a happy ending.'[92]

Despite the best efforts of those merrily leaping Brexiteers, MPs who had spotted the ground racing up towards us were desperately trying to open our collective parachute. By the end of the month, the number of Brexit-related votes the government had lost in Parliament had reached 15.[93]

—

But at least it was sunny. Very sunny, in fact. Unnaturally so.

That May had been the hottest ever recorded in the UK.[94] Speed restrictions were imposed on the nation's railway lines as tracks threatened to buckle[95] under temperatures that reached 35°C.[96] Across northern England, hundreds of firefighters battled multiple huge, unprecedented moorland wildfires.[97] Safety warnings were issued in London, and the capital's fire brigade said it was 'praying for rain' as hundreds struggled to contain the largest grass fire ever recorded in Britain.[98]

The country was reeling under the hottest, driest summer since records began,[99] and Friends of the Earth said, 'This is yet another bleak warning that we're racing towards catastrophic climate change,' and warned we urgently needed to refocus towards a low-carbon economy.[100]

The Tories took urgent action and approved a new runway at Heathrow airport.

Boris Johnson, who had promised his electors in Uxbridge that he would lie down 'in front of those bulldozers and stop the building, stop the construction of that third runway'[101] suddenly found he had urgent business in Afghanistan, and – tsk, wouldn't you know it? – missed his chance to vote against the runway.[102]

Theresa May, whose constituency in Maidenhead lay right under the proposed flight path, had previously opposed the idea of an expanded Heathrow. For some mystifying reason, all references to her earlier objections were deleted overnight from her personal website.[103] Probably some sort of bug. She voted for the runway.

And then the Tories scrapped plans to build a renewable tidal power plant in Swansea, which would generate clean, carbon-free energy for half of Wales. It would cost the average energy consumer £35 a year, and that's far too expensive.[104]

Costing each of us £900 in a single year for Brexit was fine, though.

Trade Minister Greg Hands resigned in opposition to the Heathrow decision.[105] Justice Minister Phillip Lee resigned in opposition to Brexit.[106] Christopher Chope didn't do either, dagnabbit – he just blocked regulation to make it illegal to point your camera up the skirts of unsuspecting women and take photos of their underwear.

The ban on so-called 'upskirting' was brought as a Private Member's Bill rather than a government White Paper, but even so, the government said it would happily back the measure. It was assumed every MP backed it too. No time was allocated to debate it because no debate was needed. It was a no-brainer.

But by now, they should have realised a man with no brain was present.

Up popped Chope, who shouted 'objection', and all of a sudden, we needed a debate, for which there was no time. Chope knew that would happen when he objected: exploiting the time limit to sabotage any form of progress had been his intention.

He was the only MP to object, time ran out, and upskirting remained legal.[107]

Later the same day, Chope used the same trick to block laws to safeguard against the excessive use of force in mental health units, and to provide better protection for police dogs and horses.[108] In November, he used the same tactic to block a bill protecting girls against female genital mutilation, the prevention of which he described as 'virtue signalling'.

What's the opposite of virtue? Oh yes: iniquity. Christopher Chope was iniquity signalling.

—

Back to the government's never-ending experiment with new ways to befuddle the educational system.

In 2010, the government had launched a programme of so-called 'studio schools', designed to focus on vocational and practical studies, and a subset of the better-known free schools.

If, as the National Audit Office had found, free schools were a 'waste of money', we're going to need an army of Susie Dents to find a suitable phrase for the much larger failure of studio schools. In the seven years since the programme was started, 56 studio schools had opened, and then 27 – one short of half of them – had either closed, announced they were closing, or had collapsed before they even opened their gates.[109]

The schools were designed for around 300 students each, so the closures interrupted the education of about 8,000 kids, and cost the taxpayer £150 million in wasted start-up costs, including millions on schools that didn't even make it to opening day.

Lord Nash – and if the name seems familiar, he's the care-homes owner who sponsored Andrew Lansley – had been appointed as academies minister, because *of course* he had. Care homes are exactly the same as schools. And while he held this post, Nash was also chair of an academy chain accountable to the government department he helped to run,[110] and his daughter – unqualified and unpaid – was appointed to draw up the school's history curriculum.[111]

But back to the Studio Schools Trust (SST), which Nash met to – in the words of the official minutes – 'review the concept of studio schools'. But David Nicoll, chair of the SST, insisted a review was 'definitely not on the agenda of any meeting I attended'. You can see the logic: if nobody is reviewing the project, the project can't possibly be a failure. As long as nobody notices the disaster, it isn't happening.

So a Freedom of Information request was made about this quantum-fluctuating review, but the FOI inevitably ran into the roadblock of heavily redacted documents that told the public nothing. Fortunately, a leak of the uncensored documents revealed Nicoll emailing Nash to 'ask again if there was any progress and/or timetable you could share regarding the studio school review'. That would be the review he had never discussed.

The Department for Education (DfE) cleared matters up. 'There has been no formal review of studio schools and we have never set out the expectation that there is one. We know that there have been challenges, which is why we will continue to look into their performance.'

So they weren't reviewing them. They were just 'looking into' them.

What does this 'looking into' consist of? the DfE was asked.

We're not telling you, the DfE replied.

Nobody voted for studio schools. Nobody voted for Lord Nash to be responsible for reviewing/not reviewing studio schools. And nobody is allowed to see the records of what he or the DfE were doing. We just have to cough up the £150 million for another one of Michael Gove's mad experiments.

Aren't you glad our children's education is in the hands of such qualified and accountable leaders?[112]

—

We had reached July. During the previous month, groups as diverse as the Society of Motor Manufacturers and Traders[113] and the British Medical Association had called for Britain to remain in the single market and customs union.[114] Investment in new car models, equipment and facilities had halved in a year,[115] and the CBI warned that the motor sector faced 'extinction' if Britain exited the customs union. There were dire warnings from air transport and tourism,[116] the National Farmers' Union,[117] bodies representing HGV drivers[118] and hauliers, fisheries,[119] the IT and technology sector,[120] energy generators,[121] higher education[122] and the City of London.[123]

Between them, these represented almost every job and supply chain in the country.

The Tories responded that they had offered state support to Nissan.[124]

There wasn't much sign of state aid for the rest of us, but Nissan had become a talisman of the success or failure of Brexit, and if that one business abandoned the country the embarrassment in Downing Street would be devastating. Even so, it was hard to see how a blank cheque for Nissan was proof of a successful policy, when the Tories said the bailout for Northern Rock was evidence of unmitigated policy failure.[125]

Yet appeals to logic didn't work any more. After a viciously divisive campaign, Leave was no longer something voters *did*, it was something they *were*. It was almost impossible to shift opinion, regardless of the overwhelming weight of evidence. Across the political spectrum, views solidified, and for Leavers within government, no form of Brexit could possibly be too hard or too damaging.

There had been countless Brexit-related crescendos to date, but the one in July was a doozie. The Cabinet and main players were summoned to the PM's country residence for a showdown. On one side, haughty, stressed-out Theresa May, offering the softest Brexit she thought she could get away with, and simultaneously scrawling red lines across every opportunity for common sense. On the other, every delusional nationalist flapdoodle you could think of, starting with Boris Johnson and David Davis.

To prove the PM meant business this time, official cars dropped ministers at the door of Chequers and then unexpectedly drove away, leaving the Cabinet in no doubt that if they didn't accept the terms on offer, they'd be walking home.[126] As the guests entered the building, they were relieved of their phones, so they couldn't take to Twitter and shitpost about the PM all day,[127] and special advisers were banned from attending, which must have compelled Chris Grayling to hold it in for the whole meeting, rather than face having to figure out for himself which way to sit on a toilet.[128]

They'd assembled to discuss a 120-page document that most of them had only seen for the first time the day before,[129] and which was at least 118 pages more Brexit detail than David Davis had ever seen gathered in one place.

In all, 29 ministers had their turn to speak, 22 in favour of the plan and seven against, including the usual suspects of Johnson, Liam Fox and Iain Duncan Smith. Andrea Leadsom opposed May's proposals but finished her speech with an assurance that, 'I will support you, Prime Minister.' David Davis disagreed with the plan but assured the room he would accept the majority view.[130]

In the end, the Cabinet assented to the plan, shook hands on it, and agreed to present a cohesive and consistent front to the nation and the world.[131]

'We have seen what happens when a team is united and gets behind their leader,' said a relieved May. 'If only people could see how united we are now.'

The ministerial cars hove into view. The ministerial phones were returned to their owners. And they all went home to begin a new, united future.

—

David Davis resigned before breakfast the next day.[132]

For all his talk of accepting the majority view of the Cabinet, it looked like he was just saying whatever he needed to avoid having to shell out for a taxi back from Chequers.[133] Davis was the dull pebble that triggered an avalanche of resignations, including a right set of absolute boulders. Boris Johnson quit, of course, because staying in the Cabinet delivered no immediate career benefit. He called the deal a 'suicide vest' – a Cabinet colleague called this comment 'disgusting' – and said Britain should scrap the 'insanity of the so-called backstop', which by 2021 he was begging the EU to extend.[134]

Steve 'beat me by the bins' Baker also resigned, as did foreign office private secretary Conor Burns, and a nondescript entity that nobody had noticed before: Chris Green.

Nope, me neither. I'm convinced he only resigned to feel alive.[135]

There followed a brief interlude in ministerial resignations about Brexit to allow Andrew Griffiths to resign about sex. Somehow – and it's hard not to be weirdly impressed by his work ethic – Griffiths had managed to send over 2,000 non-consensual sexually explicit text messages to two barmaids over a three-week period, which, if you do the maths – I mean, it takes some doing, especially when you factor in the phoneless hours he spent at Chequers.[136] He must have thumbs like The Flash and a forearm like Popeye.

That squalid bit of business dealt with, the Brexit-related resignations resumed again at full tilt: three more junior ministers and two vice chairs of the party went next. In total, Theresa May had managed to lose nine ministers in a week.

—

You could go out in the morning with a fowling piece, bag a juicy mallard, pluck it, roast it, chop it into neat strips, and serve it with Hasselback potatoes and an orange compote, and it still wouldn't be as dead a duck as May's Chequers plan was. But still she ploughed on.

Her next idea was a White Paper, which said we should definitely end freedom of movement, but also encourage freedom of movement via reciprocal arrangements that recognised the 'depth of the relationship and close ties between the peoples of the UK and the EU'.[137]

'The UK's future economic partnership should therefore provide reciprocal arrangements, consistent with the ending of free movement,' it said, and solved this conundrum by suggesting only skilled people should move from one location to another.

This, they argued, would mean more unskilled jobs would be available for British nationals. But not high-skilled jobs. Forgive my ignorance, but I'm struggling to see how ensuring *only* British nationals get to do unskilled work helps to drive up the skills and wages of British nationals.

Let's not worry about little things like that, eh?

David Davis was gone, so we needed a new Brexit minister. The role was taken by box-faced, thick-necked Play-Doh inaction-figurine Dominic Raab, who had the perfect skill set to be the minister responsible for being irresponsible. His first enthusiastic-yet-doomed stab at competence came with that White Paper on freedom of movement. It was by now commonplace for any Brexit plan to fall apart as soon as it arrived in Parliament, but this one managed to fall apart before it even got that far. The Speaker had to suspend proceedings when it was revealed the document they were debating didn't exist. It had been shown to the media at 9 a.m. that morning, of course, but not handed to any of the MPs who were debating it that afternoon.

When it did eventually turn up (along with apologies from Raab), copies had to be hurled bodily around the chamber by mooing MPs, who then had literally seconds to read it before forming an opinion. It looked like a food fight organised by cows.

Reading the White Paper made no difference: opinions were rarely based on facts or understanding any more. Hardcore Brexiteers refused utterly to countenance any sort of immigration. MPs opposed to Brexit demanded the whole thing be hurled out and another referendum held. Everybody shouted and nobody listened, and the world looked on agog.

Among those not being listened to was the Road Haulage Association (RHA), who coughed politely to get the attention of politicians too busy squabbling to do any planning, and delicately pointed out that the HGV drivers delivering bourgeois luxuries like food to our nation's shops didn't meet Raab's definition of 'skilled'. Without drivers we would have empty shelves in supermarkets. Food producers joined the RHA in warning that a reduction in EU nationals would harm our ability to grow our own food.[138]

Michael Gove responded by proposing a pilot scheme of agricultural worker visas, which offered 2,500 temporary places. Sounds a lot, but that's 4 per cent of the required workforce.[139] And even in September 2018 – before the great exodus began – the UK already had 10,000 vacancies for farm workers, fruit pickers and other supposedly unimportant people without whom supposedly important people couldn't have dinner.

The survival of the government was on a knife-edge, and it behaved increasingly irrationally. It was just over a week since nine ministers had resigned because May wanted to keep the UK more closely aligned to the EU, so when the ERG put forward amendments to make the UK *less* closely aligned, you'd expect May, having made such sacrifices, would refuse utterly. Nope. She accepted the ERG amendments without so much as a whimper.

This meant the ministers who had stuck by her after Chequers now felt betrayed, and could no longer support a bill that was the opposite of what May had just sacrificed half her Cabinet to deliver.

Only 10 days after boasting her Chequers deal beckoned in a period of unity, May effectively abandoned it to avoid the ignominy of losing yet more parliamentary votes. Three more ministers resigned in protest at a deal that now undid all it had been designed to do barely a week earlier. The PM had mislaid 12 ministers in 10 days, and even though she won the vote, she ended up celebrating because Parliament had supported something she had told everybody she was against.

Her majority was down to just three.[140]

Pro-EU Tory Dominic Grieve described the ERG's move as 'entirely malevolent'. Former minister – OK, I admit that doesn't help, because almost everybody was a former minister by now, but anyway – former minister Nicky Morgan described the ERG as 'a single-minded pressure group within the Conservative party who have had little regard for any long-term damage they cause'.[141]

She was right. Constitutional experts described the ERG as a 'party within a party', with the Brexit they supported putting the foundation of our democracy under strain.[142]

ERG leader Jacob Rees-Mogg, Napoleon Dynamite cosplaying a Victorian lamppost, happily proclaimed: 'We're the opposition now.'[143]

—

In July, the National Audit Office (NAO) published a report on the rollout of Universal Credit, which found a quarter of claims hadn't been paid in full, 40 per cent of those affected had to wait more than 11 weeks, and a fifth had waited four months.

The NAO said the Tories had 'shown a lack of regard in failing to understand the hardship faced by some claimants', and found Universal Credit was lousy value for money. But having burned through £16 billion to build the system – that's enough to form a tower of £10 notes over 100 miles tall – we were now in a position where cancelling it would cost more than finishing it. So the NAO said the government had better get it sorted out, the feckless gobshites.

I added 'feckless gobshites' myself. The rest is what the NAO said.

Esther McVey, the feckless gobshite now responsible for Universal Credit, described this official litany of humiliating and painful failure as a 'unique example of great British innovation', and told MPs, 'We are leading the world in developing this kind of person-centred system.'

In the first such letter of its kind, the NAO wrote publicly to McVey and, in a dazzling display of heroic understatement, described her behaviour as 'odd'.[144] They told her to 'clarify the facts', which led to a surreally bouncy McVey looking delighted to apologise to Parliament. It was hard to believe she understood what had just happened.

'I mistakenly said the NAO had asked for the rollout of Universal Credit to continue at a faster rate and be speeded up,' she said. 'In fact, the NAO did not say that, and I want to apologise.'[145]

Just one day later, the NAO sent her a second letter – so many precedents! – requesting a meeting to explain to McVey what they actually do, so in future she wouldn't spend so much of her waking life untethered from reason.[146]

The Ministerial Code says any minister who is found to have misled Parliament should resign or be sacked. She wasn't, obviously, because rules are for little people, and she claimed it wasn't misleading Parliament, just a simple mistake. People who make a mistake with a bus timetable and are one minute late for a benefits meeting are sanctioned. So instead of sacking McVey, how about we see how she likes 11 weeks without income for making a mistake.

—

Just like you and me, MPs had had enough of Parliament, and were just about to vacate Westminster for their summer recess when Christopher Chope decided to make a rare stupid and regressive intervention.

A motion was read out proposing that a global women's conference could use the empty parliamentary chamber while MPs were away on holiday. This was right in the middle of the #MeToo movement, and everybody wanted to be seen to support equality. The only thing at stake was an empty room. It hurt nobody, helped plenty of people, and was a wholly inoffensive idea. The motion would pass with a verbal 'aye', assuming nobody shouted 'object'.

Christopher Chope shouted 'object'. Almost every other MP in the house shouted 'shame', but rules are rules, so now the government had to set aside time and effort to debate the motion, as if there weren't more important things to worry the government than: are women allowed to sit on a misogynist's chair while he's sunning himself in Crete?[147]

Fair's fair: the Tories, as infinitely frustrated by Chope as the rest of us are, immediately resubmitted the motion for the following Wednesday, fully intending to back it. But by that time Chope, along with Desmond Swayne – he of the comedy brigadier persona, and an upholstered face the colour of Berocca-wee – had submitted further written amendments aimed at preventing those pesky womenfolk from entering Parliament.

—

Let's dash quickly through August, because nobody wants to hang around for long in this mire.

Grant Shapps had to resign from two appointments after it was discovered he'd listed his advisory role to a blockchain technology start-up as 'unpaid', when in reality he was due to be given up to £700,000 of cryptocurrency tokens for his work.

(Don't worry if you don't understand what blockchain and cryptocurrency are. Nobody does.)

Shapps explained away his resignation as chair of the All-Party Group on Blockchain with the words, 'I don't want to overstretch myself'. He was perfectly willing to overstretch himself for £700,000 of secret payments, though.[148]

—

Boris Johnson wrote an article saying Muslim women wearing burkas 'look like letter-boxes' and describing them as resembling bank robbers.[149]

Tory peer Baroness Warsi said, 'Tories are in denial on Islamophobia,'[150] and that Johnson's remarks were 'offensive and deliberately provocative, but very clever politics'.

Call me a snowflake, but I don't see what's so clever about racism.

Johnson himself claimed he was 'speaking up for liberal values', but really, he just wanted to remain in the public eye, ready to take advantage of May's weakness, and the collateral damage done to minorities was supremely unimportant to him. In Warsi's words, he was 'trying to get airtime and attention on an issue which he knows will resonate with a certain part of the Tory party'.[151]

—

Jacob Rees-Mogg, that pustulent eruption of idle xenophobia, privilege and stupidity, stuffed into the waxy corpse of an exhumed

Regency orphanage-worrier, turned up on TV to suggest it could take 50 years to see any benefits to Brexit.[152] It clearly hadn't occurred to the attenuated dolt that we'd only been in the EU for 43 years, so by his own argument we should give it another seven before we decided whether it made sense to leave. And the only age groups with a majority in favour of Brexit were those over 50, so by his reckoning every single one of them would be more than 100 years old by the time they saw any benefit.[153]

Meanwhile, the City firm co-founded by Rees-Mogg had moved two of its investment funds from London to Ireland, to protect depositors from the financial damage analysts predicted Brexit would cause.[154]

It would be crude to refer to Mr Rees-Mogg as shit-for-brains, so let's put it in terms he'd understand: he is *compost mentis*.

—

The risk of leaving the EU without any sort of trading arrangements in place was growing rapidly. Dominic Raab told the nation to 'prepare for No Deal', although it was unclear what we should do. Would press-ups help?

He claimed there would be 'short-term disruption', but he must have had his watch set to a different speed from Chancellor Philip Hammond, who later the same day released documents warning of a 7.7 per cent hit to GDP for 15 years. I guess on the timescales Jacob Rees-Mogg was operating, 15 years is short-term. You can manage 15 years without food, can't you? It'll be worth it in the end.

'They are frightened of taking responsibility for managing the economy without the crutch of the EU,' said Rees-Mogg, while moving his money into the crutch of the EU.[155]

Raab attempted to reassure the nation with some gibberish about sandwiches. 'Let me assure you that, contrary to one of the wilder claims, you will still be able to enjoy a BLT after Brexit, and there are no plans to deploy the army to maintain food supplies,' he said.

In 2021 the army was put on standby to maintain food supplies.[156]

—

In September, after nine months in the job, Northern Ireland Secretary Karen Bradley finally grasped the most basic fact about the region's politics.

'I didn't understand things like: when elections are fought, for example, in Northern Ireland,' she explained, 'people who are nationalists don't vote for unionist parties and vice versa.'

Go on, Karen, you're doing so well.

'Actually, the unionist parties fight the elections against each other in unionist communities and nationalists in nationalist communities.'[157]

Gold star and a toffee apple for Karen. Go to the top of the class. And jump off.

Meanwhile Jacob Rees-Mogg's European Research Group was censured by the Parliamentary Standards Authority after it became obvious that the £340,000 of public money it had been given was being used for political campaigning (for which public money is not provided) rather than for research (for which it is).[158]

It's not as if the clues were hard to spot. It's a struggle to find the research behind Rees-Mogg's 2017 claim that Brexit would reduce the cost of food, wine and clothes by 20 per cent.[159] If, as I suspect, it was a wild guess, he was almost accurate: the figure was right, but in the wrong direction. Farm incomes fell by 20 per cent,[160] while food commodity prices were up 17 per cent.[161]

Perhaps sensing that there might be an electoral price for this, for the first time since post-war rationing ended in 1958, the UK appointed a minister for food supplies, in the hopes of addressing widespread concerns about shortages following Brexit[162] – which drags us, screaming and kicking, back to that godawful topic. We were in the closing stretch of the year, and events sped up as we headed towards the cataclysm.

Stroppy old Theresa May suddenly declared the EU wasn't treating Britain with enough respect – a tough idea to sell, given that we'd just voted to name a submarine *Boaty McBoatface*, and Boris Johnson was the Foreign Secretary. May shrugged this off and showed how formidable we were in a combative speech that placed the blame for the Brexit impasse squarely on the heads of EU leaders.

The global markets carefully assessed Britain's formidableness, and the pound immediately suffered the biggest one-day drop for a year.

The backdrop to this latest spasm of stupidity was a summit meeting at which May rigidly insisted the festering corpse of her Chequers deal was still alive and kicking, and that it must therefore form the basis of any future negotiations. EU negotiators wearily popped another handful of Nurofen, showed May photos of her own Cabinet pissing all over the Chequers deal, and politely suggested negotiations would go better if everybody around the table could recognise reality when they saw it.[163]

Philip Hammond didn't help matters by doing an interview in which he insisted the Chequers deal was 'still alive', even though he accepted the EU would never agree to it.

Philip, if only one side signs a deal, it's dead.[164]

'Yesterday, Donald Tusk said our proposals would undermine the single market,' complained May, because the proposals *did* undermine the single market. She told the EU it was time to spell out 'what their alternative is'.[165]

Their alternative was Britain making its bloody mind up. It could be in the single market, or it could be out of it. There wasn't some middle way. There has never been an option to be a *bit* pregnant. Surely even Karen Bradley could understand such a simple concept if it was explained slowly.

But the frustration of Brexit advocates was easy to understand. The EU and Theresa May seemed to be delaying delivery because of petty debates about what Brexit meant, when to them it was perfectly clear what it meant. All they wanted was a soft Brexit, and a hard Brexit, and Norway, Norway +, Canada, Canada +, Canada ++, and Canada +++.

Also, an Australia-type deal, European Economic Area, and

European Free Trade Association, and a single market, no single market, No Deal, managed No Deal, a jobs-first Brexit, Lexit, Flexit, and a red-white-and-blue Brexit.

All Theresa May had to do was give them that, and they'd be happy. Why was it so complicated?

Fortunately, the president of the European Council helped to reduce the options available by spelling out, for the hard of thought, exactly what their offer was: the EU would retain its single market, completely unchanged, but Britain would no longer be a member. Why? Because not being a member is what we'd chosen to do. Instead, Britain would get better-than-average trading terms, and third-country status.

'From the very beginning, the EU offer has been a Canada+++ deal,' he tweeted. 'Much further-reaching on trade, internal security and foreign policy cooperation. This is a true measure of respect. And this offer remains in place.'[166]

Boris Johnson described this as 'a superb way forward'. Even Nigel Farage said the government should 'take it and run.'[167]

So naturally, the government didn't take it.

David Davis could have backed the deal on offer, but instead called for a Cabinet revolt against Theresa May, because he'd realised none of the panoply of Brexits listed above solved the Irish border problem, as he'd been warned was inevitable for the last decade.[168] There must be another solution, he thought; but the other solutions boiled down to kicking the problem down the road a few years and hoping that in the meantime the DUP and Sinn Féin would bond over a mutual love of macramé or crown green bowling.

Not much of this resembled the promises made before we had voted. The EU hadn't collapsed in the face of our might. Germany's car manufacturers hadn't raced to our shores, begging for deals. The reassurances of simplicity had transformed into broiling chaos. The massive savings had turned into a quarter-trillion-pound loss. Our grand new sovereignty had been overtaken by an undemocratic executive power-grab that bypassed Parliament. Our world-renowned pragmatism and *savoir faire* had turned into delusion, division and rancour; and not even the architects of the plan could agree what the plan was.

Meanwhile, the country was furious, whichever way you turned. Friendships collapsed. Families were split apart. Minorities were attacked. And protest marches erupted, as more than half a million Remainers took to the streets of London, demanding a second referendum now the facts were known.

To counter this, Nigel Farage held a vast counter-protest in Harrogate, attended by slightly fewer than 1,200 people in a hall that was one-third empty,[169] during which he promised a second referendum 'when we work out exactly what shape Europe's going to be and how happy we are as an independent nation'.[170]

Which raises the inevitable question: has any of this made *anybody* happier?

—

It was conference season again, that special time of the year when all the densest things you can imagine are shoved into one location, and the world prays they reach critical mass and explode.

We begin with Home Secretary Sajid Javid, who announced yet another new immigration policy – this would make it the 106th since Cameron took office, slightly more than one a month. Under this one, highly skilled people would be welcome in Britain, and those with low skills refused entry.[171] It was pointed out that his own father would fail the immigration rules Javid wanted to implement, which Javid said 'makes me very optimistic about our future'.[172] It's a strange way to tell your dad you despise him, but rather than focus on one family's private pain, let's look at the logic of what this means: if you *only* import high skills, increasingly the jobs left for the people of Britain would inevitably be low skilled, and pay less money.

A Tory immigration policy designed to push up wages would end up pushing down wages. The government truly is as thick as a Boxing Day shit.

To wit, halfwit Chris Grayling. Already battling terrible headlines after months of widespread rail delays, he managed to get lost in the conference hall and turned up late to his own speech.[173]

After last year's calamitous appearance, this time Theresa May decided to embrace her inner pissed-auntie-at-a-wedding, and on live TV, without warning any of us, she lurched into a robot dance to the strains of ABBA's 'Dancing Queen'. It was Vogon poetry in motion. In the hall, those who hadn't cringed hard enough to cause a hernia burst into rapturous applause as May told them 'austerity is over' and promised 'opportunity for all'.[174]

Except for Sajid Javid's dad, obviously.

The speech was considered a success, inasmuch as no significant parts of the structure collapsed, and the PM was still capable of basic human functions by the end. But frankly, what happened inside the conference hall meant nothing, when events outside the hall were so existentially terrible. There was – as had been widely predicted – no way past the Northern Ireland conundrum, no realistic proposal for managing trade post-Brexit, and her Chequers deal could have been easily mistaken for a fetid corpse under Norman Tebbit's patio. Even if, by some miracle, this inebriated collection of fantasists and scam artists managed to come up with a viable solution, the parliamentary arithmetic made it impossible to get any bill passed.

Analysts had predicted the government would lack the capacity to manage anything except for Brexit, but it turned out they couldn't even manage that.

—

The October conference done, we could return to the wilder shores of Brexitania.

Andrew Bridgen phoned in a radio interview with a presenter from Northern Ireland, during which the host attempted to discuss things within the observable universe, and Bridgen attempted to demonstrate you don't need to take hallucinogenic mushrooms if your brain is already muddy enough to grow its own fungus.

Northern Ireland, Bridgen claimed, would not be treated differently to the rest of the population of Britain. Oh really, said the interviewer, have you mentioned that to the government whose Brexit position paper explicitly says NI would be treated differently to the rest of Britain?

That doesn't matter, said Bridgen, because there is 'a reciprocal arrangement' between Ireland and Britain, which would mean 'as an English person I have the right to go to Ireland; I believe I can ask for a passport'.[175]

Sure. You can also ask for a centaur and a handful of magic beans. No such 'reciprocal arrangement' exists. It never has.

But Bridgen was just warming up. 'People in the Republic of Ireland can vote in the UK,' he continued, which of course they can't, because – and if Andrew is reading this, he might need to brace himself – it's a different fucking country.[176] This obscure bit of research hadn't cropped up in all the research being undertaken by the European Research Group, which was Bridgen's publicly funded day-care centre.

Rather than stick around to face questions about this remarkable misunderstanding of pretty much everything, Bridgen hung up. It is, perhaps, unsurprising to learn Bridgen's Tory colleagues describe him as being 'as thick as mash'.[177]

—

Things were going about as well as we'd come to expect. The Confederation of British Industry (CBI) reported 80 per cent of UK firms had delayed or cancelled investment as a result of Brexit. The previous year had been bad enough, when the figure was 36 per cent, but this was edging closer and closer to a complete end to all business investment. The BBC described the mood of the CBI as being 'near the point of no return', with 19 per cent of members saying it was 'too late already'.[178]

The same applied to Theresa May. Conservative Party rules stated a leadership challenge could begin if 48 members requested one from the leader of the backbench 1922 Committee. Towards the end of

October, more than 50 had publicly supported the Stand Up 4 Brexit campaign, a movement to overturn all of May's plans.[179]

The ERG deputy chairman, Steve Baker, flattered himself that he was a much sharper tool than all the rest, while still being a tool. He had once described himself as a 'numbers man',[180] and his less capable ERG colleagues had taken him at his word: Baker reckoned he had the requisite 48 votes, so he wrote his own letter of no confidence in the PM. He was immediately followed by a slew of like-minded Brexiteer MPs.

Unfortunately, in this case 'like-minded' means 'none of them can count either'. The ERG putsch was guided by the calculations of Baker, but it appeared he'd taken off his shoes and socks, got all the way to 20, and then become disoriented. They were 11 votes short, and so May staggered on, ineffectual but seemingly unstoppable, like the Terminator with his shoelaces tied together.[181]

An article in *The Times* described the mood of Tory MPs simultaneously coping with being members of a government acting like a sack of rats and also facing the reality of what they had spent a generation agitating for. Senior figures, speaking under a guise of anonymity, described Brexit as 'a poison' and 'a biblical curse'.[182]

'We are stuck in a "damned if we do, damned if we don't" bind,' said one. 'If we try to cancel Brexit, we destroy ourselves; if we go ahead with it, we destroy the country. People voted for a fantasy.'[183]

Guiding us through this was Dominic Raab, season-ticket holder to that fantasy world, who was filmed making a confession that is pretty astonishing for, y'know, a grown human man who had somehow contrived to complete a law degree at Oxford.

'I hadn't quite understood the full extent of this,' said Raab, 'but if you look at the UK and look at how we trade in goods, we are particularly reliant on the Dover–Calais crossing.'[184]

Still, he managed to be more effectual than his predecessor David Davis, and at least Raab had managed to get something in writing. In November, the deal he'd struck was ready to be presented to the Cabinet for final approval in a tense five-hour meeting.

Matt Hancock settled nerves nicely by announcing to the room he could 'not guarantee people would not die'[185] as a result of Brexit, after which Esther McVey had to be 'shouted down' by the Chief Whip after what attendees described as an 'aggressive' and 'fruity' meltdown.[186]

Yet in the end, May gained Cabinet approval, and announced to the waiting media that – praise be! – we finally had a unified approach to Brexit that everybody could get behind. The unified approach she'd announced back in July had just been a trial run, but this – well, this was the real thing. You could count on it.

The following morning, the resignations began. Ten ministers quit rather than support the thing they'd just agreed to. Jo Johnson, brother to Boris, described Brexit as a 'terrible mistake' and predicted it would lead to chaos, clearly not recognising that it already had.[187] And then Dominic Raab, the minister responsible for the deal, set a new precedent for idiocy when he resigned in protest at his own achievements.[188]

—

By now being Brexit minister was starting to look like being Defence Against the Dark Arts teacher: loads of people were having a go at the job, nobody was expected to last long, and there was a good chance you'd end up coming into contact with Voldemort's soul, who in this episode was played by Priti Patel. Perhaps to counter the inherent risks of the job, May handed it to Stephen Barclay, reasoning that at least the curse wouldn't be able to recognise him. Nobody could.

Barclay is the nonentity's nonentity, or would be, if anybody had noticed him during the voting. He is so devoid of personality that his official portrait is the curtains behind him. His DNA profile reads '404 error'. You will have forgotten Stephen Barclay exists before you reach the end of this sentence.

It had been decided that from now on, the minister responsible for negotiating with the EU would no longer focus on negotiating with the EU, because that's how mad things had become. Instead, Barclay's role was described as 'domestic preparation' – battening down the hatches for the impending disaster, despite the Leave campaign assuring us there would be only benefits.[189]

A further five ministers were reported to be on the brink of resignation, insisting this still wasn't the Brexit they imagined at 3 a.m., after gorging on an imperial pound of Stilton. They wanted negotiations to continue. Insiders claimed Michael Gove was 'tortured' over Brexit, which I think we can put down as the first tangible benefit.[190] He, along with Grayling, Penny Mordaunt, Andrea Leadsom and Liam Fox, were threatening to quit.[191]

But the EU no longer cared about the inner turmoil of the Tory party, and just wanted to get this done so they could go back to playing boules and having a functioning economy. They endorsed May's plan, calling it 'the best and only deal possible', and it was finally agreed that Britain would leave the EU on 29 March 2019.[192] All Theresa May had to do now was get Parliament to agree to it.

So off we popped for a banquet of failure in the Palace of Westminster. As an amuse-bouche, MPs found the government in contempt of Parliament because it had failed on its promise to publish the full legal advice on the Brexit deal.[193] Next, the DUP, who had taken £1 billion on a promise that they'd prop up Theresa May, decided enough was enough and voted against her.

May turned meditative. 'I never said this deal was perfect,' she told Parliament, and for once they entirely agreed with her, even though for once she didn't want them to. She tried to assert her authority, saying Brexit divisions had 'gone on long enough', and urging MPs to resolve them. So they did: they voted that if her deal failed to pass Parliament in an upcoming vote, MPs would take greater control of the process, and bypass May's tattered authority completely.[194]

The Tories lost three parliamentary votes in 63 minutes, which was a new record.

It's hardly newsworthy by this point, but at the same time this was happening, Nigel Farage quit UKIP again, this time claiming he 'did not recognise' what it had turned into.[195] Which was the thing he had turned it into.

A couple of days later, the Brexit legal advice was finally published. It warned of 'stalemate' on the Northern Irish border, and 'protracted rounds of negotiations' that would last indefinitely. And for all our chest-thumping about British power, it concluded the UK would not have the legal authority to force an end to negotiations – not because of EU intransigence, but because that's how international law works.[196] Precedent says any existing law stands until both parties agree something better, but in this case, there was nothing better.

Exactly as had been predicted since before the referendum, the Irish border made the Brexit we had been sold impossible to achieve.

—

Time for another wild spin of the Brexit Endgame Tombola, and this time we plucked out Norway +, a fresh new guess at what Leave might mean. This was suggested by Amber Rudd – now back in the Cabinet as work and pensions minister – and it meant we would keep freedom of movement, continue our subscription payments, remain in the customs union, but lose any say on any future regulations.[197]

The best solution the government could now offer was all the things Leavers hated about the EU, with the added benefit of no control at all. Everything desirable was impossible. And everything possible was undesirable.

Over a year earlier, a legal action had forced the government to offer Parliament a 'meaningful vote' on the Withdrawal Agreement. Now it became obvious May would lose that vote badly, so she delayed it, once again kicking the crisis down the road.[198] The delay was too much for most of her backbenchers, and after much wrangling and haggling, it was agreed to hold a vote of no confidence in the person now being described as the worst prime minister ever.[199]

She rushed off to meet her MPs in a desperate effort to bolster support before the vote. The only thing she had left to offer them was her demise, so she assured her MPs that she would not lead them into the next election but begged them to leave her in office long enough to complete Brexit.

'Many people praised her stamina,' said one MP.

Yes, said MP Lee Rowley. But 'stamina is not a strategy'.[200]

Her most senior aide remarked that it wasn't about who led them into the election: it was about whether changing the leader could make any difference to Brexit. And to most of the party, the answer was clear: May was absolutely terrible, but she was at least technically sane, and removing her would place this maelstrom of bullshit in the hands of somebody infinitely less capable and rational. When the vote came, she won with a majority of 83, but one-third of her own party had voted to oust her.[201]

International faith in Britain's political structures had been fragile for years, and only weeks before the confidence vote, the pound had fallen to the lowest rate for 18 months. Now it fell yet further as the world looked on in disbelief at the crumbling edifice of a once stable and mature parliamentary democracy.[202]

In the real world, the consequences of this were really hurting. Philip Alston, the United Nations special rapporteur on extreme poverty, described the disconnect between the MPs who claimed to be fighting against the metropolitan elites on behalf of ordinary people, and the effects of their battle on those ordinary people.

'There's been almost no discussion of the effect of Brexit on poverty – but poorer people will bear the brunt of the economic fallout from it. Brexit will make the economic concerns which contributed to the vote to leave the EU worse.

'The damage being done to the fabric of British society, to the sense of community... soon there will be nowhere for those in the lower income groups to go. They will find themselves living in an increasingly hostile & unwelcoming society.'[203]

—

We started the year in the magical world of Chris Grayling, so it's only fair we end there too. During 2018 the minister for transport had buggered up planes, trains and automobiles, so in December it was only natural that he turned his attention to the seas.

In preparation for the No Deal Brexit that the government assured everybody would never happen, Grayling handed a £13.8 million contract to Seaborne Freight, a terrific-sounding ferry company that had only one minor flaw: it owned no ships.

Nothing to worry about, Mr Grayling's spokesman assured us. A 'wide range of operators' had been invited to tender. Oh, good, we must surely have picked the best!

The contract document states only a single operator had put in a bid, and they had no ships.[204]

Nothing to worry about, Mr Grayling assured us. He had 'looked very carefully' at Seaborne and had 'put in place a tight contract to make sure they can deliver for us'.

The Road Haulage Association said that given Seaborne needed to source ferries, hire and train staff, and link with relevant authorities across Europe, they had an 'impossible timescale'.

Nothing to worry about, Mr Grayling assured us. He had undertaken thorough due diligence, and Seaborne knew what they were doing.

Seaborne's terms and conditions document was for a pizza delivery service.[205] Their chief executive had been forced into liquidation by HMRC,[206] and the auditors undertaking due diligence had reported they were unable to complete the process because Seaborne lacked the relevant documentation.[207]

Are we done yet? We are not.

Grayling had forgotten to tell the operator of the Channel Tunnel they could compete for the freight contracts, and as a result we ended up agreeing an out-of-court settlement, just so the witless dolt didn't have to face a prosecution for 'distortionary and anti-competitive practices'. The cost to the taxpayer? £33 million.[208]

When challenged on his record, reports say that Grayling spent a good portion of parliamentary questions attempting to divert attention to MP Jamie Stone, criticising him wildly over what Grayling asserted were terrible things being done by Stone's Scottish National Party.

Nobody had the heart to tell him that Jamie Stone is a member of the Lib Dems.[209]

2019

We Don't Trust What's Coming Next

In January it became clear the government's determination to cut corporation tax had been vastly miscalculated: they had, quite literally, got their sums wrong. Philip Hammond, the latest dingbat to be in charge of the nation's money, had got all befuddled by his times tables, and discovered his 2 per cent cut to the tax on corporate profits would actually cost the nation £6.2 billion more than we could afford.[1]

He had essentially misplaced a stack of £10 notes 41 miles high, but rather than reconsider the cuts, Hammond just pressed on regardless. Fuck it, it's only enough money to pay 30,000 nurses. Even Rupert Harrison, an adviser to George Osborne, thought it was madness, saying it was 'hard to see why further cuts to corporation tax are good value'.

But any tax cut was good value for reportedly the Cabinet's richest man.[2] A business of which he is a beneficiary used tax loopholes to pay just £5,964 in tax on £1.6 million in profits. That's an effective tax rate of 0.4 per cent.[3] And this was while he was launching what he described as a 'crackdown' on big businesses using tax loopholes to avoid paying their fair share. In the mind of patriots in the Tory party, it is always somebody else's job to contribute to the nation's upkeep.

As a result of this and other fundamental failures, 1.9 million people were reliant on food banks in 2019.[4] Since the Tories won power, food-bank use had increased 4,500 per cent.

But spare a moment to think of the real victims.

In 2015, Marion Little had acted as election agent for a Tory candidate in South Thanet during an election plagued by accusations of campaign funding fraud. Although the MP she helped was cleared of falsifying expenses, Marion Little wasn't. In January 2019, a judge said Conservative HQ had a 'culture of convenient self-deception' as he handed down a suspended sentence to Marion Little.[5]

The party of law and order organised a whip-round for Marion Little, with an email from Sir Geoffrey Clifton-Brown asking his fellow Tory MPs to fund a 'substantial present so that she and her husband can go on a short holiday'.[6]

They were too busy organising relaxing sojourns in the Algarve for convicted electoral fraudsters to pay attention to much else, so probably didn't notice that a cross-party committee of MPs recommended the government create a minister for hunger, after a UNICEF report found 19 per cent of British children were from households that struggled to buy food.

'We already provide support through free school meals,' said the government, ignoring UNICEF and packing Marion Little off to the beach for a rest after her hard work corrupting democracy.[7]

—

Preparations for Brexit began in earnest, and responsibility went to government's safest pair of hands: those attached to Chris Grayling. He put in place an emergency traffic-management system for our major ports, and then undertook a trial of its effectiveness in handling the 10,000 HGVs per day travelling along the roads of Dover. His 'stress-test' trial consisted of a piddling 89 lorries, which he had driving in circles around an abandoned airfield, before creating a fake traffic jam in a specially segregated lane on a nearby A-road. And then three hours later, they did it again.[8]

I don't know about you, but my stress is very tested. Grayling's first fiasco of the year cost us £50,000,[9] and a participating driver said, 'To be honest, it was a waste of time.'[10]

With Grayling kept busy with this idiocy, Theresa May focused on winning over her enemies on the backbenches. She knighted Dalek impersonator John Redwood, who thanked her by immediately announcing he would vote against her, and then she invited Brexiteers to a cocktail party in the state rooms of 10 Downing Street and cawed at them until they could bear no more.[11] They politely made their excuses and returned to plotting her downfall.

Nobody in the Tory ranks was going to change their mind about Brexit, or, it seemed, make up their minds about it either. Donald Tusk had to write to Theresa May, reminding her that 'we are not in a position to agree to anything that changes or is inconsistent with the Withdrawal Agreement',[12] simply because Britain was already bored by the pact we'd made, and was trying to wriggle free of it.

It was becoming hard to remember why we were doing any of this. Support for Brexit was being depleted by a combination of unavoidable truth about the vast problems we would face, bone-deep weariness with the process, and the inexorable march of time. In the referendum, the only demographic to give a majority to Leave were older voters, and they had been dying off at a rate of 1,350 per day ever since. In January we reached 'Brexit Crossover Day', the point at which this process would inevitably wipe out the Leave majority before Leave had even happened.[13] But even without the effects of that bleak and inevitable process, opinion was shifting. Polling showed just 39 per cent of us would still vote to leave the EU.[14]

We were only three months from the agreed deadline for Brexit, and still, in the words of Ken Clarke, there was 'no majority for anything'.[15] He suggested the government revoke Article 50 and delay the whole process until we knew what we wanted to do and how to do it.

But Brexiteers said they knew how to do it. They'd written it all down on a piece of paper. The problem, as they saw it, was that leaving the single market meant we would need to have customs declarations and border checks for everything entering or leaving the country.

But the solution was devastatingly simple: move the customs checks 'a reasonable distance from the border' and introduce 'alternative arrangements', which was code for: technology that doesn't exist.[16]

So that was the latest grand plan: a 200-mile-thick border containing a magic computer, and a customs officer on every factory floor in the land who would check goods before they were shoved into a lorry.

For reasons that should be obvious, this idea went in the toilet, and would have remained there if it wasn't for Kit Malthouse, who rolled up his sleeves, fished around down there, dragged it out, and beamingly presented his compromise to the world.

There were only two small obstacles between the Malthouse Compromise and success. The first was that it relied on science traditionally restricted to the Marvel Cinematic Universe, a quantum leap in technology that they expected to be delivered in the next three months by a government that had just failed to organise a traffic jam in Dover during Monday rush-hour.

The second problem was that the Malthouse Compromise was designed to serve the needs of the Tory party, and nothing beyond that. It ignored the small hindrance that we had already negotiated a Withdrawal Agreement with the EU. Kit Malthouse himself had voted for it.[17] Negotiations had taken 18 months, and we now had barely six weeks before Brexit hit us. Plus, the other 27 nations had better things to do than this bullshit. There was absolutely no possibility of the talks starting again, and you'd have to be a demented, delusional, gibbering cretin to suppose they would.

Tories from both wings loved the Malthouse Compromise. An EU official described it as 'bonkers'.[18]

—

The Tories had, in the past month, settled on a Withdrawal Agreement, then decided they hated it, and then demanded an impossible renegotiation that relied on a voodoo computer. Now it was time to face the humiliation of putting all of this to Parliament.

May had already postponed the 'meaningful vote' from December, when it became clear the government would lose, but nobody had foreseen how badly. Her defeat by a 230-vote margin was the worst parliamentary rout for over 100 years. Although May's leadership hadn't yet collapsed, it was clear she was fighting an unwinnable death-battle of parliamentary Jenga. Junior ministers Gareth Johnson, Craig Tracey and Eddie Hughes were the latest lumpen blocks to exit the stack, resigning so they could vote against themselves.[19] After the record-breaking defeat, the Tories – who had held a 98-seat majority before the Brexit referendum – next faced a motion of no-confidence, which they scraped through by just 19 votes.[20]

Politics is a minority interest, so most of the country had no idea what was going on or why, but it was even worse for EU citizens living in the UK, who still didn't have any clue what their legal position would be in just a couple of months. So the government launched its EU Settlement Scheme, a lovely piece of legislation that meant EU citizens who had lived here for more than five years now had to apply for permission to stay in their *own homes*, even though in 2016 Theresa May had told them she would guarantee their rights.[21]

Applications to keep on living in the same country as your house, job, spouse and kids cost £65 per person, and could be made via a simple and effective app, which at launch hadn't been made available for iPhones, and wasn't compatible with Android, somewhat limiting its practicality. Whoops, said the government, and did a U-turn on the £65 charge, which at least meant foreigners living, working and paying tax in Britain had the benefit of experiencing our abject failure for free.[22]

The presence of such foreigners had, of course, been central to the Brexit campaign and now, only three years too late, journalists began asking whether the claims made by Boris Johnson's campaign stood up to scrutiny, including his leaflet declaring '80 million Turks would come to this country if we stayed in the EU'.

'Actually, I didn't say anything about Turkey in the referendum,' replied the scrupulously honest Mr Johnson. 'I didn't say a thing about

Turkey. Since I made no remarks, I can't defend them. I didn't make any remarks about Turkey.'

He denied it three times, like St Peter.[23] And like St Peter, he was full of shit. Unlike Peter, however, there wasn't a whole lot of repentance.

Three weeks before the referendum, Johnson had told *The Andrew Marr Show*, 'It is the government's policy that Turkey should join the EU.'[24] A few weeks before that, Johnson, whose grandfather was Turkish, had described a hellish vision of an EU in which '77 million of my fellow Turks and those of Turkish origin can come here without any checks at all', and described this as 'mad'.[25] The same day he had written a *Telegraph* column claiming, 'It is Turkey's hand on the [immigration] tap. Erdogan, if he chooses, can allow the trickle to turn back into a flood.'[26]

—

Time for another go at passing the Withdrawal Agreement with what Theresa May called Plan B, but everybody who wasn't Theresa May called 'Plan A in disguise'.[27]

Rebadging it didn't help. It was still a dog's dinner, MPs still hated it, and Parliament continued to vote for maximal confusion. During a single afternoon, they first backed a motion saying MPs wanted to avoid a No Deal Brexit, and then rejected a motion that would ensure No Deal Brexit couldn't happen.

Meanwhile Daniel Kawczynski, the tallest MP but a midget in every way that counts, was running his own campaign to secure the supremacy of the British Parliament, which took the form of him circumventing the will of the British Parliament. He formally asked the Polish government to veto any motions to allow the extension of Article 50.[28]

While the Polish government was still googling who this pranny was, the chairman of the backbench 1922 Committee, Sir Graham Brady, put forward an amendment calling for the government to renegotiate the Northern Ireland backstop, which the EU had already refused to do, because Britain had already agreed terms. MPs naturally voted to pass that amendment, because a hazy fantasy of an indefinable future was infinitely preferable to facing the nasty reality of the mess we'd landed ourselves in.[29] And sticking to what we said last month is for wimps.

Speaking of which, Nigel Farage went viral with a typically shrill yodel of petulance at the EU Parliament, in which he said Theresa May had 'signed up to something that no country – unless it had been defeated in war – would have signed up to'.[30] The previous October he had been so much in favour of May's deal, he had urged the prime minister to 'take it and run'.[31]

Not that his target audience, readers of the *Daily Mail*, were made aware of this spectacular hypocrisy. They were just told, once again, that the floundering, chaotic, confusing mess was all the EU's fault. In a sense, you can't blame them for not knowing the truth: from January, when you visited the *Daily Mail* website, MailOnline, the Microsoft browser added a warning note reading 'this website fails to maintain basic standards of accuracy and accountability'.[32] Wikipedia had already banned the *Mail* as a source, citing its 'reputation for poor fact-checking and sensationalism'.[33]

MailOnline is Britain's most-read news website, and had been a relentless cheerleader for Brexit. And it turns out its readers were, by definition, misinformed.

—

Unsurprisingly, minor stories went largely unnoticed.

In January a study of the public trust in government produced by the Cabinet Office found austerity had 'undermined perceptions of competence and the belief that [the government is] acting fairly, openly and with integrity'.[34]

The Tories decided to take urgent action to redress this problem, so published their fair funding review of local government grants. This being the Tory definition of 'fair', it ended up with 76 per cent of Tory MPs representing an area that was getting more money, and tens of millions of pounds redirected away from deprived areas to fund wealthier constituencies.[35]

Not every Tory was still comfortable with this sort of thing. An increasingly uneasy Heidi Allen set off on a fact-finding tour of austerity Britain, and broke down in tears when confronted with the realities of hungry kids and homeless families. 'I've absolutely had enough,' she said, and announced she was determined to 'show the government this exists. Unless we blow the lid off it, my lot are not going to listen.'[36]

But the party was now dominated by people who didn't want to listen. They had completely detached themselves from evidence, reality, or any loyalty to the truth. Brexit, of course, was this process's original sin: the event that showed electoral success could be achieved by brazenly abandoning evidence, truth and shame. And it empowered every fact-denying idiot with pretensions to rule. Welcome back Daniel Kawczynski, who started February demonstrating an ignorance about the Second World War that is remarkable, considering how utterly obsessed the Brexiteers were with wartime metaphors.

Kawczynski tweeted, 'Britain helped to liberate half of Europe. She mortgaged herself up to eyeballs in process. No Marshall Plan for us only for Germany. We gave up war reparations in 1990. We put £370 billion into EU since we joined. Watch the way ungrateful EU treats us now. We will remember.'[37]

In reality, the EU was treating Britain as an independent country outside of the single market, because at the bidding of Kawczynski and his mates, that's what we had decided to be. Europe didn't force us to.

More reality: Britain helped liberate eight countries in the Second World War, but alone we liberated nothing. Alone we were fucked: starving, broke, and our army defeated across the continent. Also, even if we had singlehandedly liberated eight countries – and we hadn't – that isn't half of Europe.

And as for money: Britain got more of the Marshall Plan money than any other country (26 per cent of it), while West Germany got

11 per cent.[38] Almost all the money we got was as grants, not loans,[39] and we made our last loan repayment in 2006, not 1990.[40] There was also no source for the £370 billion claim, which appears to be entirely invented; Kawczynski refused journalists' requests for comment and refused to remove the tweet.

Disinformation by MPs was fine now.

As Heidi Allen predicted, her lot were not going to listen. Following his Marshall Plan claims, a radio journalist asked Kawczynski to discuss it; Kawczynski decided to hang up rather than learn anything.[41] Since that little run-in with reality, he first habitually disabled replies to his tweets, and then deleted his account entirely, so there was no possibility of him having to experience his falsehoods being corrected.[42]

—

In February, Jay Daniel of the Blackpool Young Conservatives was expelled for sharing a racist tweet. The party said, 'this cannot and will not be tolerated'.[43]

What was tolerated, however, had been calculated without considering the lavishly scattered wits of Nadine Dorries, who days later seemed incapable of differentiating between journalist Ash Sarkar and parliamentary candidate Faiza Shaheen, on the basis that they are both British Asian women. When she was told this teetered into 'they all look the same to me' territory, Dorries first responded with the excuse that it had nothing to do with looks, but voices – they all *sound* the same[44] – and then she tweeted, 'Apparently I'm racist because I think Chuka Umunna looks like Chris Eubank.'[45]

Oh right: so they all sound the same *and* all look the same. Got it.

—

Back to Brexit, and the Tories passed a motion telling Theresa May she had to go back to Europe and order them, in her absolutely primmest schoolmarm voice, to renegotiate the Withdrawal Agreement, which of course made absolutely no difference to the grown-ups in the other 27 nations. As far as they were concerned, Britain had agreed to the terms, and that was the end of the matter. If we were determined to machine-gun our feet, it wasn't their responsibility to provide us with Kevlar boots.

Donald Tusk said there was 'a special place in hell' for 'those who promoted Brexit without even a sketch of a plan of how to carry it out', and this made the Tories very cross.[46]

'Mr Tusk is hardly in the Aquinas class as a theologian, and he seems to have forgotten the commandment about not bearing false witness,' wrote theologian and abortion profiteer Jacob Rees-Mogg, who had earlier tweeted that a yet-to-appear Brexit benefit would 'deliver £350 million a week for the NHS'.[47] Of course, Captain False Witness has now deleted that tweet.[48]

The slanging match ate away precious days while the clock ran down towards No Deal Brexit. May headed back to Brussels, assuring us she had a 'fresh mandate, new ideas and a renewed determination', which turned out to be yet another rehash of the old 'alternative arrangements' concept: magic computers will sort it all out, but until then everybody in Ireland has to pretend the border is 200 miles thick.[49] EU leaders described her proposals as not credible; we had barely a month to go, and there was still no viable, rational, realistic way forward.

—

What were the opposition doing to stop all of this? Mostly, disintegrating.

Either Chris Eubank or Chuka Umunna – Nadine Dorries will sort out any confusion – led a group of seven Labour MPs off into the wilderness, where they were immediately joined by the three least-soiled Tory MPs: Sarah Wollaston, Heidi Allen and Anna Soubry, who gave a typically frank reason for her abandoning the Conservatives.[50] The party, she said, had been subject to 'infiltration from the hard right'.[51] She's not wrong.

They called themselves Change UK for about quarter of an hour, and then the Independent Group for Change, and then the Artist Formerly Known as Change UK, and then Unemployed. Every one of them lost their parliamentary seat at the next election, and in their absence, their former Tory colleagues, now utterly unmoored from anything resembling the centre, continued their unstoppable drift to the right.[52]

May once again delayed a vote on the final deal. Three Cabinet ministers publicly called for a delay to the Brexit deadline, but May insisted we were definitely leaving on 29 March, no ifs, no buts,[53] and then immediately agreed to a vote that would allow Brexit to be delayed.[54]

Meanwhile, the Tory assurances that No Deal wasn't anything to worry our little heads about were somewhat undermined by the revelation that there were plans to declare martial law and suspend parliamentary democracy if we left without a deal.[55]

So Palaeolithic bassoon Jacob Rees-Mogg said we should leave without a deal.[56]

Two more ministers resigned.

By March, 15 ministerial posts were vacant due to a combination of rats jumping ship and nobody else being willing to take the job.[57]

—

Chris Grayling continued his winning streak that same month, applying his special brand of fumbling ineptitude to the launch of new trains on the East Coast Main Line.

The trains had been ordered almost 10 years previously, which apparently was a bit too much of a rush for Grayling to prepare the infrastructure they needed. The new trains interfered with trackside signalling equipment and caused delays, and it turned out they'd cost twice their original estimated amount.

'These new state-of-the-art trains show our commitment to put passengers at the heart of everything,' said Grayling, boasting that the new carriages would 'carry people across Britain, from Swansea to Aberdeen and London to Inverness'.

Except: not Swansea. Grayling's service to Swansea didn't reach Swansea. The track wasn't ready.

Tut-tut, never mind. To shake this off, Grayling decided to show off some other achievements before an expectant media scrum. He proudly boarded the speedy new West Coast train service. It set off 25 minutes late, arrived 41 minutes late, and during the journey air-conditioning fluid leaked into the carriages and the cooling system had to be turned off.[58]

—

Events in Parliament were simultaneously moving at dizzying speed and sluggishly paddling through shark-infested tapioca while tied to a 10-ton weight. Nothing seemed to be happening, and it was happening very, very slowly, but somehow it was terribly exciting.

For a second time, May's Withdrawal Agreement failed to pass in the House, with a majority of 149 MPs rejecting it. The following day they voted to refuse to accept No Deal under any circumstances, despite the government ordering its own MPs to reject the motion.[59] All parliamentary discipline had collapsed.

On a third day of voting, MPs added an extra couple of loops in the Gordian knot that bound the prime minister: they voted to request a delay to Brexit but rejected a second referendum.[60]

May was now cornered. She couldn't change the deal she was putting to Parliament. She couldn't get support for it in Parliament. She couldn't leave the EU without a deal. And she couldn't ask the country to reconsider.

May began to discuss the possibility of an agreement with Labour to leave the UK permanently inside the customs union, an outcome senior Leave campaigners had said they were absolutely fine with before the referendum, but which they now decided was heresy and treason.[61]

'Never!' cried the Brexiteers, among them Mark Francois, who is as short as two thick planks and vice versa. He refused to have a second referendum simply because the situation had changed, but demanded a second confidence vote in Theresa May, because the situation had changed.[62]

Ministerial resignations became all the rage again. Some quit because they objected to delaying Brexit. Some quit because they objected to attempts to find common ground. Lord Bates, the minister for international development, resigned because he wanted to 'explore a process for restoring our national unity', and you have to admire his starry-eyed optimism, when his colleagues couldn't even agree on their reasons for resigning.[63] By mid-April a further eight ministers had gone.

The only unity appeared to be on the Remain side. A million marched in London, asking for a second referendum;[64] 4.4 million signed a petition to revoke Article 50 and remain in the EU, which was the largest petition to Parliament in history. Margaret Georgiadou, who organised the petition without any notion that it would reach such a scale, had to go into hiding after receiving multiple death threats.[65]

Lord Bates really had his work cut out.

———

In the spirit of the Jarrow Crusade, Nigel Farage organised a mighty throng to march from Sunderland to Westminster, demanding we leave the EU, which he seemingly hadn't noticed we were already trying to do.

The multitude set off, led by the heroic Nigel. It was raining, so on day two Nigel didn't turn up. Just like the Jarrow marchers a century earlier, the rest of the participants decided to make things easier for themselves by chartering a bus for 30-mile stretches.[66] Of the 350 who signed up to take part, only 100 were there by day three, and just one in seven said they planned to do the entire route.[67] Makes you proud to be British.

At the behest of a frazzled, banjaxed and bewildered Theresa May, the EU agreed to a two-week delay, but insisted the government must propose a way forward by 12 April. That was the deadline for the UK to agree to participate in elections to the European Parliament, and the EU would be damned if the democratic process of 440 million Europeans was going to be buggered up by a sack of squabbling, feral rats in Westminster.[68]

It became vital that MPs do things fast, so Parliament held a series of rapid indicative votes to try to find a consensus. It didn't help. Eight options were put to Parliament, and all eight failed to gain majority support. The closest we came to agreement was an idea to retain a 'permanent and comprehensive UK-wide customs union with the EU', which lost by just six votes.[69]

On April Fool's Day a second round of indicative votes was held, and this time the idea of a customs union lost by just three votes, and there was still no agreed way forward.[70] Yet more ministers quit, bringing the number who had resigned from May's government to 33; they were leaving at a rate of 1.5 every month.

What the hell should we do next? we wondered. Europe wasn't about to tell us. 'It is up to the UK to indicate how it plans to proceed in order to avoid a no-deal scenario,' said the Irish Taoiseach: 'The European council has agreed unanimously that the Withdrawal Agreement will not be reopened.'[71]

Official campaigning for Brexit had begun 1,133 days earlier, and there was still no plan how to do it, so inevitably the entire thing was once again kicked down the road. Brexit would now happen on 31 October, and this time we would countenance no more delays.[72] That was final.

Sure.

—

Let's revisit old friends, or if they're not available, be-tweeded badger murderer Owen Paterson.

Paterson grew up on a farm, obtained a history degree, and before entering Parliament spent his days managing a tannery,[73] so it's difficult to immediately spot what 'consultancy services' he could offer to a forensics lab.

Regardless, for some reason Paterson was being paid £100,000 per year for 16 hours' work per month acting as a consultant to Randox Laboratories, which performed forensic testing under a government contract.[74]

Randox hit the headlines back in 2017, when evidence emerged that there had been manipulation of the forensic tests they performed, which covered everything from driving offences to violent crime and sexual assaults.[75] The scandal led to over 10,000 test results having to be repeated, 42 police forces having to suspend contracts with their forensics providers, and almost 100 people having convictions quashed or their cases dropped.[76]

In April 2019, as Brexit dominated the headlines, it was revealed that Owen Paterson had lobbied the government to give contracts to the unimpeachable Randox,[77] which was almost certainly not in any way related to the £100,000 they gave to a former tannery manager, slapdash badger slaughterer and climate-change denier to help in their scientific endeavours. Paterson also wrote to ministers asking them to take steps that would benefit Lynn's Country Foods,[78] which handed Paterson £12,000 per year.[79]

Owen Paterson said he was lobbying, and as we all know, lobbying is not the same as corruption. Corruption is illegal. Lobbying isn't.

Paterson thought he'd got away with it, but he was outfoxed – a refreshing change from him being out-badgered – by the body overseeing parliamentary standards. They investigated the Randox business in 2021 and concluded 'no previous case of paid advocacy has seen so many breaches or such a clear pattern of behaviour in failing to separate private and public interest'.[80] Paterson was suspended from the House of Commons for 30 days.[81]

You or I might think that's rather mild, but to Boris Johnson the idea that actions might one day have consequences was a terrifying and alien concept. Faced with the utter horror of his friend Paterson having to sit at home watching *Loose Women* for a month while being paid a salary of £81,932 (plus expenses), Johnson did what any decent prime minister would do: tried to delay the suspension long enough for the Tories to scrap the Standards Committee,[82] and set up a more friendly regime that would let them get away with more of what I suppose we must still describe as 'lobbying'.

Parliament, lawyers, media commentators of every ilk and most of the public roared their outrage. This was a step too far, even for Johnson. There was a swift U-turn on the idea of a new committee, and Paterson resigned from Parliament in a towering huff, still protesting his innocence. At the resulting by-election in his former seat of North Shropshire, a 23,000 majority was overturned by a combination of extreme voter revulsion and tactically organised opposition parties. The Lib Dems took a seat that Tories had held for almost 200 unbroken years.[83]

—

But we still faced another couple of years of squalid opportunism and iffy donations before any of that came to pass. For example, in May 2019 it was discovered Lubov Chernukhin, the wife of one of Vladimir Putin's former ministers, had paid the Tories £30,000 to have a private dinner with Gavin Williamson, which is one of the most luridly disturbing dates it's possible to imagine.

The donation was part of a stream of money Chernukhin had directed towards the party. Even after Theresa May had pledged to 'crack down' on money from Russian sources in the wake of the Salisbury nerve-agent attack, she'd been perfectly happy to take £135,000 from Mrs Chernukhin, and then have her own private dinner with her, to which May invited along six Cabinet ministers.[84] That's 19 grand per minister, if you're wondering what our government costs.

There is no suggestion whatsoever that Mrs Chernukhin has broken any laws. She and her husband are both legal residents in this country, and as such are allowed to make political donations. Lubov Chernukhin's husband Vladimir, for example, gained a visa to live and work in the UK, in part because the banker Nathaniel Rothschild created a job for him.[85] Rothschild was at school with George Osborne and is a former member of the Bullingdon Club.[86]

In 2016 Vladimir Chernukhin was sent $8 million via the Virgin Islands by a company said to be linked to one of Putin's closest allies, Suleyman Kerimov.[87] Mr Kerimov is under sanctions by US authorities for playing 'a key role in advancing Russia's malign activities'.[88] In the three years since this money transfer, Mrs Chernukhin made 32 donations to the Tories, totalling over £1.7 million.

—

I hope her palpably strange desire to eat with Gavin Williamson lived up to her expectations, because it was to be their last opportunity for such socialising for a while. For reasons that still defy explanation, Williamson had been given the job of defence secretary, and had taken the opportunity to humiliate the nation at every turn.

His response to the Salisbury nerve-agent attack had been to tell Russia to 'shut up and go away', which we can all agree is pretty stern stuff. Sadly, Russia failed to quake to its foundations, and merely responded that Williamson suffers from 'extreme intellectual impotency'.[89]

Having brought one superpower to its knees, laughing, Williamson branched out: he accused China of being 'malign' over their use of the Huawei telecommunications system, which Britain was planning to use as part of our 5G network. China responded by saying Williamson reflected attitudes of 'deep-rooted ignorance, prejudice and anxiety'.

This was by now a majority view. But Williamson was determined to show those pesky nuclear superpowers who was boss: he made a speech announcing plans to send an aircraft carrier to the Pacific to terrify the Chinese into submission and get his face on the front page of the papers. It's unknown whether these aircraft carriers would be the ones on which the Tory defence secretary had spent so much money that we could no longer afford the aircraft to accompany them.[90]

But leave aside the bewildering notion of the Chinese being terrified by an empty vessel – in both senses. We don't know whether we were deploying our non-aircraft-carrying aircraft carriers because we didn't deploy them. Instead, Williamson's Cabinet colleagues were sent on a tour of Britain's newsrooms to reassure the public that the war games were all in Williamson's seemingly deranged imagination. A parliamentary colleague is reported to have labelled him 'Private Pike'.[91]

The defence secretary was still very cross about 5G, and the Huawei controversy rumbled on, but Williamson didn't. At the beginning of May he was suddenly sacked after Theresa May was given what she called 'compelling evidence' that Williamson had leaked information from the National Security Council. Several attendees of the Council had been questioned about the leak, but in the letter firing Williamson, May wrote: 'They have answered all questions, engaged properly, provided as much information as possible to assist with the investigation, and encouraged their staff to do the same. Your conduct has not been of the same standard as others.'

She gave him the opportunity to voluntarily resign, but he chose not to. So instead, she gave him the opportunity to be involuntarily sacked, which he was.[92]

Yet another minister was gone. The same week, the minister for trade and the Government Whip in the Lords both quit. They cited 'personal reasons', perhaps in much the same way people had personal reasons for jumping from the sloping deck of the Titanic.[93]

And so we had a new defence secretary, Penny Mordaunt, which is a real person, and not a minor Addams Family character. She brought to the role all the experience you needed for one of the great offices of state: she began her career as a magician's assistant, and since then had progressed to failing to reach the last 10 during her time on a celebrity diving show.[94] She was primarily famous for not being as ludicrous as Williamson, and for her ability to swear for 37 solid minutes without repeating herself. Britain was in safe hands.

—

Off to Llangollen for the Welsh Conservative Conference and Ritual Murder of the Prime Minister. 'Thank you, everybody, and—' began Theresa May's speech.

'Why don't you resign?' shouted the audience.

'It's great to be back in North Wales again,' she continued. 'My experience of North Wales is that everybody I meet is friendly.'

'We don't want you,' they shouted back, friendily.[95]

The friendly Tories of North Wales weren't alone. When she assumed office in 2016, May's net approval rating (the percentage of people approving of her, minus those disapproving) had stood at a healthy 12 per cent. It was now minus 49 per cent.[96] Her near total inability to control the government, failure to deliver on her party's defining promise, and her metallic, frigid and voter-repellent personality were all damaging the country, and more importantly for the Tories, they were damaging their electability. The day before she was barracked at the Welsh conference, local elections in England led to the Tories losing over 1,300 council seats, and not even May's few remaining friends in Parliament could take much more.[97]

She'd previously declared she intended to resign after her deal passed in Parliament, but after two solid years of losing every battle in the Commons, that was now about as likely as Boris Johnson agreeing to resign after he passes a lie detector test.

Graham Brady, leader of the backbench 1922 Committee and previously a staunch May loyalist, requested 'clarity' over the timetable for the PM leaving her job, and she fobbed him off for a few days.[98] But the pressure mounted: Andrea Leadsom, leader of the House of Commons, quit, her reasons being that she no longer 'believes that we will be a truly sovereign United Kingdom through the deal that is now proposed'.[99] She was convinced May's deal would create an almost permanent Northern Ireland backstop, and she absolutely refused to support such a policy – until October, when she backed Boris Johnson's deal, which did exactly the same thing.[100]

The resignation of Leadsom, who had been handsomely beaten in a leadership election by the most inept PM in living memory, shouldn't have caused much of a kerfuffle, but it was the *coup de grâce* for that most graceless of leaders.

Say what you like about Theresa May. Sure, she was a glacial, uncharismatic, unimaginative, cruel and bungling sack of elbows, imbued with all the cordiality and charm of a tin scorpion. It's true that she had exhibited no emotion as she wrongly detained and deported the Windrush generation. No tears fell as she turned her back on the Grenfell victims. She exhibited epic froideur as she blithely demolished the hopes of myriad industries. She steadfastly ignored the cries of over 5,000 migrants drowning in Europe's waters,[101] was stoic as she ruined the life chances of our young, and remained coolly dispassionate as she starved the sick of funds.

But finally, there was something tragic enough to bring tears to her eyes. As she stood in the street to announce that she'd have to stop being an absolutely abysmal prime minister and would in future merely be an exceptionally well-paid MP with a guaranteed place in the House of Lords and a multimillionaire husband who profits from tax avoiding companies,[102] she finally wept.

She would step down on 7 June.[103] This didn't exactly help with Brexit negotiations. 'We trust you, Theresa,' said Michel Barnier, but 'we don't trust what we think is coming next.'[104]

—

Thirteen candidates thought they had what it takes to lead our country, and every single one of them was wrong. Regardless, it is my solemn duty to introduce the applicants for the vacant role of prime minister.

First up: Boris Johnson, who only seemed to want the job so he would have to see less of his children. I mean fewer. He was a documented racist, sexist and homophobe, who had been sacked twice for lying, had helped to organise the planned assault and battery of a journalist, and who trundled around like he was secretly dreading a life-destroying dawn raid from a specialist branch of the Met. One of his colleagues described Boris as 'a receptacle for every wack job and loon in the Tory party',[105] which is all the explanation required for why Johnson was favourite to win.[106]

He was up against Dominic Raab, the former minister for bellowing at foreigners, who had been proud to turn his cubiform face to camera and announce that he didn't think humans should have human rights.[107] Not sure who should get them, then. Crayfish? His greatest achievement to date had been resigning in protest at his own achievements, yet even so, his bland contempt for the poor made 78-year-old Tory youngsters briefly moist, and they loved him for it.

We also faced the prospect of being led by Jeremy Hunt, whose public persona was a close match to that of a polyester-blazered assistant in a pretentious soft-furnishings shop. He had accidentally become health minister, where he spent his daylight hours auctioning your wellbeing off to – well, I'd like to say the highest bidder, but I doubt he's competent enough to get a good price. Without ever changing his absolutely horrible opinions, he'd somehow contrived to end up being thought of as the moderate candidate, because that's how far the other Tories had lurched to the right.

Poor, fragile-looking Rory Stewart had decided to stand, although few of us were sure he had the strength, and nobody thought it advisable. By now he belonged to a different party, from a different age, with different morals – by which I mean: some. He had original ideas, thought about consequences, and wasn't the slightest bit shy about telling Tories that Brexit was utter bollocks, all of which meant he had absolutely no chance of winning. But he became infinitely more huggable simply by describing his battle to beat Boris Johnson as 'Jiminy Cricket up against Pinocchio'.[108]

Fellow no-hoper Esther McVey decided to throw her hat into the ring and surprised us all by hitting the target. Her integrity, humility and willingness to put the interests of the nation ahead of her own were starkly illustrated by her decision to claim £8,750 in expenses for a personal photographer, just in case we forgot what she looked like.[109] If there's a premium on terrible ideas, I want mineral rights to her head.

Matt Hancock's assurance that No Deal Brexit 'simply won't be allowed by Parliament' singled him out as the realist candidate, an accolade he immediately ruined by claiming he was running because the party needed to 'attract younger voters'.[110] Are we confident 18-year-olds will find themselves drawn to a toe-curlingly sinister middle-aged accountant who looks like Pee-wee Herman reflected in the back of a spoon? We are not.

Andrea Leadsom was back, undeterred by her record of already being abundantly thrashed in the 2016 leadership election by the worst leader for 100 years, where Leadsom's pitch had been: 'I'm a bloody baby factory, me.' She was 53 at the time. For her second hilariously misjudged attempt at seizing power, her offering to Tory members was that we would walk away from EU negotiations, but also continue negotiating with the EU; and that she would grant rights to EU citizens living in the UK, but also prevent EU citizens from living in the UK.[111] She was all the contradictions and delusions of Brexit personified in the form of a big waxy model of Margaret Thatcher that had been leaning against a radiator for slightly too long.

Guess who else was back? Our favourite haunted Pob doll was having another go at becoming leader, despite telling us, 'I have repeatedly said that I do not want to be prime minister.'[112] There's a thin line between genius and madness, and Michael Gove appeared to have snorted that line. Even so, he was considered relatively progressive because he once grudgingly agreed that burying the planet under plastic bags might damage profits.[113]

Home Secretary Sajid Javid fancied his chances, and he had all the attributes you'd expect in a Tory leader: he was utterly unqualified but rabidly ambitious, and he'd been perfectly happy to let a British baby live, and subsequently die, in a Syrian refugee camp to garner approving headlines in the *Daily Mail*.[114] His chances of entering Downing Street were damaged because he had been a firm Remainer, but happily he had forgotten all of that, and now called himself a 'firm Leaver', because who needs beliefs when you've got an insatiable craving for power?[115]

Mark Harper's vote-winning contempt for immigrants wasn't as hard to prove as other candidates': he'd been the executor of the

'Go Home' vans policy, and he quite wrongly assumed this would be enough to overcome his complete invisibility on the public stage. A proud Brexiteer, he was such a fierce proponent of Great British exceptionalism that he had heroically attempted to sell off all our national forests,[116] and he so fully exemplified Great British competence that he had heroically failed.[117]

Kit Malthouse-Compromise stood very briefly, and then almost immediately gave up when it became obvious that he was in a party that rejected the very concept of compromise. And James Cleverly fancied himself, which is more than anybody else did. Cleverly, a stunningly successful one-man campaign to disprove nominative determinism, had to stand down after it became clear – and you should read this out loud, because it's amazing – that his colleagues thought he was even less capable than Esther McVey.[118]

Presumably just for shits and giggles, Sam Gyimah put himself forward, despite being a vocal advocate for a second referendum on Brexit, and despite being Black. He'd have had more chance of winning over the Tory membership if he'd been called Karl Che Guevara Marx and advocated a total ban on Pimm's, Saga holidays, and stories about house prices in the *Daily Express*.[119]

———

At this point in the leadership election, not much could bump Boris Johnson out of the headlines, but Mark Field managed it. In the midst of the campaign, Field was attending an event at London's Mansion House, when it was interrupted by non-violent Greenpeace protestors in ballgowns making polite speeches. As an activist in an elegant gown passed Mark Field's seat, he turned suddenly, shoved her violently against a marble pillar, and then grabbed her by the throat and frogmarched her out. The entire thing was caught on camera, there wasn't much point in denying it, and Field was suspended from his ministerial post at the Foreign Office.[120]

The previous week, Field had criticised police in Hong Kong for their 'inappropriate use of force'.

—

MPs beating up climate protestors was quite a big story, so few noticed yet another report by the special rapporteur on extreme poverty from the UN. It found poverty in the UK was a 'systematic tragedy', which was being created deliberately as a matter of policy.

'The bottom line is that much of the glue that has held British society together since the Second World War has been deliberately removed and replaced with a harsh and uncaring ethos,' it concluded.[121] The report's lead author said the Department of Work and Pensions was creating 'a digital and sanitised version of the 19th-century workhouse'.

Britain's measure for poverty didn't include the costs of housing or childcare, which as we all know are entirely voluntary extravagances, when anybody with proper entrepreneurial spirit would buckle down, sleep under a bush, and sell their kids for medical experiments. But as soon as luxuries such as a roof over your head and care for your offspring were included in calculations, the UN found 14 million of us lived in poverty.

But those were merely British human beings and were therefore less important to patriotic Tory MPs than appealing to the tiny group of patriotic Tory members who would decide the next prime minister. To win over those members in the only way he knew how, Johnson offered an immediate bribe. There would be tax cuts for the 3 million highest earners, the cost of which would be £9.6 billion.[122] That's like giving the wealthiest people in the land a stack of £10 notes 64 miles high while 14 million of us were living in systematic and deliberate poverty.

Nobody was shocked that Johnson was offering dodgy electoral bribes, but what was surprising was the sudden outbreak of competence and efficiency from the notoriously shambolic and undisciplined Boris. Colleagues claimed they were 'gobsmacked' by the lengths to which Johnson's team were going in an effort to reduce the risk of him blundering on his route to power; although when you looked at the measures taken, they could all be reduced to this: put a gag on the gibbering ape. His zookeepers were reported to have literally dragged Johnson away from groups of journalists with whom he'd been chatting before he had the chance to gaffe too severely.

His team restricted his appearances to a single interview with *The Times*,[123] and he even refused to participate in a TV debate with the other candidates, which polling showed had been won by Rory Stewart. After a knockout stage, during which Tory MPs got to vote for their favourite sociopath, the candidates were reduced to just five, and brave Sir Boris decided he felt safe enough to join in with the second debate.

Polling of the public showed Rory Stewart won that one too, so naturally Tory MPs eliminated him in the next round.[124] Two further ballots of MPs knocked out everybody except for Hunt and the uncharacteristically taciturn Johnson.

Turning up to an interview for the most important occupation in the country while operating under a vow of silence is a strange way to get the job, but he was perhaps unique in that in the middle of an absolutely silent campaign to become PM, the police had to be called.

Officers arrived at Johnson's home right in the middle of his literal job interview, after neighbours had reported a lavishly noisy and violent fight with his partner Carrie Symonds. One resident became worried after hearing a woman repeatedly screaming 'get off me' and 'get out of my flat'. Plates were smashed. Symonds shouted, 'You just don't care for anything because you're spoilt. You have no care for money or anything,' which Johnson proved wrong by showing how much he loved his MacBook: he bawled 'get off my fucking laptop', after which neighbours reported even louder crashing noises.[125]

The following day Johnson faced an interview with Iain Dale, during which he had the gall to tell the audience nobody wanted to hear about his massive, blazing, violent, police-attended nocturnal fracas with his latest girlfriend, or what was so embarrassing about the contents of his laptop.

The following week things became even stranger. During a frankly mesmerising interview with Talk Radio, Johnson was asked what he did to relax. You could almost see the internal warning flash before his eyes: do not say getting pissed and shagging, do not say getting pissed and shagging. Even at his best, which is a low bar, Johnson's speaking style could always be described as a series of erratic pauses, burbled gibberish, and ultimately unsuccessful lunges towards articulacy. But in answering the incredibly challenging 'what do you do to relax' question, his distinctive incoherence reached Olympian heights.

He began, seemingly in slow motion, with the words 'I like to paint', and immediately seemed surprised to have found his mouth had made those noises.

'I like to paint, or I make things. I have a thing where I make models of—' at which point there was a lengthy pause while his super-ego screamed 'what the fuck are you doing?' at his id; and then he plumped for 'models of buses', to the surprise of all.

The interviewer looked on with increasing disbelief that this – this – was how he'd be remembered.

'What I make is', Johnson went on, now fully committed, 'I get old, I don't know, wooden crates, and I paint them. It's a box that's been used to contain two wine bottles, right, and it will have a dividing thing. And I turn it into a bus'.[126]

No details emerged about the (presumably quite complicated) winebox-to-bus stage of the creative process, but let's leave it there, because it was already time for Johnson's next attempt at boggling the minds of the nation. Our candidate for bold new leadership chickened out of the next televised face-to-face with Hunt, so the event was cancelled on the unproven assumption that not even Jeremy Hunt could lose a debate with himself.[127] Although he had a good go, boasting that he would be delighted to inform businesses that had gone bust after Brexit that their sacrifice was worth it.[128]

It didn't help: no matter how much Hunt pretended he would

gleefully impoverish every business in the country to deliver the Tories' beloved Brexit, it was all but certain Johnson would win.[129]

Yet almost everybody who met him knew Johnson wasn't prime minister material. His subsequent failures were all entirely predictable, and heavily foreshadowed. Max Hastings, his former boss, did his best to warn us in a lengthy article during the leadership campaign.

'I have known Johnson since the 1980s, when I edited the *Daily Telegraph* and he was our flamboyant Brussels correspondent,' wrote Hastings. 'I have argued for a decade that he is unfit for national office, because it seems he cares for no interest save his own fame and gratification.'

He described Johnson as a 'tasteless joke' and predicted 'his premiership will almost certainly reveal a contempt for rules, precedent, order and stability'.

Hastings said Johnson was a 'weak character', closer to Alan Partridge than his idol, Winston Churchill, and reported Johnson's habit of issuing threats that border on blackmail when journalists tried to report his activities. These included historical attempts to intimidate Christopher Bland, former chairman of the BBC, with promises to publish revelations about Bland's private life if the BBC didn't stop reporting accurate stories about Johnson; and then further threats to Hastings himself, who said he possessed 'handwritten notes from our possible next prime minister, threatening dire consequences in print if I continued to criticise him'.[130]

Unfortunately, Hastings' concerns were only printed in the *Guardian*, which is not a paper habitually read by the only people who got to vote for our next prime minister: the one in 250 who had paid to become members of the Tory party. They didn't see the warnings and wouldn't have cared anyway. They just wanted a comedy character they called Boris, and when the voting was done, he was declared the winner.

He had gained the support of 92,153 people out of an electorate of 47 million.[131] That's just 0.19 per cent of the voting public.

Thus, in our terrific, modern and inclusive democracy, Alexander Boris de Pfeffel Johnson – a repeatedly sacked, lying, unqualified, lazy and unreliable newspaper columnist who used a fake name, wouldn't even admit how many children he had, and had attempted to take out a gagging order to prevent the public learning about his adultery or the child arising from it[132] – became the fourth successive person to start the job of prime minister without winning a general election.

When asked to express his feelings about Johnson being our prime minister, a Cabinet colleague summed it up in a single word: 'Gulp.'[133]

—

Johnson's ascendency came down to two things: his personification of a certain type of unthinking British half-heartedness, and his total disregard for the truth.

The half-heartedness is exemplified by the large section of British society that wants well-funded infrastructure but also demands tiny rates of tax and no borrowing. Johnson, unfettered by reality or honesty, told them they could have it.

These voters want endless welfare cuts, and the social safety net abolished for other families, but they don't want to have to see homeless people in the doorways of their market town, and they want to keep getting all their traditional child benefits and pensions. Johnson guaranteed it.

They want Britain to export globally, but don't want to encounter foreigners or accept trade regulations. Boris assured them this was possible. They want us to be completely independent and self-sufficient, but also want to eat kiwi fruit on Christmas Day and have cheap energy and German beer. Johnson said sure, no problem.

They long to live in a nation which is a mighty power, thumping Nazis and bossing around China, but do it without fighting any wars or having to pay for planes to put on our aircraft carriers. Johnson would do a little dance, tell a joke in cod Latin, and assure them the world respected and feared us.

If he had said any of this shit in a strong regional accent, you'd write him off as a drunken, ignorant moron. But at Eton he had perfected an artificially posh, booming speaking style, and developed 'the eccentric English persona' for which he is known,[134] and in our hidebound, class-crippled society, those tools will allow you to con every other tool you come into contact with.

He appealed to the large rump of the British – and specifically English – population which longed to feel Britain was wonderful but was prepared to make absolutely no sacrifices to keep it that way. And because Johnson didn't care about telling the truth or even recognising the choices involved, he was always happy to reassure them they could have it all.

He described this as sunny optimism. Others said it was mindless denialism. But whatever it's called, it achieved the only thing Johnson really cared about: getting him into Downing Street.

—

So what can we say about the outgoing Theresa May? Let's try to put a positive spin on this: she wasn't as bad as Boris Johnson, and she packed a lot in.

For example, in barely 12 months she had managed to go from being one of the most popular politicians in the country to a humiliating election debacle that transformed her into the least popular prime minister for at least 100 years. Credit where it's due: that's no mean feat.

Not many people can say they achieved more than Thatcher or Blair, but despite having one of the shortest premierships in a century, May delivered more ministerial resignations than either of them. Kudos.

We are a country that likes a bit of world-beating, and her parliamentary defeats were certainly that. Quite frankly I don't think there's enough national pride about what she accomplished on that score.[135]

May's crumbling, cacophonous, calamitous 2017 conference speech has rightly gone down in history as a Pythonesque comedy classic. It should be shown nightly on Dave, like that episode of *Top Gear* where something is racist and a caravan blows up.

She even managed to get to the top spot in the iTunes charts. Thatcher barely scraped into the top 10, and didn't even manage that until she was dead, which I think is cheating. Whereas May was very much alive when she scored her big hit, with a phat beat that sampled various promises she had cawed into the public realm during her time in office; it was entitled 'Liar Liar'.[136]

Those are the positives.

The negatives are enumerated in a survey of UK academics specialising in British politics and contemporary British history. Every prime minister since the Second World War was assessed and scored. Theresa May came bottom, with an average score of 2.3 out of 10. Labour's Clement Attlee came top, and in the last half-century only Blair and Brown were judged to have improved British society or our democracy – every single Tory leader had damaged those things.

Labour also had the biggest positive impact on our economy, with Blair a full 64 points ahead of his nearest Tory rival, Margaret Thatcher. Even Gordon Brown beat her by 45 points.

David Cameron and Theresa May scored worst of all. They were the only prime ministers since the Second World War to receive negative scores for every criterion measured: their impact on the UK's economy, on our society, on Britain's role in the world, our democracy, and on their own political party.[137] They had been entirely harmful to every major aspect of our nation.

We were nine years into Tory rule, and somehow, we still hadn't hit rock bottom.

Part 3
The Lightness of Being Unbearable

2019
I Thought Johnson Was Fucking Stupid

Britain was trapped in a paradox: any government competent enough to deliver Brexit… wouldn't.

In December 2015, before David Cameron lazily handed control of our fate to the zealots on his backbench, polling found only 1 per cent of Britons felt our relationship with Europe was the most important issue facing the nation.[1] By 2016 this had increased to 40 per cent, and then to 68 per cent by the time Theresa May left office.[2]

Spoiler: leaving Europe was never the most important issue facing Britain.

No, it wasn't. Shut up.

But still they pressed on, blind to all other issues. The only way things could get any bleaker was if we shoved a monumentally ill-suited, dissolute wastrel into the most important job in the country, and then cheered as he promised to deliver the worst possible solution in the shortest possible time.

Out lumbered Boris Johnson to deliver his victory speech, his vast, gormless face emerging from a clump of matted fur like a birthing video for a manatee.

'We are going to get Brexit done on 31 October,' he boomed, and in those few words set the tone for his entire premiership: ignore all complexities, lie for no reason, and be completely wrong. He continued by assuring his party of gullible rubes that if no agreement was made by the deadline, we would accept No Deal Brexit and thrive regardless. Britain would leave the EU at the end of October 'do or die'.[3]

He neither did nor died. Sorry to be the bearer of bad news.

A clutch of Johnson's less docile colleagues quit rather than serve with him. Margot James resigned so she could block the prorogation of Parliament – in essence, the cancellation of our democratic body just because it was proving inconvenient.[4] She described Johnson as 'erratic and reckless'.[5] Andrew Percy resigned in opposition to the damage Johnson would do with his cavalier acceptance of No Deal Brexit, which Percy called a 'cack-handed' move.[6]

Chancellor Philip Hammond jumped ship, as did Alan Duncan, Anne Milton, David Gauke, David Lidington – who had been de facto deputy prime minister – and Rory Stewart, the only one of the leadership candidates to have remotely impressed the general public.[7] There had been 60 ministerial resignations since the 2017 general election, which works out at one every 13 days.

Michael Gove wasn't about to quit, though. Why should he? After all, he'd finally completed his epic three-year journey from warning the country Boris Johnson was too inept, chaotic and dishonest to lead the party, to describing him as a 'great prime minister'.[8] His endorsement had been enough to get Johnson over the line, and history suggests Gove knew a thing or two about lines.

The mass resignations actually benefited the notoriously idle Johnson, because it meant he had fewer people to sack in his first reshuffle. In total, 17 ministers were replaced, including Jeremy Hunt and anybody who had ever uttered the words 'Jeremy Hunt', which thankfully didn't include the multiple major newsreaders who had called him 'Jeremy Cunt' during the previous few weeks.[9]

They did it by accident, of course. I did it on purpose.

Johnson would brook no dissent, so filled every Cabinet vacancy with a formless, spineless, thoughtless nonentity who would yield to his bidding. Matt Hancock became health secretary, and robotically echoed Johnson's pledge to 'show some love' by increasing pay for public-sector workers,[10] an idea Johnson appeared not to have communicated to his new Chancellor Sajid Javid, who declined to endorse the raise.[11]

Javid was ruthlessly efficient, but at the same time positively lavish in the number of contradictory opinions he could hold at the same time. He warned the 'UK risks sliding into nationalism',[12] and condemned 'naked populism',[13] all while proposing that a mandatory 'British values oath' must be taken by people emptying your bins.[14] The problem, as he saw it, was 'politicians with no real purpose – other than just to gather up as many votes as they can', so he backed Boris Johnson, whose grand plan for the country was…

The end of the previous sentence has not yet been discovered.

Dominic Raab might have looked like an Etch A Sketch representation of a dodgy colonel straight out of central casting, but he'd impressed Johnson with his logic-defying suggestion that Parliament should be abolished so Brexit could restore our democracy.[15] His only purpose in life is to be an internationally recognised lodestone for wrongness. If you should ever find yourself nodding along to his pronouncements, stop, make sure you have six feet of soft ground behind you, and then slap yourself unconscious. Naturally, he got one of the great offices of state, and was sent off to represent us as Foreign Secretary.

And we welcomed back Priti Patel, who approached her new role as Home Secretary with all the warmth and compassion of a Klingon backstreet abortionist. Having recently resigned after accusations she had broken the Ministerial Code, Patel showed she had learned from her mistakes by making the same mistake even better next time. Less than 48 hours after getting the job, she was embroiled in a fresh scandal, when it was revealed that she'd been paid £1,000 per hour to work at a global communications agency without getting permission from the parliamentary vetting body, which was widely criticised as a second breach of the code (although she subsequently got the permission she should have asked for in the first place).[16]

Disgrace in Tory politics doesn't seem to last very long, so not only did we have Patel back in a senior Cabinet role, but we also saw the almost instant return of Amber 'Windrush' Rudd, Grant 'Michael Green' Shapps, and Gavin 'Fuck it, let's start World War Three' Williamson.

And in charge of international trade we got the froth-weight Liz Truss, whose contortions around Brexit had made her the second most likely person in government to belong in a circus. She had been a Remain campaigner in 2016, yet in 2017 she was fiercely pro-Brexit, saying, 'I voted to Remain because I was concerned about the economy, but what we've seen since the Brexit vote is our economy has done well.'[17] A quick peek outside the window showed the economy was weaker than at any point for five years,[18] our credit rating had been downgraded yet again, and we had thrown away £250 billion in a single morning to prevent the voracious capital markets from eating us alive after the referendum result.

Truss was a member of the Adam Smith Institute and the Institute of Economic Affairs, both of which strongly support free trade, yet now she was backing a policy to stop free trade with our biggest market.[19] Unsurprisingly, it was easy to lure her into an idiot-trap, as Eddie Mair did during a blissful radio interview. Mair asked if we should have another EU referendum, and Truss said no.

'But what about people who've changed their minds?' asked Mair.

'I don't think people have changed their minds', she replied.

'*You* have.'

A slight, baffled pause before she said, 'I have, that's true,' and giggled. 'In the other way, though.'[20]

An anagram of Elizabeth Truss is 'haziest bluster'.

Laugh all you want, but the mindset that leads to Truss's interview is troubling: only one change of heart was valid, and moving further to the right was the only permissible direction of travel. The party's terror of being outflanked on the right by Nigel Farage was leading to an inexorable drift into more and more extreme positions. And as for her assertion that people hadn't changed their minds: polling evidence showed remaining in the EU was by now the far most popular preferred outcome, 11 per cent ahead of leaving without a deal.[21]

—

The ERG decided to lend a hand by proposing we jail any British citizen found to be discussing Brexit negotiations with a foreign politician.[22] More sensible heads prevailed, among which was not the one perched atop the ERG's Daniel Kawczynski. He literally offered to get himself sent to jail *under his own proposed law*, by tweeting that he was 'doing all I can to convince Polish government to veto extension of Article 50'.[23]

This kind of deep thinking had laid the earlier foundations for yet another disaster, which was still wreaking havoc in 2019.

Back in 2014 the government – against advice and widespread opposition – had allowed commercial companies to take over child-protection services for a profit. These contracts had been hoovered up by the usual suspects: the eternally competent G4S, the endlessly proficient Serco, and so on.

By the time Johnson entered office, 39 per cent of kids in foster care in England were there to make a profit for one of the giant contractors. This was more efficient, we were told, yet the average weekly cost to taxpayers was £823 for those handled privately, compared to £553 by those handled by the local authority. More than £220 million a year of profits was being made off the backs of our most vulnerable children.[24] That money, now in the pockets of the venture capitalists behind the commercial contractors, would have funded local authorities employing an additional 4,400 child social workers.

In an effort to further maximise profits, outsourced units – or as we traditionally call them, 'children' – were soon being warehoused in the cheapest possible locations. By 2019, 84 per cent of children in privatised care had been relocated outside of their local authority area. A county council in Lincolnshire sent its vulnerable kids to the delightful-sounding Cherry Blossom Children's Home, which would be lovely, except it was in Peterhead, Scotland, which was 400 miles away from any family or friends those kids might still have.[25]

And almost nobody was paying the slightest bit of attention, because the entire purpose of the nation was now Brexit.

—

Johnson started by detailing his long-promised clear, simple solution to the crisis. Never one to be stymied by consistency, he expressed four completely different solutions in a single week, assuring us each of them was the real thing.

And what were they? In essence, stone-dead concepts from the May era, over which Johnson barked one of his famous mumbo-jumbo incantations, resurrected them, and sent the zombie ideas lurching off towards Westminster, there to feed ravenously upon the body politic.

The first idea was to kick the whole thing down the road. Johnson said discussions about the Irish border should 'take place after Brexit',[26] which is a bit like saying discussions about the massive subsidence affecting your dream home should take place after you've signed the mortgage agreement, and neither MPs nor the EU were willing to countenance that lunatic idea.

Solution number two fixed the Irish backstop – the agreement that Northern Ireland would effectively remain in the single market until we thought up something else – with a sublimely simple plan. It could be 'deleted' from the Withdrawal Agreement, which was yet another of the solutions Theresa May tried, and which had also been a comprehensive failure. We'd signed an agreement. We did it voluntarily. It was too late to change, and the British weren't offering any viable alternatives anyway.

The same week, he explained solution number three: get Parliament to agree to all the things it had already subjected to record-breaking defeats, because Johnson suddenly had 'a feeling [that] common sense was breaking out' among MPs, and they were going to pass the deal any minute now.[27] Yet again: May's failure, rebadged, and a complete non-starter.

His fourth clear solution of the week was that the EU were going to reopen negotiations, and that Johnson, master of detail, would get an entirely new agreement in the two short months before his self-imposed, crazy deadline. 'If the approach of the new British prime minister is that they're going to tear up the Withdrawal Agreement, I think we're in trouble,' said Ireland's deputy prime minister, speaking for the EU and rejecting the idea that Britain could simply throw away its agreed undertakings.[28]

So after a week, all we had discovered was that Johnson's grand, clear plan for achieving Brexit was all four of the failed plans May had tried, but this time delivered by a thrasonical cretin with a head like a startled dust-bunny.

Never mind, said the government, and off to Brussels went David Frost: not the unctuous TV guy from 1960s satire, but the satire-proof adviser to Boris Johnson on all things Europe. He told EU diplomatic staff that Johnson had 'no intention' of negotiating a different agreement,[29] a claim only slightly undermined by Number 10 announcing on the same day that the government was 'ready to negotiate in good faith'.

After hours of meetings, the EU could finally tell us everything they'd learned about Johnson's big new plan.

'It was clear the UK does not have another plan,' said a senior EU diplomat. 'No Deal now appears to be the UK government's central scenario.'

Well, that couldn't possibly be true, because honest Johnson had reassured us just a couple of weeks earlier that the chances of leaving with No Deal were 'a million to one'.[30]

In preparation for the thing that definitely wasn't going to happen (but which the prime minister had sent his senior adviser to Europe to tell them he wanted, while telling British people he didn't want it at all) the government had done a study, codenamed Yellowhammer. Rumours of its contents had drifted around Whitehall for months, but it was now leaked in full, probably with the intention of terrifying MPs into agreeing to anything Johnson proposed, rather than the No Deal disaster Yellowhammer predicted.

The report described a future where Britain would have a land border with Ireland that broke the Good Friday Agreement; this would severely restrict our chances of getting the longed-for trade deal with the USA. There would also be a crisis in fishing, shortages of food and fuel, and probably medical supplies too.

We'd suffer rising inflation, catastrophic, rolling disruption to deliveries, food rotting in fields, a sudden leap in the price of social care, and businesses large and small being driven out of existence by a combination of soaring costs, labour shortages and shattered supply chains. Yellowhammer described a 'three-month meltdown' following No Deal.[31]

MPs took a look at it and shrugged. Leavers refused to believe it, and Remainers had already predicted all those things were going to happen anyway, the only difference being that Yellowhammer compressed them all into three months rather than grinding painfully on for years.

Johnson had been in office a month and had packed into it a repeat of all the failures May had eked out over her entire shambolic premiership, plus a few more of his own. So his next move was to cancel democracy.

The idea of proroguing Parliament had first appeared in Dominic Raab's head, because nature abhors a vacuum. The notion of bypassing our democracy spread like wildfire among the kind of person who was prepared to destroy absolutely everything we hold dear to deliver a Brexit they could scarcely describe, but Johnson, during his leadership campaign, had distanced himself from it, telling a meeting of Tory MPs he was 'strongly not attracted' to the notion.[32]

Perhaps if they'd dressed it in a skirt?

The thinking behind prorogation went like this: we had voted for something called Brexit, even though nobody knew what it was. But having voted for a hazy fantasy, Parliament now had to deliver it.

If Parliament couldn't do this impossible task, there was something wrong with Parliament, not with Brexit. It was a bit like voting to abolish gravity. We made our decision, and it was now the job of MPs to allow us to leap safely off high buildings.

Throughout July and August rumours grew that MPs were about to force a further extension to Brexit. Johnson said 'I'd rather be dead in a ditch' than ask for an extension, but his own ill-conceived plans and foggy understanding of what was going on meant there really wasn't any viable alternative.[33]

So suddenly, the idea of disbanding Parliament for a few weeks – quick, before they had a chance to dig a ditch for him – seemed very appealing. Johnson secretly sought legal advice about it from Geoffrey Cox, the Attorney General.[34] When news of this broke, there was a roar of condemnation from every direction at once: media, MPs, peers, newspapers, lawyers, judges and the general public. Over 1.7 million people signed a petition opposing prorogation. The Speaker of the House of Commons, John Bercow, described the idea as a 'constitutional outrage'.[35]

Jacob Rees-Mogg got dressed up nicely, put on some aftershave that probably smelled like the inside of a grandfather clock, and stalked off to Balmoral to convey Cox's legal advice to the Queen, who did her constitutionally mandatory duty: she gave her consent to prorogation, based on what she'd been told.[36] She believed Rees-Mogg's story to be true.

Not many other people did.

Impromptu protests broke out on the streets outside the Palace of Westminster[37] and legal challenges were launched.[38] Such was the division in the Tory ranks that former prime minister John Major joined with the team bringing a High Court action to stop the actions of the current prime minister.[39]

Three days before the plan to suspend Parliament was announced, Downing Street had told the media: 'The claim that the government is considering proroguing Parliament in September in order to stop MPs debating Brexit is entirely false.' Yet during the subsequent legal challenge, documents emerged showing that at the time his office made that statement, Johnson had already secretly agreed to suspension of Parliament two weeks earlier.[40]

But courts move slowly, and Johnson was fast. He simply ignored the possibility he would be found to have broken the law and damaged our constitution, and pushed ahead regardless of consequences.

When the official known as Black Rod arrived to begin the process of proroguing Parliament, the Speaker of the House of Commons found himself surrounded by opposition MPs, holding banners reading 'silenced', while he loudly denounced the suspension of democracy as an 'act of executive fiat'. The ceremony to end a session of Parliament – something that happens each time they go on holiday – always finishes in a packed House of Lords. This time it was attended by only 16 peers.[41] The other 766 boycotted it.

—

Brexit was scheduled to happen on 31 October. Parliament would return on 14 October, and would then have to scrutinise, debate, amend and vote on the most important constitutional change for at least half a century in just 11 working days.[42] This was something they'd failed to achieve in three years. And even this was predicated on the idea that by some miracle, Johnson could come back from the EU with a new deal at all.

Meanwhile, the Queen was dragged back into the melee, even though her constitutional role requires that she remains above the political fray. It seemed the legal advice reported to her hadn't been absolutely candid. People began to ask: had Johnson lied to the monarch?

It was common knowledge that he'd lied to all his wives, his family, his countless mistresses, his media employers, his parliamentary colleagues, every PM he'd worked for, his readers, the EU, any journalist who interviewed him, the population of London, every single foreign leader he'd ever met, and the entire British public. Yet some people still found it inconceivable that he would lie to the Queen.

It went to court, where the Tories had every opportunity to refute the claims of Johnson's dishonesty, and would normally be expected to submit a witness statement explaining and defending the decision they'd made. In this case, the government simply didn't bother, either because they realised the case was indefensible, or because they figured that revealing what was in their secret documents would have been even more damaging than offering no defence.[43] They decided they'd just risk the ruling.

The court unanimously found Boris Johnson had misled the Queen.[44]

—

As a child, Boris Johnson had the modest ambition to be 'World King',[45] and he'd been fortunate enough to attend a vastly privileged school, which was proud of its reputation for training future great leaders. Since then, he'd dedicated much of his life and almost all his political career to the single goal of becoming prime minister.

And it turned out he was absolute dogshit at it.

He'd already revealed he had no bright, shiny, new ideas for how to implement Brexit; just the same old nonsense, accompanied by an alarming lack of concern for what happened to other people if it all went wrong. He had lost his first six parliamentary votes, suspended democracy, brought protestors onto the streets, was accused by MPs of a constitutional coup, got sued by a previous Tory occupant of Downing Street, and was the first prime minister in history to have been found by a court to have misled the monarch.[46]

Not bad for six weeks in the job. But what else had happened in July and August?

—

Let's start with Andrea Jenkyns, who, while sitting in a chair in a Whitehall meeting room, somehow managed to give herself whiplash and concussion, which in a book full of inexplicable and bewildering events still manages to stand out as even less plicable and more wildering than almost anything else.[47]

—

James Cleverly received no reported head injuries in August, so no excuses for him celebrating the anniversary of the end of the British slave trade by claiming William Wilberforce, the abolitionist who led the campaign against slavery, had been a Tory. Wilberforce was a famously independent MP, never had any party affiliations,[48] and the bill to abolish slavery was passed under a Whig prime minister leading a national unity government of MPs from all parties.[49]

—

Ryan Henson, Conservative candidate for Bedford, wrote that Scotland being in the UK was a 'catastrophe' for the union, and England should say 'what everyone's really thinking: Scotland, it's time for you to go'. The official name of the party he represented is the Conservative and Unionist Party. 'It does not reflect my views,' said Henson about the time he wrote his views down on a piece of paper.[50]

—

Meanwhile in Westminster, the relentless pressure of delivering something everybody sane predicted would be a disaster was fraying the nerves of Tory MPs. Party loyalties couldn't hold things together as they once did. At the end of August Lord Young, who had been leader of the House of Commons under Cameron, and had been a Tory MP for over 40 years, resigned as a government spokesman. He said Johnson's behaviour 'risks undermining the role of Parliament' and wanted nothing to do with what he called our 'tinpot' prime minister.[51]

Not many people noticed his resignation, because literally minutes later the leader of the Scottish Conservatives, Ruth Davidson, startled everybody by announcing she was quitting too, citing a combination of a desire for a better work-life balance, and 'conflict over Brexit'.[52]

Two days later, at the start of September, Tory MP Leo Docherty's brother Paddy wrote an open letter to him, which read: 'I am simply appalled that this government, of which you are sadly a part, has become the principal threat to the lives and liberties of the people. Please do the decent thing, and resign.'[53]

Docherty didn't, but his colleague Phillip Lee had had enough:[54] he quit the Tories and crossed the floor of the House of Commons to become a Lib Dem, thus achieving more parliamentary success for them in two minutes than Tim Farron, Vince Cable and Jo Swinson had managed in four years.

Johnson had inherited a wafer-thin majority from May, and it vanished the moment Lee wandered over to the other side of the chamber. Once again, we had a minority government, incapable of driving policy, and deliberately doing all it could to avoid confronting the realities of Brexit.

Johnson desperately wanted a general election to create a bigger majority that would allow him to totally ignore everybody's warnings. This was, once again, exactly the same tactic May had tried. But the Fixed-term Parliaments Act meant he couldn't just call an early election: he had to get permission from MPs, and Parliament said no. Johnson blamed Labour for being unwilling to vote for an election they were certain to lose, but in truth, only 28 Labour MPs opposed the motion for an election; 288 MPs didn't even vote.[55]

He was hemmed in on every side by the red lines he'd personally drawn, by electoral mathematics, by widespread concern about the effects of his signature policy, and by his lack of control over his own party. Nothing had changed since the days of May, except now it was September, MPs were back from their enforced prorogation, and they were mightily pissed off. Multiple concurrent actions to stop a No Deal Brexit immediately kicked in.

Labour proposed a no-confidence vote in the government and suggested that Jeremy Corbyn could be installed as a caretaker prime minister with a simple mandate: pause Brexit before No Deal could happen, ask Parliament to approve a second referendum, and then call a general election and hand back power to whoever won.

Unfortunately, the three most divisive things in Britain at that time were Brexit, Jeremy Corbyn and the correct pronunciation of scone, and both MPs and the public seemed ready to fight over these issues in any pub car park you care to name. The Lib Dems refused to back the idea of an interim government of national unity if the wildly unpopular Corbyn was in charge. And Corbyn refused to hand over his one shot at the premiership or relinquish control over what he considered his own idea. So the prospect of national unity evaporated in a puff of short-termism and hubris.[56]

—

During the referendum campaign, Johnson's Vote Leave group had sent a leaflet to millions of homes, stating: 'There is a free trade zone stretching all the way from Iceland to the Russian border. We will still be part of it after we Vote Leave.' It went on to say, 'Taking back control is a careful change, not a sudden step – we will negotiate the terms of a new deal before we start any legal process to leave.'[57]

That's what Johnson promised, and that's what people believed when they voted in the referendum. Yet in September 2019, Johnson withdrew the whip from 21 of his own MPs, effectively expelling them from the parliamentary party, because they had voted to force him to do what was promised: stay in a free-trade zone and negotiate terms before leaving, rather than quit the single market and rush to No Deal in order to hit a self-imposed deadline.

The suspended MPs included Winston Churchill's grandson and eight former Tory ministers, among them Ken Clarke.[58] He had been right wing enough for Thatcher to have him in her Cabinet and had sat on Tory benches for 49 years. He now described the party as having been 'taken over by the nationalist right'.[59]

First the National Front became the BNP; then the BNP became UKIP; and now UKIP had become the Conservative Party. There was scarcely any difference in ideology or policy.[60]

The purge was supposed to prove that Johnson was fearsome, fearless, and very much in control. Many of his MPs thought it made him look like an irresponsible vandal. Just one day later, the prime minister's younger brother Jo Johnson resigned, writing on Twitter that in his internal conflict between 'family loyalty and the national interest',[61] family loyalty had come second. Boris Johnson, in the opinion of his own brother, was against the national interest.

Shortly afterwards, Boris Johnson's own sister described the PM as 'highly reprehensible'.[62]

In an effort to take control over the narrative, Sajid Javid went on TV to claim the government was 'straining every sinew' to get a deal with the EU. Amber Rudd, observing the reality of Johnson's administration from within Cabinet, expressed a different opinion.

'I no longer believe leaving with a deal is the government's main objective,' Rudd said. She quit and revealed that, regardless of Johnson's assurances that he was fighting to get an agreement with the EU by the deadline, the government was currently undertaking 'no formal negotiations'.[63]

The following week, recent Tory leadership candidate Sam Gyimah defected to the Lib Dems.[64] He'd been one of the 21 expelled, and joined Phillip Lee and Sarah Wollaston, both ex-Tories, who had also switched party in recent weeks.

May had been replaced, but the Tories still seemed to be little more than a continuous, panicky explosion of whitewash, intended – but failing – to cover up a total lack of direction and competence. And it was all accompanied by a daily roster of high-profile resignations.

Yet because it was all being done by an administration that had thrown away its own miniscule majority – and then sacked a further couple of dozen MPs in a fit of petulance – backbenchers once again had power. Parliament could now bring forward its own legislation, including a bill to delay Brexit.

The Tories went to great lengths to illustrate how little they cared about today's constitutional crisis, and made conspicuous noise about their utter disdain for the nation's democratic system, having just spent almost four decades insisting their actions were driven by a love of British parliamentary authority.

It was the most important political emergency since the Suez Crisis, but Michael Gove turned up to one debate seemingly incapable of standing straight.[65] He was seen to be swaying uncontrollably, stumbling, and eventually slumped and clung desperately to the Speaker's chair. Questions were asked about his condition: perhaps he was just tired, or had a head cold – after all, he was described as 'repeatedly sniffing, grinding his teeth and looking extremely flushed'.

Meanwhile his more cultured colleague, Jacob Rees-Mogg, chose to louchely prostrate himself across a bench in the House of Commons and take a vastly performative nap, thus to demonstrate how supremely above all this people of his class are.[66] Not for the first time, it was hard to think of Rees-Mogg as anything more than an empty persona: a physical manifestation of entitlement and stupidity, displayed for lols by bored TV execs.

It was hard to avoid the suspicion that more than one member of the government was, for one reason or another, out of their tiny minds. Oblivious to the realities, the government chose this moment to launch a mystifying ad campaign, imploring Britain to 'Get ready for Brexit'.[67]

When you visited the government website for advice on what form our personal preparations should take, it couldn't tell you a thing: there was a 'Brexit checker' tool that did next to nothing, because nobody knew what was about to happen or when. The campaign urged us to prepare for an event that by now only the truly demented believed would still occur, namely leaving the EU on 31 October. Various legislative roadblocks had made it impossible for the government to leave without a deal, yet the government couldn't agree that deal and – if Amber Rudd was correct – it wasn't even trying. The only viable road ahead was another delay.

Yet still the government blew £100 million on telling us to get ready.

Doublespeak became the norm. Parliament had passed legislation forcing the government to ask for an extension to Article 50 if no deal had been struck by 19 October, yet: 'The government will obey the law,' said Sajid Javid, 'but we'll also not ask for an extension.'

I see. Just blow into this bag, Mr Javid.

Andrew Marr conducted a testy interview with the Chancellor, desperate to get to the bottom of what the hell was going on. 'Meetings, meetings, meetings, talk, talk, talk,' said Marr. 'Not a shred of a new idea from the British government, nothing.'

'There actually are new ideas,' insisted Javid.

'So what? Tell me!'

'Anyone who knows how negotiation works knows you would not discuss them in public.'[68]

Essentially: I've done my homework, but you're not allowed to see it.

Lead EU negotiator Michel Barnier told a different story. His diaries describe years of indolence, unpreparedness and avoidance from the UK side. The first Brexit minister, David Davis, had taken a consistently 'nonchalant' approach, and throughout their months of meetings Barnier found 'as is always the case with him we rarely get into the substance of things.'[69]

Davis's insouciance was probably because he didn't think he was doing the real talks. He most likely assumed the real business was happening somewhere else, in talks between national heads of government. He could have checked, of course. All he had to do was compare notes with Boris Johnson, who, when he was still Foreign Secretary, would personally call the leaders of Germany and France in an attempt to bypass the unified EU negotiating team. Each time, they refused to take Johnson's calls. Yet we never learned our lesson, and just kept on assuming Merkel would cave any moment.

The Tories labelled this 'EU intransigence', because they always assumed there was a back-door method of getting what they wanted without having to do the difficult business of knuckling down and achieving something for themselves. Who can blame them? Their entire lives had been built around the pulling of strings to get special favours.

But the EU saw itself as a single, cohesive entity; and our leaders' fundamental inability to recognise this reality meant Britain didn't take negotiations with the EU's team seriously; not until it was far too late. We just wandered around the meeting rooms of Brussels assuming we'd find the correct string to pull any day now.

As Michel Barnier wrote of Theresa May, 'This is not really a negotiation with the EU but a far more intense negotiation, on an almost hourly basis, with her own ministers.'

The importance of detail, clarity and honesty was not a lesson Johnson had learned, and one he seemed ontologically incapable of ever learning, as shown by his continued insistence that we were leaving on 31 October, 'no ifs, no buts',[70] even while his representatives went off to Brussels to ask to delay Brexit until 31 January 2020.[71]

—

Let's take a breather, and welcome to these pages Jennifer Arcuri.

Arcuri had been a rather anonymous American-born, London-based low-level tech entrepreneur before she came to our attention in 2019. She had been introduced to Boris Johnson at a meeting of entrepreneurs back in 2011, when he was Mayor of London, and she claimed they bonded over a 'mutual interest in classical literature', although the cynics among you might conclude Johnson's interest was more related to her being a pole-dancing former model[72] with a penchant for wandering around wearing nothing but a skimpy bikini made of flags.[73]

Johnson recommended Arcuri – then a 27-year-old student – for a £100,000-a-year role running a taxpayer-funded technology company. When you or I fail to get a job we're massively underqualified to perform, we're lucky if we get a letter saying 'thanks but no thanks'. Arcuri's rather more extravagant kiss-off was the Mayor of London taking her abroad with him on three official trips[74] – overruling official advice that she didn't meet the necessary criteria[75] – and then handing her £126,000 of taxpayers' money.[76]

Ms Arcuri insisted she had 'never, ever' been the recipient of favouritism from Boris Johnson. Sure. We all get that treatment.

During their time of definitely not having an affair, Johnson would go to her flat regularly for – in her words – 'technology lessons'.[77]

Also in her words, Johnson 'asked me to show him a few things' on the pole-dancing paraphernalia in her living room.

Back at home, Johnson's then-wife Marina Wheeler was privately battling cancer and taking care of an estimated 57 per cent of his acknowledged children.[78] Out in public, her husband was battling to not have to admit that the moment Wheeler's back was turned, he'd been thrashing away on top of Jennifer Arcuri like a stranded beluga.[79]

For the second time in just three months, the police were called to investigate the prime minister, this time for misconduct in public office. However, the police found their investigation was hampered by the remarkably convenient mass deletion of vast swathes of information that should have been stored in emails and hard drives used by Johnson.[80]

—

Let's pay a visit to Desmond Swayne, the reanimated corpse of Alvin Stardust, who wrote in September that there was nothing wrong with blacking up, which he felt was an 'entirely acceptable bit of fun'.[81]

As he explained in his blog, whenever he did it – *whenever he did it* – he 'went to some trouble to be as authentic as possible'. So the *Telegraph* confronted him with a photograph of himself and his wife, with Mr Swayne painted completely charcoal black at a party.

'It is definitely my wife,' said Swayne, when shown a photo of himself and his wife.

Is that you next to her?

'It might be is all I can say,' replied a suddenly forgetful Swayne; and let's not cast aspersions. Who among us can honestly say we haven't – now and again – totally forgotten the time we painted ourselves pitch black from head to toe before going out in public?

And what did Mrs Swayne think about all of this? She 'just wanted the whole thing to go away'.[82] As do we all, Mrs Swayne.

—

As September ground to its close, nobody on earth was shocked to learn Boris Johnson was in hot water over sexual impropriety: journalist

Charlotte Edwardes had revealed that our new prime minister had not only 'inappropriately grabbed her thigh', he had also done it to another woman at the same lunchtime meeting when he was still editor of the *Spectator* magazine.[83] One groping victim per lunch isn't enough for our nation's leader.

His successor as editor of the *Spectator* – and wife of Johnson's chief adviser and superpredicting dynamo Dominic Cummings – issued a statement saying, 'Boris was a good boss and nothing like this ever happened to me.' A perfectly valid defence. Barristers often draw the attention of court to all the homes the defendant *hasn't* broken into.

Ministers were shoved out to defend the Neanderthal seduction techniques of our erotically unbridled new prime minister. They claimed – probably rightly – that none of this would affect the important stuff – elections – because non-consensually groping unsuspecting women was 'priced in' to Johnson's character, and nobody really objected to the 'pinching of a knee'.[84] Johnson hadn't pinched her knee, though: he had groped her inner thigh. In her words, he grabbed 'enough inner flesh beneath his fingers' to make her sit bolt upright in shock. But the Tories had other things they preferred to talk about, such as 'Getting Brexit Done'.

OK then: how's that going?

Don't ask.

The government lost a Supreme Court judgement, which ruled Johnson's advice to the Queen about proroguing parliament was unlawful. This time, ministers were not shoved out to defend him – Number 10 ordered them to avoid all interviews, and not to make any comments on social media.

Instead, lowly backbench cannon fodder were given their scripts and sent out to die for Johnson's honour, which is a bit like sacrificing your life for the good of Brigadoon.

Their default line roughly translated like this: 'It's unfair to blame Boris Johnson for Boris Johnson's actions. It's really complicated running a country, and it's not his fault that he's nowhere near up to the task. Anyway, he was distracted by furiously lubricious IT lessons, and too busy groping female journalists, who we've just remembered we have to reiterate he didn't grope at all, despite the witnesses. Blame Dominic Cummings, who can scheme anything and superpredict everything, but didn't superpredict the highest court in the land would rule his scheme was illegal.'

Among the things Cummings also didn't superpredict was that one Eurosceptic former Cabinet minister would break ranks and tell reporters, 'I thought [Johnson] was fucking stupid to appoint Cummings and I told him so at the time.'[85]

I don't know if they've settled on an epitaph yet, but that must surely be on the shortlist.

As the news of the Supreme Court ruling came in, it was reported Johnson had personally phoned the Queen to apologise for embarrassing her, and that the Queen had listened with interest to his pretend grovelling, and then asked her aides for advice on how she could sack him.[86]

—

Thomas Cook collapsed at the end of September, and new Transport Secretary Grant Shapps made a statement reflecting how much the government cared about the distressed travellers, the loss of an iconic business, and the risk to 22,000 jobs.

Shapps cared enough to photocopy almost an entire speech from Chris Grayling.[87] It's heart-warming stuff.

On Grayling's watch, Monarch Airlines had gone bust. Grayling had made a speech about how sad it all was, which Shapps had copied verbatim. Not just a bit. Nine whole passages, consisting of hundreds of words. He'd taken the trouble to replace the words 'Monarch Airlines' with 'Thomas Cook', and had fiddled with the number of newly unemployed people he said he cared deeply about, but otherwise: identical.

Shapps told Parliament: 'We have never had the collapse of an airline or holiday company on this scale before,' which is, word for word, what Grayling said when it happened last time.

When discovered, Shapps said, 'I wasn't aware that some of these words had been used before,' which is a pretty substantial failure to understand photocopiers or how language operates. Let me help you, Grant: all words have been used before. That's what makes them words, rather than random noises. None of them are unique.

Except 'catastrofucknuckle'. That's an original, just for you.

—

In October it was time for the now traditional exciting arrival of the party conference, and equally exciting departure of some senior Tories.

First out was Geoffrey Clifton-Brown, last seen arranging complimentary holidays for party workers found guilty of electoral fraud. Surprisingly, he didn't quit the Tory party, merely the Tory conference, and his exit was temporary. It followed what was at first described by party officials as 'a small misunderstanding'.

This was upgraded to 'totally unacceptable behaviour' when it was revealed the small misunderstanding had required the presence of both security staff and paramedics, ended in a police statement, and at one point led to the windows to the media lounge being draped in cloth to obscure whatever a fulminating Clifton-Brown was getting up to inside. He was asked to leave his own conference, and then everybody just pretended it was all normal, and no further questions were answered.[88]

We move from there to Rory Stewart, who had lovely fun in front of an audience at the Royal Albert Hall, where he read from Boris Johnson's school reports from his time at Eton. Say what you want about Eton, but the teaching staff certainly had Johnson's number.

'Boris really has adopted a disgracefully cavalier attitude,' they wrote to Johnson's father. 'He sometimes seems affronted when criticised for what amounts to a gross failure of responsibility and surprised at the same time that he was not appointed Captain of the School. He is, in fact, pretty idle.'

It goes on: 'I think he honestly believes that it is churlish of us not to regard him as an exception, one who should be free of the network of obligation which binds everyone else.'

Stewart told the audience that his reading of the letter constituted his resignation from the Conservative Party, and they all laughed. He wasn't joking. He'd had enough, and formally resigned from the party a few hours later.[89] He was the second of the recent leadership candidates to recognise the party could no longer contain the moderate centre-right.

Instead, it was festooned with characters such as Owen Paterson – of whom more shortly – and Priti Patel. Our Home Secretary and human Horcrux began October having to be literally reminded not to giggle on live television when told how much damage her policies were going to do. As Andrew Marr read out a – let's face it, pretty lengthy – list of businesses, manufacturing giants and industry groups who were begging the government to vandalise the nation a bit less, Marr had to break off to say to the Home Secretary, 'I can't see why you're laughing.'

Of course, Tory MPs totally ignored the desperate appeals from industry, and turned the entire thing into a demand that Andrew Marr apologise.[90]

While that unseemly row was eating up time and attention, Paterson was quietly closing down his private thinktank, UK 2020. Under parliamentary rules, MPs must declare the source of funds for overseas visits. But Owen Paterson had chosen to set up UK 2020 as a private company, which meant the source of his funding could be kept secret.

Somebody – and we may never know who – had paid him to make nearly a dozen overseas trips to campaign for the hardest possible Brexit. Among the speeches to right-wing political groups in the USA, he called for Britain to abandon the 'precautionary principle'. This is the rule stating that innovations must be demonstrably safe before being deployed, which Paterson felt we could do without.[91]

Perhaps somebody had pressed the reset button on his brain since the horsemeat scandal, which culminated in the very same Owen Paterson personally heading off to The Hague to demand the

Europe he hates help him to solve the crisis he had caused by slashing Britain's precautionary principles.[92] We kept expecting Paterson to learn something, but it would be easier to teach my cat to rewire a plug.

It wasn't even the first time Paterson had done this sort of funded foreign jaunt to bang on about undermining Britain's safety, merely the first time he'd been secretive about the source of the funding. Months earlier, he and fellow Brexiteer David Davis had enjoyed a week-long trip to the USA, funded to the tune of £5,300 by the E Foundation, a campaign group allegedly favouring weaker food standards in Europe.[93]

While he was busy pocketing money from lobbyists apparently committed to us eating worse food, Davis was calmly reassuring the British that Brexit would not lead to lower food standards.[94]

—

In Brussels, Boris Johnson had struck a deal with the EU. 'We've got a great new deal that takes back control,' beamed the prime minister, extolling it as an unequivocal triumph. Not everybody agreed.

'As things stand, we could not support what is being suggested,' said the DUP, which was propping up his government.

'If you try and co-opt me, I'll fuck over the government, don't push me,' said one prominent Eurosceptic.[95]

'The referendum should never have been called,' said the people of Britain in opinion polls, and by a margin of two to one.[96] Only 26 per cent thought Johnson's deal would be beneficial to Britain.[97]

Regardless, Sajid Javid said the deal was 'self-evidently in our economic interest'.[98] When asked for *real* evidence of this self-evidence, he refused to release the Treasury's analysis, which doesn't suggest it gave the deal a ringing endorsement.

Nor did the independent National Institute of Economic and Social Research, which reported the deal would leave our economy even worse off than any of the deals May had failed to sell to us. It would cost us the equivalent of the GDP of Wales being removed from our economy.[99] Johnson's plan for Brexit was the same as giving every single person in the country a 7 per cent pay cut.[100]

But it was a deal, and that was all Johnson had promised. He had never said it wouldn't be a steaming pile of horseshit. And now it existed, he wasn't going to let anything stand in its way, least of all MPs pointing out it was a whole lot more awful than the incredibly awful thing that had made his predecessor the least popular PM in a century.

He'd already tried cancelling Parliament, and probably doubted the Queen would stand for it a second time; but he could still try to render the House of Commons ineffective. His latest amazing plan was to give Parliament no time to find all the gaping flaws in his previous amazing plan, so he proposed a timetable of just three days for MPs to scrutinise the 110 pages of dense legal documentation in his agreement.[101]

Frankly, this was Christopher Chope's wet dream.

There are 650 MPs. Even if they worked 18 hours a day, this would give each MP just four minutes to debate a treaty that would define the country and its trade for a generation. And that berserk timetable assumed no time for reading it, no time to get legal advice, and that no minister was required to take up time answering questions.

It also assumed nobody would ask for any changes. One of May's attempted deals had resulted in 100 pages of amendments, each of which needed time to be debated.[102] It hadn't been possible in three years. We now had three days.

Priti Patel was asked how the new customs arrangements for Northern Ireland, as described in the Withdrawal Agreement Bill, were going to work. She replied that she was 'not going to speak about hypotheticals'.[103] But it wasn't a hypothetical; it was literally written down in the bill. Perhaps she, too, hadn't found time to read it.

For all his chest-puffing bravado, Johnson had no parliamentary majority and was at the mercy of MPs. They rejected the enforced timetable by a thumping majority. So now, in the words of the Speaker, the Withdrawal Agreement was officially 'in limbo', and time had run out. We were due to bounce out of the EU without a deal in just one week's time.[104]

Boris Johnson had forged a path into Downing Street by promising his delighted members that Brexit would happen on 31 October, 'no ifs, no buts', and assuring them he would 'rather be dead in a ditch' than ask for a delay.

He asked for a delay. The EU sighed, shrugged, and said 'sure'.[105]

Many people wanted them to say no. Hardcore Leavers wanted them to say no so we could have a rock-hard Brexit, and then they could go home and joylessly masturbate themselves into a coma while watching *Zulu* and fantasising about how mighty Britain would become now it had the same trading status as Mongolia and Turkmenistan.[106]

The most fervent wing of Remain wanted the EU to say no so they could shout 'I told you so' at the world for the rest of their lives.

And gravediggers wanted the EU to say no so they would get paid to dig the ditch Boris Johnson had promised to die in.

Thankfully we had the calming voices of the ERG to keep everybody rational. 'I think if we don't leave on 31st of October, this country will explode,'[107] said Mark Francois, once again bringing to mind one of our greatest philosophers, Thomas Hobbes.

That's the guy who coined the phrase 'Nasty, brutish and short'.

—

Two important things happened at the end of October, neither of which was the important thing we'd expected.

First, it was agreed there would now be another slightly flexible three-month delay in Britain leaving the EU. Brexit was now happening on 31 January, or sooner if Johnson could get a deal through Parliament before then.[108]

Of course, in a land that had effectively given up on truth, even that date wasn't strictly accurate. We would leave the political elements of the EU, certainly, but we would enter a 'transition period', during which we would remain a member of the single market and customs union. And even that was contentious: the UK government refused to use the term 'transition period', and insisted we call it an 'implementation period', although beyond sheer bloody-mindedness it's hard to understand why.

Regardless, this interim period was set to last until December 2020, with a clause to allow it to be extended by up to two additional years,[109] during which further delays could be requested.

This would mean the process of leaving the EU because of one opinion poll would have taken us at least eight years. Not a single person born in this century had voted for it. And by now twice as many Britons believed the referendum was a mistake than believed it was a good idea.[110]

The second important thing was that MPs finally agreed to hold a general election, which would happen on 12 December. This meant instead of scrutinising the vastly important Brexit document before them, they all went off to campaign in their constituencies.

To help ensure he could win the parliamentary vote to trigger a general election, Johnson invited back the 21 Tory MPs he'd expelled just a month earlier.[111] Five of the 21 decided they no longer wanted to be in the same party as Johnson, and chose to stand either as Lib Dems or as independent candidates at the forthcoming election. A further 12 decided they didn't even want to be in the same building as Johnson, and announced they were standing down as MPs.[112]

—

Wary of repeating the catastrophic campaign of Theresa May, who had relied on the endless, moronic repetition of a four-word slogan, 'Strong and Stable Leadership', Johnson took a radically different route. He chose a *three*-word slogan: 'Get Brexit Done'. The election was all about leaving the EU, and that was all the Tories really wanted to talk about.

For good reason. Without Brexit, they were nothing.

The Institute for Fiscal Studies (IFS) did an in-depth analysis of their election promises and found there was 'essentially nothing new in the manifesto' of the Tory party, and that the Conservatives hadn't provided any 'properly credible' prospectus for how anything would be financed.[113] They didn't really want to *do* any governing, they just wanted to *be* a government. Five months earlier, somebody had decried 'politicians with no real purpose – other than just to gather up as many votes as they can'.[114] That somebody was now Chancellor of the Exchequer in a party fighting an election with no policies.

Regardless, there was a campaign, so they had to say something. They took the tried-and-tested route of talking absolute bollocks that the papers would unquestioningly repeat ad nauseum, like free advertising for the ravings of a madman. Wall-to-wall coverage would embed Tory nonsense in the public's mind. It didn't matter that it was all a lie; it only mattered that it was a big, simple lie that could be stabbed directly into your hippocampus and stay there.

Meanwhile Labour announced something between umpteen and one squillion policies, which people nodded sagely at, broadly agreed sounded lovely, dear, and then promptly forgot.

Javid made yet another promise that austerity was about to end – this would make it the fourth major announcement of the end of austerity since 2015. Yet the IFS study found his policies would lead to an additional 14 per cent of cuts to public spending, and in the absence of 14 per cent tax increases, that meant more austerity.[115]

Johnson announced £3.7 billion to build 40 new hospitals. Experts put the cost of 40 hospitals at £24 billion.[116] But we no longer cared about experts in this country, and the 40 hospitals claim went largely unchallenged. Few paid much attention when it was revealed that 34 of the 'new hospitals' were either small-scale building projects to make minor improvements to existing hospitals, or a pot of seed money intended to attract enough private investment to get the work done. Only six hospitals would be new,[117] and to put that into context, the 1970 government built 66 hospitals.[118]

The Tories promised us 20,000 new police officers, which very nearly replaced the 21,732 police officers thrown away by – oh yes, that's right: the Tories.[119] Population increases since 2010 meant we'd end up with many fewer police per head of population than when Cameron came to power in 2010.[120]

'One thing in your manifesto is the promise to deliver 50,000 more nurses,' said Sky News.

'Yes,' said Boris Johnson.

'How many of those will actually be new?' asked Sky.

'Thirty-one thousand.'[121]

It got better: after half a decade of anti-immigrant dog-whistling, the Tory manifesto promised the nurses would be sourced via 'foreign recruitment'.[122]

And just as the election campaign kicked off, the National Audit Office found the government had once again failed to deliver a single new home, despite yet another Tory promise to build 200,000 by 2020.[123]

—

During a head-to-head televised debate between Boris Johnson and Jeremy Corbyn, Conservative HQ rebranded its Twitter account as FactCheckUK, which led to Twitter issuing a warning to the British government against any further attempts to mislead the British public.[124]

'We made it absolutely clear it is the Conservative party website,' said Tory chairman James Cleverly about the thing that wasn't a website and wasn't labelled 'Conservative Party'.[125] He insisted Tories would never stoop so low as to con people by falsely claiming to be a different organisation.

The following week the Tories published a fake Labour Manifesto website and sponsored Google to push it to the top of the search results.[126]

And the week after that, they published a video that doctored the responses of Kier Starmer to make it look as if he was incapable of answering a question. Tory MP Johnny Mercer was livid when he found out that by retweeting the video, he'd become an unwitting agent of misinformation.

'It would appear this has inexplicably been doctored at the end. I apologise and will remove it,' he tweeted. 'I will call this out – whichever side does it, including my own.'[127]

Days later the fake news video was still on his Twitter account. People asked why he hadn't deleted it as promised.

If I deleted the original, people would be saying "what video?", was the explanation he offered. The video is still there, quietly spreading misinformation. Mercer advises people who see it to 'get off Twitter'.[128]

—

Lee Anderson had a spectacularly exciting election. It started out with his delightful plans to make any council tenants who irritated him work in forced labour camps. They should be 'in the field, picking potatoes or any other seasonal vegetables, back in the tent, cold shower, lights out, six o'clock, same again the next day'.[129]

Working backwards through the Nazi handbook, next he was investigated for anti-Semitism when it was discovered he was an active member of a Facebook group supporting conspiracy theories about financier George Soros. Two other candidates were also investigated. There was Sally-Ann Hart, who had been spreading a rumour that Soros – who is Jewish – controls the EU. She also 'liked' a Nazi slogan on Facebook. And another candidate, Richard Short, contended British Jewish journalists were more loyal to Israel than their own country.[130]

But Anderson went one better: even while awaiting the outcome of an inquiry into his alleged anti-Semitism, he was confronted with the allegation he'd signed a letter containing a phrase linked to 'a far-right antisemitic conspiracy theory'[131] and sent it to the *Telegraph*.[132]

Are we finished with Lee Anderson's election? We are not. TV journalists accompanied him as he went door to door, meeting enthusiastically pro-Tory constituents. 'There is no way Labour are ever getting my vote,' said voter Steve, and then vigorously endorsed Anderson's views on forced labour camps for anybody who made him feel a bit shirty.

Unfortunately, Lee Anderson forgot he was wearing a mic for the TV cameras, so was recorded briefing voter Steve – who we should really call Lee Anderson's long-term friend Steve – before their impromptu and completely genuine encounter.

'Make out you know who I am,' Anderson told Steve. 'You know I'm the candidate, but not a friend, all right?'[133]

Those words may also apply to council tenants and Jews.

—

And then there's Boris Johnson's campaign. Where do we begin?

Let's start with the first distressing signs of Johnson's seemingly years-long Mr Benn fixation, which takes the form of him engaging in almost daily dressing-up games rather than governing the country. 'Being photographed pretending to do something' is the new 'doing something'. In this instance he posed as a builder and – just like real builders do – immediately drove a JCB through a wall while his zookeepers stood around and clapped.[134]

Johnson then held an interview with ITN during which their reporter took out his phone to show the prime minister a photo of a four-year-old boy with suspected pneumonia. He'd attended a Leeds hospital that had experienced such severe cuts they couldn't find a bed, trolley or chair for the child, so he ended up lying for hours on a pile of coats on the floor.

Johnson said, 'We have every sympathy,' refused to look at the photo, and then stole the reporter's phone.[135]

When other journalists approached him, he mouthed 'Oh, for fuck's sake' and hid in a fridge.[136] You're right to think this sounds implausible, but he plaused it anyway.

After he'd emerged from cold storage, it was back to giving us the facts. During his very first address to the nation as prime minister back in July, Johnson had said: 'I am announcing now – on the steps of Downing Street – that we will fix the crisis in social care once and for all with a clear plan we have prepared'. So now, months later, people asked what that clear plan was.

'Cross-party consensus,' Johnson replied, would 'bring forward an answer.'[137]

So the clear plan you announced on the steps of Downing Street doesn't exist? Well, never mind, at least there's consensus.

There was 'no consensus' on the social care plan, said Housing Minister Robert Jenrick.[138]

Let's leave that there and ask about the NHS. Nothing to worry about, said Johnson, because when it came to Brexit, 'The NHS is not on the table.'[139]

Maybe worry a bit, said Tory MP Nick Boles, because Boris Johnson is 'a compulsive liar who has betrayed every single person he has ever had any dealings with. He is a man with an all-consuming ego, utterly without conscience.'[140]

Well, that's reassuring. Let's move on to the Brexit deal: will there be a border in Northern Ireland?

'There will be no checks on goods from GB to Northern Ireland or Northern Ireland to GB,' said Johnson.

'There will be checks as goods head into Northern Ireland,' said a leak from the Treasury, clarifying the prime minister's words, which we may have been foolish enough to misunderstand.[141]

'There will be no forms, no checks, no barriers of any kind,' repeated a rambling and seemingly drunk Johnson in front of business leaders in Northern Ireland a few days later.[142]

A Treasury report into his deal stated there would definitely be checks and barriers, and the cumulative cost of them would be the same as a 30 per cent tariff on trade.[143]

'Actually, Northern Ireland has got a great deal. You keep free movement, you keep access to the single market and, as it says in the deal, unfettered access to the UK,' said Johnson.[144]

Wow, that does sound like a great deal! Can the rest of Britain have the same?

No!

—

It was in this spirit of absolute candour that Johnson decided not to release a report into Russian influence in British politics until after

British politics had given him another five years in power. There's not enough time, claimed the prime minister: it has to go through a 'sign-off process' before anyone can see it.[145]

The Tory chair of the Intelligence and Security Committee – which had written the report – called the decision to not publish it 'jaw-dropping',[146] and said the reasons given for not publishing were 'bogus'.[147]

But evidence already in the public realm, plus a series of leaks, drew a slightly worrying picture of why the Tories – and Johnson in particular – might want to keep things schtum. We begin with Conservative Friends of Russia, a club for Tories who thought Putin was a simply terrific chap, and which as recently as September had sent activists to Russia with the tab being picked up by the Russian cultural agency. Nothing too dodgy about that. But then it emerged that the senior Russian diplomat acting as liaison with Conservative Friends of Russia – Sergey Nalobin – was the son of a top-ranking agent in the Russian security services.[148]

Nobody should be condemned for their dad's career. The younger Nalobin may have been blameless at the time he took photos with Tory figures including John Whittingdale, David Lidington, William Hague and Boris Johnson. But then it was discovered that Nalobin lived in a Moscow apartment building known as 'FSB House' because it was where employees of the Russian spy agency FSB lived. There were reports that he was the figurehead of a five-year programme to infiltrate the Conservatives by cultivating close personal relationships. Nalobin reportedly described Boris Johnson as 'our good friend' (and that 'our' is very telling).[149]

Sergei Cristo, a Russian-born Conservative activist, said: 'Soon after arriving in London, [Nalobin] told me that his masters back in Moscow wanted to build on the relationship of Putin's United Russia party with Britain's Conservatives in the Council of Europe and that he wanted United Russia to be officially affiliated with [the Conservative] party. There was also a suggestion that UK-registered but Russian-owned companies might well be willing to make financial contributions to the Conservatives.'[150]

I'm sure that made a lot of ears prick up in the fundraising department of the Tory party.

Cristo described Conservative Friends of Russia as a 'muppet show', pointedly noting that not a single member of its committee had been remotely critical of Russia, not even when Russia was poisoning people in Salisbury, or backing massively violent conflicts in Syria and Chechnya.

Wilier figures than the abandoned candyfloss now leading the party suddenly discovered they were washing their hair on the days Conservative Friends of Russia met. Well, William Hague probably wasn't, but the group's president, Malcolm Rifkind, resigned, citing concerns about the group's behaviour and political direction; he was followed out the door by Robert Buckland and Nigel Evans.

You can see why stories suggesting the prime minister was being deliberately targeted and befriended by a likely Russian agent acting on orders from the Kremlin might not go down well during an election campaign. David Anderson, an independent member of the House of Lords and a national security expert, said, 'It invites, I'm afraid, suspicion of the government and its motives.'[151]

But what were Russia's motives?

Belgium's Institute for European Studies found a key foreign-policy objective of Russia was 'to employ a tactic of "divide and rule" whereby it either aims at weakening the centre (Brussels) by playing off one Member State against the other, or by undermining EU cohesion and coherence as a whole'.[152]

The US Center for Strategic and International Studies found 'Russia's ambition is to create a multipolar world' by weakening the West, specifically the European Union, which, due to its proximity, was a greater hindrance to the ambitious expansion of Moscow's influence than the USA could be.[153]

Basically, Russia wanted to undermine the power of the West, and specifically to divide the EU. The Kremlin saw a great opportunity when one of the major political parties in a nation riven by tabloid-driven Eurosceptic sentiment went absolutely tonto and started screaming they'd had enough of laws and stability and food. From now on, we were going to take to the high seas, and wildly buccaneer around, shacking up with every country on earth, like some kind of pirate hooker.

I'm not suggesting Russian influence was the sole reason so many Tories wanted Brexit: simply that Brexit aligned nicely with Russia's policy agenda. So they sent a questionable bunch of diplomat-spies off to London with orders to make friends with Boris Johnson, and to encourage us to get down the docks and dress pretty.

And what was the motive that drove the Tory party to unquestioningly welcome this burgeoning relationship with Russia?

Ker-ching!

In the year leading up to the 2019 election, the former Russian finance minister's wife handed over £450,000 to the Tory party.[154] Alexander Temerko, employed by Russia's defence ministry, handed the Conservatives £1.2 million. Russian billionaire Lev Mikheev – with offices next to the Kremlin – gave the party £212,000.[155]

At least another £500,000 was handed to Conservatives from Russian business executives. A London-based PR firm was employed by Putin's government to portray a positive image of Russia and did so by handing over £177,000 to the Tories. Being a PR firm, it's hard to imagine they didn't also apply their skills to influence Tory opinion.[156]

Since 2010, investigations revealed, Russians had been behind more than £3.5 million of donations to the Conservative Party. In total, nine Tory donors were reported to have been mentioned by name in the report into the threat posed by Russian interference in Britain's democracy.[157]

It's all legal. But laws are strange things. For example, in Britain it's illegal to be drunk in a pub, and an act of treason to put a stamp upside down on an envelope.[158] The legality (or otherwise) of an action doesn't tell us anything about its morality, its sense, or the motives that directed it.

—

So: quite a busy election, at the end of which Labour suffered its worst defeat since 1935[159] and Boris Johnson romped home with a majority of 80 MPs.[160]

It didn't seem to matter that he had a decades-long record of ineptitude, mendacity and indolence, or that his soul had been reduced to a paper-thin husk by being constantly, lasciviously ground against his high-grade narcissism. To his fans, his bounciness was a wonderfully invigorating political novelty that made his obvious flaws irrelevant. It seemed nothing could dent him. Where other politicians seemed heavy and dull, Johnson seemed effervescent and Tiggerish.

To his detractors, that bounciness was a puerile act. He was a one-trick pony, and his trick had been done to death. The nation deserved more than a shallow, flashy shell of a man, and we all knew that his frothy persona could be blown away in an instant by events. His ability to evade political gravity didn't make us see him as an irrepressible eruption of positivity. His bounce and lightness simply made him unbearable.

It was a bleak time for people who had predicted Brexit would be a disaster. That fight was lost, and nothing would now prevent us from departing the EU with what was, even if we were very fortunate, the fifth-best deal we'd been offered.

Bleak times too for anybody who was to the left of the Tory party, a boundary which, we soon learned, had shifted once again: the leader of Britain First – a far-right organisation described as 'neo-fascist' by CNN[161] – officially joined the Conservatives.[162]

The Tories had no discernible policy agenda beyond Brexit, a project which they assured us would be finished in just one month. God knows what they'd do with their remaining years in office, for which they had announced barely any policies, and during which they would be practically unstoppable.

'I will not let you down,' promised Johnson.[163]

'This is going to be a fantastic year for Britain.'[164]

2020

A Fantastic Year for Britain

January

On 17 November 2019, an unnamed 55-year-old in Wuhan, China, was hospitalised with what at first appeared to be a case of pneumonia that didn't respond to the usual treatments.[1] As a medical anomaly it was interesting, but interesting things happen in hospitals all the time, a fact to which George Clooney owes his career. Nothing about a solitary, slightly unusual case of pneumonia raised immediate concerns, because why would it?

Within weeks, there were dozens of cases, and doctors started comparing notes. A disturbing pattern emerged. The evidence was presented to Chinese medical authorities in the middle of December.

Wuhan, with a population of 11 million, is bigger than London and Paris combined. It's a major transportation hub, with dozens of railways and major expressways connecting the city to nine neighbouring provinces. If you set out to design the ideal location from which to spread a virus quickly, it would be hard to do better. China's authorities recognised the risk and took urgent, drastic action: to prevent further contagion, Wuhan was locked down immediately.[2]

On the last day of 2019 the outbreak was reported to the World Health Organization (WHO), and within days the WHO published a worldwide Disease Outbreak Alert.[3] By the time another week had passed, the Chinese health authorities had described the structure of what became known as Covid-19, and had shared the details with the global scientific community. The crisis was underway, and global authorities were reacting with gravity, urgency, decisiveness and alarm.

—

In Britain we didn't take a lot of notice of this, because we were all busy starting the best year ever.

Boris Johnson had celebrated winning the 2016 Brexit referendum by ignoring the country and awarding himself a big, drunken party; and after his 2019 election victory he did the same thing again, but on a grander scale. A Tory donor, David Ross, coughed up £15,000 to send Johnson off to Mustique for a well-earned rest after his exhausting five weeks of running a new government that was committed to implementing zero new policies. Johnson being Johnson, he didn't bother declaring the £15,000 as a gift, and was later found guilty of breaking rules governing MPs' declarations.[4]

Despite having immediately proven his own unsuitability for the job, Johnson put pressure on his equally unsuitable henchpersons. 'Shape up or be sacked within weeks,'[5] he told a room that contained Dominic Raab, Priti Patel, Gavin Williamson, Matt Hancock, Liz Truss, Grant Shapps, Jacob Rees-Mogg and James Cleverly, all of whom still attended Cabinet a year later.[6]

Yet despite Johnson's threats to the smorgasbord of odium and banality that gathered around his Cabinet table, vast leaps forward in competence and delivery didn't materialise. His backbenchers felt newly empowered by an 80-seat majority that meant their default setting of frenzied insurrection would no longer risk collapsing the government. They suddenly threatened a revolt over HS2. Dozens of them claimed, with some justification, that it was a 'catastrophic waste of money'. Boris Johnson gestured to that same comfortable majority of 80, knew he was safe from any insurgency, and completely ignored the rebels.[7]

It must have been a different Boris Johnson who in 2018 had called for the HS2 project to be cancelled because the £56 billion budget could be better spent elsewhere.[8] Now the budget had spiralled to £107 billion, so he suddenly thought it was worth every pound, which in this sentence means £1 per second for 3,392 years. Or £3,600 per hour, every hour since Tutankhamun died.[9] Money well spent to allow business travellers to get to Manchester one hour faster during the first time in human history when technology meant face-to-face meetings were no longer necessary.[10]

The same week: 'Protecting vulnerable children will remain our priority after Brexit,' said the PM's spokesman, just as Johnson dropped the government's guarantee of protections for vulnerable unaccompanied child refugees.[11] Tory domination of Parliament comfortably overrode objections, and they voted to shit on parentless kids fleeing war-torn regions by a majority of 348 to 252. Amnesty International said the government was doing 'deliberate and destructive' harm to children.[12]

—

On 24 January, Professor Neil Ferguson from the government's Scientific Advisory Group for Emergencies (SAGE) identified the frightening transmissibility of Covid, and told a COBRA meeting that we should immediately stop contact between people.[13] The government wasn't keen to do this – the economy was already suffering due to Brexit, but those who had fought for us to leave the EU now needed to show there would be no negative consequences. Any further economic harm would be disastrous to their major policy project, namely: winning the next election. So we stayed open. For months.

By now Covid had burst out of China, reached Europe, and was ravaging Italy. Despite this, and despite Ferguson's warnings, the UK risk level was merely raised from 'low' to 'moderate'. The chief medical officer said the government should 'plan for all eventualities',[14] so the government rushed ahead to announce a plan to crowdfund £500,000 to finish repairs on Big Ben, so it could ring as we left the EU.[15]

Brexit was Johnson's crowning glory, and his team of infallible advisers and gurus, imported into Downing Street straight from the Leave campaign, didn't want anything to cast a shadow on their moment. A deadly plague wasn't as big a deal as making Big Ben go bong, and Vote Leave supremo Daniel Hannan once again demonstrated his genius for prognostication by proclaiming: 'The coronavirus isn't going to kill you. It really isn't.'[16]

—

At 11 p.m. on 31 January, Britain finally left the EU, only 1,659 days, £200 billion in costs,[17] three prime ministers and 60 ministerial resignations[18] since John Redwood, the Oracle of Wokingham, had predicted it would be quick and easy.[19]

The cost of Brexit in the four years since the referendum was almost identical to the UK's entire combined contribution to the EU since we joined 47 years earlier.[20] Except of course, we still hadn't left at all. This was merely the start of a transition period, as defined by the deal Johnson had struck.

And what did a senior figure from Johnson's own Vote Leave campaign think of that wonderful new deal?

'It's crap. It's basically the same as May's deal.'[21]

To mark the occasion, Boris Johnson flew to the talismanic, Brexit-backing North-East of England for a celebratory Cabinet meeting on the day we finally almost (but not quite) left the EU.[22] As he landed at Newcastle Airport, the UK's first two coronavirus patients were confirmed in the city and rushed into quarantine, and if he even noticed it's hard to find any evidence.[23]

Johnson made a speech extolling Britain's newly acquired 'power of independent thought and action'.[24] Acquiring it doesn't mean using it. Between 31 January and 30 March, his government missed eight meetings or conference calls to discuss the Covid outbreak with other heads of state or health ministers.[25]

As Johnson was speaking in Sunderland, *The Lancet* medical journal issued a warning about the growing crisis: 'Outbreaks in major cities globally could become inevitable,'[26] it read, while the WHO declared Covid-19 a 'public health emergency of international concern'.[27]

—

But before we get to that, a quick detour to the exotic bookkeeping habits of mobile network operator Lycamobile, which had been entertaining and exasperating authorities in various countries for over a year. Examples of their approach to financial activity included almost being struck off twice in three years for failure to submit accounts, and managing to avoid paying any corporation tax for three years.[28]

Nothing unusual about that, in a country diligently run by the party of law, order and fierce guardianship of our nation's money. But it was tricky to immediately see why, in London, Lyca appeared to employ at least three men to drive around in an unmarked car, depositing bags containing up to £1 million in cash at various post offices. Lyca said the million pounds in cash were the result of 'day to day banking' and the deposits were sanctioned by the Post Office.[29]

Across town, HMRC were told that almost £46 million in previously undeclared Lyca turnover was suddenly unearthed by Lyca's auditors, and questions were asked.

Meanwhile in Sri Lanka, officials were investigating offshore entities in the Lyca empire, to try to establish why their name kept cropping up in connection with corruption allegations reaching the highest levels of the Sri Lankan government.[30] In 2016 Lyca's own auditors reportedly said its finances were 'so opaque' that it couldn't account for £134 million of cash and assets.[31]

Eventually, French authorities investigating suspected money laundering and tax fraud involving Lyca arrested 19 people and made a formal request for additional raids to be carried out at Lycamobile premises in London.

The British refused. When asked by the French to explain why we weren't cooperating, it was reported that HMRC candidly wrote: '[Lyca] are the biggest corporate donor to the Conservative Party.'[32]

Oh well, that's fine, then.

Lycamobile deny all wrongdoing. There doesn't appear to be a comparable statement of innocence from the Tories.

February

Even faced with an impending global pandemic, Boris Johnson couldn't be arsed to attend any of the emergency COBRA meetings.[1] He was more focused on funding his latest divorce than with the future of the nation, as Dominic Cummings recorded in his blog.

'Dom,' said Johnson to Cummings. 'I want to run something by you. Do you think it's OK if I spend a lot of time writing my Shakespeare book?'

'What do you mean?'

'This fucking divorce, very expensive. And this job. It's like getting up every morning pulling a 747 down the runway. I love writing, I love it; I want to write my Shakespeare book.'[2]

Yet despite Cummings beseeching him to stay in the office and do his fucking job, Johnson preferred to take another couple of weeks' break from being prime minister – it had, after all, been a whole month since his illegitimate holiday in a luxury private villa in Mustique. So off he buggered to the taxpayer-funded 115-room lakeside mansion of Chevening with his pregnant girlfriend Carrie Symonds,[3] from where he sent messages to Number 10 telling them Covid was no more than 'the new swine flu'. In Italy they had moved to 'war-like measures' to tackle the crisis engulfing them,[4] and the other leaders of the G7 group of economically advanced nations held urgent teleconferences to consider unified action.[5] Meanwhile what was Johnson's approach to the crisis?

'Within a month of the election,' wrote Cummings, 'he was bored with the PM job and wanted to get back to what he loves while shaking down the publishers for some extra cash.'[6]

The only event to draw Johnson's attention away from his personal whims was the annual Tory Black and White fundraising ball, at which Brexit commemorative coins were flogged off for £60,000 a pop.[7] I know what I'm going to buy with mine: £44,000 worth of euros. The event coincided with the National Security Communications Team warning that half a million Britons could die from Covid,[8] while in a comfort to us all, Dominic Cummings was spending his time writing vast, rambling blog posts and advertising for 'weirdos and misfits' to help in his project of smashing Britain's system of governance.[9] He needed weirdos to help him because, as his blog admitted, many of the decisions he was making were 'well outside [his] circle of competence'.[10]

As if to prove this, on the day Johnson posed with David Attenborough while announcing Britain would host the COP26 climate summit, Cummings took it upon himself to fire the head of COP26, who then reported that Dom had admitted he 'didn't really understand' the issue of climate change. The Cabinet committee on climate hadn't met once since it was formed four months earlier.[11] It wasn't long since Johnson had written that concern about the climate was 'without foundation',[12] although I doubt he mentioned that to Attenborough.

So environmental science wasn't one of Cummings' competencies, and virology didn't seem to be one either. Or humanity. As Italy declared a state of emergency,[13] and China entirely locked down a province of over 57 million people to protect its citizens,[14] Cummings told guests at a private party that the government's strategy on Covid was 'herd immunity, protect the economy, and if that means some pensioners die, too bad'.[15]

—

We'd had nearly 10 years of such laissez-faire contempt for matters affecting the lower orders, or requiring plans with a longer half-life than tomorrow's *Daily Mail*. As a result, the UK was suffering some of the worst poverty in Europe.

What we are still supposed to call 'Tory economic competence' had led to us having a higher proportion of children living in poverty than they had in Poland,[16] which ranked more than 20 places below us in the list of richest countries.[17] During that Conservative decade, one-third of English children had been living in poverty for at least three years running.[18] Britain's wages had fallen further than anywhere else in the OECD, except for Greece and Mexico.[19]

But we had simultaneously seen the number of millionaires increase by more than 50 per cent.[20] People over 65 – the group most likely to vote Tory – had seen their average wealth increase by 96 per cent, and now one in five of them were millionaires.[21] The richest 1,000 families had seen their wealth more than double, and now owned more than the poorest 26 million Britons combined.[22] Those richest 1,000 had increased – *increased* – their wealth by nearly £200 billion, while for the rest of us the government implemented nearly £200 billion of cumulative cuts to welfare, justice, defence, policing, infrastructure, council services, education and more.[23]

—

The Tories were so steadfastly ignoring the surging pandemic that in early February the major point of communication between the UK government and the epicentre in Wuhan was an accidental meeting between the PM's dad and the Chinese Ambassador to the UK. And we only know of this because Stanley Johnson, surely the font of his son's competence, emailed the ambassador's private concerns to UK officials, but accidentally copied in the BBC.[24]

Meanwhile his son was picking up where David Cameron left off: never mind the terrifying existential crises, it's time for some gongs to be handed out. Johnson's honours shortlist included Michael Spencer (£5 million in donations to the Tories), Jon Moynihan (£100,000 to Boris Johnson's leadership campaign) and Charles Moore (the terrifyingly Johnson-supporting editor of the *Telegraph*).

Also getting a peerage, Peter Cruddas, who had donated £50,000 to Johnson's leadership bid, handed £3 million to the Tories, and been found by a court to have offered access to the prime minister for £250,000 a pop.[25]

While Johnson was applying his full, four-second attention span to giving gold stars and ribbons to his schoolfriends and benefactors, behind the scenes the government was finally firing up the full might of the state to battle Covid. In China, it had taken just two days to quarantine an area larger than Greece, ban all cars from roads, stop all transport in or out of the province, close all shops and businesses except for those related to food or medicine, and bar anybody from leaving their home for any reason other than one hour per week for vital food shopping.[26]

In Britain, we published a poster telling people to put their tissues in the bin.[27]

Fret not: we were 'doing everything we can to protect the public', said Matt Hancock, who was both our health secretary and the answer to the question: whatever became of that volleyball from the Tom Hanks desert island movie?[28] 'The government has detailed plans for how to deal with an outbreak like this,' he claimed, and everybody wiped their brow and exhaled with deep relief. Everybody, that is, except for people who knew what those plans were.[29]

Back in October 2016 the government had carried out Exercise Cygnus, a three-day training drill to prepare for dealing with a pandemic. The report on Cygnus was shown to Cabinet, but a senior government figure said the findings were considered 'too terrifying' to be made public. 'It showed gaping holes in Britain's emergency preparedness, resilience and response plan.'[30]

The Tories then did nothing for a year, after which the National Risk Register warned the Cabinet Office: 'there is a high probability of a pandemic'. They predicted hundreds of thousands of deaths and suggested we should probably do something to avoid such an outcome. Instead, the government spent its time debating whether to scrap 300-year-old wigs and squabbling about the quantum state of its impact assessments for Brexit.

Another year sauntered by, and in 2018 a government biological security strategy produced recommendations to address the risk of pandemics. 'It was not properly implemented,' said a chief scientific adviser to the government.[31]

To free up resources to cope with figuring out what colour Brexit was, Theresa May decided to suspend the government's Threats, Hazards, Resilience and Contingency Committee (THRCC). This was bad enough, but then Boris Johnson scrapped it altogether within days of entering office, without having any discussions about virus-control planning.[32]

And then came Covid.

As the virus raged through Italy, Dominic Cummings finally got around to asking Matt Hancock if Britain's preparations for a pandemic were up to date. Hancock reassured him the 'full plans' for a pandemic were 'regularly refreshed'.[33]

Once every thousand years is 'regular'. Regularly doesn't mean recently.

'From about mid-January onwards, it was absolutely obvious that this was serious, very serious,' said the key adviser on disease modelling to the government,[34] which is why a mere *two months* after that, the prime minister finally got around to attending a COBRA meeting about the pandemic.[35] Not immediately, though. First, he decided to delay the meeting for a few days so he could have a long weekend at Chequers. Downing Street were unable to provide details of his diary for those three days, so it was unclear what vitally important thing took precedence over a global pandemic.[36]

It was two months since the WHO warned of Covid. Six months since Johnson closed the THRCC. Four years since Exercise Cygnus. And this was the moment Boris Johnson chose to tell Reuters he'd been listening to scientific advice all along, but they'd been 'slow to sound the alarm',[37] while his government quietly sold 279,000 items of our stockpiled personal protective equipment (PPE) to overseas buyers.[38]

—

Despite the news pouring out of China and Italy, the Tories decided not much was going on; the PM was busy with shagging and Shakespeare, and in the face of the rising pandemic the government kept its idiots occupied by running a Cabinet reshuffle, while in the words of Dominic Cummings, 'lots of key people were literally skiing'.[39]

Sajid Javid unexpectedly had a massive strop after clashing with Cummings, who had recently engineered the sacking of Javid's aides.

Now the Chancellor quit, saying 'no self-respecting minister' could work under such conditions.[40] No self-respecting minister could be in that Cabinet at all, a point that seemed to elude Mr Javid. He was replaced by Rishi Sunak, whose primary skill appeared to be taking his jacket off on Instagram.

But it wasn't all terrible, terrible news: we also got rid of Esther McVey, and I wouldn't be shocked if you had completely missed her contribution to public life, since she's so dense no light can escape her. She was sacked as housing minister after only eight months in the job, during which her only noticeable achievement was revealing how impressed she was with the 'whole new way of doing' architecture. Apparently, she revealed, there were now people 'doing it on a computer'.[41]

Just prior to being sacked, she had put forward her theory about why so many people were attending food banks – they were making all the wrong choices. 'When I was growing up, my parents put money into food, utility bills and the mortgage,' she said. But now people felt 'they've got to have an iPad and a phone', complained the woman who, as Secretary of State for Work and Pensions, had been personally responsible for benefits changes that required the claimant to have access to a phone and the internet.[42]

But Matt Hancock survived the reshuffle and remained health minister. This wasn't a universally popular decision: Dominic Cummings told Boris Johnson that unless he sacked Hancock, 'We are going to kill people and it's going to be a catastrophe.'[43]

March

On 3 March, SAGE told the government it should 'advise against greetings such as shaking hands and hugging'. Having heard that advice, later that same day Boris Johnson told reporters he'd visited a hospital with coronavirus patients and 'shook hands with everybody, you will be pleased to know, and I continue to shake hands'. He went on to tell the public that 'people obviously can make up their own minds' about whether to follow scientific advice.[1]

Those scientific advisers were concerned. The government 'should be sharing the data as much as possible', said Professor John Ashton of Public Health England. 'The public needs to know if [Covid] is in their area on a daily basis.' So the government decided it would only collate and release Covid information once a week.[2]

Two days later, Johnson once more demonstrated his opinion that the jury was still out on medical science, and shook hands with everybody as he made an appearance on hard-hitting news programme *This Morning*.[3] He was interviewed just after a segment in which Phillip Schofield got his head stuck in a wigwam for dogs, and it was in this solemn atmosphere that our prime minister expatiated various new theories about what to do about the pandemic.

You knew things were becoming serious because Johnson had turned up looking like he'd brushed his hair with a toffee apple, and in the course of a single, uninterrupted stream of consciousness suggested we 'take it on the chin' and 'allow the disease, as it were, to move through the population' while avoiding any 'draconian measures' and simultaneously taking 'all the measures that we can' to stop the disease.[4] If his left brain was talking to his right brain, they were speaking different languages. Neither of them seemed to be sending messages to his mouth, and his ears had downed tools in protest at all those doctors who kept bleating on about boring, finicky, joke-free shit, such as simple ways to not die.

He hazily waffled on about the multiplicity of directions he could travel, if only Holly and Phillip's sofa wasn't so damned comfortable. Surveying the options before him, Johnson appeared to want to select them all, and none of them. Margaret Thatcher's precept that 'advisers advise, ministers decide' appeared to have been taken by Boris Johnson as a challenge to be overcome: he would decide nothing, and damn the consequences.

It was now 7 March, and shit was about to speed up precipitously.

In a week there had been a 30 per cent increase in UK Covid cases.[5] Dr Rupert Read, an expert on the precautionary principle, published a briefing he'd sent to the government on 24 February, recommending they suspend air travel.[6] Airports remained open.

A month later, they still remained open, even though thousands petitioned Parliament to close them.[7] They remained open a year later, and a year after that too. We never stopped flights into the UK. After a decade of aggressively campaigning for Brexit so we could 'control our borders', the government flatly refused to control our borders against the spread of Covid. Over 130 nations introduced travel restrictions in the early days of the pandemic, but not us. 'It is very hard to understand why [Britain] persists in having this open-borders policy. It is most peculiar,' said Professor Gabriel Scally of the Royal Society of Medicine.[8]

And then health minister and exuberantly gormless flapdoodle Nadine Dorries contracted coronavirus, and suddenly the crisis was close to home. There was, by now, a moderate chance that the Tories might wake up to the threat.[9] Any day now.

By 12 March almost every country in Europe had closed schools. Not us. Only the UK and Belarus were still sending kids to school, but to be fair, the government did have more important things to deal with.[10] Newspapers had published a story about the dog belonging to Johnson's fiancée, Carrie Symonds, and she was cross about it. Downing Street staff spent the day coping with her demands that they 'deal with that'.[11]

—

The next day, 13 March, was a big one.

The WHO issued clear guidance: track and trace the outbreak urgently. 'You can't fight a virus if you don't know where it is,' said their director general.

So the UK government announced that it would 'no longer try to track and trace everybody suspected of having the virus'.[12] Instead, senior advisers suggested the nation should be encouraged to have 'chickenpox-style parties' to spread infection as much as possible.[13]

Amazingly, there were still some spineless naysayers who *didn't* think deliberately killing 100,000 people was a good plan. Almost 230 scientists wrote to the government, urging them to introduce more stringent measures, and fast. The government argued that 'people will become fed up' if they had to suffer restrictions. So far, only 21 had died, but infection numbers were doubling every couple of days.[14]

That evening, more than *three months* after WHO declared a crisis, the government finally got around to checking what their pandemic action plan was. There was a shock in store.

'There is no plan, we're in huge trouble,' Deputy Cabinet Secretary Helen MacNamara told Dominic Cummings. 'I think we're absolutely fucked. I think this country's heading for a disaster, I think we're going to kill thousands of people.'[15]

And that's without even factoring in Matt Hancock.

—

A fish rots from the head, and we were being led by Sir Plankton Churchill. Senior figures in Downing Street singled out Boris Johnson as the greatest block to the nation taking action.

'There's no way you're at war if your PM isn't there,' said one senior adviser. 'And what you learn about Boris was he didn't chair any meetings. He liked his country breaks. He didn't work weekends. It was like working for an old-fashioned chief executive in a local authority 20 years ago. There was a real sense that he didn't do urgent crisis planning. It was exactly like people feared he would be.'[16]

As week after week of government chaos, indolence and inaction rolled by, private companies and institutions took their own steps. The Premier League suspended matches. The Champions League was postponed. The Six Nations, Formula 1 and countless music and cultural events were suspended or cancelled.[17]

The cancellation of the Cheltenham Festival would have led to the loss of tens of millions of pounds, so it was fortunate for the Jockey Club that the health secretary allowed the event to go ahead, attended by 250,000 tightly packed fans.[18] The Jockey Club is located at Newmarket, where the local MP was that very same health secretary, Matt Hancock. Leading members of the Jockey Club, Cheltenham Festival and associated horse-racing figures had given Hancock £350,000 in donations.[19] Racing was one of the last sports to be suspended, and the first to return after the first lockdown ended in June.

When asked if the festival should have gone ahead, Hancock stopped counting his donations long enough to reply, 'We followed the scientific advice.'

Followed at some distance, though. SAGE's Professor Neil Ferguson had called for social distancing as early as 24 January. The editor of *The Lancet* had already called for the 'urgent implementation of social distancing and closure policies' way before the Cheltenham Festival began.[20] During the month that followed the event, hospitals covering the Cheltenham area recorded more than double the Covid deaths of other hospitals in the region.[21]

—

Having performed the most important duty of a government – protecting the income of Tory donors at the Cheltenham Festival – our leaders could finally find time to protect the rest of us. But not straight away, of course.

On the evening of 13 March, just as the pandemic action plan was discovered to have gone missing, Johnson vaguely indicated he was thinking about possibly preparing to soon announce that he *might* cancel some public events; he didn't specify what size of event, or when a lockdown might begin.[22] And he didn't issue the advice he'd been given more than a week earlier, that the elderly and vulnerable must shield.[23] Instead, the government merely suggested older people 'avoid going on cruises'.[24]

I don't know about you, but 'stay away from the *Queen Mary 2*' is at the heart of my plan for the zombie apocalypse.

There was a vacuum in governance, so rumours flooded in. It was generally assumed pubs and clubs would shut by the weekend, so the nation rushed out to pack itself into every bar it could find, stocking up on liver damage and coronavirus before the lockdown began.[25]

The next day, 14 March, Johnson's advisers told him, 'We are going to have to lock down as soon as we possibly can.' Officials advised it would be better to shut everything straight away, and then cobble together a pandemic plan after the event.[26]

Of course, 'as soon as we possibly can' is a pretty loose term, and just because the UK death toll was doubling every 24 hours didn't mean there was any reason to rush into action.[27] Italy, Spain and France had already locked down. Austria and Germany had closed. Greece had closed. Russia, Ukraine and Switzerland had shut borders and stopped flights. Most of Europe was in a high state of lockdown.[28] Not us.

A further four long, deadly days passed, and as rumours of imminent restrictions continued to spread, Dominic Cummings called the BBC's political correspondent Laura Kuenssberg to deny a lockdown was going to happen.[29]

Herd immunity was still being seriously discussed at Cabinet level, despite the British Society for Immunology publicly telling the government that such a plan wouldn't work. Six of Britain's most senior health experts wrote a public letter, saying there was 'no clear indication that the UK's response is being informed by experiences of other countries'.[30]

Those other countries were more blunt. A Harvard professor of epidemiology and infectious disease said, 'I could not believe it. My colleagues here in the US assumed that reports of the UK policy were satire.'[31]

Until mid-March, Johnson hadn't even studied the option of a stringent lockdown, such as that adopted in China.[32] Wuhan was completely locked down within two days of Covid being confirmed in the region.[33] Months on from there, and the British prime minister was still humming and hawing.

Johnson seemed incapable of dealing with reality and addicted to giving people good news – no matter how false it was – while his apathetic, distracted inaction all but guaranteed a terrible outcome. He boasted that Britain's exceptionalism meant we could 'turn the tide of coronavirus within the next 12 weeks', while his indolence and arrogance made that already impossible task vastly more difficult.[34]

—

After an eternity of fannying around, Johnson finally went on TV and announced a lockdown would begin – in three more days.[35] Pubs and restaurants were crammed to overflowing on the evening before they closed. It was a public health catastrophe beyond comprehension.

The consequences of that catastrophe were becoming very clear. There was still much to learn about Covid, but it was absolutely certain it would swamp every hospital. Reports from Italy, where the infection had landed a few weeks ahead of Britain, showed emergency services battling huge demand and exhausted medics struggling to cope. The Italian death toll had reached over 4,000 a day, and tens of thousands were infected and needing treatment.[36]

Out rushed Matt Hancock, just behind a press release, to boast of seven new Nightingale Hospitals that would save us.[37] The cost was half a billion pounds,[38] and they had the capacity to treat 10,000 Covid patients, if only we could find staff. But after a decade of cuts to training and bursaries, there were no medics or nurses spare. Even as the pandemic began, the NHS had 100,000 vacancies,[39] and we'd just lost a further 10,000 EU-born staff who quit because of Brexit.[40]

London's Nightingale Hospital cost £57.4 million, and by the time it closed had treated only a few hundred patients. The Nightingale in Birmingham cost £66 million and didn't treat a single patient throughout the entire pandemic.[41]

For the rest of the NHS, it was clear Britain needed to vastly increase supplies of two things: ventilators and PPE.

The EU had already launched a scheme to source, develop and share ventilators, and said: forget about Brexit; this shit is too important to play politics. Britain was invited to join in the scheme. Yet the UK government announced we weren't taking part because we were 'no longer a member', and would be 'making our own efforts'.

If you think it's terrible that the Tories would put Brexit posturing ahead of its own citizens breathing, you're wrong: it's worse than that. The government first claimed this had nothing to do with *our* attitudes to Brexit and told journalists it was actually Europe that had snubbed *us*, like typical scheming Johnny Foreigners. Yet as soon as the next round of frantic, self-created chaos was distracting the public, they finally admitted the truth: we didn't participate in the EU scheme because the Tories had accidentally missed the deadline.[42]

It was sheer incompetence.

The day the government admitted this, irony vacuum Boris Johnson called for 'international cooperation' on resources for Covid. Then he announced we would source 30,000 ventilators from entirely British manufacturers, including companies that had never made ventilators before.[43]

Brexit-backing friend of the PM Sir James Dyson announced he'd secured a government order to build 10,000 ventilators. He was slightly more reticent about the fact he'd exchanged text messages with Boris Johnson during negotiations, in which Johnson had volunteered to 'fix' tax changes Dyson wanted.[44]

'I am First Lord of the Treasury', wrote Johnson, 'and you can take it that we are backing you to do what you need.'[45]

You might argue that secretly discussing dodgy tax breaks so your famously patriotic billionaire chums will bother to help save a few hundred thousand of their fellow countrymen is a reasonable price to pay for 10,000 ventilators in a crisis, but Dyson's machines didn't meet the right standards anyway, and the government said they didn't want them. Dyson ended up supplying none and funded his own needless development costs.[46]

Meanwhile, people who *could* supply ventilators (but didn't have Boris Johnson's phone number) were ignored. The BBC interviewed the CEO of a ventilator manufacturer, who had a working design for machines that met all the right standards and were ready to go at a moment's notice.

'You got in touch with the government as soon as they put out the call for help a few weeks ago,' said the BBC's Emily Maitlis. 'What happened then?'

'Nothing, quite honestly.'

He was literally begging to provide the equipment we needed, with no tax breaks required, and his calls went unanswered.[47]

Boris Johnson, ever-sensitive to the suffering of others, joked his plan for building more ventilators was called 'Operation Last Gasp'[48] and, despite not bothering to order ventilators, reassured us the government was there to 'look after people, thick and thin', which must have been a relief to Mark Francois and Jacob Rees-Mogg.[49]

The bits of government action that were visible to the public were a blizzard of obfuscation. The bits we didn't see were a churning bedlam of ineptitude and stupidity. In February the UK had 5,900 ventilators. The NHS said we needed 25,000 to cope with demand. So Matt Hancock played safe and promised 30,000.[50]

But for all the Tory pretensions that Britain could be mighty in isolation, the government quickly gave up on building our own ventilators and turned to imports, claiming China would rush to our rescue by supplying 8,000 machines. We actually sourced just 800.[51]

On 19 March Matt Hancock proudly announced we had already increased ventilator numbers to 12,000. A cheer went up: we were saved. A week later the government said we had 8,175 ventilators.[52] Somehow, we'd managed to import 800 additional machines, yet ended up with 4,000 fewer. And this was still less than a third of what the NHS said were required.

Designing, sourcing and staffing the ventilators was difficult, so let's not criticise too excessively. But counting them should have been easy. On YouTube there's a horse that can count. Salamanders can count. Fish can.[53] Yet the Tories couldn't even get that bit right.

If you painted a number 7 on Matt Hancock's face, he would be physically and functionally indistinguishable from the type of spoon they use to track your order at a Harvester.

—

Maybe I'm being unfair. Maybe the government was buggering up ventilators because it was putting all its efforts into solving the crisis with PPE.

Or maybe not.

To understand how PPE got so catastrophically fucked up, we must rewind to 24 February – around the time Dominic Cummings was warning that continuing to employ Matt Hancock would lead to the deaths of thousands. On that date, the UK was invited to an emergency meeting of the European Commission to discuss joint PPE procurement, which culminated in an agreement that countries would confirm their exact requirements, and then everybody would cooperate for maximum efficiency and to save as many lives as possible.

Nobody from the UK attended that meeting. Didn't bother. Couldn't be arsed. We didn't turn up to the next one on 12 March either, or the one on 17 March.[54]

By the time we got to 19 March, almost a month after the first gathering, we finally deigned to attend a meeting; but then we decided to opt out of widescale PPE procurement anyway.[55]

That same week, the Commons Health Select Committee asked what the hell was going on with PPE, and ministers gave the assurance there was 'adequate supply to keep staff safe in the months ahead'. The government assured senior NHS managers that our 'NHS and wider health system are extremely well prepared for these types of outbreaks'.[56]

This was just delusional. Since Andrew Lansley's wildly successful tenure as in-house vandal at the NHS, nobody in government had considered the possibility that a pandemic might *not* be simple, annual flu. As a result, the small amount of PPE we had bothered to stockpile was found to be entirely inadequate for Covid.[57] Worse: over 200 million pieces of kit in our national stockpile were out of date. That included 80 per cent of respirators and 45 per cent of our PPE supply. The government had simply stopped updating stock, because there wasn't a pandemic at the time, which is a bit like not bothering to buy home insurance until your house is actually engulfed in flames.

Over 20 million expired respirators needed testing before we could deploy them, which delayed their arrival on the front line until 19 March, more than two months after coronavirus was declared an 'international emergency'.[58]

Hancock's department had wasted months, lied about our capacity, buggered up orders for more materials – and now those giant, non-existent, expired stockpiles of PPE ran out ludicrously fast. Doctors and nurses coming into constant, immediate contact with thousands of Covid patients were having to cobble together woefully inadequate protective equipment from bin bags, rubber bands, snorkel masks and polystyrene swimming-pool noodles.[59] By June, over 1,500 of those NHS staff had died from Covid.[60]

It was 61 days since the Wuhan lockdown began, and now the government paused from flogging commemorative Brexit coins and giving peerages to its biggest sponsors, and finally got stuck into an urgent procurement programme. The results of their efforts strain the bounds of satire. First, let's look at who *didn't* get a contract to supply PPE.

PPE suppliers, that's who.

'We can get hold of 500,000 masks, made for us within one day,' said the director of a UK business providing PPE. 'We actually offered our services [to the UK government] when this first happened and unfortunately our services weren't taken up, but the rest of the world did take it up.' She was selling British-made PPE masks overseas while the British government ignored her.[61]

Businesses such as hers – suppliers of real PPE – were snubbed because officials were spending all their time helping to enrich pals of the government. A National Audit Office report confirmed the Tories set up a 'high-priority VIP lane' to process applications for contracts coming in from 'government officials, ministers' offices, MPs, members of the House of Lords' and other well-connected individuals.[62] The High Court later ruled that this was unlawful, but at the time Johnson was in charge, and laws meant nothing to him.[63]

Needless to say, into the VIP lane rushed the sharks, and civil servants reported they were 'drowning' in hopelessly implausible bids for contracts, submitted by politically connected suppliers, many of whom weren't remotely capable of fulfilling the national need.[64] As a result, real suppliers were ignored, sidelined, or faced long delays in having their contracts approved.

So PPE suppliers didn't get contracts, but let's see who did.

There was Ayanda Capital, a London-based asset investment business, registered in a tax haven.[65] They were not, and have never been, a PPE manufacturer. Yet they still got a contract for £252 million to deliver PPE, of which at least £155 million might as well have been ground up and snorted by Michael Gove, because the kit they supplied 'will not be used in the NHS'. It didn't meet basic design requirements.[66]

How did they get the gig? Andrew Mills, adviser to Liz Truss, told the UK government he had secured 'exclusive rights to the full production capacity of a large factory in China to produce masks', and offered to manage the Ayanda contract via his own family business, Prospermill. We have no idea how much Prospermill syphoned off from this deal, because, according to *The Times*, just as the contracts were being agreed, Mills changed the legal status of Prospermill to that rare beast, an 'unlimited company', which meant he would never have to reveal details of his accounts.[67]

We were now 10 years into David Cameron's transparency agenda, but civil servants seemed unwilling to question any of this because – in the words of the head of new supplier sourcing – Andrew Mills had 'close ties to Department of International Trade, so wouldn't be a good outcome'.[68]

Ayanda Capital got the contract. The company issued a statement saying the masks it supplied to the NHS 'went through a rigorous technical assurance programme', yet it was later found 50 million of the masks were of the wrong standard, and couldn't be used by the NHS. Ayanda's profits increased 2,600 per cent.[69]

Let's move on to Uniserve, a logistics company, which got a PPE contract worth more than £300 million after accidentally wandering into the VIP lane. They shouldn't have been there, because they had no history of ever providing PPE; but by one of those amazing coincidences, they did happen to share an address with government minister Julia Lopez.

The health department paid Uniserve 87p per mask, but according to research the department had commissioned, the average market price for those masks on the day the order was placed was just 51p. We paid 70 per cent above the market price, and the contract was given without a tender. A health department spokesman said their 'priority has been to protect frontline health and care workers'.[70]

This doesn't explain why Uniserve also landed another £104 million contract, this time for storing PPE, rather than for handing it out to health and care workers. You might be thinking that £2 million a month seems a lot of money to store something that didn't need storing. Uniserve's profits reportedly increased 500 per cent.[71]

PestFix got a contract for £350 million to supply PPE, and apparently the Tories thought this was money well spent, despite the government's own documents describing them as a company that 'specialises in pest-control products', which had been made dormant in 2018.[72]

Clandeboye Agencies describe themselves on the Companies House website as trading in the 'wholesale of sugar, chocolate and sugar confectionery' – a sweet warehouse. It's something of a puzzle why this business got given £108 million to provide PPE,[73] seemingly 'without advertising or competitive tendering process'.[74] Clandeboye said it delivered what was ordered and that its pricing was competitive. The BBC reported that a box of the PPE gowns they supplied at – in their words – a 'competitive' cost to the taxpayer of over £1,000 was later sold on for just £5.[75]

Medpro was founded by two wealth-management consultants working in an offshore tax haven and had a share value of just £2.[76] It had also existed for just two days.[77] One of the directors proudly boasted of his years working in 'yacht management'. Tory peer Michelle Mone might have found it tricky to speak more than once during the two years she'd been claiming fees to attend the House of Lords, but she was pretty mouthy about getting a contract for Medpro.[78] She miraculously recommended them as a PPE supplier five days before the company even existed.[79] What did she say about the accusations that she and her husband were 'part of the financial consortium that backed' Medpro?[80] At the time of writing it's not clear; but it is clear that before her intervention Medpro was worth £2, and after, it was handed £200 million to deliver PPE.[81]

Meller Designs, which makes home and beauty products for Marks & Spencer, is run by David Meller, a major Tory donor and director of small government-lobby group Policy Exchange.[82] Meller was fortunate enough to have the phone number of Health Minister Lord Bethell, and put in a call. Bethell then recommended his department deal urgently with the bid for Meller's business to provide PPE.[83] Meller, the small government lobbyist, saw his business handed a not very small £148 million.[84] He didn't 'win the bid', because there was no competitive bidding process.[85] He just made a call, and then £148 million was handed over.

A spokesperson for Meller Designs said, 'We are extremely proud of the role we played at the height of the Covid-19 crisis and managed to secure more than 100m items of PPE,' and I'd be proud too if my business's turnover had increased elevenfold based on those contracts alone.[86]

Some of the contracts beggar belief. Luxe Lifestyle was handed a £26 million PPE contract despite having no employees and, according to the most recent accounts, being insolvent.[87] Initia Ventures declared itself 'dormant' in January, yet got a £48 million PPE contract in March, and according to one report never delivered a thing. A further £28 million went to a company that made shop furniture, which again, reportedly didn't deliver any PPE.[88]

In June of 2019 Aventis Solutions had assets of just £332. That's not a typo, it really was worth £332. The collection of bags for life in the cupboard under my sink is valued at more than £332. Aventis won a PPE contract worth £18 million. There's nothing wrong with giving contracts to small suppliers, but this does seem a remarkably extreme instance.[89]

A million quid went to a shoemaker in Bristol. For PPE. From a cobbler.[90]

Even if those and other contracts were providing urgently needed PPE – and in many cases, they seemingly weren't – the price we agreed to pay was often astonishing. Textile importer Jonathon Bennett had connections with the world's biggest PPE manufacturers in China, who could provide millions of items. He approached the UK government, having agreed a price of £1.70 each for PPE masks. The government instead chose to give the contract to Ayanda Capital, with its close connections to Liz Truss's advisor, for £3.10 per mask.[91]

A report from anti-corruption NGO Transparency International found one-fifth of UK government contracts awarded in response to the pandemic raised a 'red flag' for corruption.[92]

At a Downing Street press conference, the nation was told: 'If we can keep deaths below 20,000, we will have done very well in this epidemic.'[93] Well, they were half right: lots of people did very well indeed in the epidemic, just not NHS staff or patients. By the end of March, the UK death toll was 1,789[94] and the government had handed out £1.6 billion to companies directly connected to the Conservative Party.[95] That's a stack of £10 notes 45 miles high to their pals, while medics were literally being told to 'hold their breath' due to the lack of basic equipment.[96]

—

You'd be forgiven for thinking Tories wanted smaller government for the same reason the Sopranos wanted a smaller police force.

Not that this was the rationale given for their behaviour. The Tories' most commonly proffered excuse was that no government had faced anything like this before, and that in a desperate emergency, shortcuts were taken. But there are 195 countries on earth, which means 194 other leaders were facing the same challenges. We had entered 2010 with the most efficient health service on the planet. By the time the pandemic hit, the UK was among the least well-prepared of all major nations. And that wasn't because of the EU: it was down to a decade of monumental misgovernment.

And it was reflected in our mortality rate. By September 2021, the UK had over 2,000 Covid deaths per million people. Germany, with a similar population density, had half that.

Thailand had a tenth our mortality rate. So did Cambodia. There were 16 deaths per million people in Singapore.[97] Sixteen, in a country immediately next to the pandemic epicentre, with a population density 30 times greater than that of the UK, and with a higher average age too.[98]

New Zealand took the opportunity afforded by its island status, and stopped people from entering the country. They suffered five deaths per million people. Britain, also an island, didn't bother with all that border stuff, despite a decade demanding our right to do so. Our mortality rate was 400 times higher.[99]

There were important lessons to be learned here, by a government willing to absorb new information. If only we'd had one. The director of the Centre for Evidence-Based Medicine at Oxford University spelled it out for those prepared to genuinely listen to the science.

'What's been very noticeable is that we always seem to be one step behind on the policy,' he said. 'If it's not ventilators, it's tests, if it's not tests, it's PPE. It's an important lesson that we have to invest, to create overcapacity for these moments.

'We've really cut to the bone in this country far too much.'[100]

—

There was largesse for some bits of the country, though. As the underfunded NHS battled with the effects of a pandemic our government had spent years failing to prepare for and then months ignoring, that same government came up with a novel plan.

Well, I say novel: it was actually the same plan they always come up with. They gave huge piles of money to the private sector to do what the NHS was already doing, but less efficiently.

The Tories booked the entire capacity of England's private hospitals – 7,950 beds and 20,000 staff – to help cope with the huge surge in healthcare demands. The fees for those hospitals were estimated at £400 million a month. A sensible decision, you might say; and who cares about money when people are dying?

But research shows that between March 2020 and March 2021, those private contractors treated absolutely no Covid patients – not one – on 39 per cent of days. On another 20 per cent of days, they treated just one patient.

The government has thus far refused to release full figures, but few doubt the costs will exceed £4 billion. And what did we get in return? Of the 3.6 million Covid bed-days during the first year of the pandemic, those hugely expensive private institutions provided just 3,000. That's fewer than one in every thousand.[101]

—

On 17 March, around about the time the government was repeatedly failing to participate in international efforts to prepare for Covid, the Tories also decided to update the rules on discharging patients from hospitals.

NHS trusts were told to maximise the availability of critical-care beds by discharging everybody they could. Due to the decade-long assault on social care, elderly patients often 'bed-blocked' because there was nowhere to put them, other than hospital.[102] This had been largely ignored during the entire time Tories had been in office, but now the government acted. Unfortunately, they acted in the worst conceivable way. Without being tested for infection, elderly patients were unceremoniously discharged from hospitals teeming with the virus, directly into care homes packed with the most vulnerable people.

Government guidance explicitly said: 'negative tests are not required prior to transfers/admissions into the care home'.[103] No need to test for Covid, just pour highly infectious patients directly into old people's homes lacking in the most basic PPE, and hope for the best.

The best didn't show up. Infection rates soared. Some of the UK's largest care home operators repeatedly warned Matt Hancock's department about the risk,[104] but the policy went ahead anyway. Between March's 'fuck it, anything goes' guidance and February 2021, there were close to 38,000 deaths from Covid in UK care homes.[105]

In 2022 the high court ruled the policy was illegal and irrational,[106] and the plaintiff in the case – a bereaved daughter whose father had died in a care home – said Matt Hancock was a liar.[107]

—

On 27 March, Boris Johnson and Hancock tested positive for Covid, and the government – which had just blown £6.75 billion on overpriced, non-existent PPE made by dormant cobblers and empty sweet warehouses – started turning down ventilators because it said they were too expensive.[108]

They also spent the month further confusing the nation about their testing strategy. On 12 March they'd announced a 'significant expansion of coronavirus testing, with enhanced labs', and claimed that any moment now they'd be able to do 10,000 tests per day. Just one day later they said they would no longer attempt to track and trace infection, and would only offer tests to people admitted to hospitals with serious symptoms.[109]

'There comes a point in a pandemic where that is not an appropriate intervention,' they told journalists. The WHO responded instantly, announcing that its message for all countries was 'test, test, test'.

'I want to say a special word about testing, because it is so important, and as I have said for weeks and weeks, this is the way through,' responded Boris Johnson.[110] Words can be so confusing, can't they?

So, let's examine actions. Until only a few days before this, the government had chosen to use just *one* of Britain's network of laboratories to do all our Covid tests. No universities had been asked to help process tests, and 11 other qualified national labs were sitting idle. While Johnson flagrantly bullshat the nation about how he'd spent weeks insisting on the importance of testing, that solitary lab could cope with barely 500 tests per day.[111]

So suddenly, the message changed again. Of course we were going to test, the government now told us, and then Matt Hancock plucked a figure out of the air and assured us by the end of the month there would be 10 times as many tests as they'd already announced. Now, they told us, we were going to get 100,000 tests per day.[112]

April

One hundred thousand tests a day? By 5 April the UK had carried out slightly less than 200,000 tests *in total*. In Germany they had done more than four times as many.[1]

It doesn't seem to matter how shocking this floundering incompetence was, there always seemed to be something even more shocking just around the corner. On 6 April it was discovered the government had neglected to deploy more than 5,000 contact-tracing experts from local council environmental health departments. Instead, they'd boosted their own team by just 300 people. But this latest scandalous failure was almost completely unreported because news broke that Boris Johnson had been admitted to hospital.[2]

If you think the bullshit would stop because the chief bullshitter was out of action, you're wrong: Dominic 'Kryten' Raab claimed Johnson was still in charge and 'leading the nation', even as Johnson was struggling to breathe, and medics seriously considered putting him into an induced coma on a ventilator.[3]

To be brutally frank, I doubt this would have made the Tories' performance noticeably worse. A month earlier, senior members of the government had advocated the 'herd immunity' approach, and Johnson had personally appeared on live TV to propose the idea.[4] When even Donald inject-me-with-bleach Trump started calling the idea 'catastrophic' and describing it as a good concept 'if you don't mind death, a lot of death', the newly leaderless carnival of lummoxes around the Cabinet table now denied everything.

'It's been rubbish from start to finish,' said Matt Hancock when confronted with almost three months of documented – often filmed – government plans for herd immunity. 'When people write articles about all of this, I just want them to know that they're talking nonsense.'[5]

But it wasn't nonsense. It was the reason why the US-based Centers for Disease Control and Prevention found that at this point

Britain had the worst per capita death toll on earth.[6] For several long, catastrophic months, the so-called 'natural party of government' had utterly failed on every significant aspect of planning, preparation and response.

But finally – thank you, Jesus! – there was a solution. In the face of what became the sixth worst pandemic in human history, the government would arrange for the people of Britain to collectively stand on our doorsteps and clap front-line workers.[7] If the Tories really believed what they'd been preaching for the last decade, we should have clapped billionaires, and the applause would have just trickled down to nurses.[8]

Having made us all feel patriotic while their half-hearted, quarter-brained, eighth-souled ineptitude destroyed the country, the Tories' next move was to start hurling a thesaurus at truth, in the hope that a subtle adjustment in language would bend reality into a less embarrassing shape. What had once been a promise of 100,000 tests per day now became a guarantee of 25,000. When the true figures emerged – 7,500 tests per day – ministers started talking in terms of testing *capacity*. We had reached a magical *capacity* of 12,750 tests, they told us, and hoped we wouldn't notice this was slightly less than 13 per cent of what we'd once been promised. But that already pitiful capacity disguised something worse: four months since Covid broke out of China, we were testing just 8,600 people per day.[9]

At this rate, it would take 21 years to test the nation.

Almost none of this was reported. All the papers could talk about was the survival of a lazy, incompetent, mendacious dingbat from Number 10, who had taken an unavoidable crisis and turned it into a largely avoidable disaster.

'He stayed in work for you,' shouted the front page of the *Sun*. 'Now pray for him at home.'[10] To be quite honest, if he'd bunked off being PM for a few more months and just stayed in a villa in Mustique, we'd have done better, and he'd have had less chance of getting ill. Their deaths per million were one-sixth of ours.[11]

'The health of Boris is the health of the nation,'[12] declared the batshit-crazy front-page headline in the *Telegraph* while another 7,000 presumably unimportant people died.[13] His cheerleading press treated Johnson like the leader of a cult, although to be fair, he does share a lot of characteristics with one: nothing he said was true, he'd made an incomprehensibly large number of much younger women pregnant, and his tenure had culminated in countless unnecessary fatalities.

—

The government claimed it had been 'led by the science', but quite a lot of the science seemed to have gone to places the government didn't want to follow.[14] Essentially, anywhere that required hard work or vigorous action.

They had ignored expert advice over Exercise Cygnus. They had ignored half a decade of expert advice that it was crazy for Britain to have just one-third of the ICU bed capacity of Germany.[15] They ignored years of expert advice that ending NHS bursaries would reduce staff levels.[16] They ignored screams of expert advice that leaving the EU would harm the NHS.[17]

They ignored the 2018 expert advice about the risk of a pandemic from their own bio-threat consultants.[18] They ignored the expert advice as early as 26 January that 'policy- and decision-makers must act swiftly' and that we should take urgent precautions and lock down the nation.[19]

The government's default setting was demented optimism about everything difficult, combined with cynical pessimism about the public's willingness to adhere to lockdown. They were wrong in both cases. A government populated entirely by people who felt rules didn't apply to them presumed the British public would also ignore the law. Yet research showed only 2 per cent of us didn't comply very strictly with the lockdown rules,[20] and the only thing that could undermine our unity and sacrifice would be – I dunno, maybe a senior member of the government flagrantly breaking its own regulations and suffering no consequences at all.

Enter Dominic Cummings. Or rather, exit Dominic Cummings, filmed racing at speed from Downing Street on 27 March, the same day Johnson was diagnosed with Covid.[21] We didn't immediately find out the reasons for Cummings' alacrity, but eventually it all poured out, as one of the few men alive to have been found in contempt of Parliament now moved onto contempt for absolutely everybody.[22]

In fairness to Cummings, I'm simply relating to you the story he ended up telling the country.

On the day Boris Johnson announced he'd been diagnosed with Covid, Cummings, the self-styled enemy of the Islington media elite, said his wife, who works in the media,[23] had been ill in their house in Islington.[24] But she was only a bit ill, so he popped home, got himself nice and infected, then went back to Downing Street to sit in small, unventilated rooms with lots of vitally important people in the middle of a national crisis.[25]

But then he got ill too, and it was sad. He couldn't find childcare in London, even though several immediate relatives lived within three miles of him in the same city.[26] So, because he was carrying a virus that can cross a two-metre distance and kill, he immediately locked himself in a car with his wife and child and drove 264 miles to his family home in Durham.

When the story broke, and he was accused of doing things that looked bad, he said he didn't care how things looked.[27] Ministers said press outrage meant nothing: only the opinion of the people mattered. A poll showed 59 per cent of Britons wanted Cummings to resign,[28] and my guess is that the other 41 per cent hadn't yet seen the news.

So Cummings decided to show the public some respect by arriving 30 minutes late to make his explanation. He turned up looking for all the world like Lucius Malfoy after a flash fire, and began by saying he wasn't speaking for the government, which must be why he was in the Rose Garden of 10 Downing Street.

From here, the scourge of the rich, monied elite made himself extra-relatable by describing his family's sprawling country estate, multiple houses and idyllic woodlands, before moving on to saying how he'd warned about pandemics years ago on his blog.[29] However, the internet archive Wayback Machine proved that the guy who 'didn't care how things looked' had actually amended an old blog after he'd returned from Durham, inserting new material about pandemics so he'd look smarter. But not smart enough to realise that if he had warned about pandemics years ago, his subsequent years of doing nothing to prepare for one made him look incompetent or genocidal. Or both.[30]

He then told us he could 'barely stand up' when he was in Durham and was too ill to move for a week. Somehow in the middle of this he'd miraculously found the ability to drive to a nearby hospital to collect his child after a check-up. He didn't have the strength to ask members of his family to do it, even though getting their help was specifically the reason he'd driven to Durham.

A few days after that, he told us, he had begun to suffer from a condition absolutely nobody calls 'wonky eyes' and decided to test whether he could see by putting his wife and child in a car and driving them 30 miles down country roads for a nice afternoon at the local tourist attraction of Barnard Castle. On his wife's birthday.

In the world's greatest ever instance of 'if it didn't exist, they'd have to invent it', it was soon revealed that 'Barnard Castle' is 19th-century Durham slang for 'pathetic excuse'.[31]

Nevertheless, a day trip to a tourist spot was, Cummings claimed, the only way he could test whether his eyes were up to driving his family to London. His wife drives, but the most dazzlingly brilliant man in this or any other government never thought to ask her to do it. Perhaps he thought she was already in London; it would be a reasonable assumption, given that her *Spectator* article, written during their week in Durham, describes her experiences of 'the almost comical uncertainty of London lockdown';[32] and using the national press to mislead people about your location is exactly the kind of obfuscation you'd indulge in if you weren't hiding anything.

Then, having respectfully appraised the public of the true and real events, Cummings respectfully stood, respectfully threw a cup onto the table, respectfully smirked, and left.

The country threw a shit-fit. So now the government, which had thus far done the square root of fuck all to handle the pandemic, sprang into action.

Attorney General Suella Braverman said it was OK to break the law if you were acting on instinct.[33] Health Minister Matt Hancock said it was OK to endanger public health if you meant well.[34] Michael Gove said it was 'wise' to drive 30 miles down country lanes if you needed to test your eyesight.[35]

Boris Johnson said Cummings' story 'rings true' because his own eyesight was fine before coronavirus, but now he needed glasses.[36] This is mildly perplexing, because in a 2014 interview with the *Daily Mail*, Johnson said he already wore glasses cos he was 'blind as a bat'.[37] The prime minister went on to say Cummings had acted 'responsibly, legally and with integrity', and you couldn't ask for a finer judge of those attributes than Boris Johnson.[38]

Minister Douglas Ross resigned in protests at Cummings' actions.[39] A government adviser said 'more people will die' because of the lack of consequences for Cummings' breaching the law around national lockdown, and he was right.[40] Research found the 'Dominic Cummings effect' had caused a 'sudden decrease' in public trust in the lockdown, and a major increase in risky behaviours.[41] We never bounced back from that.[42]

Then, during a Downing Street press briefing, a vicar called in to ask Matt Hancock if other people who had been fined for doing exactly what Cummings did would get their fine dropped. Matt Hancock said he'd suggest it to the government.[43]

The government said no within an hour. Dominic Cummings' statement had lasted longer than that.[44]

Boris Johnson said Cummings was on his 'last chance', and that if there was one more mistake or scandal, our stern and honourable PM would ruthlessly fire his most valued adviser.[45] It was then revealed Cummings had built his Durham bolthole without seeking planning permission; that he'd avoided paying thousands of pounds of council tax on it for over 18 years; and that those back taxes were now being waived.[46] Johnson did nothing.

The official Twitter account of the UK Civil Service tweeted: 'Arrogant and offensive. Can you imagine having to work with these truth twisters?',[47] which would be the perfect last words on this matter, were it not for SAGE member Professor Stephen Reicher. He tweeted: 'I can say that in a few short minutes tonight, Boris Johnson has trashed all the advice we have given on how to build trust and secure adherence to the measures necessary to control Covid-19.

'Be open and honest, we said. Trashed. Respect the public, we said. Trashed. Ensure equity, so everyone is treated the same, we said. Trashed. Be consistent, we said. Trashed. Make clear "we are all in it together". Trashed.

'It is very hard to provide scientific advice to a government which doesn't want to listen to science. I hope, however, that the public will read our papers … and continue to make up for this bad government with their own good sense.'[48]

May

Senior health experts and virologists now told the government that 100,000 people would die if lockdown was lifted too early, so Boris Johnson sagely nodded, and then lifted lockdown too early.[1]

Those experts hadn't been given a chance to review Johnson's new advice to the nation: partly because it urgently needed to be announced on Sunday so lockdown could be lifted on Monday, and partly because the frankly dipsomaniac Johnson had boasted 'I can drink an awful lot at lunch', which doesn't immediately suggest he'd be especially focused on his job straight after the weekend.[2]

In their rush to deliver ill-founded good news, the government hadn't checked the small print, and accidentally made it illegal to drive to Wales.[3] They then made it easier to meet up with other people's parents than with your own.[4] Within hours, they issued a new batch of advice on stopping the spread of Covid, which epidemiologists immediately said would make Covid spread quicker, and which was officially ignored by Scotland, Wales, Northern Ireland[5] and dozens of English councils, including Manchester, Liverpool and Newcastle.[6]

The prime minister said we must now all go to work, but we must under no circumstances *travel* to work.[7] The nation wondered how to reconcile this bollocks with the Stay At Home rule, so the government abandoned that, and instead said we must Stay Alert, keeping our eyes peeled for a virus a 100th of the size of a grain of salt.

Sensing the public might be struggling to get a handle on this fresh helping of gibberish, Dominic Raab, the minister for bellowing at his own demons, offered clarity: he said it was fine to socialise with people outdoors, and the same day Downing Street said it wasn't fine to do this at all.[8]

The PM's own father, the overpopulation activist Stanley Johnson,[9] broke the guidelines so he could buy a paper about 'my 14th grandchild', and nobody did a thing, possibly because by this point nobody knew what the giddy screaming Jesus they were supposed to be doing anyway.[10]

Boris Johnson blamed the public for not understanding the rules, after which Andrew Bridgen appeared on TV to explain those rules, got them wrong, and had to be corrected by Piers Morgan.[11] That embarrassment out of the way, Johnson himself appeared in Parliament to explain the rules, got them wrong, and had to be corrected by the opposition.[12]

Details, schmetails. Johnson said he trusted British Common Sense, temporarily forgetting the British had chosen *Boaty McBoatface*, and also decided Boris Johnson would make a good prime minister.[13]

—

It had been hours since we'd had any confusing new plague advice, so the government said we could now go outside and mix with one other person from outside our family, but that we must wear face masks.[14] Sadly, despite valiantly giving billions in PPE orders to our very best yacht-management experts and dormant pest-control businesses, the nation had still somehow contrived to run out of those masks.[15] The Science Select Committee described our response to the crisis as 'inadequate for most of the pandemic'.[16]

Fortunately, the Tories were all over it: only the previous week, Matt Hancock had said our tracking app would be 'rolling out in mid-May', but now mid-May was here, and the app wasn't.[17] So Boris Johnson said the app – which he'd pre-emptively described as 'world-beating' – would instead be ready by 1 June.[18] Both predictions were only mildly blown off course by the revelation we'd unaccountably abandoned development of the app back in March.[19]

They had a clear explanation for this fiasco too, of course: 'There's been a bit too much focus on the app,' said the government, and now described it as a mere 'digital supplement'. Their latest plan was for humans to track everybody they'd been within two metres of in the last fortnight. The methodology, it seemed, would be as follows:

'I think I've got Covid.'

'Where have you visited?'

'Tesco.'

'When was that?'

'Ooh, 10 or 12 days ago.'

'And who did you see there?'

'Over a thousand complete strangers.'

'Well, that's all the info we need, so now we'll track them down using… magic! Jazz hands, top hat, SHIM SHA-LA-BAM!'

All we needed now were some wizards. In their absence, government job ads attracted thousands of applications from muggle contact tracers, swiftly followed by government emails telling them all to fuck off again: the roles had been put on hold 'due to a delay in the launch of the Track and Trace app itself while the government considers an alternative app'.[20]

Just to clarify the logic of this for those of you who have already pounded your head against the wall a little too vigorously: the Tories were telling us the app was the top priority, but manual tracing was *more* of a priority. So they stopped employing people to do manual tracing because they were now prioritising the app. Which they had also stopped developing.

Still keeping up?

Recruitment began again, and the Tories – obviously – outsourced top-quality staff training to the private sector; when asked how to break the news to a family that their loved one had died, the training scheme told employees to look it up on YouTube.[21]

Meanwhile ministers wouldn't reopen playgrounds because children from different households might spread disease by wiping snot on the slides.[22] But they announced they'd soon reopen primary schools, where children from different households wiped snot on literally everything. Over 1,500 schools and 18 local authorities refused to implement the policy on the grounds that the health department was now an active threat to everybody's health.[23]

But in other parts of the government, decisive action was being taken. Only 136 days after Wuhan had closed its borders,[24] the UK finally got around to announcing there would soon be a quarantine system for people coming into the UK. Soon, but not immediately. What's the hurry? We'd give everybody another couple of weeks to spread the virus first, and then quarantining would start on 8 June, unless you were coming from France, in which case you were exempt from quarantine.[25]

Why was France exempt? Not a Scooby Doo.[26]

Perhaps the problem was that rather than focusing on the pandemic, Matt Hancock was spending his days in a hot pash with lobbyist Gina Coladangelo, who had been, as the *Telegraph* put it, 'quietly appointed'[27] to scrutinise his performance as a minister.[28] She must have scrutinised him very closely, because while the nation battled with lockdowns and bewildering quasi-quarantines, she was two metres closer to lover-boy than the restrictions allowed. It's all fun and games until somebody leaks the footage to the *Sun*, at which point both of them had to resign because they were breaching social-distancing rules by playing tonsil tennis in the office.[29]

But those revelations were still a year away, and the nation was still operating under the misbegotten belief the rules mattered, even if they often breached the bounds of rationality. Case in point: the government finally provided a detailed definition of their 'strict quarantine', and it seems they allowed strictly isolated people to pop to supermarkets to buy food, to use public transport whenever they wanted to, and to move house.[30] The deadly virus would probably just wait patiently in your quarantine hotel while you did those things.

Britain had now – praise Jesus – taken back control of our borders, so of the 1.8 million people entering or returning to the UK since the pandemic began, only 273 had gone through a quarantine.[31]

Ministers defended their recent decision to ignore SAGE and relax lockdown: only 113 people had died on the day the restrictions were lifted, they said. In fact, it was 556 deaths, which was the highest for a month, but it seemed Eton only teaches you to count in money, not in human lives. Half of the SAGE committee had publicly pleaded with them not to relax the lockdown, and to be 'open and honest' with the public.

So Number 10 refused to release an uncensored report into disproportionately high incidences of Covid deaths among Black, Asian and minority ethnic people, because of 'worries about global events' such as the death of George Floyd and the rise of the Black Lives Matter movement.[32] In essence, they said there was too much racism happening right now to let them address race issues.

June

It had been weeks since we'd had any *serious* sleaze, and housing minister Robert Jenrick must have been getting antsy. He decided to overrule local planning advice, and approve a new housing development,[1] rushing to sign off the project just one day before it became eligible for a new levy that should have funded local schools and health clinics.[2]

The 2019 Tory manifesto reads: 'we will offer more homes to local families, enabling councils to use developers' contributions via the planning process'.[3] The bypassed levy was that 'developers' contribution'. Jenrick admitted his actions were 'unlawful', but he did it anyway, and it saved the property developer, billionaire Richard Desmond, £40 million.[4]

Yes, you're right: Richard Desmond *has* been a Tory donor. Good guess.

He was also a pornographer, owned the *Daily Express*, and had forced his employees to make Nazi-style '*Sieg Heil*' salutes and sing '*Deutschland über Alles*' in front of media rivals from Germany, one of whom said: 'It was the most grotesque outburst of a mix of slander and racism that I have ever been subjected to. If it had been in a public place, [Desmond] would have been arrested.'[5]

Business Minister Nadhim Zahawi reassured us that if voters wanted to raise their concerns about Jenrick's planning decisions, they could do so by paying to meet MPs at a Conservative Party fundraising event.[6] Yep: you have to donate to the Tory party before the Tory party will listen to your complaints that they only listen to people who give them money.

—

The PM now described the government's performance in tackling the pandemic as 'our apparent success'. I don't know who it was apparent to; our mortality rate was the highest in Europe, four times greater than that in Germany, and by now over 35,000 British people had died.[7]

So obviously, we reopened IKEA.[8]

But at least betwattled Health Secretary Matt Hancock finally had some good news, and peeled himself away from Coladangelo long enough to bound in front of the cameras and celebrate the government reaching a 'capacity' – very much in air-quotes – of 200,000 Covid tests per day.[9] If journalists had bothered to ask how many tests were actually *performed*, they'd have heard it was a less impressive 128,000. What's more, a single test consisted of a nasal swab and a saliva swab, and the government suddenly decided to count these as two separate tests. So, when Hancock boasted of a 200,000 test 'capacity', we had in fact tested 67,000 people: one-third of what he'd led us to believe.[10]

It was now 125 days since Britain's first Covid case.[11] We still had no tracing app; its development had been started, pointlessly stopped, and then started again, as had the recruitment of manual contact-tracing staff. The manual tracing scheme wasn't functioning properly, and many of its operators had received only two hours' training from a promised – and still insufficient – eight hours; and seemingly government ministers couldn't count.[12]

Matt Hancock laughed for one minute and 12 seconds when confronted with this on live television.[13] He then relaxed lockdown from Level 4 to Level 3, and announced plans to relax down to Level 1, 'on the advice of the Joint Biosecurity Centre,'[14] a body that at the time didn't even exist.[15]

The Chancellor said Nando's reopening was 'the good news we've all been waiting for' on the day we reached 36,000 deaths.[16] Matt Hancock said horse racing starting again was 'wonderful news'[17] on the day we reached 37,000 deaths.[18]

Wonderful for him, perhaps. He was still counting his donations of £350,000 from figures linked to the racing world.[19]

—

Parliament reopened under the wise guidance of Leader of the House Jacob Rees-Mogg, a cross between the Child Catcher and rickets. To ensure social distancing when voting, JRM instructed his fellow MPs to form a queue with two metres between each member, forming an absurd 1.3-kilometre conga line weaving unprotected around the streets of central London. Parliamentary votes often happen multiple times each day. Each time there was a vote, we held a conga.

No risk assessment had been published. There had been eight terrorist incidents in London since 2000, and almost as many attacks on MPs by members of the public as there had been attacks on members of the public by MPs. Everybody still remembered Jo Cox.

And now we had 650 defenceless MPs lined up on the streets, and Parliament even rang a bell to announce they were going to be there.

Rees-Mogg defended his farcical alternative to the safe and efficient remote ballots that worked for the House of Lords and most of the democratic bodies on earth. 'Voting while taking a sunny walk or watching television does democracy an injustice,' he said, as our parliamentarians stood around in the sun for hours, plaintively watching clips of proper democracies on their phones.[20]

—

At the 2019 general election, Boris Johnson had assured voters he had an 'oven-ready deal', and as he signed the Brexit Withdrawal Agreement in January, he described it as 'fantastic', and told the nation it would 'end years of argument and division'.[21]

By the second week in June, he was describing his deal as 'defective', and demanding negotiations start again.[22]

Thus began the latest stage in Britain's epic journey through our self-created Brexit Reality-Distortion Field. As we tumbled towards the death of trading relations with the body that bought almost 50 per cent of our exports,[23] the Tories began to negotiate a glorious-sounding new trade deal with New Zealand, which the government admitted would probably leave us even worse off.[24] Nobody should be shocked that Britons leaving the UK and being granted German citizenship had risen 2,300 per cent in just one year.[25]

But here on the much-abandoned Plague Island, there were new guidelines helping to stop the spread of the virus by making it compulsory for teachers to wear face masks on public transport while travelling to school.[26] Those guidelines were immediately undermined by other guidelines telling teachers to avoid wearing face masks once they got to school.[27]

Hancock said he was '100 per cent guided by the science'. A leading government scientist noted that his failure to enter lockdown sooner had 'cost a lot of lives', to which Matt Hancock responded there was 'a broad range of scientific opinion', and clearly, he was only being guided by the bits of science he liked.[28]

But to quote one of the Tories' best big-word-understanders, Ben Bradley: 'Science is not an exact science'.[29]

It was now the middle of June, six months into the pandemic, and despite the government knowing their policy had already killed over 13,000 elderly patients,[30] Imperial College said Covid was still 'spilling out of hospitals' and into care homes, from where it was entering the community and 'sustaining the outbreak'.[31]

Ah, said Hancock, but the government had 'now managed successfully to offer tests to every care home'.[32] That wasn't a perfectly accurate reflection of reality: only 40 per cent of care homes had been able to access testing.[33]

Meanwhile in South Korea, not a single care-home resident had died of Covid. Not one.[34]

—

The government now took full responsibility for delivering a test-and-trace service by outsourcing that responsibility to somebody else. They handed a £45 million contract to Serco, which had just been fined £1 million for multiple failures to deliver their previous massively expensive government contracts. The health minister in the department responsible for the new contract was Edward Argar, a former Serco lobbyist.[35]

To prove there was nothing corrupt about this, Boris Johnson promised 'decisions will be taken with the maximum possible transparency',[36] and then refused to provide details of the Serco fine, despite a six-month Freedom of Information battle.[37]

They'd promised our world-beating contact-tracing system would be ready by June, but ministers now said it wouldn't be ready until September, or maybe October, and would be 'imperfect'. A leaked email from the chief executive of Serco said he doubted their service would ever evolve smoothly, but he wanted to take on the job anyway so he could 'cement the position of the private sector' in the NHS.[38]

The chief executive of Serco, incidentally, is Rupert Soames: ex-Eton, ex-Bullingdon Club, and made OBE by David Cameron.[39]

Fellow Bullingdon man Boris Johnson suddenly announced he was taking 'direct control' of the handling of coronavirus.[40] It was not clear who had been in control for the previous 132 days of the outbreak, but let's not get overexcited about the transformative possibilities of the new management: it was reported Johnson took naps for as much as three hours per working day.[41]

Unsurprisingly, the UK government now had joint lowest approval rating worldwide for how they had managed coronavirus,[42] and Johnson's personal approval ratings had fallen 40 per cent in 40 days.[43]

So Johnson said he was 'very proud' of the government's response,[44] and then changed the subject again, acknowledging the 'incontrovertible, undeniable feeling of injustice' behind the rallies in support of the Black Lives Matter movement.[45]

Given his earlier claims that the people of Papua New Guinea were 'cannibals', and his decision to call Africa a 'blot' of which 'the problem is not that we were once in charge, but that we are not in charge any more',[46] he was clearly the right man to assert that racism in the UK 'cannot be ignored'.[47] And it surely wasn't the Conservatives' fault that more than two years after the Windrush scandal, only 36 of the 15,000 victims had yet received compensation from the Tory government that was responsible.[48]

Still, Johnson did his best to make an earnest, heartfelt appeal to end what he called undeniable injustice, after which, infinitely touched by his sincere entreaty, 40 Tory MPs utterly refused to take part in attempts to tackle that undeniable injustice, calling it 'Marxist, snake-oil crap'.[49]

Unbowed, Johnson said that Black Lives really did Matter, but while he now thought racism was a *bad thing*, 'I will not support or indulge those who break the law'.[50]

Dominic Cummings and Robert Jenrick still had jobs.[51]

—

Near the end of the month Boris Johnson was warned by senior police officers that it was 'total madness' to further relax the lockdown, and then did it anyway.[52] He reassured critics that he 'would not hesitate' to reintroduce restrictions if social-distancing measures weren't observed.[53] Forty-eight hours later a major incident was declared on the south coast as 500,000 people common-sensibly packed the beaches, and Johnson did bugger all about it.[54]

The government just shrugged and said it was somebody else's problem, claiming local councils had the 'power and resources' to enforce local lockdowns. Council leaders wrote to the government to explain they didn't have those legal powers at all.[55] And as for resources: after a decade of swingeing cuts to funding, eight out of every 10 English councils reported they faced the risk of bankruptcy,[56] having absorbed cuts of between 26 per cent and 50 per cent.[57]

It was clear to anybody paying attention that the toxic mix of ineptitude, ignorance, ideology and intransigence that permeated Downing Street pretty much guaranteed a resurgence of Covid cases. The presidents of the Royal Colleges of Physicians, Nurses, GPs and Surgeons wrote to the government begging for an urgent review of preparations for a second wave.[58] The government said no,[59] and instead opened pubs, clubs and what cinemas remained after their failure to give them the promised aid.[60]

They then scrapped the daily briefings that had informed us of what was going on, although it's fair to say they hadn't been helping much:[61] the UK statistics regulator issued a 'sharp reprimand' to

Matt Hancock for presenting deliberately misleading and inaccurate information to the British public.[62]

These were turbulent and challenging times, but to prove they were totally focused on the important issues, the government spent £900,000 painting a flag on the tail of Boris Johnson's plane.[63] And to prove that the Tories were competent to govern, they painted the flag upside down.[64] A year later, they bought Boris a second plane, and painted that too, cos nobody can be expected to get by with just a single Airbus.[65]

—

By now we had burned through £12 million developing our world-beating app[66] and then found it didn't work, which everybody knew it wouldn't.[67] The government's plan was predicated on Apple devices functioning in ways Apple devices aren't built to function, not even if you really want them to and have lots and lots of Union flags. Thousands of programmers warned this was the case back in May,[68] but the Tories did what the Tories do – ignored awkward reality and proven expertise – and instead they wasted £12 million and vital weeks, during which over 10,000 British people died.

In software development, if you want your code to be open source, you can upload it onto a file-sharing 'repository' website and let anybody download it. This is what the Germans did with their properly functioning contact app.

The Tories declined to use the free, open-source German code, and went for their magical, impossible, dream app instead. We eventually abandoned developing our own solution when reality refused to comply, and went with a model just like Germany used.[69]

If we had paid each of our programmers £50,000, our budget would have paid for 240 of them. The file-sharing page for the German app lists 37 participating programmers.[70]

So where did £12 million vanish to? Not the foggiest.

But rather than answer that tricky question, Tories went for their default setting of misinformation and misdirection. Boris Johnson claimed in Parliament that 'no country in the world has a working contact-tracing app'.[71] On the day he said this, there were contact-tracing apps in at least 20 countries.[72]

—

Brexit still hadn't gone away, and I'm sorry to break it to you, but Brexit will never go away. If you voted to leave the EU, you voted to enter a lifetime of wrangling chaos.

Throughout June, negotiations continued for what happened after the implementation period ended, and to make sure everybody knew what we were facing and could prepare properly, the government refused to publish its own report that predicted food, fuel and medicine shortages and huge price rises as a consequence of their own cretinous policy.[73]

None of that mattered anyway, because regardless of the havoc it would wreak, the Tories said they had to deliver Brexit: they had a duty to democracy. That's why, the same month, Tories ignored official recommendations by the Electoral Commission, and pushed ahead with changes that would lead to 9 million (mostly non-Tory) voters being removed from the electoral roll.[74]

But Conservatives insisted it was absolutely essential that they deliver their Brexit manifesto pledge to what remained of the electorate after all that deliberate disenfranchisement and avoidable death. They then broke a manifesto pledge[75] by merging the Department for International Development into the Foreign Office.[76] Johnson promised this would mean no cuts to overseas aid. Two weeks later, the Treasury asked for 'a minimum of 30 per cent cuts' to overseas aid.[77]

Having insisted on their legal obligation to deliver a Brexit the majority of Britons no longer wanted or recognised,[78] the government next announced it wanted to abolish trial by jury – the cornerstone of our legal system for a thousand years – in order to address the waiting list of half a million cases created by their own cuts to the criminal justice system.[79]

—

Despite Downing Street's heroic efforts to suppress reports into racism, racism stubbornly continued, and those who felt this wasn't necessarily a positive thing had now taken to pulling down statues celebrating prominent slavers. Excessively noisy and appalled Tory MPs, desperate to instigate a culture war, insisted removing monuments to slave traders meant we couldn't learn lessons about our history.[80]

They had also overseen the closure of 773 public libraries, and I'm prepared to place a large bet that every single one of those once contained books about history.[81]

But it is often much easier to say words than to do actions, which was reflected in the report into government progress on being carbon net zero by 2050, another manifesto pledge. Despite their best efforts (or at least the best efforts they could be bothered to do) the government was slightly off-track. Under their policies, we would reach net zero in the year 3550, a mere 1,500 years behind schedule.[82]

—

If all of this makes you simply want to leave the planet, I've got bad news for you: they fucked up space too. Brexit meant the UK was leaving the EU's Galileo satellite scheme, a vital part of the satnav system, without which Boris Johnson couldn't find his own arse with both hands and a map.

Leaving Galileo was not part of the Brexit we were promised, of course, because almost nothing was, and quitting it meant the loss of billions of pounds of investment that we'd already sunk into the service.[83] But the satellites had the EU flag on the side, and that might irritate the people of Grimsby, so we had to walk away from this vital part of our public infrastructure, road system and military capability. We were also faced with a brand new, completely avoidable multibillion-pound bill to create a new national satellite system.[84]

Surely there was a cheaper option? Why, yes, there was!

The Tories announced they'd piggyback on existing technology, and threw £500 million at OneWeb, a company that already had 72 satellites in orbit, and that everybody suddenly had to pretend hadn't just gone bankrupt because their solution didn't work.[85]

GPS requires an orbital distance of around 20,000 km, allowing each satellite to map large areas of the planet. OneWeb's orbiters were barely one-tenth that distance from us, and therefore couldn't possibly provide the service we required.

'The fundamental starting point,' said space policy expert Dr Bleddyn Bowen, 'is we've bought the wrong satellites.' Another analyst agreed: 'This situation is nonsensical,' he said. 'It looks like nationalism trumping solid industrial policy.'[86]

We would now need to create a global constellation of 648 additional low-level satellites, each covering a relatively tiny area. This would most likely be a bit of a challenge: the last time Britain launched its own independent satellite was 1971.

So to fix this stupid act of self-harm, the Tories created Space Command, a new service that sounds like somebody needs to prise the *Dan Dare* comic from our PM's clammy, pudgy fists.

The cost of the European Space Agency's Ariane rocket, used to put satellites into low orbit, is £120 million, and it's a single-use item.[87] Space Command would require hundreds of such rockets to launch over 600 satellites. No matter how you slice it, that's tens of billions of pounds. It's a stack of money hundreds of miles high. You could literally climb up that tower of cash with a satellite on your back, and gently push it into orbit.

It gets better. Space Command would be based in Fife. If Scotland votes for independence – which seems increasingly likely – our national satellite system, which we only need because we don't like foreigners or the EU, would end up being based in a foreign country that wants to become part of the EU anyway.

—

It was now three years since Grenfell, and the National Audit Office reported only 14 per cent of dangerous buildings had yet had their cladding removed.[88] Less than 1 per cent of funds to remove cladding had been paid out.[89] The UN had to warn the UK that it would breach international law over its failure to remove combustible cladding from high-rise buildings.[90]

Negligently placing the public in danger inevitably brings us back to the pandemic; and in his eternal search for fresh headlines, Boris Johnson revealed a new plan to supercharge the economy after Covid. Tories called it a £5 billion 'New Deal'.

Sounds exciting! Tell me the details.

President Roosevelt's New Deal expenditure to lift the US out of the 1930s Great Depression was 40 per cent of America's GDP.[91] Boris Johnson's was 0.2 per cent of Britain's GDP, and that was before you realised most of it wasn't new money at all. He'd simply brought forward some previously announced schemes. A key boast was his £1 billion school-building programme, spread over 10 years,[92] which was one-seventh of what the Tories had cut from the education in the previous 10 years.[93] If your polling station is in a school and you vote Tory, you might as well take a shit in the corner while you're there.

Statistics were further tortured by the Tory boast that we now had a billion pieces of PPE, a figure that was only obtained by counting each pair of gloves as two separate items.[94] Doctors would just have to treat patients one-handed. So up stepped demonic Fingerbob Jeremy Hunt, former health secretary and current pillock, who delivered a compelling and impassioned plea for the mass testing of NHS and care staff. Hunt, blessed with the soul of a hyena and the memory of a goldfish, had voted against the mass testing of NHS and care staff earlier the very same week.[95]

Unsurprisingly, the BMA reported almost one in seven doctors planned to quit or retire in response to the pressures, dangers, lies and fiascos they'd been subjected to since January.[96] More than 22,000 EU-born NHS staff had already quit the health service since the Brexit referendum,[97] and the budget for training new staff had been cut by half since 2019, the year Johnson became PM. So the likelihood of training replacements was shrinking rapidly, and we still had multiple waves of Covid to face.[98]

Johnson refused to rule out tax increases to rescue the NHS from the disastrous policies of the guy who lived in his bathroom mirror. But thankfully he did rule out tax increases for the rich (phew!) and told us that instead of clapping for nurses, we should now 'clap for bankers who make our NHS possible'.[99]

Sure. We'll get right on that, Boris. Leave it with us.

July

Rock bottom? Not even close. As we entered July, Boris Johnson nominated Chris Grayling to be chair of the Intelligence Committee.

Honestly. Chris Grayling.

The majority of members of the Intelligence Committee were Tories, so the PM probably assumed his pick would be a shoo-in. In fact, Johnson was relying on it, because the committee was about to decide whether to publish a report on Russian influence over both his government and himself. This was exactly the kind of scrutiny Johnson felt was a gross intrusion into his God-given right to do whatever he fucking wanted without any consequences, and with Grayling in charge you could all but guarantee the report would accidentally fall out of his satchel, be snatched up by a passing seagull, and get dropped into a volcano.

Sadly for Johnson, Tory MP Julian Lewis put himself forward to chair the Intelligence Committee and got the job.

'[Grayling] just wanted to be chair,' another committee member was reported as saying. 'When he wasn't chair, he obviously just started throwing his toys out of the pram. He had no interest in the subject at all, he hasn't got any background in defence or intelligence matters.'[1]

'No background in intelligence' pretty much sums up Grayling, and he resigned from the committee in a massive sulk. Johnson then kicked the victorious Lewis out of the parliamentary Conservative Party in a fit of childish pique.[2]

This sort of idiocy appeared to be catching: a July report from SAGE said Test and Trace must be improved before schools were reopened,[3] so the following day Education Minister Gavin Williamson said he would issue fines against parents who didn't send kids back to schools.[4]

And in the latest episode of *Hancock's Halfwit Hour*, the health secretary tweeted that he was 'really pleased that the Domestic Abuse Bill has been passed by Parliament'[5] the day after he voted against it.[6]

—

At the start of July, the Texas Medical Association published a table of the 37 riskiest activities in a pandemic, the most high-risk of which was 'going to a bar',[7] so our government tweeted, 'Grab a drink and raise a glass, the pubs are opening,'[8] as we recorded the third highest death toll in the world.[9]

Don't panic: the government was taking all possible precautions. The prime minister, looking like a leaking pillowcase stuffed with blancmange and Viagra, stoutly marched onto TV and asserted that 'anyone who flouts Covid rules isn't just putting us all at risk, but letting down the rest of us',[10] a quote you should commit to memory, because it might come in useful later. He then did sod all when the same week his own father once again flouted the rules, this time by flying off to his villa in Greece.

It turned out the edict about obeying rules applied to everybody except the PM's dad. And his special adviser. And his sister too, who had spent her lockdown ignoring lockdown, and travelling regularly between her homes in London and Somerset. She defended this by claiming she was an 'essential worker' because she had a column in the *Mail on Sunday*.[11]

Hey, that's essential. There was a national shortage of toilet paper.

—

The Brexit campaign had promised an end to red tape, and Boris Johnson had insisted 'emphatically' that border checks in the Irish Sea would never happen.[12] Predictably enough, in July the details of the additional red tape and Irish Sea border checks were revealed.

The international trade secretary said her own government's plans 'risk smuggling, damage to the UK's international reputation and legal challenge from the WTO', and warned we weren't remotely ready for full Brexit at the end of the transitional period.[13] Duly cautioned of the awful consequences of being ill-prepared, the government missed the deadline for extending the transition period.[14]

Dominic Raab, our perpetually stupefied cardboard cut-out of a Foreign Secretary and vehement opponent of human rights,[15] further burnished our international reputation, announcing a new policy of sanctions against regimes engaged in human-rights violations.[16] And then literally the next day, we resumed arms sales to Saudi Arabia, despite acknowledging Saudi war crimes in Yemen.[17]

—

The Tories were keen for everything to return to what they had now convinced themselves was normal, and to prove it, Rishi Sunak, who appeared to be having a go at being Chancellor during his gap year, revealed new guidelines for eating in restaurants,[18] and decided to publicise them with a photo-op of him serving customers in a restaurant without wearing a mask, thus breaking the guidelines he was there to announce.[19]

He was the best one. They kept saying he was the best one. Him.

Having spent the last few months telling us that masks were: useful, not useful, recommended, not recommended, mandatory, optional, and effective in small static spaces but not on small moving buses, the Tories now became entirely untethered from reason, and began claiming masks worked in Asia because there was a 'culture of wearing them', but 'we in Britain don't need to wear them'.[20]

A virus is an inert, mindless and technically dead engine of destruction, so it's a stretch to expect it to adhere to our cultural norms. Regardless, Desmond Swayne – who is also all those things – claimed wearing masks in shops was a 'monstrous imposition'.[21] So Michael Gove reassured him masks didn't need to be mandatory in British shops, because in Britain we could rely on 'common sense' and 'basic good manners'.[22]

The following day Gove was photographed displaying common sense and basic good manners by not wearing a mask in a shop.[23]

Inevitably, it was announced masks would become mandatory in shops, only 161 days after the SAGE committee first recommended the measure.[24] But to assuage Swayne, Gove said they wouldn't become mandatory for a further 12 days.[25] During those 12 days of delay, more than 1,000 people died.[26]

To assist with expressing their complicated ideas about the quantum state of mask protocol, the Tories now awarded (without tender) a £3 million 'coronavirus communications operation' contract to two right-wing campaigners who had worked on their 2019 election campaign.[27] Their tactic during that election had been to create deliberately shit content that was so bad people would retweet it for lols. This meant their terrible ideas, awfully expressed, and explicitly designed to confound rational debate and confuse the public, would end up being spread virally.

And this was now the team in charge of pandemic communications.

—

Off to Parliament, where on 13 July Boris Johnson indicated he hadn't even read the official report on preparations needed for a second wave of the virus, which by now was predicted to kill at least 100,000 people. Hadn't read it. Couldn't be bothered.[28]

This brand of overwhelming ignorance was now replaced by sheer negligence, as the UK opted out of the joint EU programme for advanced purchase of a vaccine, on the grounds that it all felt a bit too European.[29]

The Wellcome Trust said the EU scheme was 'not just morally right, but also the fastest way to end this pandemic'.[30] But things like morality and good outcomes were secondary considerations to the government that brought us Brexit, the gift that keeps on giving.

The latest consequence of it was a huge plot in Ashford, Kent, which the government bought to act as a customs-clearance centre to handle all the friction caused by the 'frictionless trade' Boris Johnson could 'absolutely assure you of' when he wanted your vote back in 2016.[31] The journey from the nearest port to the customs checks in Ashford is 23 miles along public roads, providing a welcome boost for Britain's burgeoning smuggling industry.[32]

The CEO of the Road Haulage Association (RHA) warned that because of Brexit border checks, an extra 220 million customs declarations would be needed each year. That's 600,000 a day. The new Ashford lorry park had a capacity of 7,000 HGVs.[33]

The RHA explained each customs declaration was 'as complicated as a tax return' and would be impossible for most businesses to manage. Not to fret, said the government, and promised it would train 50,000 customs brokers to do the job.[34] We had five months until they were needed. It typically takes 18 months to train a customs broker. And the cost of all this would be £15 billion, which is a stack of £10 notes 100 miles high.

In the same week it was revealed the number of British children admitted to hospital with malnutrition had doubled in the previous six months, and you're not alone in wondering if there might be better ways to spend £15 billion than being performatively horrible to the French.[35]

But the Tories never saw a problem they couldn't make worse, so next they announced the end of free school meals for 1.4 million of those hungry kids,[36] and then, in a dazzling display of joined-up thinking, they began handing out £10 vouchers for people to go to restaurants.[37]

The scheme was called Eat Out to Help Out, which is catchier than Leave Your Famished Kids at Home While You Risk Your Life So Wetherspoons Doesn't Go Bust. But while the Tories were doing their best to spread the virus, and simultaneously increase malnutrition in children and diabetes in adults, the Treasury Committee described the scheme as 'badly-timed and poorly-targeted', and concluded the government had basically wasted most of the £30 billion cost.[38]

That's yet another stack of tenners, this time 200 miles high. But the government wasn't done: they next launched a fantastically informative national campaign to market the phrase 'Let's Get Going',[39] which could have been promoting anything from a dog-walking service to a new constipation treatment but, it transpired, was actually to tell people we were leaving the EU.

Remember that time you didn't know Brexit was a thing, until you saw a poster with 'Let's Get Going' written on it? Well, that cost you £93 million. Happy now?

David Davis wasn't. He'd helped to negotiate the Brexit deal and then voted for that Brexit deal, but now tweeted that he was startled by the contents of the Brexit deal and wanted to negotiate it all over again.[40] Buyer's remorse – or in his case, seller's remorse – affected Dominic Cummings too, as it was reported he thought quitting the EU could be 'an error' and called the referendum a 'dumb idea'.[41] But to our rescue came Liz Truss, the kind of Foreign Secretary you'd expect to find on Gumtree. She claimed the economy would be fine after Brexit because we could sell lamb to New Zealand;[42] and in a mark of that nation's confidence in Truss, their deputy PM said Britain's leaders were 'not match fit for trade talks' and that the UK government was 'beset with inertia'.[43]

—

The next week saw the return to Parliament of Matt Hancock, explaining how the deaths of 44,830 of his fellow citizens was proof that his plans were working. Part of those plans, Matt explained, was that wearing masks in shops was mandatory, even though later the same day Number 10 told everybody wearing masks in shops *wasn't* mandatory.[44] Thankfully Schrödinger's twat, Gavin Williamson, was on hand to clear things up by saying they were both right.[45]

His colleague Rob Roberts was having his own sweepingly romantic adventures. He texted his 21-year-old intern: 'Just thought we could have some fun maybe, no strings. I might be gay but I enjoy… fun times.' She responded that she was having a 'really, really bad mental health day', to which he tenderly replied, 'I was just thinking about fun times. Maybe if you thought of them too it might help you.'[46]

He's not a trained psychiatrist, but he'll give it a go.

Speaking of rank amateurs (with the emphasis on rank), Alok Sharma, the pro-Brexit business secretary, startled the nation by suddenly telling us, 'Seamless trade is vital for our economy, boosting business, supporting jobs, and ensuring consumers get the best deal.' He was talking about seamless trade between England and Scotland, of course. He still thought abandoning seamless trade with the EU was a spiffing idea.[47]

It was in this spirit of delivering the Brexit it had promised that the government used its majority to vote against protecting the NHS from being sold;[48] then voted against protection of agriculture and food standards;[49] and then voted against Parliament having oversight of any future trade deals.[50] That's definitely what you voted for, right?

—

Back to the pandemic, where a leaked report found the world-beating test-and-trace programme was a spectacular failure.[51] Contract-tracing staff were 'making a handful of calls per month' and filling their hours with barbeques. Their managers were giving them online quizzes to keep them occupied. Over a two-day period, 471 Serco agents made just 135 calls, which is about 0.14 calls per agent per day.[52] In six weeks, Serco traced and called just 9,997 individuals for a fee of £10 billion. That's more than £1 million per phone call.[53]

Update: 45,000 dead.[54] Serco profits up 50 per cent.[55]

Dido Harding, the head of Test and Trace, said 'NHS Test and Trace is working'.[56] But it wasn't working, and it wasn't *NHS* Test and Trace either: it was outsourced. A cross-party committee of MPs later called the £37 billion we gave to private contractors an 'unimaginable' expense, but even so, we were still paying 2,500 contractors up to £6,624 a day.[57] Nobody thought this was weird or bothered to look up 'profiteering' in the dictionary.

—

Few would be shocked if we were told that the whole of this mystifying and chaotic July had been an elaborate piece of satirical performance art. Case in point: as the pandemic led to a drop in traffic and a surge in people cycling, the government launched a 'fix your bike' voucher website,[58] which broke in less than an hour.[59] Then they launched a £10 million campaign to get us to all lose weight, while still issuing £10 vouchers to encourage us to buy burgers in pubs.[60]

After that, and as a precursor to the looming parliamentary report into Russian interference in our democracy, they said the solution to espionage – and I'm really not making this up – was to ask Russia to tell us who their spies are.[61]

Priti Patel said we could ignore the 'Russia report' because the Tories had delayed its publication for nine months, so now it was nine months old, and therefore 'out of date'.[62] The report, when it finally emerged, concluded Russian intelligence had undertaken disinformation and propaganda operations that influenced the Scottish independence referendum. But it found the government didn't even bother looking into whether Russia deployed the same proven methods to the Brexit referendum.[63]

The report damned the Conservatives' 'lack of curiosity' and said our government 'avoided asking the question' about whether any of their multiple, highly placed, FSB- or Putin-adjacent Russian donors were somehow undermining our democracy.[64] Individuals or companies linked to Russia had put money in the pockets of 14 ministers in Boris Johnson's government.[65]

So we had now reached the gobsmacking stage where the head of our Intelligence and Security Committee had to warn our government not to interfere in the workings of Britain's intelligence services as they investigated interference by the Russians.[66]

Paint an upside-down flag on that act of patriotism, Boris.

—

More fun this month, as the wretched and inadequate Matt Hancock boasted he'd met his six targets for government performance.[67] Independent fact-checkers found four of those six targets were actually missed,[68] one target couldn't possibly be met because it had never even been defined,[69] and the final one 'relied on a definition [that] does not reflect practice'.[70]

Never mind all that, said Hancock, and encouraged everybody to look at how well he was doing with data for contact tracing. He said the government would provide 'full information, including the name and address of those who tested positive, to local authorities'.

Local authority heads of public health wrote: 'For weeks, minister after minister has stated that we have the data, but it's a shambles. Councils and communities are being penalised for national failures; lives have been lost and businesses have been failed.' They said local government wanted 'to control the virus but has been hampered by this national failure'.[71]

Ministers claimed the national government was focused on the larger economy. Yet the cross-party Public Accounts Committee found there was an 'astonishing failure to plan for the economic impact' of Covid.[72] The committee said, 'A competent government does not run a country on the hoof'.[73] It also said the policy of discharging patients into care homes was a 'reckless and appalling policy error', and called the government 'slow, inconsistent [and] negligent'.[74]

—

Deep-cover Transport Secretary Grant Shapps suddenly emerged to announce new quarantine rules for tourists returning from Spain, which he said was now a Covid hotspot.[75] During the previous week, there were 426 Covid deaths in the UK. In Spain, there were just 12.[76] In a world-class example of 'you couldn't make it up', Shapps was on holiday in Spain when he announced this policy change, so ended up nearly locking himself out of his own country.[77]

Incompetent liars accidentally doing acts of self-harm by preventing movement around Europe inevitably brings us to a report from the LSE, which showed Brexit would permanently shrink 16 out of the UK's 24 industrial sectors by up to 15 per cent.[78] Not for one year, but permanently.

It also said a WTO-rules Brexit, which was still on the cards if we couldn't negotiate a final deal, would be even worse, so dipshit flag enthusiast Andrea Jenkyns celebrated the encouraging news that your jobs and livelihoods were at risk with the tweet: 'WTO here we come!'[79] Fellow Tory MP Greg Hands tweeted: 'My strong advice is: take the opportunity to live abroad', clearly failing to understand what his own party's 'ending freedom of movement' policy meant.[80]

Just as MPs left Parliament for summer recess and couldn't gather in tribes to make mooing noises about it, the government quietly cut international aid by £2.9 billion. They would still hit their commitment to spend 0.7 per cent of GDP, but because Brexit made us poorer, 0.7 per cent now equated to billions less money.[81] Sunlit uplands ahoy!

Meanwhile a Nuffield Health study found that after 10 years of 'chronic under-investment', the UK was now near the bottom of the league table for health resources.[82] When Tories entered office in 2010, the NHS was the best-ranked health service on earth.

—

The dictionary definition of 'honour' is 'the quality of knowing and doing what is morally right'. Keep that in mind as you read that at the end of July Boris Johnson used the honours system to give peerages to his own brother, and to the editor of the *Telegraph*, the newspaper that provided Johnson with his most obsequious coverage.[83]

Theresa May's husband was knighted for 'political service', although an ITN investigation found 'a brief stint as chairman of Wimbledon Conservative Association was as close as he got to politics'.[84]

Yet even that makes him a political giant compared to the newly ennobled Ian Botham, an anti-immigration cricketer who bafflingly lived for years in Spain.[85] He was joined – in the Lords, not Spain – by Claire Fox, another staunch Brexit campaigner, who supported IRA bombings, never apologised, and who was now able to influence terrorism laws for the rest of her life.[86]

Also arise, Johnson's pal and now 'Baron' Evgeny Lebedev, son of a KGB spy, and the man who threw that 'anything goes' party for Johnson.[87]

Most of the new peers were leading campaigners for Brexit, and as such were viscerally opposed to unelected power and sprawling bureaucracy. They now swelled the number of our unelected parliamentarians to 797.[88] There are only 650 elected MPs.

Having created 36 new peers, Johnson said he was 'still committed to reducing the size of the House of Lords',[89] but it was starting to look like he might not be scrupulously honest, as the Office for Statistics Regulation noted that week. They said the prime minister repeatedly used statistics 'selectively, inaccurately and, ultimately, misleadingly'.[90] The Office of National Statistics revealed we'd had the worst rate of excess deaths in Europe,[91] so a chastened and newly honest Johnson hailed Britain's 'massive success' in reducing deaths, and I wondered how things could get worse.[92]

Oh, hello, Iain Duncan Smith!

Two weeks after the cost of IDS's Universal Credit rose by a further £1.4 billion, a parliamentary committee found it was still 'not fit for purpose' and needed £8 billion more.[93] It was now almost 11 years since the whispering atrocity had launched his cheap, simple, three-year programme to introduce Universal Credit. Implementation costs had risen from £2 billion to almost £20 billion, and at the current rate it would take 495 years to roll out the service.[94]

The committee found Universal Credit 'has led to an unprecedented number of people relying on food banks', which was the cue for Dominic Raab, thick as a rhino omelette, to pose for photos at a food bank, which specifically illustrated a decade of massive, deliberate and cruel governmental failure.[95]

But Iain Duncan Smith hadn't used up his entire month's supply of arrant stupidity yet. Back in October 2019, he'd voted to accelerate the passage of the Brexit Withdrawal Agreement through Parliament in just three days, specifically so it wouldn't have to face scrutiny. And in March 2020 he voted for the Withdrawal Agreement in Parliament.[96] Now it was July 2020, and he finally got around to reading the Withdrawal Agreement, saw that it would cost £160 billion, and demanded it be renegotiated.[97]

He said the details were 'buried in the fine print, unnoticed by many', which is *literally* why we needed the scrutiny he'd explicitly voted to deny Parliament.[98] But Iain will be Iain.

Iain being Iain had just cost the country almost £180 billion, which you can think of as a stack of £10 notes stretching 1,240 miles into the air, in return for a future that would be demonstrably worse.

Little of this was helping to build trust in our government, but they weren't helping themselves much either: a study found Dominic Cummings' Durham adventure was 'a key factor in the breakdown of a sense of national unity' and had cost lives.[99] A second study by a cross-party group of MPs said the failure to close airports in March had been 'inexplicable' and 'a serious mistake' that led to thousands of deaths.

So the airports were immediately and urgently left wide open.

—

It was now two months since Boris Johnson had said he was taking personal control of the crisis, and a parliamentary committee found they still 'could not identify anybody in government who was making decisions' about Covid.[100] Certainly not the prime minister: by the middle of July, seven months into the crisis, the government's top pandemic planning expert still hadn't even met Johnson.[101]

Dido Harding told a parliamentary enquiry – this time into the shambolic Covid app – that 'I absolutely don't accept that this is failure, it's the opposite'.[102] It had cost £13 million, which is £12.3 million more than the fully functioning Irish app; and then it was abandoned because it didn't work.[103]

Meanwhile, local directors of public health in Greater Manchester found out about a new lockdown affecting their city when journalists called to ask them about it. The government hadn't bothered to inform the council, but had issued a press release about the lockdown at 11.19 p.m., just 41 minutes before Manchester had to implement it for 2.8 million people.[104]

Civil servants inside Number 10 described events as 'a shit show', but the show had barely even started.[105] Unsurprisingly, after this apocalyptic spree of stupidity and ineptitude, a report found fewer than half of British adults had even a 'broad understanding' of Covid rules.[106] Equally unsurprisingly, the government didn't understand the basics either. Dominic Raab sought to reassure returning holidaymakers who might be punished by their employers for following new quarantine guidelines. 'You cannot be penalised in this country lawfully for following the rules and the law that's in place,' he told them, perfectly wrongly. The government hadn't realised their own law meant businesses *could* penalise their employees who quarantined. The actual government.[107]

Meanwhile the nation still battled the hangover from the government's previous blithering failure to understand details or acknowledge consequences. Polls showed a 60 per cent reduction in Tory support among expats living in Europe, with 'the implications of Brexit' being given as the primary reason.[108] The researchers noted that the 30 per cent upsurge in people fleeing Britain since the referendum was 'of a magnitude that you would only expect when a country is hit by a major economic or political crisis.'[109]

Insiders described the negotiations on the next phase of Brexit as 'running out of time', mostly because more than four years after the referendum, UK negotiators had only engaged with the issues 'in the last week or two',[110] and even the prime minister's father said Boris Johnson was 'living in cloud cuckoo land' about his vision for Britain after Brexit.[111]

August

This, I feel, is a great moment for us to all open our second bottle of gin.

August got off to a blistering start as Olympian mediocrity Craig Whittaker finally made the papers, with a totally unfounded claim that the 'vast majority' of people breaching lockdown rules were from minority, and specifically Muslim, backgrounds.[1] In the non-racist world of facts, 80 per cent of infections in locked-down areas were in the white British community, and a study said this should be 'a warning to the complacent white middle class'.[2]

Meanwhile, Liam Fox was back in the news, as it was revealed that stalwart defender of our national security was probably a major cause of Russian hacking into British politics. He'd used an unsecured personal email account for classified governmental business and got 451 pages of documents nicked.[3]

The great Northern Irish politician and Nobel Peace Prize winner John Hume died, and Michael Gove praised his 'integrity and wisdom' in helping to create the Good Friday Agreement.[4] Gove had previously written a 58-page pamphlet calling the Good Friday Agreement a 'moral sin' and accused those involved in the peace process of being akin to appeasing the Nazis.[5]

—

Back in March, Boris Johnson had emphasised the need to strike a balance between the nation's health and our economy. And for once he had succeeded at something: by August both our economy[6] and our Covid deaths[7] were the worst in the G7.

So just like that other great balancer, Thanos, after a bit of mass death Johnson went on a glamping holiday.[8]

Back at Whitehall, a scant eight months after the WHO alerted the world to Covid, the Tories decided the time was right to advertise for a 'Head of Pandemic Preparedness', offering a salary of £61,000.[9] For context, they'd paid somebody £53,000 to help Samantha Cameron choose what frocks to wear.[10]

It was this fanatical devotion to scrupulous fiscal responsibility that got Liz Truss out of bed in the morning. As studies showed losses from Brexit would be 178 times greater than any gains we would make from new trade deals,[11] Truss suspended trade negotiations with Japan over concerns for the fate of Stilton, of which Japan bought £102,000 worth, or the equivalent of 0.001 pence per Briton per year.[12]

Truss argued that risking the other 99.993 per cent of the deal over the fate of a few slices of cheese represented a 'symbolic win' for Britain, and while we were all contemplating the symbolic mortgage payments we'd soon have to make, she unveiled her latest visionary idea: increasing motorway speed limits to 80 mph could be the solution to all our economic woes.[13]

Really, Liz? You reckon we're losing billions a year because we're not driving fast enough? Nothing to do with Brexit?

The rest of the government was also heroically battling against reality, insisting the centralised, Serco-powered test-and-trace system remained 'world-beating' after it traced just 56 per cent of cases. Unconvinced, local councils had set up their own in-house, public-sector services in Lancashire, Liverpool and West Yorkshire, and had traced 98 per cent of cases. So after all the blather, it turned out the Conservatives' world-beating service couldn't even defeat Blackburn local council.[14]

The chief exec of NHS Providers, the membership organisation for NHS trusts in England, described the government's system as 'not fit for purpose, let alone world class', and something about that phrase brings to mind the man who dominated August: Gavin Williamson.[15]

—

To fully appreciate Williamson's latest fiasco, we must rewind to February 2020, when the lurching abomination had overruled the exam regulator, Ofqual, which had recommended holding GCSE and A-level exams in socially distanced settings. Williamson had instead simply cancelled exams in favour of results based on teacher assessments. He set teachers the exciting new task of spending hours per pupil creating estimated grades, which then had to be reviewed and approved by their headteachers.[16]

No sooner had they finished this task than Williamson changed his mind, ordering Ofqual to commission an algorithm that would invent new grades for 2020's students, based largely on statistics for different students sitting different papers in different years.[17]

The Royal Statistical Society (RSS) offered their expertise in helping ensure the algorithm performed as well as possible, but Williamson's department created legal hurdles preventing the involvement of the RSS.[18] Even so, Ofqual warned that their standardisation algorithm would be at best only 60 per cent accurate.[19]

Williamson ignored them, just as his department had ignored the RSS, and just as everybody had ignored the teachers. That's three levels of ignorance. A turducken of stupidity.

Predictably enough, the result was the biggest debacle since the last one. There was an outcry as the algorithm downgraded 40 per cent of students, and tens of thousands missed university places.[20]

Hey, at least there hadn't been grade inflation, which would lead to 'a danger pupils will be over-promoted into jobs that are beyond their competence', according to fireplace salesman-cum-Education Secretary Gavin Williamson.[21]

He couldn't even fuck up fabricated grades in a fair way. In some areas 84 per cent of state-school pupils had their grades reduced.[22] By contrast, private schools saw an average 12 per cent *improvement* in grades awarded by the software,[23] and in some subjects, 98.9 per cent of privately educated kids saw their grades increased.[24]

Williamson's first instinct was to stick to his guns, and he stamped his foot and shouted, 'No U-turn, no change,' a phrase he seemingly stole from a job more fitting to a man of his abilities: manning a tollbooth on the M6.

But multiple former Tory ministers described his tenure at Education as a 'total shambles', and events began moving fast, although not as fast as the contents of Williamson's colon.[25] He U-turned on his guarantee of no U-turns, and during the next 48 hours rattled through the following remarkable policies.

First, students were told the algorithm grades were final and couldn't be appealed. Then they were told mock exam results would be used instead, only for this decision to be reversed a few hours later.[26] Next the government said algorithm exam results *could* be appealed, at a cost of up to £150 per result.[27] When parents complained about the expense of this, the costs were shunted onto our flat-broke schools, already reeling from £7 billion of cuts. Clearly that wasn't a solution either, so finally the government announced appeals would be free, without even checking whether Ofqual had the capacity to undertake the number of appeals required.[28] Ofqual didn't.

Lord Bethell rocked up, apparently trying to help, but clearly without the foggiest notion of how to do that. He tweeted that he'd 'fluffed my A-levels' but that this 'taught me how to hustle', yet he failed to mention he'd 'hustled' his way into his hereditary position as a result of his dad dying.[29]

The Tories hadn't finished with schools. The same week, an Education Policy Institute report found pupils from wealthy backgrounds would get one-third more funds from the 'levelling up' budget than poorer pupils would.[30]

And then the government told parents their children would be safe from Covid when schools reopened[31] but that Boris Johnson would 'bulldoze schools' at which there were outbreaks, which seems a smidge excessive if schools were as safe as he'd promised they would be all that time ago, when this sentence began.[32]

To further reassure anxious parents, Williamson said there was no evidence children had caught Covid at schools, which his disordered intellect hadn't connected with the fact schools were closed.[33] An international study found pupils over 12 are just as susceptible to Covid-19 as any adult.[34] Scientists called for routine testing of teachers and pupils, but minister Nick Gibb said no, because...[35]

I have no idea why Nick Gibb said no. It was now 147 days since the WHO said 'test, test, test', and the UK government had wholeheartedly agreed.[36] Now Nick Gibb said no. End of discussion.

On the steps of 10 Downing Street the day he became PM, Boris Johnson had told the nation: 'My job is to make sure your kids get a superb education, wherever you are from. I will take personal responsibility. The buck stops here.'[37] But Johnson was still busy glamping, so instead the buck stopped at Gavin Williamson's permanent secretary, who was unceremoniously sacked, apparently for doing exactly what his boss had told him to do.[38]

Despite Williamson deploying every trick from the minister-in-trouble handbook – primarily, sacking somebody blameless – somehow he still hadn't convinced his colleagues he was up to the task. Nicholas Soames tweeted: 'What could have been in the Prime Minister's mind that led him to appoint so mere, so unreliable, so wholly unsuitable a man to one of the most important jobs in Government.'[39]

'It was as clear as day that there would be an issue,' said another disgruntled Tory backbencher, 'yet they fucked around.' A poetic soul from a newly Tory northern constituency worried that the government was 'wanking into the void', and if that's not the name of a band by midnight, what's the point of anything?[40]

It was a PR death-spiral, and an urgent search was launched for a good-news story out of the Department for Education. Somebody alighted on Williamson's January promise of 540,000 extra laptops for disadvantaged students during the lockdown. Surely that was something to boast about? Unfortunately, after almost eight months, barely any of the laptops had been delivered; 27 academy trusts had received just one computer each, to be shared between over 2,000 students.[41]

A flailing Williamson had one last desperate attempt at rescuing his reputation with core Tory voters. He issued a cheery pledge to starve 175,000 children of immigrants by stopping their free meals while their families were legally forbidden from either earning a wage or claiming benefits.[42]

And the week wasn't even done.

—

Scrupulous honesty klaxon: it was reported that property developers had given the Tories £11 million during the previous year,[43] and then, miraculously, the Tories relaxed rules on planning permission, which would massively aid those donors.[44] Among the regulations they sought to scrap was the one requiring dwellings to have at least one window.[45]

There's no need to panic, though, because Robert Jenrick was back with the words 'you can trust me on housing'. The Royal Institute of British Architects didn't trust him as far as they could spit, and said the reforms were 'shameful' and would 'lead to a generation of slum housing'.[46] Housing charity Shelter said Jenrick would make affordable housing 'extinct' and would force more than 1 million people onto housing waiting lists.[47]

Priti Patel had her own characteristic take on this, assuring us the government adding 1 million British people to the queue for housing was nothing compared to the strain on housing caused by the arrival of a couple of dozen Syrian refugees. Focus on the boats, focus on the boats. Do not look at your own government. Focus on the boats.

Patel was absolutely certain that crossing to the UK in a boat was illegal, which it wasn't and never has been.[48] She seemed entirely unconcerned that borders remained open to Covid, or that three times as many asylum seekers arrive on planes than on boats, or that almost all asylum seekers immediately apply for official asylum when they land, regardless of how they get here.[49]

She also seemed unconcerned that far from having a refugee crisis, in 2020 Britain had accepted just 0.026 per cent of the world's refugees.[50] Our numbers were half of 1 per cent[51] of those aided by Turkey.[52]

Images of Patel pugnaciously trundling around our shoreline in a borrowed tabard had made for great propaganda TV, which is all that really mattered to the government; but if your political ambition is built on ever-more furious opposition to migration, you have to up the ante constantly. So in August, Patel, Miss Trunchbull in larval form, said migrants were only coming to the UK because the French are all racist and Germans torture people,[53] and then invented a pointless new job with a pointedly exciting title.

The 'Clandestine Channel Threat Commander' was tasked with, among other impossible things, pushing migrants back out to sea so they could drown,[54] in direct contravention of international law and British Navy regulations.[55] The navy duly refused to send warships off to kill defenceless refugees in the Channel, on the quite reasonable grounds that they're defenceless refugees, and what are you, a fucking monster?

The UN described the ideas pouring out of the Home Secretary as 'troubling proposals' that would cause 'fatal incidents',[56] and a leak from inside the MoD said Patel's plans were 'inappropriate, impractical and unnecessary', had 'more holes than a slice of Swiss cheese', and were 'completely potty'.[57]

To prove she wasn't potty, Priti Patel then had a public argument about all of this with Ben & Jerry's ice cream[58].

In stepped voice of reason Sir Edward Leigh, with his own unique take on events: 'Problem with cross-Channel migrants?' he tweeted: 'We should never have lost Calais in 1558. Why not take it back?'[59]

Sure, just invade France. Totally normal.

Then Sir Edward, a vocal champion of Britain's ability to cope perfectly well without those bloody Europeans, suggested we pay the EU to manage migration for us.

If the realisation that every single one of them is a clueless bellend is making you anxious, look away now: Immigration Minister Chris Philp asked if he could re-record an interview that was being broadcast *live*, because he forgot what country he was from.[60]

—

But at least we now had Boris Johnson back, returning from his holidays just in time to deny there would be a customs border between Great

Britain and Northern Ireland. 'Over my dead body,' he said, seemingly forgetting his live body had signed an agreement that created that very customs border in the Irish Sea.[61]

He had also promised Brexit would bring lower costs and 'a bonfire of red tape,'[62] so 52 per cent of jaws hit the floor when the government quietly announced in August that they would spend £355 million to help companies in Northern Ireland deal with 'a new wave of red tape.'[63]

Perhaps feeling that this blizzard of needless and destructive admin wasn't enough, the Tories next announced they'd abolish Public Health England in the middle of a fucking pandemic, move the deckchairs around a bit, and then reopen it with a new name. Even though this new organisation didn't yet exist, they had already selected Dido Harding to lead it.[64]

When she led telecoms company TalkTalk, a trade magazine wrote of her, 'Dido Harding's utter ignorance is a lesson to us all,' and that lesson appeared to be: make friends with senior Tories. She was pals with Cameron at university. She was married to Tory MP John Penrose. She sat on the board of the Jockey Club, the body at the centre of the UK's horse-racing establishment. Wealthy members of that establishment gave tens of thousands in donations to Matt Hancock.[65]

A major Jockey Club sponsor is Randox,[66] which was paying Harding's (and for that matter, Boris Johnson's) chum Owen Paterson £100,000 per year to act as a 'consultant'.[67] Paterson lobbied the government dozens of times to give contracts to Randox, despite the company not even having the necessary equipment to do the job[68] and, lo and behold, Randox got a £133m contract to produce Covid testing kits without the contract being advertised, or any other providers being allowed to bid for the work.[69] Also involved was Lord Bethell – yes, him again – who had met with Randox and Paterson to organise the contract,[70] but had mysteriously lost all records of the discussions by the time investigators started looking.

The first time he was asked to produce his records, Bethell claimed he'd only kept them on his phone, which he had lost. A few days after that, he said he hadn't lost the phone at all, but it had become 'broken', was 'defective', had problems with its battery, its screen was too cracked to allow anybody to read things on it, and anyway, he'd given it to a family member.

Shortly after that, he signed a witness statement saying the lost, found, cracked, gifted phone wasn't even the correct phone. He'd used another one.

Can we see that phone, Lord Bethell?

He'd love to, but sadly – 'to save space' – he had deleted all the WhatsApp conversations relating to Randox.[71]

Anybody starting to feel all of this sounds a bit shady is, of course, free to report it to the prime minister's anti-corruption champion. His name is John Penrose. And he is Dido Harding's husband.[72]

———

Continuing the theme: Sajid Javid, until very recently the Chancellor, and still employed full-time as some poor fucker's MP, took a job at banking giant J. P. Morgan, cos if the last 10 years have taught us anything, it's that there's no danger in MPs or bankers not fully concentrating on what they're doing.

Under our system, any minister taking a job less than two years after leaving a government role is supposed to get approval from the Advisory Committee on Business Appointments. That committee warned Javid had 'privileged access to information', and that the former Chancellor taking the job carried risks. He took the job anyway.[73]

———

This was just one of a swarm of amazing coincidences at the heart of government. Public First, a company led by long-term friends and associates of Gove and Dominic Cummings, was by mere happenstance given a contract to help Ofqual with the exam fiasco. The contract wasn't put out to competitive tender.[74]

Gove then appointed five new non-executive directors to oversee performance and ensure probity in his own department, the Cabinet Office. Only one of these *wasn't* a long-term friend of his.[75] They included his ex-girlfriend Simone Finn, who had co-founded Francis Maude Associates. Maude himself is a former Tory MP and now businessman, who was immediately appointed by – yep – Simone Finn to conduct a review into the Cabinet Office.[76]

Gove then handed out a five-figure contract to a company tasked with asking – and please forgive me for laughing dementedly while I type this – tasked with asking Tunisians what they thought about Covid. The contract was allowed to bypass normal tender processes, because finding out whether Tunisians liked pandemics was labelled an 'urgent consultancy service'.[77]

And then Faculty AI, yet another business associated with Gove and Cummings, got handed £400,000 to analyse tweets by UK citizens, so if I vanish one dark night, tell my family I loved them.[78]

Stung by terribly unfair suggestions that any of these revelations looked unbelievably, hilariously, staggeringly corrupt, the government decided to do 'an analysis of Government contracts'. The contract for that analysis went to the cousin of Tory MP Tom Tugendhat.

By this point the whole affair was like a helix, wrapped inside a Möbius strip, encased in a corkscrew, and superglued to a spiral; but even so, Tom Tugendhat told the *Mirror* his cousin had no input into the firm he actually owned, and had won the contract because no other company could provide the service.[79]

Against this background, it's easy to see why Home Secretary (and holiday home for Voldemort's soul) Priti Patel authorised 'more painful' Tasers. Clearly, somebody was anticipating more determined rioters.[80]

But at last, a bit of good news for families bereaved by Covid. Matt Hancock made a big deal of a new £60,000 compensation package for families of NHS workers who had died fighting the pandemic while he gave their PPE budget to yacht-management experts. And then, lovingly, the Tories simultaneously stopped all other benefits to those families.[81]

—

You probably need a breather, so let's finish the month with a break from Westminster madness, and head north to visit Douglas Ross, leader of the Scottish Tories, who was reassuring voters worried that Brexit would allow the importation of food with lower standards.

'I would have no hesitation in voting against any legislation which would allow chlorinated chicken or hormone-injected beef into this country. That's a categorical assurance,' he tweeted.[82]

He then voted against legislation to keep the food standards we enjoyed as part of the EU.[83]

September

Two fun reports to start the month.

First, as a liveable future slipped ever further from our grasp, figures showed the government spent just £2,000 tackling environmental damage to the English countryside.[1] They had just spent 2,300 times that much advertising an October Brexit the entire nation already knew about, and which they subsequently postponed anyway.

And next, the National Federation of Fishermen's Organisations concluded Brexit would cost the UK's fishing fleet £64 million a year,[2] so Fisheries Minister Victoria Prentis decided to celebrate this wonderful future with a photoshoot, in which she was depicted catching mackerel with a rod that had no line, in a sea that contained no mackerel; and suddenly we had to order a fresh barrel of satire.[3]

Meanwhile the Tories announced that this wasn't the *real* Brexit after all, because none of them are. Time to reveal yet another new plan, which this time came down to simply breaking international law by ignoring the treaty they had only just signed. All five living former prime ministers opposed this illegal act.[4]

Robert Buckland, the Lord Chancellor and Britain's highest law officer, implied it was now OK to break international law.[5] Attorney General Suella Braverman agreed,[6] as did Kit Malthouse, the police minister.[7]

The Northern Ireland Secretary Brandon Lewis sought to soothe troubled brows, telling Parliament Tories would only break the law in a 'limited and specific way', which I'd love to see him try as a defence tactic in the High Court, ideally quite soon.[8] But until that day we had to make do with the demented situation in which a government that had previously sacked 21 of its own MPs for not agreeing to the Tory Brexit deal was now threatening to sack any of its MPs who insisted the Tories stick to that deal.

The same week, Foreign Secretary and irony no-fly zone Dominic Raab tweeted that Iran 'must comply with its commitments' and observe the agreements it had signed.[9]

Before another bleak visit to Plague Island, one tiny story: we were now nine months into Boris Johnson's 'levelling up' agenda, and the gap between rich and poor pupils had grown by 46 per cent.[10]

—

People still seemed distressingly keen on remaining alive, but Matt Hancock – who by now looked like a man who wept every morning in front of his frightened children – said no, we should all get back to work because there was 'little evidence' coronavirus was passed on in offices. Boris Johnson, Dominic Cummings and Hancock himself had all contracted Covid in their offices. I don't know what additional evidence he was hoping for.[11]

Regardless, while you donned an inadequate bin bag, elbow-bumped your family goodbye for ever, and trudged back to your plague-infested office, Tory MPs voted to extend their own remote working for another 11 weeks.[12] They then instructed us not to gather in groups of more than six, while they held a meeting of 50 MPs in a room with a capacity of 29.[13] Only eight minutes after their meeting adjourned, they tweeted that 'gatherings of more than 30 people are illegal'.[14]

Obviously, grouse shooting was exempt from that rule.[15] After all, what are we: French!? The 'no gatherings' ban also excluded the St Leger Festival, which made a lot of money for the horse-racing community that had been such generous benefactors of the health secretary.[16]

Halfway through September, we seemed trapped in a spiral of the same stupid, shoddy mistakes. This was partly because we were still governed by the stupid and the shoddy, not least of whom was the prime minister, who seemed to wake up with a brand-new brain every morning. One of those new brains suddenly produced an exciting-sounding and infinitely vague whim, which Johnson named Operation Moonshot. You'll be amazed to hear Johnson's half-brother sat on the board of the business that would get most of the proposed £100 billion Moonshot budget.[17]

Apart from enriching friends and family, the success of Moonshot was predicated on the notion we would soon be able to test 10 million people a day using magical technology that didn't exist, but the creation of which would be entrusted to the likes of Gavin Williamson and Chris Grayling.

A pilot scheme for this fugacious wisp of an idea produced incorrect test results more than 50 per cent of the time,[18] and the scheme would cost almost the same as the entire NHS budget. But first, they decided to spend £500 million on a pilot of Moonshot,[19] about which the BMJ said experts 'questioned the wisdom'.

Of course, that £500 million could have been spent on home testing kits, which parts of the country now ran out of.[20] Consequently, nine months into the pandemic, Britons worried about Covid were commonly being asked to trek 500 miles to find a test centre, in what many dubbed the Full Cummings Experience.[21]

—

You might wonder how this cluster of gobshites had ever managed to organise themselves enough to win power. It's simple, really: in September, King's College London completed research into the 2019 general election, which concluded the Tories had 'employed overt disinformation' with 'new levels of impunity'.[22] In short: they'd lied, and the media had turned a blind eye.

And just in case the media had any ideas about doing a better job in future, as the report came out, the government was also 'formally warned for threatening press freedom' (thus putting us in the same classification as Russia) by the Council of Europe, which the UK had co-founded in 1949 to protect human rights.[23]

So Boris Johnson suggested we opt out of human rights too.[24]

Then to cap an otherwise blisteringly successful week, the Tories voted not to implement the recommendations of their own Grenfell Tower Inquiry, because honestly, by this point, what difference would a few more avoidable deaths make?[25]

—

Off we skip to Downing Street, where chief Brexit negotiator Lord Frost prised the Calippo from the prime minister's soggy paw, wiped him down, and attempted to brief him on progress towards the oven-ready deal Johnson had assured voters he had baked and eaten months ago. It was an eye-opening experience for all present.

'It wasn't until 25 September 2020 that [Johnson] finally understood even vaguely what leaving the Customs Union meant,' recorded Dominic Cummings.

'I will never forget the look on his face when, after listening to Frost in a meeting on the final stage of the negotiation, he said, "No no no, Frosty, fuck this, what happens with a deal?" And Frost looked up from his paper and said, "PM, this is what happens with a deal, that's what leaving the Customs Union means." The PM's face was priceless. He sat back in his chair and looked around the room with appalled disbelief and shook his head.'[26]

Johnson had declared his backing for Brexit on 21 February 2016, and it wasn't until now – four years, seven months and four days later – that he understood what it was.[27]

These geniuses now had to pass the Internal Markets Bill (IMB), which broke international law, and which caused a flurry of resignations. The head of the Government Legal Department quit, as did the Advocate General for Scotland, their most senior law officer. The UK's special envoy on media freedom, Amal Clooney (yes, that one), resigned too.[28] It was soon found that hidden in the small print of the IMB was a provision that laid the ground for the UK government to break absolutely any law it wanted at any time.[29]

While attempting to reassure a naturally worried parliamentary committee that this wouldn't damage the Irish peace process, Dominic Raab, whose job it was to understand the Good Friday Agreement, admitted he hadn't actually read the Good Friday Agreement. 'It's not a novel,' he said in mitigation. True. Novels tend to be longer than 35 pages, and aren't usually vital to resolving conflicts that killed 3,600 people.[30]

—

As infections began to soar once more, the Conservatives said people would be fined £10,000 if they didn't self-isolate after getting a positive test,[31] which coincided neatly with the UK running out of Covid tests in the 10 worst-hit hotspots.[32] Within days, home testing kits ran out across the entire country, which was just a warm-up for the website for booking tests crashing because of a 'government failure to carry out proper software testing'.[33] And then Matt Hancock said the system was under strain because people kept asking for tests when they didn't know if they were infected.[34]

So this meant – deep breath – the government was going to fine you £10,000 if you didn't self-isolate after getting a test that didn't exist, but you must only ask for that test if you already knew the result.

It was at this point in proceedings that the health minister had to implore his fellow seven-year-old Cabinet ministers to stop referring to him as 'Matt WankCock',[35] and clearly excited by this new game, officials branded the prime minister's dream scheme Operation Moonfuck,[36] just as Johnson promised Parliament that Moonfuck would shortly deliver 10 million tests per day.

Three days after making that promise, Johnson told a parliamentary committee he 'didn't recognise' the figure of 10 million tests per day.[37]

Dido Harding was also having lapses. At a parliamentary committee looking into Test and Trace, she was presented with the latest shockingly awful performance figures, and said: 'I'm sorry, that's just not true. I don't know where that number is from.' It was from her own report. Page 8. In bold type.[38]

The government took its foot off the gas, although it had hardly been racing to begin with. It was nearly October, and in the biggest pandemic for a century there hadn't been a meeting of COBRA since 10 May.[39] Restrictions still existed, but only for the little folk, and the PM was described as having essentially given up on the day job and was thinking of quitting because he was worried about his personal finances. Reports – and here I must issue a trigger warning – said that the poor man had to 'pay tax', 'support four of his six [admitted] children', and 'buy his own food'.[40]

Oh, the humanity.

But you can cancel the call to Amnesty International, because it turned out he wasn't being forced to feed himself after all. Instead, the wife of a Tory donor was regularly sending her frikking butler round to Downing Street in disguise, to discreetly deliver at least £27,000 of luxury takeaways for Johnson and Carrie Symonds *in a single year*. The meals were charged at 'cost price' from a business owned by Lady Bamford, with several items marked as 'charged to LB's account'.[41] LB's husband had already handed the Tories £10 million and by some one-in-a-billion chance had ended up being made a lord by David Cameron;[42] and Johnson broke parliamentary rules once again by failing to declare the gift of food in the register of interests.[43]

But that was just the start of it. Johnson and Symonds had also splashed out £200,000 to refurbish their grace-and-favour flat above 11 Downing Street, for which the annual decorating budget is £30,000. You'd think that was pretty generous – more than the average annual wage handed over to the PM so he doesn't get bored by his chairs. But 30 grand doesn't go very far when your tastes run to £800-a-roll wallpaper, as Carrie Antoinette's did.

Deploring the 'John Lewis furniture nightmare' that poor Carrie said she had to endure, they invited in some top designers to install the kind of baroque decorative horrors that are normally only seen when intrepid reporters follow revolutionaries into a gaudy, despotic presidential compound.[44] Boris, of course, couldn't afford for his nest to be so terrifyingly vajazzled, so £52,000 emerged, undeclared, from Tory donor Lord Brownlow.[45]

Dominic Cummings described the arrangement as 'unethical, foolish, possibly illegal' and said Johnson 'almost certainly broke the rules on proper disclosure of political donations'.[46] After much wriggling, Johnson, who had apparently been unable to feed two-thirds of his acknowledged children barely a week earlier, now rummaged down the back of his florid abomination of a sofa, found fifty-odd grand to repay Brownlow, and somehow escaped serious censure.[47]

This was probably because he was the victim of yet another WhatsApp/new-phone kerfuffle, just like the one that tragically afflicted the evidence that might have clarified the events surrounding Lord Bethell. Johnson had said he had no recollection of discussing donations, but only a day after a report (mostly) exonerated him, evidence showed his story was bollocks. He'd exchanged messages with Brownlow, discussing a secret gift of £52,000 to Johnson. It was denied by the Business Minister that this had anything to do with the chance of government funding for a 'Great Exhibition' which would be organised by – and beneficial to – Brownlow's business.[48] Johnson then claimed he had not only lost track of the phone containing these messages, but sadly all the details of being given £52,000 had also fallen out of his memory.

He ended up having to issue a 'humble and sincere apology', which was to become something of a pattern over the coming year.[49]

October

To tackle rising infection rates caused by them paying us to go to the pub, the Tories now ruled that pubs had to close an hour early, seemingly under the impression that coronavirus – an inert, sub-microscopic entity with no brain or nervous system – was able to tell the time.[1] Having reassured us we were all in this together, they then exempted bars in the House of Commons from the curfew.[2]

And then, nine months into Johnson's world-beating, shit-spackled strategy of giving every vitally important contract to an underqualified mate, and every vitally important job to his mate's underqualified wife, the government finally released its long-awaited Covid app. It didn't work with NHS test results.[3] Or on 18 per cent of phones.[4] Or if you lived a bit too close to Scotland.[5]

Even when those issues were resolved, studies showed most of us weren't comfortable using the app, because we didn't trust Dominic Cummings with our data.[6] Hardly surprising: a report found Cummings' proposed 'radical changes' to our privacy laws were so iffy, they'd result in the UK being barred from selling or sharing data with countries that had proper laws; this would undermine Britain's anti-terrorism and security measures, and risk Britain's legitimate data industry, which is worth £80 billion.[7]

As the air still echoed with September's governmental screams that we must all go back to work or we'd be sacked,[8] the Tories now issued screams that we must all stay at home, or we'd be fined.[9] They denied their default setting of flailing incoherence had contributed to Britain having both the worst Covid response *and* the worst economy in Europe. No, said Johnson: it was because Brits were too 'freedom-loving' to obey the rules,[10] and to prove it, his government freedom-lovingly banned schools from using source materials that criticised capitalism.[11]

Not content with this, they also banned schools from discussing something they described as 'victim narratives',[12] which nobody could define, but which didn't seem in keeping with the core values of their national anti-bullying strategy.[13]

Johnson, that stout defender of our freedoms, had earlier tweeted 'a free press is vital in holding the government to account',[14] and now raced to replace the people holding his government to account with his most loyal cheerleaders. His old friend and unfailingly irrumating backer Charles Moore – the former editor of the *Telegraph* who had spent most of his professional life demanding the end of the BBC – was suddenly tipped to be appointed the next BBC chairman. He was on record as saying the very existence of the BBC caused 'human misery worthy of Dickens', which is going a bit far, even factoring in *Mrs Brown's Boys*.[15]

Having led a long, wearisome and mostly Gary-Lineker-centric campaign to get the BBC to cut the wages it pays to senior figures, the Tories suddenly had a change of heart. The PM advocated increasing the pay of the BBC chairman from £100,000 to £280,000 in order to secure the services of his mate Charles Moore.[16]

'Anyone who knows him knows he is open-minded, fair-minded, passionate about this country's success,'[17] said Michael Gove about Moore, the man who had written: 'The Korean sets up a grocery store, which the black then robs – that is the caricature. One explanation is that there really is something different about blacks.'

Warming to his theme, Moore went on to say he could 'detect in black youths an aggression and defiance and indifference to normal moral and social constraints. If it is true, as it surely is, that some races – the Jews are the obvious example – are highly enterprising and talented, it may also be true that some are the opposite.'[18]

He sounds charming, but just in case he inadvertently slipped into racism and needed some oversight, Johnson decided to hand chairmanship of media regulator Ofcom to yet another staunch supporter, the former *Daily Mail* editor Paul Dacre.[19] If you're unfamiliar with Dacre, he was known for shouting 'cunt' so regularly that his meetings had been nicknamed 'The Vagina Monologues',[20] and the paper he published had been banned as a reference by Wikipedia because it printed so many blatant falsehoods.[21] So he was the obvious candidate for Ofcom's role of ensuring decent and honest broadcasting.

Dacre's application was unanimously rejected by the interview panel on the grounds that he was 'not appointable' in a role that required an unbiased attitude and independence from government.[22] The government sought to adjust the rules so Dacre could apply a second time, which was almost certainly unlawful, but a court never got to test that theory: Dacre withdrew his candidacy.[23]

Even Tory backbenchers began saying it didn't look good to be so blatantly handing out jobs to your friends and former bosses, so Moore, Boris Johnson's friend and former boss, also withdrew as a candidate to be the next chairman of the BBC.[24]

Instead, the job went to Richard Sharp, who was – just let me check – oh yes, Rishi Sunak's friend and former boss.[25]

—

A week into October, and we've already covered catastrophic Covid failures, open racism, flagrant nepotism, probable illegality, attempts to undermine press freedom, and the negligent collapse of our economy: what next? Oh yes. Brexit.

Michael Gove told Parliament that only 24 per cent of businesses had made any preparations for leaving the EU, which we were due to do in under four months. Also – and really, guys, this is so minor it's barely worth mentioning – only one in three of the cross-Channel HGVs we relied upon for inconsequential things like food and medicines had the necessary paperwork. Despite having been warned of import problems repeatedly since before the referendum, only now did the Tories begin to ponder what to do about their own 'reasonable scenario' of two-day-long queues at Channel ports.[26]

After a seemingly 30-second brainstorm, they emerged with the most ludicrous solution imaginable: the answer to queues of HGVs at Dover was for Britain to have a shiny new internal border, preventing lorries from entering Kent without paperwork, and helpfully relocating those predicted queues to London, Essex, Surrey and East Sussex instead.[27] Scarcely a month after Sir Edward Leigh had urged the nation to take back Calais, we were now abandoning Margate.

The new border was scheduled to start on 1 January 2021, and it would be controlled by software that the developers admitted wouldn't be ready until two months after that, in March.[28] In the event, it wasn't ready by March either, at which point the government announced it wasn't going to be able to do border checks for at least a further six months.[29]

Gove, seemingly taken unawares by the Brexit he'd spent a decade campaigning for, admitted to MPs that a 'lack of preparation for the end of the transition period' would mean as many as 70 per cent of lorries exporting the goods on which our economy depended being turned back at the border.[30]

Of course, Gove being Gove, he hadn't even noticed the bigger problem: we had just 2,000 import permits shared between our 40,000 UK hauliers.[31] So just 5 per cent of them had permission to work. And yet when the food shortages and HGV driver crisis happened in 2021, the Tories once again seemed taken completely by surprise.

Supply and demand being what it is, the British Retail Consortium said this spectacular, avoidable and entirely predictable – in fact, entirely predicted – fiasco would add £3.1 billion to the nation's food bill in January 2021.[32] Almost everybody, including the American Embassy, predicted 'the worst kind of inflation',[33] and the LSE reported the annual cost of Brexit would be double the cost of Covid and would last indefinitely.[34]

So Rishi Sunak, the discarded early draft of an Aardman sidekick who was currently having a go at being Chancellor, decided not to look at the scary problem, and cancelled the Budget.[35] This gave J. P. Morgan such confidence in our future that they shifted £170 billion out of the UK and into Germany 'as a result of Brexit'.[36] These huge sums are hard to grasp, so perhaps it would be easier if you pictured £170 billion as a stack of £10 notes towering 1,170 miles high. And that was just the start: in the subsequent week it was announced financial services businesses operating in the UK had relocated $1.6 trillion in assets to the EU ahead of the Brexit deadline. To put that into context, the UK's entire GDP is $2.8 trillion.[37]

———

The Tories are all about providing business confidence, and who could fail to be impressed by the revelation that the government was attempting to store Covid data about 67 million people in a Microsoft Excel spreadsheet, which has a maximum capacity of 1 million records.[38] Result? Countless records of potentially infected people fell out of the computer and rolled down a grid, lost for ever.

If that wasn't a clear enough indication that the Tories couldn't do the job, a leaked official report showed the government had increased payments to consultants by 45 per cent in three years, reaching £450 million. The report concluded that outsourcing every major decision to a moneygrubbing huckster you met at boarding school had produced a government that was 'infantilised', and our standards of leadership were now 'unacceptable'.[39]

Even 125 days after announcing he would take 'direct control' of Covid, Boris Johnson, the very embodiment of that infantilisation, couldn't tell us the latest social-distancing rules, how many spreadsheet records had been lost, or explain why four different lockdown regimes existed in Greater Manchester alone. By now he was making the same mistake so often he'd given himself a repetitive strain injury.[40]

It was a bad few days for the PM, although there was a bright spot: a poll of Tory members found they thought Gavin Williamson was even shitter than their own leader. Unfortunately, they also ranked every other leading Conservative ahead of Johnson, and only 28 per cent of them thought he was up to the job. And that's his fan club.[41]

'It's like "Carry on Coronavirus", said one starstruck Tory MP, 'with Boris as Sid James and Matt Hancock as Kenneth Williams.'[42]

'[Boris Johnson] genuinely doesn't give a flying fuck what the policy is, he's never done the homework, so he doesn't know anything.

There really is no point in talking to the prime minister about policy at all', said another.[43]

A third said, 'I find myself bewildered at the clownish lack of professionalism in Downing Street,' while a fourth commented, 'If you drop something which is entirely ornamental, it tends to lose its appeal,' referring to Boris Johnson.

Finally: 'We've gone from eat out to help out, to drink up and piss off,'[44] which brings us neatly back to Rishi Sunak's scheme. A parliamentary report found paying people to go to the pub in a pandemic had cost the nation £500m and didn't do a single thing to improve the economy of the UK's hospitality sector,[45] but it did increase Covid infections by 17 per cent.[46] Although the government didn't notice that last bit because it was logging its figures in Excel.

Sunak, who at the time everyone said was the best Tory, and who still wanted everybody to believe he was the nicest one (which is a bit like being the best at stabbing dogs), had reassured us that nobody was going to go hungry as a result of Covid. While he defended his fiscally useless and actively deadly eating-out plan, he refused to cancel this month's benefit cuts for the poorest 6 million families.[47]

To counter the bad press, Sunak unveiled a new 'Job Coaches' scheme, and made the claim that being drilled for up to two hours to do jobs that didn't exist would be 'the first time that people will realise government could be helpful'.[48] That may be true of *your* government, Rishi, but don't assume it can't be done better.

Sunak, Johnson, Williamson and Gove were towering figures within the Tory movement, so it's not a great shock to find that those lower down the ranks are quite luminously foolish. In the middle of October, the Tory leader of Hertfordshire County Council (which presumably means he's the best one they've got) said the government should abolish local councils so that local councils could remain Tory.[49] Read that twice. I had to.

Meanwhile, over 50 Tory MPs confronted Johnson, concerned about the increasing length of his shortcomings and demanding a say in future policy.[50] Then they voted for the government's new Internal Market Bill, which removed their say over future policy.[51]

Theresa May said the bill, which broke international law, was 'reckless and irresponsible' and 'risks the integrity of the United Kingdom',[52] and so fierce was her opposition to the new law that she then couldn't be arsed to vote against it.[53]

Hardline Brexit cheerleader Steve Baker told the BBC many members of the Tory party were seriously concerned about 'parliamentary democracy and the rule of law'.[54] He also voted to break the rule of law.[55]

And the Lord Chancellor, the Attorney General, and the Solicitor General for England and Wales all voted *against* a clause in the bill 'requiring Ministers to respect the rule of law and uphold the independence of the Courts'.[56] Those are the nation's three most senior law officers.

So the EU, who allegedly are the bad guys in this story, had to launch a legal action to prevent us – allegedly the good guys – from acting illegally.[57]

But rather than focus on this, our government chose to spend a frankly astonishing amount of time pretending Turkey was actually British, so we wouldn't have to pay tariffs on goods coming from there. It's hard to believe the EU didn't fall for this ploy, but apparently some MEPs had access to a map and a brain, putting them streets ahead of us in this round of negotiations. We ended up paying tariffs on car parts.[58] The motor industry said this would mean £100 billion in cumulative losses and would be 'catastrophic'.[59]

—

Let us don our biohazard suits and head over to see what Priti Patel has been playing at.

In October a report found 'trust between ministers and staff is being severely eroded' by a seven-month delay in publishing the report into bullying by the Home Secretary.[60] This warranted a bit of reputational management, and her unique opening gambit was to make a speech in which she voluntarily opted to define herself as the opposite of those who 'do good'.[61]

In this, at least, the Court of Appeal agreed with Patel, and unanimously overturned her policy of removing people from the UK without giving them access to legal process or justice.[62] Their judgement could be paraphrased as: What the fuck, Patel? What the actual fuck?

Having limbered up a bit, she now announced plans to make rough sleeping 'grounds for removal of permission to be in the UK' and 'denial of legal aid'.[63] The logic of this is that if you were born overseas and now found yourself too poor to have a roof over your head, you had to find money for a lawyer, or she would shove you into the sea.

On the off-chance people decided to turn around and head back to shore, Patel suggested we garland the entire south coast with machines to generate huge waves that would increase the chance that refugees and newly dunked homeless people would drown.[64] She's like a modern-day Cnut; and that's not a typo, you just think it is.

She next suggested we ship all migrants to an uninhabited Scottish island, until it was pointed out all the ones you can land a boat on are inhabited.[65] She had modelled her plan on something Australia had done, and Australian experts were so proud of it they described it as a 'human rights disaster'.[66]

Undeterred, she proposed building concentration camps for migrants on a literal volcano in the middle of the ocean, like a fucking Bond villain.[67] Astonishingly, this idea wasn't rejected on the grounds of being demonstrably, comically insane: it was rejected because it was too expensive. So after that, she decided she wanted to catch migrants in a big net in the middle of the sea.[68] You know, just like the things even dolphins drown in.

This was all in one month, you understand. She didn't eke out the horror in a thin coat of awfulness spread across a whole lifetime, like Harold Shipman or Coldplay. This was packed into two or three weeks.

Possibly to distract from the increasing sense that the Home Secretary was a deranged monster, we were once again invited to visit the magical, spinning world of gaffe-hamster Lord Bethell, who rushed out to claim the government's appalling response to Covid would one day make us as proud as the Olympics.[69]

Covid had by now killed about as many Britons as you could fit into an Olympic stadium, so maybe that's what he meant, but who knows: the workings of his mind are inscrutable. Only the previous week he'd tried to distract from governmental cockups by claiming Covid was predominantly caused by students shagging. 'Late-night intimacy' was killing tens of thousands, he claimed, and not, for example, him and his mates being too focused on turning a penny to deliver basic standards of public safety.[70]

—

Suddenly we had two pieces of genuinely good news. No, really! Britain now had four times as many ventilators as we'd had when the virus first hit, and we had begun to help the struggling arts sector. This sounds great, and it's well worth looking into the details behind the headlines.

We could only use one-fifth of those new ventilators, because we forgot to train enough staff.[71] And the bit of the arts the government decided to help out was the highly exclusive Nevill Holt Opera Company, owned by Boris Johnson's friend and Tory donor David Ross, who is worth £700 million, so clearly needed the £100,000 government grant to 'maintain operations'. Minimal operations for an opera company is surely: not singing. They got £100,000 for that. At best, people will give me a fiver to shut up. Still, Ross was clearly keen to avoid the slightest suggestion of impropriety, so before the money was handed over, he passed control of his opera company to his son, Carl, who was still at school.[72]

So: plenty of help for the 17-year-old son of a multimillionaire Tory donor to run his luxurious little opera company, but not so much for the country's largest cinema chain, Cineworld, which in the absence of the promised state aid went bust, risking 45,000 jobs.[73]

Fortunately Work and Pensions Minister and Uncle Fester impersonator Thérèse Coffey was on hand to reassuringly offer a route to new employment: they could all become care workers, which Coffey believed could be done with 'very little training'.[74] The only kink in Coffey's otherwise brilliant plan was that in June her government had frozen funding to train care workers.[75]

—

Despite being warned of its inevitability since April, by the middle of October ministers still managed to find themselves startled by the news that infections were rising, and rushed to introduce new restrictions and regional lockdowns.[76] The local councils responsible for implementing the new plans were given – and this is not an exaggeration – *five minutes'* warning, and no additional resources whatsoever.[77]

Johnson, in a spasm of boosterism, rushed out to promise he would turn Britain into 'a new Jerusalem', and for once he was right: Jerusalem is one of the most bitterly divided places on earth.[78] Even so, his pledge to unify the nation lasted a surprisingly long time – several minutes – before he decried lawyers as 'lefty do-gooders', following hot on the cloven heels of Priti Patel.[79] The former president of the Supreme Court said that by constantly undermining the rule of law, ministers were 'going down a very slippery slope [towards] dictatorship and tyranny'.[80]

Johnson spread yet more good cheer with a speech listing all the marvellous yet vague things he was definitely going to do in the coming unspecified period of time using unspecified money that he didn't have. But he mystifyingly forgot to mention Operation Moonshot, the £100-billion centrepiece of the last Covid strategy, which he'd announced only 25 days earlier.

Unperturbed that all his previous grand plans made a mayfly look like Methuselah, he now promised wind turbines would power all UK homes within 10 years.[81] A report the very next day found that at the current rate, the government would not meet its low-carbon targets for another 700 years.[82]

—

Over at Number 11, Rishi Sunak spent the month trying to rebuild society to match the crayon sketch in his head. He had put his finger on the cause of the crises engulfing almost everything: there were too many actors. Sunak declared the jobs of thespians were 'not viable', which was mainly true because the coffee shops they predominantly worked in were closed. So now, said the Chancellor, actors should find a different livelihood, using a shiny new careers website he was launching.[83] Almost every person who used the site was immediately advised to become an actor. It was the first recommendation in almost every case.[84]

Meanwhile 250,000 businesses that were *not* closely aligned with leading Tories still weren't able to access the Covid support loans the government had promised. As for the loans that did manage to find their way to businesses – sorry, but the government got confused and forgot to track them, and it seemed likely that quite a few of them would simply evaporate.[85] Well, I say a quite a few: £26 billion. The same as a stack of £10 notes 179 miles high. Lost. Gone. Like a dream that never was.

At this point, Rishi Sunak was favourite to become the next prime minister.[86]

But it wouldn't matter, because the Tories replacing Boris Johnson would have the same effect as scraping mould off a cheese. The cheese is designed to endlessly produce more mould. It always has, it always will. The generation of mould is its foundational composition, and Rishi Sunak was just the latest iteration of intellectual fungi rising up from within. The entire cheese needed to go.

—

Even the very loyal were breaking ranks. Fraser Nelson, editor of Conservative in-house jazz mag the *Spectator*, wrote: 'Around the world, no government has been judged to do a worse job by its people, and no country has created as much debt: no matter how you look at it, we're pretty much the worst in the developed world.'[87]

Michael Gove put a different spin on events. 'Things are still looking very positive,' he proudly proclaimed, as his Brexit briefing to Parliament revealed the Tories now had a 66 per cent chance of agreeing what they'd always told us was 'the easiest deal in history'.[88]

We were now just days from the deadline for a deal, and frankly we were desperate. So after spending almost an entire decade telling us the Human Rights Act was a terrible imposition that Brexit would finally free us from, Boris Johnson was now forced to promise the EU he wouldn't rip up the Human Rights Act.[89]

I mean, good try, but useless: they just didn't believe him. Johnson's character and actions had undermined trust in anything he promised the EU, and they said he had not 'created the confidence we need to build our future relationship'.[90]

—

As Covid spiked again, Cabinet ministers began to reassure journalists about the quality of the government response: 'Local lockdowns have no effect. I don't know why we're doing them.'[91] Another said, 'There's no science behind the 10 p.m. pub curfew, it's back-of-a-fag-packet stuff.'[92]

So, with exhausting inevitability, the government introduced more local curfews on pubs.[93] Boris Johnson announced a new four-tier lockdown system, with the lowest tier being 'medium', like at McDonald's. As part of the announcement, the chief medical officer reassuringly said the plan wouldn't work.[94]

The PM addressed the country with a firm reassurance that this time, finally, the new rules were 'simple enough for anybody to understand',[95] and to prove the point, Michael Gove immediately got them wrong, although to be fair, the latest rules were something of a challenge to even the most limber and chemical-free of minds.[96] Many of the regulations seemed resplendently bananas.

You were permitted to go swimming, but not – emphatically *not* – in any places designed for swimming. If you had a six-year-old child, you could meet somebody with a three-year-old or a twelve-year-old, but nobody with another six-year-old. And you could visit a church or mosque, but only if you could be certain nothing religious was going on inside.[97]

This sort of thing should have given MPs pause, but instead they were thinking up excuses for their leader. One veteran backbencher said, 'His personal skill set, this doesn't play to it. He's not a details, manager type. He's a leader and picture painter.'

Buses on wine boxes, mostly. And if finger-painting wasn't enough to keep Johnson occupied, Dominic Cummings was reported this month to have told the PM that he'd do all the work, while Johnson should 'get on with dog walking'.[98]

Against this background, who can blame people for turning to drink? Well, I can. No sooner had the new curfew started than Hancock broke it in a House of Commons bar, where he was overheard to say: 'The drinks are on me, but Public Health England are in charge of the payment methodology, so I will not be paying anything.'[99]

Nobody had the heart to remind him he'd scrapped Public Health England two months earlier.

—

Let's do a quick round-up of the other joys October brought.

We flushed and flushed and flushed, but Gavin Williamson resurfaced again, this time with the thrilling news that he'd decided to cut by 80 per cent the number of laptops being issued to support distance learning, just in time for the new lockdown to require vastly more distance learning.[100]

Northern Ireland Minister Conor Burns told Parliament: 'Our manifesto was clear. We will not compromise our animal welfare and food standards,'[101] after which Tory MPs voted against guarantees of food standards,[102] then used an obscure rule to deny Parliament the chance to ban imports of chlorinated chicken.[103]

And as if we hadn't suffered enough, Robert Jenrick was back again. Against all odds, he'd been handed control over £3.6 billion and told to fairly redistribute it as part of a scheme to aid the 101 most deprived towns. He handed the maximum grant of £25 million to his own constituency, which wasn't even in the list of 101 most deprived towns. In fact, it's the 270th most deprived town.[104]

Jenrick had a simple explanation for this tiny administrative flub. He, Jenrick, had not made the decision about funds for his constituency. He was totally innocent. The decision was made by his colleague, Jake Berry. Berry also got money for his constituency, and that decision had been made by – you guessed it – Robert Jenrick.[105]

Yet the Tories had a plan to replenish the nation's coffers after Jenrick and his mates had done their worst. They noisily announced a brand new 'digital tax' to get tech companies like Amazon to pay their fair share into the nation's bank account. A few days later the Tories rather more quietly murmured the news that they'd made Amazon exempt from the Amazon tax.[106]

While the government excused the richest man on the planet from paying tax, NHS staff were polled on whether, in recognition of their heroic efforts to fight Covid, they would prefer to be given a badge or a snack box,[107] and it was reported that two out of three hospices would have to make redundancies due to funding cuts.[108]

—

Operation Moonshot was back in the news, or would have been if the news bothered to cover things like the Tories still paying more than 200 private consultants up to £7,360 per day each to work on a project that had been effectively cancelled.[109] We were still handing billions to private suppliers to do a hazily defined thingumabob that we'd already proved didn't produce any useful results. Jolly Boris Johnson had chosen this over other things he could have done with a few billion quid, such as feeding kids, so now the Tories, fresh from their promise to 'work around the clock to ensure nobody goes hungry', cancelled the meals provided to our 600,000 poorest children.[110]

Enter footballer Marcus Rashford, who launched a campaign to stop the government from starving half a million children at Christmas in one of the richest countries that has ever existed. The campaign won Rashford an MBE, which led to the bizarre spectacle of a prime minister congratulating somebody on the award they'd received for stopping *his own policies*.[111]

Vicky Ford, the actual children's minister, was one of 332 Tories who voted not to feed children.[112] In case you didn't think things could get any more unbelievable, so did Tory MP Jo Gideon, who was chair of the charity Feeding Britain, which campaigns to end food poverty and hunger in the UK. They effectively sacked her.[113]

Gary Sambrook said it was fine for kids to not eat during their weeks away from school, because they had 'been benefiting from free school meals during term time'.[114] Gary might be surprised to learn that children require food on quite a regular basis.

Selaine Saxby said if businesses were caught helping to feed hungry children, she 'very much hopes they will not be seeking any further government support'.[115]

Ben Bradley, who once had to apologise for suggesting the involuntary sterilisation of the poor, said feeding children would simply 'increase their dependency'. On food. Yeah, wean the little bastards off it: it'll do them good in the end, which will be in around three agonising weeks.[116]

But Bradley hadn't finished. A few weeks earlier he'd boasted of his humanitarian desire to 'fight for working-class white boys who'd been left behind', and now, having voted to starve them, he found himself scrabbling around for justification.[117] He claimed his vote was because food vouchers for children would only end up being spent in brothels and crack dens. I can't claim to be an expert, but I'd be surprised if many crack dens run a tuck shop that accepts food vouchers. Regardless, Bradley insisted he knew kids who lived in such crack dens and brothels.

So rather than help them to a better life, he decided to starve their friends.[118]

Paul Scully waved away the grumbling parents of kids with grumbling bellies and said, 'Children have been going hungry under Labour for years,' seemingly confused about who had been in power for a decade.[119] That attempt to blame Labour for Tory policy didn't work, so next up was Nicky Morgan, who argued that she'd only voted to starve 600,000 children because a Labour MP called Tory MPs 'scum' after they'd just voted to starve 600,000 children.[120]

Checkmate, so-called logic.

One last attempt to shift blame. Marcus Rashford's experience of poverty in secondary school 'took place entirely under a Labour government' said ace Tory and terrible mathematician David Simmonds. Rashford was 11 when Tories came into power, making David Simmonds are rare example of ad hominem self-harm.[121]

Brendan Clarke-Smith voted to starve kids, then felt we should move the debate on, and demanded 'more action to tackle the real causes of child poverty'.[122] So at once the government cut the minimum wage for furloughed people. They would now receive two-thirds of the money the government said was the absolute minimum it is possible to survive on.[123]

Rishi Sunak, who made this decision and was, remember, the nicest Tory, had celebrated when the first lockdown ended, tweeting, 'I can't wait to get back to the pub.'[124] As a result of the nicest Tory voting to starve kids, his local pub barred him for life.[125]

Now take a moment to consider this: MPs get their food and drink subsidised. A £30 meal in a parliamentary restaurant costs MPs £12.75.[126] In 2018 this subsidy cost the taxpayer £4.4 million.[127] I can't find any record of Tories like Ben Bradley or Jo Gideon voting to abolish it.

Long story short: the Tories said they couldn't spend £120 million feeding children, but they *could* spend £522 million on their Eat Out scheme, which its own report said contributed 'negligible amounts' to the hospitality economy, and which drove up infection rates, making lockdown inevitable, and forcing more people to need money the government now refused to give them.

—

Britain had only just unpacked our collective slide rules in an effort to work out what the fuck was going on with the new restrictions, when – if you'll excuse the jumbled metaphors – all of a sudden ministers started shuffling the deck once again, and yesterday's scatological explosion of lockdown directives were replaced with an entirely new beshitting of the national bed.[128]

Boris Johnson sought to clarify matters by describing the financial support people could claim during the new lockdown. 'Whatever happens,' he said, 'nobody gets less than 93 per cent of their current income,' which is a lovely headline, but not even slightly true: people were getting a maximum of 67 per cent.[129]

But the PM hadn't finished: he assured us he would 'stop at nothing' to support people in Tier 3 areas.[130] So Andy Burnham, the Mayor of Manchester, which had just been moved into Tier 3 due to rising infection numbers, asked the government for a £90 million support package. That's one-sixth of the budget for the Eat Out programme that had increased those infection numbers in the first place. We were quite literally spending more on causing harm than on fixing it.

Manchester needed £90 million. The government, which would stop at nothing, stopped at £60 million. Manchester said, how about £65 million? The Tories said no.

Fine, said Burnham, we'll take the £60 million.

So the Tories gave Manchester £22 million, and told the press Burnham was 'being unreasonable.'[131] That was £7.85 per person. The supremely dodgy £25 million gift to Robert Jenrick's small, wealthy constituency amounted to £237 per person.

—

It's absolutely fine to scream occasionally while reading this book.

Inevitably, such screams bring us back to Brexit, where we discover Boris Johnson's oven-ready deal had skipped the middleman and gone straight into the toilet. The PM told the nation we should get ready for No Deal, and it was reported he was 'startled by the EU insistence' that he stick to the agreements that he, personally, had insisted the EU sign up to.[132]

Now Johnson argued we should have an Australian-type deal with the EU. It was quickly explained to the PM that Australia didn't have a comprehensive trade deal with the EU, so the next time he was asked, Johnson, master of detail, said we should have a Canada-style deal instead.[133]

The Canada/EU deal included an arbitration mechanism that Boris Johnson had already rejected and so, after a dizzying few hours chasing reality in small circles, the vision of our future became an Australian-type deal again.

That idea lasted scarcely a day before Alok Sharma was asked in a radio interview: what was the difference between the No Deal the government abhorred and Australian deal the government loved?

Nothing, he said. They were the same thing.[134]

The Tories had said we must Get Brexit Done to boost business confidence. Business seemed unconvinced. The head of the CBI and head of the Federation of Small Businesses warned the UK was not ready for what was coming.[135] The chairman of Tesco predicted months of food shortages and delivery problems.[136] The chairman of the Royal Institute for International Affairs said, 'It now seems likely that Brexit will lead to the breakup of the UK.'[137]

An anagram of Get Brexit Done is 'being extorted'.

And then, bewilderingly, Captain Kirk got involved. William Shatner beamed down to try to explain to an uncaring Britain that Brexit meant smaller overseas businesses importing into the UK now had to pay £1,000 just to file the forms to register for VAT, and therefore would likely stop trading with us.[138]

If you think that doesn't make a lot of sense, here's something that doesn't make even more: an all-bishop finale to October.

John Sentamu, the Archbishop of York, was denied the traditional peerage on his retirement, ending a custom that dates back to King

Richard II in the 14th century. I don't know if it's worth mentioning – I'm sure nobody in the Tory party had even noticed – but Sentamu was the first Black archbishop Britain had ever had.[139] Sadly, it seems the Tories couldn't find space for him – in fact, they said they urgently needed to 'limit the size of the House of Lords', having spent July packing it with 36 close relatives, racists, terrorism-apologists and cricketers.[140]

Meanwhile half a dozen of Sentamu's fellow archbishops appealed to the Tories not to breach international law with their Internal Markets Bill, which seems like an eminently reasonable thing to ask. It's the law. Please don't break it. Who could argue?[141]

I'll tell you who: self-styled 'Brexit hardman' and evangelical Christian Steve Baker, who argued that *of course* the bishops were entitled to their views, but if they persisted in having the views they were entitled to, they should be thrown out of the House of Lords, and then the entire Church of England, of which the Queen is the head, should be disestablished.[142]

November

In a not-at-all-obvious attempt to distract attention from the rolling PR disaster that was the school meals vote, 112 Tory MPs – 98 per cent of whom had just voted to let children starve at Christmas – wrote to Keir Starmer to complain of the 'widespread abuse' they received as a result of Angela Rayner calling one of them 'scum'.[1] They must have been unable to find a pen and paper when there was a 375 per cent increase in Islamophobic incidents after Boris Johnson referred to Muslim women as 'letterboxes' and 'bank robbers'.[2]

Matt Hancock, that ever-dependable master of detail, went on radio and assured the nation the government desperately wanted to resolve the whole 'starving kids' kerfuffle – not by feeding kids, obviously, but by claiming the Tories had opened 'lines of communication' between Boris Johnson and Marcus Rashford.

Rashford denied there had been any such contact.[3]

In the absence of an ethical government, McDonald's stepped in, providing a million free meals over half term, and proving to the Tories that it is possible for clowns to make moral decisions; yet still this maelstrom of witless gobshitery spun ever faster.[4]

After demanding local councils 'build, build, build', Michael Gove now personally stepped in to oppose building in his constituency.[5] If you were 50 years old, you had now spent 20 per cent of your life watching the Tories endlessly repeat the same utter bollocks about their commitment to housebuilding. There's a fine line between spin and bullshit, and that is just one of many lines Michael Gove has caused to disappear.

Meanwhile his reputedly clean and sober Cabinet colleagues now confirmed they were going to start charging 20 per cent VAT on PPE, in the middle of a fucking pandemic.[6] Don't worry, the government said, because care homes can claim back that VAT. We know this stuff. We're all over the details. Trust us.

But we didn't, and with good reason. The government's own advice website said, 'Care homes are unlikely to be able to recover any VAT on PPE.'[7]

As the Tories carelessly added 20 per cent to the cost of basic protection for nursing staff, their world-beating test-and-trace service achieved dizzying new heights: out of 268 million records, just 104 cases had been pursued.[8] It's hard to believe it could get worse, but now, only 211 days after South Korea started mandatory tests and quarantine at its airports, the Tories finally got around to announcing Britain would do the same.

Deaths per million in South Korea: 70.

Deaths per million in the UK: 2,160.[9]

Obviously – because we're not animals or, God help us, Belgians – bankers and hedge-fund managers would be exempt from any new quarantine.[10]

—

Suddenly, seemingly out of the blue, the prime minister was sacked. No, not him: the real one.

Dominic Cummings was seen leaving Number 10 by the front door, carrying a box with his possessions in it, a bit like absolutely nobody does except in a movie. Johnson's Svengali had made a mistake fatal to his career. No, not calling the real prime minister 'dithering' and 'indecisive'.[11] No, not squandering the government's political capital with his endless sniping and awful relationships with ministers and journalists. No, not undermining public support for lockdowns with his bonkers eye-test claims, leading to thousands of unnecessary deaths.

The big mistake was briefing against Carrie Symonds, and for that he was gone, in perhaps a unique example of something he hadn't superpredicted with stunning accuracy. It was the funniest thing to happen to Dominic Cummings since that time he was attacked by a squirrel that leaped from a bin at Alton Towers.[12]

Symonds, who was just as democratically elected as Cummings, had blocked the promotion of Lee Cain, an old Cummings ally from the Leave campaign, and this led to an almighty internal row. Cummings allegedly briefed the press against Symonds, got the full Rasputin treatment, and off he went, leaving behind him (according to reports), 'a void at the heart of Downing Street'.[13]

So what else is new?

Meanwhile the prime minister we were still stuck with, Boris Johnson, was forced to self-isolate after testing positive for Covid again.[14] The word 'forced' is key here: aides reported that he took so little notice of the regulations that they had to set up 'a kind of puppy gate' to prevent his constant habit of simply leaving his rooms and wandering around Downing Street, infecting everybody.

'There was a pattern throughout,' they said. 'He just simply did not think about following the rules. They were not for him'.[15]

December

Tory MPs hoped Cummings' departure was a chance to rebuild relationships inside Parliament. 'Because of coronavirus, [MPs] have not been able to attend parties and functions with the PM and see his good side,' said one, but in news that might disappoint that backbencher, it turns out that wasn't strictly true. He just hadn't been invited.

But we'll come to that. First, because we're heading into the final straight of this crooked decade, let's take one last visit to feckless polyp David Cameron.

After leaving office in 2016, the former prime minister had taken a job with his new best friend, the large pile of money belonging to financier Lex Greensill, from which Cameron derived share options worth tens of millions of pounds. When the pandemic hit, Greensill Capital teetered on the brink of collapse, and Cameron's nest egg looked set to turn green and rot. Something had to be done, so Cameron oiled himself up and squeezed out of his absurd squillionaire's woodshed for just long enough to further sully his dismal reputation.

While the government idly let huge high-street chains go bust, with the cost of hundreds of thousands of ordinary prole-type jobs, ministers were only too glad to take calls from Cameron, who popped the cloak of secrecy back on and lobbied them to give Greensill the 'largest possible allocation of government-backed loans'.

Cameron encouraged Matt Hancock to go for 'private drinks' with Lex Greensill,[1] while Rishi Sunak – at this point bewailing that a tragic bout of extreme indifference prevented him from saving thousands of jobs at Cineworld – texted Cameron to say he had 'pushed the team' at the Treasury to splurge as much money as possible on Cameron's favourite billionaire.[2]

So deep were the links that Greensill, in an echo of the whole Liam Fox/Adam Werritty scandal, even carried business cards describing him as an 'official adviser' to Number 10.[3] Meanwhile the government's chief commercial officer was testing how conflicted an interest could become, simultaneously working for both the UK civil service and Greensill, with the full knowledge and permission of the Cabinet Office.[4] Public Interests and Private Interests had by now happily merged into one, and then as soon as nobody was looking, Private Interests went feral, strangled Public Interests, and dumped its limp body in a layby on the A31 near Shitterton.

When this latest dip into abject squalor became known, Tory MPs voted en masse to prevent the creation of a cross-party parliamentary committee to look into corrupt lobbying.[5] Unsurprisingly, voting to let their mates get away with murder simply led to more murder.

Meet Matt Hancock's friend, neighbour and local pub landlord Alex Bourne, who had zero experience of producing medical supplies, but made up for it with lashings of enthusiasm about getting his hands on fat piles of public cash. Via a series of secretive WhatsApp messages, Bourne ended up getting a health department PPE contract worth £40 million.[6]

No, no, no, protested all those involved: Bourne didn't get a contract at all. That was merely a 'fabrication pushed by the Labour Party'.[7] We were assured Hancock and Bourne weren't even friends. They had never even been to one another's homes, and the contract went to an unrelated third-party company called Alpha Laboratories.

That last part is technically true, but it was reported that the contract Hancock's department gave to Alpha Labs explicitly states that their manufacturing would be outsourced to Alex Bourne's business.[8] And if Hancock was such a stranger to Bourne's home, why did he have a photo of it hanging on the wall in his office?[9]

I'd like to pitch a TV show where Tory MPs tell ludicrous stories to excuse their greed. It'll be called *I'm-All-Right-Jackanory*.

—

You might wonder how they got to be like this. All of them, I mean, not just the unsettling Hancock and undeserving Cameron. How does a person do these things, day in, day out, while their nation battles the sixth worst pandemic in recorded history, and how do they still consider themselves to be remotely moral or decent?

An excuse regularly tendered is that they don't realise they're evil; that this sort of behaviour seems commonplace to most Tory MPs. Every success they'd achieved since they were packed off to prep school was a result of pulling strings, rubbing shoulders, scratching backs, fiddling with knobs, or nobbing with fiddlers. Sleaze and venality ran through them like a stick of Blackpool rock, and the culprits were unaware of how bad they'd become.

The major flaw in the argument that *They Don't Know Any Better* is that it's a fat load of donkey balls: if they didn't know this stuff was wrong, they wouldn't spend so much of their time (and our money) trying to cover it all up. Case in point: Priti Patel.

It gives me no pleasure to tell you this, but Priti Patel is a horrid witch. She persisted in her hobby of inventing stupid new ways to make refugees catastrophically miserable or conveniently dead, even though the Public Accounts Committee found her immigration policies were entirely based on 'anecdote, assumption and prejudice'.[10] The report concluded she had 'no idea' what was actually being achieved by her annual £400 million expenditure on being grotesquely awful to those in desperate need. Parliamentary investigations into her activities had been able to reveal no useful results, simply 'the wreckage that the Home Office's ignorance caused'.[11]

But she didn't care about little things like results. She was far too busy spending over £340,000 of public money attempting to cover up the wreckage caused by her own relentless bullying.[12]

Philip Rutnam, the permanent secretary in her department, had accused her of running a 'vicious and orchestrated campaign' against him after he challenged her abuse and mistreatment of staff, and upon first reading the headlines my heart went out to the poor lawyers tasked with proving a member of this government was capable of competently orchestrating *anything*. Regardless, the government delayed publication of the report into Patel's personal behaviour for months, and it's easy to speculate why: a rare outbreak of shame. When the report finally emerged, it concluded Patel's 'approach on occasions has amounted to behaviour that can be described as bullying'.[13]

Her conduct was so bad, she had literally caused senior personnel to collapse during a display of her very best shrieking and browbeating, and her actions at the Home Office weren't a temporary lapse either. It had gone on for years. The Department for Work and Pensions, at which she worked in 2015, ended up paying £25,000 in compensation to officials rather than go through a tribunal into the accusations of Patel's bullying.[14]

But finally the truth was out. She was found – yet again – to have broken the Ministerial Code, for which she'd been forced to resign in the past, and which traditionally meant a minister had to quit.[15] Finally, justice!

Or not.

Boris Johnson simply ignored the report's findings, vetoed ministerial rules, and instead of Patel being sacked, Johnson's ethics advisor – which was a bit like being Shane MacGowan's dental hygienist – lost his job. And Philip Rutnam, who had stood up to Patel's intimidation, won £340,000 for unfair dismissal.

Laws and integrity didn't matter to Johnson, who continued methodically dismantling the norms of decent behaviour, probity in public office, and our hard-won democratic standards. The Institute for Government said his decision on Patel had 'fatally undermined the Ministerial Code', which I guess we can mark down as the latest in a very, very long line of avoidable deaths.[16]

—

By December 2020 those deaths exceeded 80,000.[17] The latest month-long lockdown – called too late and lifted too early – had temporarily slowed the rate of infection, but Johnson was keen to lift further restrictions so he could be seen to 'save Christmas', even though the bloom in infections that followed gave Britain one of the highest death rates in the world by the end of January 2021.[18]

As Christmas approached and cases increased once again, Boris Johnson had sombrely told the rest of the nation that we could mix at work, but 'this Christmas it's vital that everyone exercises the greatest possible personal responsibility'. London went into higher levels of restrictions, and official guidelines stated 'you must not have a work Christmas lunch or party'.[19]

That evening, there was a Christmas party in 10 Downing Street, with around 50 people packed 'cheek by jowl' into a small room.

When news of the shindig – still, at that point, assumed to be an isolated incident – eventually emerged a year later in December 2021, somebody had to explain it away to a Radio 4 audience that broke new records for looking caustically at a radio over the top of their glasses. That person was science minister George Freeman, and we should spare a thought for him, because it sounds like he could do with the donation.

Freeman's strategy was to tell adult human beings that just because everybody had got pissed in Downing Street at Christmas and held a Secret Santa, that didn't mean it had been an office Christmas party. And even if it was, it all happened within the guidelines that also banned it. And also, it didn't happen.

The challenge of storing three contradictory lies in a single, meagre mind quickly overwhelmed poor George, and he began to babble. There hadn't even been a party, he said, but he had been 'told by those who were there that all the guidance was followed'. At the party that hadn't happened.

He probably went away confident he'd put the whole issue to bed, but over the coming days details of more parties emerged. It was claimed they happened regularly because 'Carrie's addicted to them' (as if it could all be blamed on some ditzy woman rather than her noble husband), and they included a rip-roaring knees-up on the night Dominic Cummings was sacked.[20] While the government still urbanely dismissed these gatherings as impromptu work meetings, photos showed London mayoral candidate Shaun Bailey crammed among a group of drunken Number 10 staffers, raising glasses, wearing party hats and sprawling across the floor next to a trestle table lined with prearranged – yet purportedly impromptu – plates of hot catered food.[21]

To the surprise of all of us, it turned out they *could* organise a piss-up.

More images showed Johnson, Cummings and 15 other people breaching social distancing guidelines, knocking back cheese and wine in the Downing Street garden during the May lockdown, at which point guidelines said you could only meet one person outdoors. And even Rishi Sunak could work out 15 was more than one. Klaxons sounded, and the government, in increasing alarm, assured us it was another 'work meeting', which might explain the presence of the PM, but not of Carrie Symonds.

Ah, said the PM's spokesman, she was there because it was 'her garden'.

Did she have security clearance for attending reassuringly pissed-up prime ministerial meetings?

'I won't get into that', said the spokesman.[22]

Johnson was still reeling from the realisation it might not have been a smart idea to have a photographer on hand to snap evidence of every time his home hosted something illegal, but the next day brought even worse news for him. Earlier in the year the government had announced they would spend £100,000 to employ a prime ministerial spokesperson, Allegra Stratton, and had blown £2.6 million on three plinths, two flags and a small amount of offensively orange wood panelling from which she could mouth Johnson's lies for him. The media room was scrapped before it had ever been used, and by 2021 Johnson was using it to watch Bond movies in the evenings.[23]

But in the interim, Allegra Stratton had used the room to rehearse her act. She never actually held a press conference, but the one she was filmed practising was good enough: footage reached the press of her laughing with colleagues about the 'not socially distanced' parties that George Freeman had just sold his soul to deny.[24] Both she and Shaun Bailey resigned, and any hope of future public adherence to government guidelines vanished like a fart in the wind.

For months, the position of Boris Johnson was that nothing had happened; and if it had happened, he hadn't known about it. He was asked in parliament to 'tell the House whether there was a party in Downing Street on 13 November', and replied, 'No, but I'm sure whatever happened the guidance and the rules were followed at all times'.[25] Yet photos showed him attending the parties, raising a glass and grinning as he delivered speeches to rooms packed with staff, every one of whom was breaching the guidelines.[26] So cramped were some of the parties that people had to sit on one another's laps, and it was reported that an event Johnson attended wasn't a drinks party until the PM 'instigated it'.[27]

Over the course of many months we endured the slow drip, drip, drip of revelations about these revelries, as a morose stream of abject, sullied and inconsequential backbench nonentities were sent out to defend the indefensible. With (depressingly few) honourable exceptions, they seemed happy to let the shite the prime minister was generating pass through every one of them before it reached the public, like a sort of Tory Human Centipede, with Johnson at the front of a stitched-up, crawling conga of bullshit.

The Conservatives quickly fell into a pattern of presenting a palpably false denial, followed by a retreat into a small admission, and then another temporary denial.

There were no gatherings, they said.

OK, there were gatherings, but not parties.

Yes, there were parties, but not *organised* parties.

Fine, they were organised, but the PM didn't know about them.

Sure, he knew about them, but he didn't attend them.

OK, he attended them, but only because he'd been 'ambushed by cake'.[28]

Yes, he ate cake (you half-expected them to say), but he didn't kill any hookers.

The parties – for there had been many – could be traced throughout the entire pandemic. On the day Oliver Dowden, the adenoidal Morph cosplayer who was pretending to be party chairman, told the public at a press briefing: 'You can meet one person outside of your household in an outdoor, public place provided that you stay two metres apart,' around 100 Downing Street staff were invited to a drunken shindig.[29] Regular get-togethers were organised under the title 'wine-time Friday', and so much was consumed it had to be brought into Number 10 in a wheely suitcase, while a dedicated 34-bottle drinks fridge was purchased.[30]

They gave up denying parties happened, and moved onto the defence that attendees of these parties should be cut some slack because of how much people in government had suffered.

What: was some of the wine screw-top?

Johnson produced bizarre justifications. When confronted with groups of people knocking back vats of wine, eating catered canapés, running a fucking DJ set,[31] and getting so pissed in the garden that they broke his own kids' swing, the prime minister reassured us he had figured out this *wasn't* a business meeting in a mere 25 minutes.[32]

Mind you, after his weekends with Lebedev, it's possible his threshold for recognising debauchery was pretty high.

Or maybe he didn't go at all. He simultaneously denied everything and insisted he hadn't got a clue, and would have to wait until a senior civil servant, Sue Gray, produced a report to confirm his whereabouts on the nights in question. Until then, he seemingly wanted us to believe he was capable of running a country but couldn't be sure what room he was in until somebody held an inquiry into it. While that inquiry rolled on, Johnson took a glorious opportunity to pack in a few more lies to the House of Commons and the country.

'All the guidelines were observed,' he said, and, 'I can tell you once again that I certainly broke no rules.'[33]

By now it was pretty much a given that he'd bullshit the press and public without a second – or even a first – thought. However

Parliament is a different beast: it has rules about lies, as Boris Johnson should know, because – never short of chutzpah – he'd actually written the introduction to that very rule book. In the foreword to the Ministerial Code, Johnson had explained that to regain the trust of a jaded public after Brexit, 'we must uphold the very highest standards of propriety – and this code sets out how we must do so'.

Central to the code is the rule that 'ministers who knowingly mislead Parliament will be expected to offer their resignation', and having put his name to that directive, Johnson then went to parliament and allowed the following words to fall out of his baloney-hole: 'What I can tell the right honourable and learned gentleman is that all guidance was followed completely in No 10.'

Guess what: it wasn't.

But the prime minister wasn't finished. After the video of a laughing Allegra Stratton had emerged, Johnson made a prepared statement to the House, in which he said, 'I am sickened myself and furious about that, but I repeat what I have said: I have been repeatedly assured that the rules were not broken. I repeat that I have been repeatedly assured since these allegations emerged that there was no party.'

There were at least 12 parties, and he'd personally attended at least three of them, including an ABBA-themed bash reportedly thrown in his Downing Street flat on the night of his birthday, the noise of which could be heard all over the building.[34]

Two other parties had been held on the eve of Prince Philip's funeral in April 2021, a spartan ceremony that saw the isolated Queen adhering strictly to social distancing rules while mourning the loss of the man she'd been married to for 73 years. Over in Downing Street they were downing shots. This led to absolute scenes as – for the second time – Boris Johnson had to phone the Queen and apologise, while still pretending he didn't know if the thing he was apologising for had even happened.[35] Then the rozzers got involved, although in a way that would be unrecognisable to most people who are subject to criminal inquiries. The Metropolitan Police started sending questionnaires to over 100 witnesses (and potential attendees) rather than the more traditional method of hauling them in for questioning. And even then, reports emerged that the police had somehow neglected to send Johnson one of the key questionnaires, leading to suggestions he'd escaped justifiable penalties because the police forgot to ask him any questions.[36]

Twelve events were formally – if partially – investigated by the Met, and in a tour-de-farce performance, Boris Johnson was handed a £50 fixed penalty notice for breaching the very lockdown rules that he had set. His wife Carrie and Rishi Sunak were also fined.[37]

The *Observer* has asserted – and no one seems to have proved otherwise – that under Boris Johnson, 10 Downing Street has become the most law-breaking address in Britain, with 126 fines handed down.[38] Johnson himself has become the first sitting prime minister in our history to have been found guilty of breaking the law in office.[39]

The Sue Gray report emerged shortly after the police fines, and revealed further sordid details. The shindigs had sometimes gone on until 4am, with attendees being given prior instructions on how to sneak out to avoid being detected by the media. Partygoers were also warned not to 'wave around' bottles of wine, because of the presence of photographers: the party was scheduled to kick off immediately after a press briefing urging the country to follow Covid rules.[40]

Staggering attendees had accidentally leaned on a panic button during one party, and the police rushed to attend, only to find Downing Street staff packed illegally into a room, getting illegally pissed during a lockdown that forbade social gatherings. Somehow, no arrests were made.[41]

At another party a fight had broken out, and shindigs had resulted in cleaners being asked to tackle red wine and vomit sprayed around the seat of government.[42] Those cleaners had been serially treated with 'a lack of respect' by Downing Street staff,[43] as had security personnel who were mocked when they attempted to stop a party in full flow.[44]

It was reported that one illegal Christmas party included a jolly-sounding section where a prize was awarded for 'Sexist of the Year,[45] and that the event to mark the departure of Number 10 communications director Lee Cain 'wasn't a leaving do' until Johnson had arrived and personally kickstarted festivities by pouring drinks for everybody.[46]

As the accusations, investigations and fines dug the government's hole deeper and deeper, Tory MPs sullied themselves seemingly without limit to defend the feckless gobshite they'd staked their careers on. They fell back on claiming all of this was mere 'fluff' (Jacob Rees-Mogg),[47] that it's not as if 'pole dancers' were present (Michael Fabricant),[48] or that nobody gets sacked for receiving speeding tickets (Brandon Lewis).[49]

And it's true, nobody gets sacked for a speeding ticket. But you do lose the right to drive if you get 126 of the bloody things, so it was hardly a rationale for Johnson and his enablers still having the keys to Downing Street.

Backbencher Alexander Stafford moved past denial and into clemency, suggesting we should forgive Boris Johnson 'as a Christian country',[50] which sounds lovely, but coincided with Johnson issuing a 'disgraceful slur' against the Archbishop of Canterbury, who had questioned the ethics of the UK's asylum policy.[51]

Fittingly, in the race to debase, nobody debased as effectively as Johnson, who – having proudly written the stirring introduction to the Ministerial Code – was faced with the probability that he'd be found to have breached that code by lying to parliament. All on his own, without reference to any MPs or other authority, he suddenly took it upon himself to remove from the code his own injunction that ministers should 'uphold the very highest standards of propriety', probably because it was obvious he hadn't.[52] He also watered down the code so ministers no longer had to resign for lying to parliament,[53] which will come in handy if he survives long enough for the standards committee to rule he lied to parliament.[54]

His attempts to tweak the rules for his own benefit was a repeat of his failed approach to the Owen Paterson affair: a frenzy of flailing desperation to avoid consequences, while all normal national leadership ground to a halt.[55] The most important function of government became the survival of the prime minister, and the public were urged to believe it was right and proper for Allegra Stratton to resign for joking about illegal parties, but entirely wrong for Boris Johnson to resign for *going to* those parties.

The most commonly parroted gibberish was that the parties and their attendant lies to parliament and the public didn't matter, since Johnson had 'got the big calls right' on Covid.[56]

But did he?

An epidemiological study found that if he'd called the first lockdown one week earlier – as he was advised to do – there would have been 34,000 fewer deaths. Two weeks earlier would have saved up to 43,000 lives[57] – that's twice as many dead Britons as we clocked up on the first day of the Somme.[58] Johnson's advisers had urged him to lock down on 14 March[59] but didn't do so until nine days later, on 23 March.[60] In the subsequent year, as the Tories turned the seat of government into a frat house,[61] 175,000 people lost their lives, and we ended up having to create an entirely new governmental department whose primary role seemed to be preventing the prime minister from getting pissed while driving a country.[62]

It's easy to place the blame for all of this at the clumbidextrous feet of one catastrophic man. Boris Johnson is, without question, an indolent, graceless, bullshitting narcissist, utterly devoid of morals and hopelessly unsuited to office. Britain's official Seven Principles of Public Life – Selflessness, Integrity, Objectivity, Openness, Accountability, Honesty and Leadership – read like you'd find them in a thesaurus as the antonym of Johnson's character.[63]

But how realistic is it for us to believe this was all done by him alone? Dominic Raab was stand-in prime minister for weeks while Johnson was hospitalised with Covid. Hancock took pains to be photographed constantly in Downing Street, burnishing his deluded self-image as an effective man of action. Each day, ministers took turns to stand in the Downing Street briefing room and speak to the nation. Truss was there regularly. Patel was there. The entire Cabinet, their entire entourage.

Are we truly expected to believe not one of these senior figures, who will doubtless continue to vie for power in coming years, noticed countless parties,[64] often with hundreds of invited guests and suitcases of wine trundling around the corridors of power, or being hurled up its walls? It's inconceivable that nobody knew this was happening. Surely they are all either deaf and blind, or servile and debased liars.

I could probably have saved a lot of time and just written that last sentence rather than an entire book. But a book you wanted, and a book you got; and now you're at the finale – or very nearly. At long last, we reached the end of 2020, which we can all agree was the most fantastic of years, just as Boris Johnson had promised. Well done for getting this far, and your reward is to go back to the beginning and start again.

Don't panic: I don't mean 2010 again. We're going further back than that, to see how this all began.

Part 4
A Perpetual Vortex of Agitation

A Perpetual Vortex of Agitation

At Christmas 1834, the statesman and politician Robert Peel delivered his Tamworth Manifesto, laying down the founding principles of a new politics for Britain.[1] His movement would not undertake radical, sudden changes but would embrace a 'careful review of institutions' and deliver 'judicious reform' once it was certain its plans would ensure 'the correction of proved abuses and the redress of real grievances'. It would bring about constancy, responsibility, substance and modest change; no longer would Britons live in 'a perpetual vortex of agitation'.

With that pledge to the nation, Peel conjured into life the modern Conservative Party.

At the end of 2020 we reached the milestone of 10 successive years of Conservative rule. During that decade there have never been more than 365 Tory MPs. This book names 156 of them in its by-no-means-comprehensive account of demonstrable lies, relentless incompetence, epic waste, serial corruption, sexual and physical assaults, official police investigations, illegal drug use, excessive alcohol consumption, addition to registers of sex pests, antidemocratic practices, abuse of power, dereliction of duty, hundreds of thousands of avoidable deaths, and repeated attempts to instigate the mass slaughter of small woodland creatures.

That's almost half of them. Tory MPs, I mean, not woodland creatures. And that number doesn't even include the various peers, donors, councillors, relatives, mistresses, tarantulas and advisers swept up in the maelstrom of transgression and despondency.

Imagine any other political party, or perhaps a union, at which over 40 per cent of senior officials had committed those offences. Can you begin to conceive of the media and public outrage? For God's sake, we had a month of shouting when Labour's Diane Abbott drank a mojito from a can on a train.[2]

Whereas under the Tories we've trashed international norms, breached election law countless times, lost the trust of our global allies, auctioned our democracy to the highest bidders, crashed our health service, undermined our educational system, demolished our welfare safety net, weakened our military, ruined our credit status, condemned our young to a desperate future, and killed 120,000 people before the pandemic even started.[3]

Britain's productivity is now 20 per cent lower than it would have been, had it continued the trend bequeathed to the Tories by Labour.[4] A decade of wage stagnation and shambolic governance means by 2026, real wages in the UK will be lower than they were in 2008.[5] Failures to tackle housing mean a record number of young adults now live with their parents.[6]

Tory rule has brought about the slowest recovery from a recession since records began.[7] Even before the pandemic, life expectancy was falling across much of the UK.[8] Investment crashed.[9] Racism soared.[10] Homelessness rose 250 per cent,[11] and we've gone from 40,000 people needing food banks each year to over 2.5 million.[12]

State debt had risen by 40 per cent even before factoring in Covid; and then the inept and late decision to prioritise the economy over health in a pandemic led to Britain having one of the highest death tolls on earth, but also the worst economic performance of any comparable major nation.

Meanwhile the government handed out towering piles of money that would stretch – quite literally – into outer space; not once, but over and over again. Party donors got it. Friends in the media got it. Landlords got it. Chums from Eton got it. It seems the only thing that had prevented us from becoming a banana republic before now was fictitious EU regulations about bananas.

In that Tory decade we've had three prime ministers, not one of whom started the job having won an election. There have been ministerial resignations by the hundred, and MPs doing a grand tour of every scandal you can imagine, and several you really don't want to. They started with basic lies and hypocrisy – which no longer raise an eyebrow, let alone demand an honourable resignation – and moved swiftly through a Heinz 57 varieties of terrible behaviour.

They ran two national referendums – or three if you're in Scotland, in which case: run, run like hell. In one of those referendums the Tories campaigned against their own promises of democratic reforms, and the other became the most pointless, divisive and damaging political rupture in living memory. Brexit has turned into a biblical curse, a rolling, unstoppable, slow-motion catastrophe that will stain our nation and impoverish our people for years to come. We're starting to recognise what a huge mistake it is: a 2022 poll found 64 per cent felt Brexit had been negative for the country, including one-third of former Leave voters.[13]

Yet our government's furious contempt for our neighbours during the entire process makes it vanishingly unlikely they would accept us back any time soon. We are trapped, victims of a scam perpetrated by spittle-flecked fanatics and implemented by vapid, overpromoted schoolboys, playing at politics until they've made enough wealthy contacts to let them cash in.

As for the second half of the Conservative and Unionist Party's name – Unionist – most of Scotland don't want to be ruled by the British government, and nobody, literally nobody, in Northern Ireland voted for a Tory MP at all.

The fact that the general public is so ignorant or accepting of this should be a cause for national shame. It's become normalised. For most of his time in public life, people chuckled at Johnson's antics, and his jokes were the highlight of many news reports. Yet it's not just him: the depth of anti-talent on the Tory benches is simply horrific.

Whether you like their politics or not, we once had a heavyweight Tory Cabinet that included Michael Heseltine, Chris Patten, David Mellor, Virginia Bottomley, Douglas Hurd, Ken Clarke and John Major. Now we have Liz Truss, Grant Shapps, Nadine Dorries, Rishi Sunak and Priti Patel, locked in a fearsome tussle over the award for Most Over-Promoted Mediocrity; and we count ourselves lucky Grayling and Williamson have finally gone.

The decline in ministerial standards has been precipitous. Many felt Thatcher's Tories were just plain evil, and John Major's party was sleazy and incompetent. Cameron's were too posh to understand how the real world worked, while May's Tories had no guiding purpose, and simply drifted from crisis to crisis as the nation drummed their fingers and waited for the leader to fall over.

Boris Johnson's Tories somehow managed to be all of that at once. From his lack of beliefs and direction sprang near-constant political chaos. In 2020 alone Johnson performed 18 major policy U-turns.[14] He was his own worst enemy, and nobody was more surprised about that than me.

How did it come to this? We must be mad. I mean that quite literally, because in a rational country David Cameron would have remained where he started: the PR guy for a local daytime TV channel. Theresa May would be the deputy head of a primary school in special measures. Nigel Farage would be a shift manager at a branch of Wetherspoons in Cleethorpes, and Boris Johnson would be a children's entertainer on administrative leave pending the outcome of a tribunal.

But we aren't in a rational country: we're in a country where the rules no longer apply. The last decade has been indistinguishable from a rollercoaster drawn by M. C. Escher, composed entirely of nauseating descents. Meanwhile the nation has heaved a weary sigh of relief at the demise of each iteration of their pointless, ghastly ministers, only to watch each one be replaced by something even worse – and then vote for them all over again.

Robert Peel's new party was designed to conserve stability. That's not a great ambition in life but it is, at least, a doctrine. His modern Conservative descendants have no doctrine but greed and conserve nothing except dominance. The entire purpose of them now is to be in power, and to use that power to manipulate political norms with the goal of helping Tories secure more power a year from now.

Once in office, they don't govern, not in a sense that would be recognisable to leaders from previous decades. They simply indulge, to an increasing and repulsive degree, in open and shameless corruption. We tend to fight shy of using that word in Britain, partly because we're scared of being sued, and partly because we still tend to think it's something that only happens in dodgy rogue nations far from supposedly civilised London.

But it isn't. Selling peerages is corruption. Giving vast public contracts to unqualified and unworthy pals from the school rugger team is corruption. VIP lanes to pap great wodges of cash into the voracious mouths of a company your mate owns is corruption. Giving public cash to your mistress, taking fat stacks of secret dosh to make your life more disgustingly self-indulgent, jetting away for freebie luxury holidays discreetly funded by billionaires with indistinct motives… all corruption. There's no other word.

But if you look at the achievements of the last few years, that's practically all they've done. There's frankly little that's been constructive. Much destruction, sure, but no building. And there is no grand plan still waiting to be revealed. Don't wait for one. It's not coming. Johnson had claimed Levelling Up was his 'defining mission',[15] but Levelling Up means shit all if you're not going to level somebody else down, and the Tories will absolutely refuse to redistribute the wealth of their ageing core vote.

I can already hear detractors insisting this book is simply a prolonged whine from the losing side, and that an elected government has the right to pursue an agenda. But before it can pursue an agenda, a government first needs to *have* an agenda.

With the exception of Brexit, the Tories have none. And they still can't define Brexit. Johnson's administration was handed a blank cheque in 2019, to which they've been adding zeroes ever since. Not one of us voted for most of his administration's subsequent major policies, because Johnson's manifesto makes no mention of them. It's government on the hoof, and today's every announcement reeks of being a desperate attempt to distract from yesterday's disaster. What is the agenda, beyond the political survival of a tiny clique around the PM?

A government has a greater responsibility than its own survival and gratification, a lesson from Robert Peel's foundational tract that today's Tories have simply forgotten. The resident of Number 10 has a responsibility to our democracy: to maintain it, and protect it, and not simply reduce it to a solitary referendum on a solitary day, from which dictatorial power emerges. Governments should be custodians of the fundamentals without which a parliamentary democracy fails: integrity, honesty, accountability, and the requirement of those in power to uphold laws and institutions – and to strengthen the public's faith in them.

But there is no responsibility, no plan, no policy agenda, no Tory path to a brighter future. Rather than a programme for government, the Tories increasingly engage in a flailing ballet of opportunistic gimmicks, each one born of paranoia and desperation, and each one granted the lifespan of a mayfly. I remain undecided if Johnson was the cause of this, or if it is an emergent behaviour arising from a deeper malaise in the party, of which Johnson is merely the most obvious recent example. Perhaps it's both.

Regardless of the cause, what the public experiences is a relentless, chaotic scream of bewildering announcements which – if we accept the precarious proposition that there is a design at all – seem designed to merely wrongfoot voters, and persuade them that there is no such thing as truth, and that all politicians are as bad as each other.

Let me tell you something: truth exists. Plans exist. Consequences exist. And all politicians are *not* the same.

It has always been in the interests of bad, lying, corrupt politicians to make you doubt those things. For venal leaders, the claim that their opponents are 'just as bad' is merely a cheap way to sow doubt in the electorate's mind. If nobody else is any better, voters might as well stick with what they've got.

But that's bollocks. A better politics *can* be found, and it *really* matters, not just in the abstract sense. Fighting for that alternative is patriotic, a hell of a lot more patriotic than flags are. The left – or at least anybody who isn't actively from the right – are commonly accused of lacking patriotic fervour, but wrapping yourself in a flag is a meaningless, shallow gesture if you don't do anything to look after the country it represents.

Patriotism is about caring for your fellow citizens – all of them, not just the ones who buy peerages. It is about decently funding our national institutions and investing in our collective futures. It involves delivering a full and enriching education for the next generation, and providing decent care and respite for the elderly and vulnerable.

It's about ensuring we have a capable and well-founded health service, a justice system that is open to all – and which applies equally to all. Patriotism is about ensuring equality of life chances, and the possibility of a home and a family. It recognises that it doesn't matter what colour, faith, gender or sexuality you are: every person in Britain is equally British, and division demeans us all.

But simply being British isn't enough. We live on this planet with billions of other people, and we have to make it work. So patriotism is building sound and convivial relationships with our neighbours and allies. It is tackling global climate change in congress with the entire world, not seeking ways to screw our rivals and condemn our grandkids to a terrifying heat death.

Patriotism is about crushing corruption and fostering decency, rather than the other way around. Those things are patriotic. Not flags. Fuck your flags. Flags are just the wrapping paper around those things, and nothing more. Yet increasingly they're wrapped around a hollowed-out nation.

The good of the public, our futures, the country, our neighbours, our allies and the world – under the Tories those things have become secondary considerations to vacuous nationalism and the acquisition of power, if they're considered at all.

The distinguishing features of the Conservative Party after a decade in office are: the deification of Winston Churchill; relentless agitation for a distracting culture war; and the corruption of our national institutions and resources for private gain. The main tool for delivering this has been chaos, behind which their malefaction has run riot. And it will continue to be like this until enough of us demand better.

If I believed in God, I'd pray for an end to this. But God isn't listening, and not enough of the public are either. Until one or the other wakes up, a perpetual vortex of agitation is where we are all doomed to live.

Notes

Part 1: The Wrong Walk to Freedom
2010: Take Up the Cudgels

1   'UK unemployment increases to 2.51 million', BBC, 12 May 2010, www.bbc.co.uk/news/
    10109965
2   'Cadbury agrees Kraft takeover bid', BBC, 19 January 2010, news.bbc.co.uk/1/hi/business
    /8467007.stm
3   '2009 full year top ten best-selling cars in Britain', Car Sales Statistics, 20 June 2011,
    www.best-selling-cars.com/britain-uk/2009-full-year-top-ten-best-selling-cars-in-britain
4   'List of MPs who stood down at the 2010 United Kingdom general election', Wikipedia, last
    edited on 14 March 2022, en.wikipedia.org/wiki/List_of_MPs_who_stood_down_at_
    the_2010_United_Kingdom_general_election
5   'Public sector net debt expressed as a percentage of gross domestic product in the
    United Kingdom from 1920/21 to 2021/22', Statista, last updated 22 February 2022,
    www.statista.com/statistics/282841/debt-as-gdp-uk
6   'UK National Debt Charts', ukpublicspending.co.uk, www.ukpublicspending.co.uk/
    debt_brief.php
7   'Public sector net debt expressed as a percentage of gross domestic product in the United
    Kingdom from 1920/21 to 2021/22'
8   Matthew Keep, *The budget deficit: A short guide*, House of Commons Library, 4 April 2022,
    commonslibrary.parliament.uk/research-briefings/sn06167
9   Ibid.
10 'Cameron lashes out at banks', City A.M., 6 October 2021,
    www.cityam.com/cameron-lashes-out-banks
11 Patrick Hennessy, 'Tories plan £14bn cuts to red tape', *Telegraph*, 12 August 2007,
    www.telegraph.co.uk/news/uknews/1560100/Tories-plan-14bn-cuts-to-red-tape.html
12 Rt Hon John Redwood MP and Simon Wolfson, *Freeing Britain to Compete:
    Equipping the UK for Globalisation*, Submission to the Shadow Cabinet, August 2007,
    image.guardian.co.uk/sys-files/Politics/documents/2007/08/17/ECPGcomplete.pdf
13 Adam Lusher, '"He is capable of awful cruelty. He is a Vulcan, not a human being"',
    Telegraph, 3 April 2005, www.telegraph.co.uk/news/uknews/1487009/He-is-capable-of-
    awful-cruelty.-He-is-a-Vulcan-not-a-human-being.html
14 'Gordon Brown "mortified" by his "bigoted woman" slur', BBC, 28 April 2010,
    news.bbc.co.uk/1/hi/uk_politics/election_2010/8649853.stm
15 David Cameron, 'A new politics: We need a massive, radical redistribution of power',
    Guardian, 25 May 2009, www.theguardian.com/commentisfree/2009/may/25/
    david-cameron-a-new-politics
16 Ben Lucas, 'General Election 2010 – what about the issues?', RSA, 27 April 2010,
    www.thersa.org/comment/2010/04/general-election-2010---what-about-the-issues
17 'The Conservative manifesto at a glance', *Guardian*, 13 April 2010,
    www.theguardian.com/politics/2010/apr/13/conservative-manifesto-at-a-glance

18 George Parker, 'Cameron struggles to prevent Tories "banging on about Europe"', *FT*, 13 May 2013, www.ft.com/content/75f0ea96-bbc3-11e2-a4b4-00144feab7de

19 Gaby Hinsliff, 'Cameron softens crime image in "hug a hoodie" call', *Guardian*, 9 July 2006, www.theguardian.com/politics/2006/jul/09/conservatives.ukcrime

20 Adam Vaughan, 'Ten years after "hug a husky", what is David Cameron's green legacy?', *Guardian*, 20 April 2016, www.theguardian.com/environment/blog/2016/apr/20/david-cameron-hug-a-husky-green-legacy-10-years

21 Patrick Wintour and Polly Curtis, 'Election 2010: Gordon Brown pledges to fight £6bn Tory cuts', *Guardian*, 24 April 2010, www.theguardian.com/politics/2010/apr/24/election-2010-gordon-brown-cuts

22 Carl Emmerson, Christine Farquharson and Paul Johnson (eds.), *The IFS Green Budget*, Institute for Fiscal Studies, October 2018, www.ifs.org.uk/uploads/publications/budgets/gb2018/GB2018.pdf

23 Andy McSmith, 'George Osborne: A silver spoon for the golden boy', *Independent*, 19 June 2010, www.independent.co.uk/news/people/profiles/george-osborne-a-silver-spoon-for-the-golden-boy-2004814.html

24 'Spending Review 2010: George Osborne wields the axe', BBC, 20 October 2010, www.bbc.co.uk/news/uk-politics-11579979

25 Emily Mee, 'Decade in Review: A look back at what happened in 2010', Sky, 31 December 2019, news.sky.com/story/decade-in-review-a-look-back-at-what-happened-in-2010-11888443

26 Press Association, 'UK could face Greece-style unrest over spending cuts, warns Nick Clegg', *Guardian*, 16 March 2010, www.theguardian.com/politics/2010/mar/16/uk-greece-style-unrest-nick-clegg-spending-cuts

27 'Spending Review 2010: George Osborne wields the axe', BBC, 20 October 2010, www.bbc.co.uk/news/uk-politics-11579979

28 'Annual growth of gross domestic product in the United Kingdom from 1949 to 2022', Statista, last updated 21 June 2022, www.statista.com/statistics/281734/gdp-growth-in-the-united-kingdom-uk

29 Jonathan Owen, 'Recovery of UK economy is the slowest since records began, say unions', *Independent*, 2 August 2015, www.independent.co.uk/news/uk/home-news/recovery-uk-economy-slowest-ever-say-unions-10432717.html

30 HM Treasury, *Budget 2010*, 22 June 2010, assets.publishing.service.gov.uk/government/uploads/system/uploads/attachment_data/file/248096/0061.pdf

31 'Public sector net debt expressed as a percentage of gross domestic product in the United Kingdom from 1920/21 to 2021/22', Statista, last updated 22 February 2022, www.statista.com/statistics/282841/debt-as-gdp-uk

32 Ibid.

33 'Fawcett Society in legal challenge to "unfair" Budget', BBC, 1 August 2010, www.bbc.co.uk/news/uk-10833190

34 Press Association, 'Fawcett Society loses court challenge to legality of budget', *Guardian*, 6 December 2010, www.theguardian.com/world/2010/dec/06/fawcett-society-loses-court-challenge-budget

35 'Spending Review 2010: George Osborne wields the axe'

36 'Theresa May's letter to the chancellor', *Guardian*, 3 August 2010, www.theguardian.com/politics/interactive/2010/aug/03/theresa-may-letter-chancellor-cuts

37 Vikram Dodd, 'Budget cuts could break equality laws, Theresa May warned chancellor', *Guardian*, 3 August 2010, www.theguardian.com/politics/2010/aug/03/budget-cuts-equality-theresa-may

38 'Have the Conservatives brought in £70 billion worth of tax cuts?', Full Fact, 20 March 2017, fullfact.org/economy/have-conservatives-brought-70-billion-worth-tax-cuts

39 Jack Peat, 'Poorest families pay 47.6% of their income in tax as top earners hive off wealth to tax havens', The London Economic, 30 May 2019, www.thelondoneconomic.com/news/poorest-families-pay-47-6-of-their-income-in-tax-as-top-earners-hive-off-wealth-to-tax-havens-134130

40 Glen Owen, 'The coalition of millionaires: 23 of the 29 members of the new cabinet are worth more than £1m... and the Lib Dems are just as wealthy as the Tories', *Daily Mail*, 23 May 2010, www.dailymail.co.uk/news/election/article-1280554/The-coalition-millionaires-23-29-member-new-cabinet-worth-1 million--Lib-Dems-just-wealthy-Tories.html

41 Ian Dunt, '2010: Year in review – part one', politics.co.uk, 1 January 2010, www.politics.co.uk/comment-analysis/2010/01/01/2010-year-in-review-part-one

42 'Conservative-Liberal Democrat coalition rule (2010–15)', Britannica, www.britannica.com /place/United-Kingdom/Conservative-Liberal-Democrat-coalition-rule-2010-15

43 'UK productivity continues lost decade', BBC, 5 April 2019, www.bbc.co.uk/news/business-47826195

44 Ian Dunt, '2010: Year in review – part one'

45 Nick McDermott, 'The gaffer's gaffes', Guardian, 30 October 2003, www.theguardian.com/ politics/2003/oct/30/conservatives.uk

46 Ibid.

47 BBC Press Office, 'Newsnight reveals inaccuracies in Iain Duncan Smith's CV', BBC press release, 19 December 2002, www.bbc.co.uk/pressoffice/pressreleases/stories/2002/12_ december/19/newsnight_ids_cv.shtml

48 Ibid.

49 Nyta Mann, 'Section 28 compromise avoids a crisis', BBC, 16 January 2003, news.bbc.co.uk /1/hi/uk_politics/2664163.stm

50 Nick McDermott, 'The gaffer's gaffes'

51 Ibid.

52 Andrew Porter and Rosa Prince, 'Pensions shake-up could see most people working into their seventies', Telegraph, 23 June 2010, web.archive.org/web/20100626100158/http:// www.telegraph.co.uk/news/newstopics/politics/7850626/Pensions-shake-up-could-see-most-people-working-into-their-seventies.html

53 Barbara Petrongolo and John Van Reenen, 'The level of youth unemployment is at a record high', LSE, 5 July 2011, blogs.lse.ac.uk/politicsandpolicy/youth-unemployment

54 Department for Work & Pensions, The Work Programme, December 2012, www.dwp.gov.uk/docs/the-work-programme.pdf

55 'New style JSA amounts', Disability Rights UK, www.disabilityrightsuk.org/contribution-based-jsa-amounts

56 'National minimum wage amounts in the United Kingdom from 1999 to 2022, by wage category', Statista, last updated 20 June 2022, www.statista.com/statistics/280483/ national-minimum-wage-in-the-uk

57 Shiv Malik, 'Sick and disabled braced for enforced work-for-benefits programme', Guardian, 30 November 2012, www.theguardian.com/politics/2012/nov/30/sick-disabled-work-benefits-programme

58 Emily Dugan, 'Thousands with degenerative conditions classified as "fit to work in future" –despite no possibility of improvement', Independent, 23 October 2014, www.independent.co.uk/news/uk/politics/thousands-degenerative-conditions-classified-fit-work-future-despite-no-possibility-improvement-9811910.html

59 Jason Beattie, 'Iain Duncan Smith to press ahead with plans to cut support for disabled and chronically ill', Mirror, 14 October 2015, www.mirror.co.uk/news/uk-news/iain-duncan-smith-press-ahead-6628337

60 Ibid.

61 Frances Ryan, 'Iain Duncan Smith thinks he can cure disabled people as if by magic', Guardian, 24 October 2014, www.theguardian.com/commentisfree/2014/oct/24/iain-duncan-smith-disabled-ms-parkinsons-dwp

62 'Universal Credit introduced', press release from Department for Work and Pensions and The Rt Hon Iain Duncan Smith MP, 5 October 2010, www.gov.uk/government/news/ universal-credit-introduced

63 Hannah Richardson, 'Thousands of depression cases "linked to universal credit"', BBC, 28 February 2020, www.bbc.co.uk/news/education-51664792

64 Amelia Gentleman, 'Universal credit pilot to launch with only a few dozen claimants', Guardian, 26 April 2013, www.theguardian.com/society/2013/apr/26/universal-credit-pilot-launch

65 Amelia Gentleman, 'Teething troubles on day one of universal credit pilot scheme', Guardian, 29 April 2013, www.theguardian.com/society/2013/apr/29/universal-credit-pilot-scheme

66 Michael Buchanan, 'Universal credit rollout delayed yet again', BBC, 16 October 2018, www.bbc.co.uk/news/uk-45870553

67   Rajeev Syal and Rowena Mason, 'Labour says universal credit will take 495 years to roll out as costs rise £3bn', *Guardian*, 25 June 2015, www.theguardian.com/society/2015/jun/25/labour-says-universal-credit-will-take-495-years-to-roll-out-as-costs-rise-3bn

68   Hannah Richardson, 'Universal Credit "could cost more than current benefits system"', BBC, 15 June 2018, www.bbc.co.uk/news/education-44468437

69   Patrick Butler, 'Cost of rolling out universal credit rises by £1.4bn, say auditors', *Guardian*, 10 July 2020, www.theguardian.com/society/2020/jul/10/cost-of-rolling-out-universal-credit-rises-by-14bn-say-auditors

70   James Moore, 'Universal credit plunges kids into poverty and 120,000 have died because of austerity – but Jacob Rees-Mogg wants more cuts', *Independent*, 16 November 2017, www.independent.co.uk/voices/nhs-austerity-cuts-120000-deaths-universal-credit-only-get-worse-a8058231.html

71   Simon Hoggart, 'Simon Hoggart's 2010 political review: heroes and zeroes in year of change', *Guardian*, 17 December 2010, www.theguardian.com/politics/2010/dec/17/simon-hoggart-political-review-2010

72   Peter Walker, 'Tory peer Howard Flight apologies over poor people "breeding" comments', *Guardian*, 25 November 2010, www.theguardian.com/politics/2010/nov/25/howard-flight-rebuked-no-10-poor-people-breeding

73   Ian Jack, 'Rees-Mogg's roots tell a true Conservative tale – just not the one he wants us to hear', *Guardian*, 22 January 2022, www.theguardian.com/commentisfree/2022/jan/22/jacob-rees-mogg-roots-conservative-mp

74   Scotsman Reporter, 'Looking back: When a young Jacob Rees-Mogg campaigned in Scotland with his nanny', *Scotsman*, 4 September 2019, www.scotsman.com/news/politics/brexit/looking-back-when-young-jacob-rees-mogg-campaigned-scotland-his-nanny-1408562

75   'Sajid Javid: From risky business to business secretary', Euromoney, 13 May 2015, www.euromoney.com/article/b12km259jtpqtd/sajid-javid-from-risky-business-to-business-secretary

76   Permanent Subcommittee on Investigations, *Wall Street and the Financial Crisis: Anatomy of a Financial Collapse*, United States Senate, 13 April 2011, www.hsgac.senate.gov/imo/media/doc/PSI%20REPORT%20-%20Wall%20Street%20&%20the%20Financial%20Crisis-Anatomy%20of%20a%20Financial%20Collapse%20(FINAL%205-10-11).pdf

77   Richard Partington, 'John McDonnell questions chancellor's suitability for office', *Guardian*, 5 August 2019, www.theguardian.com/politics/2019/aug/05/john-mcdonnell-questions-chancellors-suitability-for-office

78   'Sajid Javid: Parliamentary career', MPs and Lords, UK Parliament, members.parliament.uk/member/3945/career

79   Brian Groom, 'Young minister has the skills to climb to the top in Westminster', *FT*, 10 July 2014, www.ft.com/content/027bd85e-0290-11e4-a68d-00144feab7de

80   Becky Barrow, 'Ebay bidders go wild for April 8 memorabilia', *Telegraph*, 9 April 2005, www.telegraph.co.uk/news/uknews/1487452/Ebay-bidders-go-wild-for-April-8-memorabilia.html

81   Ian Parker, 'Paths of glory', *New Yorker*, 7 November 2010, www.newyorker.com/magazine/2010/11/15/paths-of-glory-ian-parker

82   'Mark Reckless MP sorry for being "too drunk to vote"', BBC, 11 July 2010, www.bbc.co.uk/news/10590725

83   'The Rt Hon Elizabeth Truss MP', Gov.uk, www.gov.uk/government/people/elizabeth-truss

84   Dale Bassett, Thomas Cawston, Laurie Thraves and Elizabeth Truss, *A new level*, Reform, June 2009, web.archive.org/web/20120406100248/http://www.reform.co.uk/pages/2152/view

85   Press Association, 'Tory Elizabeth Truss faces deselection vote in two weeks over affair', *Guardian*, 5 November 2009, www.theguardian.com/politics/2009/nov/05/elizabeth-truss-deselection-affair

86   Jamie Doward, 'Minister worked as spin doctor for tobacco giant that paid workers £15 a month', *Guardian*, 31 May 2015, www.theguardian.com/business/2015/may/30/priti-patel-worked-as-spin-doctor-tobacco-firm-burma-scandal

87   'Q&A: Tuition fees', BBC, 14 September 2011, www.bbc.co.uk/news/education-11483638

88 Seeta Bhardwa, "'I feel conned": UK students on soaring rates of student debt', Times Higher Education, 13 July 2017, www.timeshighereducation.com/student/blogs/i-feel-conned-uk-students-soaring-rates-student-debt

89 'Distribution of median and mean income and tax by age range and gender, 2010–11', A National Statistics Publication, 2012, assets.publishing.service.gov.uk/government/uploads/system/uploads/attachment_data/file/267112/table3-2-1.xls

90 Angela Harrison, 'Violence at Tory HQ overshadows student fees protest', BBC, 10 November 2010, www.bbc.co.uk/news/education-11726822

91 Jeevan Vasagar, 'Universities alarmed by 40% cut to teaching budgets', Guardian, 20 October 2010, www.theguardian.com/education/2010/oct/20/spending-review-university-teaching-cuts

92 Liberal Democrats, 'Liberal Democrats: Say goodbye to broken promises', YouTube, 13 April 2010, www.youtube.com/watch?v=jTLR8R9JXz4

93 Simon Hoggart, 'Simon Hoggart's 2010 political review: heroes and zeroes in year of change'

94 Harry Mount, 'The students and police I saw toder were utterly dignified', Telegraph, 10 November 2010, web.archive.org/web/20101112094136/http://blogs.telegraph.co.uk/culture/harrymount/100048723/the-students-and-police-i-saw-today-were-utterly-dignified

95 OECD, Education at a Glance 2019, 2019, www.oecd.org/education/education-at-a-glance/EAG2019_CN_GBR.pdf

96 Sam Courtney-Guy, 'Higher education in England among world's most expensive, report says', Metro, 10 September 2019, www.metro.co.uk/2019/09/10/higher-education-england-among-worlds-expensive-report-says-10719210

97 David Leigh and Rob Evans, 'Salaries soar for heads of British universities', Guardian, 14 March 2010, www.theguardian.com/education/2010/mar/14/university-heads-vice-chancellor-salaries

98 Jamie Johnson, 'Average university vice chancellor now earns more than £250k for the first time, as majority given pay rises in last year despite criticism', Telegraph, 12 February 2019, www.telegraph.co.uk/news/2019/02/12/average-university-vice-chancellor-now-earns-250k-first-time

99 Jeevan Vasagar, Amelia Hill and Afua Hirsch, 'Public anger grows over scrapped school-building programme', Guardian, 8 July 2010, www.theguardian.com/education/2010/jul/08/schools-building-michael-gove-public-anger

100 Jessica Shepherd, 'Michael Gove apologises for blunders in cancelled school project list', Guardian, 8 July 2010, www.theguardian.com/politics/2010/jul/08/michael-gove-cancelled-school-projects

101 Ian Liddell-Grainger, 'Why I campaign', accessed 28 June 2022, liddellgrainger.org.uk/campaigns/why-i-campaign

102 Hélène Mulholland and Paul Owen, 'Tory MP plans march against Michael Gove's education cuts', Guardian, 8 July 2010, www.theguardian.com/politics/2010/jul/08/tory-mp-march-downing-street-michael-gove-cuts

103 'The national curriculum', Gov.uk, accessed 28 June 2022, www.gov.uk/national-curriculum

104 James Carr, 'Five free schools cost more than £30m, new figures show', Schools Week, 4 February 2020, schoolsweek.co.uk/five-free-schools-cost-more-than-30m-new-figures-show

105 Jess Staufenberg, 'Revealed: The hidden cost of free schools', Schools Week, 26 January 2018, schoolsweek.co.uk/revealed-the-hidden-cost-of-free-schools

106 James Carr, 'Five free schools cost more than £30m, new figures show'

107 'Harris Westminster Sixth Form', Wikipedia, last edited on 18 October 2021, en.wikipedia.org/wiki/Harris_Westminster_Sixth_Form

108 Jeevan Vasagar, 'Free school plan comes at a price for voluntary groups', Guardian, 17 January 2011, www.theguardian.com/education/2011/jan/17/young-free-school-groups-refugees

109 'West London Free School', Wikipedia, last edited on 3 March 2022, en.wikipedia.org/wiki/West_London_Free_School

110 James Carr, 'Five free schools cost more than £30m, new figures show'

111 'Free school (England)', Wikipedia, last edited on 12 June 2022, en.wikipedia.org/wiki/Free_school_(England)

112 Sally Weale, 'Free schools policy under fire as another closure announced', *Guardian*, 25 April 2018, www.theguardian.com/politics/2018/apr/25/free-schools-policy-under-fire-as -yet-another-closure-announced-plymouth

113 Jess Staufenberg, 'Revealed: The hidden cost of free schools'

114 James Carr, 'Five free schools cost more than £30m, new figures show'

115 'Number of people receiving three days' worth of emergency food by Trussell Trust foodbanks in the United Kingdom from 2008/09 to 2021/22', Statista, 11 May 2022, www.statista.com/statistics/382695/uk-foodbank-users

116 Warwick Mansell, 'The 60% extra funds enjoyed by England's free school pupils', *Guardian*, 25 August 2015, www.theguardian.com/education/2015/aug/25/extra-funds-free-schools- warwick-mansell

117 Antony Mason, 'New research shows austerity is favouring older voters at the expense of the young', Intergenerational Foundation, 23 November 2015, www.if.org.uk/2015/11/23 /new-research-shows-austerity-is-favouring-older-voters-at-the-expense-of-the-young

118 'Average UK savings by age', Occam Investing, occaminvesting.co.uk/average-savings-by- age-in-the-uk-savings-statistics

119 Antony Mason, 'New research shows austerity is favouring older voters at the expense of the young'

120 Chris Curtis, 'The demographics diving Britain', YouGov, 25 April 2017, www.yougov.co.uk /topics/politics/articles-reports/2017/04/25/demographics-dividing-britain

121 Christopher Hope, 'Local people to get powers to veto excessive council tax rises, Eric Pickles to say today', *Telegraph*, 30 July 2010, www.telegraph.co.uk/news/politics/7917021/ Local-people-to-get-powers-to-veto-excessive-council-tax-rises-Eric-Pickles-to-say-today. html

122 Polly Curtis, 'Eric Pickles unveils biggest council budget cuts in recent times', *Guardian*, 13 December 2010, www.theguardian.com/politics/2010/dec/13/eric-pickles-council- budget-cuts

123 Patrick Butler, '"Territorial injustice" may rise in England due to council cuts – study', *Guardian*, 9 October 2018, www.theguardian.com/society/2018/oct/09/territorial-injustice- on-rise-england-due-to-council-cuts-study

124 David Cameron, 'Full text of David Cameron's speech', *Guardian*, 8 October 2009, www.the guardian.com/politics/2009/oct/08/david-cameron-speech-in-full

125 'MP: Long hours justify second home claim', BBC, 27 March 2009, news.bbc.co.uk/1/hi/ programmes/question_time/7967561.stm

126 Larry Elliott, 'Budget will cost 1.3m jobs – Treasury', *Guardian*, 29 June 2010, www.theguardian.com/uk/2010/jun/29/budget-job-losses-unemployment-austerity

127 Benjamin Kentish, 'Number of new social homes being built down 90% since Tories came to power in 2010', *Independent*, 19 June 2018, www.independent.co.uk/news/uk/politics/ social-housing-uk-labour-tories-2010-election-government-building-council- houses-a8406626.html

128 Esteban Ortiz-Ospina and Max Roser, 'Homelessness', Our World in Data, 2017, www.ourworldindata.org/homelessness-rise-england

129 Cassie Barton and Wendy Wilson, *Rough sleeping (England)*, UK Parliament, House of Commons Library, 23 April 2022, commonslibrary.parliament.uk/research-briefings/sn0 2007; 'How many people are homeless in the UK? And what can you do about it?', The Big Issue, 29 April 2022, www.bigissue.com/latest/social-activism/how-many-people-are- homeless-in-the-uk-and-what-can-you-do-about-it

130 Alex Firth, 'Every child in the UK deserves a safe and secure home', Human Rights Watch, 14 December 2020, www.hrw.org/news/2020/12/14/every-child-uk-deserves-safe-and-secu re-home

131 James Randerson, 'Cameron: I want coalition to be the "greenest government ever"', *Guardian*, 14 May 2010, www.theguardian.com/environment/2010/may/14/cameron-wan ts-greenest-government-ever

132 Juliette Jowit, 'Spending review: "Greenest government ever" reserves worst cuts for Defra', *Guardian*, 20 October 2010, www.theguardian.com/environment/2010/oct/20/spending-re view-cuts-environment

133 Sabrina Weiss, 'The UK's big flooding problem is only going to get worse', *Wired*, 26 June 2019, www.wired.co.uk/article/flooding-in-uk-weather-defence

134 'Spending Review 2010: George Osborne wields the axe', BBC

135 Juliette Jowit, 'Spending review: "Greenest government ever" reserves worst cuts for Defra'

136 *2010 to 2015 government policy: flooding and coastal change*, policy paper, 2010 to 2015 Conservative and Liberal Democrat coalition government, 8 May 2015, www.gov.uk/government/publications/2010-to-2015-government-policy-flooding-and-coastal-change/2010-to-2015-government-policy-flooding-and-coastal-change

137 Sally Weale, 'Youth services suffer 70% funding cut in less than a decade', *Guardian*, 20 January 2020, www.theguardian.com/society/2020/jan/20/youth-services-suffer-70-funding-cut-in-less-than-a-decade

138 'Youth services cut by 70% since 2010: £880mcut from services for young people since Tories came to power', Labour, 15 April 2019, labour.org.uk/press/youth-services-cut-70-since-2010-880m-cut-services-young-people-since-tories-came-power

139 Andrew Johnson, Ian Griggs and Brian Brady, 'Now it's the age of the knife', *Independent*, 3 February 2008, www.independent.co.uk/news/uk/crime/now-it-s-the-age-of-the-knife-777548.html

140 'Cameron "hoodie" speech in full', BBC, 10 July 2006, news.bbc.co.uk/1/hi/5166498.stm

141 Sally Weale, 'Youth services suffer 70% funding cut in less than a decade'

142 Dave Hill, 'Boris Johnson: Met records big increase in young people injured by knives on his watch', *Guardian*, 12 July 2011, www.theguardian.com/politics/davehillblog/2011/jul/12/boris-johnson-rise-knife-crime-injuries-of-young-people

143 'Leading article: Bridging the Tory credibility gap', *Independent*, 25 March 2009, www.independent.co.uk/voices/editorials/leading-article-bridging-the-tory-credibility-gap-1653322.html

144 Alan Travis, 'Spending review 2010: Policing and criminal justice cut by 20%', *Guardian*, 20 October 2010, www.theguardian.com/politics/2010/oct/20/spending-review-police-cuts

145 Rachel Schraer, 'Have police numbers dropped?', BBC, 26 July 2019, www.bbc.co.uk/news/uk-47225797

146 Amelia Hill, '"Hostile environment": the hardline Home Office policy tearing families apart', *Guardian*, 28 November 2017, www.theguardian.com/uk-news/2017/nov/28/hostile-environment-the-hardline-home-office-policy-tearing-families-apart

147 Simon Hattenstone, 'Why was the scheme behind May's "Go Home" vans called Operation Vaken?', *Guardian*, 26 April 2018, www.theguardian.com/commentisfree/2018/apr/26/theresa-may-go-home-vans-operation-vaken-ukip

148 'Farage attacks "nasty" immigration posters', BBC, 25 July 2013, www.bbc.co.uk/news/uk-politics-23450438

149 Alan Travis, '"Go home" vans resulted in 11 people leaving Britain, says report', *Guardian*, 31 October 2013, www.theguardian.com/uk-news/2013/oct/31/go-home-vans-11-leave-britain

150 Peter Walker, 'Government faces high court challenge over "right to rent" scheme', *Guardian*, 6 June 2018, www.theguardian.com/uk-news/2018/jun/06/government-faces-high-court-challenge-right-rent-scheme

151 Amelia Hill and Diane Taylor, 'Right to Rent scheme ruled incompatible with human rights law', *Guardian*, 1 March 2019, www.theguardian.com/uk-news/2019/mar/01/right-to-rent-scheme-ruled-incompatible-with-human-rights-law

152 May Bulman, 'Austerity measures and hostile environment "entrenching racism" in UK, says UN', *Independent*, 15 June 2019, www.independent.co.uk/news/uk/home-news/austerity-racism-hostile-environment-xenophobia-un-report-rapporteur-immigration-bame-a8959866.html

153 Satbir Singh, 'The hostile environment is indefensible. Now we know it's unlawful too', *Guardian*, 25 November 2020, www.theguardian.com/commentisfree/2020/nov/25/hostile-environment-unlawful-ehrc-report-windrush-scandal-policy

154 Jack Peat, 'Theresa May: "We can deport first and hear appeals later"', The London Economic, 19 April 2018, www.thelondoneconomic.com/news/theresa-may-we-can-deport-first-and-hear-appeals-later-86745

155 'The "hostile environment"', the 3 million, www.the3million.org.uk/hostile-environment

156 Diane Taylor, 'Disabled Briton held in immigration removal centre for four months', *Guardian*, 4 April 2018, www.theguardian.com/uk-news/2018/apr/04/disabled-briton-held-immigration-removal-centre-four-months

157 'Bangor man detained for four months in deportation centre due to be released', *Bangor Aye*, 6 April 2018, www.thebangoraye.com/bangor-man-detained-four-months-deportation-centre-due-released

158 Alan Travis, 'ID cards scheme to be scrapped within 100 days', *Guardian*, 27 May 2010, www.theguardian.com/politics/2010/may/27/theresa-may-scrapping-id-cards

159 'Cannock Jobcentre to close as Government closes 22 UK offices', BusinessLive, 30 May 3013, www.business-live.co.uk/economic-development/cannock-jobcentre-close-government-closes-3921099

160 Denis Campbell, 'David Cameron faces pressure as NHS waiting times grow', *Guardian*, 19 April 2012, www.theguardian.com/society/2012/apr/19/david-cameron-pressure-nhs-waiting-times

161 Patrick Collinson, 'One in 65 UK adults now a millionaire, figures show', *Guardian*, 27 August 2015, www.theguardian.com/uk-news/2015/aug/27/number-of-millionaires-in-uk-rises-by-200000

162 'The scale of ecoenmic inequality in the UK', The Equality Trust, www.equalitytrust.org.uk/scale-economic-inequality-uk

163 Will Hutton, 'Cameron, Alexander, Osborne, Clegg: how the austerity "quad" sold their souls', *Guardian*, 16 May 2021, www.theguardian.com/commentisfree/2021/may/16/austerity-quad-sold-their-souls-cameron-osborne-alexander-clegg

164 'United Kingdom / Government debt (2010)', Eurostat, www.google.com/search?q=national+debt+uk+2010; 'United Kingdom / Government debt (2011)', Eurostat, www.google.com/search?q=national+debt+uk+2011

165 Daniel Boffey, 'Recession is a good time to boost profits, says Cameron aide', *Guardian*, 11 May 2013, www.theguardian.com/business/2013/may/11/young-recession-cheap-labour

166 Patrick Wintour, 'Lord Young resigns over recession gaffe', *Guardian*, 19 November 2010, www.theguardian.com/politics/2010/nov/19/lord-young-resigns-recession

167 Todd Cardy, 'Offensive Young returns to favour', Growth Business, 19 October 2011, www.growthbusiness.co.uk/offensive-young-returns-to-favour-1676553

168 Ibid.

169 Daniel Boffey, 'Recession is a good time to boost profits, says Cameron aide'

170 Robert Booth, 'David Cameron accused of being dishonest over links with "Conservative madrasa"', *Guardian*, 5 May 2010, www.theguardian.com/politics/2010/may/05/young-britons-foundation-david-cameron

171 Ibid.

172 Allegra Stratton, 'Tory bill attempts to water down minimum wage', *Guardian*, 13 May 2009, www.theguardian.com/politics/2009/may/13/minimum-wage-tory-bill

173 Leo Hickman, 'Cabal of climate sceptics to descend on UK parliament', *Guardian*, 26 October 2010, www.theguardian.com/environment/blog/2010/oct/25/climate-fools-day-sceptics-parliament?INTCMP=SRCH

174 Amy Willis, 'General Election 2010: who are the newspapers backing?', *Telegraph*, 2 May 2010, www.telegraph.co.uk/news/election-2010/7664387/General-Election-2010-who-are-the-newspapers-backing.html

175 'BBC's Craig Oliver replacing Andy Coulson at No 10', BBC, 2 February 2011, www.bbc.co.uk/news/uk-politics-12348159

176 'About This Week', BBC, news.bbc.co.uk/1/hi/programmes/this_week/about_the_show/default.stm

177 'The Daily Politics', Programme Index, BBC, genome.ch.bbc.co.uk/9cbf839c7ce94567853a1c53d3f680f5

178 Freddy Mayhew, 'Daily Politics editor Robbie Gibb leaving BBC for new role as Prime Minister's head of communications', PressGazette, 6 July 2017, www.pressgazette.co.uk/daily-politics-editor-robbie-gibb-leaving-bbc-for-new-role-as-prime-ministers-head-of-communications

179 'Nick Robinson: Northern, arsey, confrontational', *Independent*, 18 September 2006, www.independent.co.uk/news/media/nick-robinson-northern-arsey-confrontational-416446.html

180 Peter Dominiczak, 'A history of Conservative university associations', *Telegraph*, 14 May 2014, www.telegraph.co.uk/news/politics/10828746/A-history-of-Conservative-university-associations.html

181 Benjamin Kentish, 'BBC journalist James Landale turns down job working as Theresa May's head of communications', *Independent*, 5 July 2017, www.independent.co.uk/news/uk/politics/ames-landale-theresa-may-job-turn-down-bbc-head-communications-prime-minister-number-10-downing-street-a7824291.html

182 Mike Berry, 'Hard Evidence: how biased is the BBC?', The Conversation, 23 August 2013, orca.cf.ac.uk/140008/1/hardevidence_berry.pdf

2011: Fornicating Hippies

1 Sharlene Goff and George Parker, 'Diamond says time for remorse is over', *FT*, 11 January 2011, www.ft.com/content/d4f02d66-1d84-11e0-a163-00144feab49a

2 'RBS chief Stephen Hester to get £963,000 bonus', BBC, 26 January 2012, www.bbc.co.uk/news/business-16751691

3 'Cameron gets tough on bankers with promise to block RBS bonus', *The Times*, 12 November 2011, www.thetimes.co.uk/article/cameron-gets-tough-on-bankers-with-promise-to-block-rbs-bonus-t5wd7hcztb3

4 James Lyons, 'Conservative party links to fat cat bankers revealed by Daily Mirror investigation', *Mirror*, 10 January 2011, www.mirror.co.uk/news/uk-news/conservative-party-links-fat-cat-103271

5 Vincent Moss, 'Fury over Tory Party fundraising ball sponsored by mega-rich bankers', *Mirror*, 30 January 2011, www.mirror.co.uk/news/uk-news/fury-over-tory-party-fundraising-107529

6 Nicholas Watt and Jill Treanor, 'Revealed: 50% of Tory funds come from City', *Guardian*, 8 February 2011, www.theguardian.com/politics/2011/feb/08/tory-funds-half-city-banks-financial-sector

7 Vincent Moss, 'Fury over Tory Party fundraising ball sponsored by mega-rich bankers'

8 Jill Treanor, 'Bob Diamond grilled by MPs – blog', *Guardian*, 11 January 2011, www.theguardian.com/business/blog/2011/jan/11/bob-diamond-bank-bonuses-mps

9 Jill Treanor, 'Barclays chief Bob Diamond takes home £17m in pay, shares and perks', *Guardian*, 9 March 2012, www.theguardian.com/business/2012/mar/09/barclays-chief-bob-diamond-pay

10 Jill Treanor, 'Bank levy to raise £2.5bn a year but bigger banks could still gain', *Guardian*, 21 October 2010, www.theguardian.com/business/2010/oct/21/bank-levy-to-raise-two-billion-pounds

11 D. Clark, 'Number of people using food banks in the UK 2008–2022', Statista, 11 May 2022, www.statista.com/statistics/382695/uk-foodbank-users

12 Patrick Wintour and Nick Davies, 'Andy Coulson resigns as phone-hacking scandal rocks Downing Street', *Guardian*, 21 January 2011, www.theguardian.com/media/2011/jan/21/andy-coulson-resigns-david-cameron

13 'Andy Coulson quits Number 10', *Telegraph*, 21 January 2011, www.telegraph.co.uk/news/politics/david-cameron/8274940/Andy-Coulson-quits-Number-10.html

14 Robert Booth, Hélène Mulholland and Vikram Dodd, 'Pressure mounts on David Cameron over Andy Coulson's security level', *Guardian*, 21 July 2011, www.theguardian.com/media/2011/jul/21/david-cameron-andy-coulson-security-vetting

15 Molly Fitzpatrick, 'How to watch TV like a world leader', *Guardian*, 24 July 2014, www.theguardian.com/tv-and-radio/2014/jul/24/the-wire-obama-seinfeld-scalia-tv-leader

16 Robert Booth, Hélène Mulholland and Vikram Dodd, 'Pressure mounts on David Cameron over Andy Coulson's security level'

17 James Robinson and Polly Curtis, 'Andy Coulson reportedly paid by News International when hired by Tories', *Guardian*, 23 August 2011, www.theguardian.com/media/2011/aug/23/andy-coulson-news-international-tories

18 'David Cameron to make more government data available', BBC, 31 May 2010, www.bbc.co.uk/news/10195808

19 Nick Davies and Amelia Hill, 'Missing Molly Dowler's voicemail was hacked by News of the World', *Guardian*, 4 July 2011, www.theguardian.com/uk/2011/jul/04/milly-dowler-voicemail-hacked-news-of-world

20 'List of victims of the News International phone hacking scandal', Wikipedia, last edited on 26 May 2022, en.wikipedia.org/wiki/List_of_victims_of_the_News_International_phone_hacking_scandal

21 Nick Davies and Amelia Hill, 'News of the World targeted phone of Sarah Payne's mother', *Guardian*, 28 July 2011, www.theguardian.com/media/2011/jul/28/phone-hacking-sarah-payne

22 Helen Pidd, 'Adam Smith and Frédéric Michel: an intimate correspondence', *Guardian*, 25 April 2012, www.theguardian.com/politics/2012/apr/25/adam-smith-frederic-michel-correspondence

23 Joe Murphy and Nicholas Cecil, 'Murdoch emails scandal claims adviser to Jeremy Hunt as its first victim', *Evening Standard*, 25 April 2012, www.standard.co.uk/news/politics/murdoch-emails-scandal-claims-adviser-to-jeremy-hunt-as-its-first-victim-7677923.html

24 Iain Martin, 'The night I saw Jeremy Hunt hide behind a tree before dinner with James Murdoch...', CAPX, 26 February 2016, capx.co/the-night-i-saw-jeremy-hunt-hide-behind-a-tree

25 John Harris, 'How the phone-hacking scandal unmasked the British power elite', *Guardian*, 18 July 2011, www.theguardian.com/media/2011/jul/18/phone-hacking-british-power-elite

26 Reuters Staff, 'UPDATE 1-UK's Osborne had 16 meetings with Murdoch execs', Reuters, 26 July 2011, www.reuters.com/article/britain-osborne-idUSL6E7IQ1IS20110726

27 'UK: David Cameron admits to riding Rebekah Brooks' police horse', *The World*, 2 March 2012, www.pri.org/stories/2012-03-02/uk-david-cameron-admits-riding-rebekah-brooks-police-horse

28 James Robinson and Polly Curtis, 'Andy Coulson reportedly paid by News International when hired by Tories'

29 Ian Katz, 'David Cameron and Rebekah Brooks: a special relationship', *Guardian*, 14 July 2011, www.theguardian.com/commentisfree/2011/jul/14/cameron-brooks-special-relationship

30 'David Cameron statement in response to the Leveson Inquiry report', *Guardian*, 29 November 2012, www.theguardian.com/media/2012/nov/29/leveson-inquiry-david-cameron-statement

31 'News of the World to close amid hacking scandal', BBC, 7 July 2011, www.bbc.co.uk/news/uk-14070733

32 Dan Sabbagh and Lisa O'Carroll, 'Rebekah Brooks took £10.8m compensation from News Corp', *Guardian*, 12 December 2012, www.theguardian.com/uk/2012/dec/12/rebekah-brooks-news-corp

33 'Human capital estimates in the UK: 2004 to 2018', Office for National Statistics, 28 October 2019, www.ons.gov.uk/peoplepopulationandcommunity/wellbeing/articles/humancapitalestimates/2004to2018

34 Freddy Mayhew, 'The biggest newspaper groups in the UK: Rothermere and Murdoch control two thirds of market', *PressGazette*, 18 August 2020, www.pressgazette.co.uk/biggest-news-groups-uk

35 Severin Carrell, 'Salmond hails "historic" victory as SNP secures Holyrood's first ever majority', *Guardian*, 6 May 2011, www.theguardian.com/politics/2011/may/06/scottish-elections-salmond-historic-victory-snp

36 Jessica Shepherd, 'Nadine Dorries: Teenage girls should be taught how to say no to sex', *Guardian*, 4 May 2011, www.theguardian.com/politics/2011/may/04/nadine-dorries-teenage-girls

37 Guy Lodge and Glenn Gottfried, 'In 2005 not a single MP was returned with active majority support amongst their local citizens', LSE Blog, 10 January 2011, blogs.lse.ac.uk/politicsandpolicy/first-past-the-post-no-longer-fit-for-purpose

38 'Analysis: Millions of votes go to waste as parties need "wildly" different number of votes per MP', Electoral Reform Society, 13 December 2019, www.electoral-reform.org.uk/latest-news-and-research/media-centre/press-releases/analysis-millions-of-votes-go-to-waste-as-parties-need-wildly-different-number-of-votes-per-mp

39 Liam D. Anderson, 'Voters per MP: why First Past The Post failed', openDemocracy, 21 May 2015, www.opendemocracy.net/en/opendemocracyuk/voters-per-mp-why-first-past-post-failed

40 Simon Jeffery, 'Election 2010: How much is your vote worth?', *Guardian*, 9 April 2010, www.theguardian.com/politics/blog/2010/apr/09/election-2010-website-vote

41 'Elections in the United Kingdom', Wikipedia, last edited on 8 July 2022, en.wikipedia.org/wiki/Elections_in_the_United_Kingdom

42 D. Clark, 'Share of votes in UK elections 1918–2019', Statista, 13 August 2021, www.statista.com/statistics/717004/general-elections-vote-share-by-party-uk

43 'Timeline of British governments since 1900', Institute for Government, www.instituteforgovernment.org.uk/charts/timeline-british-governments-1900

44 Patrick Wintour, 'AV reform is "inherently unfair", says David Cameron', *Guardian*, 18 February 2011, www.theguardian.com/politics/2011/feb/18/av-reform-david-cameron

45 '250 million reasons to say no to AV: Why our country can't afford it', NOtoAV, web.archive.org/web/20110311045010/http://votemay5th.notoav.org/documents/the-cost-of-AV.pdf

46 Samira Shackle, '"No campaign used made-up figures", says David Blunkett', *New Statesman*, 5 May 2011, www.newstatesman.com/blogs/the-staggers/2011/05/campaign-figure-blunkett

47 'England riots: Maps and timeline', BBC, 15 August 2011, www.bbc.co.uk/news/uk-14436499

48 Tim Adams, 'England riots: justice grinds on as courts sit through the night', *Guardian*, 14 August 2011, www.theguardian.com/uk/2011/aug/14/riots-courts-justice-metropolitan-police

49 Peter Oborne, 'The moral decay of our society is as bad at the top as the bottom', *Telegraph*, 11 August 2011, web.archive.org/web/20160325141128/http://blogs.telegraph.co.uk/news/peteroborne/100100708/the-moral-decay-of-our-society-is-as-bad-at-the-top-as-the-bottom

50 'London Riots Survey', Online fieldwork: 10–11 August 2011, web.archive.org/web/2012101 7193956/http://www.comres.co.uk/polls/Ios_SM_LondonRiots_12thAugust11.pdf

51 James Meikle, 'Nick Clegg: police funding cuts will not change despite riots', *Guardian*, 11 August 2011, www.theguardian.com/politics/2011/aug/11/nick-clegg-police-funding-cuts-riots

52 'England riots: Broken society is top priority – Cameron', BBC, 15 August 2011, www.bbc.co.uk/news/uk-politics-14524834

53 'Riots: Miliband blames "me first" culture', BBC, 12 August 2011, www.bbc.co.uk/news/uk-politics-14503023

54 'England riots: Broken society is top priority – Cameron', BBC

55 Nick Parker, 'Ex-PM David Cameron blows ANOTHER £25,000 on second shed, this time for his Cornish clifftop getaway', *Sun*, 10 August 2018, www.thesun.co.uk/news/6983328/ex-pm-david-cameron-blows-another-25000-on-second-shed-this-time-for-his-cornish-clifftop-getaway

56 'Benefits cap "could make 40,000 families homeless"', 4 News, 3 July 2011, www.channel4.com/news/benefits-cap-could-make-40-000-families-homeless

57 'Full text of letter from the office of Eric Pickles', *Guardian*, 2 July 2011, www.theguardian.com/politics/2011/jul/02/full-text-letter-eric-pickles-welfare-reform

58 Ibid.

59 Home Office and The Rt Hon Theresa May MP, 'Securing borders: Home Secretary's oral statement on suspensions in UK Border Force', Oral statement to Parliament, Gov.uk, 7 November 2011, www.gov.uk/government/speeches/securing-borders-home-secretarys-or al-statement-on-suspensions-in-uk-border-force

60 Alan Travis, 'Brodie Clark tells MPs: Theresa May destroyed my reputation', *Guardian*, 15 November 2011, www.theguardian.com/uk/2011/nov/15/brodie-clark-theresa-may-reputation

61 Press Association, 'UK Border Agency expects to axe 5,000 jobs', *Guardian*, 9 November 2010, www.theguardian.com/uk/2010/nov/09/uk-border-agency-axe-jobs

62 Steve Doughty, 'Immigration "boosted the UK population by 1.75m in just eight years"', *Daily Mail*, 19 May 2011, www.dailymail.co.uk/news/article-1388472/UK-immigration-boosted-population-1-75m-8-years.html

63 Sarah O'Grady, 'Migrant workers flooding Britain', *Express*, 27 May 2011, www.express.co.uk/news/uk/249097/Migrant-workers-flooding-Britain

64 'Theresa May should relax border checks, says Keith Vaz', BBC, 26 July 2012, www.bbc.co.uk/news/uk-politics-18985273

65 Home Office and The Rt Hon Theresa May MP, 'Securing borders: Home Secretary's oral statement on suspensions in UK Border Force'

66 'Head of US border force Brodie Clark suspended', BBC, 5 November 2011, www.bbc.co.uk/news/uk-15601988

67   Independent Chief Inspector of Borders and Immigration, 'Inspection report on border security checks, February 2012', Gov.uk, 20 February 2012, www.gov.uk/government/publications/inspection-report-on-border-security-checks-february-2012

68   'David Cameron to make more government data available', BBC

69   'Inquiry into the provision of UK Border Controls', Home Affairs Committee, www.parliament.uk, prepared 19 January 2012, publications.parliament.uk/pa/cm201012/cmselect/cmhaff/1647/164703.htm

70   'Theresa May should relax border checks, says Keith Vaz', BBC

71   'Queen's Speech – Identity Documents Bill', Number10.gov.uk, 25 May 2010, web.archive.org/web/20100528110952/http://www.number10.gov.uk/queens-speech/2010/05/queens-speech-identity-documents-bill-50641

72   UK Border Agency, *Annual Report and Accounts 2011–12 (For the year ended 31 March 2012)*, 12 July 2012, assets.publishing.service.gov.uk/government/uploads/system/uploads/attachment_data/file/257136/annual-report-11-12.pdf

73   'Labour Market Statistics, October 2011', Office for National Statistics, 12 October 2011, webarchive.nationalarchives.gov.uk/20160109123912/http://www.ons.gov.uk/ons/rel/lms/labour-market-statistics/october-2011/statistical-bulletin.html

74   Katie Allen, 'UK unemployment total hits highest in 17 years', *Guardian*, 12 October 2011, www.theguardian.com/business/2011/oct/12/uk-unemployment-highest-17-years

75   Gerri Peev, 'PM's aide attacked over call to axe maternity pay', *Daily Mail*, 19 July 2011, www.dailymail.co.uk/news/article-2019627/Steve-Hilton-Axe-maternity-leave-boost-econ omy-says-Cameron-guru.html

76   Nicholas Watt, 'Steve Hilton policy leaks show Downing Street divide over David Cameron aide', *Guardian*, 28 July 2011, www.theguardian.com/politics/2011/jul/28/steve-hilton-polic ies-coalition-split

77   'Steve Hilton: the barefoot revolutionary', MoneyWeek, 12 March 2012, moneyweek.com /30718/profile-of-steve-hilton-57946

78   'Labour Market Statistics, October 2011', Office for National Statistics, webarchive.national archives.gov.uk/20160109123912/http://www.ons.gov.uk/ons/rel/lms/labour-market-statistics/october-2011/statistical-bulletin.html

79   Polly Curtis, 'Reality check: how much did the banking crisis cost taxpayers?', *Guardian*, news blog, www.theguardian.com/politics/reality-check-with-polly-curtis/2011/sep/12/reality-check-banking-bailout

80   'Labour Market Statistics, October 2011', Office for National Statistics

81   Polly Curtis, 'Reality check: is this generation bust?', *Guardian*, news blog, www.theguardian.com/politics/reality-check-with-polly-curtis/2011/oct/12/unemployment-unemployment-and-employment-statistics

82   Reuters Staff, 'Super rich hold $32 trillion in offshore havens', Reuters, 22 July 2012, www.reuters.com/article/us-offshore-wealth-idUSBRE86L03U20120722

83   Patrick Kingsley, 'Are the Occupy London protesters just a bunch of "hippies"', *Guardian*, 28 November 2011, www.theguardian.com/uk/2011/nov/28/occupy-london-boris-johnson

84   Hélène Mulholland, 'Occupy protesters accuse Boris Johnson of defending the rich', *Guardian*, 16 November 2011, www.theguardian.com/politics/2011/nov/16/occupy-london-boris-johnson-defending-rich

85   Polly Curtis, 'Has 2011 really been the busiest year for news in recent memory?', *Guardian*, 28 December 2011, www.theguardian.com/politics/reality-check-with-polly-curtis/2011 /dec/28/has-2011-been-a-busy-news-year

86   Mike Brewer, James Browne and Robert Joyce, *Child and Working-Age Poverty from 2010 to 2020*, Institute for Fiscal Studies, October 2011, www.ifs.org.uk/comms/comm121.pdf

87   Wenchao Jin, Robert Joyce, David Phillips and Luke Sibieta, *Poverty and Inequality in the UK: 2011*, Institute for Fiscal Studies, May 2011, www.ifs.org.uk/comms/comm118.pdf

88   Decca Aitkenhead, '2011: the year in review', *Guardian*, 30 December 2011, www.theguardi an.com/uk/2011/dec/30/2011-end-of-year-review

89   'Fuel poverty kills more people than road accidents', *Mirror*, 20 October 2011, www.mirror.co.uk/news/uk-news/fuel-poverty-kills-more-people-86673

90   'Budget 2011: Corporation Tax to be cut to 23% by 2014', BBC, 23 March 2011, www.bbc.co.uk/news/business-12828434

91 D. Clark, 'Corporation tax receipts in the UK 2000–2021', Statista, 27 July 2022,
    www.statista.com/statistics/284319/united-kingdom-hmrc-tax-receipts-corporation-tax
92 'Budget 2011: Corporation Tax to be cut to 23% by 2014', BBC
93 'UK unemployment increases to 2.62m', BBC, 16 November 2011, www.bbc.co.uk/news/
    business-15747103
94 Emily Dugan, 'Exclusive: Salaries for top executives are rocketing "out of control"',
    Independent, 15 May 2011, www.independent.co.uk/news/business/news/exclusive-
    salaries-top-executives-are-rocketing-out-control-2284397.html
95 Oliver Wright, 'Revealed: how the City bankrolls Tory party', Independent, 9 February 2011,
    www.independent.co.uk/news/uk/politics/revealed-how-city-bankrolls-tory-party-
    2208668.html
96 James Kirkup, 'Defence Secretary Liam Fox used expenses to pay his best man Adam
    Werritty', Telegraph, 10 October 2011, www.telegraph.co.uk/news/newstopics/mps-expen
    ses/conservative-mps-expenses/8817286/Defence-Secretary-Liam-Fox-used-expenses-to-
    pay-his-best-man-Adam-Werritty.html
97 Rupert Neate, 'Liam Fox faces questions for allowing former flatmate access to MoD',
    Guardian, 4 October 2011, www.theguardian.com/politics/2011/oct/04/liam-fox-national-
    security-threat
98 James Chapman and James White, 'Fox admits friend Adam Werritty was present during
    18 trips overseas and visited him at MoD 22 times', Daily Mail, 10 October 2011, www.daily
    mail.co.uk/news/article-2047217/Liam-Fox-admits-Adam-Werritty-18-trips-overseas-
    visited-MoD-22-times.html
99 'Full list of meetings between Liam Fox and Adam Werritty', Guardian, blog, 10 October
    2011, www.theguardian.com/politics/datablog/2011/oct/10/liam-fox-and-adam-werritty-
    links-liamfox
100 Nick Hopkins and Simon Bowers, 'Not just Dubai: Liam Fox met Adam Werritty 18 times
    around the world', Guardian, 10 October 2011, www.theguardian.com/politics/2011/oct/10
    /liam-fox-met-adam-werritty-around-world?intcmp=239
101 Brian Brady, 'Liam Fox, Adam Werritty, and the curious case of Our Man in Tel Aviv',
    Independent, 27 November 2011, www.independent.co.uk/news/uk/politics/liam-fox-
    adam-werritty-and-curious-case-our-man-tel-aviv-6268640.html
102 Nick Robinson, 'Liam Fox: why he might go', BBC, 14 October 2011, www.bbc.co.uk/news
    /uk-politics-15304433
103 Rupert Neate, 'Fresh questions over company that funded Adam Werritty's jet-set life',
    Guardian, 16 October 2011, www.theguardian.com/uk/2011/oct/16/adam-werritty-
    liam-fox-pargav
104 Rupert Neate, 'Charity created by Liam Fox axed after watchdog issues criticism',
    Guardian, 5 October 2011, www.theguardian.com/politics/2011/oct/05/charity-liam-
    fox-axed-watchdog
105 Dan Milmo, Caroline Davies, Polly Curtis and Hélène Mulholland, 'Strikes over public
    sector pensions hit services across UK as 2 million walk out', Guardian, 30 November 2011,
    www.theguardian.com/society/2011/nov/30/strikes-public-sector-pensions-impact
106 Hélène Mulholland, 'David Cameron admits day of action was "obviously a big strike"',
    Guardian, 1 December 2011, www.theguardian.com/society/2011/dec/01/david-cameron-
    obviously-big-strike?newsfeed=true
107 'Public sector strike hits services and schools', BBC, 30 June 2011, www.bbc.co.uk/news/uk-
    13967580
108 'Public sector strike proving damp squib – David Cameron', BBC, 30 November 2011,
    www.bbc.co.uk/news/uk-politics-15966120
109 Andy McSmith, 'Public sector strikes: the day Michael Gove took his place on the picket
    line', Independent, 10 July 2014, www.independent.co.uk/news/uk/politics/michael-gove-
    strike-day-when-teachers-are-criticised-walk-out-photo-shows-education-minister-picket-
    line-9597723.html
110 Dan Milmo, Caroline Davies, Polly Curtis and Hélène Mulholland, 'Strikes over public
    sector pensions hit services across UK as 2 million walk out'
111 Hélène Mulholland, 'David Cameron admits day of action was "obviously a big strike"'
112 Hélène Mulholland and agencies, 'Public sector strikes: government drops deadline for
    pension talks', Guardian, 1 December 2011, www.theguardian.com/society/2011/dec/01/pu
    blic-sector-strikes-deadline-talks

113 Ibid.

114 Hélène Mulholland, 'Tory party suspends Nadine Dorris', *Guardian*, 6 November 2012, www.theguardian.com/politics/2012/nov/06/nadine-dorries-im-a-celebrity

115 Louise Mensch, 'Nadine Dorries has demeaned the role of an MP', *Guardian*, Opinion, 7 November 2012, www.theguardian.com/commentisfree/2012/nov/07/nadine-dorries-celebrity-mp

116 Peter Walker, Jim Waterson and Aubrey Allegretti, 'Nadine Dorries appointed culture secretary in reshuffle', *Guardian*, 15 September 2021, www.theguardian.com/politics/2021/sep/15/nadine-dorries-appointed-culture-secretary-in-reshuffle

117 Huffington Post UK, 'Homelessness risk for 35,000 people by Christmas, charity warns', *Huffington Post*, 1 January 2012, www.huffingtonpost.co.uk/2011/11/01/homelessness-risk-for-350_n_1069027.html

118 Ian Traynor, Nicholas Watt, David Gow and Patrick Wintour, 'David Cameron blocks EU treaty with veto, casting Britain adrift in Europe', *Guardian*, 9 December 2011, www.theguardian.com/world/2011/dec/09/david-cameron-blocks-eu-treaty

119 Ibid.

120 Anthony Wells, 'New YouGov and ComRes polls', UK Polling Report, 31 October 2011, ukpollingreport.co.uk/blog/archives/date/2011/10

121 Ian Traynor, Nicholas Watt, David Gow and Patrick Wintour, 'David Cameron blocks EU treaty with veto, casting Britain adrift in Europe'

2012: Badgers Moved the Goalposts

1 Anthony Horowitz, 'I always defended Michael Gove. Then I met him', *Spectator,* 15 March 2013, www.spectator.co.uk/article/i-always-defended-michael-gove-then-i-met-him

2 'Gove intrigue over "use of private e mails for official business"', *The Times*, 21 September 2011, www.thetimes.co.uk/article/gove-intrigue-over-use-of-private-e-mails-for-official-business-8bj58qmzl6z

3 Jeevan Vasagar, 'Michael Gove aides accused of deleting government correspondence', *Guardian,* 2 March 2012, www.theguardian.com/politics/2012/mar/02/michael-gove-email-private-account

4 Andrew Woodcock, 'Michael Gove loses FOI battle over emails', *Independent,* 2 March 2012, www.independent.co.uk/news/uk/politics/michael-gove-loses-foi-battle-over-emails-7485313.html

5 Andy McSmith, 'Tony Blair may be an admirer of Ukrainian mills, but not on the basis of British ones he's visited', *Independent,* 26 October 2012, www.independent.co.uk/voices/comment/tony-blair-may-be-admirer-ukrainian-mills-not-basis-british-ones-he-s-visited-8228721.html

6 Jeevan Vasagar, 'Michael Gove aides accused of deleting government correspondence'

7 Ibid.

8 Jane Merrick, 'Secret memo shows Michael Gove's plan for privatisation of academies', *Independent,* 10 February 2013, www.independent.co.uk/news/education/education-news/secret-memo-shows-michael-gove-s-plan-privatisation-academies-8488552.html

9 Ibid.

10 Mike Baker, 'Gove's academies: 1980s idea rebranded?', BBC, 1 August 2010, www.bbc.co.uk/news/education-10824069

11 Hélène Mulholland, 'Michael Gove tells academies they can hire unqualified teaching staff', *Guardian,* 27 July 2012, www.theguardian.com/education/2012/jul/27/gove-academies-unqualified-teaching-staff

12 'Converting maintained schools to academies', National Audit Office, 22 February 2018, www.nao.org.uk/press-release/converting-maintained-schools-toacademies

13 'Peter Cruddas', *Forbes*, 3 January 2012, www.forbes.com/profile/peter-cruddas

14 'Tory Peter Cruddas sold access to PM, Sunday Times alleges', BBC, 25 March 2012, www.bbc.co.uk/news/uk-politics-17501618

15 Press Association, 'Peter Cruddas wins £180,000 damages in Sunday Times libel case', *Guardian,* 31 July 2013, www.theguardian.com/politics/2013/jul/31/peter-cruddas-damages-libel-sunday-times

16 Roy Greenslade, 'Appeal court reduces damages award against Sunday Times to £50,000', 17 March 2015, www.theguardian.com/media/greenslade/2015/mar/17/appeal-court-reduces-damages-award-against-sunday-times-to-50000

17 Justin Parkinson, 'Peter Cruddas: PM overrules watchdog with Tory donor peerage', BBC, 22 December 2020, www.bbc.co.uk/news/uk-politics-55414981

18 Ibid.

19 Ibid.

20 Mark Kleinman, 'CMC tycoon Cruddas hands £50,000 to Johnson leadership bid', Sky News, 7 June 2019, news.sky.com/story/cmc-tycoon-cruddas-hands-50-000-to-johnson-leadership-bid-11736804

21 Jim Pickard, 'Blue Sky thinking in overdrive – Steve Hilton's most "out-there" ideas', FT, 27 July 2011, www.ft.com/content/c2704a29-ee72-3bf6-95f7-479f07e5b77e

22 Patrick Wintour, 'Steve Hilton's parting shots: £25bn in cuts and a broadside at the civil service', Guardian, 16 May 2012, www.theguardian.com/politics/2012/may/16/cameron-adviser-steve-hilton-leaves?newsfeed=true

23 Jim Pickard, 'Blue Sky thinking in overdrive – Steve Hilton's most "out-there" ideas'

24 Iain Watson, 'Steve Hilton's civil service attack uncovers coalition tensions', BBC, 18 May 2012, www.bbc.co.uk/news/uk-politics-18111271

25 Patrick Wintour, 'Steve Hilton's parting shots: £25bn in cuts and a broadside at the civil service'

26 Michael Burton, 'Understanding Britain's lost decade', LSE, 10 February 2022, blogs.lse.ac.uk/europpblog/2022/02/10/understanding-britains-lost-decade

27 'Public sector net debt expressed as a percentage of gross domestic product in the United Kingdom from 1920/21 to 2021/22', Statista, February 2022, www.statista.com/statistics/282841/debt-as-gdp-uk

28 Patrick Collinson, 'Budget 2012: the highlights and lowlights', Guardian, 23 March 2012, www.theguardian.com/money/2012/mar/23/budget-2012-highlights-lowlights

29 Juliette Jowit, 'Top rate tax cut would have "very large cost"', Guardian, 3 May 2012, www.theguardian.com/politics/2012/may/03/top-tax-rate-cut-large-cost

30 Nick Robinson, 'Budget 2012: Will the "granny tax" backlash last?', BBC, 22 March 2012, www.bbc.co.uk/news/uk-politics-17477822

31 Michelle McGagh, 'Budget 2012: "granny tax" to cost pensioners £259 a year', City Wire, 21 March 2012, citywire.co.uk/investment-trust-insider/news/budget-2012-granny-tax-to-cost-pensioners-259-a-year/a576400?section=money

32 Patrick Wintour, 'David Davis calls on government to rethink charity tax relief plans', Guardian, 12 April 2012, www.theguardian.com/politics/2012/apr/12/david-davis-charity-tax-relief

33 Patrick Wintour, 'Tax relief cap: church and Cate Blanchett join chorus of anger', Guardian, 13 April 2012, www.theguardian.com/society/2012/apr/13/tax-relief-church-cate-blanchett

34 Reuters Staff, 'Bank levy hike offset by corporation tax cut – BBA', Reuters, 21 March 2012, www.reuters.com/article/uk-britain-banks-budget-idUKLNE82K05420120321

35 'Budget 2012: Osborne announces new corporation tax', BBC, 21 March 2012, www.bbc.co.uk/news/av/uk-politics-17461244

36 Dan Milmo, 'Corporation tax rate cut to 21% in autumn statement', Guardian, 5 December 2012, www.theguardian.com/uk/2012/dec/05/corporation-tax-rate-cut-autumn-statement

37 'Omnishambles named word of the year by Oxford English Dictionary', BBC, 13 November 2012, www.bbc.co.uk/news/uk-politics-20309441

38 Patrick Wintour and Martin Wainwright, 'Pasty row hots up for David Cameron', Guardian, 29 March 2012, www.theguardian.com/politics/2012/mar/29/pasty-row-david-cameron

39 'Government does U-turn over "Cornish pasty tax"', BBC, 28 May 2012, www.bbc.co.uk/news/uk-politics-18244640

40 'Tax relief limit on charity to be axed in fresh U-turn', BBC, 31 May 2012, www.bbc.co.uk/news/uk-politics-18278253

41 Hélène Mulholland, 'Ministers "preparing for rethink on charity tax relief"', Guardian, 29 May 2012, www.theguardian.com/society/2012/may/29/ministers-rethink-charity-tax-relief

42 Press Association, 'MPs pass "granny tax" despite Labour appeals', Guardian, 19 April 2012, www.theguardian.com/politics/2012/apr/19/granny-tax-passes-commons

43 'Public satisfaction with the NHS', The King's Fund, www.kingsfund.org.uk/projects/public-satisfaction-nhs

44 'How much is the "NHS market system" costing?', Full Fact, 31 March 2014, fullfact.org/
    health/how-much-nhs-market-system-costing www.theguardian.com/society/2010/mar/30
    /nhs-management-costs-spending (now at 14% of budget)
45 'NHS: "patient-centred" reform means 24,500 job losses', Channel 4 News, 19 January 2011,
    www.channel4.com/news/nhs-patient-centred-shake-up-means-24-500-job-losses
46 Nick Triggle, 'NHS ranked "number one" health system', BBC, 14 July 2017, www.bbc.co.uk
    /news/health-40608253
47 Eric C. Schneider, Dana O. Sarnak, David Squires, Arnav Shah, and Michelle M. Doty,
    'Mirror, Mirror 2017: International Comparison Reflects Flaws and Opportunities for
    Better U.S. Health Care', The Commonwealth Fund, interactives.commonwealthfund.org
    /2017/july/mirror-mirror
48 David A. Squires, 'The U.S. Health System in Perspective: A Comparison of Twelve
    Industrialized Nations', The Commonwealth Fund, July 2011, www.commonwealthfund.org/
    sites/default/files/documents/___media_files_publications_issue_brief_2011_jul_1532_
    squires_us_hlt_sys_comparison_12_nations_intl_brief_v2.pdf
49 Ashley Cowburn, 'Boris Johnson pushed for private involvement in NHS and insurance
    based healthcare, newly unearthed article shows', Independent, 28 November 2019,
    www.independent.co.uk/news/uk/politics/boris-johnson-nhs-private-insurance-
    healthcare-general-election-tories-a9225061.html
50 Nick Sommerland, 'Exposed: 12 worrying links between Tories and private healthcare
    industry', Mirror, 2 December 2019, www.mirror.co.uk/news/politics/exposed-12-
    worrying-links-between-21013592
51 Ashley Cowburn, 'Boris Johnson pushed for private involvement in NHS and insurance
    based healthcare, newly unearthed article shows'
52 Kirsty Walker, 'Tory Health spokesman accepted £21,000 donation from private health
    firm boss', Daily Mail, 15 January 2010, www.dailymail.co.uk/news/article-1243579/
    Andrew-Lansley-embroiled-cash-influence-row-accepting-21-000-donation-Care-UK-
    chairman-John-Nash.html
53 Holly Watt, 'Two major Conservative donors appointed to government', Telegraph, 11
    January 2013, www.telegraph.co.uk/news/newstopics/mps-expenses/9794202/Two-major-
    Conservative-donors-appointed-to-government.html
54 Kirsty Walker, 'Tory Health spokesman accepted £21,000 donation from private health
    firm boss'
55 Ibid.
56 Nigel Edwards, 'The risks of NHS reorganisation: lessons from history', Nuffield Trust, 20
    February 2020, www.nuffieldtrust.org.uk/news-item/the-risks-of-nhs-reorganisation-lesso
    ns-from-history
57 Health and Social Care Act 2012: Chapter 7, www.legislation.gov.uk/ukpga/2012/7/pdfs/uk
    pga_20120007_en.pdf
58 Health and Care Social Act 2012: Exxplanatory Notes, www.legislation.gov.uk/ukpga/2012/
    7/notes/data.pdf
59 National Health Service Act,1946, www.legislation.gov.uk/ukpga/1946/81/pdfs/ukpga_194
    60081_en.pdf
60 Chris Smyth and Rachel Sylvester, 'NHS reforms our worst mistake, Tories admit', The Times,
    13 October 2014, www.thetimes.co.uk/article/nhs-reforms-our-worst-mistake-tories-admit-
    tqs6tz55mvk
61 'Changes to the Health and Social Care Bill: competition', The King's Fund, www.kingsfund.
    org.uk/projects/reforming-the-health-bill-index/competition-reform
62 Randeep Ramesh, 'Hundreds of contracts signed in "biggest ever act of NHS privatisation"',
    Guardian, 3 October 2012, www.theguardian.com/society/2012/oct/03/private-contracts-
    signed-nhs-privatisation
63 'Myth four: the NHS has too many managers', The King's Fund, www.kingsfund.org.uk/
    projects/health-and-social-care-bill/mythbusters/nhs-managers
64 'NHS: "patient-centred" reform means 24,500 job losses', Channel 4 News, 19 January 2011,
    www.channel4.com/news/nhs-patient-centred-shake-up-means-24-500-job-losses
65 'More than 160,000 nurses have quit NHS since 2010/11, data show', ITV News, 27 March
    2019, www.itv.com/news/2019-03-27/more-than-160-000-nurses-have-quit-nhs-since-
    2010-11-data-shows

66 'Fatally flawed: Yes to the NHS Internal Market – No to the External Market', Lord David Owen, 31 March 2011, http://www.lorddavidowen.co.uk/fatally-flawed-yes-to-the-nhs-internal-market-%E2%80%93-no-to-the-external-market

67 *Understanding the New NHS – A Guide for everyone working and training within the NHS*, NHS Buckinghamshire, 23 July 2014, www.buckinghamshireccg.nhs.uk/understanding-the-new-nhs-a-guide-for-everyone-working-and-training-within-the-nhs/

68 'How funding for the NHS in the UK has changed over a rolling ten year period', The Health Foundation, 31 October 2015, www.health.org.uk/chart-how-funding-for-the-nhs-in-the-uk-has-changed-over-a-rolling-ten-year-period

69 'How much is the "NHS market system" costing?', Full Fact, 31 March 2014, www.fullfact.org/health/how-much-nhs-market-system-costing; Denis Campbell, 'NHS spends 14% of budget on management, MPs reveal', *Guardian*, 30 March 2010, www.theguardian.com/society/2010/mar/30/nhs-management-costs-spending

70 Chris Smyth and Rachel Sylvester, 'NHS reforms our worst mistake, Tories admit', *The Times*, 13 October 2014, www.thetimes.co.uk/article/nhs-reforms-our-worst-mistake-tories-admit-tqs6tz55mvk

71 John Appleby, 'British Social Attitudes survey 2011: public satisfaction with the NHS and its services', The King's Fund, 17 July 2012, www.kingsfund.org.uk/publications/british-social-attitudes-survey-2011

72 George Eaton, 'Will Lansley be "taken out and shot"?', *New Statesman*, 7 February 2012, www.newstatesman.com/blogs/the-staggers/2012/02/lansley-shot-taken-sylvester

73 Press Association, 'David Cameron's 'calm down, dear' call causes outrage – video', *Guardian*, 27 April 2011, www.theguardian.com/politics/video/2011/apr/27/david-cameron-calm-down-dear

74 Kailash Chand, '"NHS reforms our worst mistake"? Coming from Tories this is too little too late', Open Democracy, 13 October 2014, www.opendemocracy.net/en/ournhs/nhs-reforms-our-worst-mistake-coming-from-tories-this-is-too-little-too-late

75 Patrick Dunleavy, 'With a likely cost of £4 billion, the Health and Social Care Bill has all the hallmarks of an avoidable policy fiasco', *LSE*, 24 January 2012, blogs.lse.ac.uk/politicsandpolicy/hsc-bill-policy-fiasco

76 Independent Staff, 'House of Lords appointments: The new unelected peers promoted by David Cameron', *Independent*, 28 August 2015, www.independent.co.uk/news/uk/politics/house-of-lords-appointments-the-new-unelected-peers-promoted-by-david-cameron-10476080.html

77 'Lord Nash', Gov.uk, www.gov.uk/government/people/lord-nash

78 'Care UK/Practice Plus Group', NHS Support Federation, web.archive.org/web/20210303030402/www.nhsforsale.info/private-providers/care-uk-new

79 Haroon Siddique, 'Antisocial behaviour: Eric Pickles insists troubled families are not victims', *Guardian*, 11 June 2012, www.theguardian.com/society/2012/jun/11/antisocial-behaviour-eric-pickles-victims

80 Haroon Siddique, 'David Cameron left daughter behind after pub visit', *Guardian*, 11 June 2011, www.theguardian.com/politics/2011/jun/11/david-cameron-daughter-behind-pub

81 *Liberal Democrat Manifesto 2010*, Liberal Democrats, 2010, web.archive.org/web/20111219211028/http://network.libdems.org.uk/manifesto2010/libdem_manifesto_2010.pdf

82 Nicholas Watt and Patrick Wintour, 'House of Lords reform: senior Tories threaten rebellion', *Guardian*, 19 April 2012, www.theguardian.com/politics/2012/apr/19/house-of-lords-reform-tories

83 Jessica Henry, 'House of Lords - reform or retain?', YouGov, 10 May 2012, yougov.co.uk/topics/politics/articles-reports/2012/05/10/house-lords-reform-your-views

84 'Hybrid Bills', UK Parliament, www.parliament.uk/about/how/laws/bills/hybrid

85 James Landale, 'Lords reform: How the Commons war will be fought', BBC, 10 July 2012, www.bbc.co.uk/news/uk-politics-18782379

86 Andrew Grice, 'Coalition shaken as Cameron ducks out of vote on Lords', *Independent*, 11 July 2011, www.independent.co.uk/news/uk/politics/coalition-shaken-as-cameron-ducks-out-of-vote-on-lords-7932344.html

87 Robert Winnett and Robertwinnett, 'David Cameron retreats on House of Lords reform', *Telegraph*, 2 August 2012, www.telegraph.co.uk/news/politics/david-cameron/9447897/David-Cameron-retreats-on-House-of-Lords-reform.html

88 Phillip Inman, 'IMF slashes UK economic growth forecast', *Guardian*, 17 July 2012, www.theguardian.com/business/2012/jul/16/imf-slashes-uk-economic-growth-forecast

89 D. Clark, 'Annual growth of gross domestic product in the United Kingdom from 1949 to 2022', Statista, March 2022, www.statista.com/statistics/281734/gdp-growth-in-the-united-kingdom-uk

90 Hélène Mulholland, 'Coe pays tribute to Labour for delivering Olympics to London', *Guardian*, 2 October 2012, www.theguardian.com/politics/2012/oct/02/coe-tribute-labour-olympics

91 'Chinese media attacks Boris Johnson for being "rude, arrogant and disrespectful" at Olympic ceremony', *Daily Mail*, 27 August 2008, www.dailymail.co.uk/news/article-10490 36/Chinese-media-attacks-Boris-Johnson-rude-arrogant-disrespectful-Olympic-ceremony.html

92 Ibid.

93 Robert Booth and Nick Hopkins, 'London 2012 Olympics: G4S failures prompt further military deployment', *Guardian*, 24 July 2012, www.theguardian.com/uk/2012/jul/24/london-2012-olympics-g4s-military

94 Nicholas Watt, Hélène Mulholland and Owen Gibson, 'Mitt Romney's Olympics blunder stuns No 10 and hands gift to Obama', *Guardian*, 27 July 2012, www.theguardian.com/world/2012/jul/26/mitt-romney-olympics-blunder

95 'G4S staff hit out over Olympics security "shambles"', BBC, 18 July 2012, www.bbc.co.uk/news/uk-18877744

96 International Olympic Committee, 'Factsheet London 2012 Facts and Figures', November 2012, stillmed.olympic.org/media/Document%20Library/OlympicOrg/IOC/Olympic_Ga mes/Olympic_Legacy/London_2012/Legacy/EN_London_2012_Facts_and_Figures.pdf

97 Nick Hopkins, 'Army warns Olympic Games recovery will take two years', *Guardian*, 13 August 2012, www.theguardian.com/uk/2012/aug/13/army-olympic-games-recovery-two-years

98 Alice Gribbin, 'Nick Buckles: "My leadership style? 'No excuses'"', *New Statesman*, 17 April 2012, web.archive.org/web/20140603173356/https://www.newstatesman.com/business/2012/04/nick-buckles-g4s-interview

99 Euan Ferguson, '2012 review: it was the best of times. It was the worst of times …', *Guardian*, 29 December 2012, www.theguardian.com/uk/2012/dec/29/2012-review-best-worst

100 'UK: Increased annual pay for G4S chief despite London 2012 games fiasco', *East Anglian Daily Times*, 15 April 2013, www.eadt.co.uk/news/business/uk-increased-annual-pay-for-g4s-chief-despite-london-2012-2079620

101 'Number of people receiving three days' worth of emergency food by Trussell Trust foodbanks in the United Kingdom from 2008/09 to 2021/22', Statista, 2022, www.statista.com/statistics/382695/uk-foodbank-users

102 'Boris Johnson left hanging on zip wire during Olympic event', BBC, 1 August 2012, www.bbc.co.uk/news/uk-england-london-19079733

103 'Media reaction to London 2012 Olympic opening ceremony', BBC, 28 July 2012, www.bbc.co.uk/news/uk-19025686

104 Nicholas Watt and Kim Willsher, 'Tory MP Aidan Burley ruled "stupid" but not antisemitic for Nazi stag party', *Guardian*, 22 January 2014, www.theguardian.com/world/2014/jan/21/tory-mp-aidan-burley-nazi-stag-party-france-offensive-not-antisemitic

105 'MP attacks "leftie Ceremony"', ITV News, 27 July 2012, www.itv.com/news/story/2012-07-27/twitter-anger-after-conservative-mp-aidan-burley-tweets-about-most-leftie-opening-ceremony

106 'David Cameron attacks "idiotic" criticism from Aidan Burley MP', BBC, 30 July 2012, www.bbc.co.uk/news/uk-politics-19046448

107 Samuel Osborne, 'Danny Boyle claims Tories tried to axe NHS celebration in London 2012 Olympics opening ceremony', *Independent*, 10 July 2016, www.independent.co.uk/news/uk/politics/danny-boyle-nhs-celebration-tories-london-2012-olympics-opening-ceremony-a7 129186.html

108 Nicola Bartlett and Oliver Milne, 'Olympic legacy of 2012 in tatters as Tory cuts force leisure facilities to close', *Mirror*, 6 December 2018, www.mirror.co.uk/news/politics/olympic-legacy-2012-tatters-tory-13697973

109 Benjamin Kentish, 'Tories accused of ruining London Olympic legacy as just 1 in 100 sixth-formers from poor backgrounds doing sport in school', *Independent*, 27 July 2019, www.independent.co.uk/news/uk/politics/tory-party-london-olympics-sport-school-sixth-form-pe-exercise-a9023766.html

110 'George Osborne Booed By Paralympic Crowd', Sky News, 3 September 2013, news.sky.com/story/george-osborne-booed-by-paralympic-crowd-10471153

111 Robert Winnett, 'Police log reveals details of Andrew Mitchell's "pleb" rant', *Telegraph*, 24 September 2014, www.telegraph.co.uk/news/politics/conservative/9563847/Police-log-reveals-details-of-Andrew-Mitchells-pleb-rant.html

112 'Chief Whip in four-letter tirade at Downing St police "must quit"', *Evening Standard*, 21 September 2012, www.standard.co.uk/news/uk/chief-whip-in-fourletter-tirade-at-downing-st-police-must-quit-8162493.html

113 '"Plebgate" PC Keith Wallis jailed for a year', BBC, 6 February 2014, www.bbc.co.uk/news/uk-politics-26064536

114 'Andrew Mitchell "probably called police plebs", judge rules', BBC, 27 November 2014, www.bbc.co.uk/news/uk-30235009

115 Ben Chu, 'Review of the economy in 2012: This was not supposed to happen', *Independent*, 22 December 2012, www.independent.co.uk/news/business/analysis-and-features/review-economy-2012-was-not-supposed-happen-8424651.html

116 'Triple-dip recession: Does it matter?', BBC, 24 April 2013, www.bbc.co.uk/news/business-22277955

117 Aaron O'Neill, 'Annual growth of real GDP in the United States of America from 1930 to 2021', Statista, 21 June 2022, www.statista.com/statistics/996758/rea-gdp-growth-united-states-1930-2019

118 Ben Chu, 'UK economy in grip of most feeble recovery on modern record, says IFS', *Independent*, 14 March 2018, www.independent.co.uk/news/business/analysis-and-features/uk-economy-latest-updates-feeble-recovery-record-spring-statement-ifs-recession-philip-hammond-a8255756.html

119 Larry Elliot, 'UK recovery has been weaker than in US, Germany, France and Canada', *Guardian*, 11 March 2012, www.theguardian.com/business/economics-blog/2012/mar/11/uk-economic-recovery-slow

120 David N.F. Bell and David G. Blanchflower, 'Underemployment in the UK revisited', *National Institute Economic Review*, No. 224, May 2013, journals.sagepub.com/doi/pdf/10.1177/002795011322400110

121 'U.K. Unemployment Rate 1991-2022', MacroTrends, www.macrotrends.net/countries/GBR/united-kingdom/unemployment-rate

122 'Underemployment affects 10.5% of UK workforce', BBC, 28 November 2012, www.bbc.co.uk/news/business-20509189

123 Caroline Gall, 'One in Ten - a statistic, a reminder', BBC, 12 August 2009, news.bbc.co.uk/1/hi/england/west_midlands/8196911.stm

124 Noah Daponte-Smith, 'Is David Cameron Really A One-Nation Conservative?', *Forbes*, 2 June 2015, www.forbes.com/sites/noahdapontesmith/2015/06/02/is-david-cameron-really-a-one-nation-conservative/?sh=30af2f1c7c3b

125 Juliet Jowit, 'Conservative conference: squeezed middle gives way to strivers', *Guardian*, 8 October 2012, www.theguardian.com/politics/2012/oct/07/conservative-conference-squeezed-middle-strivers

126 'George Monbiot', Goodreads, www.goodreads.com/quotes/554523-if-wealth-was-the-inevitable-result-of-hard-work-and

127 Peter Kellner, 'George Osborne', Britannica, www.britannica.com/biography/George-Osborne

128 Cahal Milmo, 'Revealed: how Cameron is related to the Queen', *Independent*, 5 December 2005, www.independent.co.uk/news/uk/politics/revealed-how-cameron-related-queen-869 2928.html

129 Adam Withnall, 'David Cameron's father and senior Tories named in Panama Papers leak', *Independent*, 4 April 2016, www.independent.co.uk/news/uk/politics/david-cameron-father-and-senior-tory-figures-named-in-panama-papers-leak-a6967116.html

130 Juliette Garside, 'Fund run by David Cameron's father avoided paying tax in Britain', *Guardian*, 4 April 2016, www.theguardian.com/news/2016/apr/04/panama-papers-david-cameron-father-tax-bahamas

131 Megan Samrai, 'How much Eton College and other top Berkshire private schools cost', *Berkshire Live*, 12 November 2021, www.getreading.co.uk/news/reading-berkshire-news/how-much-eton-college-top-22135881

132 'Why are universities, churches and private schools charities?', How Charities Work, howcharitieswork.com/about-charities/what-is-a-charity/why-are-universities-churches-and-private-schools-charities

133 '"Off our heads" - David Cameron reveals pot-smoking school days', Sky News, 16 September 2019, news.sky.com/story/off-our-heads-david-cameron-reveals-pot-smoking-school-days-11809147

134 May Bulman, 'More than 60% of Oxford University students went to private or grammar school, figures show', *Independent*, 24 September 2014, www.independent.co.uk/news/uk/home-news/oxford-university-cambridge-state-school-socially-inclusive-ethnicity-sunday-times-guide-david-lammy-a8551036.html

135 Michael Ashcroft and Isabel Oakeshott, *Call Me Dave: The Unauthorised Biography of David Cameron*, Biteback Publishing, London, 2015.

136 Miranda Norris, 'Oxford's Bullingdon Club: Most shocking moments', *Oxford Mail*, 16 May 2021, www.oxfordmail.co.uk/news/19306048.oxfords-bullingdon-club-shocking-moments

137 'MPs' expenses list reveals David Cameron "used the system" to claim £21,000 in a year to pay his mortgage', *Evening Standard*, 4 April 2008, www.standard.co.uk/hp/front/mps-expenses-list-reveals-david-cameron-used-the-system-to-claim-ps21-000-in-a-year-to-pay-his-mortgage-7286588.html

138 Rajeev Syal, 'George Osborne's mortgage on paddock paid by taxpayers', *Guardian*, 7 December 2012, www.theguardian.com/politics/2012/dec/07/taxpayers-paid-george-osborne-paddock-mortgage

139 'Oral Answers to Questions: Matt Hancock Excerpts', Parallel Parliament, 29 October 2012, www.parallelparliament.co.uk/mp/matt-hancock/debate/Commons/2012-10-29/debates/1210294000002/OralAnswersToQuestions

140 Ibid.

141 'National Minimum Wage and National Living Wage rates', Gov.uk, www.gov.uk/national-minimum-wage-rates

142 'Panorama to focus on Zenos, Morrisons and subcontracting', FE Week, 2 April 2012, feweek.co.uk/2012/04/02/panorama-to-focus-on-zenos-morrisons-and-subcontracting

143 Nick Linford, 'Elmfield Training founder slapped with six-year ban for £1m withdrawal', FE Week, 30 January 2016, feweek.co.uk/elmfield-training-founder-slapped-with-six-year-ban-for-1m-withdrawal

144 Mehdi Hasan, 'Why Is Climate Change Denier Owen Paterson Still in His Job?', *Huffington Post*, 11 February 2014, www.huffingtonpost.co.uk/mehdi-hasan/uk-floods-owen-paterson_b_4767153.html

145 Damian Carrington, 'David Cameron: this is the greenest government ever', *Guardian*, 26 April 2012, www.theguardian.com/environment/2012/apr/26/david-cameron-greenest-government-ever

146 'Badgers "moved goalposts" says minister Owen Paterson', BBC, 9 October 2013, www.bbc.co.uk/news/uk-england-24459424

147 'Marriage (Same Sex Couples) Bill — Third Reading — 21 May 2013', The Public Whip, 21 May 2013, www.publicwhip.org.uk/division.php?date=2013-05-21&number=11&display=allpossible

148 Joe Murphy, 'Anti-homosexual Section 28 was right for schools, says Tory MP', *Evening Standard*, 10 December 2012, www.standard.co.uk/news/politics/antihomosexual-section-28-was-right-for-schools-says-tory-mp-8398942.html

149 Emma Innes, 'Harrow East MP Bob Blackman at heart of national newspaper storm', *Harrow Times*, 17 December 2012, www.harrowtimes.co.uk/news/10112195.harrow-east-mp-bob-blackman-at-heart-of-national-newspaper-storm

150 Alex Hern, 'David Davies MP: I'm not bigoted, I punched a gay man', *New Statesman*, 10 December 2012, http://www.newstatesman.com/politics/2012/12/david-davies-mp-im-not-bigoted-i-punched-gay-man

151 'Services gay ban lifted', BBC, 12 January 2000, http://news.bbc.co.uk/1/hi/uk_politics/599810.stm

152 'Gay marriage: Deal to allow bill to proceed in Parliament', BBC, 20 May 2013, www.bbc.co.uk/news/uk-politics-22588954

153 'Gay marriage debate in quotes', *Guardian*, 6 February 2013, www.theguardian.com/society /2013/feb/06/gay-marriage-debate-in-quotes

154 'Exclusive: Defence Secretary Philip Hammond links incest with same-sex marriage', *Pink News*, 28 January 2013, www.pinknews.co.uk/2013/01/28/exclusive-defence-secretary-philip-hammond-links-incest-with-same-sex-marriage

155 Patrick Wintour, 'Tory backlash against same-sex marriage', *Guardian*, 10 December 2012, www.theguardian.com/society/2012/dec/10/gay-marriage-tory-backlash

2013: Mad, Swivel-Eyed Loons

1 'Introducing gay marriage one of my proudest moments: former PM David Cameron', *Shropshire Star*, 14 September 2019, www.shropshirestar.com/news/uk-news/2019/09/14/ introducing-gay-marriage-one-of-my-proudest-moments-former-pm-david-cameron

2 Kitty Donaldson [@kitty_donaldson], Twitter, 7 January 2013, twitter.com/kitty_donaldson /status/288317378163507201

3 'U.K. Debt to GDP Ratio 1990-2022', Macrotrends, www.macrotrends.net/countries/GBR /united-kingdom/debt-to-gdp-ratio

4 Jamie Doward and Taytula Burke, 'Britain 2013: children of poor families are still left behind', *Guardian*, 24 August 2013, www.theguardian.com/society/2013/aug/24/ child-poverty-britain-40-years-failure; *Child and working-age poverty from 2010 to 2020*, Joseph Rowntree Foundation, October 2011, www.jrf.org.uk/sites/default/files/jrf/migrated/ files/children-adult-poverty-welfare-summary.pdf

5 Patrick Collinson, 'One in 65 UK adults now a millionaire, figures show', *Guardian*, 27 August 2015, www.theguardian.com/uk-news/2015/aug/27/number-of-millionaires-in-uk-rises-by-200000

6 Hilary Osborne, 'Real wages fall back to 2003 levels in UK', *Guardian*, 13 February 2013, www.theguardian.com/money/2013/feb/13/real-wages-fall-back-2003-levels-uk-ons

7 Matthew Whittaker and Alex Hurrell, 'Low Pay Britain 2013', Resolution Foundation, 4 September 2013, www.resolutionfoundation.org/publications/low-pay-britain-2013

8 Patrick Wintour and Juliette Jowit, 'Spending review: government expects 490,000 public sector job cuts', *Guardian*, 19 October 2010, www.theguardian.com/politics/2010/oct/19/sp ending-review-document-job-cuts

9 'New style JSA amounts', Disability Rights UK, 11 April 2022, www.disabilityrightsuk.org /contribution-based-jsa-amounts

10 'Median annual earnings for full-time employees in the United Kingdom from 1999 to 2021', Statista, October 2021, www.statista.com/statistics/1002964/average-full-time-annual-earnings-in-the-uk

11 'Key events for 2013: the year in data', *Guardian*, www.theguardian.com/news/datablog/20 13/jan/04/key-events-2013-year-in-data

12 David Bovill, 'Annual Survey of Hours and Earnings: 2013 Provisional Results', Office for National Statistics, 12 December 2013, www.ons.gov.uk/employmentandlabourmarket/ peopleinwork/earningsandworkinghours/bulletins/annualsurveyofhoursandearnin gs/2013-12-12

13 Tom de Castella, 'Have train fares gone up or down since British Rail?', BBC, 22 January 2013, www.bbc.co.uk/news/magazine-21056703

14 'Key events for 2013: the year in data', *Guardian*

15 'Rail privatisation is "great train robbery", finds CRESC report', University of Manchester, 7 June 2013, www.manchester.ac.uk/discover/news/rail-privatisation-is-great-train-robbery-finds-cresc-report

16 Paul Salveson, 'Getting back on track: an alternative to private railways', Red Pepper, 1 October 2013, www.redpepper.org.uk/getting-back-on-track-an-alternative-to-private-railways

17 Wikipedia, 'Andrew Bridgen', Last edited: 3 July 2022, en.wikipedia.org/wiki/ Andrew_Bridgen

18 Martin Williams, 'After the duck house ... where MPs' expenses went next', *Guardian*, 17 March 2016, www.theguardian.com/politics/2016/may/17/mps-expenses-martin-williams-parliament-ltd

19 'Tory MP Chope calls Commons staff "servants"', Sky News, 17 January 2013, news.sky.com/story/tory-mp-chope-calls-commons-staff-servants-10457575

20 'Findus beef lasagne contained up to 100% horsemeat, FSA says', BBC, 7 February 2013, www.bbc.co.uk/news/uk-21375594

21 Holly Watt, 'Owen Paterson becomes new Environment Secretary', *Telegraph*, 4 September 2012, www.telegraph.co.uk/news/politics/9520174/Owen-Paterson-becomes-new-Environment-Secretary.html

22 Tom Bawden, 'Environment Secretary Owen Paterson has yet to be briefed on climate change by chief scientist Sir Ian Boyd', *Independent*, 30 October 2013, www.independent.co.uk/news/uk/politics/environment-secretary-owen-paterson-has-yet-to-be-briefed-on-climate-change-by-chief-scientist-sir-ian-boyd-8912738.html

23 Damian Carrington, 'UK climate change spend almost halved under Owen Paterson, figures reveal', *Guardian*, 27 January 2014, www.theguardian.com/environment/2014/jan/27/uk-climate-change-owen-paterson

24 Will Hutton, 'The meat scandal shows all that is rotten about our free marketeers', *Guardian*, 17 February 2013, www.theguardian.com/commentisfree/2013/feb/17/horsemeat-scandal-is-tory-party-crisis

25 Felicity Lawrence and John Domokos, 'Horsemeat company regularly mixed horse in with beef, say Polish workers', *Guardian*, 24 May 2013, www.theguardian.com/uk/2013/may/24/horsemeat-beef-meat-dutch-factory

26 Prime Minister's Office, 10 Downing Street, 'Letter from the Prime Minister on cutting red tape', Gov.uk, 7 April 2011, www.gov.uk/government/news/letter-from-the-prime-minister-on-cutting-red-tape

27 Department for Environment, Food & Rural Affairs and The Rt Hon Owen Paterson MP, 'Owen Paterson statement following Europol meeting in the Hague on horse meat – 14 February', Gov.uk, 14 February 2013, www.gov.uk/government/news/owen-paterson-statement-following-europol-meeting-in-the-hague-on-horse-meat-14-february

28 'George Osborne: Mais Lecture - A New Economic Model', SayIt, 24 February 2010, conservative-speeches.sayit.mysociety.org/speech/601526

29 'Enoch Powell 1912–98 British Conservative politician', *Oxford Essential Quotations (4 ed.)*, Oxford Univesrity Press, Oxford, 2016, www.oxfordreference.com/view/10.1093/acref/9780191826719.001.0001/q-oro-ed4-00008596

30 Will Hutton, 'Cameron, Alexander, Osborne, Clegg: how the austerity "quad" sold their souls', *Guardian*, 16 May 2021, www.theguardian.com/commentisfree/2021/may/16/austerity-quad-sold-their-souls-cameron-osborne-alexander-clegg

31 Patrick Wintour, 'George Osborne warned: protecting AAA credit rating is lost cause', *Guardian*, 6 December 2012, www.theguardian.com/politics/2012/dec/06/george-osborne-credit-rating-lost-cause

32 'Rating: United Kingdom Credit Rating', Country Economy, countryeconomy.com/ratings/uk

33 Aubrey Allegretti, 'Nick Clegg announced 5p plastic bag charge from a dogging spot, ex-press officer reveals', *Huffington Post*, 4 March 2016, www.huffingtonpost.co.uk/2016/03/04/nick-clegg-announced-5p-p_n_9382810.html

34 Emily Dugan, '"Big lie" behind the bedroom tax: Families trapped with nowhere to move face penalty for having spare room', *Independent*, 5 August 2013, www.independent.co.uk/news/uk/politics/big-lie-behind-bedroom-tax-families-trapped-nowhere-move-face-penalty-having-spare-room-8745597.html

35 Ian Duncan Smith, 'Britain cannot afford the spare room subsidy', *Telegraph*, 7 March 2013, www.telegraph.co.uk/news/politics/9914373/Britain-cannot-afford-the-spare-room-subsidy.html

36 Patrick Butler, 'Welfare reform: household benefit cap Q&A', *Guardian*, 23 January 2013, www.theguardian.com/politics/2012/jan/23/welfare-reform-benefit-cap-questions-answers?intcmp=239

37 Kamran Hussain, 'Review of British Politics 2013', *Huffington Post*, 2 March 2014, www.huffingtonpost.co.uk/kamran-hussain/british-politics-2013_b_4485261.html

38 'Number of people receiving three days' worth of emergency food by Trussell Trust foodbanks in the United Kingdom from 2008/09 to 2021/22', Statista, 2022, www.statista.com/statistics/382695/uk-foodbank-users

39 Chi Chi Izundu, 'Ding Dong! The Witch Is Dead headed for the Top 10', BBC, 10 April 2013, www.bbc.co.uk/news/newsbeat-22093181

40 'U.K. Unemployment Rate 1991-2022', Macrotrends, www.macrotrends.net/countries/ GBR/united-kingdom/unemployment-rate

41 Richard Simmons, 'Five reasons why the relationship between Gove and lawyers is going to be messy', ProQuest, 11 May 2015, www.proquest.com/docview/1747881095

42 'Universal Declaration of Human Rights', United Nations, www.un.org/en/about-us/ universal-declaration-of-human-rights

43 Stephen Cobb, 'Legal aid reform: its impact on family law', *Journal of Social Welfare and Family Law*, 19 April 2013, 25(1), pp. 3–19, www.tandfonline.com/doi/abs/10.1080/096490 69.2013.774607

44 The Secret Barrister, *The Secret Barrister: Stories of the Law and How It's Broken*, Picador, London, 2018.

45 'The Criminal Legal Aid (Remuneration) (Amendment) Regulations 2016', Legislation.gov. uk, www.legislation.gov.uk/uksi/2016/313/schedule/3/made?view=plain

46 Daniel Lewman and Faith Gordon, 'Legal aid at 70: how decades of cuts have diminished the right to legal equality', The Conversation, 29 July 2019, theconversation.com/legal-aid-at-70-how-decades-of-cuts-have-diminished-the-right-to-legal-equality-120905

47 Owen Bowcott, 'Covid has undermined chronically under-funded justice system', *Guardian*, 10 January 2021, www.theguardian.com/law/2021/jan/10/covid-has-undermined-uks-chro nically-under-funded-justice-system

48 Amanda Sime, 'Access to justice without legal aid in family proceedings and how we can help', Canter Levin & Berg Solicitors, 16 January 2020, canter-law.co.uk/access-to-justice-without-legal-aid-in-family-proceedings-and-how-we-can-help

49 Owen Bowcott and Pamela Duncan, 'Half of magistrates courts in England and Wales closed since 2010', *Guardian*, 27 January 2019, www.theguardian.com/law/2019/jan/27/half-of-magistrates-courts-in-england-and-wales-closed-since-tories-elected

50 Dominic Gilbert, 'Legal aid advice network 'decimated' by funding cuts', BBC, 10 December 2018, www.bbc.co.uk/news/uk-46357169

51 Owen Bowcott, 'Law Society takes action over cuts to legal aid fees', *Guardian*, 25 January 2018, www.theguardian.com/law/2018/jan/25/law-society-takes-action-over-cuts-to-legal-aid-fees

52 'Judicial Review Reform', Ministry of Justice, March 2021, assets.publishing.service.gov.uk /government/uploads/system/uploads/attachment_data/file/975301/judicial-review-reform-consultation-document.pdf

53 Jessica Elgot, 'From court fees to a books ban: Chris Grayling's short-lived justice policies', *Guardian*, 26 July 2017, www.theguardian.com/politics/2017/jul/26/from-court-fees-to-a-books-ban-chris-grayling-short-lived-justice-policies

54 'Legal aid cuts for prisoners', Howard League for Penal Reform, howardleague.org/legal-work/legal-aid-cuts-for-prisoners

55 'Revealed: The total number of wrongful convictions made in the UK', The University of Law, 15 September 2020, www.law.ac.uk/about/press-releases/wrongful-convictions

56 Her Majesty's Prison and Probation Service, 'Wormwood Scrubs Prison', Gov.uk, 2 June 2020, www.gov.uk/guidance/wormwood-scrubs-prison

57 Alan Travis and Owen Bowcott, 'Cuts to legal aid for prisoners ruled unlawful', *Guardian*, 10 April 2017, www.theguardian.com/law/2017/apr/10/cuts-legal-aid-for-prisoners-unlawful-court-of-appeal

58 Jessica Elgot, 'From court fees to a books ban: Chris Grayling's short-lived justice policies', *Guardian*, 26 July 2017, www.theguardian.com/politics/2017/jul/26/from-court-fees-to-a-books-ban-chris-grayling-short-lived-justice-policies

59 Amy Walker, 'Watchdog condemns Grayling's "costly" probation changes', *Guardian*, 1 March 2019, www.theguardian.com/society/2019/mar/01/watchdog-slams-extremely-costly-probation-changes

60 Jamie Doward, 'Chris Grayling's privatisation of probation service "a disaster"', *Guardian*, 30 June 2019, www.theguardian.com/politics/2019/jun/30/chris-grayling-probation-privatisation-disaster

61 'Michael Gove moves to justice in post-election reshuffle', BBC, 10 May 2015, www.bbc.co.uk/news/election-2015-32679004

62 Simon Hoggart, 'Simon Hoggart's 2010 political review: heroes and zeroes in year of change', *Guardian*, 17 December 2010, www.theguardian.com/politics/2010/dec/17/simon-hoggart-political-review-2010

63 'Profile: UKIP leader Lord Pearson', BBC, 17 August 2010, www.bbc.co.uk/news/uk-1099 6751

64 Asa Bennett, '10 policies Ukip would prefer to forget', *Telegraph*, 23 March 2015, www.telegraph.co.uk/news/politics/ukip/11489357/10-policies-Ukip-would-prefer-to-forget.html

65 Rowena Mason, 'Nigel Farage disowns Ukip's entire 2010 election manifesto', *Guardian*, 24 January 2014, www.theguardian.com/politics/2014/jan/23/nigel-farage-ukip-2010-election-manifesto

66 Lennøx, 'pleurigloss', Urban Dictionary, 25 September 2020, www.urbandictionary.com/define.php?term=pleurigloss

67 Grammar Wizard, 'Octarine', Urban Dictionary, 5 September 2004, www.urbandictionary.com/define.php?term=Octarine

68 'Local elections: Nigel Farage hails results as a "game changer"', BBC, 3 May 2013, www.bbc.co.uk/news/uk-politics-22382098

69 Matthew J. Goodwin, *New British Fascism: Rise of the British National Party*, Routledge, London and New York, 2011.

70 Toby Nangle [@toby_n], Twitter, 7 December 2020, twitter.com/toby_n/status/1335884489 004900352

71 James Robinson, Tara Conlan and Mark Sweney, 'BBC relief turns to anxiety as public say Nick Griffin was "picked-on"', *Guardian*, 23 October 2009, www.theguardian.com/politics/2009/oct/23/bbc-anxiety-nick-griffin

72 Matthew Goodwin, 'Just how much media coverage does UKIP get?', *New Statesman*, 11 November 2013, www.newstatesman.com/politics/2013/11/just-how-much-media-coverage-does-ukip-get

73 Nick Reilly, 'Nigel Farage is about to set the record for the most Question Time appearances this century', *Yahoo News*, 21 February 2018, uk.news.yahoo.com/nigel-farage-set-record-question-time-appearances-century-155615416.html

74 Matthew Goodwin, 'Just how much media coverage does UKIP get?'

75 Gary Gibbon, 'Tory MP threatens Cameron with water clock torture', *Channel 4 News*, 21 May 2013, www.channel4.com/news/by/gary-gibbon/blogs/tory-mp-threatens-cameron-with-water-clock-torture

76 Nicholas Watt, 'David Cameron ally: Tory activists are mad, swivel-eyed loons', *Guardian*, 18 May 2018, www.theguardian.com/politics/2013/may/18/david-cameron-ally-activists-loons

77 Gary Gibbon, 'Tory MP threatens Cameron with water clock torture'

78 Rowena Mason, 'Ukip's Godfrey Bloom sparks row after "joke" branding women "sluts"', *Guardian*, 20 September 2013, www.theguardian.com/politics/2013/sep/20/ukip-godfrey-bloom-calls-women-sluts

79 'David Cameron: EU referendum bill shows only Tories listen', BBC, 14 May 2013, www.bbc.co.uk/news/uk-politics-22530655

80 Robert Watts, 'Conservative MPs launch attempt to bring back death penalty, privatise the BBC and ban burka', *Telegraph*, 20 June 2013, www.telegraph.co.uk/news/politics/10133076/Conservative-MPs-launch-attempt-to-bring-back-death-penalty-privatise-the-BBC-and-ban-burka.html

81 Rowena Mason, 'Patrick Mercer made one of worst ever breaches of rules, watchdog finds', *Guardian*, www.theguardian.com/politics/2014/may/01/patrick-mercer-tory-mp-worst-ever-breaches-rules

82 Nicholas Watt, 'MP Patrick Mercer resigns Commons seat in wake of lobbying allegations', *Guardian*, 29 April 2014, www.theguardian.com/politics/2014/apr/29/patrick-mercer-suspended-house-of-commons

83 'Patrick Mercer MP: "Use water cannon if necessary"', BBC, 9 August 2011, www.bbc.co.uk/news/av/uk-14456971

84 'Creationist church remains resolute in pursuit of free school', National Secular Society, www.secularism.org.uk/creationist-church-remains-resol.html

85 Holly Watt and Claire Newell, 'Cash for questions: Patrick Mercer no stranger to controversy', *Telegraph*, 29 April 2014, www.telegraph.co.uk/news/politics/conservative/10092624/Cash-for-questions-Patrick-Mercer-no-stranger-to-controversy.html

86 'Top Tory axed over Army race row', BBC, 8 March 2007, http://news.bbc.co.uk/1/hi/uk_politics/6431005.stm

87 Rowena Mason, 'Patrick Mercer made one of worst ever breaches of rules, watchdog finds', *Guardian*, 1 May 2014, www.theguardian.com/politics/2014/may/01/patrick-mercer-tory -mp-worst-ever-breaches-rules

88 Holly Watt and Claire Newell, 'Cash for questions: Patrick Mercer no stranger to controversy'

89 Ned Simons, 'Patrick Mercer calls David Cameron an "arse" and a "despicable creature"', *Huffington Post*, 12 January 2012, www.huffingtonpost.co.uk/2011/11/12/patrick-mercer-david-cameron-arse-despicable-creature_n_1090108.html

90 Datablog, 'Government spending by department, 2011-12: get the data', *Guardian*, www.the guardian.com/news/datablog/2012/dec/04/government-spending-department-2011-12

91 'Departments of State', *London Gazzette*, 9 October 2015, Issue 61375, p. 18926, www.thegazette.co.uk/London/issue/61375/page/18926

92 '"Honest mistake": Jeremy Hunt sorry for failure to declare luxury flats purchase', *Guardian*, 13 April 2018, www.theguardian.com/politics/2018/apr/13/jeremy-hunt-sorry-for-luxury -flat-purchase-errors

93 Datablog, 'Government spending by department, 2011-12: get the data'

94 Patrick Wintour, Nicholas Watt and Juliette Jowit, 'Autumn statement: growth and NHS figures jolt George Osborne', *Guardian*, 4 December 2012, www.theguardian.com/uk/2012 /dec/04/autumn-statement-nhs-george-osborne

95 Damian Carrington, 'Badger cull ruled legal in England', *Guardian*,12 July 2012, www.theguardian.com/environment/2012/jul/12/badger-cull-legal-high-court

96 'Nigel Evans quits as deputy speaker amid sex charges', BBC, 11 September 2013, www.bbc.co.uk/news/uk-24042797

97 Amelia Hill and Owen Bowcott, '"It's completely wrong": falsely accused Tory MP attacks legal aid cuts', *Guardian*, 27 December 2018, www.theguardian.com/law/2018/dec/27/its-completely-wrong-falsely-accused-tory-mp-attacks-legal-aid-cuts

98 'Legal Aid, Sentencing and Punishment of Offenders Act 2012', The Public Whip, 5 December 2012, www.publicwhip.org.uk/division.php?date=2012-12-05&house=common s&number=116

99 Amelia Hill and Owen Bowcott, '"It's completely wrong": falsely accused Tory MP attacks legal aid cuts', *Guardian*, 27 December 2018, www.theguardian.com/law/2018/dec/27/its-completely-wrong-falsely-accused-tory-mp-attacks-legal-aid-cuts

100 'Nigel Evans', TheyWorkForYou, www.theyworkforyou.com/mp/10190/nigel_evans/ ribble_valley/votes#welfare

101 Ibid.

102 Ian Johnston, 'UN investigator Raquel Rolnik calls for Government's "bedroom tax" to be axed', *Independent*, 11 September 2013, www.independent.co.uk/news/uk/politics/un-inves tigator-raquel-rolnik-calls-government-s-bedroom-tax-be-axed-8807678.html

103 'Conservatives protest to UN over "bedroom tax" report', BBC, 11 September 2013, www.bbc.co.uk/news/uk-politics-24046094

104 Jennifer Rankin and Patrick Butler, 'Winter deaths rose by almost a third in 2012-13', *Guardian*, 26 November 2013, www.theguardian.com/uk-news/2013/nov/26/winter-deaths-rose-third

105 'Fuel Poverty levels in England, 2013', Fuel Poverty statistics, June 2015, assets.publishing. service.gov.uk/government/uploads/system/uploads/attachment_data/file/437955/Fuel_ Poverty_levels_in_England_2013.pdf

106 'Tory chairman Grant Shapps admits he had second job while an MP', ITV News, 16 March 2015, www.itv.com/news/2015-03-16/tory-chairman-grant-shapps-admits-he-had-second-job-while-an-mp

107 Randeep Ramesh, 'Grant Shapps admits he had second job as "millionaire web marketer" while MP', *Guardian*, 15 March 2015, www.theguardian.com/politics/2015/mar/15/grant-shapps-admits-he-had-second-job-as-millioniare-web-marketer-while-mp

108 Holly Watt, 'Offshore company backs crowdfunding firm run by minister's brother', *Guardian*, 7 January 2017, www.theguardian.com/politics/2017/jan/06/offshore-company-backs-ministers-brothers-crowdfunding-firm-matt-chris-hancock

109 Jemima Kelly, 'What's the story, blockchain Tory?', *FT*, 18 February 2022, www.ft.com/content/37b8c103-b044-435e-98cd-58a87d37041e

110 Rupert Neate, '£3.3bn Royal Mail privatisation pushed through ahead of possible strike', *Guardian*, 27 September 2013, www.theguardian.com/uk-news/2013/sep/27/royal-mail-3bn-pound-valuation-flotation

111 'Sir John Major calls for windfall tax on energy profits', BBC, 22 October 2013, www.bbc.co.uk/news/uk-politics-24621391

112 William Jordan, 'Two-thirds of public oppose Royal Mail sell-off', YouGov.com, 11 July 2013, yougov.co.uk/topics/politics/articles-reports/2013/07/11/two-thirds-public-oppose-royal-mail-sell

113 Rupert Neate, 'Royal Mail sale: ministers set to go where Thatcher feared to tread', *Guardian*, 29 April 2013, www.theguardian.com/uk/2013/apr/29/royal-mail-sale-thatcher

114 Rupert Neate, 'Royal Mail sale: ministers set to go where Thatcher feared to tread'

115 Djuna Thurley, 'Royal Mail Pension Plan', UK Parliament, 18 July 2013, commonslibrary.parliament.uk/research-briefings/sn04940

116 Simon Jenkins, 'There was only one loser in this Royal Mail privatisation: the taxpayer', *Guardian*, 1 April 2014, www.theguardian.com/commentisfree/2014/apr/01/royal-mail-privatisation-taxpayer-loser

117 Graham Hiscott, 'Royal Mail sell-off: Goldman Sachs admits share price will almost double and predicts redundancies at postal service', *Mirror*, 28 November 2013, www.mirror.co.uk/money/city-news/royal-mail-sell-off-goldman-sachs-2862934

118 'Royal mail share price', Google.com, accessed on 1 June 2021, www.google.com/search?q=royal+mail+share+price

119 Simon Jenkins, 'There was only one loser in this Royal Mail privatisation: the taxpayer', *Guardian*, 1 April 2014, www.theguardian.com/commentisfree/2014/apr/01/royal-mail-privatisation-taxpayer-loser

120 'History of Lindisfarne Priory', English Heritage, www.english-heritage.org.uk/visit/places/lindisfarne-priory/history

121 Simon Read, 'Government sells £900 million in student loans to debt collection company', *Independent*, 26 November 2013, www.independent.co.uk/student/news/government-sells-ps900-million-student-loans-debt-collection-company-8961790.html

122 'Lib Dem MP John Leech disappointed at delay to Alan Turing pardon bill', *Pink News*, 2 December 2013, www.pinknews.co.uk/2013/12/02/lib-dem-mp-john-leech-disappointed-at-delay-to-alan-turing-pardon-bill

2014: Lagoons of Urine

1 Steven Swinford, 'David Cameron: TV crime dramas show need for "snooper's charter"', *Telegraph*, 30 January 2014, www.telegraph.co.uk/news/uknews/crime/10608439/David-Cameron-TV-crime-dramas-show-need-for-snoopers-charter.html

2 Rowena Mason and Patrick Wintour, 'David Cameron refuses to back bonus cap for Royal Bank of Scotland', *Guardian*, 15 January 2014, www.theguardian.com/business/2014/jan/15/david-cameron-bonus-cap-royal-bank-of-scotland

3 Jaya Narain, 'Anger as Crystal Methodist returns to manse: Former Co-op Bank boss "living rent-free" in £300,000 home', *Daily Mail*, 13 January 2014, www.dailymail.co.uk/news/article-2538346/Former-Co-op-Bank-boss-Paul-Flowers-living-rent-free-300-000-home.html

4 Matthew Drake, 'Top Tory MP resigns as Ministerial aide following claims he paid male escort for sex and drugs', *Mirror*, 30 March 2014, www.mirror.co.uk/news/uk-news/tory-mp-mark-menzies-resigns-3300512

5 Edward Malnick, 'Tory MP Mark Menzies quits as ministerial aide over gay sex claims', *Telegraph*, 29 March 2014, www.telegraph.co.uk/news/politics/10732427/Tory-MP-Mark-Menzies-quits-as-ministerial-aide-over-gay-sex-claims.html

6 John Ferguson, 'Royal Bank fatcats award themselves £23million bonus packages after £8.2billion loss', *Daily Record*, 8 March 2014, www.dailyrecord.co.uk/news/uk-world-news/royal-bank-fatcats-award-themselves-3219434

7 'UKIP suspends councillor who blamed flooding on gay marriage', BBC, 19 January 2014, www.bbc.co.uk/news/uk-25802437

8 S. Arrhenius, 'On the influence of carbonic acid in the air upon the temperature of the earth', 1897, The Astronomical Society of the Pacific, 9(54), iopscience.iop.org/article/10.1086/121158

9   Sabrina Weiss, 'The UK's big flooding problem is only going to get worse', *Wired*, 26 June 2019, www.wired.co.uk/article/flooding-in-uk-weather-defence

10 'Spending Review 2010: George Osborne wields the axe', BBC, 20 October 2010, www.bbc.co.uk/news/uk-politics-11579979

11 'UK: Wettest Winter In 250 Years (Infographic)', Climate State, 27 February 2014, climatestate.com/2014/02/27/wettest-winter-in-250-years-infographic

12 'UK floods: PM says money 'no object' in relief effort', BBC, 11 February 2014, www.bbc.co.uk/news/uk-26131515

13 Richard Davies, 'UK Floods – 2013 to 2014 Winter Floods Caused £1.3 Billion Damage', Flood List, 2 March 2016, http://floodlist.com/dealing-with-floods/uk-floods-2013-2014-winter-flood-damage-costs

14 'UK floods: Call for Budget funding increase for defences', BBC, 26 February 2014, www.bbc.co.uk/news/uk-politics-26348220

15 'Number of people receiving three days' worth of emergency food by Trussell Trust foodbanks in the United Kingdom from 2008/09 to 2021/22', Statista, 11 May 2022, www.statista.com/statistics/382695/uk-foodbank-users

16 'Rise in food banks not due to welfare reforms says UK minister', BBC, 14 May 2014, www.bbc.co.uk/news/uk-scotland-scotland-politics-27402400

17 'MPs grant powers to close local hospitals', BBC, 11 March 2014, www.bbc.co.uk/news/health-26531807

18 Andy Worthington, 'Rare Good News for the NHS: Government Accepts Lords Amendment Removing Hospital Closure Clause from Care Bill', Andy Worthington, 15 May 2014, http://www.andyworthington.co.uk/2014/05/15/rare-good-news-for-the-nhs-government-accepts-lords-amendment-removing-hospital-closure-clause-from-care-bill

19 Andrew Grice, 'Maria Miller resigns: Sajid Javid appointed new Culture Secretary following expenses row', *Independent*, 9 April 2014, www.independent.co.uk/news/uk/politics/culture-secretary-maria-miller-resigns-amid-expenses-row-9247795.html

20 'Maria Miller apologises for handling of expenses inquiry', BBC, 3 April, www.bbc.co.uk/news/uk-politics-26865695

21 Andrew Grice, 'Maria Miller resigns: Sajid Javid appointed new Culture Secretary following expenses row'

22 Ibid.

23 Oliver Wright, 'Michael Fabricant: Llamas, incest, bestiality, and the demise of the Tories' Deputy Chairman', *Independent*, www.independent.co.uk/news/people/profiles/michael-fabricant-llamas-incest-bestiality-and-demise-tories-deputy-chairman-9255151.html

24 'Hillsborough Wikipedia posts were "sickening", Cabinet Office says', BBC, 25 April 2014, www.bbc.co.uk/news/uk-england-merseyside-27165844

25 'Osborne wants above-inflation minimum wage rise', BBC, 16 January 2014, www.bbc.co.uk/news/uk-politics-25766558

26 'National minimum wage: response to Low Pay Commission 2014 report', Gov.uk, 12 March 2014, www.gov.uk/government/publications/national-minimum-wage-response-to-low-pay-commission-2014-report

27 'Feature: History of apprenticeships dating back to days of Elizabeth 1st', FE Week, 11 March 2016, feweek.co.uk/history-of-apprenticeships

28 Education and Skills Funding Agency, 'Withdrawal of apprenticeship frameworks', Gov.uk, 7 July 2020, www.gov.uk/government/publications/removal-of-apprenticeship-frameworks

29 'Specification of apprenticeship standards for England (SASE)', Gov.uk, 7 March 2013, www.gov.uk/government/publications/specification-of-apprenticeship-standards-for-england

30 'Specification of apprenticeship standards for England (SASE)', Gov.uk

31 'Register of end-point assessment organisations', Gov.uk, 5 April 2018, www.gov.uk/guidance/register-of-end-point-assessment-organisations

32 '5 reasons you should consider becoming an End-Point Assessor', Protocol, 24 January 2019, www.protocol.co.uk/employment-advice/5-reasons-you-should-consider-becoming-an-end-point-assessor

33 'Salaries and benefits', Department for Education, Teaching, getintoteaching.education.gov.uk/salaries-and-benefits

34 UK Parliament, 'Planned changes to minimum school funding: Schools affected by constituency', 11 September 2019, commonslibrary.parliament.uk/proposed-changes-to-minimum-school-funding-schools-affected-by-constituency (£5000 / 38 weeks education)

35 'Apprenticeships and traineeships', Gov.uk, 26 November 2020, explore-education-statistics.service.gov.uk/find-statistics/apprenticeships-and-traineeships/2019-20

36 'Cameron: Newark win shows economic message hitting home', BBC, 6 June 2014, www.bbc.co.uk/news/uk-politics-27728789

37 UK Parliament, 'General Election 2019: Which party received the most donations?', 24 January 2020, commonslibrary.parliament.uk/general-election-2019-which-party-received-the-most-donations

38 'Cameron: Newark win shows economic message hitting home', BBC, 6 June 2014, www.bbc.co.uk/news/uk-politics-27728789

39 George Parker, Kiran Stacey and Hugh Carnegy, 'Ukip and Front National lead populist earthquake', FT, 26 May 2014, www.ft.com/content/aad578e8-e463-11e3-a73a-00144feabdc0

40 Rowena Mason and Shiv Malik, 'Alarm sounded on anti-Roma rhetoric as door opens to more EU workers', Guardian, 1 January 2014, www.theguardian.com/uk-news/2013/dec/31/mps-anti-roma-rhetoric-romania-bulgaria

41 Alex Andreou, 'The immigration invasion that never was', Guardian, 2 January 2014, www.theguardian.com/commentisfree/2014/jan/02/immigration-invasion-bulgarians-romanians-uk

42 Caroline Davies and Shiv Malik, 'Welcome to Luton: Romanian arrival greeted by two MPs and a media scrum', Guardian, 1 January 2014, www.theguardian.com/uk-news/2014/jan/01/luton-romanian-arrival-mps-media

43 'Supreme Court rules "deport first, appeal later" policy unlawful', Deighton Pierce Glynn, 15 June 2022, dpglaw.co.uk/supreme-court-rules-deport-first-appeal-later-policy-unlawful

44 'David Cameron's EU speech: full text', BBC, 28 November 2014, www.bbc.co.uk/news/uk-politics-30250299

45 Dan Sabbagh, Luke Harding and Harry Davies, 'Lubov Chernukhin: Tories' tennis-bidding, record-setting donor', Guardian, 27 February 2020, www.theguardian.com/politics/2020/feb/27/lubov-chernukhin-tories-tennis-record-donor-uk-russia

46 Catherine Belton, 'In British PM race, a former Russian tycoon quietly wields influence', Reuters, 19 July 2019, www.reuters.com/investigates/special-report/britain-eu-johnson-russian

47 Adrian Pearson, 'Newcastle-based Russian millionaire Alexander Temerko at exclusive Cameron bash', Chronicle Live, 6 July 2014, www.chroniclelive.co.uk/news/north-east-news/newcastle-based-russian-millionaire-alexander-temerko-7370497

48 'Tennis match with Cameron auctioned off for £160,000', BBC, 4 July 2014, www.bbc.co.uk/news/uk-politics-28158479

49 'Reshuffle: 6 ways Cameron's "rise of the women" is a damp squib', The Huffington Post, 16 July 2014, www.huffingtonpost.co.uk/2014/07/16/cameron-women-reshuffle-cabinet_n_5590451.html

50 Sophy Ridge, 'Cameron's reshuffle: gender isn't the only thing women MPs have to offer', Telegraph, 14 July 2014, www.telegraph.co.uk/women/womens-politics/10966193/David-Cameron-Cabinet-reshuffle-2014-gender-isnt-all-women-MPs-have-to-offer.html

51 Jerry Hayes [@jerryhayes1], Twitter, 12 July 2014, twitter.com/jerryhayes1/status/488016650424569856

52 Joe Murphy, 'PM accused of abuse of honours system as "shuffled" ministers are put up for knighthoods', Evening Standard, 16 July 2014, www.standard.co.uk/news/politics/david-cameron-honours-system-abuse-reshuffle-knighthoods-9609014.html

53 William Cash, 'David Cameron's decision to sack Owen Paterson will send rural voters flooding to Ukip', Spectator, 22 July 2014, www.spectator.co.uk/article/david-cameron-s-decision-to-sack-owen-paterson-will-send-rural-voters-flooding-to-ukip

54 'Michael Gove move not a demotion, says David Cameron', BBC, 15 July 2014, www.bbc.co.uk/news/uk-politics-28302487

55 Catherine Baksi, 'Buckland appointment "an insult to lawyers"', Law Society Gazette, 21 July 2014, www.lawgazette.co.uk/practice/buckland-appointment-an-insult-to-lawyers/5042318.article

56 Nicholas Watt, 'Liz Truss: leave lawnmower in the shed to protect UK's bees', *Guardian*, 4 November 2014, www.theguardian.com/environment/2014/nov/04/bees-uk-protect-liz-truss-pollinating-lawnmower

57 Damian Carrington, 'UK suspends ban on pesticides linked to serious harm in bees', *Guardian*, 23 July 2015, www.theguardian.com/environment/2015/jul/23/uk-suspends-ban-pesticides-linked-serious-harm-bees

58 '"Postcode lottery" for homeopathic treatment', *Kent News*, 12 October 2007, web.archive.org/web/20160806103257/http://www.kentnews.co.uk/news/postcode_lottery_for_homeopathic_treatment_1_1033474

59 James Tapsfield, 'London Mayor Boris Johnson seeks 'safe' Tory seat in election', *Independent.ie*, 26 August 2014, www.independent.ie/world-news/europe/london-mayor-boris-johnson-seeks-safe-tory-seat-in-election-30538320.html

60 Chris Johnton, 'Boris Johnson selected to stand for Tories in Uxbridge and South Ruislip', *Guardian*, 12 September 2014, www.theguardian.com/politics/2014/sep/12/boris-johnson-tory-candidate-uxbridge-south-ruislip

61 mindlessgonzoALT, 'HIGNFY Mastermind Instances', YouTube, 23 July 2017, www.youtube.com/watch?v=cZAy-tybIPQ (6:00)

62 James Ball, 'All the times Boris Johnson flat-out lied', *iNews*, 8 July 2020, inews.co.uk/news/uk/times-boris-johnson-flat-lied-130475

63 Sam Knight, 'The Empty Promise of Boris Johnson', *New Yorker*, 13 July 2019, www.newyorker.com/magazine/2019/06/24/the-empty-promise-of-boris-johnson

64 Boris Johnson, 'I'm no longer Nasty, but please stop lying about Nice', *Telegraph*, 17 October 2002, www.telegraph.co.uk/comment/personal-view/3582944/Im-no-longer-Nasty-but-please-stop-lying-about-Nice.html

65 Martin Fletcher, 'Boris Johnson peddled absurd EU myths – and our disgraceful press followed his lead', *New Statesman*, 1 July 2016, www.newstatesman.com/politics/uk/2016/07/boris-johnson-peddled-absurd-eu-myths-and-our-disgraceful-press-followed-his

66 Letters, 'Biography of Boris from Bullingdon to Brussels', *Guardian*, 25 June 2019, www.theguardian.com/politics/2019/jun/25/biography-of-boris-from-bullingdon-to-brussels

67 Jennifer Rankin and Jim Waterson, 'How Boris Johnson's Brussels-bashing stories shaped British politics', *Guardian*, 14 July 2019, www.theguardian.com/politics/2019/jul/14/boris-johnson-brussels-bashing-stories-shaped-politics

68 'Boris Johnson: "The boy who wanted to be world king"', BBC, 24 July 2019, www.bbc.co.uk/news/av/uk-politics-49088773

69 Martin Fletcher, 'Boris Johnson peddled absurd EU myths – and our disgraceful press followed his lead', *New Statesman*, 1 July 2016, www.newstatesman.com/politics/uk/2016/07/boris-johnson-peddled-absurd-eu-myths-and-our-disgraceful-press-followed-his

70 Kate Lyons, 'The 10 best Euro myths – from custard creams to condoms', *Guardian*, 23 June 2016, www.theguardian.com/politics/2016/jun/23/10-best-euro-myths-from-custard-creams-to-condoms

71 'Boris Johnson v Andrew Tyrie on EU coffin and lorry claims', BBC, 23 March 2016, www.bbc.co.uk/news/av/uk-politics-35887003

72 Jane Merrick, 'Boris Johnson's kipper stunt based on incorrect information about EU rules, experts say', *iNews*, 18 July 2018, inews.co.uk/news/brexit/boris-johnson-brexit-fake-news-accusation-eu-kipper-rules-315568

73 Peter Stubley, 'Boris Johnson: The most infamous lies and untruths by the Conservative leadership candidate', *Independent*, 25 May 2019, www.independent.co.uk/news/uk/politics/boris-johnson-lies-conservative-leader-candidate-list-times-banana-brexit-bus-a8929076.html

74 Patrick Worrall, 'Boris Johnson falsely claims he "didn't say anything about Turkey" in the referendum campaign', Channel 4 News, www.channel4.com/news/factcheck/factcheck-boris-johnson-falsely-claims-he-didnt-say-anything-about-turkey-in-the-referendum-campaign

75 Patrick Hennessy and Melissa Kite, 'Howard sacks "devastated' Boris Johnson over affair"', *Telegraph*, 14 November 2004, www.telegraph.co.uk/news/uknews/1476560/Howard-sacks-devastated-Boris-Johnson-over-affair.html

76   'UK Statistics Authority statement on the use of official statistics on contributions
     to the European Union', UK Statistics Authority, 27 May 2016, uksa.statisticsauthority.
     gov.uk/news/uk-statistics-authority-statement-on-the-use-of-official-statistics-on-
     contributions-to-the-european-union
77   Peter Stubley, 'Boris Johnson: The most infamous lies and untruths by the Conservative
     leadership candidate'
78   'Mark Reckless defects to UKIP from Tories', BBC, 27 September 2014, www.bbc.co.uk/
     news/uk-politics-29394697
79   Matt Payton, 'Ukip's Douglas Carswell is the least trustworthy MP while Diane Abbott is
     most patronising, survey finds', Independent, 29 June 2016, www.independent.co.uk/news
     /uk/politics/ukip-s-douglas-carswell-least-trustworthy-mp-while-diane-abbott-most-
     patronising-survey-finds-a7107381.html
80   'Tory MP Douglas Carswell defects to UKIP and forces by-election', BBC, 28 August 2014,
     www.bbc.co.uk/news/uk-politics-28967904
81   'MPs to repay more than 1m in expenses', The Lowestoft Journal, 4 February 2010,
     www.lowestoftjournal.co.uk/news/mps-to-repay-more-than-1 million-in-expenses-282044
82   Dominic Gover, 'Douglas Carswell and the £650 "Love Seat" Which Mired Ukip MP in
     Expenses Scandal', International Business Times, 28 August 2014, www.ibtimes.co.uk/
     douglas-carswell-650-love-seat-which-mired-ukip-mp-expenses-scandal-1462995
83   'AB Produce near Measham risks losing licence over "urine" smell', BBC, 14 August 2014,
     www.bbc.co.uk/news/uk-england-leicestershire-28785285
84   AB Farms, AB Produce PLC, abproduce.co.uk
85   Holly Watt, 'Mark Simmonds: Expenses system gave Foreign Office minister a £500,000 lift',
     Telegraph, 11 August 2014, www.telegraph.co.uk/news/newstopics/mps-expenses/11026474
     /Mark-Simmonds-Expenses-system-gave-Foreign-Office-minister-a-500000-lift.html
86   'Mark Simmonds and why £89,435 (and the rest) is not enough to live on', Guardian, 12
     August 2014, www.theguardian.com/politics/shortcuts/2014/aug/12/mark-simmonds-why-
     salary-not-enough
87   'Allowances by MP - Mark Simmonds', www.parliament.co.uk, mpsallowances.parliament
     .uk/mpslordsandoffices/hocallowances/allowances-by-mp/mark-simmonds
88   Steven Swinford, 'How taxpayers helped fund £1m home of minister who can't live
     on MP's pay', Telegraph, 12 August 2014, www.telegraph.co.uk/news/newstopics/
     mps-expenses/conservative-mps-expenses/11029709/How-taxpayers-helped-fund-1m-
     home-of-minister-who-cant-live-on-MPs-pay.html
89   Ibid.
90   Ian Burbidge, 'James Duddridge in £11,000 benefits row over hotel expense', Echo, 16
     September 2014, www.echo-news.co.uk/news/local_news/11475436.james-duddridge-in
     -11000-benefits-row-over-hotel-expense
91   Patrick Wintour and Rowena Mason, 'Lady Warsi resigns over UK's "morally indefensible"
     stance on Gaza', Guardian, 5 August 2014, www.theguardian.com/politics/2014/aug/05/
     lady-warsi-resigns-government-gaza-stance
92   Lord Ashcroft, 'How Scotland voted, and why', Lord Ashcroft Polls, 19 September 2014,
     lordashcroftpolls.com/2014/09/scotland-voted
93   'SNP membership trebles following indyref', Herald, 1 October 2014,
     www.heraldscotland.com/news/13182725.snp-membership-trebles-following-indyref
94   Fraser Nelson, 'Brooks Newmark quits after sending explicit photos of himself in paisley
     pyjamas', Spectator, 27 September 2014, www.spectator.co.uk/article/brooks-newmark-
     quits-after-sending-explicit-photos-of-himself-in-paisley-pyjamas
95   Matt Payton, 'Has Tory sleaze made paisley pyjamas sexy? Marks & Spencer sells
     out after Brooks Newmark scandal', Metro, 28 September 2014, metro.co.uk/2014/09/
     28/has-tory-sleaze-made-paisley-pyjamas-sexy-marks-spencer-sells-out-after-brooks-
     newmark-scandal-4885274
96   Ibid.
97   Steve Anderson, 'Brooks Newmark resigns: Minister caught in sex sting to quit as MP
     over new scandal', Independent, 12 October 2014, www.independent.co.uk/news/brooks-
     newmark-resigns-minister-caught-sex-sting-quit-mp-over-new-scandal-9789165.html
98   'Brooks Newmark: I have been a complete fool, says Conservative ex-minister', BBC, 28
     September 2014, www.bbc.co.uk/news/uk-politics-29399636

99 "'Flog" home owners who leave bins in road, says Eric Pickles', *Telegraph*, 16 December 2014, www.telegraph.co.uk/news/politics/11297687/Flog-home-owners-who-leave-bins-in-road-says-Eric-Pickles.html

100 Heather Saul, 'Equal pay: Seven male Tory MPs vote against bill to make big companies reveal gender pay gap', *Independent*, 16 December 2014, web.archive.org/web/20150425151006/http://www.independent.co.uk/news/uk/politics/equal-pay-seven-male-tory-mps-vote-against-bill-to-make-big-companies-reveal-gender-pay-gap-9928964.html

101 'Nazi stag MP Aidan Burley "caused deep offence", report finds', BBC, 22 January 2014, www.bbc.co.uk/news/uk-politics-25836506

2015: A Statesman or a Twat?

1 Steve Baker, 'Wycombe MP in Combat Academy shock (2/2)', YouTube, 18 January 2015, www.youtube.com/watch?v=HwVd7XDyZgM

2 Steve Baker, 'Wycombe MP in Combat Academy shock (1/2)', YouTube, 18 January 2015, www.youtube.com/watch?v=I-QfqXaVWks

3 Press Assocation, 'I want to slap David Cameron, Nick Clegg admits', *Telegraph*, 30 January 2015, www.telegraph.co.uk/news/politics/nick-clegg/11381391/I-want-to-slap-David-Cameron-Nick-Clegg-admits.html

4 Rowena Mason, 'David Cameron under growing pressure over TV debates', *Guardian*, 14 January 2015, www.theguardian.com/politics/2015/jan/14/pressure-on-cameron-over-tv-debates

5 'Cameron denies "running scared" of TV election debates', BBC, 5 March 2015, www.bbc.co.uk/news/uk-politics-31745808

6 'Election 2015: Seven-party TV debate plan announced', BBC, 23 January 2015, www.bbc.co.uk/news/uk-politics-30955379

7 Rob Merrick, 'Housebuilding figures under Conservatives lowest since the Second World War', *Independent*, 1 January 2019, www.independent.co.uk/news/uk/politics/england-house-building-record-second-world-war-conservative-government-home-a8706776.html

8 Tamsin Rutter, '2015 in housing: 12 months of growing crisis', *Guardian*, 29 December 2015, www.theguardian.com/housing-network/2015/dec/29/2015-housing-12-months-growing-crisis

9 'House prices at 10 times salary', This is Money, 15 January 2009, www.thisismoney.co.uk/money/mortgageshome/article-1610770/House-prices-at-10-times-salary.html

10 Rajeev Syal, 'Tories fail to build any of 200,000 starter homes promised in 2015, says watchdog', *Guardian*, 5 November 2019, www.theguardian.com/society/2019/nov/05/tories-broke-pledge-on-starter-homes-in-2015-manifesto-report-says

11 Tamsin Rutter, '2015 in housing: 12 months of growing crisis'

12 Richard Partington, 'Home ownership among young adults has "collapsed", study finds', *Guardian*, 16 February 2018, www.theguardian.com/money/2018/feb/16/homeownership-among-young-adults-collapsed-institute-fiscal-studies

13 Ibid.

14 Tamsin Rutter, '2015 in housing: 12 months of growing crisis'

15 Liam Kelly, 'What the latest statistics tell us about housing – in six charts', *Guardian*, 26 February 2015, www.theguardian.com/housing-network/2015/feb/26/english-housing-survey-2015-in-charts

16 Tamsin Rutter, '2015 in housing: 12 months of growing crisis'

17 D. Clark, 'Government expenditure on housing benefit in the UK 2000–2021', Statista, 1 April 2022, www.statista.com/statistics/283949/housing-benefit-united-kingdom-uk-government-spending

18 Tom de Castella, 'Self-build: should people build their own homes?', BBC, 19 July 2011, www.bbc.co.uk/news/magazine-14125196

19 James Lyons, 'Land grubbers: David Cameron faces claims wealthy donors are influencing policy on planning laws', *Mirror*, 28 March 2012, www.mirror.co.uk/news/uk-news/tory-sleaze-david-cameron-faces-774353

20 Peter Geoghegan and Jenna Corderoy, 'Exclusive: Property tycoons gave Tories more than £11m in less than a year', openDemocracy, 26 June 2020, www.opendemocracy.net/en/dark-money-investigations/exclusive-property-tycoons-gave-tories-more-than-11m-in-less-than-a-year

21 Helena Bengtsson, Emma Hartley and Rajeev Syal, 'Number of MPs who earn from renting
    out property rises by a third', *Guardian*, 6 May 2015, www.theguardian.com/politics/2015
    /may/06/number-of-mps-who-earn-from-renting-out-property-rises-by-a-third

22 Rowena Mason, 'Cameron appoints second gay-marriage opponent to Equalities Office',
    Guardian, 12 May 2015, www.theguardian.com/politics/2015/may/12/david-cameron-
    appoints-another-gay-marriage-opponent-to-equalities-office

23 Owen Bennett, 'Tory MP Tobias Ellwood apologies after claiming his £90k salary left him
    "watching the pennies"', *Huffington Post*, 20 July 2015, www.huffingtonpost.co.uk/2015/07
    /20/tory-mp-tobias-ellwood-pennies_n_7830784.html

24 'MPs named over written-off expenses', BBC, 10 September 2015, www.bbc.co.uk/news/
    uk-politics-34200969

25 Ashitha Nagesh, 'A Tory MP might have quoted Goebbels in defence of the government's
    surveillance bill', *Metro*, 5 November 2015, metro.co.uk/2015/11/05/a-tory-mp-might-
    have-quoted-goebbels-in-defence-of-the-governments-surveillance-bill-5481457

26 'Tory apologises over "joke" about turning Scots into "slaves"', *Herald Scotland*, 7 June 2015,
    www.heraldscotland.com/news/13411808.tory-apologises-joke-turning-scots-slaves

27 Ben Riley-Smith, 'Expenses and sex scandal deleted from MPs' Wikipedia pages by
    computers inside Parliament', *Telegraph*, 26 May 2015, www.telegraph.co.uk/news/general-
    election-2015/11574217/Expenses-and-sex-scandal-deleted-from-MPs-Wikipedia-pages-
    by-computers-inside-Parliament.html

28 Edward Malnick, 'Ministers' red boxes chauffeured around in official cars', *Telegraph*,
    6 January 2014, www.telegraph.co.uk/news/politics/10526813/Ministers-red-boxes-
    chauffeured-around-in-official-cars.html

29 D. Clark, 'Number of people using food banks in the UK 2008–2022', Statista, 11 May 2022,
    www.statista.com/statistics/382695/uk-foodbank-users

30 Patrick Butler, 'Council cuts: the burden falls again on the north and the inner cities',
    Guardian, 14 January 2015, www.theguardian.com/society/patrick-butler-cuts-blog/2015
    /jan/14/council-cuts-burden-falls-again-on-north-and-inner-cities

31 Ibid.

32 Peter Hetherington, 'Bluff diamond', *Guardian*, interview, 2 July 2008,
    www.theguardian.com/society/2008/jul/02/localgovernment.localgovernment

33 Matthew Weaver, '"Cash for access": the main allegations', *Guardian*, 23 February 2015,
    www.theguardian.com/politics/2015/feb/23/cash-for-access-allegations-jack-straw-
    malcolm-rifkind

34 'Malcolm Rifkind', TheyWorkForYou, accessed on 28 July 2022, www.theyworkforyou.com
    /mp/11660/malcolm_rifkind/kensington

35 Claire Newell, Edward Malnick, Christopher Hope, Luke Heighton and Lyndsey Telford,
    'Jack Straw and Sir Malcolm Rifkind did offer cash for access', *Telegraph*, 21 December 2015,
    www.telegraph.co.uk/news/investigations/jack-straw-and-sir-malcolm-rifkind-did-offer-
    cash-for-access

36 Jack Blanchard, 'Malcolm Rifkind: I am entitled to more than £67k salary', *Mirror*, 23
    February 2015, www.mirror.co.uk/news/uk-news/malcolm-rifkind-am-entitled-more-521
    8827

37 Lizzie Dearden, '"Cash for access" scandal: Sir Malcolm Rifkind suspended from the
    Conservative Party', *Independent*, 23 February 2015, www.independent.co.uk/news/uk/pol
    itics/cash-for-access-scandal-sir-malcolm-rifkind-suspended-from-the-conservative-party
    -10064817.html

38 James Gallagher, 'NHS reorganisation was disastrous, says King's Fund', BBC, 6 February
    2015, www.bbc.co.uk/news/health-31145600

39 'David Cameron "won't serve third term" if re-elected', BBC, 24 March 2015,
    www.bbc.co.uk/news/uk-politics-32022484

40 Daniel Boffey, 'Revealed: the link between life peerages and party donations', *Guardian*,
    21 March 2015, www.theguardian.com/politics/2015/mar/21/revealed-link-life-peerages-
    party-donations

41 'Hedge fund donors', Electorial Commission; FT research, accessed on 28 July 2022,
    media.ft.com/cms/c3f0d088-2107-11e1-8a43-00144feabdc0.pdf

42 Daniel Boffey, 'Revealed: the link between life peerages and party donations'

43 Jenny Cosgrave, 'UK finally finishes paying for World War I', CNBC, 9 March 2015,
    www.cnbc.com/2015/03/09/uk-finally-finishes-paying-for-world-war-i.html

44 'The story of social housing', Shelter, accessed on 28 July 2022, england.shelter.org.uk/support_us/campaigns/story_of_social_housing

45 'UK economic growth slows to 0.3%', BBC, 28 April 2015, www.bbc.co.uk/news/business-32493745

46 Stephen Machin, 'Real wages and living standards: the latest UK evidence', LSE, blog, 26 March 2015, blogs.lse.ac.uk/politicsandpolicy/real-wages-and-living-standards

47 Alex Bryson and John Forth, *The UK's Productivity Puzzle*, IZA Discussion Papers, No. 9097, Institute for the Study of Labor (IZA), Bonn, 2015, www.econstor.eu/bitstream/104 19/111549/1/dp9097.pdf

48 'Growth, 2008–13', LSE, blog, accessed on 28 July 2022, blogs.lse.ac.uk/politicsandpolicy/files/2015/03/Machin-Fig-3.jpg

49 'UK economic growth slows to 0.3%', BBC

50 William Jordan, 'Health overtakes immigration as an issue for voters', YouGov, 15 April 2015, yougov.co.uk/topics/politics/articles-reports/2015/04/15/health-tops-immigration-second-most-important-issu

51 Jonathan Owen, 'Recovery of UK economy is the slowest since records began, say unions', *Independent*, 2 August 2015, www.independent.co.uk/news/uk/home-news/recovery-uk-economy-slowest-ever-say-unions-10432717.html

52 Paul Evans, 'NHS privatisation soars 500% in the last year, finds in-depth new study', openDemocracy, 30 April 2015, www.opendemocracy.net/en/ournhs/nhs-privatisation-soars-500-in-last-year-finds-indepth-new-study

53 Will Dahlgreen, 'Nationalise energy and rail companies, say public', YouGov, 4 November 2013, yougov.co.uk/topics/politics/articles-reports/2013/11/04/nationalise-energy-and-rail-companies-say-public

54 'The history of strikes in the UK', Office for National Statistics, 21 September 2015, www.ons.gov.uk/employmentandlabourmarket/peopleinwork/employmentand employeetypes/articles/thehistoryofstrikesintheuk/2015-09-21

55 'Labour disputes in the UK: 2015', Office for National Statistics, 2 August 2016, www.ons.gov.uk/employmentandlabourmarket/peopleinwork/workplacedisputesand workingconditions/articles/labourdisputes/2015

56 'Trade Union Bill: Ministers deny "attack on workers' rights"', BBC, 15 July 2015, www.bbc.co.uk/news/uk-politics-33529248

57 'Election 2010: National Results after 650 of 650', BBC, accessed on 28 July 2022, news.bbc.co.uk/1/shared/election2010/results/

58 'Electoral statistics, UK: March 2020', Office for National Statistics, 5 January 2021, www.ons.gov.uk/peoplepopulationandcommunity/elections/electoralregistration/bulletins/electoralstatisticsforuk/march2020

59 Andy McSmith, 'Public sector strikes: The day Michael Gove took his place on the picket line', *Independent*, 10 July 2014, www.independent.co.uk/news/uk/politics/michael-gove-on-strike-on-day-when-teachers-are-criticised-for-walkout-photo-shows-education-minister-on-picket-line-9597723.html

60 Caroline Mortimer, 'General Election 2015: David Cameron forgets if he's an Aston Villa or West Ham fan', *Independent*, 25 April 2015, www.independent.co.uk/news/uk/politics/generalelection-2015-david-cameron-forgets-if-he-s-aston-villa-or-west-ham-fan-10203685.html

61 David Cameron [@David_Cameron], Twitter, 4 May 2015, twitter.com/david_cameron/status/595112367358406656?lang=en

62 James Moore, 'Universal credit plunges kids into poverty and 120,000 have died because of austerity – but Jacob Rees-Mogg wants more cuts', *Independent*, 16 November 2017, www.independent.co.uk/voices/nhs-austerity-cuts-120000-deaths-universal-credit-only-get-worse-a8058231.html

63 Benjamin Kentish, 'Tory MP Mark Menzies interviewed by police over claims he got dog drunk and started brawl with friend', *Independent*, 29 May 2017, www.independent.co.uk/news/uk/politics/conservative-mp-mark-menzies-got-dog-drunk-street-brawl-fylde-thames-valley-police-a7761486.html

64 Ibid.

65 'Fylde: 2015 General Election', MPs and Lords, UK Parliament, accessed on 28 July 2022, members.parliament.uk/constituency/3491/election/369

66　'Crowded phone box is record-breaker', *Guardian*, 19 August 2003, www.theguardian.com/uk/2003/aug/19/sillyseason.media

67　Sarah Ann Harris, 'Nigel Farage's 7 failed attempts to become an MP', *Huffington Post*, 20 April 2017, www.huffingtonpost.co.uk/entry/nigel-farage-mp-elected-general-election-2017_uk_58f885f8e4b070a11750524e

68　'Farage stays as UKIP leader after resignation rejected', BBC, 11 May 2015, www.bbc.co.uk/news/uk-politics-32696505

69　Damien Gayle, 'Tenant evictions reach six-year high amid rising rents and benefit cuts', *Guardian*, 14 May 2015, www.theguardian.com/money/2015/may/14/tenant-evictions-reach-six-year-high-rising-rents-benefit-cuts

70　Tamsin Rutter, '2015 in housing: 12 months of growing crisis', *Guardian*, 29 December 2015, www.theguardian.com/housing-network/2015/dec/29/2015-housing-12-months-growing-crisis

71　Liam Kelly, 'Housing and budget: what you need to know', *Guardian*, 9 July 2015, www.theguardian.com/housing-network/2015/jul/09/housing-budget-what-you-need-to-know

72　'Corporation tax rates around the world. How much do companies pay?', *Guardian*, blog, accessed on 28 July 2022, www.theguardian.com/news/datablog/2011/feb/21/corporation-tax-rates-world#data

73　'2010 Chapter 13', Finance Act 2010, legislation.gov.uk, www.legislation.gov.uk/ukpga/2010/13/enacted

74　'Budget 2015: Osborne unveils National Living Wage', BBC, 8 July 2015, www.bbc.co.uk/news/uk-politics-33437115

75　Rajeev Syal, 'HMRC staff braced for thousands of job cuts as 137 tax offices to close', *Guardian*, 12 November 2015, www.theguardian.com/politics/2015/nov/12/hmrc-staff-braced-for-thousands-of-job-cuts-if-tax-offices-close

76　Liam Kelly, 'Housing and budget: what you need to know'

77　'A guide to Inheritance Tax', Money Advice Service, accessed on 28 July 2022, www.moneyadviceservice.org.uk/en/articles/a-guide-to-inheritance-tax%23when-do-you-have-to-pay-inheritance-tax

78　Damien Gayle, 'Anti-austerity protests: tens of thousands rally across UK', *Guardian*, 20 June 2015, www.theguardian.com/world/2015/jun/20/tens-thousands-rally-uk-protest-against-austerity

79　'Draw up 40% cuts plans, George Osborne tells Whitehall departments', BBC, 21 July 2015, www.bbc.co.uk/news/uk-politics-33610801

80　Carl Emmerson, 'Two parliaments of pain: the UK public finances 2010 to 2017', Institute for Fiscal Studies, 2 May 2017, ifs.org.uk/publications/9180

81　D. Clark, 'National debt as a percentage of GDP in the UK 1920–2022', Statista, 22 February 2022, www.statista.com/statistics/282841/debt-as-gdp-uk

82　Sarah Vine, 'I'm proof a nanny CAN make you a worse mum', *Daily Mail*, 22 July 2015, www.dailymail.co.uk/debate/article-3170220/SARAH-VINE-m-proof-nanny-make-worse-mum.html#nf

83　Kat Lay, 'Gove can't get x ray at weekend', *The Times*, 23 July 2015, www.thetimes.co.uk/article/gove-cant-get-x-ray-at-weekend-ngc3fxfz03z

84　Jasper Jackson, 'Telegraph misled readers over NHS x-ray service, press watchdog finds', *Guardian*, 20 November 2015, www.theguardian.com/media/2015/nov/20/telegraph-misled-readers-over-nhs-x-ray-service-press-watchdog-finds

85　'Pay for doctors', NHS, accessed on 28 July 2022, www.healthcareers.nhs.uk/explore-roles/doctors/pay-doctors

86　'Job Search', Aldi, accessed on 28 July 2022, www.aldirecruitment.co.uk/job-search?tag=Store-Manager

87　Denis Campbell, 'Junior doctors overwhelmingly vote for NHS strikes', *Guardian*, 19 November 2015, www.theguardian.com/society/2015/nov/19/nhs-strikes-junior-doctors-vote-action-bma

88　Ashley Cowburn, 'Welfare office made up quotes from "happy benefits claimants"', *The Times*, 19 August 2015, www.thetimes.co.uk/article/welfare-office-made-up-quotes-from-happy-benefits-claimants-pjq38j57x32

89 Peter Dominiczak, 'Thousands of benefit claimants died after being declared "fit for work"', *Telegraph*, 27 August 2015, www.telegraph.co.uk/news/politics/11828097/Thousands-of-benefit-claimants-died-after-being-declared-fit-for-work.html

90 Jon Stone, 'Legally binding child poverty targets to be scrapped, Iain Duncan Smith says', *Independent*, 1 July 2015, www.independent.co.uk/news/uk/politics/unsustainable-legally-binding-child-poverty-targets-be-scrapped-iain-duncan-smith-says-10358111.html

91 Ibid.

92 Frances Perraudin, Rowena Mason and Graham Ruddick, 'The new peerages and the new House of Lords – full list', *Guardian*, 27 August 2015, www.theguardian.com/politics/2015/aug/27/the-new-peerages-and-the-new-house-of-lords-full-list

93 Jim Pickard and Robert Wright, 'Priti Patel scandal turns spotlight on Stuart Polak', *FT*, 8 November 2017, www.ft.com/content/383e5caa-c4a2-11e7-b2bb-322b2cb39656

94 Douglas Murray, 'Mass immigration will DESTROY Britain if we don't act now, blasts DOUGLAS MURRAY', *Express*, 28 August 2015, www.express.co.uk/comment/expresscomment/601232/Mass-immigration-destroy-the-UK-we-dont-act-now

95 Matt Chorley, 'Britain is a "magnet for migrants" as number of foreigners with right to work hits 820,000 including 220% rise in Romanians', *Daily Mail*, 4 June 2015, www.dailymail.co.uk/news/article-3110649/Britain-magnet-migrants-number-foreigners-right-work-hits-820-000-including-220-rise-Romanians.html

96 Anil Dawar, 'In the heart of England: Shock pics that prove UK's migrant invasion is OUT OF CONTROL', *Express*, 11 June 2015, www.express.co.uk/news/uk/583611/Pictures-shocking-migrants-invasion

97 Alan Travis, 'The only "migrant madness" is the tabloid pretence about events in Calais', *Guardian*, 30 July 2015, www.theguardian.com/uk-news/2015/jul/30/the-only-migrant-madness-is-the-tabloid-pretence-about-events-in-calais

98 Amelia Gentleman, 'The horror of the Calais refugee camp: "We feel like we are dying slowly"', *Guardian*, 3 November 2015, www.theguardian.com/world/2015/nov/03/refugees-horror-calais-jungle-refugee-camp-feel-like-dying-slowly

99 'Channel tunnel: "2,000 migrants" tried to enter', BBC, 28 July 2015, www.bbc.co.uk/news/world-europe-33689473

100 Gill Plimmer, 'UK falls short of 24,000 nurses due to cuts and immigration rules', *FT*, 7 June 2015, www.ft.com/content/beb7831a-0b77-11e5-8937-00144feabdc0

101 Haroon Siddique, 'New immigration rules will cost the NHS millions, warns nursing union', *Guardian*, 22 June 2015, www.theguardian.com/society/2015/jun/22/new-immigration-rules-cost-nhs-millions-nursing

102 Helena Smith, 'Shocking images of drowned Syrian boy show tragic plight of refugees', *Guardian*, 2 September 2015, www.theguardian.com/world/2015/sep/02/shocking-image-of-drowned-syrian-boy-shows-tragic-plight-of-refugees

103 'IOM counts 3,771 migrant fatalities in Mediterranean in 2015', International Organization for Migration, 5 January 2016, www.iom.int/news/iom-counts-3771-migrant-fatalities-mediterranean-2015

104 ANSA, 'Migrant deaths: 19,000 in Mediterranean in past 6 years', InfoMigrants, 9 October 2019, www.infomigrants.net/en/post/20055/migrant-deaths-19-000-in-mediterranean-in-past-6-years

105 James Souter, 'Why the UK has a special responsibility to protect its share of refugees', The Conversation, 15 May 2015, theconversation.com/why-the-uk-has-a-special-responsibility-to-protect-its-share-of-refugees-41773

106 Alan Travis, 'Home secretary hardens refusal to accept EU resettlement programme', *Guardian*, 11 May 2015, www.theguardian.com/politics/2015/may/11/home-secretary-theresa-may-eu-emergency-resettlement-programme-theresa-may

107 'Syrian refugees appeal', unicef, www.unicef.org/appeals/syrian-refugees

108 James Souter, 'Why the UK has a special responsibility to protect its share of refugees'

109 Alan Travis, 'Home secretary hardens refusal to accept EU resettlement programme'

110 'David Cameron: UK to accept "thousands" more Syrian refugees', BBC, 4 September 2015, www.bbc.co.uk/news/uk-34148913

111 Harry Cockburn, 'Third of councils in England refuse to take in Syrian refugees', *Independent*, 7 July 2016, www.independent.co.uk/news/uk/third-councils-england-refuse-take-resettle-syrian-refugees-a7125856.html

112 Ibid.

113 David Cameron [@David_Cameron], Twitter, 13 September 2015, twitter.com/
David_Cameron/status/642984909980725248
114 James Blitz, 'Biggest UK defence cuts since cold war', *FT*, 18 October 2010, www.ft.com/
content/80eff352-daa6-11df-81b0-00144feabdc0
115 Carl Emmerson, 'Two parliaments of pain: the UK public finances 2010 to 2017'
116 Christina R. Victor, 'The health of homeless people in Britain', *European Journal of Public
Health*, 1997, 7, pp. 398–404, academic.oup.com/eurpub/article-pdf/7/4/398/1462995/7-4-
398.pdf
117 Rowena Mason and Tom Phillips, 'Cameron biography: Ashcroft makes new debauchery
claims about student days', *Guardian*, 21 September 2015, www.theguardian.com/politics
/2015/sep/21/david-cameron-pig-head-lord-ashcroft-unofficial-biography-drug-taking-
claims
118 Robert Booth and Jane Martinson, 'Lord Ashcroft's Cameron biography bears hallmarks
of revenge job', *Guardian*, 21 September 2015, www.theguardian.com/politics/2015/sep/
21/lord-ashcrofts-cameron-biography-bears-hallmarks-of-revenge-job
119 Will Gore, 'Call Me Dave: Four extraordinary and utterly unverified claims from the
David Cameron book', *Independent*, 23 September 2015, www.independent.co.uk/news/
media/call-me-dave-four-extraordinary-and-utterly-unverified-claims-david-cameron-
book-10512989.html
120 Hazel Sheffield, 'David Cameron pig allegations could harm UK productivity', *Independent*,
21 September 2015, www.independent.co.uk/news/business/news/david-cameron-pig-
allegations-could-harm-uk-productivity-10511347.html
121 mikez2605, 'Is there actually any evidence of David Cameron doing the typical "Bullingdon
Club" things?', Reddit, 6 May 2015, www.reddit.com/r/unitedkingdom/comments/353tmf
/is_there_actually_any_evidence_of_david_cameron
122 Sophie McBain, 'Smashing job chaps: exclusive inside look at Bullingdon Club', *Oxford
Student*, 12 January 2005, web.archive.org/web/20090806051215/http://www.oxfordstudent.
com/ht2006wk0/Features/smashing_job_chaps%3A_exclusive_inside_look_at_bullingdon_club
123 Ben Turner, 'What is the Chernobyl Exclusion Zone?', Live Science, 3 February 2022,
www.livescience.com/chernobyl-exclusion-zone
124 Joe Churcher and Dan Bloom, 'David Cameron FINALLY comments publicly on
PigGate and says he's "too busy" to sue Lord Ashcroft', *Mirror*, 28 September 2015,
www.mirror.co.uk/news/uk-news/david-cameron-finally-comments-publicly-6529563
125 Francesca Infante and Richard Marsden, 'Three-holidays Dave and his very dubious choice
of footwear: PM poses in a battered pair of sandals as he chillaxes on another break', *Daily
Mail*, 19 August 2014, www.dailymail.co.uk/news/article-2728683/Chillaxing-David-
Cameron-Cornwall-FIFTEENTH-holiday-Prime-Minister.html
126 Frances Perraudin, 'Tory MP's filibuster blocks bill to give carers free hospital parking',
Guardian, 30 October 2015, www.theguardian.com/society/2015/oct/30/tory-mps-
filibuster-blocks-bill-to-give-carers-free-hospital-parking
127 Ibid.
128 Matt Coyle, 'Hospital car parking charges – how much does it cost and where
can I park for free?', *Sun*, 19 December 2019, www.thesun.co.uk/news/10518573/
hospital-car-parking-charges-cost/
129 'Philip Davies Expense Claims', Parallel Parliament, accessed on 29 July 2022, www.parallel
parliament.co.uk/mp/philip-davies/expenses
130 Chris Young, 'Shipley MP Philip Davies defends latest filibustering criticism after 52
minute speech by saying "it takes as long as it takes"', Telegraph & Argus, 22 November
2015, www.thetelegraphandargus.co.uk/news/14095746.shipley-mp-philip-davies-defends-
latest-filibustering-criticism-after-52-minute-speech-by-saying-it-takes-as-long-as-it-takes
131 Jon Stone, 'Tory MPs block bill to give first aid training to children by
talking non-stop until debate ends', *Independent*, 20 November 2015,
www.independent.co.uk/news/uk/politics/tory-mps-block-bill-to-give-first-aid-training-
to-children-by-talking-until-time-runs-out-a6742251.html
132 Jamie Grierson, 'Conservative activist Elliott Johnson killed himself, coroner rules',
Guardian, 31 May 2016, www.theguardian.com/politics/2016/may/31/conservative-
activist-elliott-johnson-killed-himself-coroner-rules

133 Robert Booth, "'Tory madrasa" preaches radical message to would-be MPs',
   Guardian, 6 March 2010, www.theguardian.com/world/2010/mar/06/tory-madrasa-young-
   britons-foundation

134 Lucy Fisher and Billy Kenber, 'Young Tatler Tory activists "were drunk and chaotic"', *The
   Times*, 3 December 2015, www.thetimes.co.uk/article/young-tatler-tory-activists-were-
   drunk-and-chaotic-j3m28zttnwf

135 Lucy Fisher and Billy Kenber, 'Tatler Tory activists "were drunk and chaotic"',
   The Times, 3 December 2015, www.thetimes.co.uk/article/tatler-tory-activists-
   were-drunk-and-chaotic-bjbk5cx7l

136 Jamie Grierson and Rowena Mason, 'Conservative party "must come clean" over Mark
   Clarke bullying allegations', *Guardian*, 20 November 2015, www.theguardian.com/politics
   /2015/nov/20/conservative-party-must-come-clean-over-mark-clarke-bullying-allegations

137 Jeremy Wilson, 'A Tory Minister admitted to an affair with a junior party member after
   fearing he'd be blackmailed', Insider, 16 November 2015, www.businessinsider.com/robert-
   halfon-admits-affair-with-alexandra-paterson-because-of-blackmail-2015-11?r=US&IR=T

138 Rajeev Syal, Jamie Grierson and Rowena Mason, 'Tory activist "blackmailed" days before
   giving sexual harassment evidence', *Guardian*, 20 November 2015, www.theguardian.com
   /uk-news/2015/nov/20/tory-activist-sexual-harassment-evidence-victim-blackmail

139 'Tories "were aware of bullying claims"', BBC, 20 November 2015, www.bbc.co.uk/news/
   uk-politics-34886069

140 Simon Usborne, 'David Cameron invited "Tatler Tory" Mark Clarke to tea party at
   Chequers', *Independent*, 23 November 2015, www.independent.co.uk/news/uk/politics/
   david-cameron-invited-tatler-tory-mark-clarke-to-tea-party-at-chequers-a6745726.html

141 Jack Blanchard, 'Grant Shapps trousered £8,000 taxpayer-funded "goodbye" after Tatler
   Tory bullying scandal', *Mirror*, 18 August 2016, www.mirror.co.uk/news/uk-news/grant-sha
   pps-trousered-8000-taxpayer-8660576

142 Daniel Boffey and Jamie Grierson, 'Grant Shapps resigns over bullying scandal: "the buck
   should stop with me"', *Guardian*, 28 November 2015, www.theguardian.com/politics/2015
   /nov/28/grant-shapps-resigns-over-bullying-scandal

143 Jamie Grierson, 'Lady Warsi letter warning Tory party chair Grant Shapps of bullying by
   aide', *Guardian*, 27 November 2015, www.theguardian.com/politics/2015/nov/27/lady-war
   si-letter-warning-tory-party-chair-grant-shapps-of-bullying-by-aide

144 'Tory chairman Lord Feldman "given bullying dossier in 2010"', BBC, 9 December 2015,
   www.bbc.co.uk/news/av/uk-politics-35047730

145 Christopher Hope, "'Tatler Tory" Mark Clarke could face private prosecution after CPS say
   he will not face assault charges', *Telegraph*, 10 February 2016, www.telegraph.co.uk/news
   /politics/conservative/12150947/Tatler-Tory-Mark-Clarke-could-face-private-prosecution
   -after-CPS-say-he-will-not-face-assault-charges.html?onwardjourney=584162_c1

146 Frances Perraudin and Jamie Grierson, 'Mark Clarke expelled from Conservative party for
   life over bullying claims', *Guardian*, 18 November 2015, www.theguardian.com/politics/20
   15/nov/18/mark-clarke-expelled-from-conservative-party-for-life-over-bullying-cliams

147 Joseph Watts, 'Tories rocked by new "bullying" storm as MP Lucy Allan accused
   of "vicious" abuse of sick staff member', *Evening Standard*, 17 December 2015,
   www.standard.co.uk/news/politics/tories-rocked-by-new-bullying-storm-as-mp-lucy-
   allan-accused-of-vicious-abuse-of-sick-staff-member-a3139526.html

148 'Telford MP Lucy Allan defends adding death threat', BBC, 7 December 2015,
   www.bbc.co.uk/news/uk-england-35027252

2016: Nonsense on Stilts

1   'The Daily Courant', Wikipedia, last edited on 21 July 2022, en.wikipedia.org/wiki/
   The_Daily_Courant

2   Adam Rasmi, 'Only 1% of Brits cared much about the EU before the 2016 Brexit vote',
   Quartz, 10 October 2019, qz.com/1725402/only-5-per cent-of-brits-cared-about-the-eu-
   before-brexit

3   Dominic Ponsford, 'Rothermere: "DMGT remains committed to journalism"', *Press Gazette*,
   21 January 2009, archive.ph/20120907084414/http://www.pressgazette.co.uk/story.asp?
   storycode=42877

4 'Tax free: Rupert Murdoch's zero status', BBC, 25 March 1999, news.bbc.co.uk/1/hi/special_report/1999/02/99/e-cyclopedia/302366.stm; Chris Tryhorn, 'Who are the Barclay brothers?', *Guardian*, 23 June 2004, www.theguardian.com/media/2004/jun/23/pressan dpublishing.business; Dan Cancian, 'How much is Daily Mail owner Lord Rothermere worth?', IBT, 7 October 2017, www.ibtimes.co.uk/how-much-daily-mail-owner-lord-rothe rmere-worth-1628099; Tom de Castella, 'Who are the Barclay brothers?', BBC, 20 February 2015, www.bbc.co.uk/news/magazine-31517392; Bernard Keane, 'Tax dodging News Corp continues to rip Australia off – and is subsidised by taxpayers to do so', Crikey., 11 December 2020, www.crikey.com.au/2020/12/11/news-corp-tax-dodging

5 Pan Pylas, 'Britain's EU Journey: When Thatcher turned all euroskeptic', AP News, 23 January 2020, apnews.com/article/brexit-business-international-news-europe-margaret-thatcher-64855d1ff67454443db5132bdfb22ea6

6 Jonathan Maitland, 'Howezat! The day a "dead sheep" turned into a roaring lion', *Guardian*, 15 November 2020, www.theguardian.com/politics/2020/nov/15/geoffrey-howe-dead-sheep-turned-roaring-lion

7 Jim Waterson, 'David Cameron called a c*** in David Cameron's favourite TV show', BuzzFeed News, 23 January 2016, www.buzzfeed.com/jimwaterson/david-cameron-called-a-c-in-david-camerons-favourite-tv-show

8 'Did MPs vote against forcing homes to be made fit to live in?', Full Fact, 26 June 2017, fullfact.org/economy/did-mps-vote-against-homes-having-be-made-fit-live-in

9 Jon Stone, 'Landlord Tory MP Philip Davies says law requiring homes be fit for human habitation is an unnecessary burden', *Independent*, 16 October 2015, www.independent.co.uk/news/uk/politics/landlord-tory-mp-philip-davies-law-requiring-homes-be-fit-human-habitation-unnecessary-a6696931.html

10 Indy100 Staff, 'These are the 72 MPs that voted against making homes fit for human habitation', indy100, 15 June 2017, www.indy100.com/news/72-mps-vote-human-habitation-living-standards-private-landlords-grenfell-tower-7790891

11 Lyndsey Telford and Luke Heighton, 'The MPs who topped up their salaries with £1,600-an-hour second jobs', *Telegraph*, 22 February 2015, www.telegraph.co.uk/news/inv estigations/11428075/The-MPs-who-topped-up-their-salaries-with-1600-an-hour-second-jobs.html

12 Andy McSmith, 'Geoffrey Cox: Tory MP has expenses claim for 49p pint of milk rejected by Commons', *Independent*, 14 January 2016, www.independent.co.uk/news/uk/politics/geoffrey-cox-tory-mp-has-expenses-claim-49p-pint-milk-rejected-commons-a6813131.html

13 Nicola McCafferty, 'Cameron: Pay back greedy expenses or go', *Express*, 12 May 2009, www.express.co.uk/news/uk/100615/Cameron-Pay-back-greedy-expenses-or-go

14 Nicholas Watt, 'David Cameron claimed over £1,000 a month on second home', *Guardian*, 10 December 2009, www.theguardian.com/politics/2009/dec/10/david-cameron-mps-expenses

15 Martin Williams, 'After the duck house … where MP's expenses went next', *Guardian*, 17 May 2016, www.theguardian.com/politics/2016/may/17/mps-expenses-martin-williams-parliament-ltd

16 Matt Turner, 'Ben Bradley MADE UP claims about his local authority using an Indian call centre while he was a Tory councillor', Evolve Politics, 28 February 2018, evolvepolitics.com/ben-bradley-made-claims-local-authority-using-indian-call-centre-tory-councillor

17 'Ben Bradley', IPSA, accessed on 3 August 2022, www.theipsa.org.uk/mp-staffing-business -costs/your-mp/ben-bradley/4663

18 'EU vote: Where the cabinet and other MPs stand', BBC, 22 June 2016, www.bbc.co.uk/news/uk-politics-eu-referendum-35616946

19 Patrick Wintour, 'EU referendum: Stuart Rose will chair campaign to keep Britain in the union', *Guardian*, 9 October 2015, www.theguardian.com/politics/2015/oct/09/stuart-rose-will-chair-campaign-to-keep-britain-in-the-eu

20 'Sir Stuart Rose', crunchbase, accessed on 3 August 2022, www.crunchbase.com/person/sir-stuart-rose

21 Elizabeth Day, 'Marks & Spencer's Stuart Rose: "I'm like a £3.49 chicken jalfrezi! It's got punch, it's got zest, and it's just fabulous to be with"', *Guardian*, 31 May 2009, www.theguardian.com/business/2009/may/31/marks-and-spencer-stuart-rose

22   Annie Brown, 'Boris Johnson's refusal to reveal number of kids by different women shows his hypocrisy', *Daily Record*, 30 April 2020, www.dailyrecord.co.uk/news/scottish-news/boris-johnsons-refusal-reveal-number-21949371

23   Guardian News, 'Boris Johnson knocks over boy in rugby match in Japan', YouTube, 15 October 2015, www.youtube.com/watch?v=IBt8AoLBCoo

24   Dan Bloom, 'Pro-EU chief Lord Rose forgets the name of his own referendum campaign', *Mirror*, 25 January 2016, www.mirror.co.uk/news/uk-news/pro-eu-chief-lord-rose-7242443

25   Zoe Wood, 'Stuart Rose: anger at politicians and mistrust of big business drove leave vote', *Guardian*, 24 June 2016, www.theguardian.com/business/2016/jun/24/stuart-rose-anger-at-politicians-mistrust-of-big-business-leave-vote-referendum-remain

26   'Danny Alexander launches Ginger Rodent beer', BBC, 9 November 2012, www.bbc.co.uk/news/uk-scotland-highlands-islands-20272937

27   Matthew Weaver, 'Thousands of porn images on Damian Green's computer, says detective', *Guardian*, 1 December 2017, www.theguardian.com/politics/2017/dec/01/damian-green-thousands-of-pornographic-images-on-computer-says-detective

28   'About the campaign', Why Vote Leave, www.voteleavetakecontrol.org/campaign.html

29   'Leading Brexiteer Lord Lawson applies for French residency', BBC, 1 June 2018, www.bbc.co.uk/news/uk-politics-44313941

30   Andrew Learmonth, 'Tory contender Leadsom was "worst minister ever", says civil servants who worked with her', *The National*, 5 July 2016, www.thenational.scot/news/14903779.tory-contender-leadsom-was-worst-minister-ever-say-civil-servants-who-worked-with-her

31   Dan Milmo, 'City financier Peter Cruddas donates £1m for campaign to leave EU', *Guardian*, 20 November 2015, www.theguardian.com/politics/2015/nov/20/city-financier-peter-cruddas-donates-1m-for-campaign-to-leave-eu

32   David Hellier, 'Why are hedge funds supporting Brexit?', *Guardian*, 6 November 2015, www.theguardian.com/business/2015/nov/06/why-are-hedge-funds-supporting-brexit

33   Jack Rear, 'Brexit leaders: who is Brexiteer Peter Hargreaves and why did he want the UK to quit the EU?', Verdict, 4 August 2017, www.verdict.co.uk/peter-hargreaves-brexit

34   'Short (finance)', Wikipedia, last edited on 2 July 2022, en.wikipedia.org/wiki/Short_(finance)

35   'Pound plunges after Leave vote', BBC, 24 June 2016, www.bbc.co.uk/news/business-36611512

36   James Salmon and Darren Boyle, 'Brexit buccaneer rakes in £220million: Hedge fund tycoon declares he "may be the winner" after betting on stock value falling', *Daily Mail*, 25 June 2016, www.dailymail.co.uk/news/article-3659328/Brexit-buccaneer-rakes-220million-Hedge-fund-tycoon-declares-winner-betting-stock-value-falling.html

37   David Woode, 'Tory donor bets £300 million on losses for UK firms after no-deal Brexit', *i News*, 8 October 2020, inews.co.uk/news/tory-donor-bets-300-million-on-losses-for-uk-firms-after-no-deal-brexit-322326

38   Andrew MacAskill, Ben Martin and Maiya Keidan, 'Exclusive: Leading Brexit donors say Britain will reverse decision to leave EU', Reuters, 11 January 2019, www.reuters.com/article/uk-britain-eu-donors-exclusive-idUKKCN1P50UU

39   Tom McTague, 'EU referendum: Sensible Eurosceptics being put off by "angry, unintelligent mob", says senior Tory', *Independent*, 10 January 2016, www.independent.co.uk/news/uk/politics/eu-referendum-sensible-eurosceptics-being-put-angry-unintelligent-mob-says-senior-tory-a6804036.html

40   Ted Jeory, 'Farage's fascist past? Nigel boasted about his NF initials and sang "gas them all", claims schoolfriend', *Independent*, 14 May 2019, www.independent.co.uk/news/uk/politics/nigel-farage-fascist-nazi-song-gas-them-all-ukip-brexit-schoolfriend-dulwich-college-a7185236.html

41   '"Dear Nigel… I wish your teenage fascist views had been dealt with. History could have been very different"', *Independent*, 13 May 2019, www.independent.co.uk/news/uk/politics/nigel-farage-open-letter-schoolfriend-brexit-poster-nazi-song-dulwich-college-gas-them-all-a7185336.html

42   James Tapsfield, 'David Cameron vows to bulldoze "sink estates where poverty and crime has become entrenched"', *Mirror*, 9 January 2016, www.mirror.co.uk/news/uk-news/david-cameron-vows-bulldoze-sink-7150006

43 Matt Fish, 'Cameron's talk of "sink estates" at PMQs hides the reality behind the council housing in the UK', *Independent*, 14 January 2016, www.independent.co.uk/voices/camer on-s-talk-sink-estates-pmqs-hides-reality-behind-council-housing-uk-a6812836.html

44 Pete Jeffreys, 'Non-starter homes', Shelter, 26 August 2015, blog.shelter.org.uk/2015/08/non -starter-homes

45 Julia Jollewe, 'First-time buyers need to earn £77,000 a year to live in London', *Guardian*, 4 May 2015, www.theguardian.com/business/2015/may/04/first-time-buyers-need-to-earn-77000-a-year-to-live-in-london?CMP=gu_com

46 Erin Yurday, 'Average household savings & wealth UK 2022', NimbleFins, 6 July 2022, www.nimblefins.co.uk/savings-accounts/average-household-savings-uk

47 'Iain Duncan Smith: Are we in this together?', Why Vote Leave, 10 May 2016, www.voteleavetakecontrol.org/iain_duncan_smith_are_we_in_this_together.html

48 'David Cameron's Muslim women policy "lazy and misguided"', BBC, 18 January 2016, www.bbc.co.uk/news/uk-35345903

49 Matt Oliver, 'Exclusive: Prime Minister David Cameron clashes with Oxfordshire County Council over cuts to frontline services', Oxford Mail, 11 November 2015, www.oxfordmail.co.uk/news/13948252.exclusive-prime-minister-david-cameron-clashes-oxfordshire-county-council-cuts-frontline-services

50 Rowena Mason, 'David Cameron's mother signs petition against cuts to children's services', *Guardian*, 8 February 2016, www.theguardian.com/politics/2016/feb/08/david-camerons-mother-signs-petition-against-cuts-to-childrens-services

51 Daniel Martin, 'Top ranking Tory activist quits the party in fury at David Cameron's failures on EU and immigration saying he is "glad Mrs Thatcher cannot see what her party has become"', *Daily Mail*, 19 February 2016, www.dailymail.co.uk/news/article-3453837 /Top-ranking-Tory-activist-quits-party-fury-David-Cameron-s-failures-EU-immigration-saying-glad-Mrs-Thatcher-party-become.html

52 Rowena Mason, 'Labour furious as 83% of fund to ease council cuts will go to Conservative authorities', *Guardian*, 10 February 2016, www.theguardian.com/society/2016/feb/10/labour-furious-fund-ease-council-cuts-conservative-authorities

53 Ibid.

54 Louise Haigh, 'The Conservatives are so committed to the Northern Powerhouse they've moved it to London', *New Statesman*, 31 January 2016, www.newstatesman.com/politics/economy/2016/01/conservatives-are-so-committed-northern-powerhouse-theyve-moved-it-london

55 William Hague, 'An old hand remembers …', *Guardian*, 21 February 2003, www.theguardian.com/politics/2003/feb/21/williamhague

56 'Archie Norman', Gov.uk, www.gov.uk/government/people/archie-norman

57 'Philp, Chris', politics.co.uk, www.politics.co.uk/reference/chris-philp

58 'Q & A with Helen', Conservatives, 26 March 2015, www.helenwhately.org.uk/news/q-helen

59 Louise Haigh, 'The Conservatives are so committed to the Northern Powerhouse they've moved it to London'

60 Statista Research Department, 'Prime office rental prices in selected European cities Q4 2021', Statista, 23 June 2022, www.statista.com/statistics/431672/commercial-property-prime-rents-europe

61 Jeremy Armstrong, 'Tories target student doctor grants and declare class war on hopefuls from poor backgrounds', *Mirror*, 5 February 2016, www.mirror.co.uk/news/uk-news/tories-target-student-doctor-grants-7318234

62 Sophie Borland and Jack Doyle, 'Fury after Osborne axes student grants for nurses and imposes apprenticeships levy on biggest firms "that will hit wages"', *Daily Mail*, 26 November 2015, www.dailymail.co.uk/news/article-3334382/Fury-Osborne-axes-student-grants-nurses-imposes-apprenticeships-levy-biggest-firms-hit-wages.html

63 Alex Turnbull, 'Nursing degree applications down 30% as RCN warns Long-term Plan in danger', Independent Nurse, 8 February 2019, www.independentnurse.co.uk/news/nursing-degree-applications-down-30-as-rcn-warns-long-term-plan-in-danger/208889

64 Alexandra Sims, 'Autumn statement: Grants for student nurses to be scrapped and replaced with loans', *Independent*, 25 November 2015, www.independent.co.uk/news/uk/politics/autumn-statement-grants-student-nurses-be-scrapped-and-replaced-loans-a6748446.html

65 Andrew Gregory, 'Tory cuts trapping 8,500 healthy patients in hospital as "bed-blocking" crisis costs NHS £1bn a year', *Mirror*, 5 February 2016, www.mirror.co.uk/news/uk-news/tory-cuts-trapping-8500-healthy-7312244

66 Gemma Mitchell, 'NHS nurse vacancies in England rise to more than 43,000', Nursing Times, 8 October 2019, www.nursingtimes.net/news/workforce/nhs-nurse-vacancies-in-england-rise-to-more-than-43000-08-10-2019

67 Tim Sculthorpe, 'Conservative MPs dismiss David Cameron's renegotiation efforts as a failure and mark dozens of policies as "not attempted" or only "partially achieved"', *Daily Mail*, 22 February 2016, www.dailymail.co.uk/news/article-3458552/Conservative-MPs-dismiss-David-Cameron-s-renegotiation-efforts-failure-mark-dozens-policies-not-attempted-partially-achieved.html

68 'The full text: Boris Johnson's previously secret article backing Britain in the EU', *Evening Standard*, 16 October 2016, www.standard.co.uk/news/politics/boris-johnson-s-article-backing-britain-s-future-in-the-eu-a3370296.html

69 Robert Winnett and Boris Johnson, 'Quitting the EU won't solve our problems, says Boris Johnson', *Telegraph*, 12 May 2013, www.telegraph.co.uk/news/politics/10052646/Quitting-the-EU-wont-solve-our-problems-says-Boris-Johnson.html

70 '55 years of European legislation', Dimiter Toshkov, www.dimiter.eu/Eurlex.html

71 Simon Heffer, 'Even Boris's senior colleagues dread Tory activists handing him the keys to Downing Street', *New Statesman*, 4 March 2016, www.newstatesman.com/politics/uk/2016/03/even-boris-s-senior-colleagues-dread-tory-activists-handing-him-keys-downing

72 Nicholas Watt and Ian Traynor, 'EU referendum: No 10 rejects the idea of second vote if UK decides to leave', *Guardian*, 22 February 2016, www.theguardian.com/politics/2016/feb/22/eu-referendum-no-10-rejects-idea-of-second-plebiscite-if-uk-votes-to-leave

73 Ibid.

74 'After the Agreement', Northern Ireland Assembly', education.niassembly.gov.uk/post_16/snapshots_of_devolution/gfa/after

75 Greg Evans, 'Jacob Rees-Mogg calls billboard featuring his quote on a second referendum "fundamentally dishonest"', indy100, 2 March 2019, www.indy100.com/news/jacob-rees-mogg-brexit-billboard-second-referendum-quote-bristol-response-8755986

76 Interviews by Declan Harvey and Greg Dawson, words by Emma Brant, 'Scottish referendum: How first vote went for 16/17-year-olds', BBC, 19 September 2014, www.bbc.co.uk/news/newsbeat-29279384

77 'In some respects the Brexit referendum was a violation of human rights', LSE, blog, 9 February 2017, blogs.lse.ac.uk/europpblog/2017/02/09/brexit-referendum-human-rights

78 'Boris Johnson: Brexit would not affect Irish border', BBC, 29 February 2016, www.bbc.co.uk/news/uk-northern-ireland-35692452

79 'Pound hits lowest level against dollar since 2009', BBC, 22 February 2016, www.bbc.co.uk/news/business-35628733

80 Katie Allen and Jill Treanor, 'Moody's warns Brexit would risk UK's credit rating', *Guardian*, 22 February 2016, www.theguardian.com/business/2016/feb/22/moodys-warns-on-brexit-risk-to-uk-credit-rating-eu-referendum

81 James Crisp, 'Boris' dad: I respect Brexiteers but will vote Remain', Euractiv, 14 June 2016, www.euractiv.com/section/uk-europe/news/mon-boris-dad-eu-must-dump-euro-and-control-migration-if-britain-votes-remain

82 Gary Gibbon, 'Boris Johnson throws Tory MPs into panic', 4 News, 22 February 2016, www.channel4.com/news/by/gary-gibbon/blogs/boris-johnson-throws-tory-mps-panic

83 Rowena Mason, 'Tory minister "wanted UK pensioners to be low-wage fruit pickers"', *Guardian*, 14 March 2016, www.theguardian.com/uk-news/2016/mar/14/tory-minister-wanted-uk-pensioners-to-be-low-wage-fruit-pickers

84 Jon Stone, 'Tories say they support ban on satire about Parliament footage', *Independent*, 3 March 2016, www.independent.co.uk/news/uk/politics/parliament-satire-ban-house-commons-charlie-brooker-tories-a6909391.html

85 'Personal Independence Payment – PIP Assessment – What is the PIP test?', Turn2us, www.turn2us.org.uk/Benefit-guides/Personal-Independence-Payment-Test/What-is-the-PIP-test

86 Jon Stone, 'PIP cuts: The disability benefit cuts that sparked a Tory civil war', *Independent*, 21 March 2016, www.independent.co.uk/news/uk/politics/disability-benefit-cuts-what-pip-u-turn-george-osborne-why-a6943976.html

87 Ibid.
88 HM Treasury and The Rt Hon George Osborne, 'Budget 2016: some of the things we've announced', Gov.uk, 16 March 2016, www.gov.uk/government/news/budget-2016-some-of-the-things-weve-announced
89 HM Revenue & Customs, 'Changes to Capital Gains Tax rates', Gov.uk, 16 March 2016, www.gov.uk/government/publications/changes-to-capital-gains-tax-rates
90 HM Revenue & Customs, 'Corporation Tax: main rate', Gov.uk, 8 July 2015, www.gov.uk/government/publications/corporation-tax-main-rate
91 'Economy: 1988 Budget (Lawson 5)', Margaret Thatcher Foundation, www.margaretthatcher.org/document/111449
92 Jessica Morris, 'Budget 2016: Chancellor George Osborne delivers tax relief to the UK North Sea oil and gas industry', City A.M., 16 March 2016, www.cityam.com/budget-2016-chancellor-george-osborne-delivers-tax-breaks-to-the-uk-north-sea-oil-and-gas-industry
93 Rowena Mason, 'David Cameron at centre of "get rid of all the green crap" storm', Guardian, 21 November 2013, www.theguardian.com/environment/2013/nov/21/david-cameron-green-crap-comments-storm
94 Anthony Reuben, 'Budget 2016: Growth forecasts cut for next five years', BBC, 16 March 2016, www.bbc.co.uk/news/business-35822365
95 D. Clarke, 'National debt as a percentage of GDP in the UK 1920–2022', Statista, 22 February 2022, www.statista.com/statistics/282841/debt-as-gdp-uk
96 'Three Tory MPs, including Zac Goldsmith, asked to stand down as patrons of disability charities', ThirdSector, 18 March 2016, www.thirdsector.co.uk/three-tory-mps-including-zac-goldsmith-asked-stand-down-patrons-disability-charities/policy-and-politics/article/1388050
97 Amelia Gentleman, 'It is simply no longer possible to be disabled and a Tory, says angry activist', Guardian, 21 March 2016, www.theguardian.com/politics/2016/mar/21/huge-injustice-conservative-disability-graeme-ellis-labour
98 Mikey Smith, '11 sickest Tory on Tory burns as Iain Duncan Smith's resignation plunges party into civil war', Mirror, 20 March 2016, www.mirror.co.uk/news/uk-news/11-sickest-tory-tory-burns-7595481
99 Rowena Mason and Anushka Asthana, 'How the Iain Duncan Smith resignation crisis unfolded', Guardian, 20 March 2016, www.theguardian.com/politics/2016/mar/20/how-the-iain-duncan-smith-resignation-crisis-unfolded
100 'Tory civil war sparked by resignation – in quotes', Guardian, 20 March 2016, www.theguardian.com/politics/2016/mar/20/iain-duncan-smith-tory-civil-war-quotes-shocking
101 Mikey Smith, 'Nadine Dorries slams Iain Duncan Smith for begging her to vote for disability cuts before resigning', Mirror, 19 March 2016, www.mirror.co.uk/news/uk-news/nadine-dorries-slams-iain-duncan-7587749
102 Andrew Sparrow, 'Iain Duncan Smith slams "unfair" budget – as it happened', Guardian, 20 March 2016, www.theguardian.com/politics/live/2016/mar/20/iain-duncan-smiths-resignation-fallout-politics-live
103 'Stephen Crabb: "No further plans" for welfare cuts', BBC, 21 March 2016, www.bbc.co.uk/news/uk-politics-35863776
104 Martin Shipton, 'Welsh Conservative leader received nearly £100,000 farming subsidy from the EU in a year', WalesOnline, 15 March 2016, www.walesonline.co.uk/news/politics/welsh-conservative-leader-received-nearly-11040379
105 Martin Shipton and Dan Bloom, 'Brexit-backing top Tory rakes in £100,000 of EU subsidies to family farm', Mirror, 15 March 2016, www.mirror.co.uk/news/uk-news/brexit-backing-top-tory-rakes-7563139
106 'Boris Johnson refloats Thames Estuary airport plan', BBC, 20 March 2016, www.bbc.co.uk/news/uk-england-35855676
107 Heather Saul, 'Boris Johnson's £60m cable cars used regularly by just four commuters', Independent, 21 November 2013, www.independent.co.uk/news/uk/politics/boris-johnson-s-ps60m-cable-cars-used-regularly-just-four-commuters-8954646.html
108 Damien Gayle, 'Former Tory MP's scathing Boris Johnson attack deepens party rift', Guardian, 26 March 2016, www.theguardian.com/politics/2016/mar/26/matthew-parris-boris-johnson-london-mayor-times-attack

109 Matthew Parris, 'Tories have got to end their affair with Boris', *The Times*, 26 March 2016, www.thetimes.co.uk/article/tories-have-got-to-end-their-affair-with-boris-35lc9p06w

110 John Crace, '"All very interesting, Boris. Except none of it is really true, is it?"', *Guardian*, 23 March 2016, www.theguardian.com/politics/2016/mar/23/very-interesting-boris-johnson-brexit-treasury-select-committee

111 Mikey Smith, 'Tories sneak out Land Registry sell-off at 5pm the night before Easter holiday', *Mirror*, 25 March 2016, www.mirror.co.uk/news/uk-news/tories-sneak-out-land-registry-7624668

112 Jason Beattie, 'Polls show massive opposition to George Osborne's privatisation plan – and even Tory voters are against it', *Mirror*, 10 December 2015, www.mirror.co.uk/news/uk-news/polls-shows-massive-opposition-george-6990108

113 Mikey Smith, 'Tories sneak out Land Registry sell-off at 5pm the night before Easter holiday'

114 Sean O'Neill, 'All bidders for the Land Registry have links to tax havens', *The Times*, 26 May 2016, www.thetimes.co.uk/article/all-bidders-for-the-land-registry-have-links-to-tax-havens-q9vfqw029

115 Mikey Smith, 'Tory MP and wife used taxpayer-backed Help to Buy loan to snap up new constituency house', *Mirror*, 9 March 2016, www.mirror.co.uk/news/uk-news/tory-mp-wife-used-taxpayer-7449766

116 'A.J.W.B. TRAVEL LIMITED', Gov.uk, find-and-update.company-information.service.gov.uk/company/04951501/officers

117 'Register of Members' Interests', They Work For You, last updated 11 July 2022, www.theyworkforyou.com/mp/11915/peter_bone/wellingborough#register

118 Mikey Smith, 'Tory MP and wife used taxpayer-backed Help to Buy loan to snap up new constituency house'

119 Sebastian Shakespeare, 'Model Rosie, Sam Cam's Girl Friday paid by taxpayers: "Special adviser" being paid £53,000 to organise PM's wife's diary and wardrobe', *Daily Mail*, 7 April 2016, www.dailymail.co.uk/news/article-3527314/Model-Rosie-Sam-Cam-s-Girl-Friday-paid-taxpayers-Special-adviser-paid-53-000-organise-PM-s-wife-s-diary-wardrobe.html

120 D. Clarke, 'Number of people using food banks in the UK 2008–2022', Statista, 11 May 2022, www.statista.com/statistics/382695/uk-foodbank-users

121 Andrew Woodcock, 'Foreign minister breaks ranks to voice support for ousted Pakistani PM Imran Khan', *Independent*, 11 April 2022, www.independent.co.uk/news/uk/politics/zac-goldsmith-imran-khan-pakistan-b2055520.html

122 Owen Jones, 'Forgive and forget Zac Goldsmith's racist campaign? No chance', *Guardian*, 7 May 2016, www.theguardian.com/commentisfree/2016/may/07/zac-goldsmith-racist-campaign-london

123 Ashley Cowburn, 'Zac Goldsmith critcised by former Tory minister Baroness Warsi over Sadiq Khan 7/7 London terror bus image', *Independent*, 1 May 2016, www.independent.co.uk/news/uk/politics/zac-goldsmith-london-mayor-campaign-sadiq-khan-baroness-warsi-a7009126.html

124 Siobhan Fenton, 'Zac Goldsmith accused of "racial profiling" voters again in London Mayor campaign', *Independent*, 28 March 2016, www.independent.co.uk/news/uk/politics/zac-goldsmith-accused-racial-profiling-voters-again-london-mayor-campaign-a6956556.html

125 Ashley Cowburn, 'Zac Goldsmith critcised by former Tory minister Baroness Warsi over Sadiq Khan 7/7 London terror bus image'

126 Dave Hill, *Zac Versus Sadiq: The fight to become London Mayor*, Double Q, 2016, p. 99.

127 Adam Bienkov, 'Boris Johnson says his articles calling black people "piccaninnies" with "watermelon smiles" and gay men "bumboys" were "wholly satirical"', Insider, 30 June 2019, www.businessinsider.com/boris-johnson-defends-his-offensive-articles-about-black-and-gay-people-2019-6?r=US&IR=T

128 Fred Attewill, 'Johnson eats his words after cannibal gaffe', *Guardian*, 9 September 2006, www.theguardian.com/politics/2006/sep/09/uk.conservatives

129 'Boris says sorry over "blacks have lower IQs" article in the Spectator', *Evening Standard*, 2 April 2008, www.standard.co.uk/news/mayor/boris-says-sorry-over-blacks-have-lower-iqs-article-in-the-spectator-6630340.html

130 Adam Bienkov, 'Boris Johnson abandons pledge to hold inquiry into Islamophobia in the Conservative party', Insider, 27 June 2019, www.businessinsider.com/boris-johnson-drops-pledge-to-hold-conservative-islamophobia-inquiry-2019-6?r=US&IR=T

131 Frances Perraudin, 'Boris Johnson claimed Islam put Muslim world "centuries behind"', Guardian, 15 July 2019, www.theguardian.com/politics/2019/jul/15/boris-johnson-islam-muslim-world-centuries-behind-2007-essay

132 Alexandra Topping, 'Boris Johnson criticised for suggesting women go to university to find husband', Guardian, 8 July 2013, www.theguardian.com/politics/2013/jul/08/boris-johnson-women-university-husband

133 'Boris Johnson's verbal gaffes', Telegraph, 28 October 2010, www.telegraph.co.uk/news/politics/london-mayor-election/mayor-of-london/8095693/Boris-Johnsons-verbal-gaffes.html

134 Adam Bienkov, 'Boris Johnson's sexist and homophobic articles about "hot totty" and "tank-topped bumboys" revealed', Insider, 5 January 2018, www.businessinsider.com/boris-johnson-women-gay-people-sexism-bumboys-totty-toby-young-2018-1?r=US&IR=T

135 'Boris Johnson: The liberal cosmopolitan case to Vote Leave', Why Vote Leave, 9 May 2016, www.voteleavetakecontrol.org/boris_johnson_the_liberal_cosmopolitan_case_to_vote_leave.html

136 Adam Bienkov, 'Boris Johnson's sexist and homophobic articles about "hot totty" and "tank-topped bumboys" revealed'

137 Ibid.

138 Holly Watt, 'Tory donors' links to offshore firms revealed in leaked Panama Papers', Guardian, 4 April 2016, www.theguardian.com/news/2016/apr/04/tory-donors-links-to-off shore-firms-revealed-in-leaked-panama-papers

139 Juliette Garside, 'Fund run by David Cameron's father avoided paying tax in Britain', Guardian, 4 April 2016, www.theguardian.com/news/2016/apr/04/panama-papers-david-cameron-father-tax-bahamas

140 Rowena Mason, 'David Cameron says not enough is being done to tackle tax evasion', Guardian, 30 September 2015, www.theguardian.com/business/2015/sep/30/david-camer on-tax-evasion-british-overseas-territories

141 Juliette Garside, 'Fund run by David Cameron's father avoided paying tax in Britain'

142 Martha M. Hamilton, 'Panamian law firm is gatekeeper to vast flow of murky offshore secrets', ICIJ, 3 April 2016, www.icij.org/investigations/panama-papers/20160403-mossack-fonseca-offshore-secrets

143 Robert Booth, Holly Watt and David Pegg, 'David Cameron admits he profited from father's Panama offshore trust', Guardian, 7 April 2016, www.theguardian.com/news/2016/apr/07/david-cameron-admits-he-profited-fathers-offshore-fund-panama-papers

144 Stephen Castle and Kimiko de Freytas-Tamura, 'David Cameron leads a call to thwart financial corruption', New York Times, 12 May 2016, www.nytimes.com/2016/05/13/world/europe/britain-cameron-corruption.html

145 Heather Stewart, 'Cameron stepped in to shield offshore trusts from EU tax crackdown in 2013, Guardian, 7 April 2016, www.theguardian.com/politics/2016/apr/07/david-cameron-offshore-trusts-eu-tax-crackdown-2013

146 Matt Broomfield, 'David Cameron offshore fund: PM still stalling on tax returns four years after he was "relaxed and happy" about publishing them', Independent, 8 April 2016, www.independent.co.uk/news/uk/politics/panama-papers-david-cameron-publish-tax-returns-offshore-fund-a6974146.html

147 'David Cameron: A shameless Tory snob', Mirror, 26 January 2012, www.mirror.co.uk/news/uk-news/david-cameron-a-shameless-tory-snob-197490

148 'David Cameron's mother gave PM £200,000 gift', BBC, 10 April 2016, www.bbc.co.uk/news/uk-politics-36007718

149 Jack Blanchard, 'David Cameron's Cabinet of millionaires face mounting pressure to publish their tax returns', Mirror, 10 April 2016, www.mirror.co.uk/news/uk-news/david-camerons-cabinet-millionaires-face-7726539

150 Matt Payton, 'Panama papers: Sir Alan Duncan MP says critics of David Cameron are low-achievers who hate the rich', Independent, 12 April 2016, www.independent.co.uk/news/uk/politics/panama-papers-sir-alan-duncan-mp-speaking-defence-david-cameron-critcised-decrying-low-achievers-who-hate-anyone-hint-wealth-a6979826.html

151 Rowena Mason, 'George Osborne's tax return summary reveals £198,000 income', *Guardian*, 11 April 2016, www.theguardian.com/politics/2016/apr/11/george-osborne-tax-return-reve als-198000-income

152 Juliette Garside, 'Benefit fraud or tax evasion: row over the Tories' targets', *Guardian*, 13 April 2016, www.theguardian.com/uk-news/2016/apr/13/benefit-or-tax-evasion-row-over-the-tories-targets

153 Reuters Staff, 'UK tax agency must report full scale of tax avoidance-lawmakers', Reuters, 4 November 2015, www.reuters.com/article/uk-britain-tax-lawmakers-idUKKCN0ST00 M20151104

154 Richard Murphy, 'HMRC recovers up to £97 for every £1 it spends on tax investigations', Tax Research UK, 16 January 2015, www.taxresearch.org.uk/Blog/2015/01/16/hmrc-recovers-up-to-97-for-every-1-it-spends-on-tax-investigations

155 Reuters Staff, 'UK tax agency must report full scale of tax avoidance-lawmakers'

156 Richard Murphy, 'New report: The tax gap is £119.4 billion and rising', Tax Research UK, 22 September 2014, www.taxresearch.org.uk/Blog/2014/09/22/new-report-the-tax-gap-is-119-4-billion-and-rising

157 Michael Buchanan, 'Reality Check: How much benefit money is lost to fraud?', BBC, 5 June 2017, www.bbc.co.uk/news/election-2017-39980793

158 Mikey Smith, 'David Cameron drags warring Tories to Thick of It-style "away day" in bid to calm tensions', *Mirror*, 15 April 2016, www.mirror.co.uk/news/uk-news/david-cameron-drags-warring-tories-7755614

159 Ibid.

160 Jason Beattie, 'John Whittingdale faces fresh questions about his confuct after Tory donor riddle', *Mirror*, 25 April 2016, www.mirror.co.uk/news/uk-news/john-whittingdale-faces-fresh-questions-7826908

161 'No, Electric Jukebox isn't a joke. But it probably should be.', Music Business Worldwide, 16 October 2015, www.musicbusinessworldwide.com/no-electric-jukebox-isnt-a-joke-but-it -probably-should-be

162 Jason Beattie, 'John Whittingdale faces fresh questions about his confuct after Tory donor riddle'

163 'Labour calls to curb John Whittingdale's powers after escort relationship', 13 April 2016, www.bbc.co.uk/news/uk-politics-36031743

164 Oliver Wright, 'John Whittingdale admits to taking free dinner with performers at lapdance club', *Independent*, 19 April 2016, www.independent.co.uk/news/uk/politics/john-whittingdale-admits-taking-free-dinner-performers-lapdance-club-a6991051.html

165 Ed Howker and Guy Basnett, 'The inside story of the Tory election scandal', *Guardian*, 23 March 2017, www.theguardian.com/news/2017/mar/23/conservative-election-scandal-victory-2015-expenses

166 Peter Oborne, 'Culture of dishonesty that's eating away the soul of the Tory party', *Daily Mail*, 23 April 2016, www.dailymail.co.uk/debate/article-3554828/PETER-OBORNE-Culture-dishonesty-s-eating-away-soul-Tory-party.html

167 Mikey Smith, 'Tory Zac Goldsmith utterly baffled by pint of lager', *Mirror*, 29 April 2016, www.mirror.co.uk/news/uk-news/tory-zac-goldsmith-utterly-baffled-7860135

168 Kamal Ahmed, 'UK economy "could be 6% smaller" after EU exit, warns Treasury', BBC, 17 April 2016, www.bbc.co.uk/news/business-36068892

169 Nicholas Bloom, Scarlet Chen and Paul Mizen, 'Rising Brexit uncertainty has reduced investment and employment', Vox EU, 16 November 2018, voxeu.org/article/rising-brexit-uncertainty-has-reduced-investment-and-employment

170 Ed McMillan-Scott [@EdMcMillanScott], Twitter, 16 April 2021, mobile.twitter.com/ EdMcMillanScott/status/1383115234102161408/photo/1; 'List of Question Time episodes', Wikipedia, last edited on 30 July 2022, en.wikipedia.org/wiki/List_of_Question_Time_episodes#2018

171 The Secret Tory [@secrettory12], Twitter, 19 September 2021, mobile.twitter.com/ secrettory12/status/1439698092668882945

172 Joe Sommerlad, 'What does the energy price cap mean for you?', 2 August 2022, www.independent.co.uk/news/uk/home-news/uk-energy-price-cap-b2115557.html; 'About fuel poverty', End Fuel Poverty Coalition, www.endfuelpoverty.org.uk/about-fuel-poverty

173 Katie Dickinson, 'MPs react after Vote Leave economist admits Brexit would "mostly eliminate manufacturing"', Chronicle Live, 2 May 2016, www.chroniclelive.co.uk/news/north-east-news/mps-react-after-vote-leave-11269819

174 Heather Stewart, 'Britain remaining in EU is "better for the world", says Japanese prime minister', Guardian, 5 May 2016, www.theguardian.com/politics/2016/may/05/japan-prime-minister-britain-eu-shinzo-abe

175 Jules Johnston, 'Boris Johnson compares EU to Nazi superstate', Politico, 15 May 2016, www.politico.eu/article/boris-johnson-compares-eu-to-nazi-superstate-brexit-ukip

176 'Johnson "has gone too far"', day.kyiv.ua, day.kyiv.ua/en/article/topic-day/johnson-has-gone-too-far

177 Nicholas Soames [@NSoames], Twitter, 15 May 2016, twitter.com/nsoames/status/731754354680696832

178 Jerry Hayes, 'Soames is a national treasure make him leader of the House', Jerry Hayes, 22 May 2016, www.jerryhayes.co.uk/articles/soames-is-a-national-treasure-make-him-leader-of-the-house

179 Andrew Sparrow, 'UK statistics chief says Vote Leave £350m figure is misleading', Guardian, 27 May 2016, www.theguardian.com/politics/2016/may/27/uk-statistics-chief-vote-leave-350m-figure-misleading

180 'UK Statistics Authority statement on the use of official statistics on contributions to the European Union', UK Statistics Authority, 27 May 2016, uksa.statisticsauthority.gov.uk/news/uk-statistics-authority-statement-on-the-use-of-official-statistics-on-contributions-to-the-european-union

181 Patrick Worrall, 'Boris Johnson falsely claims he "didn't say anything about Turkey" in the referendum campaign', 4 News, 18 January 2019, www.channel4.com/news/factcheck/factcheck-boris-johnson-falsely-claims-he-didnt-say-anything-about-turkey-in-the-referendum-campaign

182 Vote Leave, 'What the EU "tourist deal" means', Research Gate, www.researchgate.net/figure/What-the-EU-tourist-deal-means-Britains-new-border-is-with-Syria-and-Iraq-Source_fig2_328941178

183 Anthony Reuben and Peter Barnes, 'Reality Check: Checking the Vote Leave leaflet', BBC, 11 April 2016, www.bbc.co.uk/news/uk-politics-eu-referendum-36014941

184 UK Trade & Investment, Department for Business, Innovation & Skills, Prime Minister's Office, et al., 'UK and China agree £14 billion of trade and investment deals', Gov.uk, press release, 17 June 2014, www.gov.uk/government/news/uk-and-china-agree-14-billion-of-trade-and-investment-deals

185 Anthony Reuben and Peter Barnes, 'Reality Check: Checking the Vote Leave leaflet'

186 'Reality Check: How many EU nationals lives in the UK?', BBC, 8 July 2016, www.bbc.co.uk/news/uk-politics-uk-leaves-the-eu-36745584

187 Richard Portes, '"I think the people of this country have had enough of experts"', London Business School, 9 May 2017, www.london.edu/think/who-needs-experts

188 Emilio Casalicchio, '15 things Vote Leave promised on Brexit – and what it got', Politico, 24 December 2020, www.politico.eu/article/15-things-uk-vote-leave-promised-on-brexit-and-what-it-got

189 'Brexit: the Digby Jones Jobs Lost Index is launched', Yorkshire Bylines, 2 October 2020, yorkshirebylines.co.uk/politics/brexit-the-digby-jones-jobs-lost-index-is-launched

190 'Brexit Job Loss Index: 436,296 jobs lost as of 31 January 2020', SmallBusinessPrices.co.uk, smallbusinessprices.co.uk/brexit-index

191 'Grayling: No Brexit lorry checks at Dover', BBC, 15 March 2018, www.bbc.co.uk/programmes/p06197wy

192 Jack Wright, 'Huge 66-acre post-Brexit lorry park in Kent is STILL being built and won't be ready until February – while HGV customs facility in France was finished MONTHS ago', Daily Mail, 30 December 2020, www.dailymail.co.uk/news/article-9098377/Brexit-Huge-66-acre-lorry-park-Kent-built.html

193 'Brexit: Dover inland border checkpoint planned on farmland', BBC, 2 January 2021, www.bbc.co.uk/news/uk-england-kent-55514651

194 'David Davis gives a speech making the case for Brexit', Rt Hon David Davis MP, 26 May 2016, www.daviddavismp.com/david-davis-gives-a-speech-making-the-case-for-brexit

195 DanHannan, 'Daniel Hannan on Channel 4 News discussing Britain's EU referendum', YouTube, 14 May 2015, www.youtube.com/watch?v=zzykce4oxII

196 Daniel Hannan [@DanielJHannan], Twitter, 1 September 2015, twitter.com/danieljhannan
/status/638644981549395968?lang=en
197 Matt Kelly, 'Here's an A to Z list of Brexit lies', *GQ*, 15 February 2019, www.gq-magazine.
co.uk/article/list-of-brexit-lies
198 'Boris Johnson: Brexit would not affect Irish border', BBC
199 'Vote Leave, and take back control: speech by Theresa Villiers', Theresa Villiers,
14 April 2016, www.theresavilliers.co.uk/news/vote-leave-and-take-back-control-speech-
theresa-villiers
200 Steve Bloomfield, 'No deal is against the will of the people – and here's the proof', *Prospect*,
29 January 2019, www.prospectmagazine.co.uk/politics/no-deal-is-against-the-will-of-the-
people-and-heres-the-proof
201 Garry Kasparov [@Kasparov63], Twitter, 13 December 2016, twitter.com/kasparov63/stat
us/808750564284702720?lang=en-GB
202 'Media coverage of the EU Referendum (report 1)', Centre for Research in Communication
and Culture, Loughborough University, blog, 23 May 2016, blog.lboro.ac.uk/crcc/
eu-referendum/media-coverage-eu-referendum-report-1
203 'Queen's Speech 2016: From prison reforms to spaceports', The Week, 18 May 2016,
www.theweek.co.uk/72700/queens-speech-2016-five-things-we-can-expect
204 'Cornwall could host UK's £150, commercial spaceport', BBC, 16 May 2016, www.bbc.co.uk
/news/av/uk-politics-36303741
205 'Executive Team', Diabetes UK, web.archive.org/web/20080523183630/http://
www.diabetes.org.uk/About_us/How-we-are-governed/Executive-team
206 Adam Withnall, 'Tory minister Penny Mordaunt "plain and simple lying" over Turkey
joining EU', *Independent*, 22 May 2016, www.independent.co.uk/news/uk/politics/penny-
mordaunt-andrew-marr-uk-veto-tory-minister-accused-flat-out-lying-over-turkey-joining-
eu-a7041956.html
207 Josh Pettitt, 'Tory party in open civil war as MP calls for David Cameron to resign live on
air', *Sun*, 29 May 2016, www.thesun.co.uk/archives/politics/1222588/tory-party-in-open-
civil-war-as-mp-calls-for-david-cameron-to-resign-live-on-air
208 Ibid.
209 Daniel Boffey, 'Gove and Johnson claim Brexit is way to realise PM's dream of one-nation
Britain', *Guardian*, 4 June 2016, www.theguardian.com/politics/2016/jun/04/
gove-jonson-brexit-one-nation-britain
210 'New style JSA amounts', Disability Rights UK, www.disabilityrightsuk.org/contribution-
based-jsa-amounts
211 Joshua Nevett, 'Sarah Wollaston: Top Tory MP Brexit campaigner set to SWITCH to
Remain over fears for NHS, *Mirror*, 8 June 2016, www.mirror.co.uk/news/uk-news/
sarah-wollaston-top-tory-mp-8145398
212 Jamie Ross, 'John Major launches extraordinary attack on "court jester" Boris Johnson',
BuzzFeed News, 5 June 2016, www.buzzfeed.com/jamieross/nonsense-on-stilts
213 Tim Shipman, 'The Interview: Boris Johnson, Chief Brexiteer', *The Times*, 12 June 2016,
www.thetimes.co.uk/magazine/the-sunday-times-magazine/the-interview-boris-johnson-
chief-brexiteer-jpt7plmzv
214 Tom Peck, 'EU referendum: British public wrong about nearly everything, survey shows',
Independent, 10 June 2016, www.independent.co.uk/news/uk/politics/eu-referendum-
british-public-wrong-about-nearly-everything-survey-shows-a7074311.html
215 'List of sovereign states in Europe by GDP (nominal)', Wikipedia, last edited on 29 July
2022, en.wikipedia.org/wiki/List_of_sovereign_states_in_Europe_by_GDP_(nominal)
216 'The perils of perception and the EU', Ipsos, 9 June 2016, www.ipsos.com/ipsos-mori/en-uk
/perils-perception-and-eu
217 Ibid.
218 Economic Consulting Team, 'The fiscal impact of immigration on the UK', Oxford
Economics, 18 September 2018, www.oxfordeconomics.com/recent-releases/
8747673d-3b26-439b-9693-0e250df6dbba
219 'The perils of perception and the EU', UK in a Changing Europe, 9 June 2016, ukandeu.ac
.uk/the-perils-of-perception-and-the-eu
220 Jamie Smyth, 'How Australia's points-based immigration system works', *FT*, 1 June 2016,
www.ft.com/content/04c7142e-27e2-11e6-8ba3-cdd781d02d89

221 Alan Travis, 'Brexiters are missing the point of Australian-style immigration', *Guardian*, 1 June 2016, www.theguardian.com/uk-news/2016/jun/01/brexiters-missing-point-australian-style-immigration-conservatives

222 Esther Zuckerman, 'There are just 100 fully grown cod left in the North Sea', *The Atlantic*, 17 September 2012, www.theatlantic.com/international/archive/2012/09/there-are-just-100-fully-grown-cod-left-north-sea/323579

223 Katie Dickinson, 'MPs react after Vote Leave economist admits Brexit would "mostly eliminate manufacturing"'

224 'Brexit referendum vote caused an increase in hate crime', IZA Newsroom, 14 December 2020, newsroom.iza.org/en/archive/research/brexit-referendum-vote-caused-an-increase-in-hate-crime

225 Crispin Dowler, 'Privatising the seas: how the UK turned fishing rights into a commodity', Unearthed, 7 March 2019, unearthed.greenpeace.org/2019/03/07/fishing-brexit-uk-fleetwood

226 'Letters: Britain at fault for Brexit fishing woes', *Guardian*, 25 October 2020, www.theguardian.com/commentisfree/2020/oct/25/britain-at-fault-for-brexit-fishing-woes-letters

227 Rowena Mason, Jessica Elgot and Rajeev Syal, 'Osborne on ropes after "punishment budget" plan infuriates Tory MPs', *Guardian*, 15 June 2016, www.theguardian.com/politics/2016/jun/15/osborne-britain-eu-more-important-career-tory-mps

228 Jessica Elgot, 'Boris Johnson will make TV apology if Brexit triggers recession', *Guardian*, 21 June 2016, www.theguardian.com/politics/2016/jun/21/boris-johnson-will-make-tv-apology-if-brexit-triggers-recession

229 'Brexit analysis', Office for Budget Responsibility, last updated 26 May 2022, obr.uk/forecasts-in-depth/the-economy-forecast/brexit-analysis/#assumptions

230 Heather Stewart and Rowena Mason, 'Nigel Farage's anti-migrant poster reported to police', *Guardian*, 16 June 2016, www.theguardian.com/politics/2016/jun/16/nigel-farage-defends-ukip-breaking-point-poster-queue-of-migrants

231 Matt Dathan, 'Nigel Farage in racism storm over Brexit poster showing thousands of male refugees and warning country is at "breaking point"', *Daily Mail*, 16 June 2016, www.dailymail.co.uk/news/article-3644716/Nigel-Farage-racism-storm-Brexit-poster-showing-thousands-male-refugees-warning-country-breaking-point.html

232 Brendan Harkin [@brendanjharkin], Twitter, 16 June 2016, twitter.com/brendanjharkin/status/743388925834702848

233 Andrew Sparrow 'Nigel Farage: parts of Britain are "like a foreign land"', *Guardian*, 28 February 2014, www.theguardian.com/politics/2014/feb/28/nigel-farage-ukip-immigration-speech

234 'Jo Cox: Man jailed for "terrorist" murder of MP', BBC, 23 November 2016, www.bbc.co.uk/news/uk-38079594

235 Joe Mellor, '"I've just donated the steam off my piss" Tory abuse for murdered Jo Cox', The London Economic, 22 June 2016, www.thelondoneconomic.com/news/ive-just-donated-the-steam-off-my-piss-tory-abuse-for-murdered-jo-cox-29941

236 James Moncur, 'Boris Johnson causes chaos at daughter's St Andrews University graduation after unveiling EU vote poster during ceremony', *Daily Record*, 23 June 2016, www.dailyrecord.co.uk/news/scottish-news/boris-johnson-causes-chaos-daughters-8267228

237 'EU Referendum: Results', BBC, www.bbc.co.uk/news/politics/eu_referendum/results

238 Statista Research Department, 'Unemployment rate of the UK 1971–2022', Statista, 27 July 2022, www.statista.com/statistics/279898/unemployment-rate-in-the-united-kingdom-uk

239 Annette Walling and Gareth Clancy, 'Underemployment in the UK labour market', *Economic & Labour Market Review*, 4(2), February 2010, link.springer.com/content/pdf/10.1057/elmr.2010.21.pdf

240 'UK labour market: October 2015', Office for National Statistics, 14 October 2015, www.ons.gov.uk/employmentandlabourmarket/peopleinwork/employmentandemployeetypes/bulletins/uklabourmarket/2015-10-14

241 Ben Chapman, 'UK salaries less than they were 12 years ago, official figures reveal', *Independent*, 27 October 2016, www.independent.co.uk/news/business/news/uk-salaries-less-wages-down-inequality-ons-statistics-a7381671.html

242 'Austerity is racialized, gendered, and classed – always!', Central European University, 28 November 2016, spp.ceu.edu/article/2016-11-28/austerity-racialized-gendered-and-classed-always

243 *Cutting away at our children's futures: how austerity is affecting the health of children, young people and families*, BMA, September 2016, www.bma.org.uk/media/2060/cutting-away-at-our-childrens-futures-austerity-child-health-guuk-2016.pdf

244 'Reality Check: Did a million people use food banks?', BBC, 4 November 2016, www.bbc.co.uk/news/uk-politics-37875675

245 Lizzy Buchan, 'Education spending slashed by £7bn since 2011 with children "paying price for austerity", says Labour', *Independent*, 14 January 2019, www.independent.co.uk/news/uk/politics/labour-angela-rayner-funding-cuts-department-education-damian-hinds-a8726151.html

246 Jeevan Vasagar, 'Universities alarmed by 40% cut to teaching budgets', *Guardian*, 20 October 2010, www.theguardian.com/education/2010/oct/20/spending-review-university-teaching-cuts

247 Kaamil Ahmed, '"A hammer blow": how UK overseas aid cuts affect the world's most vulnerable', *Guardian*, 3 June 2021, www.theguardian.com/global-development/2021/jun/03/a-hammer-blow-how-uk-overseas-aid-cuts-affect-the-worlds-most-vulnerable

248 'Marriage (Same Sex Couples) Bill – Third Reading – 21 May 2013 at 18:59', The Public Whip, www.publicwhip.org.uk/division.php?date=2013-05-21&number=11&display=allpossible

249 Denis Campbell, 'Greensill lobbying: how did David Cameron target the NHS?', *Guardian*, 18 April 2021, www.theguardian.com/business/2021/apr/18/greensill-lobbying-how-did-david-cameron-target-the-nhs

250 Rowena Mason, 'David Cameron hums a merry tune as he hands over to Theresa May', *Guardian*, 11 July 2016, www.theguardian.com/politics/2016/jul/12/david-cameron-hums-a-merry-tune-as-he-hands-over-to-theresa-may

Part 2: The Bewilderness Years
2016: It's an Utter Fiasco

1 'Pound plunges after Leave vote', BBC, 24 June 2016, www.bbc.co.uk/news/business-36611512

2 'Statement from the Governor of the Bank of England following the EU referendum result', Bank of England, 24 June 2016, www.bankofengland.co.uk/news/2016/june/statement-from-the-governor-of-the-boe-following-the-eu-referendum-result

3 'Neolithic Revolution', Wikipedia, last edited on 26 July 2022, en.wikipedia.org/wiki/Neolithic_Revolution

4 Matt Egan, 'Brexit crash wiped out a record $3 trillion. Now what?', CNN Business, 28 June 2016, money.cnn.com/2016/06/27/investing/brexit-consequences-2-trillion-lost/index.html

5 'The UK's EU membership fee', Full Fact, 8 July 2019, fullfact.org/europe/our-eu-membership-fee-55-million

6 Zane Schwartz, 'What were Google's most frequent U.K. searches after Brexit?', Maclean's, 24 June 2016, www.macleans.ca/politics/worldpolitics/what-were-googles-most-frequent-searches-after-brexit

7 'Ratings agencies downgrade UK credit rating after Brexit vote', BBC, 27 June 2016, www.bbc.co.uk/news/business-36644934

8 Matt Payton, 'Racist hate crimes increase five-fold in week after Brexit vote', *Independent*, 1 July 2016, www.independent.co.uk/news/uk/crime/racism-hate-crimes-increase-brexit-eu-referendum-a7113091.html

9 'Brexit referendum vote caused an increase in hate crime', IZA Newsroom, 14 December 2020, newsroom.iza.org/en/archive/research/brexit-referendum-vote-caused-an-increase-in-hate-crime

10 'Boris Johnson's victory speech: "we can find our voice in the world again"', *Spectator*, 24 June 2016, www.spectator.co.uk/article/boris-johnson-s-victory-speech-we-can-find-our-voice-in-the-world-again-

11 Ibid.

12   Rajeev Syal, 'Boris Johnson says "no need for haste" to start EU exit negotiations', *Guardian*, 24 June 2016, www.theguardian.com/politics/2016/jun/24/boris-johnson-no-need-haste-eu-exit-negotiations

13   Gaby Hinsliff, 'A pyrrhic victory? Boris Johnson wakes up to the costs of Brexit', 24 June 2016, www.theguardian.com/politics/2016/jun/24/a-pyrrhic-victory-boris-johnson-wakes-up-to-the-costs-of-brexit

14   Ibid.

15   GoogleTrends [@GoogleTrends], Twitter, 24 June 2016, twitter.com/GoogleTrends/status /746303118820937728

16   Frances Perraudin, 'Iain Duncan Smith backtracks on leave side's £350m NHS claim', *Guardian*, 26 June 2016, www.theguardian.com/politics/2016/jun/26/eu-referendum-brexit-vote-leave-iain-duncan-smith-nhs

17   Adam Taylor, 'Brexit campaign wipes website clear, sparking speculation it is hiding its promises', *Washington Post*, 27 June 2016, www.washingtonpost.com/news/worldviews/ wp/2016/06/27/brexit-campaign-wipes-website-clear-sparking-speculation-it-is-hiding-its-promises

18   Jon Stone, 'British public still believe Vote Leave "£350million a week to EU" myth from Brexit referendum', *Independent*, 28 October 2018, www.independent.co.uk/news/uk/ politics/vote-leave-brexit-lies-eu-pay-money-remain-poll-boris-johnson-a8603646.html

19   'Guide to the Conservative leadership race: May v Leadsom', BBC, 8 July 2016, www.bbc.co.uk/news/uk-politics-36618738; 'Electoral statistics, UK: 2019', Office for National Statistics, 22 May 2020, www.ons.gov.uk/peoplepopulationand community/elections/electoralregistration/bulletins/electoralstatisticsforuk/2019

20   Gaby Hinsliff, 'Michael made an odd assassin – but then Boris was a strange Caesar', *Guardian*, 30 June 2016, www.theguardian.com/politics/2016/jun/30/michael-made-an-odd-assassin-but-then-boris-was-a-strange-caesar

21   Graeme Culliford, 'Boris Johnson's decision to play cricket day after Brexit victory cost him chance to be PM, reveals book on the secrets of Tory bust-up', *Sun*, 28 August 2016, www.thesun.co.uk/news/1684920/boris-johnsons-decision-to-play-cricket-day-after-brexit-victory-cost-him-chance-to-be-pm-reveals-book-on-the-secrets-of-tory-bust-up

22   Ibid.

23   Boris Johnson, 'I cannot stress too much that Britain is part of Europe – and always will be', *Telegraph*, 26 June 2016, www.telegraph.co.uk/politics/2016/06/26/i-cannot-stress-too-much-that-britain-is-part-of-europe--and-alw

24   Christopher Hope, 'Boris Johnson hails Brexit victory – full statement', *Telegraph*, 24 June 2016, www.telegraph.co.uk/news/2016/06/24/boris-johnson-hails-brexit-victory---full-statement

25   Boris Johnson, 'I cannot stress too much that Britain is part of Europe – and always will be'

26   Alasdair Sandford, '"No Article 50 for now": Britain in no rush towards Brexit door', Euronews, 27 June 2016, www.euronews.com/2016/06/27/no-article-50-for-now-britain-in-no-rush-towards-brexit-door

27   Boris Johnson, 'I cannot stress too much that Britain is part of Europe – and always will be'

28   Alex Spence, 'Rupert Murdoch's support for Boris Johnson comes with a warning', Politico, 29 June 2016, www.politico.eu/blogs/on-media/2016/06/brexit-eu-referendum-rupert-murdochs-support-for-boris-johnson-comes-with-a-warning

29   Tom McTague and Alex Spence, 'A very British betrayal', Politico, 30 June 2016, www.politico.eu/article/a-very-british-betrayal-michael-gove-boris-johnson

30   Will Worley, 'Sarah Vine's leaked email to Michael Gove over Boris Johnson fears – read it in full', *Independent*, 30 June 2016, www.independent.co.uk/news/uk/politics/sarah-vine-michael-gove-leaked-email-full-boris-johnson-tory-leadership-contest-latest-a7109861.html

31   'Michael Gove and Theresa May head five-way Conservative race', BBC, 30 June 2016, www.bbc.co.uk/news/uk-politics-36671336

32   Jessica Elgot and Peter Walker, 'Michael Gove to stand for Conservative party leadership', *Guardian*, 30 June 2016, www.theguardian.com/politics/2016/jun/30/michael-gove-to-stand-for-conservative-party-leadership

33   Rowena Mason and Heather Stewart, 'Gove's thunderbolt and Boris's breaking point: a shocking Tory morning', *Guardian*, 30 June 2016, www.theguardian.com/politics/2016/ jun/30/goves-thunderbolt-boris-johnson-tory-morning

34 Heather Stewart, 'Michael Gove to set out Tory leadership stall after forcing out Boris Johnson', *Guardian*, 1 July 2016, www.theguardian.com/uk-news/2016/jun/30/gove-ambush-is-swift-and-fatal-for-johnsons-hopes-of-leading-tories

35 Mary Dejevsky, 'Revealed: Fox's best man and his ties to Iran's opposition', *Independent*, 16 October 2011, www.independent.co.uk/news/uk/politics/revealed-fox-s-best-man-and-his-ties-to-iran-s-opposition-2371352.html

36 'Defence review: David Cameron unveils armed forces cuts', BBC, 19 October 2010, www.bbc.co.uk/news/av/uk-11578747

37 'Stephen Crabb', YouGov, yougov.co.uk/topics/politics/explore/public_figure/Stephen_Crabb

38 Henry Mance and George Parker, 'Andrea Leadsom seeks to play down pro-EU comments', *FT*, 4 July 2016, www.ft.com/content/5ec81170-4101-11e6-b22f-79eb4891c97d

39 Rowena Mason and Anushka Asthana, 'Ken Clarke caught on camera ridiculing Conservative leadership candidates', *Guardian*, 5 July 2016, www.theguardian.com/politics/2016/jul/05/ken-clarke-caught-camera-ridiculing-tory-leadership-candidates-theresa-may-michael-gove

40 Ashley Cowburn, 'Andrea Leadsom attacked by Tory MPs over "vile" and "insulting" comments on Theresa May's childlessness', *Independent*, 11 July 2016, www.independent.co.uk/news/uk/politics/andrea-leadsom-theresa-may-vile-insulting-children-conservative-leadership-tory-a7128311.html

41 Ibid.

42 Rowena Mason, Robert Booth and Amelia Gentleman, 'Nigel Farage resigns as Ukip leader after "achieving political ambition" of Brexit', *Guardian*, 4 July 2016, www.theguardian.com/politics/2016/jul/04/nigel-farage-resigns-as-ukip-leader

43 Harry Cole [@MrHarryCole], Twitter, 21 April 2017, twitter.com/MrHarryCole/status/855363016367513602

44 'Theresa May launches Conservative leadership bid: "Brexit means Brexit" – video', *Guardian*, 30 June 2016, www.theguardian.com/politics/video/2016/jun/30/theresa-may-launches-conservative-leadership-bid-brexit-means-brexit-video

45 Anushka Asthana, 'Theresa May to rule out return of border checks between UK and Ireland', *Guardian*, 25 July 2016, www.theguardian.com/uk-news/2016/jul/25/theresa-may-rule-out-return-border-checks-between-uk-ireland

46 Ashley Cowburn, 'Theresa May says she has an "open mind" over Brexit negotiations', *Independent*, 27 July 2016. www.independent.co.uk/news/uk/brexit-theresa-may-negotiations-eu-referendum-result-leave-europe-a7158516.html

47 John Redwood, 'Getting out of the EU can be quick and easy – the UK holds most of the cards in any negotiation', John Redwood's Diary', blog, 17 July 2016, johnredwoodsdiary.com/2016/07/17/getting-out-of-the-eu-can-be-quick-and-easy-the-uk-holds-most-of-the-cards-in-any-negotiation

48 Valur Grettisson, '36 bankers, 96 years in jail', *Reykjavik Grapevine*, 7 February 2018, grapevine.is/news/2018/02/07/36-bankers-96-years-in-jail

49 James Kirkup and Robert Winnett, 'Families must accept share of blame for Britain's woes', *Telegraph*, 3 May 2012, www.telegraph.co.uk/finance/newsbysector/banksandfinance/9244414/Families-must-accept-share-of-blame-for-Britains-woes.html

50 Jim Pickard, Vanessa Houlder and Madison Marriage, 'Tax experts call for "rethink" of UK corporation tax in Budget', *FT*, 19 November 2017, www.ft.com/content/a159deba-cb98-11e7-aa33-c63fdc9b8c6c

51 CSPAN [@cspan], Twitter, 13 July 2016, twitter.com/cspan/status/753339899755974656?ref_src=twsrc%5Etfw

52 'Boris Johnson is a liar with his back to the wall, says French FM', BBC, 14 July 2016, www.bbc.co.uk/news/world-europe-36795502

53 'Boris Johnson is foreign secretary: the world reacts', BBC, 14 July 2016, www.bbc.co.uk/news/world-36790977

54 Zia Weise, 'Boris Johnson praises his "Turkish washing machine" as he attempts to woo Erdogan in Ankara', *Telegraph*, 27 September 2016, www.telegraph.co.uk/news/2016/09/27/boris-johnson-praises-his-beautiful-turkish-washing-machine-as-h

55 'Regional Assemblies (Preparations) Bill', Part of the debate – in the House of Commons at 5:08 pm on 26th November 2002, TheyWorkForYou, www.theyworkforyou.com/debates/?id=2002-11-26.201.7

56 Albert Evans, "'We're in a mess": Painful moment David Davis has previous quotes about Brexit read out to him', *iNews*, 20 March 2019, inews.co.uk/news/brexit/david-davis-emma-barnett-bbc-5-live-brexit-secretary-271148

57 David Davis [@DavidDavisMP], Twitter, 4 February 2016, twitter.com/DavidDavisMP/sta tus/695208361625796608?ref_src=twsrc%5Etfw%7Ctwcamp%5Etweetembed%7Ctwterm %5E695208361625796608%7Ctwgr%5E%7Ctwcon%5Es1_&ref_url=https%3A%2F%2F www.newstatesman.com%2Fpolitics%2Fbrexit%2F2018%2F07%2Fall-times-david-davis-said-brexit-was-simple

58 Media Mole, 'All the times David Davis said that Brexit was simple', *New Statesman*, 9 July 2018, www.newstatesman.com/politics/brexit/2018/07/all-times-david-davis-said-brexit-was-simple

59 'Britain "too lazy and fat", says Trade Secretary Liam Fox', BBC, 10 September 2016, www.bbc.co.uk/news/uk-politics-37324491

60 Andrew Gimson, 'Profile: Gavin Williamson, the "baby-faced assassin" who is now Chief Whip', ConservativeHome, 14 September 2016, www.conservativehome.com/highlights/ 2016/09/profile-gavin-williamson-the-baby-faced-assassin-who-is-now-chief-whip.html

61 Scarlet Howes, 'Tory chief whip refuses to remove "terrifying" Westminster tarantula – as he uses it to scare backbenchers', *Mirror*, 23 November 2016, www.mirror.co.uk/news/uk-news/tory-chief-whip-refuses-remove-9317861

62 Jon Stone, 'The new International Development Secretary wanted to scrap what is now her department', *Independent*, 15 July 2016, www.independent.co.uk/news/uk/politics/ new-international-development-secretary-priti-patel-called-department-international-development-be-scrapped-a7137331.html

63 'Michael Gove: Theresa May was "right to sack me"', BBC, 9 December 2016, www.bbc.co.uk/news/uk-politics-38267368

64 Frances Gibb, 'Justice minister quits with blast at "novice" lord chancellor', *The Times*, 19 July 2016, www.thetimes.co.uk/article/justice-minister-quits-with-blast-at-novice-lord-chancellor-x99qd8xl5

65 Ian Johnston, 'Britain must urgently prepare for flooding, heatwaves and food shortages, says Government report', *Independent*, 12 July 2016, www.independent.co.uk/climate-change/news/climate-change-report-flooding-food-water-shortages-global-warming-warning-uk-must-prepare-a7131561.html

66 Ian Johnston, 'Climate change department closed by Theresa May in "plain stupid" and "deeply worrying" move', *Independent*, 14 July 2016, www.independent.co.uk/ climate-change/news/climate-change-department-killed-off-by-theresa-may-in-plain-stupid-and-deeply-worrying-move-a7137166.html

67 Peter Walker, 'Theresa May's scrapping of minister for refugees "utterly disgraceful", *Guardian*, 25 July 2016, www.theguardian.com/politics/2016/jul/25/theresa-may-scrapping -minister-syria-refugees-disgraceful

68 Jon Stone, 'David Cameron promised to take in 20,000 Syrian refugees. What have the Tories actually delivered?', *Independent*, 1 September 2016, www.independent.co.uk/news /uk/politics/syrian-refugee-crisis-refugees-british-government-20000-4000-progress-how-many-migrants-immigration-a7219971.html

69 'Modern slavery: Theresa May vows to defeat "evil"', BBC, 31 July 2016, www.bbc.co.uk/ news/uk-36934853

70 Laura Hughes, 'Stephen Crabb sent young woman sexually explicit messages after rejecting her application for role in his office', *Telegraph*, 28 October 2017, www.telegraph.co.uk/news/2017/10/28/stephen-crabb-sent-young-woman-sexually-explicit-messages-rejecting

71 Rowena Mason, 'New peer on Cameron's resignation honours list gave Tories £2.5m', *Guardian*, 5 August 2016, www.theguardian.com/politics/2016/aug/05/new-peer-on-camerons-resignation-honours-list-gave-tories-25m

72 Andrew Grice, 'David Cameron Honours list would "embarrass a medieval court"', *Independent*, 4 August 2016, www.independent.co.uk/news/uk/politics/honours-list-read-full-david-cameron-peers-knighthoods-mbes-nominations-a7172406.html

73 John Ashmore, 'Honours committee "blocks David Cameron's nomination of former Tory treasurer"', *Holyrood*, 2 August 2016, www.holyrood.com/news/view,honours-committee-blocks-david-camerons-nomination-of-former-tory-treasurer_12156.htm

74 Christopher Hope, 'David Cameron's recommendation of a peerage for Michael Spencer "holding up resignation honours list"', *Telegraph*, 22 July 2016, www.telegraph.co.uk/news /2016/07/22/david-camerons-recommendation-of-a-peerage-for-michael-spencer-h

75 May Bulman, 'David Cameron honours list: Peerage for former Tory treasurer caught up in City scandal "blocked" by honours committee', *Independent*, 2 August 2016, www.independ ent.co.uk/news/uk/politics/david-cameron-honours-list-blocked-peerage-michael-spencer-cronyism-tory-treasurer-city-scandal-a7167756.html

76 Oliver Wright and Henry Zeffman, 'Tory peers who keep a (very) low profile', *The Times*, 6 August 2016, www.thetimes.co.uk/article/tory-peers-who-keep-a-very-low-profile-jpk0t dc3n

77 Russell Taylor, 'Size of the House of Lords', House of Lords Library, UK Parliament, 29 January 2016, lordslibrary.parliament.uk/research-briefings/lln-2016-0006

78 'State of the parties', MPs and Lords, UK Parliament, accessed on 3 August 2022, members.parliament.uk/parties/Commons

79 Martin Banks, 'Brexit: Could Theresa May invoke article 50 without parliamentary approval?', *The Parliament Magazine*, 29 August 2016, www.theparliamentmagazine.eu/ne ws/article/brexit-could-theresa-may-invoke-article-50-without-parliamentary-approval

80 'Diane James becomes UKIP leader', BBC, 16 September 2016, www.bbc.co.uk/news/ uk-politics-37387162

81 'Diane James, former UKIP leader, quits party', BBC, 21 November 2016, www.bbc.co.uk /news/uk-politics-38057251

82 Dan Bloom, 'This is how the Tory Brexit Secretary REALLY spent his Big Trade Deal Day', *Mirror*, 13 September 2016, www.mirror.co.uk/news/uk-news/how-tory-brexit-secretary-really-8827013

83 Laura Hughes and Peter Foster, 'David Davis says process for leaving the EU will be the most "complicated negotiation of all time"', *Telegraph*, 12 Septemebr 2016, www.telegraph.co.uk/news/2016/09/12/david-davis-says-process-for-leaving-the-eu-will-be-the-most-com

84 Henry McDonald, 'Brexit secretary: no return to "hard" border in Ireland', *Guardian*, 1 September 2016, www.theguardian.com/uk-news/2016/sep/01/brexit-secretary-no-return-to-hard-border-in-ireland

85 Denton, Gilbert; Fahy, Tony (1993). *The Northern Ireland Land Boundary 1923–1992*. Belfast: HM Customs and Excise. OCLC 56443670.

86 Department for International Trade and The Rt Hon Elizabeth Truss MP, 'New report shows 6.5 million jobs supported by exports', press release, Gov.uk, www.gov.uk/ government/news/new-report-shows-65-million-jobs-supported-by-exports

87 'Free Trade Areas', upload.wikimedia.org/wikipedia/commons/6/6a/Free_Trade_Areas.PNG

88 Jim Edwards, 'Say goodbye to tea and carrots', Business Insider, 5 January 2019, www.busin essinsider.com/no-deal-brexit-percentage-british-food-imported-shortages-2019-1?r=US& IR=T

89 Dearbail Jordan, 'How dependent is the UK on the EU for food?', BBC, 23 December 2020, www.bbc.co.uk/news/business-55408788

90 D. Clark, 'Brexit and EU trade – statistics & facts', Statista, 28 April 2021, www.statista.com /topics/3126/brexit-and-eu-trade

91 'How important is the EU market to UK trade?', UK in a Changing Europe, updated on 1 July 2021, ukandeu.ac.uk/the-facts/how-important-is-the-eu-market-to-uk-trade

92 Femi [@Femi_Sorry], Twitter, 8 July 2021, twitter.com/Femi_Sorry/status/14132258095994 75713

93 Andrew Sparrow, 'Tories ditch budget surplus pledge and announce £3bn housebuilding plan – Politics live', *Guardian*, 3 October 2016, www.theguardian.com/politics/blog/live/20 16/oct/03/conservative-conference-philip-hammond-confirms-osbornes-austerity-timetable-has-been-dropped-politics-live?page=with:block-57f27087e4b03ca720ca2-18f#block-57f27087e4b03ca720ca218f

94 Ibid.

95 Ibid.

96 Rowena Mason, 'Theresa May's "great repeal bill": what's going to happen and when?', *Guardian*, 2 October 2016, www.theguardian.com/politics/2016/oct/02/theresa-may-great-repeal-bill-eu-british-law

97 Andrew Sparrow, 'Tories ditch budget surplus pledge and announce £3bn housebuilding plan – Politics live'
98 Ibid.
99 Phillip Inman, 'Philip Hammond to spend his way out of Brexit fallout', *Guardian*, 3 October 2016, www.theguardian.com/business/2016/oct/03/philip-hammond-to-spend-his-way-out-of-brexit-fallout
100 James Moore, 'Universal credit plunges kids into poverty and 120,000 have died because of austerity – but Jacob Rees-Mogg wants more cuts', *Independent*, 16 November 2017, www.independent.co.uk/voices/nhs-austerity-cuts-120000-deaths-universal-credit-only-get-worse-a8058231.html
101 Peter Walker, 'Philip Hammond vows to match lost EU funding for business', *Guardian*, 3 October 2016, www.theguardian.com/politics/2016/oct/03/philip-hammond-vows-to-match-lost-eu-funding-for-business
102 Jon Stone, 'Build homes with smaller rooms so young people can afford them, Tory housing minister says', *Independent*, 4 October 2016, www.independent.co.uk/news/uk/politics/housing-crisis-gavin-barwell-flats-smaller-pocket-a7344061.html
103 Statista Research Department, 'Average residential real estate square meter prices in Europe 2020, per country', Statista, 27 July 2022, www.statista.com/statistics/722905/average-residential-square-meter-prices-in-eu-28-per-country
104 'Wealth per person: Why Monaco is tops in the world', news24, 25 April 2019, www.news24.com/fin24/economy/wealth-per-person-why-monaco-is-tops-in-the-world-20190424
105 Holly Watt, 'Tory donor's firm tries to cut size of homes in town built with £30m subsidy', *Guardian*, 4 May 2015, www.theguardian.com/society/2015/may/04/developer-trying-to-cut-size-of-homes-built-with-30m-subsidy
106 Jon Stone, 'Build homes with smaller rooms so young people can afford them, Tory housing minister says'
107 'European countries by population (2022)', Worldometer, accessed on 3 August 2022, www.worldometers.info/population/countries-in-europe-by-population
108 Jon Stone, 'Build homes with smaller rooms so young people can afford them, Tory housing minister says'
109 Ibid.
110 'Sajid Javid attacks "nimbyism" as he calls for 1m new homes', BBC, 3 October 2016, www.bbc.co.uk/news/uk-politics-37540803
111 Matt Honeycombe-Foster, 'No homes built under flagship 2015 Tory housing pledge, watchdog finds', PoliticsHome, 5 November 2019, www.politicshome.com/news/article/no-homes-built-under-flagship-2015-tory-housing-pledge-watchdog-finds
112 Mikey Smith, 'The 16 most Tory things at Tory Party Conference', *Mirror*, 3 October 2016, www.mirror.co.uk/news/uk-news/16-most-tory-things-tory-8962302
113 Mikey Smith, 'Tories sip free gin and tonics as they discuss "solving poverty the Conservative way"', *Mirror* 3 October 2016, www.mirror.co.uk/news/uk-news/tories-sip-free-gin-tonics-8971173
114 Caroline Mortimer, 'Number of children in poverty increased by 250,000 under Conservatives, figures show', *Independent*, 1 October 2016, www.independent.co.uk/news/uk/politics/child-poverty-increases-low-income-families-tory-cuts-conservative-government-austerity-a7340466.html
115 Yvette Cooper, 'Just when we need the child poverty unit most, the Tories are scrapping it', *Guardian*, 21 December 2016, www.theguardian.com/commentisfree/2016/dec/21/child-poverty-unit-tories-scrapping-it-theresa-may
116 Ashley Cowburn, 'Theresa May says she has an "open mind" over Brexit negotiations'
117 Jessica Elgot, 'Liam Fox: EU nationals in UK one of "main cards" in Brexit negotiations', *Guardian*, 4 October 2016, www.theguardian.com/politics/2016/oct/04/liam-fox-refuses-to-guarantee-right-of-eu-citizens-to-remain-in-uk
118 George Parker and Kate Allen, 'David Davis brushes off Brexit retaliation fears', *FT*, 10 October 2016, www.ft.com/content/45137d44-8f0a-11e6-a72e-b428cb934b78
119 Jessica Elgot, 'Michael Gove denies stabbing Boris Johnson in the back', *Guardian*, 25 October 2016, www.theguardian.com/politics/2016/oct/25/michael-gove-denies-stabbing-boris-johnson-back-conservative-leadership-campaign

120 Dan Bloom, 'Michael Gove is BACK! Tory backstabber wins plum seat on Westminster's new Brexit Committee', *Mirror*, 26 October 2016, www.mirror.co.uk/news/uk-news/michael-gove-back-tory-backstabber-9131443

121 'UK secured Nissan investment with Brexit relief promise – source', Reuters, 27 October 2016, www.reuters.com/article/uk-britain-eu-nissan-support-idUKKCN12R1AK?edition-redirect=uk

122 James Blitz, 'Brexit Briefing: Theresa May's secret deal with Nissan', *FT*, 28 October 2016, www.ft.com/content/304e55ce-9d00-11e6-8324-be63473ce146

123 Quest Means Business, 'Why fugitive auto executive Carlos Ghosn refuses to surrender to authorities', CNN, edition.cnn.com/videos/business/2022/04/26/carlos-ghosn-fugitive-auto-executive-renault-nissan-mitsubishi-no-surrender-qmb-vpx.cnnbusiness#:~:text=Carlos%20Ghosn%2C%20the%20former%20CEO,trust%20in%20its%20judicial%20system

124 'UK secured Nissan investment with Brexit relief promise – source', Reuters

125 Rob Davies, 'Q&A: why Brexit is so important to Nissan (and Britain)', *Guardian*, 28 October 2016, www.theguardian.com/business/2016/oct/28/nissan-questions-and-answers

126 Ben Glaze, '"Shambolic Tory Brexit" slammed by Labour as PM faces fury of her own backbenchers', *Mirror*, 14 October 2016, www.mirror.co.uk/news/uk-news/shambolic-tory-brexit-slammed-labour-9033864

127 Owen Bowcott and Jessica Elgot, 'Brexit plans in disarray as high court rules parliament must have its say', *Guardian*, 3 November 2016, www.theguardian.com/politics/2016/nov/03/parliament-must-trigger-brexit-high-court-rules

128 Lizzie Dearden, 'Brexit: Theresa May's Government has "no plan" and needs up to 30,000 extra civil servants to cope – leaked report', *Independent*, 15 November 2016, www.independent.co.uk/news/uk/politics/brexit-theresa-may-government-no-plan-30000-civil-servants-cope-cabinet-split-article-50-leaked-report-memo-a7417966.html

129 'Reality Check: Who works for the EU and what do they get paid?', BBC, 24 May 2016, www.bbc.co.uk/news/uk-politics-eu-referendum-36325311

130 Lizzie Dearden, 'Brexit: Theresa May's Government has "no plan" and needs up to 30,000 extra civil servants to cope – leaked report'

131 James Cusick, 'MPs demand full investigation of hard-Brexit backing Tory "party within a party"', openDemocracy, 8 September 2017, www.opendemocracy.net/en/dark-money-investigations/mps-demand-full-investigation-of-hard-brexit-backing-tory-party-within-par

132 Andrew Rosindell MP [@AndrewRosindell], Twitter, 3 November 2016, twitter.com/AndrewRosindell/status/794154930730893312

133 Megan Davies, 'BBC Newsnight trolls Tory MP who called for "God Save the Queen" to be played on TV every night', DigitalSpy, 4 November 2016, www.digitalspy.com/tv/a813156/bbc-newsnight-trolls-tory-mp-god-save-the-queen

134 Jon Craig, 'Brexit "have our cake and eat it" note caught on camera', Sky News, 29 November 2016, news.sky.com/story/tory-brexit-plan-photographed-in-downing-street-10676337

135 Katie Allen and Peter Walker, 'Philip Hammond admits Brexit vote means £122bn extra borrowing', *Guardian*, 23 November 2016, www.theguardian.com/uk-news/2016/nov/23/philip-hammond-brexit-vote-borrowing-autumn-statement?CMP=share_btn_tw

136 'Timeline of prehistory', Wikipedia, last edited on 16 July 2022, en.wikipedia.org/wiki/Timeline_of_prehistory

137 Mikey Smith, Jack Blanchard and Dan Bloom, '11 ways we just found out exactly how badly the Tories have screwed the economy', *Mirror*, 24 November 2016, www.mirror.co.uk/news/uk-news/11-ways-just-found-out-9327673

138 D. Clark, 'Number of people using food banks in the UK 2008–2022', Statista, 11 May 2022, www.statista.com/statistics/382695/uk-foodbank-users

139 Mikey Smith, Jack Blanchard and Dan Bloom, '11 ways we just found out exactly how badly the Tories have screwed the economy'

140 James Melville, 'The doubling of the national debt: The Conservatives have "spent all the money"', *Byline Times*, 11 February 2020, bylinetimes.com/2020/02/11/the-doubling-of-the-national-debt-the-conservatives-have-spent-all-the-money

141 'National debt as a percentage of GDP in the UK 1920–2022', Statista, 22 February 2022, www.statista.com/statistics/282841/debt-as-gdp-uk

142 Mikey Smith, Jack Blanchard and Dan Bloom, '11 ways we just found out exactly how badly the Tories have screwed the economy'

143 Charlie Gall and Sarah Vesty, 'Michael Fallon's £60million folly as bumbling Tory minister axes state-of-the-art "super barracks"', *Daily Record*, 9 November 2016, www.dailyrecord.co.uk/news/scottish-news/fallon-folly-9220647

144 Caroline Mortimer, 'Tory promise to plant 11 million trees by 2020 set to be broken after just one tenth planted', *Independent*, 27 November 2016, www.independent.co.uk/news/uk/politics/conservatives-tories-plant-trees-manifesto-commitment-environment-climate-change-one-tenth-a7441871.html

145 Dan Bloom, 'Every Health Secretary of the last 20 years says Tories are failing the mentally ill', *Mirror*, 18 November 2016, www.mirror.co.uk/news/uk-news/every-health-secretary-last-20-9282877

146 Marcus Leroux and Oliver Wright, 'Liam Fox leadership backer gets role overseeing his department', *The Times*, 18 November 2016, www.thetimes.co.uk/article/liam-fox-leadership-backer-gets-role-overseeing-his-department-l08rt622r

147 Albert Evans, '"We're in a mess": Painful moment David Davis has previous quotes about Brexit read out to him'

148 Jessica Elgot, 'Theresa May calls for "red, white and blue Brexit"', *Guardian*, 6 December 2016, www.theguardian.com/politics/2016/dec/06/theresa-may-calls-for-red-white-and-blue-brexit

149 Alan Travis, 'Prisons brought to brink of collapse by Tory lord chancellors, says ex-boss', *Guardian*, 12 December 2016, www.theguardian.com/society/2016/dec/12/prisons-brought-to-brink-of-collapse-by-tory-lord-chancellors-says-ex-boss

150 Mikey Smith, 'Tory minister Liz Truss says prisons are using barking dogs to scare off drones', *Mirror*, 6 December 2016, www.mirror.co.uk/news/uk-news/liz-truss-says-prisons-using-9402972

151 'Philip Davies', Wikipedia, last edited on 1 July 2022, en.wikipedia.org/wiki/Philip_Davies

152 Jamie Grierson, 'Feminist zealots want women to have their cake and eat it, says Tory MP', *Guardian*, 12 August 2016, www.theguardian.com/politics/2016/aug/12/tory-mp-philip-davies-claims-uk-legal-system-favours-women-at-mens-rights-event

153 Ibid.

154 Katie Allen, 'UK women still far adrift on salary and promotion as gender pay gap remains a gulf', *Guardian*, 23 August 2016, www.theguardian.com/money/2016/aug/23/gender-pay-gap-average-18-per-cent-less-uk-women

155 Jon Stone, 'Here are some of the bills Tory MP Philip Davies has filibustered', *Independent*, 16 December 2016, www.independent.co.uk/news/uk/politics/philip-davies-filibuster-domestic-violence-a7479266.html

156 Anushka Asthana, 'Anti-feminist Tory MP Philip Davies elected to equalities committee', *Guardian*, 13 December 2016, www.theguardian.com/world/2016/dec/13/anti-feminist-tory-mp-philip-davies-elected-to-equalities-committee

157 Jon Stone, 'Britain could slash environmental and safety standards "a very long way" after Brexit, Tory MP Jacob Rees-Mogg says', *Independent*, 6 December 2016, www.independent.co.uk/news/uk/politics/brexit-safety-standards-workers-rights-jacob-rees-mogg-a7459336.html

158 *Workplace fatal injuries in Great Britain, 2022*, HSE, 6 July 2022, www.hse.gov.uk/statistics/pdf/fatalinjuries.pdf

159 '48,000 die due to occupational accidents yearly: Study', *Times of India*, 20 November 2017, timesofindia.indiatimes.com/business/india-business/48000-die-due-to-occupational-accidents-yearly-study/articleshow/61725283.cms

160 Jessica Elgot, 'Company boss who gave £930,000 to Tory party receives knighthood', *Guardian*, 30 December 2016, www.theguardian.com/uk-news/2016/dec/30/company-boss-david-ord-tory-donor-receives-knighthood

161 Michael Savage and Fariha Karim, 13 December 2016, 'Tory MPs back May in row over £995 leather trousers', *The Times*, www.thetimes.co.uk/article/tories-rally-to-back-pm-after-attack-on-her-1-000-trousers-zcc7m5rzs

2017: Perpetually Intoxicated and Inappropriate With Women

1   Micahel Savage, 'Angry donor threatens to stop funding Tory party', *The Times*, 7 January 2017, www.thetimes.co.uk/article/angry-donor-threatens-to-stop-funding-tory-party-dxzq 8px2m

2   Anoosh Chakelian, '"We need a stronger leader": Charlie Mullins, the millionaire plumber, pulls Tory funding', *New Statesman*, 23 January 2018, www.newstatesman.com/politics/uk /2018/01/we-need-stronger-leader-charlie-mullins-millionaire-plumber-pulls-tory-funding

3   Rajeev Syal, 'Tory donor predicts Theresa May will have to quit within two years', *Guardian*, 23 January 2017, www.theguardian.com/politics/2017/jan/23/tory-donor-charlie-mullins-predicts-theresa-may-quit-within-two-years-brexit

4   Patrick Maguire, 'Theresa May to stake Tory claim as party of social justice', *Guardian*, 8 January 2017, www.theguardian.com/politics/2017/jan/08/theresa-may-tories-party-social-justice-speech

5   Rajeev Syal, 'Tories fail to build any of 200,000 starter homes promised in 2015, says watchdog', *Guardian*, 5 November 2019, www.theguardian.com/society/2019/nov/05/tories-broke-pledge-on-starter-homes-in-2015-manifesto-report-says

6   'Britain to build 17 towns and villages to ease housing squeeze', Reuters, 2 January 2017, www.reuters.com/article/uk-britain-housing-idUKKBN14M0HG?edition-redirect=uk

7   Patrick Maguire, 'Theresa May to stake Tory claim as party of social justice', *Guardian*, 8 January 2017, www.theguardian.com/politics/2017/jan/08/theresa-may-tories-party-social-justice-speech

8   'David Cameron promises £1bn mental health "revolution"', ITV News, 11 January 2016, www.itv.com/news/2016-01-11/david-cameron-to-promise-1bn-mental-health-revolution

9   Heather Stewart, 'May adviser regrets saying benefits should only go to "really disabled" people', *Guardian*, 27 February 2017, www.theguardian.com/politics/2017/feb/27/may-adviser-george-freeman-regrets-benefits-disabled-people-anxiety

10 Andrew Sparrow and Peter Walker, 'We will reduce stigma around mental illness, says Theresa May', *Guardian*, 9 January 2017, www.theguardian.com/politics/2017/jan/09/we-will-reduce-stigma-mental-illness-theresa-may

11 Jason Beattie, 'Jeremy Hunt breaks his pledge to raise spending on mental health', *Mirror*, 2 September 2016, www.mirror.co.uk/news/uk-news/jeremy-hunt-breaks-pledge-raise-888 9117

12 'A fifth of children rejected by mental health services due to high clinical threshold', National Health Executive, 12 October 2015, www.nationalhealthexecutive.com/Health-Care-News/a-fifth-of-children-rejected-by-mental-health-services-due-to-high-clinical-threshold

13 Ryan Wilkinson, 'British Red Cross CEO defends NHS "humanitarian crisis" remarks', *Independent*, 9 January 2017, www.independent.co.uk/news/uk/home-news/nhs-british-red-cross-chief-executive-mike-adamson-defends-humanitarian-crisis-remarks-a7516751.html

14 Denis Campbell, Steven Morris and Sarah Marsh, 'NHS faces "humanitarian crisis" as demand rises, British Red Cross warns', *Guardian*, 6 January 2017, www.theguardian.com /society/2017/jan/06/nhs-faces-humanitarian-crisis-rising-demand-british-red-cross

15 'Retired British expats "outstrip European pensioners using NHS"', BBC News, 11 January 2017, www.bbc.co.uk/news/38534958

16 'Brexit rebellion avoided after "meaningful vote" offer', BBC, 7 February 2017, www.bbc.co.uk/news/uk-politics-38895007

17 'Brexit trade deal could take 10 years, says UK's ambassador', BBC, 15 December 2016, www.bbc.co.uk/news/uk-politics-38324146

18 'Sir Ivan Rogers' resignation as Britain's EU ambassador - letter in full', *Telegraph*, 3 January 2017, www.telegraph.co.uk/news/2017/01/03/sir-ivan-rogers-resignation-britains-eu-ambassador-letter

19 Paul Dallison, 'Theresa May: We're leaving the single market', Politico, 17 January 2017, www.politico.eu/article/theresa-may-were-leaving-the-single-market-brexit

20   Andrew Rawnsley, 'Mrs May as a dominatrix? Some Tories buy it, but Europe won't',
     Guardian, 22 January 2017, www.theguardian.com/commentisfree/2017/jan/
     22/theresa-may-brexit-speech-illusions

21   Henry Mance, 'Theresa May unveils plan to quit EU single market under Brexit', *FT*, 17
     January 2017, www.ft.com/content/a6b9c062-dca8-11e6-86ac-f253db7791c6

22   Danny Shaw, 'Theresa May: Home Office record-breaker', BBC, 12 July 2016,
     www.bbc.co.uk/news/uk-politics-36767844

23   Daniel Boffey, 'Boris Johnson accused of bad taste for calling Brexit "liberation"', *Guardian*,
     22 February 2017, www.theguardian.com/politics/2017/feb/22/boris-johnson-accused-of-
     bad-taste-for-calling-brexit-liberation

24   Michael Safi and Patrick Wintour, 'No 10 defends Boris Johnson over "Brexit punishment
     beatings" quip', *Guardian*, 18 January 2017,
     www.theguardian.com/politics/2017/jan/18/boris-johnson-world-war-two-punishment-
     beatings-brexit-francois-hollande

25   Guy Verhofstadt [@guyverhofstadt], Twitter, 18 January 2017, twitter.com/guyverhofstadt
     /status/821730308055846913

26   Michael Safi and Patrick Wintour, 'No 10 defends Boris Johnson over "Brexit punishment
     beatings" quip'

27   'MPs scratch their heads at bid to ban clerks' itchy wigs: Row erupts over plans to end one
     of Parliament's ancient customs', *Daily Mail*, 5 February 2017, www.dailymail.co.uk/news
     /article-4192412/MPs-scratch-heads-bid-ban-clerks-itchy-wigs.html

28   Henry Zeffman, 'Commons clerks finally granted permission to lose their wigs', *The Times*,
     7 February 2017, www.thetimes.co.uk/article/commons-clerks-finally-granted-permission-
     to-lose-their-wigs-d8xqxjlz0

29   Wikipedia, 'Duty on Hair Powder Act 1795', Last edited: 16 April 2022, en.wikipedia.org
     /wiki/Duty_on_Hair_Powder_Act_1795

30   'MPs scratch their heads at bid to ban clerks' itchy wigs: Row erupts over plans to end one
     of Parliament's ancient customs', *Daily Mail*

31   'EU deal gives UK special status, says David Cameron', BBC, 20 February 2016,
     www.bbc.co.uk/news/uk-politics-35616768

32   'David Davis MP speech "Europe: It's Time To Decide"', David Davis MP,
     www.daviddavismp.com/david-davis-mp-delivers-speech-on-the-opportunities-for-a-
     referendum-on-europe

33   Presented to Parliament by the Prime Minister by Command of Her Majesty, 'The United
     Kingdom's exit from and new partnership with the European Union', HM Government,
     February 2017, assets.publishing.service.gov.uk/government/uploads/system/uploads/
     attachment_data/file/589191/The_United_Kingdoms_exit_from_and_partnership_
     with_the_EU_Web.pdf

34   Gary Gibbon, 'Boris Johnson throws Tory MPs
     into panic', *Channel 4 News*, 22 February 2016,
     www.channel4.com/news/by/gary-gibbon/blogs/boris-johnson-throws-tory-mps-panic

35   'Brexit plan published in government White Paper', BBC, 2 February 2016, www.bbc.co.uk
     /news/uk-politics-38836906

36   Jon Henley, 'Brexit white paper: key points explained', *Guardian*, 2 February 2017, www.the
     guardian.com/politics/2017/feb/02/brexit-white-paper-key-points-explained

37   'Brexit plan published in government White Paper', BBC

38   Katie Allen and Peter Walker, 'Philip Hammond admits Brexit vote means £122bn extra
     borrowing', *Guardian*, 23 November 2016, www.theguardian.com/uk-news/2016/nov
     /23/philip-hammond-brexit-vote-borrowing-autumn-statement?CMP=share_btn_tw;
     'Statement from the Governor of the Bank of England following the EU referendum result',
     Bank of England, 24 June 2016, www.bankofengland.co.uk/news/2016/june/statement-fr
     om-the-governor-of-the-boe-following-the-eu-referendum-result

39   David Wilcock, 'Britain sets up new Brexit battle with the EU as it sets "divorce bill" it is
     willing to pay at £37.3billion - some £3.5billion LESS that Brussels is demanding as the
     cost of leaving', *Daily Mail*, 15 July 2012, www.dailymail.co.uk/news/article-9792279/Brita
     in-sets-new-Brexit-battle-offering-divorce-bill-3-5billion-Brussels-wants.html

40   'Grasping Large Numbers', EHD, www.ehd.org/science_technology_largenumbers.php

41 Nadia Drake, 'Where, exactly, is the edge of space? It depends on who you ask', National Geographic, 20 December 2018, www.nationalgeographic.com/science/article/where-is-the-edge-of-space-and-what-is-the-karman-line

42 Paul Waugh [@PaulWaugh], Twitter, 8 February 2017, twitter.com/paulwaugh/status/829459790954889216

43 'NHS protest: Tens of thousands march against "hospital cuts"', BBC, 4 March 2017, www.bbc.co.uk/news/uk-39167350

44 'Hospital cuts planned in most of England', BBC, 21 February 2017, www.bbc.co.uk/news/health-39031546

45 Jon Stone, 'Tory MP tries and fails to block anti-domestic violence bill with 91-minute speech', Independent, 24 February 2017, www.independent.co.uk/news/uk/politics/domestic-violence-istanbul-convention-bill-philip-davies-filibuster-parliament-snp-a7597686.html

46 Jon Stone, 'David Cameron promised to take in 20,000 Syrian refugees. What have the Tories actually delivered?', Independent, 1 September 2016, www.independent.co.uk/news/uk/politics/syrian-refugee-crisis-refugees-british-government-20000-4000-progress-how-many-migrants-immigration-a7219971.html

47 Harry Cockburn, 'Dubs Amendment for child refugees: Full list of MPs who voted against the scheme', Independent, 10 February 2017, www.independent.co.uk/news/uk/politics/dubs-amendment-child-refugees-full-list-mps-voted-against-tories-labour-immigration-a7573881.html

48 Jessica Elgot and Rowena Mason, 'Conservatives fined record £70,000 for campaign spending failures', Guardian, 16 March 2017, www.theguardian.com/politics/2017/mar/16/conservatives-fined-70000-for-campaign-spending-failures

49 Patrick Worrall, 'Tory election expenses defence doesn't stand up', Channel 4 News, 16 March 2017, www.channel4.com/news/factcheck/factcheck-tory-election-expenses-defence-doesnt-stand-up

50 Rob Merrick, 'Brexit: David Davis admits Government has done no economic assessment of the UK crashing out of EU without deal', Independent, 15 March 2017, www.independent.co.uk/news/uk/politics/brexit-latest-news-david-davis-no-economic-impact-assess-uk-eu-leave-no-deal-select-committee-a7630626.html

51 Paul Dallison, 'Leave campaign boss says David Davis is "thick as mince"', Politico, 17 July 2017, www.politico.eu/article/david-davis-thick-as-mince-says-brexit-boss-dominic-cummings

52 Mark D'Arcy, 'Five take-outs from the Brexit bill', BBC, 1 February 2017, www.bbc.co.uk/news/uk-politics-parliaments-38833310

53 Anushka Asthana, Heather Stewart and Peter Walker, 'May triggers article 50 with warning of consequence for UK', Guardian, 29 March 2017, www.theguardian.com/politics/2017/mar/29/theresa-may-triggers-article-50-with-warning-of-consequences-for-uk

54 'Scottish Parliament backs referendum call', BBC, 28 March 2017, www.bbc.co.uk/news/uk-scotland-39422747

55 'Scottish independence: Referendum demand "will be rejected"', BBC, 16 March 2017, www.bbc.co.uk/news/uk-scotland-39293513

56 Toby Helm, Stephen Pritchard and Michael Savage, 'Poll finds that 60% of Britons want to keep their EU citizenship', Guardian, 1 July 2017, www.theguardian.com/politics/2017/jul/01/poll-european-eu-rights-brexit

57 Wikipedia, 'Opinion polling for the 2017 United Kingdom general election', Last edited: 15 July 2022, en.wikipedia.org/wiki/Opinion_polling_for_the_2017_United_Kingdom_general_election#2017

58 Anushka Asthana, Rowena Mason and Jessica Elgot, 'Theresa May calls for UK general election on 8 June', Guardian, 18 April 2017, www.theguardian.com/politics/2017/apr/18/theresa-may-uk-general-election-8-june

59 Henry Mance, 'Theresa May loses two senior Downing St advisers in one week', FT, 21 April 2017, www.ft.com/content/b8761bc8-2688-11e7-a34a-538b4cb30025

60 Henry Mance, George Parker and Catherine Belton, 'Theresa May's leadership attacked as Deloitte pulls out of bids', FT, 21 December 2016, www.ft.com/content/a40264d2-c790-11e6-8f29-9445cac8966f

61 George Parker, 'UK lacks Brexit plan, says leaked memo', FT, 15 November 2016, www.ft.com/content/616468d6-ab03-11e6-9cb3-bb8207902122

62 Benjamin Kentish, 'Tory voters think their party is now more right-wing than Ukip, poll finds', *Independent*, 15 May 2017, www.independent.co.uk/news/uk/politics/tory-voters-more-right-wing-ukip-poll-latest-theresa-may-nigel-farage-a7737491.html

63 'Conservative MP Andrew Turner calls homosexuality "dangerous"', Sky News, 29 April 2017, news.sky.com/story/conservative-mp-andrew-turner-calls-homosexuality-dangerous-10854833

64 Matthew Holehouse, 'MP battling to save seat in "toxic" Tory rebellion after fiancee moves in with his aide', *Telegraph*, 8 January 2015, www.telegraph.co.uk/news/politics/conservative/11334299/MP-battling-to-save-seat-in-toxic-Tory-Rebellion-after-fiancee-moves-in-with-his-aide.html

65 Ben Van Der Merwe, 'Who owns the media? Top newspaper, website and magazine owners charted', *Press Gazette*,16 December 2020, pressgazette.co.uk/digital-diversity-or-age-of-consolidation-media-ownership-2020

66 Andrew Cave, 'Evgeny Lebedev spells out his vision for the Evening Standard', *Telegraph*, 2 July 2009, www.telegraph.co.uk/finance/newsbysector/mediatechnologyandtelecoms/5726062/Evgeny-Lebedev-spells-out-his-vision-for-the-Evening-Standard.html

67 John Sweeney, 'What changed to make Evgeny Lebedev no longer a security risk?', *Byline Times*, 20 August 2020, bylinetimes.com/2020/08/20/sweeney-investigates-what-changed-to-make-evgeny-lebedev-no-longer-a-security-risk

68 'Evgeny Lebedev: I am not some agent of Russia', BBC, 11 March 2020, www.bbc.co.uk/news/uk-politics-60707584

69 Benjamin Kentish, 'Zac Goldsmith accused of 'staggering hypocrisy' for standing as Conservative candidate again', *Independent*, 27 April 2017, www.independent.co.uk/news/uk/politics/zac-goldsmith-conservative-candidate-area-staggering-hypocrisy-general-election-london-mayor-jonathan-bartley-green-party-a7705396.html

70 Harriet Agerholm, 'Conservative MP says people using food banks have a "cashflow problem"', *Independent*, 30 May 2017, www.independent.co.uk/news/uk/politics/dominic-raab-conservative-mp-food-banks-cashflow-problem-esher-walton-election-2017-a7762476.html

71 'Number of people receiving three days' worth of emergency food by Trussell Trust foodbanks in the United Kingdom from 2008/09 to 2021/22', Statista, 11 May 2020, www.statista.com/statistics/382695/uk-foodbank-users

72 'UK Politics Straw tells of Lawrence report impact', BBC, 20 April 1999, http://news.bbc.co.uk/1/hi/uk_politics/323879.stm

73 'Muslims who hate us can get out, says Tory', *Scotsman*, 3 August 2005, www.scotsman.com/news/politics/muslims-who-hate-us-can-get-out-says-tory-2506382

74 Andy McSmith, 'Tory MP Gerald Howarth says Enoch Powell "was right" in notorious Rivers of Blood speech', *Independent*, 27 August 2014, www.independent.co.uk/news/uk/politics/tory-mp-gerald-howarth-says-enoch-powell-was-right-in-notorious-rivers-of-blood-speech-9693849.html

75 'Services gay ban lifted', BBC, 12 January 2000, http://news.bbc.co.uk/1/hi/uk_politics/599810.stm

76 Niamh McIntyre, 'Tories forced to admit they won't spend any new money on social housing plan', *Independent*, 14 May 2017, www.independent.co.uk/news/uk/politics/tories-admit-no-new-money-right-buy-social-housing-plan-general-election-a7735366.html

77 'How funding for the NHS in the UK has changed over a rolling ten year period', The Health Foundation, 31 October 2015, www.health.org.uk/chart/chart-how-funding-for-the-nhs-in-the-uk-has-changed-over-a-rolling-ten-year-period

78 Patrick Dunleavy, 'With a likely cost of £4 billion, the Health and Social Care Bill has all the hallmarks of an avoidable policy fiasco', LSE, 24 January 2012, blogs.lse.ac.uk/politicsandpolicy/hsc-bill-policy-fiasco

79 Charlotte England, 'Conservative manifesto 2017: All you need to know about the Tories' election pledges', *Independent*, 18 May 2017, www.independent.co.uk/news/uk/politics/conservative-manifesto-2017-all-need-know-key-points-tory-election-policies-theresa-may-a7743001.html

80 James Carr, 'Five free schools cost more than £30m, new figures show', Schools Week, 4 February 2020, schoolsweek.co.uk/five-free-schools-cost-more-than-30m-new-figures-show

81 Charlotte England, 'Conservative manifesto 2017: All you need to know about the Tories' election pledges'

82 Nicola Bartlett, 'Iain Duncan Smith's breakfast cost 557 times amount to be spent on kids' morning meals', *Mirror*, 30 May 2017, www.mirror.co.uk/news/politics/iain-duncan-smiths-breakfast-cost-10530758

83 Charlotte England, 'Conservative manifesto 2017: All you need to know about the Tories' election pledges'

84 'Should fox hunting remain illegal?', YouGov, yougov.co.uk/topics/politics/trackers/should-fox-hunting-remain-illegal

85 Charlotte England, 'Conservative manifesto 2017: All you need to know about the Tories' election pledges'

86 'BMG Research Poll: Two-thirds of people don't read political manifestos', BMG, 16 May 2017, www.bmgresearch.co.uk/bmg-research-poll-10-people-dont-know-manifesto

87 '"Dementia tax": Tories buy Google ads to stop people reading about controversy over new policy', *Independent*, 22 May 2017, www.independent.co.uk/life-style/gadgets-and-tech/news/dementia-tax-google-adverts-conservatives-stop-reading-policy-controversy-election-2017-manifesto-a7748646.html

88 Anushka Asthana and Jessica Elgot, 'Theresa May ditches manifesto plan with 'dementia tax' U-turn', *Guardian*, 22 May 2017, www.theguardian.com/society/2017/may/22/theresa-may-u-turn-on-dementia-tax-cap-social-care-conservative-manifesto

89 Aubrey Allegretti, '"Nothing has changed": A year on from Theresa May's immortal words', Sky News, 22 May 2018, news.sky.com/story/nothing-has-changed-a-year-on-from-theresa-mays-immortal-words-11381764

90 Fiona Rutherford, 'People have a lot of questions about Theresa May's "naughty" confession', Buzz Feed, 6 June 2017, www.buzzfeed.com/fionarutherford/never-have-i-ever

91 'Theresa May prompts anger after telling nurse who hasn't had pay rise for eight years: "There's no magic money tree"', *Independent*, 3 June 2017, www.independent.co.uk/news/uk/politics/theresa-may-nurse-magic-money-tree-bbcqt-question-time-pay-rise-eight-years-election-latest-a7770576.html

92 Samuel Osborne, 'Theresa May's leadership more popular than Margaret Thatcher or Tony Blair, poll reveals', *Independent*, 26 April 2017, www.independent.co.uk/news/uk/politics/theresa-may-more-popular-margaret-thatcher-tony-blair-leadership-uk-prime-minister-polls-latest-a7703591.html

93 Wikipedia, 'Opinion polling for the 2017 United Kingdom general election', Last edited: 22 July 2022, en.wikipedia.org/wiki/Opinion_polling_for_the_2017_United_Kingdom_general_election

94 Steven Erlanger and Stephen Castle, 'Theresa May loses overall majority in U.K. parliament', *New York Times*, 8 June 2017, www.nytimes.com/2017/06/08/world/europe/theresa-may-britain-election-conservatives-parliament.html

95 Jessica Elgot, 'Osborne says Theresa May is a "dead woman walking"', *Guardian*, 11 June 2017, www.theguardian.com/politics/2017/jun/11/george-osborne-says-theresa-may-is-a-dead-woman-walking

96 'UK election 2017: Conservatives lose majority', BBC, 9 June 2017, www.bbc.co.uk/news/election-2017-40209282

97 Jon Stone, 'Theresa May says she "shed a tear" on general election night', *Independent*, 13 July 2017, www.independent.co.uk/news/uk/politics/theresa-may-little-tear-2017-general-election-result-crying-sobbing-tears-david-davis-downing-street-a7838701.html

98 Owen Jones, 'There is a magic money tree. But only for the Queen and the DUP', *Guardian*, 27 January 2017, www.theguardian.com/commentisfree/2017/jun/27/magic-money-tree-queen-dup-theresa-may-northern-ireland

99 Owen Jones, 'Never mind the SNP. The real danger is if the DUP are in government', 24 April 2015, www.theguardian.com/commentisfree/2015/apr/24/snp-dup-democratic-unionist-party-government-tories-anti-scottish-coalition-homophobic

100 Ian Cobain, 'Troubled past: the paramilitary connection that still haunts the DUP', *Guardian*, 27 June 2017, www.theguardian.com/politics/2017/jun/27/troubled-past-the-paramilitary-connection-that-still-haunts-the-dup

101 'Confidence and Supply Agreement between the Conservative and Unionist Party and the Democratic Unionist Party', Gov.uk, 23 January 2020, www.gov.uk/government/publications/conservative-and-dup-agreement-and-uk-government-financial-support-for-northern-ireland/agreement-between-the-conservative-and-unionist-party-and-the-democratic-unionist-party-on-support-for-the-government-in-parliament

102 'Grasping Large Numbers', EHD, www.ehd.org/science_technology_largenumbers.php

103 D. Clark, 'Number of people receiving three days' worth of emergency food by Trussell Trust foodbanks in the United Kingdom from 2008/09 to 2021/22', Statista, 11 May 2022, www.statista.com/statistics/382695/uk-foodbank-users

104 Mark Wallace [@wallaceme], Twitter, 9 June 2017, twitter.com/wallaceme/status/873073210241105920

105 Police Community [@PolComForum], Twitter, 8 June 2017, twitter.com/PolComForum/status/873186390539988993

106 Harriet Agerholm, 'DUP politician celebrates Theresa May deal with photo of terror flag flying over Downing Street', *Independent*, 12 June 2017, www.independent.co.uk/news/uk/politics/ian-stevenson-dup-politician-uvf-flag-photo-downing-street-theresa-may-conservative-deal-a7786021.html

107 'UK election 2017: Conservatives lose majority', BBC, 9 June 2017, www.bbc.co.uk/news/election-2017-40209282

108 Ibid.

109 Tom McTague and Annabelle Dickson, 'Theresa May's strategy director and speechwriter quits', Politico, 26 July 2017, www.politico.eu/article/chris-wilkins-theresa-mays-strategy-director-and-speechwriter-quits

110 Mikey Smith, 'Theresa May aides set for £35,000 payout after quitting over botched election campaign', *Mirror*, 12 June 2017, www.mirror.co.uk/news/politics/theresa-aides-35000-payout-after-10611257

111 Rod Liddle, 'That is the worst Tory campaign ever', 27 May 2017, www.spectator.co.uk/article/this-is-the-worst-tory-campaign-ever

112 Jim Pickard and George Parker, 'Theresa May's new Downing Street team emerges', *FT*, 15 July 2017, www.ft.com/content/ac1086e6-6721-11e7-8526-7b38dcaef614

113 Josh May, 'Blow for Theresa May as Northern Powerhouse minister quits government', Politico, 14 June 2017, www.politicshome.com/news/article/blow-for-theresa-may-as-northern-powerhouse-minister-quits-government

114 Jim Pickard and James Blitz, 'Ministers leave UK Brexit department in sign of tension with May', *FT*, 13 June 2017, www.ft.com/content/273fb412-503f-11e7-a1f2-db19572361bb

115 Holly Watt, 'Conservative MP take five-star junket to Equatorial Guinea', *Telegraph*, 29 October 2011, web.archive.org/web/20111030025203/http://www.telegraph.co.uk/news/politics/8855776/Conservative-MP-take-five-star-junket-to-Equatorial-Guinea.html

116 Steve Baker, www.stevebaker.info/about/detailed-biography

117 'Brexit negotiations: Barnier rules out "concessions"', BBC, 19 June 2017, www.bbc.co.uk/news/uk-politics-40321271

118 Jon Stone, 'David Davis pictured without any notes at Brexit negotiations', *Independent*, 17 July 2017, www.independent.co.uk/news/uk/politics/david-davis-brexit-no-notes-brexit-negotiations-a7845686.html

119 Ibid.

120 Sandra Laville, 'Government-backed "red tape" group looked at EU fire safety rules on morning of Grenfell fire', *Guardian*, 22 June 2017, www.theguardian.com/uk-news/2017/jun/22/government-backed-red-tape-group-eu-fire-safety-rules-grenfell-fire

121 'Cameron aims to "kill off" health and safety culture', *Scotsman*, 6 January 2012, www.scotsman.com/news/uk-news/cameron-aims-kill-health-and-safety-culture-1648467

122 Tim Clark, 'London Building Act "would have averted Grenfell disaster"', *Construction News*, 22 June 2017, www.constructionnews.co.uk/news/knowledge-news/london-building-act-would-have-averted-grenfell-disaster-22-06-2017

123 Jim Fitzpatrick, 'Fire Sprinklers Week', UK Parliament, 6 February 2014, hansard.parliament.uk/Commons/2014-02-06/debates/14020653000002/FireSprinklersWeek

124 Sanda Laville, 'Government-backed "red tape" group looked at EU fire safety rules on morning of Grenfell fire', *Guardian*, 22 June 2017, www.theguardian.com/uk-news/2017/jun/22/government-backed-red-tape-group-eu-fire-safety-rules-grenfell-fire

125 Wikipedia, 'Grenfell Tower fire', Last edited: 20 July 2022, en.wikipedia.org/wiki/
Grenfell_Tower_fire

126 'Kensington & Chelsea Council Tax 2010–17 – Actual vs Average London Increase', RBKC
annual accounts – via @Research_Act, researchforaction.uk/wp-content/uploads/2017/08
/Screen-Shot-2017-08-04-at-15.13.54.png

127 Joel, 'Grenfell Tower and RBKC – victims of austerity? or exponents of shock doctrine?',
Research for Action, 31 July 2017, researchforaction.uk/grenfell-tower-and-rbkc-victim-of-
austerity-or-proponent-of-shock-doctrine

128 Sarah Knapton, 'Grenfell Tower refurbishment used cheaper cladding and tenants accused
builders of shoddy workmanship', *Telegraph*, 16 June 2017, www.telegraph.co.uk/news/20
17/06/16/grenfell-tower-refurbishment-used-cheaper-cladding-tenants-accused

129 'Grenfell Tower: Jacob Rees-Mogg criticised for "insulting" comments', BBC, 5 November
2019, www.bbc.co.uk/news/uk-england-london-50302573

130 Ibid.

131 Robert Mackey, 'Theresa May avoids survivors of Grenfell Tower fire during visit to scene
of disaster', The Intercept, 15 June 2017, theintercept.com/2017/06/15/theresa-may-avoids-
survivors-grenfell-tower-fire-visit-scene-disaster

132 Helena Horton and Steven Swinford, 'Gavin Barwell, Theresa May's new chief of staff,
refuses to answer questions over role in fire safety review', *Telegraph*, 16 June 2017,
www.telegraph.co.uk/news/2017/06/16/gavin-barwell-theresa-mays-new-chief-staff-
refuses-answer-questions

133 'Lakanal House Coroner Inquest', Lambeth Council, beta.lambeth.gov.uk/about-council/
transparency-open-data/lakanal-house-coroner-inquest

134 Helena Horton and Steven Swinford, 'Gavin Barwell, Theresa May's new chief of staff,
refuses to answer questions over role in fire safety review', *Telegraph*, 16 June 2017,
www.telegraph.co.uk/news/2017/06/16/gavin-barwell-theresa-mays-new-chief-staff-
refuses-answer-questions

135 LBC [@LBC], Twitter, 10 February 2021, twitter.com/LBC/status/1359521302093172741

136 'Unsafe cladding: What is it and who pays to remove it?', BBC, 13 June 2020,
www.bbc.co.uk/news/explainers-56015129

137 Helena Bengtsson, Emma Hartley and Rajeev Syal, 'Number of MPs who earn from renting
out property rises by a third', *Guardian*, 6 May 2015, www.theguardian.com/politics/2015
/may/06/number-of-mps-who-earn-from-renting-out-property-rises-by-a-third

138 'Unsafe cladding: What is it and who pays to remove it?', BBC, 13 Jun 2020, www.bbc.co.uk
/news/explainers-56015129

139 Peter Apps, 'One in six cladding leaseholders exploring bankruptcy options, survey reveals',
Inside Housing, 10 February 2021, www.insidehousing.co.uk/news/news/one-in-six-
cladding-leaseholders-exploring-bankruptcy-options-survey-reveals-69475

140 Holly Baxter, 'If only the Grenfell Tower residents had known about the magic money tree
the Queen took from this morning', *Independent*, 27 June 2017, www.independent.co.uk/vo
ices/grenfell-tower-queen-royal-family-today-cost-repair-cladding-magic-money-tree-a78
09931.html

141 'Brexit: 2018 Queen's Speech cancelled by government', BBC, 18 June 2017, www.bbc.co.uk
/news/uk-40317814

142 Sarah Boseley, 'UK public are more dissatisfied than ever with NHS, poll shows', *Guardian*,
26 June 2017, www.theguardian.com/society/2017/jun/26/uk-public-are-more-dissatisfied-
than-ever-with-nhs-poll-shows

143 May Bulman, 'Government fails to track mental health in UK prisons amid soaring suicide
and self-harm rates, report finds', *Independent*, 29 July 2017, www.independent.co.uk/news
/uk/home-news/mental-health-uk-prisons-suicide-rates-self-harm-report-national-audit-
office-hmpps-public-health-england-a7812701.html

144 Samuel Osborne, 'Theresa May poll: Satisfaction rating for Prime Minister
"worst in history" for month after general election', *Independent*, 20 July 2017,
www.independent.co.uk/news/uk/politics/conservative-government-ipsos-mori-approval-
ranking-trend-survey-popularity-a7850921.html

145 Rowena Mason, 'May orders Anne Marie Morris MP to be suspended after using N-word',
Guardian, 11 July 2017, www.theguardian.com/world/2017/jul/10/tories-urgently-
investigating-after-mp-uses-n-word-at-public-event

146 Tom Powell, 'Tory MP Jacob Rees-Mogg names sixth child Sixtus Dominic Boniface Christopher', *Evening Standard*, 5 July 2017, www.standard.co.uk/news/politics/tory-mp-jacob-reesmogg-names-sixth-child-sixtus-dominic-boniface-christopher-a3580671.html

147 Adam Smith, 'Tory MP and father-of six Jacob Rees-Mogg admits he's never changed a nappy', *Metro*, 27 July 2017, metro.co.uk/2017/07/21/tory-mp-and-father-of-six-jacob-rees-mogg-admits-hes-never-changed-a-nappy-6795660

148 Robert Wright, Andy Bounds and Gill Plimmer, 'Chris Grayling forced into late-night defence of HS2', *FT*, 17 July 2017, www.ft.com/content/d4f11b5a-6b06-11e7-b9c7-15af748b60d0

149 Aisha Majid, 'How the cost of HS2 has surged', *New Statesman*, 21 June 2021, www.newstatesman.com/politics/2021/06/how-cost-hs2-has-surged

150 Robert Wright, Andy Bounds and Gill Plimmer, 'Chris Grayling forced into late-night defence of HS2'

151 Andy Bounds, 'U-turn on rail schemes hits Northern Powerhouse plan', *FT*, 21 July 2017, www.ft.com/content/522c0f8e-6e0f-11e7-bfeb-33fe0c5b7eaa

152 Aisha Majid, 'How the cost of HS2 has surged'

153 Ashley Cowburn, 'Theresa May says she has an "open mind" over Brexit negotiations', *Independent*, 27 July 2016, www.independent.co.uk/news/uk/brexit-theresa-may-negotiations-eu-referendum-result-leave-europe-a7158516.html

154 Tom Peck, 'Theresa May's plans for EU citizens branded a "damp squib" by the European Parliament', *Independent*, 10 July 2017, www.independent.co.uk/news/uk/politics/brexit-latest-european-citizens-theresa-may-plan-damp-squib-european-parliament-guy-verhofstadt-a7832246.html

155 Ashley Cowburn, 'Conservatives abandon manifesto plan for free school breakfasts', *Independent*, 26 July 2017, www.independent.co.uk/news/uk/politics/conservatives-manifesto-general-election-2017-free-school-breakfasts-lunch-a7861836.html

156 Ashley Cowburn, 'Conservatives abandon manifesto plan for free school breakfasts', *Independent*, 26 July 2017, www.independent.co.uk/news/uk/politics/conservatives-manifesto-general-election-2017-free-school-breakfasts-lunch-a7861836.html

157 Darren Slade, 'MP Chris Chope accused of "abusing the system" after he joins with fellow Tory to put 73 bills before parliament', *Daily Echo*, 29 July 2017, www.bournemouthecho.co.uk/news/15441893.mp-chris-chope-accused-of-abusing-the-system-after-he-joins-with-fellow-tory-to-put-73-bills-before-parliament

158 Ian Sandwell, 'Oops! Tory MP Andrea Leadsom dubs Jane Austen one of our "greatest living authors" on live TV', *Digital Spy*, 20 July 2017, www.digitalspy.com/tv/a833577/tory-mp-andrea-leadsom-jane-austen-error

159 Harvey Solomon-Brady, 'GET YOUR PHIL Why has Philip Hammond quit as an MP and what was his constituency?', *Sun*, 5 November 2019, www.thesun.co.uk/news/3029328/philip-hammond-mp-former-chancellor-exchequer

160 Wikipedia, 'Dorneywood', Last updated: 27 June 2022, en.wikipedia.org/wiki/Dorneywood

161 Nick Sommerland and Jack Blanchard, 'Chancellor Philip Hammond calls nurses and cops "overpaid" while raking in £10k a month renting property', *Mirror*, 17 July 2017, www.mirror.co.uk/news/politics/chancellor-philip-hammond-calls-nurses-10811785

162 Imogen Groome, 'How much do NHS nurses earn?', *Metro*, 3 July 2017, metro.co.uk/2017/07/03/how-much-do-nhs-nurses-earn-6751022

163 Jon Craig, 'Chancellor Philip Hammond "says public sector workers overpaid"', Sky News, news.sky.com/story/chancellor-philip-hammond-says-public-sector-workers-overpaid-10950268

164 Lizze Dearden, 'Theresa May prompts anger after telling nurse who hasn't had pay rise for eight years: "There's no magic money tree"', *Independent*, 3 June 2017, www.independent.co.uk/news/uk/politics/theresa-may-nurse-magic-money-tree-bbcqt-question-time-pay-rise-eight-years-election-latest-a7770576.html

165 Jon Craig, 'Chancellor Philip Hammond "says public sector workers overpaid"', Sky News, 16 July 2017, news.sky.com/story/chancellor-philip-hammond-says-public-sector-workers-overpaid-10950268

166 Heather Stewart, 'Philip Hammond in row over "even a woman can drive a train" jibe', *Guardian*, 15 July 2017, www.theguardian.com/politics/2017/jul/15/philip-hammond-in-row-over-even-a-woman-can-drive-a-train-jibe

167 Simon Walters, '"Shrivelled PM can't function": Top Tory claims "depressed" Theresa May "struggled to engage" at recent meeting as leadership challenge rumours grow', *Daily Mail*, 16 July 2017, www.dailymail.co.uk/news/article-4700100/Depressed-Theresa-t-function-Tory-claims.html

168 Samuel Osborne, 'Conservative Party is a "failing organisation", admits Tory MP', *Independent*, 13 July 2017, www.independent.co.uk/news/uk/politics/conservative-party-failing-operation-tory-mp-bernard-jenkin-theresa-may-government-jeremy-corbyn-a7839246.html

169 Torcuil Crichton, 'Theresa May flies back from G20 summit to face "prosecco plot" from Tory MPs determined to oust her', *Daily Record*, 10 July 2017, www.dailyrecord.co.uk/news/politics/theresa-flies-back-g20-summit-10766399

170 Lucy Fisher, 'Brexit secretary David Davis only works three days a week, says former aide', *The Times*, 16 August 2017, www.thetimes.co.uk/article/david-davis-is-work-shy-and-inept-says-former-aide-james-chapman-vgc3ssvmz

171 Jon Stone, 'David Davis's former chief of staff launches extraordinary tirade against "drunk, bullying and inappropriate" Brexit chief', *Independent*, 15 August 2015, www.independent.co.uk/news/uk/politics/david-davis-brexit-drunk-diane-abbott-james-chapman-farage-john-humphrys-andrew-neil-slovakia-a7893816.html

172 Giulia Paravicini and Annabelle Dickson, 'Former aide accuses Brexit secretary David Davis of being lazy and a liar', Politico, 15 August 2017, www.politico.eu/article/james-chapman-david-davis-lazy-liar-twitter

173 Robert Wright, 'Peers censure David Davis over Lords Brexit snub', *FT*, 1 August 2017, www.ft.com/content/4be211f0-76d4-11e7-90c0-90a9d1bc9691

174 David Singleton, 'Theresa May is wildly incompetent, says top donor to "Tory Momentum"', Total Politics, 30 August 2017, www.totalpolitics.com/articles/news/theresa-may-wildly-incompetent-says-top-donor-tory-momentum

175 Benjamin Kentish, 'Young Tory activists caught discussing "gassing chavs" and "shooting peasants" in leaked WhatsApp group', *Independent*, 30 August 2017, www.independent.co.uk/news/uk/politics/tories-gassing-chavs-whatsapp-messages-group-chat-activate-members-leaked-a7921086.html

176 Karl McDonald, 'Activate: the "Tory momentum" has had a bad first week', *iNews*, 1 September 2017, inews.co.uk/light-relief/offbeat/activate-tory-momentum-bad-first-week-88146

177 John Johnston, 'EXCL Tory grassroots group Activate confirms it has shut down less than two months after launch', Politics Home, 5 June 2018, www.politicshome.com/news/article/excl-tory-grassroots-group-activate-confirms-it-has-shut-down-less-than-two-months-after-launch

178 Joe Watts, 'Conservative MP launches "Tory Glastonbury" after Jeremy Corbyn's success on the Pyramid Stage', *Independent*, 5 August 2017, www.independent.co.uk/news/uk/politics/tory-glastonbury-jeremy-corbyn-george-freeman-conservatives-theresa-may-a7878181.html

179 Paul Goodman, 'Freeman's definitely non-Glastonbury-style Conservative ideas festival', Conservative Home, 6 August 2017, www.conservativehome.com/parliament/2017/08/freemans-definitely-non-glastonbury-style-conservative-ideas-festival.html

180 Conor Sullivan, 'London Garden Bridge plans finally fall down', *FT*, 14 August 2017, www.ft.com/content/6d2f01aa-80d5-11e7-94e2-c5b903247afd

181 Alan McGuinness, 'Downing Street responds to claims Boris Johnson is seen as a "clown"', Sky News, 29 August 2017, news.sky.com/story/downing-street-responds-to-claims-boris-johnson-is-seen-as-a-clown-11011578

182 Ben Lazarus, 'BORIS IN BOTHER Boris Johnson slammed for praising a corrupt election in Kenya which has been dissolved', *Sun*, 3 September 2017, www.thesun.co.uk/news/4375342/boris-johnson-slammed-for-praising-a-corrupt-election-in-kenya-which-has-been-dissolved

183 J.D. McGregor, 'Tory MP says a memorial to men who were executed for being gay is "totally inappropriate"', Evolve Politics, 20 September 2017, evolvepolitics.com/tory-mp-says-a-memorial-to-men-who-were-executed-for-being-gay-is-totally-inappropriate

184 Richard Castle, 'Gay couple speak out after being denied dream of church wedding in Uttoxeter', *Stafford Live*, 3 July 2017, www.staffordshire-live.co.uk/news/gay-couple-speak-out-after-159562

185 Tom Peck, 'Anti-abortion MP Jacob Rees-Mogg admits profiting from sale of abortion pills', *Independent,* 1 October 2017, www.independent.co.uk/news/uk/politics/jacob-reesmogg-abortion-pills-abortion-rape-conservative-party-conference-tory-leadership-leader-a79763 86.html

186 Tom Peck, 'Jacob Rees-Mogg says rise in food bank use is "rather uplifting"', *Independent,* 14 September 2017, www.independent.co.uk/news/uk/politics/jacob-rees-mogg-uk-food-bank-uplifting-conservative-mp-leader-a7946096.html

187 Chris Giles, 'UK credit rating downgraded over Brexit uncertainty', *FT,* 22 September 2017, www.ft.com/content/3ecfa8f2-9fdc-11e7-8cd4-932067fbf946

188 Boris Johnson, 'Boris Johnson: My vision for a bold, thriving Britain enabled by Brexit', *Telegraph,* 15 September 2017, www.telegraph.co.uk/politics/0/boris-johnson-vision-for-brexit-bold-thriving-britain

189 Tom Newton Dunn, 'BREXY BEAST Boris Johnson reveals his four Brexit "red lines" for Theresa May', *Sun,* 29 September 2017, www.thesun.co.uk/news/4580334/boris-johnson-pm-brexit-red-lines

190 Tom Newton Dunn, 'WAGE BOOST Boris Johnson wants PM to deliver public sector pay rise – funded by layoffs', *Sun,* 29 September 2017, www.thesun.co.uk/news/4579862/boris-johnson-pm-pay-cap-minimum-wage

191 Michael McHugh, 'Northern Ireland grace period extensions "sensible", Boris Johnson says', *Irish News,* 8 March 2021, www.irishnews.com/news/brexit/2021/03/08/news/northern-ireland-grace-period-extensions-sensible-boris-johnson-2248443

192 Tom Newton Dunn, 'BREXY BEAST Boris Johnson reveals his four Brexit "red lines" for Theresa May'

193 Michael McHugh, 'Northern Ireland grace period extensions "sensible", Boris Johnson says'

194 Gordon Rayner, 'Theresa May expects Boris Johnson to remain as Foreign Secretary after Brexit speech', *Telegraph,* 19 September 2017, www.telegraph.co.uk/news/2017/09/19/boris-johnson-will-resign-weekend-theresa-may-goes-against-brexit

195 Benjamin Kentish, 'Boris Johnson faces calls to be sacked after "breaking Ministerial Code" with hard Brexit event', *Independent,* 29 September 2017, www.independent.co.uk/news/uk/politics/boris-johnson-brexit-sacking-ministerial-code-event-foreign-office-a7972676.html

196 Robert Wright and George Parker, 'Boris Johnson snatches conference attention from Tory unity', *FT,* 2 October 2017, www.ft.com/content/6f68d306-a6c8-11e7-ab55-27219df83c97

197 'Boris Johnson Libya "dead bodies" comment provokes anger', BBC, 4 October 2017, www.bbc.co.uk/news/uk-politics-41490174

198 Wikipedia, 'Battle of Sirte (2016)', Last edited: 22 July 2022, en.wikipedia.org/wiki/Battle_of_Sirte_(2016)

199 Patrick Wintour, 'Boris Johnson refuses to apologise for Libyan "dead bodies" remark', *Guardian,* 17 October 2017, www.theguardian.com/politics/2017/oct/17/boris-johnson-refuses-to-apologise-for-libyan-dead-bodies-remark

200 John Crace, 'Welcome to the weirdest place on Earth: the Tory party conference', *Guardian,* 6 October 2017, www.theguardian.com/uk-news/2017/oct/06/tory-conservative-party-conference-welcome-to-the-weirdest-place-on-earth

201 Kevin Maguire [@Kevin_Maguire], Twitter, 1 October 2017, twitter.com/Kevin_Maguire/status/914433577928073217

202 Henry Mance, George Parker and Robert Wright, 'Boris Johnson styles himself as "godfather of Brexit"', *FT,* 3 October 2017, www.ft.com/content/30866c52-a78b-11e7-ab55-27219df83c97

203 Ashley Cowburn, 'Jeremy Hunt ridiculed for claiming Tories "set up" the NHS', *Independent,* 3 October 2017, www.independent.co.uk/news/uk/politics/jeremy-hunt-nhs-creation-tories-health-minister-ridiculed-a7980536.html

204 Natasha Clark, 'SWEET AND SOUR Anger after Tory conference is sponsored by Tate & Lyle – despite sugar tax to crackdown on UK obesity', *Sun,* 3 October 2017, www.thesun.co.uk/news/4599678/anger-after-tory-conference-is-sponsored-by-tate-lyle-despite-sugar-tax-to-crack-down-on-uk-obesity

205 Reuters, 'Everything that went wrong during Theresa May's speech – video', *Guardian,* 5 October 2017, www.theguardian.com/politics/video/2017/oct/05/everything-that-went-wrong-during-theresa-mays-speech-video

206 Mikey Smith, 'Theresa May accused of plagiarising The West Wing in keynote speech to Conservative Party Conference', *Mirror*, 4 October 2017, www.mirror.co.uk/news/politics/theresa-accused-plagiarising-west-wing-11284766

207 Lizzie Buchan, 'Conservative party conference: Theresa May fights for survival as another cabinet minister refuses to back her', *Independent*, 1 October 2017, www.independent.co.uk/news/uk/politics/theresa-may-leadership-tories-conference-boris-johnson-sajid-javid-a79 76376.html

208 Jamie Grierson, 'Grant Shapps: from rising Tory star to plotter against the PM', *Guardian*, 6 October 2017, www.theguardian.com/politics/2017/oct/06/grant-shapps-from-rising-tory-star-to-plotter-of-may-ouster

209 Tim Shipman, 'The Shippers Awards 2010-2020: a crazy decade in politics', *The Times*, 5 January 2020, www.thetimes.co.uk/article/the-shippers-awards-2010-2020-a-crazy-decade-in-politics-xn5vs355f

210 Emma Featherstone, 'Britain is £490bn poorer than thought, reveals ONS', *Independent*, 18 October 2017, www.independent.co.uk/news/business/news/britain-490-billion-pounds-poorer-ons-figures-uk-brexit-talks-position-revision-gdp-a8002871.html

211 Wikipedia, 'Domestication of the dog', Last edited: 19 July 2022, en.wikipedia.org/wiki/Origin_of_the_domestic_dog#Bonn-Oberkassel_dog

212 Sam Coates, '40 Tory MPs on Westminster sex list', *The Times*, 31 October 2017, www.thetimes.co.uk/article/40-tory-mps-on-westminster-sex-list-cbnj97wjs

213 Fiona Simpson, 'MP sex pest scandal: 36 Tories named over sexual misconduct allegations in Tory spreadsheet of shame', *Evening Standard*, 30 October 2017, www.standard.co.uk/news/politics/leaked-spreadsheet-reveals-sexual-harassment-claims-against-36-mps-a3670961.html

214 Gordon Rayner, 'Westminster sexual harassment scandal: 36 Tory MPs accused in 'dirty dossier' as PM vows to sack ministers involved', *Telegraph*, 30 November 2017, www.telegraph.co.uk/news/2017/10/29/theresa-may-will-sack-cabinet-ministers-found-sex-pests-13-mps

215 Jack Maidment, 'Brexit minister who "sent assistant to buy sex toys" will be investigated by Cabinet Office, Jeremy Hunt reveals', *Telegraph*, 29 November 2017, www.telegraph.co.uk/news/2017/10/29/brexit-minister-sent-assistant-buy-sex-toys-will-investigated

216 Tim Sculthorpe and Scott Campbell, 'Daniel Kawczynski becomes the THIRD Tory MP referred to a disciplinary committee after he is accused of pressuring young researcher to go on a date with a wealthy businessman who was "older than her father"', *Daily Mail*, 4 November 2017, www.dailymail.co.uk/news/article-5050291/David-Cameron-adviser-named-Westminster-sleaze-scandal.html

217 Cathy Newman, 'New allegations in parliamentary sexual abuse scandal', *Channel 4 News*, 4 November 2017, www.channel4.com/news/new-allegations-in-parliamentary-sexual-abuse-scandal

218 Laura Hughes, 'Former David Cameron adviser investigated over claim he pressured woman to meet wealthy businessman', *Telegraph*, 5 November 2017, www.telegraph.co.uk/news/2017/11/05/third-tory-mp-referred-partys-investigation-committee

219 Lizzy Buchan, 'Tory MPs Stephen Crabb and Chris Pincher cleared by party over sexual harassment claims', *Independent*, 23 December 2017, www.independent.co.uk/news/uk/politics/conservatives-sexual-harassment-stephen-crabb-chris-pincher-westminster-a8126101.html

220 'Summary of the Cabinet Secretary's report on allegations about Damian Green's conduct', Gov.uk, assets.publishing.service.gov.uk/government/uploads/system/uploads/attachment_data/file/670198/SUMMARY_OF_THE_CABINET_SECRETARY_S_REPORT_ON_ALLEGATIONS_ABOUT_DAMIAN_GREEN_S_CONDUCT.pdf

221 Gordon Rayner, 'Damian Green faces calls to stand down as MP after accusation of "dirty tricks" against Kate Maltby', *Telegraph*, 24 December 2017, www.telegraph.co.uk/news/2017/12/24/damian-green-faces-calls-stand-mp-accusation-dirty-tricks-against

222 Tom Harper and Caroline Wheeler, 'Damian Green accused of "dirty tricks" over leaked text messages', *The Times*, 24 December 2017, www.thetimes.co.uk/article/damian-green-accused-of-dirty-tricks-over-leaked-text-messages-92t2jzwvj

223 'MP Dan Poulter wins damages over Sunday Times sex assault claims', BBC, 25 February 2019, www.bbc.co.uk/news/uk-england-suffolk-47358003

224 Rachel Roberts, 'Tory MP says female journalists are fuelling Westminster sex scandal and behaving like "wilting flowers"', *Independent,* 11 November 2017, www.independent.co.uk /news/uk/politics/sir-roger-gale-tory-mp-female-journalists-wilting-flowers-sex-scandal-westminster-a8050206.html

225 Anna O'Donohue, 'VIDEO: Michael Fabricant says it's unfair to accuse MPs of sexual assault if "everyone was sloshed"', *iNews,* 31 October 2017, inews.co.uk/news/uk/video-tory-mp-says-unfair-accuse-blameless-people-assault-everyone-sloshed-100767

226 Alexandra Topping, 'Ex-MP Charlie Elphicke jailed for sexual assault now claiming universal credit', *Guardian,* 19 November 2021, www.theguardian.com/politics/2021/nov /19/ex-mp-charlie-elphicke-jailed-for-sexual-assault-now-claiming-universal-credit

227 Jane Merrick, 'I won't keep my silence: Michael Fallon lunged at me after our lunch', *Guardian,* 4 November 2017, www.theguardian.com/politics/commentisfree/2017/nov/04 /michael-fallon-lunged-at-me-jane-merrick

228 Lewis Goodall [@lewis_goodall], Twitter, 2 November 2017, twitter.com/lewis_goodall/ status/926041637826023424

229 Laura Kuenssberg [@bbclaurak], Twitter, 2 November 2017, twitter.com/bbclaurak/status /926042186361311232

230 Heather Stewart [@GuardianHeather], Twitter, 2 November 2017, twitter.com/ GuardianHeather/status/926043973495422976

231 John Rentoul, 'Do the Tories have a death wish? Their fallout over Gavin Williamson could destroy the party', *Independent,* 4 November 2017, www.independent.co.uk/voices/ tories-theresa-may-conservative-gavin-williamson-sexual-harassment-scandal-westminster-andrea-leadsom-a8037486.html

232 Robert Peston [@Peston], Twitter, 2 November 2017, twitter.com/Peston/status/926047500 808704001

233 Bradley Jolly, 'Defence Secretary's pet tarantula evicted from MoD HQ', *Metro,* 10 December 2017, metro.co.uk/2017/12/10/defence-secretarys-pet-tarantula-evicted-from-mod-hq-7147572

234 Jon Stone, 'The new International Development Secretary wanted to scrap what is now her department', *Independent,* 15 July 2016, www.independent.co.uk/news/uk/politics/new-international-development-secretary-priti-patel-called-for-department-for-international-development-to-be-scrapped-a7137331.html

235 James Landale, 'Priti Patel held undisclosed meetings in Israel', BBC, 3 November 2017, www.bbc.co.uk/news/uk-politics-41853561

236 'Priti Patel suggested UK should give aid to Israeli army after secret meeting with Benjamin Netanyahu', *Telegraph,* 7 November 2017, www.telegraph.co.uk/news/2017/11/07/priti-pat el-suggested-uk-should-give-aid-israeli-army-secret

237 Jon Stone, 'EU member states unanimously reject Israel's sovereignty over Golan Heights, defying Trump and Netanyahu', *Independent,* 28 March 2019, www.independent.co.uk/ news/world/europe/israel-golan-heights-eu-trump-netanyahu-syria-middle-east-a8843311 .html

238 Rajeev Syal and Harriet Sherwood, 'Priti Patel accuses Foreign Office of briefing against her over Israel meetings', *Guardian,* 3 November 2017, www.theguardian.com/politics/2017 /nov/03/priti-patel-held-undisclosed-meetings-israel

239 'Statement from International Development Secretary Priti Patel', Gov.uk, 6 November 2017, www.gov.uk/government/news/statement-from-international-development-secretary-priti-patel

240 'Priti Patel quits cabinet over Israel meetings row', BBC, 8 November 2017, www.bbc.com /news/uk-politics-41923007

241 Patrick Grafton-Green, Nicholas Cecil and Joe Murphy, 'Priti Patel's "flight back to London" tracked by tens of thousands of people as she faces Cabinet axe', *Evening Standard,* www.standard.co.uk/news/politics/more-than-20-000-people-track-priti-patel-s-flight-back-to-london-as-she-faces-cabinet-axe-a3685576.html

242 Rajeev Syal and Anushka Asthana, 'Priti Patel forced to resign over unofficial meetings with Israelis', *Guardian,* 8 November 2017, www.theguardian.com/politics/2017/ nov/08/priti-patel-forced-to-resign-over-unofficial-meetings-with-israelis

243 Rob Merrick, 'Boris Johnson refuses to apologise for putting Nazanin Zaghari-Ratcliffe at risk of longer Iranian prison sentence', *Independent*, 7 November 2017, www.independent.co.uk/news/uk/politics/boris-johnson-nazanin-zaghari-ratcliffe-iran-refuse-apology-prison-sentence-a8042296.html

244 'Nazanin Zaghari-Ratcliffe: I should have been freed six years ago', BBC, 21 March 2020, www.bbc.co.uk/news/uk-60819018

245 Steven Swinford, 'The Brexit mutineers: At least 15 Tory MPs rebel against leave date with threat to join forces with Labour', *Telegraph*, 14 November 2017, www.telegraph.co.uk/news/2017/11/14/nearly-20-tory-mps-threaten-rebel-against-brexit-date-brutal

246 Ibid.

247 Jennifer Rankin, 'London loses EU agencies to Paris and Amsterdam in Brexit relocation', *Guardian*, 20 November 2017, www.theguardian.com/politics/2017/nov/20/london-loses-european-medicines-agency-amsterdam-brexit-relocation

248 Benjamin Kentish, 'Brexit: Tory MP John Redwood tells foreign investors to withdraw money from UK', *Independent*, 15 November 2017, www.independent.co.uk/news/uk/politics/brexit-john-redwood-tory-mp-investors-withdraw-money-uk-economy-city-london-eu-a8056771.html

249 Nigel Morris, 'Boris Johnson accused by Tory MP of "major failure of diplomacy" as UK loses court seat', *iNews*, 21 November 2017, inews.co.uk/news/politics/boris-johnson-accused-tory-mp-major-failure-diplomacy-uk-loses-court-seat-105180

250 'Impact assessments of Brexit on the UK "don't exist"', BBC, 6 December 2017, www.bbc.c.uk/news/uk-politics-42249854

251 Rob Merrick, 'Brexit: David Davis admits Government has done no economic assessment of the UK crashing out of EU without deal', *Independent*, 15 March 2017, www.independent.co.uk/news/uk/politics/brexit-latest-news-david-davis-no-economic-impact-assess-uk-eu-leave-no-deal-select-committee-a7630626.html

252 Seema Malhotra, 'David Davis boasted of his Brexit impact analysis papers. Now he wishes they didn't exist', *New Statesman*, 29 November 2017, www.newstatesman.com/politics/staggers/2017/11/david-davis-boasted-his-brexit-impact-analysis-papers-now-he-wishes-they

253 'Impact assessments of Brexit on the UK "don't exist"', BBC, 6 November 2017, www.bbc.co.uk/news/uk-politics-42249854

254 Seema Malhotra, 'David Davis boasted of his Brexit impact analysis papers. Now he wishes they didn't exist'

255 'Impact assessments of Brexit on the UK "don't exist"', BBC, 6 November 2017, www.bbc.co.uk/news/uk-politics-42249854

256 Aubrey Allegretti, 'Brexit impact assessments "do not exist", David Davis admits', Sky News, 6 December 2017, news.sky.com/story/brexit-impact-assessments-do-not-exist-david-davis-admits-11158899

257 Alex Barker, Arthur Beesley and George Parker, 'Brexit deal falls through over Irish border dispute', *FT*, 4 December 2017, www.ft.com/content/983b64e8-d8e0-11e7-a039-c64b1c09b482

258 Michael Gove, 'The British people will be in control if they dislike the Brexit deal', *Telegraph*, 8 December 2017, www.telegraph.co.uk/news/2017/12/08/british-people-will-control-dislike-brexit-deal

259 'Brexit bill: Government loses key vote after Tory rebellion', BBC, 13 December 2017, www.bbc.co.uk/news/uk-politics-42346192

260 'Bob Spink found guilty of election fraud', BBC, 1 December 2017, www.bbc.co.uk/news/uk-england-essex-42201551

261 Nicola Slawson, 'Philip Hammond causes storm with remarks about disabled workers', *Guardian*, 7 December 2017, www.theguardian.com/politics/2017/dec/07/philip-hammond-causes-storm-with-remarks-about-disabled-workers

262 Press Association, 'Theresa May "set to abandon free vote pledge on foxhunting ban"', *Guardian*, 24 November 2017, www.theguardian.com/uk-news/2017/dec/24/theresa-may-set-to-abandon-free-vote-pledge-on-foxhunting-ban

263 Nadia Khomami, 'Morecambe MP stirs row after doubting poverty claims by local schools', *Guardian*, 15 December 2017, www.theguardian.com/uk-news/2017/dec/15/morecambe-mp-stirs-row-after-doubting-poverty-claims-by-local-schools

264 National Center for Advancing Translational Sciences, 'Disease at a Glance', rarediseases.info.nih.gov/diseases/5700/rickets

265 Nadia Khomami, 'Morecambe MP stirs row after doubting poverty claims by local schools'
266 Paul Knaggs, 'Cash for questions: Tory MP ordered to apologise after breaching paid advocacy rules', Labour Heartlands, 17 September 2020, labourheartlands.com/cash-for-questions-tory-mp-ordered-to-apologise-after-breaching-paid-advocacy-rules
267 Steven Hopkins, '"National Scandal" of 128,000 children spending Christmas day homeless', Huffington Post, 6 December 2017, www.huffingtonpost.co.uk/entry/national-scandal-of-128000-children_uk_5a27a4a9e4b0c2117626c476
268 Michael Savage, 'Theresa May faces new crisis after mass walkout over social policy', Guardian, 3 December 2017, www.theguardian.com/politics/2017/dec/02/theresa-may-crisis-mass-walkout-social-policy-alan-milburn
269 Heather Stewart and Nicola Slawson, Guardian, 30 December 2017, www.theguardian.com/politics/2017/dec/29/lord-adonis-quits-as-theresa-may-infrastructure-tsar-over-brexit
270 Daniel Ferrell-Schweppenstedde, 'UK charities will lose £258m of EU money after Brexit. Where's the plan?', Guardian, 7 December 2017, www.theguardian.com/voluntary-sector-network/2017/dec/07/charities-lose-at-least-258m-after-brexit-no-government-strategy
271 'Chancellor Philip Hammond's "no unemployed" remark attacked', BBC, 19 November 2017, www.bbc.co.uk/news/uk-politics-42043710
272 'Budget 2017: Plans to build 300,000 homes a year', BBC, 19 November 2017, www.bbc.co.uk/news/business-42043084
273 Henry Mance, 'May defies cronyism charge by rewarding Tory ally in honours list', FT, 29 December 2017, www.ft.com/content/e7f34642-ebe9-11e7-8713-513b1d7ca85a

2018: An Aggressive and Fruity Meltdown

1 'Cannock Jobcentre to close as Government closes 22 UK offices', Business Insider, 13 May 2011, www.business-live.co.uk/economic-development/cannock-jobcentre-close-government-closes-3921099
2 Jamie Grierson, 'Number of supervised offenders charged with violent crimes rises 21%', Guardian, 14 October 2018, www.theguardian.com/society/2018/oct/14/number-supervised-offenders-accused-violent-crimes-rises-england-wales
3 Jamie Doward, 'Chris Grayling's privatisation of probation service "a disaster"', Guardian, 30 June 2019, www.theguardian.com/politics/2019/jun/30/chris-grayling-probation-privatisation-disaster
4 Gwyn Topham, 'Chris Grayling could face private prosecution for "dooring" cyclist', Guardian, 16 December 2016, www.theguardian.com/politics/2016/dec/16/chris-grayling-could-face-private-prosecution-for-dooring-cyclist
5 David Singleton, 'Chris Grayling gets to be Tory party chairman… for all of 27 seconds', Total Politics, 8 January 2018, www.totalpolitics.com/articles/diary/chris-grayling-gets-be-tory-party-chairman%E2%80%A6-all-27-seconds
6 'Grayling: 'No obvious passenger benefit' to Midland Main Line electrification', RTM, 23 January 2018, www.railtechnologymagazine.com/Rail-News/grayling-no-obvious-passenger-benefit-to-midland-mainline-electrification
7 'Transport spending in north of England less per head than London', BBC, 4 December 2019, www.bbc.co.uk/news/uk-england-50592261
8 Simon Calder, 'Chris Grayling grilled over rail electrification programme as delays to soaring costs', 22 January 2018, www.independent.co.uk/travel/news-and-advice/chris-grayling-rail-electrification-gwr-great-western-diesel-electric-trains-trancks-damage-a8173116.html
9 'Transport Secretary accused of lying over scrapping of rail electrification schemes', Yorkshire Post, 29 March 2018, web.archive.org/web/20190211224541/www.yorkshirepost.co.uk/news/transport-secretary-accused-of-lying-over-scrapping-of-rail-electrification-schemes-1-9087599
10 Gwyn Topham, 'The great timetable fiasco: what's gone wrong with England's railways?', Guardian, 9 June 2018, www.theguardian.com/business/2018/jun/09/uk-railways-great-timetable-fiasco-whats-gone-wrong
11 Richard Johnstone and Sam Trendall, '"The government was correct not to bail out Carillion", MPs conclude', Public Technology, 17 May 2018, www.publictechnology.net/articles/news/%E2%80%98-government-was-correct-not-bail-out-carillion%E2%80%99-mps-conclude

12   'Northern Rail disruption cost businesses "almost £38 million"', ITV News, 30 July 2018,
     www.itv.com/news/2018-07-30/northern-rail-reintroducing-75-of-cancelled-services-after-
     timetable-chaos
13   'Northern Rail disruption cost businesses "almost £38 million"', ITV News
14   Comptroller and Auditor General, 'The Thameslink, Southern and Great Northern rail
     franchise', National Audit Office, 10 January 2018, www.nao.org.uk/wp-content/uploads/
     2018/01/The-Thameslink-Southern-and-Great-Northern-rail-franchise.pdf
15   Gwyn Topham, 'The great timetable fiasco: what's gone wrong with England's railways?'
16   'Train delays: "Lack of accountability" led to rail timetable chaos', BBC, 20 September 2018,
     www.bbc.co.uk/news/business-45572736
17   Danny Shaw, 'Birmingham Prison: Government takes over from G4S', BBC, 20 August
     2018, www.bbc.co.uk/news/uk-england-birmingham-45240742
18   Owen Bennett, 'Chris Grayling berated as work begins to turn motorway into 'no deal'
     Brexit lorry park without telling residents', City A.M., 11 October 2018, www.cityam.com
     /chris-grayling-berated-work-begins-turn-motorway-into-no
19   Oliver Wright, 'Grayling put drone law on hold before Gatwick chaos', The Times, 22
     December 2018, www.thetimes.co.uk/article/grayling-put-drone-law-on-hold-before-
     gatwick-flight-chaos-9tkqck0tg
20   Gwyn Topham, 'Gatwick drone disruption cost airport just £1.4m', Guardian, 18 June 2019,
     www.theguardian.com/uk-news/2019/jun/18/gatwick-drone-disruption-cost-airport-just-
     14m
21   Ashley Cowburn, 'Chris Grayling has "wasted £2.7bn in political blunders", says Labour',
     Independent, 1 March 2019, www.independent.co.uk/news/uk/politics/chris-grayling-ferry-
     contracts-blunders-cost-a8803296.html
22   Matt Farrah, 'A quick overview of nurses' salaries in the UK in 2021', Nurses, 10
     January 2021, web.archive.org/web/20210727225527/https://www.nurses.co.uk/
     blog/a-quick-overview-of-nurses--salaries-in-the-uk-in-2021/
23   '2018 British cabinet reshuffle', Wikipedia, last edited on 1 May 2022, en.wikipedia.org/
     wiki/2018_British_cabinet_reshuffle
24   Dan Bloom, 'Theresa May "set to sack up to a quarter of her Cabinet within weeks"', Mirror,
     31 December 2017, www.mirror.co.uk/news/politics/theresa-set-sack-up-quarter-11775783
25   Nicholas Soames [@NSoames], Twitter, 8 January 2018, twitter.com/NSoames/status/95047
     2504388345857
26   Wikipedia, '2018 British cabinet reshuffle', Last edited: 1 May 2022, en.wikipedia.org/wiki
     /2018_British_cabinet_reshuffle
27   Gavin Freeguard, 'The government reshuffle, in eight charts', Institute for Government, 20
     June 2017, www.instituteforgovernment.org.uk/blog/government-reshuffle-eight-charts
28   'Maria Caulfield: MP's new women's role sparks backlash', BBC, 8 January 2018,
     www.bbc.co.uk/news/uk-politics-42608737
29   Emilio Casalicchio, 'George Osborne: Theresa May's Cabinet reshuffle is the worst in
     modern history', Politics Home, 9 January 2018, www.politicshome.com/news/article/
     george-osborne-theresa-mays-cabinet-reshuffle-is-the-worst-in-modern-history
30   Denis Campbell and Pamela Duncan, 'NHS hospitals in England record worst ever A&E
     performance', Guardian, 8 February 2018, www.theguardian.com/society/2018/feb/08/nhs-
     hospitals-england-worst-a-and-e-performance
31   Alex Therrien and Nick Triggle, 'Health secretary Jeremy Hunt sorry as A&Es struggle to
     cope', BBC, 3 January 2018, www.bbc.co.uk/news/health-42552267
32   'Rough sleeping in England rises for seventh year', BBC, 25 January 2018, www.bbc.co.uk
     /news/uk-england-42817123
33   Rowena Mason, 'Boris Johnson proposes a 22-mile bridge across the Channel', Guardian,
     19 January 2018, www.theguardian.com/politics/2018/jan/19/boris-johnson-proposes-22-
     mile-bridge-across-the-channel
34   Jonathan Morrison, 'Boris Johnson's Channel bridge could cost £120bn, warn experts', The
     Times, 19 January 2018, www.thetimes.co.uk/article/britain-should-consider-building-
     bridge-to-france-says-boris-johnson-7h3wzfp80
35   Aisha Majid, 'How the cost of HS2 has surged', New Statesman, 21 June 2021,
     www.newstatesman.com/politics/2021/06/how-cost-hs2-has-surged
36   'Grasping Large Numbers', EHD, www.ehd.org/science_technology_largenumbers.php

37   Alberto Nardelli, 'This Leaked Government Brexit Analysis Says The UK Will Be Worse
     Off In Every Scenario', *Buzz Feed News*, 29 January 2018, www.buzzfeed.com/albertonardel
     li/the-governments-own-brexit-analysis-says-the-uk-will-be?utm_term=.rkzNVerE6#.gtPb
     XNpjn
38   Grahame Allen, 'Recession and recovery', House of Commons Library Research,
     www.parliament.uk/globalassets/documents/commons/lib/research/key_issues/Key-Issues-
     Recession-and-recovery.pdf
39   Alberto Nardelli, 'This Leaked Government Brexit Analysis Says The UK Will Be Worse
     Off In Every Scenario'
40   Ibid.
41   Anushka Asthana, 'Brexit minister forced into apology for maligning civil service',
     Guardian, 1 February 2018, www.theguardian.com/politics/2018/feb/01/brexit-minister-
     steve-baker-accused-for-second-time-of-maligning-civil-service
42   Steve Baker [@SteveBakerHW], Twitter, 1 February 2018, twitter.com/SteveBakerHW/
     status/959155506655973377
43   Rachel Wearmouth, 'Rich Tory Donors Pay Ben Bradley's Legal Bills Over Corbyn Spy
     Tweet', *Huffington Post*, 9 June 2018, www.huffingtonpost.co.uk/entry/rich-tory-donors-
     foot-ben-bradleys-legal-bill-after-corbyn-spy-tweet_uk_5b1ba870e4b0adfb82696bd1
44   'Theresa May rejects EU's draft option for Northern Ireland', BBC, 28 February 2018,
     www.bbc.co.uk/news/uk-politics-43224785
45   Jon Stone, 'Brexit: EU rejects Theresa May's trade plan and warns UK will suffer "negative
     economic consequences"', *Independent*, 7 March 2018, www.independent.co.uk/news/uk
     /politics/brexit-theresa-may-trade-plan-rejected-eu-donald-tusk-uk-relations-latest-
     updates-a8243721.html
46   'The UK and EU agree terms for Brexit transition period', BBC, 19 March 2018,
     www.bbc.co.uk/news/uk-politics-43456502
47   Caitlin Morrison, 'Brexit already costing UK £800m per week, Bank of England economist
     says', *Independent*, 14 February 2019, www.independent.co.uk/news/business/news/brexit-
     cost-uk-economy-bank-england-jan-vlieghe-economist-a8779171.html?__twitter_impressi
     on=true
48   D. Clark, 'Number of people receiving three days' worth of emergency food by Trussell
     Trust foodbanks in the United Kingdom from 2008/09 to 2021/22', Statista, 11 May 2022,
     www.statista.com/statistics/382695/uk-foodbank-users
49   Wikipedia, 'Proposed UK Internet age verification system', Last edited: 22 June 2022,
     en.wikipedia.org/wiki/Proposed_UK_Internet_age_verification_system
50   Richard Partington, 'National minimum wage rise still fails to cover living costs, study
     shows', *Guardian*, 31 March 2018, www.theguardian.com/society/2018/mar/31/national-
     minimum-wage-rise-still-fails-to-cover-living-costs-study-show
51   'British workers "among worst idlers", suggest Tory MPs', BBC, 18 August 2012,
     www.bbc.co.uk/news/uk-politics-19300051
52   Benjamin Kentish, 'Gavin Williamson: Tory Defence Secretary admits to
     'kissing' trysts with married former colleague', *Independent*, 26 January 2018,
     www.independent.co.uk/news/uk/politics/gavin-williamson-cheating-defence-secretary-
     admit-romance-affair-russia-marriage-wife-a8179056.html
53   Ewen MacAskill, 'Russia should 'go away and shut up', says UK defence secretary', *Guardian*,
     15 March 2018, www.theguardian.com/politics/2018/mar/15/russia-ripping-up-the-
     international-rule-book-says-defence-secretary
54   Nia Griffith, 'Unprecedented cuts Conservatives have made to defence since 2010 – Nia
     Griffith', Labour, 16 July 2019, labour.org.uk/press/unprecedented-cuts-conservatives-
     made-defence-since-2010-nia-griffith
55   Pippa Crerar, 'Amber Rudd says police cuts not to blame for violent crime rise', Guardian, 8
     April 2018, www.theguardian.com/politics/2018/apr/08/amber-rudd-says-police-cuts-not
     -to-blame-for-violent-rise
56   Ned Simons, 'Tory Home Office Minister Victoria Atkins admits she does
     not know how many police officers there are', *Huffington Post*, 9 April 2018,
     www.huffingtonpost.co.uk/entry/tory-home-office-minister-victoria-atkins-admits-she-
     does-not-know-how-many-police-officers-there-are_uk_5acb5979e4b0337ad1e9fa8b

57 Vikram Dodd, 'Police cuts 'likely contributed' to rise in violent crime, leaked report reveals', *Guardian,* 9 April 2018, www.theguardian.com/uk-news/2018/apr/08/police-cuts-likely-contributed-to-rise-in-violent-leaked-report-reveals

58 Ned Simons, 'Tory Home Office Minister Victoria Atkins admits she does not know how many police officers there are'

59 Tony Collins, 'NHS trusts exit £27m Capita deal', Campaign4Change, 24 June 2014, ukcampaign4change.com/2014/06/24/nhs-trusts-exit-27m-capita-deal

60 Amelia Gentleman, 'Delays and disarray shatter lives of new disability claimants', *Guardian,* 27 January 2015, www.theguardian.com/society/2015/jan/27/delays-disability-benefit-pip-claimants-mps-scrutiny

61 'Capita fined £2m for CRB vetting delays', Public Finance, 22 May 2003 www.publicfinance.co.uk/news/2003/05/capita-fined-%C2%A32m-crb-vetting-delays

62 'Capita Financial fined for fraud', BBC News, 17 March 2006, http://news.bbc.co.uk/1/hi/business/4813748.stm

63 Lyndsey Telford, 'NHS hit by nurses' pay scandal', *Daily Telegraph,* 23 December 2015, Press Reader, www.pressreader.com/uk/the-daily-telegraph/20151223/281487865311121

64 Lyndsey Telford, Claire Newell, Edward Malnick and Luke Heighton, 'NHS hit by locum agency nurses' pay scandal', *Telegraph,* 22 December 2015, www.telegraph.co.uk/news/investigations/nhs-hit-by-locum-agency-nurses-pay-scandal

65 'Schools scandal hits Capita', BBC, 5 September 2002, http://news.bbc.co.uk/1/hi/business/2239095.stm

66 Simon Allin, '"Value for money" row over Capita payments', *Barnet Post,* 18 October 2021, barnetpost.co.uk/value-for-money-row-over-capita-payments

67 Chris Green and Oliver Wright, 'Capita accused of using major government contract to short-change small companies, driving some out of business', *Independent,* 10 February 2015, www.independent.co.uk/news/uk/politics/capita-accused-using-major-government-contract-short-change-small-companies-driving-some-out-business-10037349.html

68 Mark Leftly, 'Capita makes £100m in army recruitment fiasco', *Independent,* 26 June 2014, www.independent.co.uk/news/business/news/capita-makes-ps100m-army-recruitment-fiasco-9563829.html

69 Guardian Staff, '"It's inhumane": the Windrush victims who have lost jobs, homes and loved ones', *Guardian,* 20 April 2018, www.theguardian.com/uk-news/2018/apr/20/its-inhumane-the-windrush-victims-who-have-lost-jobs-homes-and-loved-ones

70 Gary Younge, 'Hounding Commonwealth citizens is no accident. It's cruelty by design', *Guardian,* 13 April 2018, www.theguardian.com/commentisfree/2018/apr/13/commonwealth-citizens-harassment-british-immigration-policy

71 Amelia Gentleman, 'Londoner denied NHS cancer care: "It's like I'm being left to die"', *Guardian,* 10 March 2018, www.theguardian.com/uk-news/2018/mar/10/denied-free-nhs-cancer-care-left-die-home-office-commonwealth

72 Nick Hopkins, 'Amber Rudd letter to PM reveals "ambitious but deliverable" removals target', *Guardian,* 29 April 2018, www.theguardian.com/politics/2018/apr/29/amber-rudd-letter-to-pm-reveals-ambitious-but-deliverable-removals-target

73 Mary Bulman, 'Home Office tells destitute Windrush woman to seek charity help to feed her child', *Independent,* 10 August 2018, www.independent.co.uk/news/uk/home-news/home-office-windrush-woman-seek-charity-help-nhs-nurse-childcare-a8482396.html

74 'Sajid Javid says Home Office's "hostile environment" towards immigrants to be reviewed after Windrush', ITV News, 3 June 2018, www.itv.com/news/2018-06-03/home-offices-hostile-environment-faces-review-after-windrush-sajid-javid

75 Harriet Agerholm, 'Windrush generation: Home Office 'set them up to fail', say MPs', *Independent,* 3 July 2018, www.independent.co.uk/news/uk/home-news/windrush-home-office-set-them-fail-mps-affairs-select-committee-a8428041.html

76 Basit Mahmood, 'Lawyers slam deportation flights to Jamaica as "appalling insult to justice"', *Metro,* 6 February 2019, metro.co.uk/2019/02/06/lawyers-slam-deportation-flights-jamaica-appalling-insult-justice-8461061

77 'Evening Standard's Evgeny Lebedev says "I am not some agent of Russia" amid peerage scrutiny', ITV News, 11 March 2022, www.itv.com/news/london/2022-03-11/lord-evgeny-lebedev-i-am-not-some-agent-of-russia

78 James Cuisk, 'Revealed: Boris, the Russian oligarch and the Page 3 model', Open Democracy, 6 July 2019, www.opendemocracy.net/en/opendemocracyuk/revealed-boris-russian-oligarch-and-page-3-model

79 Nick Hopkins, 'Morning after: Boris Johnson recovers from Lebedev's exotic Italian party', *Guardian*, 26 July 2019, www.theguardian.com/politics/2019/jul/26/boris-johnson-security-evgeny-lebedev-perugia-party

80 John Sweeney, 'What changed to make Evgeny Lebedev: No longer a security risk?', *Byline Times*, 20 August 2020, bylinetimes.com/2020/08/20/sweeney-investigates-what-changed-to-make-evgeny-lebedev-no-longer-a-security-risk

81 Tim Shipman, 'Boris Johnson "is a security risk" because of his private life, say allies of Jeremy Hunt', *The Times*, 23 June 2019, www.thetimes.co.uk/article/boris-johnson-is-a-security-risk-over-his-private-life-say-allies-of-jeremy-hunt-07l86nc8r

82 James Cuisk, 'Revealed: Boris, the Russian oligarch and the Page 3 model'

83 Nick Hopkins, 'Boris Johnson refuses to answer questions over party in Lebedev mansion', *Guardian*, 18 July 2019, www.theguardian.com/politics/2019/jul/18/boris-johnson-refuses-to-answer-questions-over-party-in-lebedev-mansion

84 James Cuisk, Number 10 abused its power by demanding cover-up of donors and friends of Boris in report on Russian influence', openDemocracy, 11 November 2019, www.opendemocracy.net/en/dark-money-investigations/number-10-abused-its-power-demanding-cover-donors-and-friends-boris-report-russian-influence

85 Nick Sommerlad, 'Dominic Raab's diary secretary caught selling sex online through sugar daddy website sparking security fears', *Mirror*, 26 April 2018, www.mirror.co.uk/news/politics/top-tory-minister-dominic-raabs-12428656

86 'England local elections 2018', BBC, www.bbc.co.uk/news/topics/cz3nmp2eyxgt/england-local-elections-2018

87 Damien Gayle, 'UK has seen 'Brexit-related' growth in racism, says UN representative', *Guardian*, 11 May 2018, www.theguardian.com/politics/2018/may/11/uk-has-seen-brexit-related-growth-in-racism-says-un-representative

88 dave [@davemacladd], Twitter, 26 January 2018, twitter.com/davemacladd/status/101163638278631424

89 Graeme Wearden, 'UK households £900 worse off since Brexit vote says Bank, but FTSE hits new high - as it happened', *Guardian*, 22 May 2018, www.theguardian.com/business/live/2018/may/22/bank-of-england-governor-mark-carney-grilling-mps-rates-uk-economy-business-live?page=with:block-5b03ecd3e4b0738b887458e6

90 Wikipedia, 'Jeremy Hosking', Last edited: 3 June 2022, en.wikipedia.org/wiki/Jeremy_Hosking

91 Best for Britain [@BestForBritain], Twitter, 29 May 2018, twitter.com/BestForBritain/status/1001432078091735040

92 Ibid.

93 'May loses 15th Lords vote on Brexit bill as peers vote to keep EU environmental standards - Politics live', *Guardian*, 16 May 2018, www.theguardian.com/politics/blog/live/2018/may/16/pmqs-may-corbyn-brexit-uk-wont-benefit-from-free-trade-deal-with-us-say-harvard-academics-politics-live

94 'May was sunniest and warmest ever recorded in the UK', ITV News, 1 June 2018, www.itv.com/news/2018-06-01/may-was-sunniest-and-warmest-on-record

95 'Temperatures reach 30C on the UK's hottest day of the year', BBC, 25 June 2018, www.bbc.co.uk/news/uk-44604782

96 'Heatwave: 2018 was the joint hottest summer for UK', BBC, 3 September 2018, www.bbc.co.uk/news/uk-45399134

97 'Winter Hill: Crews battle "aggressive" merged moorland fire', BBC, 1 July 2018, www.bbc.co.uk/news/uk-england-lancashire-44671875

98 'Wanstead Flats fire: Crews "praying for rain" amid heatwave', BBC, 16 July 2018, www.bbc.co.uk/news/uk-england-london-44848268

99 'Heatwave: 2018 was the joint hottest summer for UK', BBC, 3 September 2018, www.bbc.co.uk/news/uk-45399134

100 'Heathrow Airport: Cabinet approves new runway plan', BBC, 5 June 2018, www.bbc.co.uk/news/uk-politics-44357580

101 'Boris Johnson to fight bigger Heathrow but will not resign', BBC, 12 May 2015, www.bbc.co.uk/news/uk-politics-32703425

102 'Decade in Review: A look back at what happened in 2018', Sky News, 31 December 2019, news.sky.com/story/decade-in-review-a-look-back-at-what-happened-in-2018-11896918

103 Greg Heffer, 'Controversial Heathrow expansion gets government go-ahead', Sky News, 6 June 2018, news.sky.com/story/battle-looms-after-government-gives-go-ahead-for-heathrow-third-runway-11395738

104 '£1.3bn Swansea Bay tidal lagoon project thrown out', BBC, 25 June 2018, www.bbc.co.uk/news/uk-wales-south-west-wales-44589083

105 'Greg Hands quits as minister over Heathrow expansion', BBC, 21 June 2018, www.bbc.co.uk/news/uk-politics-44561170

106 Pippa Crerar and Peter Walker, 'Justice minister Phillip Lee resigns over Brexit policy', Guardian, 12 June 2018, www.theguardian.com/politics/2018/jun/12/justice-minister-phillip-lee-resign-over-brexit-policy

107 Peter Walker, 'Tory MP Christopher Chope blocks progress of upskirting bill', Guardian, 15 June 2018, www.theguardian.com/world/2018/jun/15/tory-mp-christopher-chope-blocks-progress-of-upskirting-bill

108 'May "disappointed" at upskirting law block', BBC, 15 June 2018, www.bbc.co.uk/news/uk-politics-44496427

109 John Dickens, 'Another studio school to close – meaning nearly half have wound up', Schools Week, 23 October 2018, schoolsweek.co.uk/another-studio-school-to-close-meaning-nearly-half-have-wound-up

110 Sonia Sodha, 'The great academy schools scandal', Guardian, 22 July 2018, www.theguardian.com/education/2018/jul/22/academy-schools-scandal-failing-trusts

111 Rajeev Syal, 'Unqualified daughter of minister teaches in his academy schools', Guardian, 12 May 2016, www.theguardian.com/education/2016/may/12/unqualified-daughter-of-minister-teaches-in-his-academy-schools

112 Pippa Allen-Kinross, 'Revealed: Uncovered emails discuss "review" of studio schools programme, but DfE still denies it happened', Schools Week, 15 September 2018, schoolsweek.co.uk/revealed-uncovered-emails-discuss-review-of-studio-schools-programme-but-dfe-still-denies-it-happened

113 'UK automotive industry urges rethink on Brexit red lines as uncertainty bites', SMMT, 26 June 2018, www.smmt.co.uk/2018/06/uk-automotive-industry-urges-rethink-on-brexit-red-lines-as-uncertainty-bites

114 Zosia Kmietowicz, 'BMA votes to oppose Brexit "as a whole" and calls for public final say on deal', BMJ, 27 June 2018, www.bmj.com/content/361/bmj.k2821

115 Caitlin Morrison, 'Investment in UK car industry halves as Brexit uncertainty bites', Independent, 26 June 2018, www.independent.co.uk/news/business/news/brexit-uk-car-industry-investment-smmt-a8417071.html

116 'BMW joins Airbus in Brexit warning', BBC, 22 June 2018, www.bbc.co.uk/news/business-44582831

117 'No-deal Brexit "catastrophic" for British farming', NFU Online, www.nfuonline.com/news/brexit-news/eu-referendum-news/no-deal-catastrophic-for-british-farming

118 Dan Roberts, 'No-deal Brexit would trigger wave of red tape for UK drivers and hauliers', Guardian, 8 February 2018, www.theguardian.com/politics/2018/feb/08/no-deal-brexit-would-trigger-wave-of-red-tape-for-uk-drivers-and-hauliers

119 Steven Morris and Rory Carroll, '"Betrayed": UK fishing industry says Brexit deal threatens long-term damage', Guardian, 28 December 2020, www.theguardian.com/politics/2020/dec/28/betrayed-uk-fishing-industry-says-brexit-deal-threatens-long-term-damage

120 Alex Hern, 'Britain's tech sector overwhelmingly opposed to Brexit', Guardian, 4 March 2016, www.theguardian.com/technology/2016/mar/04/britains-tech-sector-overwhelmingly-opposed-to-brexit

121 Adam Vaughan, 'Brexit risks energy shortages and bigger bills, peers warn', Guardian, 29 January 2018, www.theguardian.com/business/2018/jan/29/brexit-risks-energy-shortages-and-bigger-bills-peers-warn

122 'Brexit: Universities warn no deal is "biggest-ever threat"', BBC, 4 January 2019, www.bbc.co.uk/news/education-46748512

123 Will Martin, 'The City of London issued a stark warning about the future of European finance after Brexit — and the EU is listening', Business Insider, 31 July 2018, www.businessinsider.com/punitive-brexit-approach-to-city-of-london-will-hurt-eu-2018-7?r=US&IR=T

124 'UK secured Nissan investment with Brexit relief promise – source', Reuters, 27 October 2016, www.reuters.com/article/uk-britain-eu-nissan-support-idUKKCN12R1AK?edition-redirect=uk

125 Ivan Fallon, 'UK government's £37 billion bailout of Northern Rock in 2007 pays off', National News, 5 September 2017, www.thenationalnews.com/business/uk-government-s-37-billion-bailout-of-northern-rock-in-2007-pays-off-1.625760

126 Andrew Pierce, 'Suffocating heat, dark threats and the moment rebels blinked: ANDREW PIERCE tells the inside story of the fateful Brexit summit at Chequers', Daily Mail, 9 July 2019, www.dailymail.co.uk/news/article-5931637/The-inside-story-fateful-Brexit-summit-Chequers.html

127 Jason Farrell, 'Phones to be seized at Theresa May's Chequers Brexit talks amid cabinet plotting', Sky News, 6 July 2018, news.sky.com/story/phones-to-be-seized-at-theresa-mays-chequers-brexit-talks-amid-cabinet-plotting-11427649

128 Aamna Mohdin, 'The decision-making style that helps leaders survive can also thwart their legacy', Quartz, 18 July 2018, qz.com/1328805/theresa-mays-closed-decision-making-style-is-a-big-gamble-with-brexit

129 Andrew Pierce, 'Suffocating heat, dark threats and the moment rebels blinked: ANDREW PIERCE tells the inside story of the fateful Brexit summit at Chequers'

130 Ibid.

131 Ibid.

132 'Brexit: David Davis' resignation letter and May's reply in full', BBC, 9 July 2018, www.bbc.co.uk/news/uk-politics-44761416

133 Heather Stewart, 'Brexit secretary David Davis resigns plunging government into crisis', Guardian, 9 July 2018, www.theguardian.com/politics/2018/jul/08/david-davis-resigns-as-brexit-secretary-reports-say

134 'Boris Johnson compares Chequers deal to "suicide vest"', BBC, 9 September 2018, www.bbc.co.uk/news/uk-politics-45462900

135 Alex McIntyre, 'Bolton West MP Chris Green quits Department for Transport role over Brexit', The Bolton News, 9 July 2018, http://www.theboltonnews.co.uk/news/16343246.bolton-west-mp-chris-green-quits-department-for-transport-role-over-brexit

136 Alan Selby, 'Andrew Griffiths resigns over perverted demands he made in 2,000 texts sent to two barmaids', Mirror, 11 August 2018, www.mirror.co.uk/news/politics/married-tory-minister-andrew-griffiths-12919581

137 Dan Sabbagh and Peter Walker, 'Brexit white paper seeks free movement for skilled workers and students', Guardian, 12 July 2018, www.theguardian.com/politics/2018/jul/12/brexit-white-paper-seeks-free-movement-for-skilled-workers-and-students

138 Jay Rayner, 'Food and Brexit: will our cupboards be bare?', Guardian, 15 September 2018, www.theguardian.com/food/2018/sep/15/food-and-brexit-will-the-cupboard-be-bare-jay-rayner

139 Lisa O'Carroll, 'Brexit: farmers criticise temporary agricultural worker visa scheme', Guardian, 6 September 2018, www.theguardian.com/environment/2018/sep/06/government-to-issue-temporary-work-visas-to-help-uk-fruit-farmers

140 Andrew Sparrow, 'May survives Tory Brexit rebellion with narrow Commons victory – as it happened', Guardian, 16 July 2018, www.theguardian.com/politics/blog/live/2018/jul/16/brexit-mays-plan-dead-say-tory-remainers-and-leavers-jointly-ahead-of-key-votes-politics-live

141 '"We're the opposition": Rees-Mogg and his European Research Group', Guardian, 20 July 2018, www.theguardian.com/politics/2018/jul/20/opposition-jacob-rees-mogg-european-research-group-profile

142 The Constitution Blog, 'Monitor 71 — Brexit: the constitution under strain', The Constitution Union Blog, 11 March 2019, constitution-unit.com/2019/03/11/monitor-71-brexit-the-constitution-under-strain

143 '"We're the opposition": Rees-Mogg and his European Research Group', Guardian, 20 July 2018, www.theguardian.com/politics/2018/jul/20/opposition-jacob-rees-mogg-european-research-group-profile

144 Dan Bloom, Michael Pearson and Liam Thorp, 'This was the moment Esther Mcvey was forced to make a toe-curling apology after misleading parliament over Universal Credit roll out', Liverpool Echo, 4 July 2018, www.liverpoolecho.co.uk/news/local-news/moment-esther-mcvey-forced-make-14865480

145 Ibid.

146 Ibid.

147 Peter Walker, 'Tory MP who blocked upskirting bill objects to women's conference', *Guardian*, 17 July 2018, www.theguardian.com/politics/2018/jul/17/tory-mp-christopher-chope-who-blocked-upskirting-bill-objects-to-womens-conference

148 Jemima Kelly, 'Grant Shapps resigns from blockchain positions after FTAV discovers secret pay deal', *FT*, 1 August 2018, www.ft.com/content/cd8f78f8-2850-3109-b577-269eedb1e5c2

149 'Boris Johnson faces criticism over burka "letter box" jibe', BBC, 6 August 2018, www.bbc.co.uk/news/uk-politics-45083275

150 Sayeeda Warsi [@SayeedaWarsi], Twitter, 6 August 2018, twitter.com/SayeedaWarsi/status/1026456785258008576

151 'Boris Johnson "won't apologise" for burka comments', BBC, 7 August 2018, www.bbc.co.uk/news/uk-politics-45096519

152 Graeme Demianyk, 'Jacob Rees-Mogg says it could take 50 years to reap the benefits of Brexit', *Huffington Post*, 23 July 2018, www.huffingtonpost.co.uk/entry/jacob-rees-mogg-economy-brexit_uk_5b54e3b5e4b0de86f48e3566

153 Peter Moore, 'How Britain voted at the EU referendum', YouGov, 27 July 2016, yougov.co.uk/topics/politics/articles-reports/2016/06/27/how-britain-voted

154 Graeme Demianyk, 'Jacob Rees-Mogg says it could take 50 years to reap the benefits of Brexit'

155 'UK's "no-deal" Brexit plans warn of credit card fees', BBC, 23 August 2018, www.bbc.co.uk/news/uk-politics-45274972

156 Siba Jackson, 'Army "on standby" to deliver food amid shortage of lorry drivers', *Metro*, 8 August 2021, metro.co.uk/2021/08/08/army-on-standby-to-deliver-food-amid-shortage-of-lorry-drivers-15057758

157 Rory Carroll, 'Karen Bradley admits ignorance of Northern Ireland politics', *Guardian*, 7 September 2018, www.theguardian.com/politics/2018/sep/07/karen-bradley-admits-not-understanding-northern-irish-politics

158 David Pegg, Felicity Lawrence and Rob Evans, 'Tory Brexit faction censured for using public funds for campaigning', *Guardian*, 14 September 2018, www.theguardian.com/politics/2018/sep/14/tory-brexit-faction-erg-censured-for-using-public-funds-for-campaigning

159 Alix Cuthbertson, 'Brexit will REDUCE food, wine and clothes costs by 20% - Rees-Mogg fires back at Remainers', *Express*, 22 July 2017, www.express.co.uk/news/politics/831450/Jacob-Rees-Mogg-Brexit-food-wine-clothes-shoes-lower-20-per-cent

160 Fiona Harvey, 'Farm incomes fall by 20% in a year due to weather, Covid and Brexit', *Guardian*, 28 May 2021, www.theguardian.com/environment/2021/may/28/farm-incomes-fall-by-20-in-a-year-due-to-weather-covid-and-brexit

161 'Food makers are warning of price hikes – here's why', *Speciality Food Magazine*, 28 July 2021, www.specialityfoodmagazine.com/news/food-price-rise-warnings-brexit-regulations

162 Sarah Butler, 'UK appoints food supplies minister amid fears of no-deal Brexit', *Guardian*, 26 September 2018, www.theguardian.com/business/2018/sep/26/uk-appoints-food-supplies-minister-amid-fears-of-no-deal-brexit

163 Dan Sabbagh and Daniel Boffey, 'Theresa May demands respect from EU over Brexit as pound falls', *Guardian*, 21 September 2018, www.theguardian.com/politics/2018/sep/21/theresa-may-demands-respect-from-eu-in-brexit-negotiations

164 'Philip Hammond insists Chequers Brexit Agreement is still alive', LBC, 1 October 2018, www.lbc.co.uk/radio/presenters/nick-ferrari/philip-hammond-insists-chequers-is-alive

165 Dan Sabbagh and Daniel Boffey, 'Theresa May demands respect from EU over Brexit as pound falls'

166 Charles Michel [@eucopresident], Twitter, 4 October 2018, twitter.com/eucopresident/status/1047825916905357312

167 'Brexit Timeline: Key dates as the UK prepares to leave the EU', LBC, 13 April 2019, www.lbc.co.uk/hot-topics/brexit/brexit-timeline-of-key-dates

168 'Brexit: David Davis calls for cabinet rebellion over PM's plan', BBC, 14 October 2018, www.bbc.co.uk/news/uk-politics-45853384

169 'Brexit Timeline: Key dates as the UK prepares to leave the EU', LBC

170 'Farage "happy to have another referendum in 20 years"', Sky News, 20 October 2018, news.sky.com/story/farage-happy-to-have-another-referendum-in-20-years-11530869

171 'user-guide-policy-changes-mar22', Gov.uk, assets.publishing.service.gov.uk/government/ uploads/system/uploads/attachment_data/file/1010857/user-guide-policy-changes-jun21.ods

172 Jamie Grierson and Peter Walker, 'Sajid Javid backs plans for stricter citizenship rules after Brexit', *Guardian*, 2 October 2018, www.theguardian.com/uk-news/2018/oct/02/ immigrant-language-criteria-to-harden-after-brexit-says-sajid-javid

173 Jasmin Gray, 'Transport Secretary Chris Grayling ridiculed for arriving seven minutes late to his own speech', *Huffington Post*, 1 October 2018, www.huffingtonpost.co.uk/ entry/chris-grayling-late-conference-speech_uk_5bb200c7e4b0343b3dc21d08

174 'Theresa May's conference speech: what's the verdict?', *Guardian*, 3 October 2018, www.the guardian.com/commentisfree/2018/oct/03/theresa-may-conference-speech-verdict-conservative-birmingham

175 Harry Cockburn, 'Tory MP suggests all English people entitled to Irish passport', *Independent*, 17 October 2018, www.independent.co.uk/news/uk/home-news/irish-passport-england-uk-andrew-bridgen-tory-mp-brexit-border-eu-a8587286.html

176 John Spiers, 'Tory Brexiteer, Andrew Bridgen makes a fool of himself in car crash video with Stephen Nolan', YouTube, 15 October 2018, www.youtube.com/watch?v=8QzOdCq Fbfs

177 Matt Chorley, 'The Midlands Machiavelli is an assassin who'd put his weapon on expenses', *The Times*, 17 November 2018, 1www.thetimes.co.uk/article/the-midlands-machiavelli-is-an-assassin-whod-put-his-weapon-on-expenses-jsblcj3cg

178 Simon Jack, 'UK firms "near point of no return"', BBC, 21 October 2018, www.bbc.co.uk/ news/business-45931537

179 Chloe Chaplain, 'Stand Up 4 Brexit: A full list of the 50 MPs who have publicly backed the anti-Chequers campaign', *iNews*, 23 October 2018, inews.co.uk/news/brexit/stand-up-4-b rexit-a-full-list-of-the-44-mps-who-have-publicly-backed-the-anti-chequers-campaign-21 2636

180 John Crace, 'How many letters are there in ERG? Not 48, that's for sure', *Guardian*, 20 November 2018, www.theguardian.com/politics/2018/nov/20/erg-european-research-gro up-jacob-rees-mogg

181 Lucy Middleton, 'Theresa May is "11 letters away from vote of no confidence"', *Metro*, 17 November 2018, metro.co.uk/2018/11/17/theresa-may-is-11-letters-away-from-vote-of-no-confidence-8150279

182 Rachel Sylvester, 'It's still Europe that could rip the Tories apart', *The Times*, 25 July 2017, www.thetimes.co.uk/article/b34e93c0-707d-11e7-8eac-856e9b33761e

183 Josh Withey, 'Minister sums up the disaster that is Brexit in one damning sentence', indy100, 25 July 2017, www.indy100.com/news/brexit-disaster-damning-sentence-theresa-may-conservatives-destroy-the-country-7858891

184 Rob Merrick, 'Brexit secretary Dominic Raab says he "hadn't quite understood" importance of Dover-Calais crossing', *Independent*, 8 November 2018, www.independent.co.uk/news/uk/politics/brexit-latest-dominic-raab-trade-eu-france-calais-dover-economy-finance-deal-a8624036.html

185 Andrew Sparrow, 'Critics line up after May wins cabinet support – as it happened', *Guardian*, 15 November 2018, www.theguardian.com/politics/live/2018/nov/14/brexit-deal-theresa-may-conservatives-meet-decide-cabinet-politics-live?CMP=share_btn_tw&page= with:block-5beccebfe4b0772932e1ff6d#block-5beccebfe4b0772932e1ff6d

186 Sam Coates and Francis Elliot, 'Brexit: Minister in 'meltdown' at end of five-hour cabinet marathon', *The Times*, 15 November 2018, www.thetimes.co.uk/article/aef752f0-e861-11e8-a9c0-ffbf0f2a8629

187 Heather Stewart, 'Jo Johnson quits as minister over Theresa May's Brexit plan', *Guardian*, 9 November 2018, www.theguardian.com/politics/2018/nov/09/jo-johnson-quits-as-minister-over-theresa-mays-brexit-plan-boris

188 'Brexit: Dominic Raab and Esther McVey among ministers to quit over EU agreement', BBC, 15 November 2018, www.bbc.co.uk/news/uk-politics-46219495

189 'Stephen Barclay named new Brexit Secretary', BBC, 16 November 2018, www.bbc.co.uk/news/uk-46241693

190 Kate Ferguson, 'Has Gove turned down the Brexit job? Face of Vote Leave "refused May's offer unless he is allowed to go back to Brussels and renegotiate the deal"', *Daily Mail*, 15 November 2018, www.dailymail.co.uk/news/article-6394295/Michael-Gove-refused-Mays-offer-Brexit-Secretary-unless-renegotiate-deal.html

191 Terri-Ann Williams, 'The gang of five's ultimatum: Change the EU deal or we quit. Michael Gove and his four fellow Cabinet Brexiteers plot from within to renegotiate Theresa May's draft agreement', *Daily Mail*, 17 November 2018, www.dailymail.co.uk/news/article-64003 73/Michael-Gove-leads-four-Cabinet-Brexiteers-brink-resignation.html

192 'EU leaders agree UK's Brexit deal at Brussels summit', BBC, 25 November 2018, www.bbc.co.uk/news/uk-46334649

193 'Theresa May suffers three Brexit defeats in Commons', BBC, 5 December 2018, www.bbc.co.uk/news/uk-politics-46446694

194 Pippa Crerar, 'Humiliation for Theresa May during 63 minutes of mayhem that left Brexit talks in chaos', *Mirror*, 5 December 2018, www.mirror.co.uk/news/uk-news/humiliation-theresa-during-63-minutes-13686191

195 'Former leader Nigel Farage quits UKIP', BBC, 4 December 2018, www.bbc.co.uk/news/uk-politics-46448299

196 'Brexit: Legal advice warns of Irish border "stalemate"', BBC, 5 December 2018, www.bbc.co.uk/news/uk-politics-46451970

197 'Brexit Timeline: Key dates as the UK prepares to leave the EU', LBC

198 Ibid.

199 Hamish MacPherson, 'Is Theresa May the worst PM in history? Yes she is ... this is why', *National*, 25 May 2019, www.thenational.scot/news/17664101.theresa-may-worst-pm-history-yes

200 Jessica Elgot, 'The last-minute pledges and promises that helped May survive leadership challenge', *Guardian*, 12 December 2018, www.theguardian.com/politics/2018/dec/12/how-may-won-over-the-waiverers-to-survive-leadership-challenge

201 Andrew Sparrow, 'May survives confidence vote with a majority of 83 – as it happened', *Guardian*, 13 December 2018, www.theguardian.com/politics/live/2018/dec/12/tory-mps-trigger-vote-of-no-confidence-in-may-amid-brexit-uncertainty-politics-live?page=with:block-5c119e37e4b039b33ff8e25b#block-5c119e37e4b039b33ff8e25b

202 'Brexit Timeline: Key dates as the UK prepares to leave the EU', LBC

203 Hardeep Matharu [@Hardeep_Matharu], Twitter, 16 November 2018, twitter.com/Hardeep_Matharu/status/1063519062548983810

204 'Grayling defends no-deal Brexit ferry contract', BBC, 2 January 2019, www.bbc.co.uk/news/business-46735303

205 Ben Quinn, 'Brexit freight ferry firm appears all geared up – to deliver pizzas', *Guardian*, 3 January 2019, www.theguardian.com/politics/2019/jan/03/brexit-freight-ferry-firm-appears-all-geared-up-to-deliver-pizzas

206 Naomi Rovnick, James Blitz and Jim Pickard, 'Pressure grows on Grayling over Seaborne Freight and bosses', *FT*, 4 January 2019, www.ft.com/content/2e51c74c-1035-11e9-acdc-4d9976f1533b

207 Ashley Cowburn, 'Brexit: Theresa May faces questions after claiming ferry due diligence done by consultancy firm - despite officials already admitting it "could not complete tests"', *Independent*, 13 February 2019, www.independent.co.uk/news/uk/politics/brexit-theresa-may-no-deal-ferry-contract-chris-grayling-pmqs-corbyn-labour-a8777431.html

208 Dominic Brady, 'Grayling agrees £33m out of court settlement with Eurotunnel', Public Finance, 1 March 2019, www.publicfinance.co.uk/news/2019/03/grayling-agrees-ps33m-out-court-settlement-eurotunnel

209 John Crace, 'Failing Grayling never requires any help to make a fool of himself', *Guardian*, 11 October 2018, www.theguardian.com/politics/2018/oct/11/failing-grayling-transport-secretary-never-requires-help-make-fool-himself

2019: We Don't Trust What's Coming Next

1 Richard Partington, 'UK corporation tax cut to cost billions more than thought', *Guardian*, 28 January 2019, www.theguardian.com/politics/2019/jan/28/uk-corporation-tax-cut-to-cost-billions-more-than-thought

2 Gabriel Pogrund, 'Philip Hammond needs spreadsheet to keep track of his 14 new jobs', *The Times*, 6 September 2020, www.thetimes.co.uk/article/philip-hammond-needs-spreadsheet-to-keep-track-of-his-14-new-jobs-tvndfph6b

3 Jamie Nimmo, 'Hypocrite? Chancellor's firm pays paltry tax bill as Hammond tells web giants to pay "fair share"', This Is Money, 12 January 2019, www.thisismoney.co.uk/money/news/article-6585187/Hypocrite-Chancellors-firm-pays-paltry-tax-bill-Hammond-tells-web-giants-pay-fair-share.html

4 D. Clark, 'Number of people receiving three days' worth of emergency food by Trussell Trust foodbanks in the United Kingdom from 2008/09 to 2021/22', Statista, 11 May 2020, www.statista.com/statistics/382695/uk-foodbank-users

5 Rajeev Syal, 'Tory official convicted of falsifying expenses in race against Farage', *Guardian*, 19 January 2019, www.theguardian.com/politics/2019/jan/09/craig-mackinlay-tory-mp-cleared-breaking-2015-general-election-expenses-rules

6 Rob Powell, 'Tories set up fund to give convicted aide a "short holiday"', Sky News, 16 January 2019, news.sky.com/story/conservative-mps-set-up-holiday-fund-for-convicted-tory-agent-11609064

7 'MPs want hunger minister role introduced', BBC, 10 January 2019, www.bbc.co.uk/news/education-46810707

8 'More than 100 lorries rehearse for "no-deal" Brexit Dover congestion', Sky News, 7 January 2019, news.sky.com/story/more-than-100-lorries-rehearse-for-no-deal-brexit-dover-congestion-11600853

9 Dan Bloom, Ben Ashton and Chessum, 'Cost of "farcical" pre-Brexit lorry convoy trial from Manston Airport to Port of Dover revealed', *Kent Live*, 7 January 2019, www.kentlive.news/news/kent-news/cost-farcical-pre-brexit-lorry-2403273

10 Lisa O'Carroll, 'No-deal Brexit rehearsal in Kent "a waste of time"', *Guardian*, 7 January 2019, www.theguardian.com/politics/2019/jan/07/no-deal-brexit-rehearsal-tests-traffic-congestion-in-kent

11 Jane Merrick, 'Theresa May serves up cocktails and knighthoods before Brexit showdown', *CNN*, 7 January 2019, edition.cnn.com/2019/01/07/opinions/brexit-may-merrick-gbr-intl/index.html

12 'Brexit Timeline: Key dates as the UK prepares to leave the EU', *LBC*, 13 April 2019, www.lbc.co.uk/hot-topics/brexit/brexit-timeline-of-key-dates

13 'Brexit: What Is "Crossover Day" And When Is It?', *LBC*, 19 January 2019, www.lbc.co.uk/politics/the-news-explained/what-is-brexit-crossover-day

14 Jane Merrick, 'Theresa May serves up cocktails and knighthoods before Brexit showdown'

15 'Ken Clarke Tells Matt Frei Why Article 50 Should Be Revoked', *LBC*, 5 January 2019, www.lbc.co.uk/radio/presenters/matt-frei/ken-clarke-revoke-article-50/

16 Fiach Kelly and Cliff Taylor, 'Malthouse compromise: an idea whose time has come – and gone', *Irish Times*, 31 January 2019, www.irishtimes.com/news/ireland/irish-news/malthouse-compromise-an-idea-whose-time-has-come-and-gone-1.3776471

17 'Queen's Speech — Programme for Government — Leaving the European Union', They Work For You, 24 October 2019, www.theyworkforyou.com/divisions/pw-2019-10-24-11-commons/mp/25346

18 Jennifer Rankin, '"Bonkers": what the EU thinks of the Malthouse compromise', *Guardian*, 4 February 2019, www.theguardian.com/politics/2019/feb/04/bonkers-what-the-eu-thinks-of-the-malthouse-compromise

19 Daniel Mackrell, 'All of the conservative MPs who have resigned because of Brexit', *Metro*, 26 March 2019, metro.co.uk/2019/03/26/conservative-mps-resigned-brexit-9019322

20 'May's government survives no-confidence vote', BBC, 16 January 2019, www.bbc.co.uk/news/uk-politics-46899466

21 Ashley Cowburn, 'Theresa May says she has an "open mind" over Brexit negotiations', *Independent*, 27 July 2016, www.independent.co.uk/news/uk/brexit-theresa-may-negotiations-eu-referendum-result-leave-europe-a7158516.html

22 'EU citizen settled status process a shambles as thousands struggle to apply', *LBC*, 21 January 2019, www.lbc.co.uk/hot-topics/brexit/eu-citizen-settled-status-process-a-shambles

23 Patrick Worrall, 'Boris Johnson falsely claims he "didn't say anything about Turkey" in the referendum campaign', Channel 4 News, 18 January 2019, www.channel4.com/news/factcheck/factcheck-boris-johnson-falsely-claims-he-didnt-say-anything-about-turkey-in-the-referendum-campaign

24 Andrew Marr Show Transcript, Andrew Marr Show with Boris Johnson, Conservative Leave Campaign, 5 June 2016, http://news.bbc.co.uk/1/shared/bsp/hi/pdfs/05061602.pdf

25 Peter Henn, 'Boris accuses PM of talking "b******s" over EU', *Express*, 18 April 2016, www.express.co.uk/news/politics/661980/Boris-Cameron-EU-referendum-Turkey

26 Boris Johnson, 'Angela Merkel is now silencing German satirists to please Erdogan. This is what the EU has wrought', *Telegraph*, 17 April 2016, www.telegraph.co.uk/news/2016/04/17 /angela-merkel-is-now-silencing-german-satirists-to-please-erdoga

27 'Brexit Timeline: Key dates as the UK prepares to leave the EU', *LBC*

28 Karl McDonald, 'Daniel Kawczynski: Tory MP asks Poland to block Article 50 extension – and force no-deal Brexit', *iNews*, 22 January 2019, inews.co.uk/news/brexit/daniel-kawczyn ski-poland-no-deal-brexit-article-50-block-extension-249158

29 'Brexit amendments: What did MPs vote on and what were the results?', BBC, 29 January 2019, www.bbc.co.uk/news/uk-politics-46959545

30 'Nigel Farage's speech to European parliament that's gone viral', *LBC*, 3 February 2019, www.lbc.co.uk/radio/presenters/nigel-farage/speech-to-parliament-gone-viral

31 'Brexit Timeline: Key dates as the UK prepares to leave the EU', *LBC*

32 Jim Waterson, 'Don't trust Daily Mail website, Microsoft browser warns users', *Guardian*, 23 January 2019, www.theguardian.com/media/2019/jan/23/dont-trust-daily-mail-website-microsoft-browser-warns-users

33 Jasper Jackson, 'Wikipedia bans Daily Mail as "unreliable" source', *Guardian*, 8 February 2017, www.theguardian.com/technology/2017/feb/08/wikipedia-bans-daily-mail-as-unreliable-source-for-website

34 Mikey Smith, 'Tory austerity undermined trust in Government says damning leaked official study', *Mirror*, 17 January 2019, www.mirror.co.uk/news/politics/breaking-tory-aust erity-undermined-trust-13870939

35 Patrick Butler, 'Plan to redirect inner-city funds to Tory shires "a stitch-up"', *Guardian*, 20 January 2019, www.theguardian.com/society/2019/jan/20/ministry-of-housing-plans-to-re direct-inner-city-funds-to-tory-shires-branded-stitch-up

36 Robert Booth, '"I've absolutely had enough": Tory MP embarks on anti-austerity tour', *Guardian*, 24 January 2019, www.theguardian.com/society/2019/jan/24/ive-absolutely-had-enough-tory-mp-embarks-on-anti-austerity-tour

37 James Felton [@JimMFelton], Twitter, 3 February 2019, twitter.com/DKShrewsbury/status/ 1091728290337959936

38 'Pro-Brexit MP makes "totally false" claim about Europe after WW2 on Twitter', *Shropshire Star*, 2 February 2019, www.shropshirestar.com/news/uk-news/2019/02/02/pro-brexit-mp-makes-totally-false-claim-about-europe-after-ww2-on-twitter

39 Andrew Neil [@afneil], Twitter, 2 February 2019, twitter.com/afneil/status/1091756315871 973376

40 'Pro-Brexit MP makes "totally false" claim about Europe after WW2 on Twitter', *Shropshire Star*

41 Talk TW [@TalkTV], Twitter, 3 February 2019, twitter.com/talkRADIO/status/1092093761 570652160?ref_src=twsrc%5Etfw

42 @DKShrewsbury, Twitter, twitter.com/DKShrewsbury

43 'Young Blackpool Conservative expelled for racist tweets', BBC, 5 February 2019, www.bbc.co.uk/news/uk-england-lancashire-47134818

44 'Nadine Dorries accused of thinking "brown women look the same"', BBC, 4 February 2019, www.bbc.co.uk/news/newsbeat-47120879

45 Nadine Dorries [@NadineDorries], Twitter, 9 April 2013, twitter.com/NadineDorries/ status/321618304567488512

46 'Donald Tusk: Special place in hell for Brexiteers without a plan', BBC, 6 February 2019, www.bbc.co.uk/news/uk-politics-47143135

47 Newsdesk, 'Rees-Mogg: Post-Brexit windfall should be used to honour £350m NHS pledge', *Jersey Evening Post*, 14 November 2017, jerseyeveningpost.com/news/uk-news/2017/11/14 /rees-mogg-post-brexit-windfall-should-be-used-to-honour-350m-nhs-pledge

48 Twitter, twitter.com/Jacob_Rees_Mogg/status/930408942588583936

49 'Brexit: Theresa May "determined" to leave EU in March', BBC, 3 February 2019, www.bbc.co.uk/news/uk-politics-47105990

50   Heather Stewart, Jessica Elgot and Rowena Mason, 'Conservative split as rebels denounce grip of hardline Brexiters', *Guardian*, 21 February 2019, www.theguardian.com/politics/ 2019/feb/20/tory-mps-defect-independent-group-soubry-allen-wollaston

51   Joseph Locker, 'Anna Soubry says she agrees with the "values and principles" of Chris Leslie as she leaves the Tories', *Nottinghamshire Live*, 20 February 2020, www.nottinghampost.com/news/local-news/anna-soubry-says-agrees-values-2564550

52   Jon Sharman, 'Independent Group For Change disbands after losing every MP at general election', *Independent*, 19 December 2019, www.independent.co.uk/news/ uk/politics/independent-group-for-change-uk-election-results-mps-anna-soubry-chuka-umunna-a9254166.html

53   Rajeev Syal, 'Theresa May delays meaningful vote on final Brexit deal', *Guardian*, 24 February 2019, www.theguardian.com/politics/2019/feb/24/theresa-may-postpones-meaningful-vote-on-final-brexit-deal

54   'Theresa May offers MPs Brexit delay vote', BBC, 26 February 2019, www.bbc.co.uk/news/uk-politics-47373996

55   Matt Foster, 'Government "planning for martial law" under emergency no-deal Brexit preparations', *Civil Service World*, 28 January 2019, www.civilserviceworld.com/professions/ article/government-planning-for-martial-law-under-emergency-nodeal-brexit-preparat ions

56   Dennis Kefalakos, 'A backbencher Tory MP threatens both EU and UK with a no-deal Brexit', *The European Sting*, 18 February 2019, europeansting.com/2019/02/18/a-tory-back bencher-threatens-both-eu-and-uk-with-no-deal-brexit

57   Jasmin Gray, '15 government vacancies open as Theresa May runs out of MPs to call on', *Huffington Post*, 27 March 2019, www.huffingtonpost.co.uk/entry/15-vacancies-government-theresa-may-brexit_uk_5c9b6c73e4b07c88662e8276

58   Gwyn Topham, 'Delays and drips mark Great Western Railway's new train launch', *Guardian*, 16 October 2017, www.theguardian.com/uk-news/2017/oct/16/delays-and-drips -mark-great-western-railways-new-train-launch

59   'MPs vote against a no-deal Brexit under "any circumstance"', *LBC*, 13 March 2019, www.lbc.co.uk/hot-topics/brexit/mps-vote-against-a-no-deal-brexit-under-any-circum

60   'MPs vote to request Brexit delay - but reject second referendum: all of the results', *LBC*, 14 March 2019, www.lbc.co.uk/hot-topics/brexit/mps-request-brexit-delay-reject-second-refer endum

61   Oliver Wright, 'Brexit: May deal has customs union in all but name, Tories tell Corbyn', *The Times*, 5 April 2019, www.thetimes.co.uk/article/brexit-may-deal-has-customs-union-in-all -but-name-tories-tell-corbyn-35m5h9ptw

62   Graham Lithgow [@GrahamLithgow], Twitter, 8 April 2019, twitter.com/grahamlithgow/ status/1115259420374708225

63   Michael Bates [@BatesMichaelW], Twitter, 23 April 2019, twitter.com/BatesMichaelW/ status/1120750271515246596

64   'Brexit march: Million joined Brexit protest, organisers say', BBC, 23 March 2019, www.bbc.co.uk/news/uk-politics-47678763

65   Sarah Marsh, 'Woman behind Brexit petition to revoke article 50 receives death threats', *Guardian*, 23 March 2029, www.theguardian.com/politics/2019/mar/23/more-than-4-million-people-sign-petition-to-revoke-article-50-brexit

66   Gerard Tubb, 'Nigel Farage will not complete Brexit Betrayal march despite urging supporters to join him', Sky News, 18 March 2019, news.sky.com/story/nigel-farage-will-not-complete-brexit-betrayal-march-despite-urging-supporters-to-join-him-11666858

67   Ibid.

68   'Brexit: Departure date pushed back by at least two weeks', BBC, 22 March 2019, www.bbc.co.uk/news/uk-politics-47663031

69   Peter Walker, 'MPs reject all alternative Brexit options', *Guardian*, 27 March 2019, www.theguardian.com/politics/2019/mar/27/mps-reject-all-alternative-brexit-options

70   Josh Holder, Antonio Voce and Seán Clarke, 'How did your MP vote in the indicative votes?', *Guardian*, 1 April 2019, www.theguardian.com/politics/ng-interactive/2019/apr/01/how-did-each-mp-vote-on-the-second-round-of-indicative-votes

71   Juno McEnroe, 'Ireland "must support Brexit extension"', *Irish Examiner*, 29 March 2019, www.irishexaminer.com/news/arid-30914321.html

72 'Brexit: UK and EU agree delay to 31 October', BBC, 11 April 2019, www.bbc.co.uk/news/uk-politics-47889404

73 Damian Carrington, 'Owen Paterson: true blue countryman putting wind up green campaigners', *Guardian*, 11 October 2012, www.theguardian.com/politics/2012/oct/11/owen-paterson-environment-guardian-profile

74 Nigel Nelson, 'Tory politician earns £100,000 a year from company at centre of drug test tampering scandal', *Mirror*, 27 May 2017, www.mirror.co.uk/news/politics/tory-politician-earns-100000-year-10512284

75 Matthew McConville, 'Randox Scandal', Irvingslaw, www.irvingslaw.com/randox-scandal

76 'Randox forensics inquiry: Forty drug-driving offences quashed', BBC, 6 December 2018, www.bbc.co.uk/news/uk-england-manchester-46466710

77 Rob Evans, David Pegg and Felicity Lawrence, 'MP Owen Paterson lobbied government for firm he worked for', *Guardian*, 7 April 2019, www.theguardian.com/politics/2019/apr/07/mp-owen-paterson-lobbied-government-for-firm-he-worked-for

78 Rob Evans, Felicity Lawrence and David Pegg, 'Revealed: Owen Paterson lobbied for firms he was paid to advise', *Guardian*, 30 September 2019, www.theguardian.com/politics/2019/sep/30/revealed-owen-paterson-lobbied-for-firms-he-was-paid-to-advise

79 Nigel Nelson, 'Tory politician earns £100,000 a year from company at centre of drug test tampering scandal', *Mirror*, 27 May 2017, www.mirror.co.uk/news/politics/tory-politician-earns-100000-year-10512284

80 Ibid.

81 Aubrey Allegretti, 'MP Owen Paterson faces suspension for breaking lobbying rules', *Guardian*, 26 October 2021, www.theguardian.com/politics/2021/oct/26/owen-paterson-faces-suspension-breaking-lobbying-rules

82 'Owen Paterson: Government faces backlash over new conduct rules plan', BBC, 4 November 2021, www.bbc.co.uk/news/uk-politics-59158469

83 'Tories lose North Shropshire seat they held for 115 years', BBC, 17 December 2021, www.bbc.co.uk/news/uk-england-shropshire-59693102

84 'Wife of ex-Putin ally has dinner with PM and six Cabinet ministers', ITV News, 1 May 2019, www.itv.com/news/2019-05-01/wife-of-ex-putin-ally-has-dinner-with-pm-and-six-cabinet-ministers

85 Sean O'Neill, 'Lubov Chernukhin: Quiet Russian's £1.7m makes her top female Tory donor', *The Times*, 18 July 2020, www.thetimes.co.uk/article/lubov-chernukhin-quiet-russians-1-7m-makes-her-top-female-tory-donor-z2c00bcxl

86 Steve Busfield, 'George Osborne, Nat Rothschild and the curious case of a Bullingdon Club picture', *Guardian*, 26 October 2008, www.theguardian.com/news/blog/2008/oct/26/george-osborne-nat-rothschild

87 Ben Ellery, 'Tory top donor Lubov Chernukhin linked to Putin oligarch', *The Times*, 22 September 2022, www.thetimes.co.uk/article/tory-top-donor-lubov-chernukhin-linked-to-putin-oligarch-ngrmk5p8s

88 'FinCEN Files: Tory donor Lubov Chernukhin linked to $8m Putin ally funding', BBC, 21 September 2021, www.bbc.co.uk/news/uk-54228079

89 'Russians taunt "Gavin Williamson the wench" as West is united', *Evening Standard*, 16 March 2018, www.standard.co.uk/news/uk/russians-taunt-gavin-williamson-the-wench-as-west-is-united-a3791831.html

90 David Axe, 'Britain spent so much on two giant aircraft carriers, it can't afford planes or escorts', *Forbes*, 28 June 2020, www.forbes.com/sites/davidaxe/2020/06/28/britain-spent-so-much-on-two-giant-aircraft-carriers-it-cant-afford-planes-or-escorts/?sh=61d3037d5bcc

91 Henry Zeffman, 'Philip Hammond's allies take aim at 'Private Pike' minister Gavin Williamson', *The Times*, 4 December 2017, www.thetimes.co.uk/article/philip-hammond-s-allies-take-aim-at-private-pike-minister-gavin-williamson-777z808w5

92 Heather Stewart, Dan Sabbagh and Peter Walker, 'Gavin Williamson: "I was tried by kangaroo court – then sacked"', *Guardian*, 1 May 2019, www.theguardian.com/politics/2019/may/01/gavin-williamson-sacked-as-defence-secretary-over-huawei-leak

93 Laura Hughes, 'Rona Fairhead and Zahida Manzoor quit government', *FT*, 7 May 2019, www.ft.com/content/e3e0c44c-70e2-11e9-bf5c-6eeb837566c5

94 'Penny Mordaunt: From a magician's assistant to the UK's first female defence secretary', Sky News, 2 May 2019, news.sky.com/story/penny-mordaunt-magicians-assistant-to-uks-first-female-defence-secretary-11708973

95   Ruth Mosalski, 'Theresa May was heckled and told to quit at the Welsh Conservative party conference', *Wales Online*, 3 May 2019, www.walesonline.co.uk/news/politics/theresa-heckled-told-quit-welsh-16221299

96   Cath Levett and Seán Clarke, 'Theresa May: a political obituary in five charts', *Guardian*, 7 June 2019, www.theguardian.com/politics/2019/jun/07/theresa-may-a-political-obituary-in-five-charts

97   'Local elections: Results in maps and charts', BBC, 3 May 2019, www.bbc.co.uk/news/uk-politics-48091592

98   'Brexit: 1922 Committee seeks clarity on Theresa May departure', *Irish Times*, 11 May 2019, www.irishtimes.com/news/world/uk/brexit-1922-committee-seeks-clarity-on-theresa-maydeparture-1.3889228

99   Andrew Sparrow and Latifa Yedroudji, 'May "could announce departure date on Friday" – as it happened', *Guardian*, 23 May 2019, www.theguardian.com/politics/blog/live/2019/may/22/brexit-latest-news-may-statement-mps-deal-pmqs-gove-suggests-planned-vote-on-withdrawal-agreement-bill-could-be-shelved-live-news

100 Andrea Leadsom, 'Back Boris's deal or Brexit will be the boxset that never ends', *Daily Mail*, 5 October 2019, www.dailymail.co.uk/debate/article-7541893/ANDREA-LEADSOM-Boriss-deal-Brexit-boxset-never-ends.html

101 'Why the UK has a special responsibility to protect its share of refugees', The Conversation, 15 May 2015, theconversation.com/why-the-uk-has-a-special-responsibility-to-protect-its-share-of-refugees-41773

102 Ted Jeory and Jon Stone, 'Theresa May's husband is a senior executive at a $1.4tn investment fund that profits from tax avoiding companies', *Independent*, 13 July 2016, www.independent.co.uk/news/uk/politics/theresa-may-philip-may-amazon-starbucks-google-capital-group-philip-morris-a7133231.html

103 'Theresa May quits: UK set for new PM by end of July', BBC, 24 May 2019, www.bbc.co.uk/news/uk-politics-48395905

104 Andrew Rawnsley, 'Chief of Staff by Gavin Barwell review – Theresa May's one true blue', *Guardian*, 19 September 2019, www.theguardian.com/books/2021/sep/19/chief-of-staff-by-gavin-barwell-review-theresa-mays-one-true-blue

105 Michael Savage, 'How Boris Johnson 2.0 was born', *Guardian*, 9 June 2019, www.theguardian.com/politics/2019/jun/09/how-boris-johnson-bounced-back-tory-leadership

106 Olivia Tobin, 'Tory leadership candidates 2019: The 11 MPs in the running to succeed Theresa May', *Evening Standard*, 4 June 2019, www.standard.co.uk/news/politics/tory-leadership-candidates-the-11-mps-in-the-running-to-succeed-theresa-may-a4158596.html

107 Rob Merrick, 'Dominic Raab said "I don't support the Human Rights Act" ahead of being put in charge of overhaul', *Independent*, 17 September 2021, www.independent.co.uk/news/uk/politics/dominic-raab-human-rights-act-reshuffle-b1921962.html

108 Olivia Tobin, 'Tory leadership candidates 2019: The 11 MPs in the running to succeed Theresa May'

109 Simon Murphy, 'Esther McVey claimed £8,750 in expenses for personal photographer', *Guardian*, 12 June 2019, www.theguardian.com/politics/2019/jun/12/esther-mcvey-expensed-thousands-of-pounds-for-personal-photographer

110 Olivia Tobin, 'Tory leadership candidates 2019: The 11 MPs in the running to succeed Theresa May'

111 Andrea Leadsom MP [@andrealeadsom], Twitter, 1 February 2020, twitter.com/andrealeadsom/status/1223555911861575680

112 'Michael Gove and Theresa May head five-way Conservative race', BBC, 30 June 2016, www.bbc.co.uk/news/uk-politics-36671336

113 'Plastic carrier bags: Gove sets out new measures to extend charge', Gov.uk, 27 September 2018, www.gov.uk/government/news/plastic-carrier-bags-gove-sets-out-new-measures-to-extend-charge

114 Patrick Greenfield, 'Sajid Javid accused of "human fly-tipping" in Shamima Begum case', *Guardian*, 31 May 2019, www.theguardian.com/uk-news/2019/may/31/sajid-javid-accused-shamima-begum-case-syria

115 Olivia Tobin, 'Tory leadership candidates 2019: The 11 MPs in the running to succeed Theresa May'

116 'Our Forest', *The Forest of Dean and Wye Valley Review*, 17 November 2010, www.theforestreview.co.uk/news/our-forest-199579

117 'Sale of forests in England scrapped', BBC, 17 February 2011, www.bbc.co.uk/news/av/uk-12491144

118 Aubrey Allegretti, 'James Cleverly pulls out of Tory leadership race due to lack of support', Sky News, 4 June 2019, news.sky.com/story/james-cleverly-pulls-out-of-tory-leadership-race-11734600

119 Olivia Tobin, 'Tory leadership candidates 2019: The 11 MPs in the running to succeed Theresa May'

120 Patrick Greenfield, Caroline Davies and Dan Sabbagh, 'Mark Field suspended as minister after grabbing climate protester by neck', Guardian, 21 June 2019, www.theguardian.com/politics/2019/jun/21/mark-field-suspended-as-minister-after-grabbing-climate-protester-by-neck

121 'Poverty in the UK is "systematic" and "tragic", says UN special rapporteur', BBC, 22 May 2019, www.bbc.co.uk/news/uk-48354692

122 Rowena Mason, 'Boris Johnson promises tax cut for 3m higher earners', Guardian, 10 June 2019, www.theguardian.com/politics/2019/jun/10/boris-johnson-promise-tax-cut-raise-40p-threshold

123 Rowena Mason and Heather Stewart, '"Not the Boris we're used to": Johnson's ruthlessly organised bid for PM', Guardian, 9 June 2019, www.theguardian.com/politics/2019/jun/09/boris-johnson-kept-from-media-in-ruthlessly-organised-campaign

124 John Rentoul [@JohnRentoul], Twitter, 18 June 2019, twitter.com/JohnRentoul/status/1140924710890479616

125 Jim Waterson, 'Boris Johnson: police called to loud altercation at potential PM's home', Guardian, 21 June 2019, www.theguardian.com/politics/2019/jun/21/police-called-to-loud-altercation-at-boris-johnsons-home

126 Kate Lyons, '"Mesmerising": Boris Johnson's bizarre model buses claim raises eyebrows', Guardian, 26 June 2019, www.theguardian.com/politics/2019/jun/26/mesmerising-boris-johnsons-bizarre-model-buses-claim-raises-eyebrows

127 'Tory leadership race: Sky set to cancel Johnson-Hunt debate', BBC, 24 June 2019, www.bbc.com/news/uk-politics-48744724

128 Michael Savage, 'Fears grow over Boris Johnson win as Hunt challenge fades', Guardian, 6 July 2019, www.theguardian.com/politics/2019/jul/06/boris-johnson-win-fears-hunt-challenge-fades-tories-conservatives

129 Ibid.

130 Max Hastings, 'I was Boris Johnson's boss: he is utterly unfit to be prime minister', Guardian, 24 June 2019, www.theguardian.com/commentisfree/2019/jun/24/boris-johnson-prime-minister-tory-party-britain

131 Wikipedia, 'Boris Johnson', Last edited: 15 July 2022, en.wikipedia.org/wiki/Boris_Johnson#2019_Conservative_Party_leadership_election

132 Josh Halliday, 'Public has right to know Boris Johnson fathered child during affair, court rules', Guardian, 21 May 2013, www.theguardian.com/politics/2013/may/21/boris-johnson-fathered-child-affair; Gaby Hinsliff, 'Boris Johnson sacked by Tories over private life', Guardian, 14 November 2004, www.theguardian.com/politics/2004/nov/14/uk.conservatives

133 Michael Savage, 'Fears grow over Boris Johnson win as Hunt challenge fades', Guardian, 6 July 2019, www.theguardian.com/politics/2019/jul/06/boris-johnson-win-fears-hunt-challenge-fades-tories-conservatives

134 Sonia Purnell, Just Boris: Boris Johnson: The Irresistible Rise of a Political Celebrity, Aurum Press Ltd, London, 2011.

135 'Theresa May: Premiership in six charts', BBC, 24 May 2019, www.bbc.co.uk/news/uk-politics-48308302

136 Sam Saeed, 'Theresa May "Liar liar" song tops UK charts', Politico, 31 May 2017, www.politico.eu/article/theresa-may-liar-liar-song-tops-uk-charts

137 Jonathan Este, 'Theresa May joint worst post-war prime minister, say historians and politics professors in new survey', The Conversation, 6 July 2021, theconversation.com/theresa-may-joint-worst-post-war-prime-minister-say-historians-and-politics-professors-in-new-survey-163912

Part 3: The Lightness of Being Unbearable
2019: I Thought Johnson Was Fucking Stupid

1   Barry Richards, 'British people hardly ever thought about the EU before Brexit, now it dominates their lives', *The Conversation*, 9 October 2019, theconversation.com/british-peo ple-hardly-ever-thought-about-the-eu-before-brexit-now-it-dominates-their-lives-123784

2   Sarah Prescott-Smith, 'Which issues will decide the general election?', You Gov, 7 November 2019, yougov.co.uk/topics/politics/articles-reports/2019/11/07/which-issues-will-decide-general-election

3   'Boris Johnson wins race to be Tory leader and PM', BBC, 23 July 2019, www.bbc.co.uk/news/uk-politics-49084605

4   Rebecca Speare-Cole, 'Margot James resigns as minister after voting against Government', *Evening Standard*, 18 July 2019, www.standard.co.uk/news/politics/margot-james-resigns-as-digital-minister-after-voting-against-government-a4193206.html

5   Jonathan Walker, 'Former Tory Minister Margot James: Boris is "erratic and reckless" and he's "shifted the party massively to the right"', *Birmingham Mail*, 4 September 2019, www.birminghammail.co.uk/black-country/former-tory-minister-margot-james-16863447

6   Rob Merrick, 'Brexit news: UK trade envoy quits in protest over no-deal policy threatening £800m Canada agreement', *Independent*, 21 July 2019, www.independent.co.uk/news/uk /politics/brexit-news-latest-trade-envoy-quit-deal-canada-a9012421.html

7   'David Lidington latest to resign from Government over Boris Johnson's no-deal Brexit approach', *iNews*, 24 July 2019, inews.co.uk/news/politics/david-lidington-resigns-boris-johnson-no-deal-brexit-317857

8   Alain Tolhurst, 'Michael Gove reverses opposition to Boris Johnson saying he would make a "great Prime Minister"', *Politics Home*, 16 July 2019, www.politicshome.com/news/article/ michael-gove-reverses-opposition-to-boris-johnson-saying-he-would-make-a-great-prime-minister

9   Will Bedingfield, 'Here's why people can't stop calling Jeremy Hunt the C-word', *Wired*, 13 June 2019, www.wired.co.uk/article/jeremy-hunt-mp

10   Steven Swinford, 'Tory leadership race: Boris Johnson to boost pay for public sector staff', *The Times*, 1 July 2019, www.thetimes.co.uk/article/tory-leadership-race-boris-johnson-to-boost-pay-for-public-sector-staff-vz879qs7w

11   Elizabeth Burden, 'Sajid Javid wants keys for No 11 after backing Boris Johnson for Tory leader', *The Times*, 8 July 2019, www.thetimes.co.uk/article/sajid-javid-wants-keys-for-no-11-after-backing-favourite-3bl7r3t89

12   Lizzie Dearden, 'Sajid Javid warns "UK risks sliding into nationalism" amid growing threat from far right', *Independent*, 19 July 2019, www.independent.co.uk/news/uk/home-news /far-right-tommy-robinson-sajid-javid-ukip-britain-first-violence-brexit-a9012006.html

13   Aubrey Allegretti, 'Sajid Javid warns against UK succumbing to "naked populism"', Sky News, 1 October 2018, news.sky.com/story/sajid-javid-warns-against-uk-succumbing-to-naked-populism-11514014

14   Chris York, 'British values oath proposed by Sajid Javid', Issues Online, www.issuesonline.co.uk/articles/british-values-oath-proposed-by-sajid-javid

15   Damien Gayle, 'Brexit: suspending parliament should not be ruled out, says Dominic Raab', *Guardian*, 8 June 2019, www.theguardian.com/politics/2019/jun/08/suspending-parliament-should-not-be-ruled-out-says-dominic-raab

16   Jamie Grierson, 'Priti Patel accused of breaching ministerial code for second time', *Guardian*, 26 July 2019, www.theguardian.com/politics/2019/jul/26/priti-patel-accused-of-breaching-ministerial-code-for-second-time

17   'Liz Truss', Politics.co.uk, www.politics.co.uk/reference/elizabeth-truss

18   Ben Chu, 'UK economy grew at weakest pace in five years in 2017, says new forecast', *Independent*, 12 January 2018, www.independent.co.uk/news/business/news/uk-economy-growth-gdp-rise-weak-2017-forecast-pwc-brexit-city-london-a8155296.html

19   'Liz Truss', Politics.co.uk

20   Peter Stefanovic [@PeterStefanovi2], Twitter, 3 August 2019, twitter.com/peterstefanovi2/ status/1157710250969063424?lang=en

21   'Have UK voters changed their minds on Brexit?', BBC, 17 October 2019, www.bbc.co.uk /news/uk-politics-50043549

22 Harry Cole, 'Tory MPs push for law threatening JAIL for any British citizen who undermines Government negotiations abroad', *Daily Mail*, 19 October 2019, www.dailymail.co.uk/news/article-7591983/amp/Tory-MPs-push-law-threatening-JAIL-British-citizens-undermine-Government-talks-abroad.html

23 Twitter, twitter.com/DKShrewsbury/status/1185990368795463680

24 Ray Jones, 'Outsourcing children's services isn't just wrong – it's a waste of money', *Guardian*, 7 August 2019, www.theguardian.com/society/2019/aug/07/outsourcing-childrens-services-wrong-waste-money

25 Martin Barrow [@MartinBarrow], Twitter, 13 July 2021, mobile.twitter.com/MartinBarrow/status/1414852584704196608?s=19

26 'Boris Johnson and Jeremy Hunt: The Andrew Neil interviews fact-checked', BBC, 12 July 2019, www.bbc.co.uk/news/uk-politics-48965645

27 Rowena Mason, 'Boris Johnson: odds of no-deal Brexit are "a million-to-one against"', *Guardian*, 27 June 2019, www.theguardian.com/politics/2019/jun/26/boris-johnson-chances-of-no-deal-brexit-are-a-million-to-one-against

28 Peter Walker, 'Boris Johnson's Brexit plans under threat from ministers' resignations', *Guardian*, 21 July 2019, www.theguardian.com/politics/2019/jul/21/ministers-resignations-could-disrupt-boris-johnson-brexit-plans

29 Daniel Boffey and Rowena Mason, 'Boris Johnson has no intention of renegotiating Brexit deal, EU told', *Guardian*, 5 August 2019, www.theguardian.com/politics/2019/aug/05/no-deal-brexit-is-boris-johnsons-central-scenario-eu-told

30 Kate Holton, Elizabeth Piper, Andrew MacAskill, 'Boris Johnson says chances of no-deal Brexit are "a million-to-one"', Reuters, 26 June 2019, www.reuters.com/article/uk-britain-eu-leader-idUKKCN1TR1IX

31 Rosamund Urwin and Caroline Wheeler, 'Operation Chaos: Whitehall's secret no-deal Brexit preparations leaked', *The Times*, 18 August 2019, www.thetimes.co.uk/article/operation-chaos-whitehalls-secret-no-deal-brexit-plan-leaked-j6ntwvhll

32 Kaisha Langton, 'Brexit SHUTDOWN: Boris Johnson threatens to drag the Queen into Brexit delay', *Express*, 13 June 2019, www.express.co.uk/news/politics/1140058/brexit-deadlock-boris-johnson-queen-elizabeth-ii-house-of-commons-shutdown

33 'Boris Johnson: "I'd rather be dead in a ditch" than ask for Brexit delay', BBC, 5 September 2019, www.bbc.co.uk/news/av/uk-politics-49601128

34 Toby Helm and Heather Stewart, 'Boris Johnson seeks legal advice on five-week parliament closure ahead of Brexit', *Guardian*, 24 August 2019, www.theguardian.com/politics/2019/aug/24/johnson-seeks-legal-advice-parliament-closure

35 Kate Proctor, 'Boris Johnson's move to prorogue parliament "a constitutional outrage", says Speaker', *Guardian*, 28 August 2019, www.theguardian.com/politics/2019/aug/28/boris-johnsons-move-to-prorogue-parliament-a-constitutional-outrage-says-speaker

36 Steven Swinford and Henry Zeffman, 'Prorogation of parliament: Months of planning climaxed in budget flight to Balmoral', *The Times*, 29 August 2019, www.thetimes.co.uk/article/prorogation-of-parliament-months-of-planning-climaxed-in-budget-flight-to-balmoral-vjkk5c099

37 Aamna Mohdin, Maya Wolfe-Robinson and Marvel Kalukembi, '"Stop the coup": Protests across UK over Johnson's suspension of parliament', *Guardian*, 29 August 2019, www.theguardian.com/politics/2019/aug/28/protests-sparked-by-boris-johnsons-plan-to-suspend-parliament

38 Toby Helm, 'I'll take you to court to block a no-deal Brexit, Gina Miller tells Boris Johnson', *Guardian*, 14 July 2019, www.theguardian.com/politics/2019/jul/14/gina-miller-legal-action-block-no-deal-brexit-boris-johnson

39 Rob Merrick, 'Boris Johnson secretly agreed to suspend parliament two weeks before denying it would happen, Downing St documents reveal', *Independent*, 3 September 2019, www.independent.co.uk/news/uk/politics/boris-johnson-prorogue-parliament-brexit-dominic-cummings-email-court-scotland-a9089911.html

40 Ibid.

41 Sara C Nelson, 'Parliament Prorogued: Scuffles and bursts of song as MPs protest shutdown', *Huffington Post*, 10 September 2019, www.huffingtonpost.co.uk/entry/parliament-prorogued-songs-and-protests-at-shutdown-ceremony_uk_5d7731dfe4b075210231d45f

42 Jen Kirby, 'Boris Johnson just suspended Parliament over Brexit. Here's what's going on', *Vox*, 28 August 2019, www.vox.com/2019/8/28/20836579/boris-johnson-brexit-parliament-prorogue

43 David Allen Green, 'The curious incident of the missing witness statement', *FT*, 6 September 2019, www.ft.com/content/11983298-d08e-11e9-99a4-b5ded7a7fe3f

44 David Allen Green, 'Scottish judges decide Boris Johnson misled the Queen', *FT*, 11 September 2019, www.ft.com/content/12097e7c-d47f-11e9-8367-807ebd53ab77

45 www.bbc.co.uk/news/av/uk-politics-49088773

46 Ibid.

47 Tim Wyatt, 'Tory MP suffers concussion after falling off chair', *Independent*, 1 August 2019, www.independent.co.uk/news/uk/politics/andrea-jenkyns-whiplash-concussion-chair-fall-a9030691.html

48 Angus Young, 'Backlash over Conservative Party chairman James Cleverly's wrong William Wilberforce claim', *Hull Live*, 5 August 2019, www.hulldailymail.co.uk/news/hull-east-yorkshire-news/james-cleverly-conservative-party-william-3174768

49 David [@bingaddick], Twitter, 4 August 2019, twitter.com/bingaddick/status/11577983796 21158912

50 Chaminda Jayanetti, 'England would be better off without Scotland, Tory candidate said', *Guardian*, 4 August 2019, www.theguardian.com/politics/2019/aug/04/tory-candidate-says-english-taxpayers-fleeced-by-scotland

51 Dan Bloom, 'Lord Young quits Tory government in protest at Boris Johnson's Brexit shutdown', *Mirror*, 29 August 2019, www.mirror.co.uk/news/politics/breaking-lord-young-quits-tory-19027759

52 Libby Brooks, 'Ruth Davidson quits as Scottish Tory leader citing Brexit and family', *Guardian*, 29 August 2019, www.theguardian.com/politics/2019/aug/29/ruth-davidson-quits-as-scottish-tory-leader

53 Paddy Docherty, 'An open letter to my brother the Tory MP: resign from this rogue government', *Guardian*, 3 September 2019, www.theguardian.com/commentisfree/2019/sep/03/open-letter-brother-resign-government-no-deal-brexit

54 Kate Proctor, Peter Walker and Heather Stewart, 'Phillip Lee quits Tories, leaving government without a majority', *Guardian*, 3 September 2019, www.theguardian.com/politics/2019/sep/03/phillip-lee-quits-tories-leaving-government-without-a-majority

55 'Boris Johnson's call for general election rejected by MPs', BBC, 4 September 2019, www.bbc.co.uk/news/uk-politics-49584907

56 'Brexit: Corbyn plans to call no-confidence vote to defeat no-deal', BBC, 15 August 2019, www.bbc.co.uk/news/uk-politics-49352250

57 'Vote Leave (2016) - "Taking back control is a careful change, not a sudden step"', Digital Spy, 18 July 2020, digitalspy.com/discussion/2290566/vote-leave-2016-taking-back-control-is-a-careful-change-not-a-sudden-step

58 Anna Mikhailova, 'Boris Johnson to strip 21 Tory MPs of the Tory whip in parliamentary bloodbath', *Telegraph*, 4 September 2019, www.telegraph.co.uk/politics/2019/09/04/parliament-whip-removed

59 Times News, 'Ken Clarke: Tory party taken over by the nationalist right', YouTube, 8 November 2019, www.youtube.com/watch?v=V3LI3O9lW3o

60 Matthew J. Goodwin, *New British Fascism: Rise of the British National Party*, Routledge, London and New York, 2011.

61 Joe Murphy and Nicholas Cecil, 'Jo Johnson quits: Boris Johnson's brother resigns over "tension" between "family loyalty and national interest"', *Standard*, 5 September 2019, www.standard.co.uk/news/politics/jo-johnson-quits-as-mp-amid-unresolvable-tension-between-family-loyalty-and-national-interest-a4229691.html

62 www.independent.co.uk/news/uk/politics/boris-johnson-jo-cox-death-parliament-debate-rachel-latest-a9121646.html

63 'Amber Rudd quits cabinet blaming Brexit inaction', BBC, 8 September 2019, www.bbc.co.uk/news/uk-politics-49623737

64 George Parker, 'Ex-Tory MP Sam Gyimah defects to Lib Dems', *FT*, 14 September 2019, www.ft.com/content/b55384e6-d723-11e9-8f9b-77216ebe1f17

65 Tom D. Rogers, 'Michael Gove accused of being "drunk or on drugs" as he sways and stumbles during crucial Commons debate', Evolve Politics, 26 September 2019, evolvepolitics.com/watch-michael-gove-accused-of-being-drunk-or-on-drugs-as-he-sways-and-stumbles-during-crucial-commons-debate

66 Anoosh Chakelian, 'Why it matters that Jacob Rees-Mogg was reclining in the House of Commons', New Statesman, 4 September 2019, www.newstatesman.com/politics/uk-politics/2019/09/why-it-matters-jacob-rees-mogg-was-reclining-house-commons

67 Stephen Lepitak, 'British Government's £100m Brexit advertising campaign revealed', The Drum, 1 September 2019, www.thedrum.com/news/2019/09/01/british-government-s-10 0m-brexit-advertising-campaign-revealed

68 Jonathan Read, 'Sajid Javid: "The government will obey the law, but we'll also not ask for an extension"', The New European, 8 September 2019, www.theneweuropean.co.uk/ brexit-news-sajid-javid-on-andrew-marr-show-55886

69 Jonathan Powell, 'My Secret Brexit Diary by Michel Barnier review – a British roasting', Guardian, 25 September 2021, www.theguardian.com/books/2021/sep/25/my-secret-brexit-diary-by-michel-barnier-review-a-british-roasting

70 Jonathan Read, 'Government has spent more than £250,000 on "get ready for Brexit" Facebook adverts', The New Statesman, 15 September 2019, www.theneweuropean.co.uk/ brexit-news-facebook-advert-spend-on-get-ready-for-brexit-56378

71 'Brexit delay: How is Article 50 extended?', BBC, 28 October 2019, www.bbc.co.uk/news/uk -politics-47031312

72 Amie Gordon, 'Boris Johnson "dropped pole-dancing friend Jennifer Arcuri like a stone" after she defended City trader later jailed for 14 years over Libor rate-rigging scandal', Daily Mail, 26 September 2019, www.dailymail.co.uk/news/article-7506791/Boris-Johnson-dropped-pole-dancing-friend-Jennifer-Arcuri-like-stone.html

73 David Brown, 'Boris Johnson's friend Jennifer Arcuri flags up her plans for a general election 2019 tour', The Times, 31 October 2019, www.thetimes.co.uk/article/boris-johnsons-friend-jennifer-arcuri-flags-up-her-plans-for-a-general-election-2019-tour-jz066nmf0

74 Chris Baynes, 'Jennifer Arcuri admits she feels "betrayed" by Boris Johnson, amid pole dancing revelations in extraordinary live TV interview', Independent, 7 October 2019, www.independent.co.uk/news/uk/politics/boris-johnson-jennifer-arcuri-gmb-interview-good-morning-britain-affair-allegations-a9145631.html

75 Matthew Weaver, 'Boris Johnson will not face criminal inquiry over Jennifer Arcuri', Guardian, 21 May 2020, www.theguardian.com/politics/2020/may/21/boris-johnson-will-not-face-criminal-inquiry-over-jennifer-arcuri

76 Chris Baynes, 'Jennifer Arcuri admits she feels "betrayed" by Boris Johnson, amid pole dancing revelations in extraordinary live TV interview'

77 Neil Sears, Sam Greenhill and Guy Adams, 'Boris Johnson only came round to mine for technology lessons, says ex-model who received thousands in public money', Daily Mail, 24 September 2019, www.dailymail.co.uk/news/article-7500453/Ex-model-said-Boris-John son-came-round-technology-lessons.html

78 Matthew Moore, 'I put off test that spotted my cervical cancer, says Boris Johnson's wife Marina Wheeler', The Times, 12 August 2019, www.thetimes.co.uk/article/i-put-off-test-th at-spotted-my-cervical-cancer-says-pm-s-wife-qdnzt7mm3

79 John Dunne, 'Jennifer Arcuri admits four year affair with Boris Johnson', Evening Standard, 28 March 2021, www.standard.co.uk/news/uk/jennifer-arcuri-boris-johnson-affair-b9266 66.html

80 Lizzie Dearden, 'Boris Johnson and Jennifer Arcuri investigation hampered by deleted evidence, watchdog says', Independent, 21 May 2020, www.independent.co.uk/ news/uk/politics/boris-johnson-jennifer-arcuri-criminal-investigation-news-deleted-evidence-a9527081.html

81 Lizzy Buchan, 'Tory MP says blackface is an 'entirely acceptable bit of fun' after admitting wearing racist makeup', Independent, 27 September 2019, www.independent.co.uk/news/uk /politics/desmond-swayne-blackface-tory-mp-racist-james-brown-justin-trudeau-a91230 06.html

82 Victoria Ward and Christopher Hope, 'Exclusive picture: Tory MP Sir Desmond Swayne "blacked up" as soul singer James Brown', *Telegraph*, 30 September 2019, www.telegraph.co.uk/news/2019/09/30/tory-mp-sir-desmond-swayne-pictured-blacked-soul-singer-james

83 Peter Walker, Kate Proctor, Heather Stewart and Frances Perraudin, 'Boris Johnson denies groping allegation after backing from Javid', *Guardian*, 30 September 2019, www.theguardian.com/politics/2019/sep/30/sajid-javid-backs-boris-johnson-on-groping-allegations

84 Kate Proctor and Frances Perraudin, 'Boris Johnson groping allegation haunts Tory conference', *Guardian*, 30 September 2019, www.theguardian.com/politics/2019/sep/30/boris-johnson-groping-allegation-haunts-tory-conference

85 Rowena Mason and Heather Stewart, 'Tory Brexiters rally around Johnson after supreme court defeat', *Guardian*, 24 September 2019, www.theguardian.com/politics/2019/sep/24/tory-brexiters-rally-around-johnson-after-supreme-court-defeat

86 Cahal Milmo, 'Queen "sought advice" on sacking Prime Minister, source claims', *iNews*, 29 September 2019, inews.co.uk/news/uk/queen-sought-advice-sacking-prime-minister-344801

87 Gwyn Topham, 'Grant Shapps lifts sections of speech from Chris Grayling', *Guardian*, 25 September 2019, www.theguardian.com/politics/2019/sep/25/grants-shapps-lifts-sections-of-speech-from-chris-grayling

88 Kate Proctor, 'Senior Tory MP asked to leave party conference after incident', *Guardian*, 1 October 2019, www.theguardian.com/politics/2019/oct/01/police-called-tory-conference-mp-geoffrey-clifton-brown

89 Zamira Rahim, 'Boris Johnson showed "disgracefully cavalier" attitude to studies, school letter reveals', *Independent*, 4 October 2019, www.independent.co.uk/news/uk/politics/boris-johnson-rory-stewart-eton-college-letters-live-a9142711.html

90 Jen Mills, 'Priti Patel told "I don't know why you're laughing" over Brexit fears', *Metro*, 13 October 2019, metro.co.uk/2019/10/13/priti-patel-told-dont-know-laughing-brexit-fears-10910403

91 David Pegg, Rob Evans and Felicity Lawrence, 'Owen Paterson to close private thinktank that paid for overseas trips', *Guardian*, 27 October 2019, www.theguardian.com/politics/2019/oct/27/owen-paterson-to-close-private-thinktank-that-paid-for-his-foreign-trips

92 'Owen Paterson statement following Europol meeting in the Hague on horse meat – 14 February', Gov.uk, 14 February 2013, www.gov.uk/government/news/owen-paterson-statement-following-europol-meeting-in-the-hague-on-horse-meat-14-february

93 Rob Evans, Felicity Lawrence and David Pegg, 'US agribusiness lobbyists paid for trip by David Davis', *Guardian*, 21 December 2018, www.theguardian.com/politics/2018/dec/21/us-agribusiness-lobbyists-paid-for-trip-by-david-davis

94 Anoosh Chakelian, 'A close reading of David Davis' delusional Telegraph piece on Brexit', *New Statesman*, 2 January 2018, www.newstatesman.com/politics/2018/01/close-reading-david-davis-delusional-telegraph-piece-brexit

95 Jennifer Rankin and Rowena Mason, 'Boris Johnson gets his deal and a slap on the back in Brussels', *Guardian*, 17 October 2019, www.theguardian.com/politics/2019/oct/17/boris-johnson-gets-deal-backslapping-brussels-eu-summit-brexit

96 Toby Helm, 'Brexit referendum should never have been called, say majority of voters', *Guardian*, 26 October 2019, www.theguardian.com/politics/2019/oct/26/opinium-poll-observer-uk-voters-regret-brexit-referendum-conservative-lead-over-labour

97 Ibid.

98 Heather Stewart, 'Sajid Javid refuses to assess economic dangers of Brexit plan', 21 October 2019, *Guardian*, www.theguardian.com/politics/2019/oct/21/sajid-javid-refuses-to-assess-economic-dangers-of-brexit-plan

99 Matt Honeycombe-Foster, 'Boris Johnson's Brexit deal worse for economy than Theresa May's, new analysis shows', *Politics Home*, 30 October 2019, www.politicshome.com/news/article/boris-johnsons-brexit-deal-worse-for-economy-than-theresa-mays-new-analysis-shows

100 'Johnson's Brexit leaves UK's economy worse off than May's', UK In A Changing Europe, 13 October 2019, ukandeu.ac.uk/johnsons-brexit-leaves-uk-economy-worse-off-than-mays

101 Heather Stewart and Daniel Boffey, 'MPs reject Boris Johnson's attempt to fast-track Brexit deal', *Guardian*, 22 October 2019, www.theguardian.com/politics/2019/oct/22/mps-reject -boris-johnsons-attempt-to-fast-track-brexit-deal

102 Marc D'Arcy, 'Five take-outs from the Brexit bill', BBC, 1 February 2017, www.bbc.co.uk/ news/uk-politics-parliaments-38833310

103 Eleni Courea [@elenacourea], Twitter, 23 October 2019, twitter.com/EleniCourea/ status/1187005885358444553

104 Heather Stewartand Daniel Boffey, 'MPs reject Boris Johnson's attempt to fast-track Brexit deal', *Guardian*, 22 October 2019, www.theguardian.com/politics/2019/oct/22/mps-reject-boris-johnsons-attempt-to-fast-track-brexit-deal

105 Aubrey Allegretti, 'EU has agreed Brexit delay until January 2020 - Donald Tusk', Sky News, 29 October 2019, news.sky.com/story/eu-has-agreed-brexit-delay-until-january-2020-tusk-11847480

106 Wikimedia, upload.wikimedia.org/wikipedia/commons/6/6a/Free_Trade_Areas.PNG

107 James Randerson, '9 slippery Brexit pledges', Politico, 1 November 2019, www.politico.eu/ article/9-slippery-brexit-pledges

108 Aubrey Allegretti, 'EU has agreed Brexit delay until January 2020 - Donald Tusk'

109 'Brexit transition period', Institute for Government, www.instituteforgovernment.org.uk/ explainers/brexit-transition-period

110 Toby Helm, 'Brexit referendum should never have been called, say majority of voters', *Guardian*, 26 October 2019, www.theguardian.com/politics/2019/oct/26/opinium-poll-observer-uk-voters-regret-brexit-referendum-conservative-lead-over-labour

111 Rowena Mason, 'Brexit: Parliament breaks deadlock with vote for 12 December election', *Guardian*, 30 October 2019, www.theguardian.com/politics/2019/oct/29/uk-general-election-confirmed-for-12-december-after-brexit-stalemate

112 Serina Sandhu, 'Tory rebels: the MPs who have lost the whip, defected or said they won't stand in the next general election', *iNews*, 9 September 2019, inews.co.uk/news/politics/ tory-rebels-mps-lost-whip-resigned-stand-general-election-candidates-brexit-335016

113 Phillip Inman and Julia Kollewe, 'IFS manifesto verdict: neither Tories nor Labour have credible spending plan', *Guardian*, 28 November 2019, www.theguardian.com/ business/2019/nov/28/ifs-manifesto-verdict-neither-tories-nor-labour-have-credible-spending-plan

114 Aubrey Allegretti, 'Sajid Javid warns against UK succumbing to "naked populism"', Sky News, 1 October 2018, news.sky.com/story/sajid-javid-warns-against-uk-succumbing-to-naked-populism-11514014

115 www.standard.co.uk/news/politics/tax-rises-coming-whoever-wins-the-election-leading-economists-warn-a4299121.html

116 Denis Campbell, 'Johnson's "40 new hospitals" pledge costed at up to £24bn', *Guardian*, 8 December 2019, www.theguardian.com/politics/2019/dec/08/boris-johnson-40-new-hospitals-pledge-costed

117 Peter Walker and Denis Campbell, 'Most of Boris Johnson's promised 40 new hospitals will not be totally new', *Guardian*, www.theguardian.com/society/2020/oct/02/johnsons-37bn-for-40-new-hospitals-in-england

118 'A hospital plan for England and Wales', The Health Foundation, navigator.health.org.uk/ theme/hospital-plan-england-and-wales

119 'Have police numbers dropped?', BBC, 26 July 2019, www.bbc.co.uk/news/uk-47225797

120 Patrick Worrall, 'Are the Conservatives putting 20,000 police on the streets?', Channel 4 News, 13 November 2019, www.channel4.com/news/factcheck/factcheck-are-the-conservatives-putting-20000-police-on-the-streets

121 Ashley Cowburn, 'Boris Johnson admits only 31,000 of Tories' 50,000 "more" nurses are actually new', *Independent*, 8 December 2019, www.independent.co.uk/ news/uk/politics/boris-johnson-tories-new-nurses-promise-50000-31000-a9237676.html

122 'Conservative Party manifesto 2019: 13 key policies explained', BBC, 24 November 2019, www.bbc.co.uk/news/election-2019-50524262

123 Rajeev Syal, 'Tories fail to build any of 200,000 starter homes promised in 2015, says watchdog', *Guardian*, 5 November 2019, www.theguardian.com/society/2019/nov/05/tories-broke-pledge-on-starter-homes-in-2015-manifesto-report-says

124 Alain Tolhurst, 'Twitter warns Tories after they rebrand official account as "FactcheckUK" during leaders debate', *Politics Home,* 19 November 2019, www.politicshome.com/news/article/twitter-warns-tories-after-they-rebrand-official-account-as-factcheckuk-during-leaders-debate

125 Alex Barker and Hannah Murphy, 'Conservative party's "factcheck UK" Twitter stunt backfires', *FT,* 19 November 2019, www.ft.com/content/0582a0d0-0b1f-11ea-b2d6-9bf4d1957a67

126 James Hockaday, 'Tories launch "fake Labour manifesto" website despite "FactCheckUK" backlash', *Metro,* 21 November 2019, metro.co.uk/2019/11/21/tories-launch-fake-labour-manifesto-website-despite-factcheckuk-backlash-11194311

127 Johnny Mercer [@JohnnyMercerUK], Twitter, 5 November 2019, twitter.com/JohnnyMercerUK/status/1191855472485240835

128 Johnny Mercer [@JohnnyMercerUK], Twitter, 6 November 2019, twitter.com/JohnnyMercerUK/status/1192003867568988160

129 '"Nuisance" council tenants "should live in tents" says Ashfield Tory candidate', BBC, 19 November 2019, www.bbc.co.uk/news/election-2019-50474572

130 Kate Proctor, 'Tories investigate three candidates over alleged antisemitism', *Guardian,* 7 December 2019, www.theguardian.com/politics/2019/dec/07/tories-investigate-three-candidates-over-alleged-antisemitism

131 Sarah Manavis, 'What is cultural Marxism? The alt-right meme in Suella Braverman's speech in Westminster', *New Statesman,* 22 October 2018, www.newstatesman.com/politics/2018/10/what-cultural-marxism-alt-right-meme-suella-bravermans-speech-westminster

132 'Tory MPs and peers warned over use of the term "cultural Marxism"', *The Jewish Chronicle,* 24 November 2020, www.thejc.com/news/uk/tory-mps-and-peers-warned-over-use-of-the-term-cultural-marxism-1.508974

133 Zoe Drewett, 'Tory candidate forgets he's on microphone and asks friend to pose as supporter', *Metro,* 26 November 2019, metro.co.uk/2019/11/26/tory-candidate-forgets-microphone-asks-friend-pose-supporter-11219511

134 Lizzy Buchan, 'Boris Johnson smashes union flag branded JCB "Brexit" digger through piles of boxes in bizarre campaign event', *Independent,* 10 December 2019, www.independent.co.uk/news/uk/politics/boris-johnson-brexit-wall-video-election-jcb-digger-boxes-watch-a9240801.html

135 'Boris Johnson takes ITV reporter's phone after refusing to look at photo of boy on hospital floor', ITV News, 9 December 2019, www.itv.com/news/calendar/2019-12-09/boris-johnson-takes-itv-reporter-s-phone-after-refusing-to-look-at-photo-of-boy-on-hospital-floor

136 *Guardian News,* 'Boris Johnson hides in fridge to avoid TV interview', YouTube, 11 December 2019, www.youtube.com/watch?v=Lp9XoiFbZcI

137 John Pring, 'Election 2019: Johnson backtracks on promised social care plan', Disability News Service, 28 November 2019, www.disabilitynewsservice.com/election-2019-johnson-backtracks-on-promised-social-care-plan

138 John Pring, 'Cabinet minister admits "no consensus" on social care, despite Johnson's pledge', Disability News Service, 31 October 2019, www.disabilitynewsservice.com/cabinet-minister-admits-no-consensus-on-social-care-despite-johnsons-pledge

139 Reuters, '"The NHS is not on the table": Boris Johnson denies Labour claims – video', *Guardian,* 27 November 2019, www.theguardian.com/politics/video/2019/nov/27/the-nhs-is-not-on-the-table-boris-johnson-denies-labour-claims-video

140 Jack Peat, 'Former Tory MP calls Johnson a "compulsive liar" who has betrayed "every single person he has ever had any dealings with"', *London Economic,* 11 November 2019, www.thelondoneconomic.com/politics/former-tory-mp-calls-johnson-a-compulsive-liar-who-has-betrayed-every-single-person-he-has-ever-had-any-dealings-with-166907

141 James Blitz, Jim Pickard and George Parker, 'Leaked Northern Ireland paper puts Boris Johnson's honesty under spotlight', *FT,* 6 December 2019, www.ft.com/content/1775961a-1814-11ea-8d73-6303645ac406

142 Heather Stewart, Jennifer Rankin and Lisa O'Carroll, 'Johnson accused of misleading public over Brexit deal after NI remarks', *Guardian,* 8 November 2019, www.theguardian.com/politics/2019/nov/08/boris-johnson-goods-from-northern-ireland-to-gb-wont-be-checked-brexit

143 James Blitz, Jim Pickard and George Parker, 'Leaked Northern Ireland paper puts Boris Johnson's honesty under spotlight'

144 Heather Stewart, Jennifer Rankin and Lisa O'Carroll, 'Johnson accused of misleading public over Brexit deal after NI remarks'
145 Seth Thévoz and Peter Geoghegan, 'Revealed: Russian donors have stepped up Tory funding', openDemocracy, 5 November 2019, www.opendemocracy.net/en/dark-money-investigations/revealed-russian-donors-have-stepped-tory-funding
146 Dan Sabbagh and Luke Harding, 'PM accused of cover-up over report on Russian meddling in UK politics', Guardian, 4 November 2019, www.theguardian.com/politics/2019/nov/04/no-10-blocks-russia-eu-referendum-report-until-after-election
147 Seth Thévoz and Peter Geoghegan, 'Revealed: Russian donors have stepped up Tory funding'
148 Luke Harding, 'Tory blushes deepen over activities of Conservative Friends of Russia', Guardian, 30 November 2012, www.theguardian.com/politics/2012/nov/30/activities-of-conservative-friends-of-russia
149 Dan Sabbagh and Luke Harding, 'PM accused of cover-up over report on Russian meddling in UK politics'
150 Luke Harding, 'Tory blushes deepen over activities of Conservative Friends of Russia'
151 Dan Sabbagh and Luke Harding, 'PM accused of cover-up over report on Russian meddling in UK politics'
152 Sijbren de Jong, 'Confuse, Divide and Rule - How Russia Drives Europe Apart', IES Policy Brief Issue, University of Pittsburgh, March 2016, http://aei.pitt.edu/77652
153 Mira Milosevich, 'Russia's Westpolitik and the European Union', Centre for Strategic & International Studies, 8 July 2021, www.csis.org/analysis/russias-westpolitik-and-european-union
154 Adam Payne and Adam Bienkov, 'Boris Johnson's Conservative Party has received a surge in cash from Russian donors', Business Insider, 6 November 2019, www.businessinsider.com/boris-johnsons-conservatives-receive-surge-in-cash-from-russians-2019-11?r=US&IR=T
155 Seth Thévoz and Peter Geoghegan, 'Revealed: Russian donors have stepped up Tory funding'
156 Adam Payne and Adam Bienkov, 'Boris Johnson's Conservative Party has received a surge in cash from Russian donors'
157 Tom Harper and Caroline Wheeler, 'Russian Tory donors named in secret report', The Times, 10 November 2019, www.thetimes.co.uk/article/russian-tory-donors-named-in-secret-report-z98nqpkx0
158 Jamie Pellman, '10 weird UK laws people break every day', Britton & Time, 9 November 2020, brittontime.com/2020/11/09/10-weird-uk-laws-people-break-every-day
159 'General election 2019: "Worst night for Labour since 1935"', BBC, 13 December 2019, www.bbc.co.uk/news/av/election-2019-50768605
160 Jon Henley, 'Boris Johnson wins huge majority on promise to "get Brexit done"', Guardian, 13 December 2019, www.theguardian.com/politics/2019/dec/13/bombastic-boris-johnson-wins-huge-majority-on-promise-to-get-brexit-done
161 Brian Klaas, 'Donald Trump's Britain First retweets must be the final straw', CNN, 20 November 2018, edition.cnn.com/2017/11/29/opinions/donald-trump-has-gone-too-far-again-brian-klaas-opinion/index.html
162 Jon Sharman, 'Britain First leader officially joins Conservative Party: "Boris Johnson is like us"', Independent, 19 December 2019, www.independent.co.uk/news/uk/politics/paul-golding-conservatives-britain-first-boris-johnson-muslim-women-letterboxes-a9254061.html?__twitter_impression=true
163 Jon Henley, 'Boris Johnson wins huge majority on promise to "get Brexit done"'
164 Boris Johnson [@BorisJohnson], Twitter, 13 December 2019, twitter.com/borisjohnson/status/1212679425629859840

2020: A Fantastic Year for Britain

January

1 Jeanna Bryner, '1st known case of coronavirus traced back to November in China', Live Science, 14 March 2020, www.livescience.com/first-case-coronavirus-found.html
2 'China coronavirus: Lockdown measures rise across Hubei province', BBC, 23 January 2020, www.bbc.com/news/world-asia-china-51217455

3   'Listings of WHO's response to COVID-19', World Health Organization, last updated on 29 January 2021, www.who.int/news/item/29-06-2020-covidtimeline

4   George Grylls, 'Boris Johnson cleared of wrongdoing over £15,000 Mustique holiday', *The Times*, 8 July 2021, www.thetimes.co.uk/article/boris-johnson-cleared-of-wrongdoing-over-15-000-mustique-holiday-pt325hmj8

5   Toby Helm and Michael Savage, 'Johnson to cabinet: shape up or I'll sack you within weeks', *Guardian*, 18 January 2020, www.theguardian.com/politics/2020/jan/18/boris-johnson-warns-cabinet-shape-up-or-be-sacked

6   'Second Johnson ministry', Wikipedia, last edited on 24 June 2022, en.wikipedia.org/wiki/Second_Johnson_ministry#February_2020_%E2%80%93_September_2021

7   Richard Vaughan, 'Tory MPs threaten mutiny over Boris Johnson's decision to give HS2 the go-ahead', *iNews*, 30 January 2020, inews.co.uk/news/politics/tory-mps-mutiny-boris-johnson-hs2-decision-trains-392235

8   Jack Simpson, 'HS2: Boris calls for £56bn line to be stopped', Construction News, 1 October 2018, www.constructionnews.co.uk/civils/contracts-civils/hs2-boris-calls-for-56bn-line-to-be-stopped-01-10-2018

9   'Tutankhamun', Wikipedia, last edited on 26 June 2022, en.wikipedia.org/wiki/Tutankhamun

10 'HS2: What is the route, when will it be finished and what will it cost?', BBC, 18 November 2021, www.bbc.co.uk/news/uk-16473296

11 Amelia Gentleman, Lisa O'Carroll, Peter Walker and Libby Brooks, 'MPs vote to drop child refugee protections from Brexit bill', *Guardian*, 8 January 2020, www.theguardian.com/world/2020/jan/08/mps-vote-to-drop-child-refugee-protections-from-brexit-bill

12 Amnesty International UK, 'UK Government "deliberately and destructively" preventing child refugees from reuniting with their families – new report', press release, 11 January 2020, www.amnesty.org.uk/press-releases/uk-government-deliberately-and-destructively-preventing-child-refugees-reuniting

13 Jonathan Calvert, George Arbuthnott and Jonathan Leake, 'Coronavirus: 38 days when Britain sleepwalked into disaster', *The Times*, 19 April 2020, www.thetimes.co.uk/article/coronavirus-38-days-when-britain-sleepwalked-into-disaster-hq3b9tlgh

14 Department of Health and Social Care, 'Statement from the 4 UK Chief Medical Officers on novel coronavirus', press release, Gov.uk, 30 January 2020, www.gov.uk/government/news/statement-from-the-four-uk-chief-medical-officers-on-novel-coronavirus

15 Jim Pickard, '"Bung a bob" for a Big Ben Brexit bong, says Boris Johnson', *FT*, 14 January 2020, www.ft.com/content/3abfa026-36ea-11ea-a6d3-9a26f8c3cba4

16 Otto English [@Otto_English], Twitter, 4 August 2021, mobile.twitter.com/Otto_English/status/1423044555646058497

17 'Has the "cost of Brexit" amounted to more than the UK's total net contributions over 47 years?', Full Fact, 23 January 2020, fullfact.org/europe/online-cost-brexit-net-contributions

18 'List of departures from the second May ministry', Wikipedia, last edited on 11 March 2022, en.wikipedia.org/wiki/List_of_departures_from_the_second_May_ministry

19 'Getting out of the EU can be quick and easy – and the UK holds most of the cards in any negotiation', John Redwood's Diary, 17 July 2016, johnredwoodsdiary.com/2016/07/17/getting-out-of-the-eu-can-be-quick-and-easy-the-uk-holds-most-of-the-cards-in-any-negotiation

20 Niall McCarthy, 'Brexit costs nearly match UK's total EU contributions', Statista, 20 January 2020, www.statista.com/chart/20544/forecast-cost-of-brexit-compared-to-the-uks-eu-budget-contributions

21 Tim Shipman, 'Covid-scarred No 10 sees Brexit no deal as a doddle', *The Times*, 23 August 2020, www.thetimes.co.uk/article/covid-scarred-no-10-sees-brexit-no-deal-as-a-doddle-sx57kqmn6

22 Joe Mellor, 'Video shows moment Boris Johnson steps off plane in Newcastle on day coronavirus was confirmed in the city', The London Economic, 31 January 2020, www.thelondoneconomic.com/news/video-shows-moment-boris-johnson-steps-off-plane-in-newcastle-on-day-coronavirus-was-confirmed-in-city-176003

23 Ibid.

24 Heather Stewart, Daniel Boffey and Rajeev Syal, 'Boris Johnson promises Brexit will lead to national revival', *Guardian*, 31 January 2020, www.theguardian.com/politics/2020/jan/31/boris-johnson-promises-brexit-will-lead-to-national-revival

25 Stephen Grey and Andrew MacAskill, 'Special Report: Johnson listened to his scientists about coronavirus – but they were slow to sound the alarm', Reuters, 7 April 2020, www.reuters.com/article/us-health-coronavirus-britain-path-speci-idUSKBN21P1VF

26 Prof Joseph T Wu, PhD, Kathy Leung, PhD, Prof Gabriel M Leung, MD, 'Nowcasting and forecasting the potential domestic and international spread of the 2019-nCoV outbreak originating in Wuhan, China: a modelling study', The Lancet, 395(10225), pp. 689–697, 29 February 2020, www.thelancet.com/journals/lancet/article/PIIS0140-6736(20)30260-9/fulltext

27 Nicola Davis, 'Coronavirus: what other public health emergencies has the WHO declared?', Guardian, 30 January 2020, www.theguardian.com/global/2020/jan/30/coronavirus-what-other-public-health-emergencies-has-the-who-declared

28 Rajeev Syal and Solomon Hughes, 'Lycamobile is Tories' top corporate donor – but pays no corporation tax', Guardian, 4 June 2012, www.theguardian.com/politics/2012/jun/04/lycamobile-tories-biggest-corporate-donor

29 Heidi Blake, Michael Gillard, Tom Warren, Jane Brady and Richard Holmes, 'This Tory donor was secretly filmed dropping cash-stuffed rucksacks at post offices', BuzzFeed, 5 October 2015, www.buzzfeed.com/heidiblake/this-tory-donor-was-secretly-filmed-dropping-cash-stuffed-ru

30 Ibid.

31 Solomon Hughes and Rob Evans, 'Major Tory donor Lycamobile embroiled in three diputes with HMRC', Guardian, 2 February 2020, www.theguardian.com/money/2020/feb/02/major-tory-donor-lycamobile-embroiled-in-three-disputes-with-hmrc

32 Heidi Blake, Tom Warren, Richard Holmes and Jane Bradley, 'The UK refused to raid a company suspected of money laundering, citing its Tory donations', BuzzFeed, 19 April 2018, www.buzzfeed.com/heidiblake/uk-refused-to-raid-lycamobile-citing-its-tory-donations

February

1 Dan Bloom and Ben Glaze, 'Boris Johnson staying inside his Kent country house instead of visiting Storm Dennis victims', Kent Live, 17 February 2020, www.kentlive.news/news/kent-news/boris-johnson-staying-inside-kent-3858070

2 Alix Culbertson, 'Dominic Cummings claims Boris Johnson was writing Shakespeare book instead of dealing with COVID', Sky News, 12 November 2021, news.sky.com/story/dominic-cummings-claims-boris-johnson-was-writing-shakespeare-book-instead-of-dealing-with-covid-12467178

3 Mikey Smith, 'Boris Johnson's country manor getaway with Carrie Symonds as coronavirus crisis grew', Mirror, 19 April 2020, www.mirror.co.uk/news/politics/coronavirus-boris-johnsons-country-manor-21891035

4 Alessandro Miani, Ernesto Burgio, Prisco Piscitelli, Renato Lauro and Annamaria Colao, 'The Italian war-like measures to fight coronavirus spreading: re-open closed hospitals now', eClinicalMedicine, 21, 27 March 2020, www.thelancet.com/pdfs/journals/eclinm/PIIS2589-5370(20)30064-X.pdf

5 Reuters Staff, 'G7 Health ministers to discuss coronavirus on Monday – Italy', Reuters, 3 February 2020, www.reuters.com/article/china-health-g7-italy-idINL8N2A320C

6 Dominic Cummings, 'Risk, aggression, Brexit and Article 16', Dominic Cummings substack, 12 November 2021, dominiccummings.substack.com/p/risk-aggression-brexit-and-article

7 Sophia Sleigh, 'Brexit Day coins sell for £60k at Tory Black and White ball', Evening Standard, 26 February 2020, www.standard.co.uk/news/politics/brexit-day-coins-sell-for-ps60k-at-tory-black-and-white-ball-a4372076.html

8 Chris Kitching, 'Coronavirus "could kill 500,00 Brits and infect 80%" as thousands face mass GP testing', Mirror, 27 February 2020, www.mirror.co.uk/news/uk-news/coronavirus-could-kill-500000-infect-21578658

9 Alex Morales, 'Boris Johnson's top aide seeks "weirdos and misfits" to change British government', Japan Times, 3 January 2020, www.japantimes.co.jp/news/2020/01/03/world/politics-diplomacy-world/boris-johnsons-top-aide-seeks-weirdos-misfits-change-british-government

10 Ibid.

11 Rowena Mason and Fiona Harvey, 'Boris Johnson doesn't get climate change, says sacked COP 26 head', *Guardian*, 4 February 2020, www.theguardian.com/environment/2020/feb/04/sacked-cop-26-chair-claire-oneill-berates-boris-johnson-over-climate-record

12 Dave Keating, 'Four years ago, Boris Johnson said climate concern was "without foundation"', *Forbes*, 5 February 2020, www.forbes.com/sites/davekeating/2020/02/05/four-years-ago-boris-johnson-said-climate-concern-was-without-foundation/?sh=630e49806954

13 Tom Kington, 'Italy declares state of emergency after two coronavirus cases are confirmed', *The Times*, 31 January 2020, www.thetimes.co.uk/article/italy-declares-state-of-emergency-after-two-coronavirus-cases-are-confirmed-r8xlpfqmw

14 Emma Graham-Harrison and Lily Kuo, 'China's coronavirus lockdown strategy: brutal but effective', *Guardian*, 19 March 2020, www.theguardian.com/world/2020/mar/19/chinas-coronavirus-lockdown-strategy-brutal-but-effective

15 Ian Sinclair and Rupet Read, '"A national scandal" A timeline of the UK government's woeful response to the coronavirus crisis', *Byline Times*, 11 April 2020, bylinetimes.com/2020/04/11/a-national-scandal-a-timeline-of-the-uk-governments-woeful-response-to-the-coronavirus-crisis

16 Sarah Boseley, 'Austerity blamed for life expectancy stalling for first time in century', *Guardian*, 25 February 2020, www.theguardian.com/society/2020/feb/24/austerity-blamed-for-life-expectancy-stalling-for-first-time-in-century

17 'Richest European countries 2022', World Population Review, accessed on 30 June 2022, worldpopulationreview.com/country-rankings/richest-european-countries

18 'Ending child poverty', The Children's Society, www.childrenssociety.org.uk/what-we-do/our-work/ending-child-poverty

19 Sarah Boseley, 'Austerity blamed for life expectancy stalling for first time in century'

20 D. Clark, 'Number of dollar millionaires among adult population in the United Kingdom (UK) from 2012 to 2020', Statista, 10 December 2021, www.statista.com/statistics/434012/population-of-dollar-millionaires-in-the-united-kingdom-uk

21 Nikou Asgari, 'One in five UK baby boomers are millionaires', *FT*, 9 January 2019, www.ft.com/content/c69b49de-1368-11e9-a581-4ff78404524e

22 Juliette Garside, 'Recession rich: Britain's wealthiest double net worth since crisis', *Guardian*, 26 April 2015, www.theguardian.com/business/2015/apr/26/recession-rich-britains-wealthiest-double-net-worth-since-crisis

23 Patrick Butler, 'Welfare spending for UK's poorest shrinks by £37bn', *Guardian*, 23 September 2018, www.theguardian.com/politics/2018/sep/23/welfare-spending-uk-poorest-austerity-frank-field; D. Clark, 'Public sector expenditure on tertiary education in the United Kingdom from 2009/10 to 2020/21', Statista, 17 September 2021, www.statista.com/statistics/298902/higher-education-spending-uk; Tom Harris, Louis Hodge and David Phillips, 'English local government funding: trends and challenges in 2019 and beyond', Institute for Fiscal Studies, 13 November 2019, ifs.org.uk/publications/14563; Nia Griffith, 'Unprecedented cuts Conservatives have made to defence since 2010 – Nia Griffith', Labour, 16 July 2019, labour.org.uk/press/unprecedented-cuts-conservatives-made-defence-since-2010-nia-griffith; *UK Defence in Numbers 2019*, Ministry of Defence UK, 2019, assets.publishing.service.gov.uk/government/uploads/system/uploads/attachment_data/file/919361/20200227_CH_UK_Defence_in_Numbers_2019.pdf; 'Justice spending is down 25% since 2010, not 40%', Full Fact, 18 February 2020, fullfact.org/law/justice-spending-rachel-shabi; 'Supplementary estaimte 2020–21: Estimates memorandum', Ministry of Justice, accessed 30 June 2022, committees.parliament.uk/publications/4947/documents/52560/default; Lizzy Buchan, 'Education spending slashed by £7bn since 2011 with children "paying pricefor austerity", says Labour', *Independent*, 14 January 2019, www.independent.co.uk/news/uk/politics/labour-angela-rayner-funding-cuts-department-education-damian-hinds-a8726151.html; Carl Emmerson, Christine Farquharson and Paul Johnson (eds.), *The IFS Green Budget*, Institute for Fiscal Studies, October 2018, www.ifs.org.uk/uploads/publications/budgets/gb2018/GB2018.pdf

24 Ross Hawkins, 'Boris Johnson's father spoke to Chinese ambassador about coronavirus', BBC, 6 February 2020, www.bbc.co.uk/news/uk-politics-51394044

25   Steven Swinford, 'Peter Cruddas and Daniel Hannan among Tory donors and Brexit rebels
     on Johnson's peerage list', *The Times*, 7 February 2020, www.thetimes.co.uk/article/peter-
     cruddas-and-daniel-hannan-among-tory-donors-and-brexit-rebels-on-johnsons-peerage-
     list-5j9jzwq2k
26   Emma Graham-Harrison and Lily Kuo, 'China's coronavirus lockdown strategy: brutal but
     effective'
27   Tania Snuggs, 'Coronavirus: "We can all play our part" – UK public health campaign offers
     advice to stop spread', Sky News, 2 February 2020, news.sky.com/story/coronavirus-we-
     can-all-play-our-part-government-campaign-offers-advice-to-stop-the-spread-11924298
28   Ibid.
29   Ibid.
30   Ian Sinclair and Rupet Read, '"A national scandal" A timeline of the UK government's
     woeful response to the coronavirus crisis'
31   Ibid.
32   *Telegraph* Reporters, 'Boris Johnson "scrapped cabinet pandemic committee six months
     before coronavirus hit UK"', *Telegraph*, 13 June 2020, www.telegraph.co.uk/politics/2020/06
     /13/boris-johnson-scrapped-cabinet-pandemic-committee-six-months
33   Aubrey Allegretti, 'Dominic Cummings' timeline of the early days of the Covid crisis',
     Guardian, 26 May 2021, www.theguardian.com/politics/2021/may/26/dominic-cummings-
     timeline-of-coronavirus-crisis
34   Ian Sinclair and Rupet Read, '"A national scandal" A timeline of the UK government's
     woeful response to the coronavirus crisis'
35   Sunita Patel-Carstairs, 'Coronavirus "likely to become more significant" across UK, Boris
     Johnson warns', Sky News, 2 March 2020, news.sky.com/story/coronavirus-uk-must-be-pre
     pared-for-widespread-transmission-of-covid-19-11947743
36   Kate Proctor, 'Boris Johnson will not hold coronavirus crisis meeting until Monday',
     Guardian, 28 February 2020, www.theguardian.com/politics/2020/feb/28/boris-johnson-
     not-to-hold-coronavirus-crisis-meeting-cobra-until-monday
37   Stephen Grey and Andrew MacAskill, 'Special Report: Johnson listened to his scientists
     about coronavirus – but they were slow to sound the alarm', Reuters, 7 April 2020,
     www.reuters.com/article/us-health-coronavirus-britain-path-speci-idUSKBN21P1VF
38   Jonathan Calvert, George Arbuthnott and Jonathan Leake, 'Coronavirus: 38 days when
     Britain sleepwalked into disaster', *The Times*, 19 April 2020, www.thetimes.co.uk/
     article/coronavirus-38-days-when-britain-sleepwalked-into-disaster-hq3b9tlgh
39   Aubrey Allegretti, 'Dominic Cummings' timeline of the early days of the Covid crisis'
40   'Cabinet reshuffle: Sajid Javid resigns as chancellor', BBC, 14 February 2020,
     www.bbc.co.uk/news/uk-politics-51491662
41   Harriet Brewis, 'Housing minister Esther McVey mocked for saying "3D architects"
     are now building homes "on computers"', *Evening Standard*, 30 September 2019,
     www.standard.co.uk/news/politics/housing-minister-esther-mcvey-mocked-for-saying-3d-
     architects-are-now-building-homes-on-computers-a4250356.html
42   Liam Thorp, 'All the worst things sacked cabinet minister Esther McVey has said', *Liverpool
     Echo*, 14 February 2020, www.liverpoolecho.co.uk/news/liverpool-news/worst-things-
     sacked-cabinet-minister-17744638
43   Aubrey Allegretti, 'Dominic Cummings' timeline of the early days of the Covid crisis'

March

1   Rowena Mason, 'Boris Johnson boasted of shaking hands on day Sage warned not to',
    Guardian, 5 May 2020, www.theguardian.com/politics/2020/may/05/boris-johnson-
    boasted-of-shaking-hands-on-day-sage-warned-not-to
2   Matthew Weaver, Haroon Siddique and Amy Walker, 'Move to weekly UK coronavirus
    updates criticised by experts', *Guardian*, 4 March 2020, www.theguardian.com/world/2020
    /mar/04/move-to-weekly-uk-coronavirus-updates-criticised-by-experts
3   Rowena Mason, 'Boris Johnson boasted of shaking hands on day Sage warned not to'
4   Ian Sinclair and Rupert Read, '"A National Scandal" A timeline of the UK government's
    woeful response to the Coronavirus crisis', *Byline Times*, 11 April 2020, bylinetimes.com/20
    20/04/11/a-national-scandal-a-timeline-of-the-uk-governments-woeful-response-to-the-
    coronavirus-crisis

5   'UK reports 30% rise of coronavirus cases to 273, third death', CGNT, 9 March 2020,
    news.cgtn.com/news/2020-03-09/UK-reports-30-rise-of-coronavirus-cases-to-273-third-
    death-OI7UVY0YAU/index.html
6   Rupert J Read, 'What would a precautionary approach to the coronavirus look like?',
    Medium, 7 March 2020, medium.com/@rupertjread/what-would-a-precautionary-
    approach-to-the-coronavirus-look-like-155626f7c2bd
7   'Close down all UK airports & seaports to prevent further spreading of Covid-19', UK
    Government and Parliament, petition.parliament.uk/petitions/300932
8   Pilita Clark, Robin Harding, Guy Chazan, Daniel Dombey, Christian Shepherd, Laura
    Hughes, Aime Williams, David Blood and Bob Haslett, 'Britain's open borders make
    it a global outlier in coronavirus fight', FT, 16 April 2020, www.ft.com/content/91
    dea18f-ad0e-4dcb-98c3-de836b1ba79b
9   Charles Hymas, Camilla Tominey and Anna Mikhailova, 'Nadine Dorries diagnosed
    with coronavirus, and officials may have to test Boris Johnson', Telegraph, 11 March 2020,
    www.telegraph.co.uk/news/2020/03/10/nadine-dorries-infected-coronavirus
10 Guardian Staff, 'How do coronavirus containment measures vary across Europe?',
    Guardian, 16 March 2020, www.theguardian.com/world/2020/mar/12/how-do-
    coronavirus-containment-measures-vary-across-europe
11 Aubrey Allegretti, 'Dominic Cummings' timeline of the early days of the Covid crisis',
    Guardian, 26 May 2021, www.theguardian.com/politics/2021/may/26/dominic-cummings-
    timeline-of-coronavirus-crisis
12 Sarah Boseley, 'WHO urges countries to "track and trace" every Covid-19 case', Guardian,
    13 March 2020, www.theguardian.com/world/2020/mar/13/who-urges-countries-to-track-
    and-trace-every-covid-19-case#img-1
13 Aubrey Allegretti, 'Dominic Cummings' timeline of the early days of the Covid crisis'
14 Pallab Ghosh, 'Coronavirus: Some scientists say UK virus strategy is "risking lives"', BBC,
    14 March 2020, www.bbc.co.uk/news/science-environment-51892402
15 Aubrey Allegretti, 'Dominic Cummings' timeline of the early days of the Covid crisis'
16 Jonathan Calvert, George Arbuthnott and Jonathan Leake, 'Coronavirus: 38 days when
    Britain sleepwalked into disaster', The Times, 19 April 2020, www.thetimes.co.uk/article/
    coronavirus-38-days-when-britain-sleepwalked-into-disaster-hq3b9tlgh
17 Andy Gregory, 'Coronavirus: Main events cancelled in UK and around the world',
    Independent, 15 March 2020, www.independent.co.uk/news/uk/home-news/coronavirus-
    uk-cancelled-sport-music-festivals-events-latest-postponed-a9402811.html
18 Nick Sommerlad, 'Cheltenham Festival: Questions over Matt Hancock's racing links and
    lockdown timing', Mirror, 19 July 2020, www.mirror.co.uk/news/politics/matt-hancocks-ra
    cing-links-raise-22381789
19 Emer O'Toole, 'Matt Hancock given £350k from figures linked to Cheltenham Festival', The
    National, 20 July 2020, www.thenational.scot/news/18594722.matt-hancock-given-350k-
    figures-linked-cheltenham-festival
20 Larry Elliott and Ben Quinn, 'Budget: Sunak to pledge billions to soften Covid-19 impact
    as virus reaches Downing Street', Guardian, 10 March 2020, www.theguardian.com/uk-
    news/2020/mar/10/budget-sunak-to-pledge-billions-to-soften-covid-19-impact
21 Nick Sommerlad, 'Cheltenham Festival: Questions over Matt Hancock's racing links and
    lockdown timing'
22 Heather Stewart, 'UK to ban mass gatherings in coronavirus U-turn', Guardian, 13
    March 2020, www.theguardian.com/world/2020/mar/13/uk-to-ban-mass-gatherings-in-
    coronavirus-u-turn
23 Aubrey Allegretti, 'Dominic Cummings' timeline of the early days of the Covid crisis'
24 Heather Stewart, 'UK to ban mass gatherings in coronavirus U-turn'
25 Tariq Tahir, 'They drink it's all over: Brits ignore pleas to avoid pubs on final night before
    nationwide lockdown begins', Sun, 20 March 2020, www.thesun.co.uk/news/11220599
    /brits-hit-pubs-plea-coronavirus
26 Aubrey Allegretti, 'Dominic Cummings' timeline of the early days of the Covid crisis'
27 'Coronavirus: UK deaths double in 24 hours', BBC, 14 March 2020, www.bbc.co.uk/news
    /uk-51889957
28 'Europe edging towards total coronavirus lockdown', Aljazeera, 16 March 2020, www.aljaze
    era.com/economy/2020/3/16/europe-edging-towards-total-coronavirus-lockdown

29 Ian Sinclair and Rupert Read, '"A National Scandal" A timeline of the UK government's woeful response to the Coronavirus crisis'
30 Ibid.
31 Ibid.
32 Stephen Grey and Andrew MacAskill, 'Special Report: Johnson listened to his scientists about coronavirus - but they were slow to sound the alarm', Reuters, 7 April 2020, www.reuters.com/article/us-health-coronavirus-britain-path-speci-idUSKBN21P1VF
33 Ewan Somerville, 'Coronavirus China: When did Wuhan lockdown begin and for how long?', Evening Standard, 8 April 2020, www.standard.co.uk/news/world/wuhan-lockdown-start-date-how-long-a4409866.html; Ian Sinclair and Rupert Read, '"A National Scandal" A timeline of the UK government's woeful response to the Coronavirus crisis'
34 Peter Walker, 'Boris Johnson: UK can turn tide of coronavirus in 12 weeks', Guardian, 19 March 2020, www.theguardian.com/world/2020/mar/19/boris-johnson-uk-can-turn-tide-of-coronavirus-in-12-weeks
35 Institute for Government Analysis, 'Timeline of UK coronavirus lockdowns, March 2020 to March 2021', www.instituteforgovernment.org.uk/sites/default/files/timeline-lockdown-web.pdf
36 Lucia Binding, 'Coronavirus: Italy deaths leap by 627 to 4,032 - biggest rise in 24 hours', Sky News, 21 March 2020, news.sky.com/story/coronavirus-italy-deaths-leap-by-627-to-4-032-biggest-rise-in-24-hours-11961174
37 Rebecca Gilroy, 'New temporary coronavirus hospital in name of Florence Nightingale revealed', Nursing Times, 24 March 2020, www.nursingtimes.net/news/coronavirus/new-temporary-coronavirus-hospital-in-name-of-florence-nightingale-revealed-24-03-2020
38 Nick Carding, 'Revealed: Nightingale hospitals to cost half a billion pounds in total', HSJ, 20 January 2021, www.hsj.co.uk/finance-and-efficiency/revealed-nightingale-hospitals-to-cost-half-a-billion-pounds-in-total/7029345.article
39 Siva Anandaciva, 'Was building the NHS Nightingale hospitals worth the money?', The Kings Fund, 5 May 2021, www.kingsfund.org.uk/blog/2021/04/nhs-nightingale-hospitals-worth-money
40 Michael Savage, 'NHS winter crisis fears grow after thousands of EU staff quit', Guardian, 24 November 2019, www.theguardian.com/society/2019/nov/24/nhs-winter-crisis-thousands-eu-staff-quit
41 Nick Carding, 'Revealed: Nightingale hospitals to cost half a billion pounds in total'
42 Rowena Mason and Lisa O'Carroll, 'No 10 claims it missed deadline for EU ventilator scheme', Guardian, 26 March 2020, www.theguardian.com/world/2020/mar/26/no-10-boris-johnson-accused-of-putting-brexit-over-breathing-in-covid-19-ventilator-row
43 Ibid.
44 'Dyson lobbying row: Boris Johnson makes "no apology" for seeking ventilators', BBC, 21 April 2021, www.bbc.co.uk/news/uk-politics-56832486
45 'Boris Johnson told Sir James Dyson by text he would "fix" tax issue', BBC, 21 April 2021, www.bbc.co.uk/news/uk-politics-56819137
46 Rob Davies, 'Dyson will not supply ventilators to NHS to treat Covid-19', Guardian, 24 April 2020, www.theguardian.com/world/2020/apr/24/dyson-will-not-supply-ventilators-to-nhs-to-treat-covid-19
47 Ian Sinclair and Rupert Read, '"A National Scandal" A timeline of the UK government's woeful response to the Coronavirus crisis'
48 Stephen Paton, 'Boris Johnson makes "last gasp" joke about lack of ventilators amid pandemic', The National, 17 March 2020, www.thenational.scot/news/18310479.boris-johnson-makes-last-gasp-joke-lack-ventilators-amid-pandemic
49 Gary Gibbon, 'Boris Johnson declares "war" on coronavirus', Channel 4 News, 17 March 2020, www.channel4.com/news/boris-johnson-declares-war-on-coronavirus
50 Stefan Simanowitz [@StefSimanowitz], Twitter, 26 March 2020, twitter.com/StefSimanowitz/status/1243073827392950274
51 Rob Davies, 'The inside story of the UK's NHS coronavirus ventilator challenge', Guardian, 4 May 2020, www.theguardian.com/business/2020/may/04/the-inside-story-of-the-uks-nhs-coronavirus-ventilator-challenge
52 Stefan Simanowitz [@StefSimanowitz], Twitter, 26 March 2020, twitter.com/StefSimanowitz/status/1243073827392950274

53   Jason G Goldman, 'Animals that can count', BBC, 28th November 2012, www.bbc.com/future/article/20121128-animals-that-can-count

54   Daniel Boffey, 'Timeline of UK's coronavirus PPE shortage', *Guardian*, 13 April 2020, www.theguardian.com/politics/2020/apr/13/timeline-of-uks-coronavirus-ppe-shortage

55   Ibid.

56   Peter Foster and Sarah Neville, 'How poor planning left the UK without enough PPE', *FT*, 1 May 2020, www.ft.com/content/9680c20f-7b71-4f65-9bec-0e9554a8e0a7

57   Ibid.

58   Channel 4 News Investigations Teams, 'Revealed: PPE stockpile was out-of-date when coronavirus hit UK', *Channel 4 News*, 4 May 2020, www.channel4.com/news/revealed-ppe-stockpile-was-out-of-date-when-coronavirus-hit-uk

59   Sophia Ankel, 'Photos show how shortages are forcing doctors and nurses to improvise coronavirus PPE from snorkel masks, pool noodles, and trash bags', Business Insider, 23 April 2020, www.businessinsider.com/photos-show-doctors-nurses-improvising-due-to-lack-of-ppe-2020-4

60   Luke Haynes, 'Hancock denies PPE shortages caused any of 1,500 NHS staff deaths from COVID-19', *GP*, 10 June 2021, www.gponline.com/hancock-denies-ppe-shortages-caused-1500-nhs-staff-deaths-covid-19/article/1718813

61   Stefan Simanowitz [@StefSimanowitz], Twitter, 24 March 2020, twitter.com/StefSimanowitz/status/1242536002197037057

62   David Conn, Russell Scott and David Pegg, 'Firm with mystery investors wins £200m of PPE contracts via "high-priority lane"', *Guardian*, 21 December 2020, www.theguardian.com/world/2020/dec/21/firm-with-mystery-investors-wins-200m-of-ppe-contracts-via-high-priority-lane

63   Haroon Siddique, 'Use of "VIP lane" to award Covid PPE contracts unlawful, high court rules', *Guardian*, 12 January 2022, www.theguardian.com/politics/2022/jan/12/use-of-vip-lane-to-award-covid-ppe-contracts-unlawful-high-court-rules

64   David Pegg, 'VIP lane for Covid suppliers left UK civil servants "drowning" in non-credible bids', *Guardian*, 22 April 2021, www.theguardian.com/politics/2021/apr/22/vip-lane-for-covid-suppliers-left-uk-civil-servants-drowning-in-non-credible-bids

65   'PPE masks not fit for purpose', Good Law Project, 6 August 2020, goodlawproject.org/update/ppe-masks-not-fit-for-purpose

66   George Greenwood and Billy Kenber, 'Andrew Mills: Adviser behind bungled £250m mask contract hides earnings', *The Times*, 21 January 2021, www.thetimes.co.uk/article/andrew-mills-adviser-behind-bungled-250m-mask-contract-hides-earnings-0lwgbx0g5

67   Ibid.

68   Mikey Smith, 'Bank "suspended" Matt Hancock's PPE deal payments fearing "VIPs" could be fraudsters', *Mirror*, 18 May 2021, www.mirror.co.uk/news/politics/bank-suspended-matt-hancocks-ppe-24135963

69   Martin Williams and Adam Bychawski, 'Record profits for firm involved in bungled £250m PPE deal', openDemocracy, 1 October 2021, www.opendemocracy.net/en/dark-money-investigations/record-profits-for-firm-involved-in-bungled-250m-ppe-deal

70   Joel Hills, 'Revealed: The company given £800m of Covid PPE contracts by Government without open tender', ITV News, 19 December 2020, www.itv.com/news/2020-12-18/revealed-the-company-given-800m-of-covid-ppe-contracts-by-government-without-open-tender

71   'REVEALED: Profits jumped 500% at Uniserve after firm landed "VIP" contracts', Good Law Project, 4 October 2021, goodlawproject.org/update/uniserve-profits-500-vip-contracts

72   Ibid.

73   Ibid.

74   Bimpe Archer, 'Sweet company awarded huge PPE contract to make final delivery', *Irish News*, 25 July 2020, www.irishnews.com/news/northernirelandnews/2020/07/25/news/sweet-company-awarded-huge-ppe-contract-to-make-final-delivery-2015610

75   'PPE for health service that cost taxpayer £1k sold on for £5', BBC, 14 November 2021, www.bbc.co.uk/news/uk-northern-ireland-59651994

76 Sam Bright, 'Government Awards £122 million PPE contract to One-Month-Old Firm', *Byline Times*, 14 September 2020, bylinetimes.com/2020/09/14/government-awards-122-million-ppe-contract-to-one-month-old-firm
77 Caroline Lucas, 'Letter to Health Minister about PPE contracts', www.carolinelucas.com/caroline/parliament/letter/letter-to-health-minister-about-ppe-contracts
78 Oliver Wright and Henry Zeffman, 'Tory peers who keep a (very) low profile', *The Times*, 6 August 2016, www.thetimes.co.uk/article/tory-peers-who-keep-a-very-low-profile-jpk0t dc3n
79 David Conn and Paul Lewis, 'Michelle Mone referred company for PPE contracts five days before it was incorporated', *Guardian*, 7 January 2022, www.theguardian.com/politics/2022/jan/07/michelle-mone-referred-company-for-ppe-contracts-five-days-before-it-was-incorporated
80 David Conn, Paul Lewis and Harry Davies, 'Tory peer Michelle Mone secretly involved in PPE firm she referred to government', *Guardian*, 6 January 2022, www.theguardian.com/world/2022/jan/06/tory-peer-michelle-mone-involved-ppe-medpro-government-contracts
81 Sam Bright, 'Government Awards £122 million PPE contract to One-Month-Old Firm'
82 'EXCLUSIVE: 4 more VIP-lane companies revealed', Good Law Project, 29 April 2021, goodlawproject.org/update/awarded-contracts-vip-lane
83 Rob Evans, 'Tory donor lobbied minister to speed up his £65m PPE deal', *Guardian*, 1 April 2021, www.theguardian.com/world/2021/apr/01/tory-donor-lobbied-minister-to-speed-up-his-65m-ppe-deal
84 Sam Bright, 'Firm owned by Conservative donor NETS additional £81.8 Million Government PPE Deals', *Byline Times*, 18 September 2020, bylinetimes.com/2020/09/18/firm-meller-designs-conservative-donor-nets-millions-government-ppe-deals
85 Ibid.
86 Ibid.
87 'EXCLUSIVE: 4 more VIP-lane companies revealed', Good Law Project
88 Caroline Lucas, 'Letter to Health Minister about PPE contracts'
89 Stephen Delahunty, 'Recruitment firm defends £18 million PPE contract', *Byline Times*, 17 July 2020, bylinetimes.com/2020/07/17/recruitment-firm-defends-18-million-ppe-contract
90 Caroline Lucas, 'Letter to Health Minister about PPE contracts'
91 David Rose, 'The £6.75billion PPE debacle: Dossier reveals ministers UNDERBOUGHT then threw fortunes at protective clothing - much of which was overpriced or can never be used', *Daily Mail*, 30 October 2020, www.dailymail.co.uk/news/article-8898907/amp/Dossier-reveals-ministers-UNDERBOUGHT-threw-6-75billion-protective-clothing.html?ito=native_share_article-masthead&__twitter_impression=true
92 Gareth Iacobucci, 'Covid-19: One in five government contracts had signs of possible corruption, report finds', *BMJ*, 23 April 2021, 373 n1072 doi:10.1136/bmj.n1072, https://www.bmj.com/content/373/bmj.n1072
93 Laura Hughes and Michael Pooler, 'Health official says UK can keep coronavirus deaths below 20,000', 28 March 2020, *FT*, www.ft.com/content/814321f0-00d8-49fb-92eb-b7161ff747f7
94 Matthew Weaver, 'UK coronavirus death toll reaches 1,789 amid data reporting concerns', *Guardian*, 31 March 2020, www.theguardian.com/world/2020/mar/31/uk-coronavirus-death-toll-reaches-1789-amid-data-reporting-concerns
95 Gareth Iacobucci, 'Covid-19: One in five government contracts had signs of possible corruption, report finds'
96 Ian Sinclair and Rupert Read, '"A National Scandal" A timeline of the UK government's woeful response to the Coronavirus crisis'
97 'Coronavirus (COVID-19) deaths worldwide per one million population as of April 26, 2022, by country', Statista, 26 April 2022, www.statista.com/statistics/1104709/coronavirus-deaths-worldwide-per-million-inhabitants
98 'Singapore Population', Worldometers, www.worldometers.info/world-population/singapore-population www.worldometers.info/world-population/uk-population
99 'Coronavirus (COVID-19) deaths worldwide per one million population as of April 26, 2022, by country', Statista
100 Rob Davies, 'The inside story of the UK's NHS coronavirus ventilator challenge', *Guardian*, 4 May 2020, www.theguardian.com/business/2020/may/04/the-inside-story-of-the-uks-nhs-coronavirus-ventilator-challenge

101 Denis Campbell, 'Private hospitals treated just eight Covid patients a day during pandemic
     – report', 7 October 2021, www.theguardian.com/world/2021/oct/07/private-hospitals-
     treated-eight-covid-patients-a-day-during-pandemic-says-report
102 'Bed blocking - what is it, and is it paralysing the NHS?', Full Fact, 24 July 2013, fullfact.org
     /health/bed-blocking-what-it-and-it-paralysing-nhs
103 'Yes, patients were discharged to care homes without Covid-19 tests', Full Fact, 16 June
     2020, fullfact.org/health/coronavirus-care-homes-discharge
104 Robert Booth, 'Matt Hancock "was warned of Covid care home risk in March 2020"',
     Guardian, 9 June 2021, www.theguardian.com/society/2021/jun/09/matt-hancock-was-
     warned-of-covid-care-home-risk-in-march-2020
105 Sarah Scobie, 'Covid-19 and the deaths of care home residents', Nuffield Trust,
     17 February 2021, www.nuffieldtrust.org.uk/news-item/covid-19-and-the-deaths-of-care-
     home-residents
106 Robert Booth, Guardian, 'Covid care home discharge policy was unlawful, says court',
     27 April 2020, www.theguardian.com/world/2022/apr/27/covid-discharging-untested-
     patients-into-care-homes-was-unlawful-says-court
107 'COVID-19: Matt Hancock "lied" when he said care homes were protected in lockdown,
     victim's daughter says', Sky News, 27 April 2022, news.sky.com/story/covid-19-daughter-of-
     care-home-victim-says-government-claims-of-protective-ring-were-a-lie-12599939
108 Aubrey Allegretti, 'Dominic Cummings' timeline of the early days of the Covid crisis'
109 Sarah Boseley, 'WHO urges countries to 'track and trace' every Covid-19 case'
110 Ian Sinclair and Rupert Read, "A National Scandal" A timeline of the UK government's
     woeful response to the Coronavirus crisis'
111 Pilita Clark, Clive Cookson and Laura Hughes, 'How the UK got coronavirus testing
     wrong', FT, 27 March 2020, www.ft.com/content/fa747fbd-c19e-4bac-9c37-d46afc9393fb
112 Ian Sinclair and Rupert Read, "A National Scandal" A timeline of the UK government's
     woeful response to the Coronavirus crisis'

April

1   Ian Sinclair and Rupert Read, "A National Scandal" A Timeline of the UK Government's
    Woeful Response', Byline Times, 11 April 2020, bylinetimes.com/2020/04/11/a-national-
    scandal-a-timeline-of-the-uk-governments-woeful-response-to-the-coronavirus-crisis
2   'Coronavirus: Boris Johnson admitted to hospital over virus symptoms', BBC, 6 April 2020,
    www.bbc.co.uk/news/uk-52177125
3   Luke Harding, Rowena Mason, Dan Sabbagh, Mattha Busby, Denis Campbell and Owen
    Bowcott, 'Boris Johnson and coronavirus: the inside story of his illness', Guardian, 17 April
    2020, www.theguardian.com/world/2020/apr/17/boris-johnson-and-coronavirus-inside-
    story-illness
4   Robert Peston, 'British government wants UK to acquire coronavirus "herd immunity",
    writes Robert Peston', ITV News, 12 March 2020, www.itv.com/news/2020-03-12/british-
    government-wants-uk-to-acquire-coronavirus-herd-immunity-writes-robert-peston
5   Hardeep Matharu, 'A "Distraction" of the Government's own making – why "Herd
    Immunity" won't go away', 7 April 2020, bylinetimes.com/2020/04/06/the-coronavirus-
    crisis-a-distraction-of-the-governments-own-making-why-herd-immunity-wont-go-away
6   Green Molly [@GreenPartyMolly], Twitter, 11 April 2020, twitter.com/greenpartymolly/stat
    us/1248881858148007936?s=21
7   Wikipedia, 'List of epidemics', Last edited: 11 July 2022, en.wikipedia.org/wiki/List_of_
    epidemics
8   'Clap for our Carers - sports stars come together to clap for the NHS', BBC, 26 March 2020,
    www.bbc.co.uk/sport/av/football/52056181
9   Alexandra Topping and Niamh McIntyre, 'UK records biggest daily rise in coronavirus
    deaths', Guardian, 1 April 2020, www.theguardian.com/world/2020/apr/01/uk-records-
    biggest-daily-rise-in-coronavirus-deaths
10 Helen Miller [@MsHelicat], Twitter, 7 April 2020, twitter.com/MsHelicat/status/124762376
    3769864194

11 'Saint Vincent and the Grenadines: Covid new deaths per million', Global Eonomy, www.theglobaleconomy.com/Saint-Vincent-and-the-Grenadines/covid_new_deaths_per_million; 'St. Vincent & Grenadines population', worldometer, www.worldometers.info/world-population/saint-vincent-and-the-grenadines-population

12 'Support for PM during coronavirus battle leads Wednesday's papers', ITV News, 8 April 2020, www.itv.com/news/2020-04-08/what-the-papers-say-april-8

13 'UK Coronavirus death toll rises to 7,097 as number of cases passes 60,000', ITV News, 8 April 2020, www.itv.com/news/2020-04-08/uk-coronavirus-death-toll-rises-to-7-097-as-number-of-cases-passes-60-000

14 Hannah Devlin and Sarah Boseley, 'Scientists criticise UK government's "following the science" claim', Guardian, 23 April 2020, www.theguardian.com/world/2020/apr/23/scientists-criticise-uk-government-over-following-the-science

15 Press Association, 'UK "has fewer hospital beds per person than most European countries"', Guardian, 16 April 2014, www.theguardian.com/society/2014/apr/16/britain-fewer-hospital-beds-european-oecd

16 'Student bursary cut "may worsen NHS staff shortages"', BBC, 25 May 2016, www.bbc.co.uk/news/health-36336830

17 Matthew Smith, 'Majority of healthcare workers expect Brexit to harm NHS', YouGov, 20 January 2020, yougov.co.uk/topics/health/articles-reports/2020/01/20/majority-healthcare-workers-expect-brexit-harm-nhs

18 Ian Sinclair and Rupert Read, '"A National Scandal" A Timeline of the UK Government's woeful response to the Coronavirus crisis', Byline Times, 11 April 2020, bylinetimes.com/20 20/04/11/a-national-scandal-a-timeline-of-the-uk-governments-woeful-response-to-the-coronavirus-crisis

19 Joseph Norman, Yaneer Bar-Yam, and Nassim Nicholas Taleb, 'Systemative risk of pandemic via novel pathogens – Coronovirus: A Note', New England Complex Systems Institute, 26 January 2020, necsi.edu/systemic-risk-of-pandemic-via-novel-pathogens-coronavirus-a-note

20 'The lockdown and social norms: why the UK is complying by consent rather than compulsion', LSE Blogs, 27 April 2020, blogs.lse.ac.uk/politicsandpolicy/lockdown-social-norms

21 Mikey Smith, 'Dominic Cummings spotted running away as Boris Johnson tests positive for coronavirus', Mirror, 27 March 2020, www.mirror.co.uk/news/politics/dominic-cummings-spotted-running-away-21766210

22 Rajeev Syal, 'Dominic Cummings found in contempt of parliament', Guardian, 27 March 2019, www.theguardian.com/politics/2019/mar/27/commons-report-rules-dominic-cummings-in-contempt-of-parliament

23 'Mary Wakefield', Much Rack, muckrack.com/mary-wakefield

24 Emma Bartholomew, 'Cummings: "Gang threatened to kill everyone in my Islington home"', Islington Gazette, 26 May 2021, www.islingtongazette.co.uk/news/cummings-gang-threatened-to-break-into-islington-home-8006274

25 'Dominic Cummings: Did he break lockdown rules?', BBC, 28 May 2020, www.bbc.co.uk/news/uk-politics-52784290

26 Guardian Staff, 'The lockdown breach questions Dominic Cummings has yet to clarify', Guardian, 25 May 2020, www.theguardian.com/politics/2020/may/25/dominic-cummings-press-conference-leaves-questions-unanswered

27 Milo Boyd, 'Dominic Cummings breaks cover to say he "doesn't care" how lockdown travel looks', Mirror, 23 May 2020, www.mirror.co.uk/news/politics/breaking-dominic-cummings-breaks-cover-22074482

28 Charlie Cooper, 'British public wants Dominic Cummings to resign, poll says', Politico, 26 May 2020, www.politico.eu/article/dominic-cummings-poll-british-public-wants-resign

29 'Dominic Cummings: Full transcript of Boris Johnson aide's statement from Downing Street', Independent, 25 May 2020, www.independent.co.uk/news/uk/politics/dominic-cummings-statement-speech-transcript-durham-full-text-read-lockdown-a9531856.html

30 'Coronavirus: Why did Dominic Cummings say he predicted it?', BBC, 26 May 2020, www.bbc.co.uk/news/business-52808059

31 Courtney Pochin, 'Barnard Castle means "pathetic excuse" in Durham slang that's over 150-years-old', Mirror, 26 May 2020, www.mirror.co.uk/news/uk-news/barnard-castle-means-pathetic-excuse-22086879

32 Jim Waterson, 'Quarantine article by Dominic Cummings' wife reported to regulator', *Guardian*, 28 May 2020, www.theguardian.com/politics/2020/may/28/quarantine-article -by-dominic-cummings-wife-reported-to-regulator

33 Owen Boycott, 'Attorney general faces calls to resign after she defends Dominic Cummings', *Guardian*, 25 May 2020, www.theguardian.com/politics/2020/may/25/attorney-general- faces-calls-to-resign-defends-dominic-cummings-suella-braverman

34 Ashley Cowburn, 'Matt Hancock repeatedly refuses to say whether Dominic Cummings "did the right thing"', *Independent*, 28 May 2020, www.independent.co.uk/news/uk/politics /matt-hancock-dominic-cummings-durham-lockdown-coronavirus-a9536016.html

35 Lizzy Buchan, 'Coronavirus: Michael Gove claims Dominic Cummings "wise" to drive to Barnard Castle to test eyesight', 26 May 2020, www.independent.co.uk/news/uk/politics/ coronavirus-michael-gove-dominic-cummings-barnard-castle-boris-johnson-a9532276.html

36 Jen Mills, 'Boris Johnson says coronavirus has affected his eyesight', *Metro*, 25 May 2020, metro.co.uk/2020/05/25/boris-johnson-says-coronavirus-has-affected-eyesight-12756577

37 Tamara Cohen, 'I'm blind as a bat, says Boris Johnson: London Mayor admits to needing his glasses to see anything around the house', *Daily Mail*, 20 October 2014, www.dailymail .co.uk/news/article-2799562/i-m-blind-bat-says-boris-johnson-london-mayor-admits-need ing-glasses-house.html

38 Peter Walker, 'Boris Johnson backs Dominic Cummings in face of Tory calls for chief aide to resign', *Guardian*, 24 May 2020, www.theguardian.com/politics/2020/may/24/boris- johnson-backs-dominic-cummings-in-face-of-tory-calls-for-chief-aide-to-resign

39 'Dominic Cummings: Minister Douglas Ross quits over senior aide's lockdown actions', BBC, 26 May 2020, www.bbc.co.uk/news/uk-politics-52806086

40 Ross McGuinness, 'Government adviser says 'more people will die' because of Boris Johnson's defence of Dominic Cummings', Yahoo, 25 May 2020, uk.news.yahoo.com/government- adviser-boris-johnson-dominic-cummings-092400841.html

41 Jon Stone, 'Researchers identify "Cummings effect" undermining public trust in government during lockdown', *Independent*, 6 August 2020, www.independent.co.uk/news /uk/politics/dominic-cummings-effect-trust-coronavirus-covid-19-durham-barnard- castle-a9658411.html

42 Sarah Knapton, '"Dominic Cummings effect" has led to major loss of confidence in Government, study reveals', *Telegraph*, 6 August 2020, www.telegraph.co.uk/politics/2020 /08/06/dominic-cummings-effect-has-led-major-loss-confidence-government

43 'Vicar's query over lockdown travel fines challenges Matt Hancock', *Guardian*, 27 May 2020, www.theguardian.com/world/2020/may/26/vicars-query-over-lockdown-travel-fines- challenges-hancock

44 Jack Maidment and Sebastian Murphy-Bates, 'Robert Jenrick says the Government will NOT review lockdown fines issued to people travelling for childcare reasons less than 24 hours after Matt Hancock said he would consider it in wake of Dominic Cummings row', *Daily Mail*, 27 May 2020, www.dailymail.co.uk/news/article-8360533/Vicar-Matt-Hancock- spot-disappointed-minister-wont-look-lockdown-fines.html

45 Anna MacSwan, 'Boris Johnson warns Dominic Cummings is on "last chance" and won't allow another mistake', *Mirror*, 31 May 2020, www.mirror.co.uk/news/politics/boris-johnson-warns-dominic-cummings-22114537

46 Matthew Weaver, 'Dominic Cummings allowed to avoid backdated council tax on second home', *Guardian*, 14 October 2020, www.theguardian.com/politics/2020/oct/14/dominic- cummings-must-pay-council-tax-on-second-home-in-durham

47 Peter Walker, '"Truth twisters": rogue civil service tweet causes storm', *Guardian*, 24 May 2020, www.theguardian.com/politics/2020/may/24/can-you-imagine-having-to-work- with-these-truth-twisters

48 Rajeev Syal, Matthew Weaver and Peter Walker, 'Johnson's defence of Cummings sparks anger from allies and opponents alike', *Guardian*, 24 May 2020, www.theguardian.com/ politics/2020/may/24/boris-johnson-defence-dominic-cummings-anger-from-allies-and- opponents-alike

May

1   'Ten things you need to know today: Sunday 10 May 2020', *The Week*, 10 May 2020, www.theweek.co.uk/daily-briefing/106944/ten-things-you-need-to-know-today-sunday-10-may-2020

2   Lamiat Sabin, 'Boris Johnson boasts: "I can drink an awful lot at lunch, like my icon Winston Churchill"', *Independent*, 15 October 2014, www.independent.co.uk/news/people/news/boris-johnson-boasts-i-can-drink-an-awful-lot-at-lunch-just-like-my-icon-winston-churchill-9793478.html

3   'International travel to and from Wales: coronavirus', Llywodraeth Cymru Welsh Government, first published 4 October 2021, last updated 18 March 2022, gov.wales/rules-international-travel-and-wales-coronavirus; 'Coronavirus: "Do not drive from England to Wales to exercise"', BBC, 11 May 2020, www.bbc.co.uk/news/uk-wales-52614204.amp

4   Heather Stewart and Richard Adams, 'Groups of up to six people allowed to meet in England from Monday', *Guardian*, 28 May 2020, www.theguardian.com/world/2020/may/28/groups-up-to-six-people-allowed-meet-england-monday-coronavirus-lockdown-easing; Claire Schofield, 'Can I see family and friends in lockdown? UK coronavirus rules on meeting other households explained', *iNews*, 13 July 2020, inews.co.uk/news/can-see-family-friends-coronavirus-lockdown-rules-uk-households-426773

5   David Hunter, 'If we follow Boris Johnson's advice, coronavirus will spread', *Guardian*, 11 May 2020, www.theguardian.com/commentisfree/2020/may/11/boris-johnson-advice-coronavirus-spread-work

6   Freddie Whittaker, 'The rebel councils: Government's schools plan in doubt as 27 town halls raise safety concerns', Schools Week, 21 May 2020, schoolsweek.co.uk/the-rebel-councils-governments-schools-plan-in-doubt-as-27-town-halls-raise-safety-concerns

7   Emma Reynolds, Rob Picheta, Nada Bashir and Arnaud Siad, 'Boris Johnson accused of botching announcement of new UK lockdown rules', *CNN*, 11 May 2020, edition.cnn.com/2020/05/11/uk/uk-coronavirus-boris-johnson-gbr-intl/index.html

8   Thomas Colson, 'People are very confused by Boris Johnson's attempt to loosen the UK coronavirus lockdown', Business Insider, 11 May 2020, www.businessinsider.com/people-are-confused-by-boris-johnson-new-uk-coronavirus-guidelines-2020-5

9   Taryn Tarrant-Cornish, 'We need to limit UK population growth to protect the environment, Stanley Johnson demands', *Express*, 11 Januray 2018, www.express.co.uk/news/politics/903061/Stanley-Johnson-population-growth-environment-Newsnight-Caroline-Lucas-Green

10 Faye Brown, 'Boris Johnson's dad admits he broke lockdown to find out name of grandson', *Metro*, 8 May 2020, metro.co.uk/2020/05/08/boris-johnsons-dad-admits-broke-lockdown-find-name-grandson-12672918

11 Rory Sullivan, '"You haven't got a clue": Piers Morgan attacks Tory MP who gives confused advice over visiting family', *Independent*, www.independent.co.uk/news/uk/home-news/piers-morgan-andrew-bridgen-gmb-rules-lockdown-social-distancing-video-a9507976.html

12 Novara Media, 'Boris Johnson Lies TWICE At PMQs', YouTube, 14 May 2020, www.youtube.com/watch?v=EpGwvjiNd1o

13 Tom Peck, 'What if Boris Johnson isn't just lazy? What if he really is this bad?', *Independent*, 12 May 2020, www.independent.co.uk/voices/boris-johnson-coronavirus-lockdown-exit-speech-stay-alert-a9509236.html

14 'New guidance on face coverings for the general public in Hertfordshire', NHS, hertsvalleys ccg.nhs.uk/news/articles/new-guidance-face-coverings-general-public-hertfordshire

15 Tara Lagu, Rachel Werner and Andrew W. Artenstein, 'Why don't hospitals have enough masks? Because coronavirus broke the market', *Washington Post*, 21 May 2020, www.washingtonpost.com/outlook/2020/05/21/why-dont-hospitals-have-enough-masks-because-coronavirus-broke-market

16 Selina McKee, 'UK's coronavirus testing capacity has been "inadequate", Committee finds', *Pharma Times Online*, 19 May 2020, http://www.pharmatimes.com/news/uks_coronavirus_testing_capacity_has_been_inadequate,_committee_finds_1340515

17 Dan Sabbagh, Frances Perraudin, Heather Stewart and Peter Walker, 'Plans for contact-tracing in doubt as app not ready until June', *Gurdian*, 20 May 2020, www.theguardian.com/world/2020/may/20/uk-plans-for-contact-tracing-in-doubt-as-app-not-ready-until-june

18 'Coronavirus: Track and trace system in place from June – PM', BBC, 20 May 2020, www.bbc.co.uk/news/uk-52741331

19 Dan Sabbagh, Frances Perraudin, Heather Stewart and Peter Walker, 'Plans for contact-tracing in doubt as app not ready until June', *Guardian*, 20 May 2020, www.theguardian.com/world/2020/may/20/uk-plans-for-contact-tracing-in-doubt-as-app-not-ready-until-june

20 Heather Stewart, Frances Perraudin and Alex Hern, 'Coronavirus: contact-tracing applicants in England wrongly told hiring paused', *Guardian*, 18 May 2020, www.theguardian.com/politics/2020/may/17/uk-contact-tracing-applicants-wrongly-told-hiring-paused-in-latest-misstep

21 Frances Perraudin, '"No one had any idea": Contact tracers lack knowledge about Covid-19 job', *Guardian*, 20 May 2020, www.theguardian.com/world/2020/may/20/no-one-had-any-idea-contact-tracers-lack-knowledge-about-covid-19-job

22 'Coronavirus: Can I visit all council-run parks now?', BBC, 30 May 2020, www.bbc.co.uk/news/uk-northern-ireland-52834202

23 'No 10 retreats as rebellion over schools gathers pace', *Guardian*, 19 May 2020, www.theguardian.com/world/2020/may/19/up-to-1500-english-primary-schools-to-defy-1-june-reopening-plan

24 'Wuhan lockdown: A year of China's fight against the Covid pandemic', BBC, 22 January 2021, www.bbc.co.uk/news/world-asia-china-55628488

25 Alistair Smout and Kylie MacLellan, 'UK to introduce quarantine for international arrivals from June 8', Reuters, 22 May 2020, www.reuters.com/article/us-health-coronavirus-britain-idUSKBN22Y0S2

26 'Coronavirus: French arrivals exempt from UK quarantine plans', BBC, 11 May 2020, www.bbc.co.uk/news/business-52610594

27 Steve Bird, 'Gina Coladangelo: the millionaire lobbyist quietly appointed to top government roles', *Telegraph*, 15 July 2021, www.telegraph.co.uk/politics/2021/06/25/gina-coladangelo-met-matt-hancock-decades-quietly-appointed

28 Rajeev Syal, 'Whitehall non-executive jobs "pay up to 14 times more than junior nurses"', *Guardian*, 29 June 2021, www.theguardian.com/politics/2021/jun/29/whitehall-non-executive-jobs-pay-more-than-junior-nurses

29 'Matt Hancock affair: Health secretary apologises for breaking social distancing guideline', BBC, 25 June 2021, www.bbc.co.uk/news/uk-politics-57612441

30 'Coronavirus: Quarantine plans for UK arrivals unveiled', BBC, 23 May 2021, www.bbc.co.uk/news/uk-52774854

31 Jamie Grierson, 'UK government under fire after "big influx" of Covid-19 cases from Europe revealed', *Guardian*, 5 May 2020, www.theguardian.com/world/2020/may/05/just-273-people-arriving-in-uk-in-run-up-to-lockdown-quarantined

32 Rowena Mason Deputy and Haroon Siddique, 'Boris Johnson urged to publish BAME Covid-19 review immediately', *Guardian*, 2 June 2020, www.theguardian.com/world/2020/jun/02/boris-johnson-urged-to-publish-bame-covid-19-review-immediately

June

1 Jon Sharman, 'Robert Jenrick showed "apparent bias" in approving Conservative Party donor's housing development', *Independent*, 27 May 2020, www.independent.co.uk/news/uk/politics/robert-jenrick-bias-tower-hamlets-westferry-printworks-richard-desmond-no rthern-shell-a9534941.html

2 Henry McDonald, 'Call for inquiry into why senior Tory helped donor avoid £40m tax', *Guardian*, 20 May 2020, www.theguardian.com/politics/2020/may/30/call-for-inquiry-into-why-senior-tory-robert-jenrick-helped-donor-avoid-40m-tax

3 'Offer more homes to local families', Vote for Policies, tracker.voteforpolicies.org.uk/policies/offer-more-homes-to-local-families

4 Henry McDonald, 'Former Tory donor's housing project "unlawfully approved to avoid £40m hit"', *Guardian*, 27 May 2020, www.theguardian.com/politics/2020/may/27/richa rd-desmond-housing-project-unlawfully-approved-robert-jenrick-isle-dogs-london-avoid-40m-hit

5 Michael Leidig, 'Labour expresses "contempt" for Desmond', *Guardian*, 23 April 2004, www.theguardian.com/media/2004/apr/23/dailyexpress.pressandpublishing1

6   Peter Walker, 'Minister suggests voters could raise planning issues at Tory fundraisers', *Guardian*, 25 June 2020, www.theguardian.com/politics/2020/jun/25/minister-suggests-voters-could-raise-planning-issues-tory-fundraisers

7   Frank Langfitt and Rob Schmitz, 'Coronavirus pandemic tests leadership styles in UK, Germany', 21 May 2020, www.npr.org/2020/05/21/859991289/coronavirus-pandemic-tests-leadership-styles-in-u-k-germany

8   'Coronavirus: Ikea to begin reopening stores', BBC, 22 May 2020, www.bbc.co.uk/news/business-52774436

9   'Coronavirus: UK exceeds 200,000 testing capacity target', BBC, 31 May 2020, www.bbc.co.uk/news/health-52871772

10   Rosa Ellis, 'Coronavirus in the UK: how many people are really being tested?', *The Times*, 25 May 2020, www.thetimes.co.uk/article/coronavirus-in-the-uk-how-many-people-are-really-being-tested-0ln33dp7n

11   Evie Aspinall, 'COVID-19 Timeline', BFPG, 8 April 2022, bfpg.co.uk/2020/04/covid-19-timeline

12   Sophie Charara, 'England's contact tracers are unprepared, confused and bored', *Wired*, 29 May 2020, www.wired.co.uk/article/nhs-coronavirus-contact-tracing-calls

13   Sky News, 'IN FULL: Hancock laughs off claims UK test and trace rushed to distract from Cummings COVID-19 row', YouTube, 28 May 2020, www.youtube.com/watch?v=8Zx4_07livE

14   'Paper for SAGE small group: COVID-19 Alert level change criteria', 25 May 2020, assets.publishing.service.gov.uk/government/uploads/system/uploads/attachment_data/file/950765/s0573-covid-19-alert-level-change-criteria.pdf

15   'Joint Biosecurity Centre', Gov.uk, www.gov.uk/government/groups/joint-biosecurity-centre

16   Ready For Rishi [@RishiSunak], Twitter, 27 May 2020, twitter.com/rishisunak/status/1265592505724256257

17   Matt Hancock [@MattHancock], Twitter, 30 May 2020, twitter.com/MattHancock/status/1266758277041401857

18   'Cumulative number of coronavirus (COVID-19) deaths in the United Kingdom (UK)', Statista, 5 May 2020, www.statista.com/statistics/1109595/coronavirus-mortality-in-the-uk

19   Emer O'Toole, 'Matt Hancock given £350k from figures linked to Cheltenham Festival', *National*, 20 July 2020, www.thenational.scot/news/18594722.matt-hancock-given-350k-figures-linked-cheltenham-festival

20   Lisa O'Carroll, 'MPs join 90-minute-long queue to vote to end virtual voting', *Guardian*, 2 June 2020, www.theguardian.com/politics/2020/jun/02/mps-join-90-minute-long-queue-to-vote-to-end-virtual-voting

21   Kate Procter and Daniel Boffey, '"Fantastic moment": Boris Johnson signs Brexit withdrawal deal', *Guardian*, 24 January 2020, www.theguardian.com/politics/2020/jan/24/sombre-eu-leaders-sign-brexit-withdrawal-agreement

22   Stefan Boscia, 'Boris Johnson wants to change "defective" Brexit withdrawal agreement', *City A.M.*, www.cityam.com/boris-johnson-wants-to-change-defective-brexit-withdrawal-agreement

23   'Does the EU need us more than we need them?', BBC, 23 December 2018, www.bbc.co.uk/news/business-46612362

24   Jon Stone, 'Brexit trade deal with New Zealand will have "close to zero" benefit to UK economy, government admits', *Independent*, 17 June 2020, www.independent.co.uk/news/uk/politics/brexit-trade-deal-new-zealand-economy-jacinda-ardern-a9571421.html

25   Philip Oltermann, 'Britons receiving German citizenship rose 2,300% last year', *Guardian*, 3 June 2020, www.theguardian.com/politics/2020/jun/03/britons-applying-for-german-citizenship-up-2300-last-year

26   'Coronavirus: Face coverings compulsory on public transport in England', BBC, 15 June 2020, www.bbc.co.uk/news/uk-53045386

27   'COVID-19: Latest advice for colleges', Sixth Form College Association, www.sixthformcolleges.org/380/news-and-comment/post/47/covid-19-latest-advice-for-colleges

28   'Coronavirus: Lockdown delay "cost a lot of lives", says science adviser', BBC, 7 June 2020, www.bbc.co.uk/news/uk-politics-52955034

29   Becca Monaghan, 'Tory MP roasted for saying "science is not an exact science"', indy100, 30 November 2021, www.indy100.com/viral/tory-mp-roasted-science-isn-t-exact-b1966869

30   Sebastian Payne, 'The spectre of lonely care home deaths hangs over the government', *FT*, 14 June 2020, www.ft.com/content/cd62bbf0-a73a-11ea-92e2-cbd9b7e28ee6

31   Ian Sample, 'Covid-19 spilling out of hospitals and care homes, says UK expert', *Guardian*, 2 June 2020, www.theguardian.com/world/2020/jun/02/covid-19-spilling-out-of-hospitals-and-care-homes-says-uk-expert

32   Matt Honeycombe-Foster, 'Matt Hancock says Government has hit target to offer coronavirus test kits to every care home', *Politics Home*, 8 June 2020, www.politicshome.com/news/article/row-as-matt-hancock-says-government-has-hit-target-to-offer-test-kits-every-care-home

33   Selina Rajan and Martin Mckee, 'Learning From the Impacts of COVID-19 on Care Homes in England: A Pilot Survey', LTC Responses to Covid-19, 9 June 2020, ltccovid.org/2020/06/09/learning-from-the-impacts-of-covid-19-on-care-homes-in-england-a-pilot-survey

34   Shaun Lintern, 'Coronavirus: Global experts tell MPs how they avoided UK's care home crisis', *Independent*, 19 May 2020, www.independent.co.uk/news/health/coronavirus-uk-care-homes-mps-hospitals-deaths-a9522006.html

35   Diane Taylor, 'Serco wins Covid-19 test-and-trace contract despite £1m fine', *Guardian*, 6 June 2020, www.theguardian.com/world/2020/jun/06/serco-wins-covid-19-test-and-trace-contract-despite-1m-fine

36   Mike Maloney, 'Johnson pledges "maximum transparency" over lockdown easing', *Worcester News*, 27 April 2020, www.worcesternews.co.uk/news/18407902.johnson-pledges-maximum-transparency-lockdown-easing

37   Diane Taylor, 'Serco wins Covid-19 test-and-trace contract despite £1m fine'

38   Sarah Marsh, 'NHS test-and-trace system "not fully operational until September"', *Guardian*, 4 June 2020, www.theguardian.com/society/2020/jun/04/nhs-track-and-trace-system-not-expected-to-be-operating-fully-until-september-coronavirus

39   'Serco Group plc Executive Committee', Serco, www.serco.com/about/executive-committee

40   Christopher Hope, 'Exclusive: Boris Johnson takes back control of coronavirus crisis with Downing Street shake-up', *Telegraph*, 2 June 2020, www.telegraph.co.uk/politics/2020/06/02/exclusive-boris-johnson-takes-back-control-coronavirus-crisis

41   Dan Bloom, 'No10 says it's "completely untrue" Boris Johnson needs 3-hour naps during the day', *Mirror*, 7 June 2020, www.mirror.co.uk/news/politics/no10-says-its-completely-untrue-22152332

42   Jack Peat, 'UK government now has joint-lowest approval rating in the world for handling of coronavirus', *London Economic*, 8 June 2020, www.thelondoneconomic.com/politics/uk-government-now-has-joint-lowest-approval-rating-in-the-world-for-handling-of-coronavirus-190383

43   James Tapsfield, 'Boris Johnson's approval rating has dived by 40 POINTS to turn negative in under two months amid backlash over coronavirus testing, care homes, and lockdown easing', *Daily Mail*, 4 June 2020, www.dailymail.co.uk/news/article-8388643/Boris-Johnsons-approval-rating-dived-40-POINTS-April.html

44   *Channel 5 News*, 'Boris Johnson takes "direct control" of coronavirus crisis', Facebook, www.facebook.com/watch/live/?ref=watch_permalink&v=561149971260872

45   Heather Stewart, '"I hear you": Boris Johnson to Black Lives Matter protesters', *Guardian*, 8 June 2020, www.theguardian.com/us-news/2020/jun/08/i-hear-you-boris-johnson-to-black-lives-matter-protesters

46   Jon Stone, 'Boris Johnson said colonialism in Africa should never have ended and dismissed Britain's role in slavery', *Independent*, 13 June 2020, www.independent.co.uk/news/uk/politics/boris-johnson-colonialism-africa-british-empire-slavery-a9564541.html

47   Heather Stewart, '"I hear you": Boris Johnson to Black Lives Matter protesters'

48   Amelia Gentleman and Peter Walker, 'Windrush claimants "tip of the iceberg" as payout struggle continues', *Guardian*, 9 February 2020, www.theguardian.com/uk-news/2020/feb/09/windrush-scandal-wrongly-designated-illegal-immigrants

49   Daniele Fiandaca, 'MPs are refusing unconscious bias training. Perhaps there's a real reason why', *City A.M.*, 29 September 2020, www.cityam.com/why-mps-should-refuse-unconscious-bias-training

50   Fleet Street Fox, 'Boris Johnson has vowed to crack down on rioters. He knows all about that - he is one of them', *Mirror*, 10 June 2020, www.mirror.co.uk/news/politics/boris-johnson-vowed-crackdown-riot-22168892

51 Henry McDonald, 'Former Tory donor's housing project "unlawfully approved to avoid £40m hit"', *Guardian*, 27 May 2020, www.theguardian.com/politics/2020/may/27/richa rd-desmond-housing-project-unlawfully-approved-robert-jenrick-isle-dogs-london-avoid-40m-hit

52 Mark Townsend and Nosheen Iqbal, 'Ministers ignored police chiefs' warning over risks of lifting lockdown in England', *Guardian*, 27 June 2020, www.theguardian.com/world/2020/jun/27/ministers-ignored-police-chiefs-warning-over-risks-of-lifting-lockdown-in-eng land

53 'Covid-19 Update Volume 677: debated on Tuesday 23 June 2020', UK Parliament, 3 June 2020, hansard.parliament.uk/commons/2020-06-23/debates/7E464B41-46ED-4FA9-BAFD-28EC7B3DA230/Covid-19Update

54 'Bournemouth beach: "Major incident" as thousands flock to coast', BBC, 25 June 2020, www.bbc.co.uk/news/uk-england-dorset-53176717

55 Dan Sabbagh, 'Councils warn they have no legal powers to enforce "local lockdowns"', *Guardian*, 15 June 2020, www.theguardian.com/world/2020/jun/15/councils-warn-they-have-no-legal-powers-to-enforce-local-lockdowns

56 Patrick Butler, 'Eight out of 10 English councils at risk of bankruptcy, says study', *Guardian*, 23 June 2020, www.theguardian.com/society/2020/jun/23/at-least-8-in-10-english-councils-need-help-to-avoid-going-bankrupt

57 Will Hulme, 'Local authorities' budgets are roughly 26% lower since 2010', Full Fact, 29 June 2017, fullfact.org/economy/local-authorities-budgets

58 'UK health leaders urge government to prepare for second wave of covid-19', BMJ, 23 June 2020, www.bmj.com/company/newsroom/uk-health-leaders-urge-government-to-prepare-for-second-wave-of-covid-19

59 John Johnston, 'Coronavirus: Senior Tory MP backs medics' call for review of UK's readiness for second wave', *Politics Home*, 24 June 2020, www.politicshome.com/news/article/coronavirus-senior-tory-mp-backs-medics-calls-for-review-of-uks-readiness-for-second-wave

60 Tim Hanlon, 'England to reopen pubs and cinemas from 4 July', CGTN, 24 June 2020, news.cgtn.com/news/2020-06-23/Boris-Johnson-Pubs-and-cinemas-can-reopen-from-July-4--RyR2Iph69O/index.html

61 'Coronavirus: Daily Downing Street press conference scrapped', BBC, 23 June 2020, www.bbc.co.uk/news/uk-politics-53155905

62 Laura Hughes and Chris Giles, 'Matt Hancock criticised by regulator over UK coronavirus testing figures', *FT*, 2 June 2020, www.ft.com/content/2c32d72f-8bf3-4a46-8c2a-8781721cc0db

63 Aubrey Allegretti, '"Union Jack paint job" for Boris Johnson's plane to cost £900,000', Sky News, 17 June 2020, news.sky.com/story/plan-to-rebrand-pm-plane-will-cost-900-000-12008735

64 Sian Elvin, 'Is the Union Flag upside down on Boris Johnson's £900,000 plane?', *Metro*, 26 June 2020, metro.co.uk/2020/06/26/union-flag-upside-boris-johnsons-900000-plane-12905817

65 Tom Batchelor, 'Government acquires second, brand new "Brexit jet" for Boris Johnson painted red, white and blue', *Independent*, 22 March 2021, www.independent.co.uk/news/uk/politics/government-plane-union-flag-paint-livery-b1820418.html

66 Hannah Crouch, 'Tory peer reveals NHS contact-tracing app has cost £11.8m to date', *Digital Health*, 23 June 2020, www.digitalhealth.net/2020/06/nhs-contact-tracing-app-cost

67 Matt Burgess, 'Why the NHS Covid-19 contact tracing app failed', *Wired*, 19 June 2020, www.wired.co.uk/article/nhs-tracing-app-scrapped-apple-google-uk

68 Alex Hern and Dan Sabbagh, 'Critical mass of Android users crucial for NHS contact-tracing app', *Guardian*, 6 May 2020, www.theguardian.com/world/2020/may/06/critical-ma ss-of-android-users-needed-for-success-of-nhs-coronavirus-contact-tracing-app

69 Dan Sabbagh and Alex Hern, 'UK abandons contact-tracing app for Apple and Google model', *Guardian*, 18 June 2020, www.theguardian.com/world/2020/jun/18/uk-poised-to-abandon-coronavirus-app-in-favour-of-apple-and-google-models

70 'corona-warn-app / cwa-app-andriod', GitHub, github.com/corona-warn-app/cwa-app-android/issues/478

71 'Coronavirus: Does anyone have a working contact-tracing app?', BBC, 25 June 2020, www.bbc.co.uk/news/53168438

72 Patrick Worrall, 'Boris Johnson repeats claim that no country has a functioning Covid-19 tracing app', Channel 4 News, 24 June 2020, www.channel4.com/news/factcheck/factcheck-boris-johnson-repeats-claim-that-no-country-has-a-functioning-covid-19-tracing-app

73 Rob Merrick, 'Boris Johnson told to come clean on food and medicine shortage risks from no-deal Brexit', *Independent,* 22 June 2020, www.independent.co.uk/news/uk/politics/boris-johnson-brexit-trade-talks-no-deal-food-medicine-shortage-a9578991.html

74 Rob Merrick, 'Around 9m voters missing from electoral rolls as ministers ignore calls for change', *Independent,* 21 June 2020, www.independent.co.uk/news/uk/politics/voter-registration-electoral-roll-conservatives-government-boundary-changes-a9575451.html

75 Paul Abernethy, 'What the Conservatives manifesto says about international development', Bond, 26 November 2019, www.bond.org.uk/news/2019/11/what-the-conservatives-manifesto-says-about-international-development

76 Amy Jones and Harry Yorke, 'Boris Johnson scraps overseas aid department, heralding end to "giant cashpoint in the sky"', *Telegraph,* 16 June 2020, www.telegraph.co.uk/politics/2020/06/16/lockdown-uk-news-update-boris-johnson

77 William Worley, 'Exclusive: DFID seeks cuts of up to 30% on aid project', Devex, 30 June 2020, www.devex.com/news/exclusive-dfid-seeks-cuts-of-up-to-30-on-aid-projects-97600

78 'In hindsight, do you think Britain was right or wrong to vote to leave the European Union?', Statista, July 2022, www.statista.com/statistics/987347/brexit-opinion-poll

79 John Hyde, 'Legislation to abolish some jury trials could be passed within weeks', *The Law Society Gazette,* 23 June 2020, www.lawgazette.co.uk/news/legislation-to-abolish-some-jury-trials-could-be-passed-within-weeks/5104739.article

80 Moya Lothian-McLean, 'Tory MP ridiculed after getting basic facts about Auschwitz completely wrong', indy100, 10 June 2020, www.indy100.com/news/auschwitz-simon-clarke-tory-statue-slave-trader-9558886

81 Alison Flood, 'Britain has closed almost 800 libraries since 2010, figures show', *Guardian,* 6 December 2019, www.theguardian.com/books/2019/dec/06/britain-has-closed-almost-800-libraries-since-2010-figures-show

82 Fiona Harvey, 'UK's net zero pledge: what has been achieved one year on?', *Guardian,* 24 June 2020, www.theguardian.com/environment/2020/jun/24/uks-net-zero-pledge-what-has-been-achieved-one-year-on

83 Martyn Warwick, 'Troubled OneWeb satellite system now fully owned by the UK government and Bharti', Telecom TV, 23 November 2020, www.telecomtv.com/content/access-evolution/bankrupt-oneweb-satellite-system-now-fully-owned-by-the-uk-government-and-bharti-40288

84 Alex Hern, '"We've bought the wrong satellites": UK tech gamble baffles experts', *Guardian,* 26 June 2020, www.theguardian.com/science/2020/jun/26/satellite-experts-oneweb-investment-uk-galileo-brexit

85 Martyn Warwick, 'Troubled OneWeb satellite system now fully owned by the UK government and Bharti'

86 Alex Hern, '"We've bought the wrong satellites": UK tech gamble baffles experts'

87 Gary Brown and William Harris, 'How Satellites Work' Howstuffworks.com, science. howstuffworks.com/satellite10.htm

88 Samuel Osborne, 'Government falling behind on its promise to strip dangerous cladding three years after Grenfell Tower fire, says NAO report', *Independent,* 19 June 2020, www.independent.co.uk/news/uk/home-news/grenfell-tower-fire-cladding-aluminium-composite-material-national-audit-office-a9574176.html

89 Graeme Demianyk, 'Less than 1% of government funds to remove cladding from private buildings paid out', *Huffington Post,* 19 June 2020, www.huffingtonpost.co.uk/entry/cladding-national-audit-office_uk_5eebc25ec5b6674372348207

90 Robert Booth, 'UK could be breaking international law over cladding, says UN', *Guardian,* 28 June 2020, www.theguardian.com/society/2020/jun/28/uk-could-be-breaking-international-law-over-cladding-says-un

91 'Which Was Bigger: The 2009 Recovery Act or FDR's New Deal?', Federal Reserve Bank of St Louis, 20 May 2017, www.stlouisfed.org/on-the-economy/2017/may/which-bigger-2009-recovery-act-fdr-new-deal

92 Kate Proctor and Richard Adams, 'Johnson pledges £1bn school rebuilding programme for England', *Guardian,* 28 June 2020, www.theguardian.com/education/2020/jun/28/johnson-pledges-1bn-over-10-years-for-school-rebuilding-in-england

93 Lizzy Buchan, 'Education spending slashed by £7bn since 2011 with children "paying price for austerity"', says Labour', *Independent*, 14 January 2019, www.independent.co.uk/news /uk/politics/labour-angela-rayner-funding-cuts-department-education-damian-hinds-a872 6151.html

94 Hayley Dixon, 'PPE: Government counted each glove as single item to reach one billion total, investigation shows', *Telegraph*, 28 April 2020, www.telegraph.co.uk/politics/2020/04 /28/ppe-government-counted-glove-single-item-reach-one-billion-total

95 Claire Anderson, 'Jeremy Hunt sparks fury as he calls for NHS testing despite voting against it', *Express*, 30 June 2020, www.express.co.uk/news/uk/1302889/jeremy-hunt-radio-4-testing-nhs-staff-coronavirus

96 Andrew Woodcock, 'Coronavirus: NHS facing shortage of doctors before second wave arrives as thousands set to quit, warns medics union', *Independent*, 29 June 2020, www.inde pendent.co.uk/news/uk/politics/coronavirus-uk-winter-second-wave-nhs-hospital-staff-shortage-a9588041.html

97 Andrew Woodcock, 'More than 22,000 EU nationals have left NHS since Brexit referendum, figures show', *Independent*, 10 December 2019, www.independent.co.uk/news /uk/politics/brexit-eu-citizens-nhs-crisis-migration-boris-johnson-hospital-health-a92397 91.html

98 Alan Selby, 'Hundreds of millions cut from NHS job training despite dire nurse shortages', *Mirror*, 11 May 2019, www.mirror.co.uk/news/politics/hundreds-millions-cut-nhs-job-152 48004

99 Rob Merrick, 'Coronavirus: Boris Johnson says we must also "clap for bankers who make our NHS possible"', *Independent*, 30 June 2020, www.independent.co.uk/news/uk/politics /boris-johnson-nhs-clap-bankers-coronavirus-a9593266.html

July

1 Eleni Courea, '"Sulking" Chris Grayling quits intelligence committee', *The Times*, 29 August 2019, www.thetimes.co.uk/article/sulking-chris-grayling-quits-intelligence-committee-99z pwv269

2 'Russia report: New intelligence committee chair loses Tory whip', BBC, 16 July 2020, www.bbc.co.uk/news/uk-politics-53422010

3 Hannah Devlin and Haroon Siddique, 'Improve test and trace before schools reopen, Sage report says', *Guardian*, 26 June 2020, www.theguardian.com/world/2020/jun/26/improve-test-and-trace-before-schools-reopen-sage-report-says

4 Kate Forrester, 'Gavin Williamson says parents will be fined if they fail to send children back to school', *Politics Home*, 29 June 2020, www.politicshome.com/news/article/gavin-williamson-says-parents-will-be-fined-if-they-fail-to-send-children-back-to-school

5 Matt Hancock [@MattHancock], Twitter, 7 July 2020, twitter.com/matthancock/status/1280 383422347837440?lang=en

6 'Domestic Abuse Bill — New Clause 22 — Immigration — Victims of Domestic Abuse — Right to Rent — Access to Benefits', TheyWorkForYou, www.theyworkforyou.com/ divisions/pw-2020-07-06-72-commons

7 David Doolittle, 'What's More Risky, Going to a Bar or Opening the Mail?', Texas Medical Association, 2 July 2020, www.texmed.org/TexasMedicineDetail.aspx?id=53977

8 Kevin Rawlinson, '"Raise a glass": UK Treasury faces backlash after hailing pubs reopening', *Guardian*, 2 July 2020, www.theguardian.com/global/2020/jul/02/uk-treasury-faces-backlash-after-hailing-pubs-reopening-on-saturday

9 Tom Phillips, 'Brazil overtakes UK with world's second-highest Covid-19 death toll', *Guardian*, 12 June 2020, www.theguardian.com/world/2020/jun/12/brazil-coronavirus-death-toll-second-highest

10 'Prime Minister's statement on coronavirus (COVID-19): 3 July 2020', 3 July 2020, Gov.uk, www.gov.uk/government/speeches/prime-ministers-statement-on-coronavirus-covid-19-3-july-2020

11 'Boris Johnson's sister Rachel defends lockdown journeys between her two residences', News18, 1 June 2020, www.news18.com/news/world/boris-johnsons-sister-rachel-defends-lockdown-journeys-between-her-two-residences-2647923.html

12 Lisa O'Carroll, 'Barnier rejects Johnson's claims over Irish Sea trade checks', *Guardian*, 27 January 2020, www.theguardian.com/politics/2020/jan/27/customs-checks-needed-on-irish-sea-trade-after-brexit-eu

13 Lisa O'Carroll, 'Liz Truss warns Boris Johnson over Brexit border plans', *Guardian*, 8 July 2020, www.theguardian.com/politics/2020/jul/08/liz-truss-warns-boris-johnson-over-brexit-border-plans

14 Georgina Wright, 'The June deadline for Brexit extension has passed – but the UK could still buy more time', Institute for Government, 9 July 2020, www.instituteforgovernment.org.uk/blog/june-deadline-brexit-extension-uk-buy-more-time

15 Rob Merrick, 'Dominic Raab said "I don't support the Human Rights Act" ahead of being put in charge of overhaul', *Independent*, 17 September 2021, www.independent.co.uk/news/uk/politics/dominic-raab-human-rights-act-reshuffle-b1921962.html

16 'UK announces first sanctions under new global human rights regime', Gov.uk, 6 July 2020, www.gov.uk/government/news/uk-announces-first-sanctions-under-new-global-human-rights-regime

17 Naomi Ackerman, 'UK to resume arms sales to Saudi Arabia as "possible" war crimes in Yemen were "isolated incidents", government announces', *Standard*, 7 July 2020, www.standard.co.uk/news/politics/saudi-arabia-arms-sales-uk-government-yemen-war-crimes-a4491306.html

18 UK Health Security Agency, 'Reducing the spread of respiratory infections, including COVID-19, in the workplace', Gov.uk, 1 April 2020, www.gov.uk/guidance/working-safely-during-covid-19/restaurants-pubs-bars-nightclubs-and-takeaway-services

19 Ben Quinn, '"No masks": Wagamama criticised over Rishi Sunak photo op', *Guardian*, 9 July 2020, www.theguardian.com/politics/2020/jul/09/no-masks-wagamama-criticised-over-rishi-sunak-photo-op

20 Aubrey Allegretti, 'Coronavirus: Tory MP Sir Desmond Swayne attacks face masks in shops order', Sky News, 14 July 2020, news.sky.com/story/coronavirus-tory-mp-sir-desmond-swayne-attacks-face-masks-in-shops-order-12028541

21 Matt Honeycombe-Foster, 'Watch: Tory MP Desmond Swayne rails against "monstrous imposition" of compulsory face masks and says he won't go shopping', *Politics Home*, 14 July 2020, www.politicshome.com/news/article/watch-tory-mp-desmond-swayne-rails-against-monstrous-imposition-of-compulsory-face-masks-and-says-he-wont-go-shopping

22 'Coronavirus: I trust people's sense on face masks – Gove', BBC, 12 July 2020, www.bbc.co.uk/news/uk-53381000

23 Rob Merrick, 'Coronavirus: Michael Gove photographed in Pret without a face mask, despite telling public it is "good sense"', *Independent*, 14 July 2020, www.independent.co.uk/news/uk/politics/face-mask-gove-coronavirus-shops-pret-a9619141.html

24 'Addendum to the fourth SAGE meeting on Covid-19, 4 February 2020', Gov.uk, 4 February 2020, https://assets.publishing.service.gov.uk/government/uploads/system/uploads/attachment_data/file/888771/S0372_Fourth_SAGE_meeting_on_Wuhan_Coronavirus__WN-CoV__.pdf

25 'Coronavirus: Face masks and coverings to be compulsory in England's shops', BBC, 14 July 2020, www.bbc.co.uk/news/uk-politics-53397617

26 'COVID-19 Daily Announced Deaths Archive', NHS England, www.england.nhs.uk/statistics/statistical-work-areas/covid-19-daily-deaths/covid-19-daily-announced-deaths-archive

27 Sam Bright, 'Right-wing propaganda pair paid £3 million', *Byline Times*, 15 July 2020, bylinetimes.com/2020/07/15/right-wing-propaganda-pair-paid-3-million-to-run-coronavirus-communications

28 Peter Walker, 'Boris Johnson indicates at PMQs he has not read winter coronavirus report', *Guardian*, 15 July 2020, www.theguardian.com/politics/2020/jul/15/boris-johnson-indicates-at-pmqs-he-has-not-read-winter-coronavirus-report

29 Rajeev Syal, 'UK health minister did not see 2017 pandemic report until Guardian story', *Guardian*, 14 July 2020, www.theguardian.com/world/2020/jul/14/uk-health-minister-did-not-see-2017-pandemic-report-until-guardian-story

30 'Coronavirus: UK opts out of EU Covid-19 vaccine scheme', BBC, 10 July 2020, www.bbc.co.uk/news/uk-politics-53361906

31 Simon Jenkins, 'The Tories' latest Brexit plans expose frictionless trade as a fiction', *Guardian*, 13 July 2020, www.theguardian.com/commentisfree/2020/jul/13/the-tories-latest-brexit-plans-expose-frictionless-trade-as-a-fiction

32 Robert Wright, 'Ashford residents resign themselves to the realities of Brexit', *FT*, 17 July 2020, www.ft.com/content/8f1f213c-4aeb-4ebc-b4d7-61e7909c3a79

33 Joe Mellor, 'Brexit: The size of Lorry park to hold 7,000 trucks has been calculated and it's huge', *The London Economic*, 28 September 2020, www.thelondoneconomic.com/politics/brexit-the-size-of-lorry-park-to-hold-7000-trucks-has-been-calculated-and-its-huge-20 3357

34 BBC Newsnight [@BBCNewsnight], Twitter, 14 July 2020, twitter.com/BBCNewsnight/status/1283166179847278592

35 Editorial, 'The Guardian view on England's hungry children: the indigestible truth', *Guardian*, 13 July 2020, www.theguardian.com/commentisfree/2020/jul/13/the-guardian-view-on-englands-hungry-children-the-indigestible-truth

36 Sally Weale, 'England's free school meals scheme to close for new claims over summer', *Guardian*, 14 July 2020, www.theguardian.com/uk-news/2020/jul/14/englands-free-school-meals-scheme-to-close-for-new-claims-over-summer

37 HM Revenue & Customs, 'Get a discount with the Eat Out to Help Out Scheme', Gov.uk, 15 July 2020, www.gov.uk/guidance/get-a-discount-with-the-eat-out-to-help-out-scheme

38 'Rishi Sunak defends furlough bonus scheme', BBC, 15 July 2020, www.bbc.co.uk/news/business-53421888

39 Steve Anglesey, 'BREXITEERS OF THE WEEK: Joan Collins hit by Brexit after claiming it would be "good for us"', *New European*, 16 July 2020, www.theneweuropean.co.uk/brexit-news-steve-anglesey-on-brexiteers-of-the-week-joan-collins-87056

40 David Davis [@DavidDavisMP], Twitter, 13 July 2020, twitter.com/daviddavismp/status/1282632952032133123?lang=en

41 Martina Bet, 'Dominic Cummings' bombshell Brexit confession exposed: "Leaving could be an error"', *Express*, 24 July 2020, www.express.co.uk/news/uk/1313818/brexit-news-eu-uk-trade-barnier-frost-dominic-cummings-boris-johnson-spt

42 'Our food standards campaign: The journey so far', Countryside Online, www.countrysideonline.co.uk/back-british-farming/back-british-farming-our-latest-activity/food-standards-petition/our-food-standards-campaign-the-journey-so-far

43 Ashley Cowburn, 'UK "not match-fit" for post-Brexit trade talks, says New Zealand's deputy prime minister', *Independent*, 12 August 2020, www.independent.co.uk/news/uk/politics/brexit-new-zealand-uk-talks-winston-peters-boris-johnson-a9667416.html

44 Greg Heffer, 'Coronavirus: Number 10 contradicts Health Secretary Matt Hancock on face mask rules after sandwich shop confusion', Sky News, 15 July 2020, news.sky.com/story/coronavirus-number-10-contradicts-health-secretary-matt-hancock-on-face-mask-rules-after-sandwich-shop-confusion-12029134

45 Liam James, 'Make face masks mandatory in secondary schools, teachers' union urges', *Independent*, 27 July 2020, www.independent.co.uk/news/education/face-masks-schools-latest-government-guidlines-reopening-nasuwt-gmb-a9640101.html

46 Jeremy Vine [@theJeremyVine], Twitter, 21 July 2020, twitter.com/thejeremyvine/status/1285611296101216259?lang=en

47 Alok Sharma [@AlokSharma_RDG], Twitter, 17 July 2020, twitter.com/aloksharma_rdg/status/1284141814195388416?lang=en

48 Harrison Jones, 'MPs vote against plan to protect NHS from US in trade deal', *Metro*, 22 July 2020, metro.co.uk/2020/07/22/mps-vote-plan-protect-nhs-us-trade-deal-13022079

49 Henry Goodwin, 'Gove branded "liar" as MPs vote down animal welfare amendment', *The London Economic*, 21 July 2020, www.thelondoneconomic.com/politics/gove-branded-liar-as-mps-vote-down-animal-welfare-amendment-195601

50 Kate Devlin, 'Brexit: Tory backbenchers defeated in attempt to put any future trade deals through parliament', *Independent*, 21 July 2020, www.independent.co.uk/news/uk/politics/brexit-trade-bill-parliament-vote-mps-eu-leave-a9629396.html

51 Josh Halliday, 'Test and trace failing to contact thousands in England's worst-hit areas', *Guardian*, 22 July 2020, www.theguardian.com/world/2020/jul/22/test-and-trace-system-in-england-failing-to-contact-thousands

52 Sarah Marsh and Molly Blackall, 'England's contact tracers "making handful of calls" a month', *Guardian*, 5 August 2020, www.theguardian.com/world/2020/aug/05/englands-contact-tracers-making-handful-of-calls-a-month?CMP=Share_iOSApp_Other

53 Elisabeth Mahase, 'Covid-19: Local health teams trace eight times more contacts than national service', *BMJ*, 22 June 2020, www.bmj.com/content/369/bmj.m2486

54 'UK coronavirus death toll increase by 155 to 44,391', ITV News, 7 July 2020, www.itv.com/news/2020-07-07/uk-coronavirus-death-toll-increase-by-155-to-44391

55 Joanna Partridge, 'Serco expects 50% jump in profits on back of Covid contracts', *Guardian*, 20 June 2020, www.theguardian.com/business/2021/jun/30/serco-expects-jump-in-profits-covid-contracts-nhs

56 Sarah Marsh and Molly Blackall, 'England's contact tracers "making handful of calls" a month'

57 Rob Merrick, 'Scathing report blasts "unimaginable" £37bn cost of coronavirus test and trace system', *Independent*, 10 March 2021, www.independent.co.uk/news/uk/politics/coronavirus-test-trace-dido-harding-report-b1814714.html

58 'Government Fix your Bike Voucher Scheme', Active Together, 29 July 2020, www.active-together.org/news/2020/07/government-fix-your-bike-voucher-scheme

59 '"Fix your bike" website crashes as scheme launches in England', BBC, 29 July 2020, www.bbc.co.uk/news/uk-53576008

60 Denis Campbell, Peter Walker and Haroon Siddique, 'Boris Johnson to unveil £10m ad campaign to cut obesity in England', *Guardian*, 25 July 2020, www.theguardian.com/society/2020/jul/25/boris-johnson-to-unveil-10m-ad-campaign-to-cut-obesity-in-england

61 Helen Warrell and George Parker, 'UK pledges tougher spy laws in wake of Russia report', *FT*, 22 July 2020, www.ft.com/content/8ee121ae-0736-483d-9b92-1b275c00c23e

62 'Patel flags new laws against foreign spying as concerns continue over Russia', *Guernsey Press*, 24 July 2020, guernseypress.com/news/uk-news/2020/07/24/patel-flags-new-laws-against-foreign-spying-as-concerns-continue-over-russia

63 Simon Murphy, 'UK report on Russian interference: key points explained', *Guardian*, 21 July 2020, www.theguardian.com/world/2020/jul/21/just-what-does-the-uk-russia-report-say-key-points-explained

64 John Silk, 'Russia report damning of UK government's "lack of curiosity"', DW, 21 July 2020, www.dw.com/en/russia-report-damning-of-uk-governments-lack-of-curiosity/a-54252429

65 Adam Payne, '14 ministers in Boris Johnson's government received funding from donors linked to Russia', Business Insider, 23 July 2020, www.businessinsider.com/russia-report-donors-boris-johnson-conservative-party-2020-7

66 Dan Sabbagh, 'Julian Lewis warns Dominic Cummings not to politicise ISC inquiries', *Guardian*, 22 July 2020, www.theguardian.com/uk-news/2020/jul/22/julian-lewis-warns-dominic-cummings-not-to-politicise-isc-inquiries

67 Full Fact [@FullFact], Twitter, 21 July 2020, mobile.twitter.com/FullFact/status/1285507164912656384

68 Pippa Allen-Kinross, 'Has the government really hit 100,000 tests a day, and what happens next?', Full Fact, 1 May 2020, fullfact.org/health/coronavirus-100k-tests

69 Abbas Panjwani, 'Government misses one of its Covid-19 test targets', Full Fact, 16 April 2020, fullfact.org/health/coronavirus-test-targets

70 Leo Benedictus, 'Did the government meet its Covid-19 test targets?', 10 July 2020, fullfact.org/health/six-test-targets

71 Helen Pidd and Josh Halliday, 'Coronavirus data failing local authorities, health bosses in England say', *Guardian*, 24 July 2020, www.theguardian.com/world/2020/jul/24/coronavirus-data-failing-local-authorities-england-health

72 Rajeev Syal, 'UK failed to plan for economic impact of flu-like pandemic, says watchdog', *Guardian*, 23 July 2020, www.theguardian.com/world/2020/jul/23/uk-failed-to-plan-for-economic-impact-of-flu-like-pandemic-says-watchdog

73 Ibid.

74 'Releasing patients to care homes without coronavirus tests a "reckless and appalling error"', ITV News, 29 July 2020, www.itv.com/news/2020-07-29/releasing-patients-to-care-homes-without-tests-a-reckless-and-appalling-error

75 Department for Transport and Foreign & Commonwealth Office, 'Spain removed from travel corridors exemption list', Gov.uk, 25 July 2020, www.gov.uk/government/news/spain-removed-from-travel-corridors-exemption-list

76 Abbas Panjwani, 'You were more likely to catch Covid-19 in Spain than the UK in late July', Full Fact, 10 August 2020, fullfact.org/online/spain-uk-covid-comparison

77 Lewis Goodall, [@lewis_goodall], Twitter, 25 July 2020, mobile.twitter.com/lewis_goodall /status/1287121460050501639

78 Lisa O'Carroll, 'Brexit will deliver double shock to UK economy, study finds', Guardian, 28 July 2020, www.theguardian.com/politics/2020/jul/28/brexit-will-deliver-double-shock-to-uk-economy-study-finds-coronavirus

79 Andrea Jenkyns [@andreajenkyns], Twitter, 22 July 2020, mobile.twitter.com/ andreajenkyns/status/1285835784701042689

80 Julian Shea, [@juliansheasport], Twitter, 24 July 2020, mobile.twitter.com/juliansheasport/ status/1286557766098792448

81 Jon Stone, 'UK government quietly cuts international aid by £2.9 billion as MPs leave parliament for summer', Independent, 23 July 2020, www.independent.co.uk/news/uk/politi cs/uk-government-tories-cut-foreign-international-aid-billions-budget-coronavirus-a9633 516.html?amp

82 Denis Campbell, 'Lack of beds and staff will hamper NHS in clearing backlog, says study', Guardian, 24 July 2020, www.theguardian.com/society/2020/jul/24/lack-of-beds-and-staff-will-hamper-nhs-in-clearing-backlog-says-study

83 Simon Murphy and Jim Waterson, 'Evgeny Lebedev, Jo Johnson and Ian Botham among 36 peerage nominations', Guardian, 31 July 2020, www.theguardian.com/politics/2020/jul/31/ evgeny-lebedev-jo-johnson-and-ian-botham-among-36-peerage-nominations-boris

84 'Philip May: The banker husband and Theresa's "real rock"', ITV News, 12 July 2016, www.itv.com/news/2016-07-12/philip-may-the-banker-husband-and-theresas-real-rock

85 'Ian Botham buys in Almeria', Country Life, 22 December 2007, www.countrylife.co.uk/ news/ian-botham-buys-in-almeria-35751

86 Sophia Sleigh, 'Claire Fox row: Labour calls on Boris Johnson to block former Brexit Party MEP's peerage for failure to apologise over IRA bombing "support"', Evening Standard, 5 August 2020, www.standard.co.uk/news/politics/claire-fox-blocked-peerage-ira-warrington -bombings-a4517291.html

87 Glen Owen, 'Media tycoon Evgeny Lebedev denies having files of compromising material on Boris Johnson after Prime Minister's enemies claimed information was gathered at star-studded party in Italy', Daily Mail, 16 November 2019, www.dailymail.co.uk/news/article -7693423/Media-tycoon-Evgeny-Lebedev-denies-having-files-compromising-material-Boris-Johnson.html

88 Thomas Brown, 'House of Lords membership: A snapshot in June 2020', UK Parliament, 24 June 2020, lordslibrary.parliament.uk/house-of-lords-membership-in-june-2020

89 Peter Walker and Ben Quinn, 'Boris Johnson "still committed to Lords reduction" despite 36 peerages', Guardian, 3 August 2020, www.theguardian.com/politics/2020/aug/03/no-10-boris-johnson-pm-still-committed-lords-reduction-despite-36-peerages

90 Patrick Butler and Kevin Rawlinson, 'Boris Johnson repeatedly used inaccurate child poverty figures', Guardian, 30 July 2020, www.theguardian.com/politics/2020/jul/30/boris-johnson-repeatedly-used-inaccurate-child-poverty-figures

91 Andrew Sparrow and Aamna Mohdin, 'UK coronavirus live: England had highest levels of excess deaths in Europe in first half of 2020, ONS says – as it happened', Guardian, 30 July 2020, www.theguardian.com/world/live/2020/jul/30/uk-coronavirus-live-news-covid-19-latest-updates-isolation-period

92 Imogen Braddick, 'Johnson hails nation's "massive success" in reducing deaths after Britain tops Europe for highest level of excess fatalities', Evening Standard, 30 July 2020, www.standard.co.uk/news/uk/boris-johnson-success-uk-top-europe-excess-deaths-a4512661.html?amp

93 Patrick Butler, 'Universal credit needs £8bn overhaul, says cross-party report', Guardian, 31 July 2020, www.theguardian.com/society/2020/jul/31/universal-credit-needs-8bn-overhaul-says-cross-party-report

94 Rajeev Syal and Rowena Mason, 'Labour says universal credit will take 495 years to roll out as costs rise £3bn', Guardian, 25 June 2015, www.theguardian.com/society/2015/ jun/25/labour-says-universal-credit-will-take-495-years-to-roll-out-as-costs-rise-3bn

95 Gregor Young, 'Anger as Dominic Raab posts food bank selfie on Twitter', *The National*, 25 July 2020, www.thenational.scot/news/18607295.anger-dominic-raab-posts-food-bank-selfie-twitter

96 James Mates, [@jamesmatesitv], Twitter, 3 August 2020, mobile.twitter.com/jamesmatesitv /status/1290400459841327105

97 Ian Duncan Smith MP [@MPainDS], Twitter, 3 August 2020, mobile.twitter.com/MPIain DS/status/1290292766514135040

98 Ian Duncan Smith MP [@MPainDS], Twitter, 3 August 2020, mobile.twitter.com/MPIain DS/status/1290292767852118016

99 Patrick Butler, 'Cummings trips damaged UK lockdown unity, study suggests', *Guardian*, 30 July 2020, www.theguardian.com/politics/2020/jul/30/cummings-saga-damaged-uk-unity-covid-19-study-suggests

100 Jamie Grierson, 'Lack of special border measures before UK coronavirus lockdown was "serious mistake"', *Guardian*, 5 August 2020, www.theguardian.com/politics/2020/aug/ 05/lack-of-special-border-measures-before-uk-coronavirus-lockdown-was-serious-mistake

101 Andy Gregory, 'Architect of UK's coronavirus lockdown Neil Ferguson says he has never met Boris Johnson', *Independent*, 31 July 2020, www.independent.co.uk/news/uk/politics /neil-ferguson-architect-coronavirus-lockdown-boris-johnson-a9648576.html

102 Hugh Pym [BBCHughPym], Twitter, 4 August 2020, mobile.twitter.com/BBCHughPym/ status/1290696344886292488

103 Rory Carroll, 'Cheap, popular and it works: Ireland's contact-tracing app success', *Guardian*, 20 July 2020, www.theguardian.com/world/2020/jul/20/cheap-popular-and-it-works-irelands-contact-tracing-app-success

104 Denis Campbell and Kate Proctor, 'Two U-turns and a lot of chaos: it's been a painful week for Boris Johnson', *Guardian*, 1 August 2020, www.theguardian.com/world/2020/aug/01 /two-u-turns-and-lot-of-chaos-its-been-a-painful-week-for-boris-johnson

105 Ibid.

106 'Less than half of people in England understand current lockdown rules', UCL, 31 July 2020, www.ucl.ac.uk/news/2020/jul/less-half-people-england-understand-current-lockdown-rules

107 Pippa Allen-Kinross, 'It's not true that employees who have to quarantine cannot be "penalised"', Full Fact, 29 July 2020, fullfact.org/health/coronavirus-quarantine-penalise-employees

108 Neil Vowles, 'Overseas voters' decisive Brexit-fuelled shift from Conservatives casts doubt on government Votes For Life pledge', University of Sussex, 4 August 2020, www.sussex.ac.uk/broadcast/read/52513

109 Lisa O'Carroll, 'Number of UK citizens emigrating to EU has risen by 30% since Brexit vote', *Guardian*, 4 August 2020, www.theguardian.com/politics/2020/aug/04/number-of-uk-citizens-emigrating-to-eu-has-risen-by-30-since-brexit-vote

110 Daniel Boffey, 'UK negotiators have only engaged with issues "in last week or two", says EU', *Guardian*, 29 July 2020, www.theguardian.com/politics/2020/jul/29/uk-negotiators-have-only-engaged-with-issues-in-last-week-or-two-says-eu

111 Oliver Wright, 'Prime minister is in cloud cuckoo land on EU trade deal, says his father Stanley Johnson', *The Times*, 3 August 2020, www.thetimes.co.uk/article/pm-in-cloud-cuckoo-land-on-trade-says-father-hpp80wtxw

August

1 Peter Walker and Josh Halliday, 'Tory MP condemned for claim BAME people breaching lockdown most', *Guardian*, 31 July 2020, www.theguardian.com/world/2020/jul/31/tory-mp-craig-whittaker-condemned-claim-bame-people-most-covid-19-lockdown-breaches

2 Helen Pidd, Josh Halliday and Amy Walker, 'Manchester Covid outbreak "a warning to complacent white middle class"', *Guardian*, 3 August 2020, www.theguardian.com/world /2020/aug/03/coronavirus-80-new-cases-trafford-among-white-community

3 Dan Sabbagh, 'Russians hacked Liam Fox's personal email to get US-UK trade dossier', *Guardian*, 3 August 2020, www.theguardian.com/politics/2020/aug/03/classified-documents-on-us-uk-trade-talks-hacked-from-liam-fox-emails

4 Michael Gove [@MichaelGove], Twitter, 3 August 2020, twitter.com/michaelgove/status/12 9024417072936550?lang=en

5   Oli Dugmore, 'The document that proves Michael Gove is unfit for high office', Joe, www
    .joe.co.uk/news/michael-gove-good-friday-agreement-peace-process-northern-ireland-23
    5438
6   Richard Partington, 'UK to plunge into deepest slump on record with worst GDP drop of
    G7', Guardian, 9 August 2020, www.theguardian.com/business/2020/aug/09/uk-to-fall-
    into-deepest-slump-on-record-with-worst-fall-in-gdp-among-g7
7   'Coronavirus: UK worst hit among major economies', BBC, 26 August 2020,
    www.bbc.co.uk/news/business-53918568
8   Archie Bland, 'Inside the tent: who was Boris Johnson's holiday guest?', Guardian, 21
    August 2020, www.theguardian.com/politics/2020/aug/21/inside-the-tent-who-is-boris-
    johnsons-holiday-guest
9   Kit Heren, 'Government hiring Head of Pandemic Preparedness six months into
    coronavirus outbreak', Evening Standard, 13 August 2020, www.standard.co.uk/news/uk/
    government-hire-head-pandemic-preparedness-coronavirus-a4524021.html
10 Sebastian Shakespeare, 'Model Rosie, Sam Cam's Girl Friday paid by taxpayers: 'Special
    adviser' being paid £53,000 to organise PM's wife's diary and wardrobe', Daily Mail, 7 April
    2017, www.dailymail.co.uk/news/article-3527314/Model-Rosie-Sam-Cam-s-Girl-Friday-
    paid-taxpayers-Special-adviser-paid-53-000-organise-PM-s-wife-s-diary-wardrobe.html
11 Jon Stone, 'UK's Brexit losses more than 178 times bigger than trade deal gains',
    Independent, 7 November 2021, www.independent.co.uk/news/uk/politics/brexit-trade-
    deals-australia-new-zealand-b1959478.html
12 Emer O'Toole, 'Anger as UK's trade talks with Japan halt over Liz Truss's love of stilton', The
    National, 11 August 2020, www.thenational.scot/news/18643808.anger-uks-trade-talks-
    japan-halt-liz-trusss-love-stilton
13 Christopher Hope, 'Increase motorway speed limit to 80mph to drive Britain's productivity,
    says Government minister', Telegraph, 30 September 2018, www.telegraph.co.uk/politics/20
    18/09/30/increase-motorway-speed-limit-80mph-drive-britains-productivity/?WT.mc_id=
    tmg_share_tw
14 John Harris, 'England's contact-tracing saga is at the heart of the government's failures',
    Guardian, 11 August 2020, www.theguardian.com/world/2020/aug/11/englands-test-and-
    trace-saga-is-at-the-heart-of-the-governments-coronavirus-failures
15 'Good, rapid, progress but still a way to go to be fit for purpose, let alone world class', NHS
    Providers, 11 June 2020, nhsproviders.org/news-blogs/news/good-rapid-progress-but-still-
    a-way-to-go-to-be-fit-for-purpose-let-alone-world-class
16 'Written statement from Chair of Ofqual to the Education Select Committee ', Gov.uk, 2
    September 2020, www.gov.uk/government/news/written-statement-from-chair-of-ofqual-
    to-the-education-select-committee
17 'GCSE resits: students to receive "calculated" grades', TES Magazine, 20 March 2020,
    www.tes.com/news/gcse-resits-students-receive-calculated-grades
18 Jessica Murray, 'Royal Statistical Society hits back at Ofqual in exams algorithm row',
    Guardian, 24 August 2020, www.theguardian.com/education/2020/aug/24/royal-statistical-
    society-hits-back-at-ofqual-in-exams-algorithm-row
19 Jon Coles [@JonColes01], Twitter, 13 August 2020, twitter.com/JonColes01/status/1293919
    819805241345
20 'A-levels and GCSEs: How did the exam algorithm work?', BBC, 20 August 2020,
    www.bbc.co.uk/news/explainers-53807730
21 'Students are not at risk of being promoted "beyond their competence", but our government
    is', Independent, 14 August 2020, www.independent.co.uk/voices/letters/levels-exam-
    results-gavin-williamson-education-brexit-coronavirus-face-masks-fine-a9670551.html
22 Josh Halliday, '"I feel cheated": Rotherham students struggle to make sense of exam grades',
    Guardian, 13 August 2020, www.theguardian.com/education/2020/aug/13/i-feel-cheated-
    rotherham-students-struggle-to-make-sense-of-exam-grades
23 Will Hazell, 'A-level results 2021: Private schools see huge rise in A* grades as "inequality"
    gap with state sector grows', iNews, 10 August 2021, inews.co.uk/news/education/a-level-
    results-2021-inequality-private-schools-biggest-rise-teachers-top-grade-1144049
24 'A-level private school subjects see "rampant" inflation', TES Magazine, 16 August 2020,
    www.tes.com/news/coronavirus-A-level-private-school-subjects-see-rampant-inflation

25   Elisa Menendez, 'Tories call for Gavin Williamson to resign as exam U-turn branded "utter shambles"', *Metro*, 18 August 2020, metro.co.uk/2020/08/18/calls-gavin-williamson-1314 1949

26   Ben Quinn, 'UK exams debacle: how did this year's results end up in chaos?', *Guardian*, 17 August 2020, www.theguardian.com/education/2020/aug/17/uk-exams-debacle-how-did-results-end-up-chaos

27   Aaron Walawalkar and Mattha Busby, 'Schools can appeal against A-level and GCSE grades for free, says Williamson', *Guardian*, 15 August 2020, www.theguardian.com/education/20 20/aug/15/schools-can-appeal-a-level-and-gcse-grades-for-free-says-gavin-williamson

28   Andy Gregory, 'Government to cover cost of all A-level and GCSE results appeals in England, Gavin Williamson says', *Independent*, 15 August 2020, www.independent.co.uk /news/education/schools-level-gcse-appeals-free-gavin-williamson-resign-ofqual-england-a9671816.html

29   Arj Singh, 'Hereditary Tory peer suggests "grit and perseverance" more important than A-levels', *Huffington Post*, 14 August 2020, www.huffingtonpost.co.uk/entry/a-levels-lord-bethell-tory_uk_5f367d4dc5b65bbd8c8be966

30   Sally Weale, '"Levelling up" school funding policy favours wealthy pupils – study', *Guardian*, 7 August 2020, www.theguardian.com/education/2020/aug/07/levelling-up-school-funding-policy-favours-wealthy-pupils-study

31   'Coronavirus: Parents to be told schools safe for September return', BBC, 16 August 2020, www.bbc.co.uk/news/education-53795439

32   William Cole, 'Councils can BULLDOZE contaminated homes and crush cars as a last resort under new laws to stop second wave of coronavirus', *Daily Mail*, 5 August 2020, www.dailymail.co.uk/news/article-8593993/Councils-BULLDOZE-contaminated-homes-resort-stop-second-wave-coronavirus.html

33   'Coronavirus: Little evidence of Covid transmission in schools, says Williamson', BBC, 10 August 2020, www.bbc.co.uk/news/uk-53718066

34   Neil Henderson [@hendopolis], Twitter, 10 August 2020, mobile.twitter.com/hendopolis/st atus/1292939139567034373?s=19

35   Nicola Davis, 'Scientists urge routine Covid testing when English schools reopen', *Guardian*, 10 August 2020, www.theguardian.com/education/2020/aug/10/scientists-urge-routine-covid-testing-when-english-schools-reopen

36   'WHO head: "Our key message is: test, test, test"', BBC, 16 March 2020, www.bbc.co.uk/news/av/world-51916707

37   '"Never mind the backstop, the buck stops here": Boris launches his premiership with domestic focus', *Spectator*, 24 July 2019, www.spectator.co.uk/article/-never-mind-the-back stop-the-buck-stops-here-boris-launches-his-premiership-with-domestic-focus

38   'Chief education civil servant Jonathan Slater sacked after exams row', BBC, 26 August 2020, www.bbc.co.uk/news/uk-politics-53920146

39   Nicholas Soames [@NSoames], Twitter, 17 August 2020, twitter.com/nsoames/status/12954 00108599713792

40   Isabel Hardman, 'Tory MPs have given their leaders the benefit of the doubt. Until now', *Guardian*, 16 August 2020, www.theguardian.com/commentisfree/2020/aug/16/tory-mps-have-given-their-leaders-the-benefit-of-the-doubt-until-now

41   Rachel Wearmouth, 'Exclusive: 27 academy trusts given just ONE free laptop each from government', *Huffington Post*, 18 August 2020, www.huffingtonpost.co.uk/entry/exclusive-27-academy-trusts-handed-just-1-free-laptop-despite-gavin-williamson-pledge-to-help-disadvantaged_uk_5f3ba21bc5b61100c3ac316d

42   Amelia Hill, 'Migrant children face hunger over free school meal restrictions', *Guardian*, 14 August 2020, www.theguardian.com/uk-news/2020/aug/14/migrant-children-face-hunger-over-free-school-meal-restrictions

43   Peter Geoghegan and Jenna Corderoy, 'Exclusive: Property tycoons gave Tories more than £11m in less than a year', openDemocracy, 26 June 2020, www.opendemocracy.net/en/dark-money-investigations/exclusive-property-tycoons-gave-tories-more-than-11m-in-less-than-a-year

44   Will Hurst, 'Sweeping reforms will give new schemes "automatic" planning permission', *Architects' Journal*, 3 August 2020, www.architectsjournal.co.uk/news/sweeping-reforms-will-give-new-schemes-automatic-planning-permission

45 'Ministers ignored "slums of the future" warnings, says adviser', BBC, 4 August 2020, www.bbc.co.uk/news/uk-politics-53650657

46 'Robert Jenrick denies planning system overhaul which could lead to "slum housing" is designed to "help the big boys"', ITV News, 6 August 2020, www.itv.com/news/2020-08-05/row-over-governments-drive-to-cut-planning-red-tape

47 Chloe Chaplain, 'Affordable housing will 'become extinct' with new loosened rules for developers, warns charity', *iNews*, 6 August 2020, inews.co.uk/news/politics/affordable-housing-planning-rules-extinct-572663

48 Priti Patel [@pritipatel], Twitter, 7 August 2020, twitter.com/pritipatel/status/129171361121 2247041

49 Louise Callaghan, 'No need to risk the channel — migrants take the air route', *The Times*, 1 August 2021, www.thetimes.co.uk/article/no-need-to-risk-the-channel-migrants-take-the-air-route-l7pxr20wl

50 Natalie Bennett, [@natalieben], Twitter, 18 August 2021, twitter.com/natalieben/status/142 7961893969334274

51 Jolyon Rubinstein [@JolyonRubs], Twitter, 30 November 2021, mobile.twitter.com/JolyonRubs/status/1465607194251038721?s=19

52 '10 Years On, Turkey Continues Its Support for an Ever-Growing Number of Syrian Refugees', The World Bank, 22 June 2021, www.worldbank.org/en/news/feature/2021/06/22/10-years-on-turkey-continues-its-support-for-an-ever-growing-number-of-syrian-refugees

53 Lizzie Dearden, 'Channel crossings: Priti Patel tells MPs migrants believe France is a "racist country" after 1,000 arrive in 10 days', *Independent*, 16 August 2020, www.independent.co.uk/news/uk/politics/channel-crossings-migrants-priti-patel-france-racist-country-a9672821.html

54 'Home Secretary appoints small boat commander', Gov.uk, 9 August 2020, www.gov.uk/government/news/home-secretary-appoints-small-boat-commander

55 Diane Taylor, 'UK plan to use navy to stop migrant crossings is unlawful, lawyers warn', *Guardian*, 7 August 2020, www.theguardian.com/world/2020/aug/07/uk-plan-to-use-navy-to-stop-migrant-crossings-is-unlawful-lawyers-warn

56 Lizze Dearden, 'Channel crossings: No plans for Royal Navy to block migrants after UN warns ships could cause "fatal incidents"', *Independent*, 15 August 2020, www.independent.co.uk/news/uk/home-news/channel-crossings-navy-ships-migrants-france-un-mod-a9672236.html

57 Henry Goodwin, '"Completely potty" to deploy navy to tackle migrant crossings', *The London Economic*, 7 August 2020, www.thelondoneconomic.com/politics/completely-potty-to-deploy-navy-to-tackle-migrant-crossings-197288

58 Graeme Demianyk, 'Priti Patel is arguing with an ice-cream company over migrant crossings', *Huffington Post*, 11 August 2020, www.huffingtonpost.co.uk/entry/priti-patel-ben-and-jerrys-migrant-crossings_uk_5f32f143c5b6960c066d669e

59 Twitter, mobile.twitter.com/EdwardLeighMP/status/1292781286231289857

60 Adrian Zorzut, 'Tory immigration minister asks to re-record live TV interview after forgetting which country he is from', *New European*, 12 August 2020, www.theneweurope an.co.uk/brexit-news-priti-patel-s-junior-minister-makes-embarassing-gaffe-on-live-89316

61 'Johnson says Irish Sea trade border "over my dead body"', ITV News, 14 August 2020, www.itv.com/news/utv/2020-08-13/irish-sea-trade-border-over-my-dead-body-says-johnson

62 Oliver Dowden, 'Boris Johnson orders a "bonfire" of red tape to give small firms a bigger slice of Government contracts after Brexit', *Telegraph*, 4 November 2019, www.telegraph.co.uk/politics/2019/11/04/boris-johnson-orders-bonfire-red-tape-give-small-firms-bigger

63 Jill Lawless, 'UK to spend millions to ease Brexit red tape for N Ireland', *AP News*, 7 August 2020, apnews.com/article/global-trade-boris-johnson-northern-ireland-brexit-business-2d 6b7f443e42134b7670b7edb6d7df43

64 Aubrey Allegretti, 'Coronavirus: Public Health England to be scrapped - with Dido Harding picked to lead its replacement', Sky News, 18 August 2020, news.sky.com/story/cor onavirus-public-health-england-to-be-scrapped-health-secretary-confirms-12051592

65 Emer O'Toole, 'Matt Hancock given £350k from figures linked to Cheltenham Festival', *National*, 20 July 2020, www.thenational.scot/news/18594722.matt-hancock-given-350k-figures-linked-cheltenham-festival

66 'Randox Health are the official sponsors of the Randox Health Grand National and The Jockey Club's official health partner', The Jockey Club, www.thejockeyclub.co.uk/about-us /our-present/group-partners/randox-health

67 Guy Adams, 'MP Owen Paterson blames a Commons inquiry that found him guilty of using his position for financial gain for his wife's suicide but was he a greedy politician on the make... or tragically naive?', *Daily Mail*, 27 October 2021, www.dailymail.co.uk/news/article-10134297/GUY-ADAMS-Owen-Paterson-greedy-MP-make-tragically-naive.html

68 Jane Clinton, 'Owen Paterson row: Randox won £133m Covid testing contract despite lacking equipment', *iNews*, 7 November 20201, inews.co.uk/news/politics/owen-paterson -randox-133m-covid-testing-contract-despite-lacking-equipment-1288605

69 George Monbiot, 'The government's secretive Covid contracts are heaping misery on Britain', *Guardian*, 21 October 2020, www.theguardian.com/commentisfree/ 2020/oct/21/government-covid-contracts-britain-nhs-corporate-executives-test-and-trace

70 Anneliese Dodds [@AnnalieseDodds], Twitter, 26 November 2021, mobile.twitter.com/AnnalieseDodds/status/1464293261045112832

71 David Rose, 'Tory peer Lord Bethell changes his story AGAIN over £90m Covid contracts as he admits deleting phone messages because he wrongly believed they were backed up', *Daily Mail*, 7 November 2021, www.dailymail.co.uk/news/article-10175591/Tory-peer-Lord-Bethell-changes-story-90m-Covid-contracts.html

72 Martin Williams and Peter Geoghegan, 'UK's anti-corruption tsar accused of defending COVID "cronyism"', openDemocracy, 25 March 2021, www.opendemocracy.net/en/dark-money-investigations/uk-anti-corruption-john-penrose-sinister-defence-government-covid-cronyism

73 'Sajid Javid: Why has the ex-chancellor been allowed to work for JP Morgan?', BBC, 19 August 2020, www.bbc.co.uk/news/uk-politics-53821907

74 David Conn, 'Firm linked to Gove and Cummings hired to work with Ofqual on A-levels', *Guardian*, 20 August 2020, www.theguardian.com/education/2020/aug/20/firm-linked-to-gove-and-cummings-hired-to-work-with-ofqual-on-a-levels

75 Mia Hunt, 'Gove recruits longstanding allies as UK Cabinet Office non-execs', Global Government Forum, 4 May 2020, www.globalgovernmentforum.com/gove-recruits-longst anding-allies-as-uk-cabinet-office-non-execs

76 Sebastian Payne, 'Government launches review of Cabinet Office', *FT*, 20 August 2020, www.ft.com/content/5eeab074-9de8-45e5-9749-86898a089a69

77 Mikey Smith, 'Michael Gove's department alone spent £50m on consultants and marketing during Covid-19 crisis', *Mirror*, 21 August 2020, www.mirror.co.uk/news/politics/michael-goves-department-alone-spent-22559150

78 David Pegg, 'Government paid Vote Leave AI firm to analyse UK citizens' tweets', *Guardian*, 10 August 2020, www.theguardian.com/world/2020/aug/10/government-paid-vote-leave-ai-firm-to-analyse-uk-citizens-tweets

79 'Michael Gove's department alone spent £50m on consultants and marketing during Covid-19 crisis', *Mirror*, 21 August 2020, www.mirror.co.uk/news/politics/michael-goves-department-alone-spent-22559150

80 Richard Ford, 'Priti Patel approves Taser "that is more painful"', *The Times*, 25 August 2020, www.thetimes.co.uk/article/priti-patel-approves-taser-7-that-is-more-painful-3rx0r76ww

81 Patrick Butler, 'UK families bereaved by Covid-19 lose eligibility for welfare benefits', *Guardian*, 21 August 2020, www.theguardian.com/society/2020/aug/21/uk-families-bereaved-by-covid-19-lose-eligibility-for-welfare-benefits

82 Meka Beresford, 'Scottish Conservative leader Douglas Ross "would vote against" US trade deal over chlorinated chicken import', *iNews*, 30 August 2020, inews.co.uk/news/politics/scottish-conservative-leader-douglas-ross-would-vote-against-us-trade-deal-over-chlorinated-chicken-imports-613829

83 'Trade Bill — New Clause 11 — Standards for Imported Agricultural Goods After Transition Period for Leaving the European Union', They Work For You, 20 July 2020, www.theyworkforyou.com/divisions/pw-2020-07-20-79-commons

September

1   Patrick Barkham, 'Littering epidemic in England as government spends just £2k promoting Countryside Code', *Guardian*, 26 August 2020, www.theguardian.com/uk-news/2020/aug /26/littering-epidemic-england-countryside-code

2   '"Opportunity squandered!" Fisheries say Brexit wasted as industry hit with £300m losses', *Express*, 30 September 2020, www.express.co.uk/news/politics/1498867/brexit-news-fishing-latest-eu-trade-deal-cost-update

3   Jack Wright, 'Twitter users accuse Tory fisheries minister of PR stunt after claiming she had NO line on rod in picture boasting about a good day catching mackerel', *Daily Mail*, 1 September 2020, www.dailymail.co.uk/news/article-8685835/Twitter-users-accuse-fisheries-minister-PR-stunt-claiming-NO-line-rod-picture.html

4   'Fifth ex-PM speaks out against post-Brexit bill', BBC, 14 September 2020, www.bbc.co.uk /news/uk-politics-54145202

5   'Brexit: Buckland says power to override Withdrawal Agreement is 'insurance policy', BBC, 13 September 2020, www.bbc.co.uk/news/uk-politics-54137643

6   James Johnson, 'Suella Braverman under pressure over role in plans to override Brexit Withdrawal Agreement', *Daily Echo*, 13 September 2020, www.dailyecho.co.uk/news/18717 486.suella-braverman-pressure-role-plans-override-brexit-withdrawal-agreement

7   Sophia Sleigh, 'Kit Malthouse admits Government could be breaking international law with plans to override Brexit treaty', *Evening Standard*, 14 September 2020, www.standard.co.uk/news/politics/kit-malthouse-admits-government-breaking-international-law-a4546536.html

8   'Northern Ireland Secretary admits new bill will "break international law"', BBC, 8 September 2020, www.bbc.co.uk/news/uk-politics-54073836

9   Dominic Raab [@DominicRaab], Twitter, 10 September 2020, twitter.com/dominicraab/ status/1304060029105037312

10 Richard Adams, 'Gap between rich and poor pupils in England "grows by 46% in a year"', *Guardian*, 1 September 2020, www.theguardian.com/education/2020/sep/01/disadvantaged-and-bame-pupils-lost-more-learning-study-finds

11 Kit Heren, 'Matt Hancock insists no reason not to go back to work as "little evidence" coronavirus is passed on in offices', *Evening Standard*, 19 August 2020, www.standard.co.uk /news/uk/matt-hancock-no-reason-not-to-go-back-to-work-coronavirus-a4528871.html

12 Heather Stewart, 'MPs call on Jacob Rees-Mogg to extend hybrid parliament system', *Guardian*, 28 August 2020, www.theguardian.com/politics/2020/aug/28/mps-call-on-jacob-rees-mogg-extend-hybrid-parliament-system

13 'Boris Johnson warns against large gatherings – minutes after meeting "50 MPs"', *Huffington Post*, 4 September 2020, www.huffingtonpost.co.uk/entry/coronavirus-tories-boris-johnson-distancing_uk_5f523026c5b62b3add3f4452

14 UK Prime Minister [@10DowningStreet], Twitter, 2 September 2020, twitter.com/10DowningStreet/status/1301206016126849024

15 Owen Bowcott, Severin Carrell and Amy Walker, 'Coronavirus: hunting exempt from "rule of six" restrictions in England', *Guardian*, 15 September 2020, www.theguardian.com/uk-news/2020/sep/14/hunting-in-england-exempt-from-rule-of-six-covid-19-restrictions

16 'Coronavirus: St Leger horse racing risk "too great" for Doncaster', BBC, 28 August 2020, www.bbc.co.uk/news/uk-england-south-yorkshire-53945641

17 Sebastian Shakespeare, 'Will Max give his half-brother Boris Johnson a shot in the arm? Prime Minister sibling joins advisory board of health company that has branched into coronavirus testing', *Daily Mail*, 10 September 2020, www.dailymail.co.uk/tvshowbiz/ article-8720407/SEBASTIAN-SHAKESPEARE-Max-half-brother-Boris-Johnson-shot-arm .html

18 Josh Halliday and Sarah Boseley, 'Operation Moonshot: rapid Covid test missed over 50% of cases in pilot', *Guardian*, 5 November 2020, www.theguardian.com/world/2020/nov/05 /operation-moonshot-rapid-covid-test-missed-over-50-of-cases-in-pilot

19 Ibid.

20 Josh Halliday and Helen Pidd, 'Coronavirus tests run out in north-east England as cases surge', *Guardian*, 4 September 2020, www.theguardian.com/world/2020/sep/04/covid-tests-running-out-in-north-east-england-gateshead-as-cases-surge

21 Laura Keay, 'Coronavirus: Britons told to travel as far as 500 miles for COVID-19 tests as system struggles to cope', Sky News, 10 September 2020, news.sky.com/story/coronavirus-britons-told-to-travel-as-far-as-500-miles-for-covid-19-tests-as-system-struggles-to-cope-12067581

22 Lizzie Dearden, 'Conservative Party used disinformation "with new level of impunity" during 2019 general election, report finds', Independent, 24 August 2020, www.independent.co.uk/news/uk/politics/conservative-party-disinformation-2019-general-election-a9682566.html

23 Jon Stone, 'Council of Europe issues media freedom alert over UK government blacklisting of investigative journalists', Independent, 6 September 2020, www.independent.co.uk/news/uk/politics/press-freedom-uk-government-council-europe-alert-boris-johnson-priti-patel-a9706741.html

24 Peter Stubley, 'Boris Johnson "plans to opt out of human rights laws" amid Brexit row', Independent, 13 September 2020, www.independent.co.uk/news/uk/politics/brexit-human-rights-act-uk-europe-convention-boris-johnson-b433013.html

25 Nathaniel Barker, 'Grenfell survivors "outraged" after government votes down inquiry recommendations amendment', Inside Housing, 8 September 2020, www.insidehousing.co.uk/news/news/grenfell-survivors-outraged-after-government-votes-down-inquiry-recommendations-amendment-67809

26 Dominic Cummings, 'Risk, aggression, Brexit and Article 16', Dominic Cummings substack, 12 November 2021, dominiccummings.substack.com/p/risk-aggression-brexit-and-article

27 Nicholas Watt, 'Boris Johnson to campaign for Brexit in EU referendum', Guardian, 21 February 2016, www.theguardian.com/politics/2016/feb/21/boris-johnson-eu-referendum-campaign-for-brexit-david-cameron

28 Owen Bowcott and Daniel Boffey, 'Amal Clooney quits UK envoy role over "lamentable" Brexit bill', Guardian, 18 September 2020, www.theguardian.com/world/2020/sep/18/amal-clooney-quits-uk-envoy-role-over-lamentable-brexit-bill

29 Raphael Hogarth, 'The Internal Market Bill breaks international law and lays the ground to break more law', Institute for Government, www.instituteforgovernment.org.uk/blog/internal-market-bill-breaks-international-law

30 Emma DeSouza [@EmmaandJDeSouza], Twitter, 16 September 2020, twitter.com/EmmandJDeSouza/status/1306319236583903234

31 Toby Helm, Michael Savage and Robin McKie, '£10,000 fines warning for failing to self-isolate as England Covid infections soar', Guardian, 20 September 2020, www.theguardian.com/world/2020/sep/19/10000-fines-warning-for-failing-to-self-isolate-as-covid-infections-soar

32 Josh Halliday and Steven Morris, 'People in England's 10 worst-hit Covid-19 hotspots unable to get tests', Guardian, 15 September 2020, www.theguardian.com/world/2020/sep/14/people-in-englands-10-worst-hit-covid-hotspots-unable-to-get-tests

33 'Anger as government admits test and trace website coding error', Schools Week, schoolsweek.co.uk/anger-as-government-admits-test-and-trace-website-coding-error

34 Jennifer Hassan, 'Britain's health secretary says the asymptomatic don't need tests. Critics say that sends a mixed message', Washington Post, 9 September 2020, www.washingtonpost.com/world/2020/09/09/britains-health-secretary-says-asymptomatic-dont-need-tests-many-experts-say-otherwise

35 Jack Peat, 'Minister's mocking nickname for Matt Hancock sends social media into meltdown', The London Economic, 21 September 2020, www.thelondoneconomic.com/news/ministers-mocking-nickname-for-matt-hancock-sends-social-media-into-meltdown-202264

36 Katy Balls, '"Operation Moonshot? More like operation moonf**k": Mutiny brewing as Tory MPs look ahead to a miserable Christmas', iNews, 12 September 2020, inews.co.uk/opinion/columnists/operation-moonshot-analysis-tory-mutiny-brewing-coronavirus-rules-christmas-643803

37 Mikey Smith, 'Boris Johnson squirms away from 10 million tests a day figure in "moonshot" plan', Mirror, 16 September 2020, www.mirror.co.uk/news/politics/boris-johnson-squirms-away-10-22694567

38 Science and Technology Committee, parliamentlive.tv, 17 September 2020, parliamentlive.tv/event/index/52ee1eec-a2bf-403d-a27d-7bba077ebfcc?in=15:48:28&out=15:49:20

39 Luke O'Reilly, 'Sadiq Khan says Cobra hasn't met since May 10 and he hasn't spoken to Boris Johnson in four months', *Evening Standard,* 18 September 2020, www.standard.co.uk /news/politics/sadiq-khan-cobra-boris-johnson-may-10-a4550651.html

40 Nigel Nelson, 'Boris Johnson "plans to resign next spring after complaining about £150k salary"', *Mirror,* 17 October 2020, www.mirror.co.uk/news/politics/boris-johnson-plans-resign-next-22863780

41 Gregory Kirby and Simon Walters, 'Butler on a "Boris bike" smuggled £27,000 of organic takeaways at "cost price" into No.10 for PM (under his real first name Alex) and Carrie Symonds over eight months - and some "was paid for by wife of rich Tory donor"', *Daily Mail,* 21 May 2021, www.dailymail.co.uk/news/article-9606217/Butler-smuggled-27-000-organic-takeaways-No-10-paid-wife-Tory-donor.html

42 'JCB chief Bamford and Brian Paddick among 30 new peers', BBC, 1 August 2013, www.bbc.co.uk/news/uk-politics-23529208

43 Jen Mills, 'Butler "smuggled £27,000 of organic food into Downing Street for Boris"', *Metro,* 22 May 2021, metro.co.uk/2021/05/22/butler-smuggled-27000-of-organic-food-into-downing-street-for-boris-14628328

44 Faye Brown, 'Boris Johnson's "£840-a-roll" wallpaper "keeps falling down"', *Metro,* 19 May 2021, metro.co.uk/2021/05/19/boris-johnsons-840-a-roll-downing-street-wallpaper-falling-down-14605970

45 George Grylls, 'Donor gave Boris Johnson £53k to decorate flat', *The Times,* 27 August 2021, www.thetimes.co.uk/article/donor-gave-boris-johnson-53k-to-decorate-flat-65ppn095t

46 '"Mad and totally unethical": Dominic Cummings hits out at Boris Johnson', *Guardian,* 23 April 2021, www.theguardian.com/politics/2021/apr/23/dominic-cummings-launches-attack-on-boris-johnson

47 Sophie Morris, 'Conservative accounts reveal party donor Lord Brownlow paid more than £52,000 towards PM's flat refurbishment', Sky News, 26 August 2021, news.sky.com/story /conservative-accounts-reveal-party-donor-lord-brownlow-paid-more-than-52-000-towards-pms-flat-refurbishment-12391214

48 Catherine Neilan, 'Tory donor's idea for Great Exhibition 2.0 "wasn't taken forward", says No. 10 — but something very similar was', *Insider,* 6 January 2022, www.insider.com/ boris-johnson-pushed-festival-like-flat-donor-brownlow-2022-1

49 Alexandra Rogers, 'Ethics Chief accepts Boris Johnson's "humble and sincere apology" over mislaid WhatsApps', *Huffington Post,* 6 January 2022, www.huffingtonpost.co.uk/ entry/boris-johnson-humble-and-sincere-apology-accepted-lord-geit-downing-street-flat_uk_61d6db31e4b0bb04a64185ae

October

1 Jessica Elgot, Vikram Dodd and Peter Walker, 'Coronavirus: pubs and restaurants across England to be forced to shut at 10pm', *Guardian,* 21 September 2020, www.theguardian.com/world/2020/sep/21/pubs-and-restaurants-across-england-to-be-forced-to-shut-at-10pm

2 Clea Skopeliti, 'Parliament bars exempt from 10pm curfew', *Independent,* 28 September 2020, www.independent.co.uk/news/uk/home-news/parliament-bars-curfew-exempt-commons-workplace-canteen-pubs-b665366.html

3 Zoe Tidman and Rob Merrick, 'Coronavirus: "Extraordinary" flaw leaves NHS app unable to process tens of thousands of test results', *Independent,* 27 September 2020, www.independent.co.uk/news/health/nhs-coronavirus-covid-app-test-results-nhs-hospitals-phe-labs-trace-b617947.html

4 Alex Hern, 'Users report issues as Covid-19 app launches in England and Wales', *Guardian,* 24 September 2020, www.theguardian.com/world/2020/sep/24/users-report-issues-as-covid-19-app-launches-in-england-and-wales

5 'Covid-19: Test and trace app incompatibility angers cross-border residents', BBC, 2 October 2020, www.bbc.co.uk/news/uk-england-54384743

6 Alex Hern, 'Contact-tracing app for England and Wales "hampered by loss of public trust"', *Guardian,* 21 September 2020, www.theguardian.com/world/2020/sep/21/covid-coronavirus-contact-tracing-app-hampered-lack-trust

7   Daniel Boffey, 'Dominic Cummings' data law shake-up a danger to trade, says EU',
     Guardian, 25 September 2020, www.theguardian.com/politics/2020/sep/25/dominic-
     cummings-data-law-shake-up-a-danger-to-trade-says-eu

8   Gordon Rayner, Camilla Tominey and Charles Hymas, '"Go back to work or risk losing
     your job": Major drive launched to get people returning to the office', *Telegraph*, 27 August
     2020, www.telegraph.co.uk/news/2020/08/27/go-back-work-risk-losing-job-major-drive-
     launched-get-people

9   Department for Health and Social Care, 'New legal duty to self-isolate comes into force
     today', Gov.uk, 28 September 2020,
     www.gov.uk/government/news/new-legal-duty-to-self-isolate-comes-into-force-today

10   BBC Politics [@BBCPolitics], Twitter, 22 September 2020, twitter.com/bbcpolitics/status/13
     08388554389811205

11   Mattha Busby, 'Schools in England told not to use material from anti-capitalist groups',
     Guardian, 27 September 2020, www.theguardian.com/education/2020/sep/27/uk-schools-
     told-not-to-use-anti-capitalist-material-in-teaching

12   Aamna Mohdin, 'Legal threat over anti-capitalist guidance for schools in England',
     Guardian, 1 October 2020, www.theguardian.com/education/2020/oct/01/legal-threat-
     governments-anti-capitalist-guidance-schools-political

13   'Bullying at school', Gov.uk, www.gov.uk/bullying-at-school

14   Boris Johnson [@Boris Johnson], Twitter, 5 September 2020, twitter.com/BorisJohnson/
     status/1302217031241138177

15   Alex Barker, 'BBC braced for more turbulence as arch critic is tipped for top job', *FT*, 23
     September 2020, www.ft.com/content/fb6aff0b-2be4-48d3-aa63-3c6258422a9a

16   Jack Peat, 'Boris Johnson wanted to "triple the pay" of the BBC chairman
     in order to entice Charles Moore', *The London Economic*, 20 October 2020,
     www.thelondoneconomic.com/news/boris-johnson-wanted-to-triple-the-pay-of-the-bbc-
     chairman-in-order-to-entice-charles-moore-206222

17   Ibid.

18   Jim Waterson, 'Charles Moore rules himself out of running to be BBC chairman', *Guardian*,
     4 October 2020, www.theguardian.com/media/2020/oct/04/charles-moore-rules-himself-
     out-running-for-bbc-chairman-role

19   Andy Gregory, 'Boris Johnson "asks former Daily Mail editor Paul Dacre to chair Ofcom"',
     Independent, 27 September 2020, www.independent.co.uk/news/uk/politics/boris-johnson-
     paul-dacre-ofcom-charles-moore-bbc-b627465.html

20   Sarah Phillips, 'The Daily Mail: a very, very brief guide', *Daily Mail*, 27 March 2012,
     www.theguardian.com/media/shortcuts/2012/mar/27/daily-mail-very-very-brief-guide

21   Jasper Jackson, 'Wikipedia bans Daily Mail as "unreliable" source', *Guardian*, 8 February
     2017, www.theguardian.com/technology/2017/feb/08/wikipedia-bans-daily-mail-as-
     unreliable-source-for-website

22   Alex Barker, George Parker and Nic Fildes, 'Boris Johnson orders rerun of search for
     Ofcom chair after Paul Dacre rejected', *FT*, 27 May 2021, www.ft.com/content/71bdca31-
     285a-48ac-b2a8-89946372b22c

23   'Paul Dacre: a rigged appointment', Good Law Project, 11 November 2021,
     goodlawproject.org/news/paul-dacre-a-rigged-appointment

24   Haroon Siddique, 'Idea of Charles Moore as BBC chair "beyond the pale", says Tory MP',
     Guardian, 29 September 2020, www.theguardian.com/media/2020/sep/29/idea-of-charles-
     moore-as-bbc-chair-beyond-the-pale-says-tory-mp

25   Archie Bland, 'Rishi Sunak's adviser Richard Sharp to be next BBC chair', *Guardian*, 6
     January 2021, www.theguardian.com/media/2021/jan/06/former-goldman-sachs-banker-
     richard-sharp-to-be-next-bbc-chairman

26   Adam Payne, 'Only a quarter of UK businesses say they are ready for Brexit, with less
     than 4 months to go', *Insider*, 23 September 2020, www.businessinsider.com/quarter-of-
     businesses-ready-for-brexit-michael-gove-says-2020-9

27   Oliver Wright, 'British lorries will need permit to enter Kent after Brexit', *The Times*,
     24 September 2020, www.thetimes.co.uk/article/british-lorries-will-need-permit-to-enter-
     kent-977kpnwlq

28   David Molloy, 'Brexit border software developers warn of delays', BBC, 27 October 2020,
     www.bbc.co.uk/news/technology-54706263

29 Peter Foster, Daniel Thomas, Jonathan Eley and George Parker, 'UK pushes back full Brexit border checks by another six months', *FT*, 11 March 2020, www.ft.com/conte nt/4c07eaab-4650-418c-b7c9-1b7dba7a2a9f

30 Adam Forrest, 'Brexit: Kent border plan ridiculed, as road haulage chiefs say checks "won't work"', *Independent*, 24 September 2020, www.independent.co.uk/news/uk/politics/kent-border-checks-brexit-permits-gove-plan-ridiculed-b571525.html

31 Milly Vincent, '"We need toilets all down the M20": Fears 39,000 lorries will be BLOCKED from bringing key goods to the UK and Kent will turn into a huge car park if Brexit trade talks collapse', *Daily Mail*, 14 October 2020, www.dailymail.co.uk/news/article-8838549 /We-need-portaloos-M20-Fears-39-000-lorries-BLOCKED-bringing-key-goods-UK.html

32 'Shoppers could pay more after no-deal Brexit', BBC, 25 September 2020, www.bbc.co.uk /news/business-54287283

33 Dave [@davemacladd], Twitter, 26 June 2018, twitter.com/davemacladd/status/1011636382 786314240

34 John van Reenan, 'The cost of Brexit is likely to be more than double that of COVID – it must be delayed', LSE, 22 October 2020, blogs.lse.ac.uk/brexit/2020/10/22/the-cost-of-brexit-is-likely-to-be-more-than-double-that-of-covid-it-must-be-delayed

35 'Autumn Budget cancelled for 2020 due to COVID-19 crisis', TaxAssist Accountants, 24 September 2020, www.taxassist.co.uk/resources/news/autumn-budget-cancelled-for-2020-due-to-covid-19-crisis

36 Lawrence White and Abhishek Manikandan, 'JPMorgan to move $230 billion of assets to Germany ahead of Brexit – source', Reuters, 23 September 2020, www.reuters.com/article /jp-morgan-brexit-idINKCN26E2CP

37 Bloomberg and Viren Vaghela, 'Banks are moving $1.6 trillion in assets out of the U.K. ahead of Brexit cutoff', *Fortune*, 1 October 2020, fortune.com/2020/10/01/banks-trillions-jobs-brexit-move

38 Alex Hern, 'Covid: how Excel may have caused loss of 16,000 test results in England', *Guardian*, 6 October 2020, www.theguardian.com/politics/2020/oct/05/how-excel-may-have-caused-loss-of-16000-covid-tests-in-england

39 Rajeev Syal, 'Brexit drives government consultancy fees to £450m in three years', *Guardian*, 6 October 2020, www.theguardian.com/politics/2020/oct/06/brexit-drives-government-consultancy-fees-to-450m-in-three-years

40 Adam Forrest, '"People are furious": Coronavirus rule confusion sees "red wall" revolt in north east England', *Independent*, 5 October 2020, www.independent.co.uk/news/uk/ politics/coronavirus-rules-north-east-england-pubs-red-wall-conservatives-b696261.html

41 Paul Goodman, 'Our Cabinet League Table. The Prime Minister falls into negative territory', conservativehome, 3 October 2020, www.conservativehome.com/thetorydiary/20 20/10/our-cabinet-league-table-the-prime-minister-falls-into-negative-territory.html

42 Heather Stewart and Simon Murphy, '"Carry on coronavirus": shine has come off Johnson as Tory conference begins', *Guardian*, 2 October 2020, www.theguardian.com/politics/2020 /oct/02/carry-on-coronavirus-shine-has-come-off-johnson-as-tory-conference-begins-party-turmoil

43 Harry Lambert, 'The end of the affair: how Tory MPs are falling out of love with Boris Johnson', *New Statesman*, 1 October 2020, www.newstatesman.com/politics/uk-politics/2020/10/end-affair-how-tory-mps-are-falling-out-love-boris-johnson

44 BBC Newsnight [@BBCNewsnight], Twitter, 6 October 2020, twitter.com/BBCNewsnight /status/1313606994629189634

45 Phillip Inman, '"Eat out to help out" did not boost hospitality sector finances – poll', *Guardian*, 1 October 2020, www.theguardian.com/business/2020/oct/01/eat-out-to-help-out-failed-boost-finances-uk-hospitality-industry

46 '"Eat Out to Help Out" scheme drove new COVID-19 infections up by between 8 and 17%, new research finds', The University of Warwrick, 30 October 2020, warwick.ac.uk/fac/ soc/economics/research/centres/cage/news/30-10-20-eat_out_to_help_out_scheme_ drove_new_covid_19_infections_up_by_between_8_and_17_new_research_finds

47 Andrew Woodcock, '"Red wall" seats to take brunt of welfare cuts, as 6 million families set to lose £1,000', *Independent*, 3 October 2020, www.independent.co.uk/news/uk/politics/ris hi-sunak-resolution-foundation-universal-credit-covid-b749216.html

48 Tom Kibasi, 'Sunak must realise that job coaches are useless when there are no jobs to be had', *Guardian*, 5 October 2020, www.theguardian.com/commentisfree/2020/oct/05/sunak-job-coaches-jobs-economy-chancellor-party-conference-speech

49 Robert Booth, 'Abolish district councils to help shore up "red wall", suggests top Tory', *Guardian*, 28 September 2020, www.theguardian.com/politics/2020/sep/28/abolish-district-councils-labour-red-wall-tory

50 Harrison Jones, 'Boris facing "northern revolt" as 50 Tory MPs demand lockdown "exit map"', *Metro*, 27 October 2020, metro.co.uk/2020/10/27/boris-facing-northern-revolt-as-50-tory-mps-demand-lockdown-exit-map-13485149

51 'UK Internal Market Bill violates the rule of law and threatens to undermine devolution arrangements, says Committee', UK Parliament, 16 October 2020, committees.parliament.uk/committee/172/constitution-committee/news/120102/uk-internal-market-bill-violates-the-rule-of-law-and-threatens-to-undermine-devolution-arrangements-says-committee

52 Greg Heffer, 'Brexit: Theresa May attacks "reckless" Internal Market Bill and warns of "untold damage" to UK', Sky News, 21 September 2020, news.sky.com/story/brexit-theresa-may-attacks-reckless-internal-market-bill-and-warns-of-untold-damage-to-uk-12078256

53 Nick Eardley [@nickeardleybbc], Twitter, 29 September 2020, twitter.com/nickeardleybbc/status/1311041072546619392

54 Meral Hussein-Ece [@meralhece], Twitter, 30 September 2020, mobile.twitter.com/meralhece/status/1311216480030265344

55 Joanna Taylor, 'All of the MPs who just voted to break international law', indy100, 15 September 2020, www.indy100.com/news/mps-vote-break-international-law-internal-market-bill-brexit-boris-johnson-9710391

56 'United Kingdom Internal Market Bill', UK Parliament, 29 September 2020, hansard.parliament.uk/Commons/2020-09-29/debates/96A7BFAF-F6AD-409C-86EC-4799A382727D/UnitedKingdomInternalMarketBill#division-29392

57 Reuters Staff, 'EU launches legal case against UK over Internal Market Bill', Reuters, 1 October 2020 www.reuters.com/article/us-britain-eu-vonderleyen-idUKKBN26M5FS

58 Rob Merrick, 'Brexit blow to car industry as EU rejects crucial UK plan to avoid export tariffs', *Independent*, 30 September 2020, www.independent.co.uk/news/uk/politics/brexit-uk-car-industry-eu-tariffs-exports-b712615.html

59 Lisa O'Carroll, 'UK carmakers face higher tariffs as EU rejects component plea', *Guardian*, 30 September 2020, www.theguardian.com/politics/2020/sep/30/uk-carmakers-face-higher-tariffs-as-eu-rejects-component-plea-brexit

60 Rajeev Syal, 'Priti Patel bullying inquiry delay "eroding trust" within Whitehall', *Guardian*, 2 October 2020, www.theguardian.com/politics/2020/oct/02/priti-patel-bullying-inquiry-delay-eroding-trust-within-whitehall

61 Jemma Slingo, 'Patel lashes out at "lefty lawyers" in asylum speech', *Law Society Gazette*, 5 October 2020, www.lawgazette.co.uk/news/patel-lashes-out-at-lefty-lawyers-in-asylum-speech/5105870.article

62 Diane Taylor, 'Appeal court quashes UK policy of removing migrants with little warning', *Guardian*, 21 October 2020, www.theguardian.com/politics/2020/oct/21/appeal-court-quashes-uk-policy-of-removing-migrants-unlawfully

63 Jamie Grierson, 'Foreign rough sleepers face deportation from UK post-Brexit', *Guardian*, 21 October 2020, www.theguardian.com/uk-news/2020/oct/21/foreign-rough-sleepers-face-deportation-from-uk-post-brexit

64 Chloe Chaplain, 'From moving migrants to Ascension Island to a wave machine in the Channel, all the leaked proposals considered by Priti Patel', *iNews*, 1 October 2020, inews.co.uk/news/politics/priti-patel-migrants-ascension-island-wave-machine-english-channel-home-office-leaks-proposals-672558

65 The Jouker, 'Which Scottish island will Priti Patel want to put asylum seekers on?', *The National*, 1 October 2020, www.thenational.scot/news/18763966.scottish-island-will-priti-patel-want-put-asylum-seekers

66 Helen Davidson, 'UK offshore detention proposal could create "human rights disaster", Australian experts warn', *Guardian*, 1 October 2020, www.theguardian.com/uk-news/2020/oct/01/uk-offshore-detention-proposal-could-create-human-rights-disaster-australian-experts-warn

67 David Wilcock, Jack Elsom and Jack Maidment, 'Downing Street fails to rule out sending asylum seekers trying to enter Britain to a remote SCOTTISH ISLAND after it emerged Priti Patel considered sending migrants 4,000 miles to Atlantic outcrop', *Daily Mail*, 30 September 2020, www.dailymail.co.uk/news/article-8787455/Priti-Patel-looked-sending-asylum-seekers-tiny-volcanic-islands.html

68 Jamie Grierson, 'Home Office may use nets to stop migrant boats crossing Channel', *Guardian*, 11 October 2020, www.theguardian.com/world/2020/oct/11/home-office-considers-using-nets-to-stop-migrant-boats-crossing-channel

69 Andrew Woodcock, 'Coronavirus: UK will be "extremely proud" of its response, like the Olympics, claims Lord Bethell', *Independent*, 4 October 2020, www.independent.co.uk/news/uk/politics/coronavirus-lord-bethell-proud-olympics-b784784.html

70 'Minister blames "late-night intimacy" for spreading Covid-19', *Express & Star*, 25 September 2020, www.expressandstar.com/news/uk-news/2020/09/25/minister-blames-late-night-intimacy-for-spreading-covid-19

71 Kimberley Hackett, 'Critical care: "There aren't enough ICU nurses for UK's 30,000 ventilators"', NursingStandard, 5 October 2020, web.archive.org/web/20201023023356/https://rcni.com/nursing-standard/newsroom/news/critical-care-there-arent-enough-icu-nurses-uks-30000-ventilators-167556

72 Sebastian Shakespeare, '£650m Carphone Warehouse tycoon lands bail-out for opera charity', *Mail Online*, 13 October 2020, www.dailymail.co.uk/tvshowbiz/article-8837059/650m-Carphone-Warehouse-tycoon-lands-bail-opera-charity.html

73 'Cineworld lowers curtain on US, UK theatres: 45,000 left jobless', *Aljazeera*, 5 October 2020, www.aljazeera.com/economy/2020/10/5/45000-unemployed-as-cineworld-lowers-curtain-on-us-uk-theatres

74 Ben Glaze and Dan Bloom, 'DWP chief Therese Coffey suggests sacked cabin crew go work in care', *Mirror*, 8 October 2020, homeswww.mirror.co.uk/news/politics/dwp-chief-therese-coffey-suggests-22811510

75 Sarah Clarke, 'Care staff "dismayed" over freeze on social care workforce training fund', Home Care Insight, 3 June 2020, www.homecareinsight.co.uk/care-staff-dismayed-over-freeze-on-social-care-workforce-training-fund

76 Tom Jefferson and Carl Heneghan, 'Covid 19 – Epidemic "Waves"', CEBM, 30 April 2020, www.cebm.net/covid-19/covid-19-epidemic-waves

77 Josh Halliday, 'Councils given five minutes' notice of local lockdown confirmation', *Guardian*, 2 October 2020, www.theguardian.com/politics/2020/oct/02/councils-given-five-minutes-notice-of-local-lockdown-confirmation

78 Jessica Elgot and Heather Stewart, 'Covid can change UK like "new Jerusalem" of 1940s, Johnson claims', *Guardian*, 6 October 2020, www.theguardian.com/politics/2020/oct/06/covid-can-change-uk-like-1940s-new-jerusalem-johnson-claims

79 Owen Bowcott, 'Legal profession hits back at Johnson over "lefty lawyers" speech', *Guardian*, 6 October 2020, www.theguardian.com/law/2020/oct/06/legal-profession-hits-back-at-boris-johnson-over-lefty-lawyers-speech

80 Owen Bowcott, 'Brexit strategy risks UK "dictatorship", says ex-president of supreme court', *Guardian*, 7 October 2020, www.theguardian.com/law/2020/oct/07/brexit-strategy-puts-uk-on-slippery-slope-to-tyranny-lawyers-told

81 'Boris Johnson: Wind farms could power every home by 2030', BBC, 6 October 2020, www.bbc.co.uk/news/uk-politics-54421489

82 Fiona Harvey, 'UK "will take 700 years" to reach low-carbon heating under current plans', *Guardian*, 8 October 2020, www.theguardian.com/environment/2020/oct/08/uk-will-take-700-years-to-reach-low-carbon-heating-under-current-plans

83 Kirsten McStay, 'James McAvoy hits out at Rishi Sunak suggesting "job retraining" as he campaigns to "Save the Arts"', *Daily Record*, 13 October 2020, www.dailyrecord.co.uk/entertainment/james-mcavoy-hits-out-rishi-22836587

84 Kris Tatum, 'What job does the UK Government think you should do? Take the test to find out', *York Press*, 8 October 2020, www.yorkpress.co.uk/news/national/uk-today/18777870.job-government-think-take-test-find

85 '"It's unacceptable": 250,000 SMEs struggle to access bounce-back loans', *Guardian*, 7 October 2020, www.theguardian.com/business/2020/oct/07/its-unacceptable-smes-unable-to-access-bounce-back-loans

86   John Johnston, 'Rishi Sunak favourite among public to replace Boris Johnson if
     coronavirus forces him to step back', *Politics Home*, 29 March 2020, www.politicshome.com
     /news/article/rishi-sunak-favourite-among-public-to-replace-boris-johnson-if-he-
     becomes-ill-new-poll
87   Fraser Nelson, 'Where's Boris?', *Spectator*, 19 September 2020, www.spectator.co.uk/article
     /the-missing-leader-boris-johnson-needs-to-find-his-purpose-again
88   Lisa O'Carroll, 'Gove says UK has "66% chance" of Brexit deal amid breakthrough',
     Guardian, 7 October 2020, www.theguardian.com/politics/2020/oct/07/eu-needs-clear-
     sign-uk-will-get-real-in-brexit-talks-says-irish-minister
89   Daniel Boffey, 'Boris Johnson set for compromise on Human Rights Act – EU sources',
     Guardian, Daniel Boffey, www.theguardian.com/politics/2020/oct/07/boris-johnson-set-
     to-make-compromise-on-human-rights-act-eu-sources
90   Daniel Boffey and Lisa O'Carroll, 'Brexit: Boris Johnson has undermined trust in UK
     government, says EU', *Guardian*, 9 September 2020, www.theguardian.com/politics/2020
     /sep/09/brexit-claim-boris-johnson-responding-to-barnier-threat-called-fake-news-
91   Josh Halliday, 'Local Covid lockdowns in England having limited effect, says minister',
     Guardian, 8 October 2020, www.theguardian.com/world/2020/oct/08/local-covid-
     lockdowns-england-robert-jenrick-virus
92   Jack Elsom, 'Boris Johnson's 10pm pubs curfew was based on "back of a fag packet
     calculations" and "NOT advocated by SAGE" - despite ministers insisting they are
     "following the science"', *Daily Mail*, 26 September 2020, www.dailymail.co.uk/news/article-
     8775199/Boris-Johnsons-10pm-pubs-curfew-based-fag-packet-calculations.html
93   Rob Davies, 'Pubs, bars and restaurants report Covid curfew sales dive', *Guardian*, 1
     October 2020, www.theguardian.com/business/2020/oct/01/pubs-bars-restaurants-covid-
     curfew-sales-plunge-uk
94   Kate Devlin, 'Coronavirus: Chris Whitty "not confident" that top tier lockdown restrictions
     will work', *Independent*, 12 October 2020, www.independent.co.uk/news/uk/politics/corona
     virus-three-tier-system-lockdown-chris-whitty-boris-johnson-b995460.html
95   'Covid: Sage scientists called for short lockdown weeks ago', BBC, 13 October 2020,
     www.bbc.co.uk/news/uk-54518002
96   Simon Murphy and Archie Bland, 'Ministers add to confusion over England Covid
     lockdown rules', *Guardian*, 3 November 2020, www.theguardian.com/world/2020/nov/03
     /ministers-prompt-confusion-over-england-covid-coronavirus-lockdown-rules
97   Peter Walker, 'Deciphering the quirks of England's second Covid lockdown rules', *Guardian*,
     3 November 2020, www.theguardian.com/uk-news/2020/nov/03/deciphering-the-quirks-
     of-englands-second-covid-lockdown-rules
98   Luke McGee, 'Fear sets in that Boris Johnson's Brexit government is ill equipped to handle
     a pandemic', CNN, 11 October 2020, lite.cnn.com/en/article/h_3d4d7c4e8cff1919b86566b
     579407f0e
99   Tom Gillespie, 'Coronavirus: Matt Hancock denies breaching 10pm drinking curfew
     in Commons bar', Sky News, 11 October 2020, news.sky.com/story/coronavirus-matt-
     hancock-denies-breaching-10pm-drinking-curfew-in-commons-bar-12101358
100 Donna Ferguson and Aaron Walawalkar, 'Laptop allocation for England's schools slashed
     by 80%', *Guardian*, 24 October 2020, www.theguardian.com/education/2020/oct/24/
     englands-schools-to-receive-fewer-laptops-for-distance-learning
101 'Trade Agreements', UK Parliament, 12 February 2020, questions-statements.parliament.uk
     /written-questions/detail/2020-02-12/15042
102 Oliver Wright and Callum Jones, 'Brexit: No 10 snubs tougher food rules to keep trade
     deals on the menu', *The Times*, 8 October 2020, www.thetimes.co.uk/article/brexit-no-10-
     snubs-tougher-food-rules-to-keep-trade-deals-on-the-menu-vdhks5262
103 Rob Merrick, 'Brexit: Anger as ministers use obscure rule to deny MPs a vote on blocking
     chlorinated chicken imports', *Independent*, 11 October 2020, www.independent.co.uk/news
     /uk/politics/brexit-chlorinated-chicken-eu-mps-boris-johnson-b914047.html
104 George Grylls, 'Robert Jenrick "selected own constituency for £25m funding"', *The Times*,
     10 October 2020, www.thetimes.co.uk/article/robert-jenrick-selected-own-constituency-
     for-25m-funding-zx2qd2tgz
105 Rajeev Syal, 'Robert Jenrick admits approving funds for town in Jake Berry's constituency',
     Guardian, 11 October 2020, www.theguardian.com/politics/2020/oct/11/robert-jenrick-
     admits-approving-funds-for-town-in-jake-berrys-constituency

106 Mark Sweney, 'Amazon to escape UK digital services tax that will hit smaller traders', *Guardian*, 14 October 2020, www.theguardian.com/technology/2020/oct/14/amazon-to-escape-uk-digital-services-tax-that-will-hit-smaller-traders

107 'NHS staff "insulted" by "badge or snack box" pandemic reward', Nursing Notes, 19 October 2020, nursingnotes.co.uk/news/nhs-staff-insulted-by-badge-or-snack-box-pandemic-reward

108 Daniel Hewitt, 'Covid: Two thirds of hospices facing redundancies as government help runs out', ITV, 19 October 2020, www.itv.com/news/2020-10-19/covid-two-thirds-of-hospices-facing-redundancies-as-government-help-runs-out

109 Ben Spencer, 'Test & trace consultants are being paid £7,360 a DAY each: Fury as private sector company is handed cash equivalent of £1.5 million annual salary for coronavirus tracking', *Daily Mail*, 14 October 2020, www.dailymail.co.uk/news/article-8841107/Test-trace-consultants-paid-7-360-DAY-Fury-private-sector-company-handed-cash.html

110 Ian Quinn, 'Free school meals: how government has botched the scheme', *The Grocer*, 15 June 2020, www.thegrocer.co.uk/supermarkets/free-school-meals-how-government-botched-the-scheme/645341.article

111 Eleanor Langford, 'Boris Johnson "congratulates" Marcus Rashford after footballer forces U-turn on free school meal funding', *Politics Home*, 16 June 2020, www.politicshome.com/news/article/boris-johnson-phones-marcus-rashford-after-footballer-forces-pm-to-uturn-on-funding-free-kids-meals-this-summer

112 Karl MacDonald, 'Who voted against free school meals extension? How your MP voted when Marcus Rashford campaign was defeated', *iNews*, 25 October 20220, inews.co.uk/news/politics/free-school-meals-vote-who-voted-against-how-my-mp-marcus-rashford-campaign-733881

113 Rebecca Cooney, 'Food poverty charity removes MPs from board after trustee votes against extending free school meals', *Third Sector*, 28 October 2020, www.thirdsector.co.uk/food-poverty-charity-removes-mps-board-trustee-votes-against-extending-free-school-meals/governance/article/1698465

114 Johnathan Walker, 'Free school meals row continues as Conservative MP Gary Sambrook says children are fed in term time', *Birmingham Live*, 23 October 2020, www.birminghammail.co.uk/news/midlands-news/free-school-meals-debate-continues-19152476

115 Sarah Turnnidge, 'Tory MP says she hopes businesses who feed hungry kids won't seek government support', *Huffington Post*, 24 October 2020, www.huffingtonpost.co.uk/entry/selaine-saxby-free-school-meals-businesses-government-support_uk_5f93fae7c5b6a2e1fb619d2a

116 Kate Ng, '"Not as simple as you make out": Tory MP tells Marcus Rashford free school meals increases "dependency" on state', *Independent*, 21 October 2020, www.independent.co.uk/news/uk/home-news/marcus-rashford-free-school-meals-ben-bradley-commons-vote-b1204921.html

117 'Fighting for white working class boys', Conservatives, 29 July 2020, www.benbradleyformansfield.com/news/fighting-white-working-class-boys

118 Amy Walker, 'Ben Bradley urged to apologise over free school meals tweets', *Guardian*, 24 October 2020, www.theguardian.com/education/2020/oct/24/ben-bradley-under-pressure-to-apologise-over-free-school-meals-tweets

119 'WATCH: "Children have been going hungry for years," says minister', *Labour List*, 21 October 2021, labourlist.org/2020/10/watch-children-have-been-going-hungry-for-years-says-minister

120 Harriet Brewis, 'Nicky Morgan tells Question Time that school meals motion might have got more votes if Tory MP hadn't been called scum', *Standard*, 23 October 2020, www.standard.co.uk/news/politics/nicky-morgan-question-time-free-school-meals-scum-a4572681.html

121 'Tory MPs attack celebrity free school meal campaigners', BBC, 21 October 2020, www.bbc.co.uk/news/education-54620118

122 Emily White, 'MP under fire for speech against free meals for poorest children', *Lincolnshire Live*, 23 October 2020, www.lincolnshirelive.co.uk/news/local-news/brendan-clarke-smith-school-meals-4630006

123 'Covid-19: UK workers to get 67% of pay if firms told to shut', BBC, 9 October 2020, www.bbc.co.uk/news/uk-54481817

124 Rishi Sunak [@RishiSunak], Twitter, 23 June 2020, twitter.com/rishisunak/status/12754245
49476208640
125 'Rishi Sunak "barred for life" from pub in his constituency over vote against free school
meals', ITV, 23 October 2020, www.itv.com/news/2020-10-23/rishi-sunak-barred-for-life-
from-pub-in-his-constituency-over-vote-against-free-school-meals
126 Jack Peat, 'Inside the Members' Dining Room: Where a £30 meal costs MPs just £12.75',
The London Economic, 12 January 2021, www.thelondoneconomic.com/politics/inside-the-
members-dining-room-where-a-30-meal-costs-mps-just-12-75-216257
127 Alice Scarsi, '"It is BAFFLING!" Fury as taxpayers forced to pay £4.4 MILLION so MPs can
get a cheap meal', *Express*, 25 July 2018, www.express.co.uk/news/uk/994245/taxpayers-parl
iament-expenses-taxpayers-alliance-outrage
128 Nadine Dorries [@NadineDorries], Twitter, 1 November 2020, twitter.com/NadineDorries
/status/1322909509355003910
129 Dan Bloom and Oliver Milne, 'Boris Johnson quietly corrects his false claim about
Universal Credit', *Mirror*, 16 October 2020, www.mirror.co.uk/news/politics/boris-johnson-
quietly-corrects-false-22858774
130 Jane Merrick, 'Manchester lockdown: What the Government is offering the city in its
ultimatum on Tier 3 Covid', *iNews*, 20 October 2020, restrictionsinews.co.uk/news/politics
/manchester-lockdown-tier-3-covid-restrictions-government-ultimatum-offer-731331
131 Daniel O'Mahony, 'Andy Burnham and Greater Manchester leaders shown Government's
Tier 3 decision on live TV', *Evening Standard*, 20 October 2020, www.standard.co.uk/news
/politics/watch-andy-burnham-press-conference-tier-3-a4572347.html
132 Peter Young, 'Britain and Europe still fishing in troubled waters', *Tribune*, 27 October 2020,
http://www.tribune242.com/news/2020/oct/27/peter-young-britain-and-europe-still-
fishing-troub
133 Oli Smith, 'Brexit BLUFF: Ridge calls out Boris' empty no deal threat after talks 'magically
restart'', *Express*, 25 October 2020, www.express.co.uk/news/politics/1352019/Brexit-news-
Sophy-Ridge-Boris-Johnson-Michel-Barnier-no-deal-threat-latest-vn
134 LBC [@LBC], Twitter, 19 October 2020, twitter.com/LBC/status/1318118951663161344
135 Richard Partington, 'UK economy not ready for no-deal Brexit, say business leaders',
Guardian, 16 October 2020, www.theguardian.com/politics/2020/oct/16/uk-economy-no-
deal-brexit-business-cbi-boris-johnson-covid
136 Deirdre Hipwell, Matthew Miller, and Anna Edwards, 'Tesco chairman warns Brits may
face food shortages after Brexit', *Bloomberg UK*, 16 October 2020, www.bloomberg.com/ne
ws/articles/2020-10-16/tesco-chairman-warns-brits-may-face-food-shortages-after-brexit
137 'Britain and E.U. form Brexit deal, averting a chaotic breakup', PBS, 24 December 2020,
www.pbs.org/newshour/show/britain-and-e-u-form-brexit-deal-averting-a-chaotic-bre
akup
138 Oliver Wright, 'It's VAT, Jim, but not as we know it: William Shatner laments post-Brexit
rules', *The Times*, 22 October 2020, www.thetimes.co.uk/article/its-vat-jim-but-not-as-we-
know-it-william-shatner-laments-post-brexit-rules-5t26rdd6k
139 Harriet Sherwood, 'John Sentamu peerage snub criticised as "institutional prejudice"',
Guardian, 18 October 2020, www.theguardian.com/uk-news/2020/oct/18/john-sentamu-
peerage-snub-criticised-as-institutional-prejudice
140 David Davis [@DavidDavisMP], Twitter, 18 October 2020, twitter.com/daviddavismp/
status/1317760414218883072
141 Harriet Sherwood, 'UK archbishops urge ministers not to breach international law
over Brexit', *Guardian*, 18 October 2020, www.theguardian.com/world/2020/oct/18/uk-
archbishops-urge-ministers-not-to-breach-international-law-over-brexit
142 Patrick Maguire, '"Divisive bishops" could force Johnson to cut ties with Church, says
MP', *The Times*, 20 October 2020, www.thetimes.co.uk/article/pm-could-sever-ties-with-
interfering-bishops-says-steve-baker-cpxkgbdx7

November

1   Aaron Walawalkar, 'Tory MPs faced abuse after "scum" incident, party chair says', *Guardian*,
24 October 2020, www.theguardian.com/politics/2020/oct/24/tory-mps-suffered-abuse-
following-scum-incident-party-chair-says

2   Lizzie Dearden, 'Islamophobic incidents rose 375% after Boris Johnson compared Muslim women to "letterboxes", figures show', *Independent*, 2 September 2019, www.independent.co.uk/news/uk/home-news/boris-johnson-muslim-women-letterboxes-burqa-islamphobia-rise-a9088476.html

3   Joe Murphy, Nicholas Cecil, Sophia Sleigh and Luke O'Reilly, 'Free school meals row: Marcus Rashford contradicts Matt Hancock's claims about talks with Boris Johnson', *Standard*, 26 October 2020, www.standard.co.uk/news/politics/rashford-boris-johnson-communication-matt-hancock-uturn-tweet-a4572930.html

4   Dan Keane, 'MACS A MILLION: McDonald's offers 1 MILLION free meals for families as Marcus Rashford calls for school kids to be fed over half-term', *Sun*, 23 October 2020, www.thesun.co.uk/news/13005599/mcdonalds-1-million-free-meals-families-rashford-half-term

5   'Gove opposes housing proposal in his constituency despite Govt push to "build, build, build"', SP Broadway, www.spbroadway.com/politics-of-planning/gove-opposes-housing-proposal-in-his-constituency-despite-govt-push-to-build-build-build

6   Rob Davies, 'Treasury confirms it is to end VAT waiver on PPE in UK', *Guardian*, 23 October 2020, www.theguardian.com/business/2020/oct/23/treasury-confirms-it-is-to-end-vat-waiver-on-ppe-in-uk

7   'VAT zero rating for personal protective equipment', Gov.uk, 25 March 2021, www.gov.uk/government/publications/vat-zero-rating-for-personal-protective-equipment/vat-zero-rating-for-personal-protective-equipment

8   Mattha Busby, 'Pub and restaurant check-in data hardly used by England's health officials', *Guardian*, 24 October 2020, www.theguardian.com/world/2020/oct/24/pub-and-restaurant-check-in-data-hardly-used-by-englands-health-officials

9   'Coronavirus (COVID-19) deaths worldwide per one million population as of April 26, 2022, by country', Statista, 26 April 2022, www.statista.com/statistics/1104709/coronavirus-deaths-worldwide-per-million-inhabitants

10 Jim Pickard and Philip Georgiadis, 'Quarantine exemption proposed for short business trips to England', *FT*, 24 November 2020, www.ft.com/content/1c429bdf-dddf-49f2-91c7-fc2c7f1f897a

11 Gordon Rayner, 'Dominic Cummings exits Number 10 with parting shot at Boris Johnson', *Telegraph*, 14 November 2020, www.telegraph.co.uk/politics/2020/11/13/dominiccummings-exits-number-10-parting-shot-boris-johnson

12 Otto English, 'THE ODYSSEAN PROJECT: In Search of Dominic Cummings (Part One)', *Byline Times*, 9 January 2020, bylinetimes.com/2020/01/09/the-odyssean-project-in-search-of-dominic-cummings-part-one

13 Peter Walker, Dan Sabbagh and Rajeev Syal, 'Boris Johnson boots out top adviser Dominic Cummings', *Guardian*, 13 November 2020, www.theguardian.com/politics/2020/nov/13/dominic-cummings-has-already-left-job-at-no-10-reports

14 'Boris Johnson self-isolating after MP tests positive for Covid-19', BBC, 16 November 2020, www.bbc.co.uk/news/uk-politics-54954698

15 Steven Swinford, Oliver Wright and Henry Zeffman, '"Wine-time Fridays": Boozy culture where Downing Street staff slept off hangovers on sofas', *The Times*, 15 January 2021, www.thetimes.co.uk/article/06aa6e6e-7569-11ec-89e9-22d3d9c31ba2

December

1   Kalyeena Makortoff, Michael Savage and Ben Butler, 'Cameron "lobbied senior Downing St aide and Matt Hancock" to help Greensill', *Guardian*, 10 April 2021, www.theguardian.com/politics/2021/apr/10/revealed-david-cameron-stood-to-gain-from-218m-greensill-trust

2   Peter Walker, 'Rishi Sunak told David Cameron he had "pushed the team" over Greensill', *Guardian*, 8 April 2021, www.theguardian.com/politics/2021/apr/08/rishi-sunak-told-david-cameron-he-had-pushed-the-team-over-greensill

3   Peter Walker, 'What is the Greensill lobbying scandal and who is involved?', *Guardian*, 14 April 2021, www.theguardian.com/business/2021/apr/14/what-is-greensill-lobbying-scandal-who-involved

4   Jessica Elgot, Kalyeena Makortoff and Rajeev Syal, 'Civil servant advised
     Greensill while working in Whitehall, says watchdog', *Guardian*, 13 April 2021,
     www.theguardian.com/politics/2021/apr/13/civil-servant-advised-greensill-while-working-
     in-whitehall-says-watchdog
5   Peter Walker, 'Tories close ranks to block broader inquiry into Greensill scandal', Guardian,
     14 April 2021, www.theguardian.com/business/2021/apr/14/boris-johnson-does-not-rule-
     out-more-officials-having-greensill-links
6   Tom Batchelor, 'Matt Hancock urged to "set record straight" over pub landlord's NHS
     Covid contract', *Independent*, 2 December 2021, www.independent.co.uk/news/uk/politics
     /matt-hancock-covid-contract-alex-bourne-b1968161.html
7   Felicity Lawrence, 'Pressure on Hancock over pub landlord's Covid deal', Guardian, 1
     December 2021, www.theguardian.com/politics/2021/dec/01/matt-hancock-says-labours-
     covid-contract-claims-rubbish
8   Jo Maugham [@JolyonMaugham], Twitter, 1 December 2021, mobile.twitter.com/
     JolyonMaugham/status/1465927760069672961
9   Jo Maugham, [@JolyonMaugham], Twitter, 1 December 2021, mobile.twitter.com/
     JolyonMaugham/status/1465927734069280768
10   'Home Office "has no idea" of the impact of immigration policies', UK Parliament,
     18 September 2020, committees.parliament.uk/committee/127/public-accounts-
     committee/news/119248/home-office-has-no-idea-of-the-impact-of-immigration-policies
11   Rajeev Syal, 'Home Office "bases immigration policies on anecdotes and prejudice" – MPs',
     Guardian, 18 September 2020, www.theguardian.com/politics/2020/sep/18/home-office-
     policies-based-anecdotes-prejudice-damning-report
12   Abbi Garton-Crosbie, 'Priti Patel: Home Office spent £370,000 on bullying claim', *The
     National*, 8 July 2020, www.thenational.scot/news/19430373.priti-patel-home-office-spent-
     370-000-bullying-claim
13   Jamie Grierson, 'Priti Patel bullying inquiry: why was it held and what did it find?',
     Guardian, 20 November 2020, www.theguardian.com/politics/2020/nov/20/priti-patel-
     bullying-inquiry-why-was-it-held-and-what-did-it-find
14   Ibid.
15   'Priti Patel: Bullying inquiry head quits as PM backs home secretary', BBC, 20 November
     2020, www.bbc.co.uk/news/uk-politics-55016076
16   Catherine Haddon, 'The handling of the Priti Patel bullying inquiry has fatally
     undermined the Ministerial Code', Institute for Government, 20 November 2020,
     www.instituteforgovernment.org.uk/blog/priti-patel-bullying-inquiry-undermined-
     ministerial-code
17   'Covid-19: UK sees over 80,000 excess deaths during pandemic', BBC, 22 December 2020,
     www.bbc.co.uk/news/health-55411323
18   James O'Brien [@mrjamesob], Twitter, 1 December 2021,
     mobile.twitter.com/mrjamesob/status/1465965904294989828
19   Ros Atkins [@BBCRosAtkins], Twitter, 2 December 2021, twitter.com/BBCRosAtkins/stat
     us/1466494479142113282
20   Pippa Crerar, 'Boris Johnson "broke Covid lockdown rules" with
     Downing Street parties at Xmas', *Mirror*, 30 November 2021,
     www.mirror.co.uk/news/politics/boris-johnson-broke-covid-lockdown-25585238
21   PA Media, 'Met to contact two people over party for Shaun Bailey at Conservative HQ',
     Guardian, 16 December 2021, www.theguardian.com/politics/2021/dec/16/met-to-contact-
     two-people-over-party-for-shaun-bailey-at-conservative-hq
22   Pippa Crerar [@PippaCrerar], Twitter, 20 December 2021, twitter.com/PippaCrerar/status
     /1472907231460999168
23   Lucy Campbell, 'Boris Johnson used £2.6m Downing Street briefing room to watch new
     Bond film', *Guardian*, 22 October 2021, www.theguardian.com/politics/2021/oct/22/boris-
     johnson-used-26m-downing-street-briefing-room-to-watch-new-bond-film
24   Peter Walker, Aubrey Allegretti and Jamie Grierson, 'PM accused of lying after No 10
     officials caught joking about Christmas party', *Guardian*, 7 December 2021, www.theguardi
     an.com/politics/2021/dec/07/leaked-video-shows-no-10-officials-joking-about-holding-
     christmas-party
25   BBC Politics [@BBCPolitics], Twitter, 8 December 2021, twitter.com/BBCPolitics/status/14
     68563160827568130

26 Peter Walker, 'Five Partygate quotes that show No 10 staff knew they were in the wrong', *Guardian*, 25 May 2022, www.theguardian.com/politics/2022/may/25/five-partygate-quotes-that-show-no-10-staff-knew-they-were-in-the-wrong

27 Aubrey Allegretti, 'No 10 officials say party attended by Johnson so cramped people sat on each other's laps', *Guardian*, 24 May 2022, www.theguardian.com/politics/2022/may/24/no-10-officials-tell-cramped-conditions-party-attended-boris-johnson-partygate

28 Léonie Chao-Fong, 'Tory MP says Johnson was "ambushed with a cake" on his birthday', *Guardian*, 26 January 2022, www.theguardian.com/politics/2022/jan/26/ambushed-with-a-cake-defence-of-boris-johnson-inspires-mirth

29 Paul Brand, 'Email proves Downing Street staff held drinks party at height of lockdown', ITV, 10 January 2022, www.itv.com/news/2022-01-10/email-proves-downing-street-staff-held-drinks-party-at-height-of-lockdown

30 Pippa Crerar, 'Boris Johnson's "wine time Fridays" - No10 staff held drinks EVERY week during pandemic', *Mirror*, 14 January 2022, www.mirror.co.uk/news/politics/boris-johnsons-wine-time-fridays-25951853

31 Dan Bloom, 'Inside Downing Street party with "suitcase of wine", DJ and broken kid's swing', *Mirror*, 14 January 2022, www.mirror.co.uk/news/politics/inside-downing-street-party-suitcase-25945525

32 Reuters, 'UK police issue 126 fines as Downing Street "partygate" inquiry ends', *Euronews*, 20 May 2022, www.euronews.com/2022/05/19/uk-britain-politics-police

33 Jessica Elgot, 'Seven occasions when Boris Johnson denied No 10 broke Covid rules', *Guardian*, 11 January 2022, www.theguardian.com/world/2022/jan/11/seven-occasions-when-boris-johnson-denied-no-10-broke-covid-rules

34 Aubrey Allegretti, 'Music from "Abba party" could be heard all over No 10, says Cummings', *Guardian*, 31 May 2022, www.theguardian.com/politics/2022/may/31/music-from-abba-party-could-be-heard-all-over-no-10-says-cummings

35 Heather Stewart, Rowena Mason, Jessica Murray and Steven Morris, 'No 10 apologises to Queen over parties on eve of Prince Philip funeral', *Guardian*, 14 January 2022, www.theguardian.com/politics/2022/jan/14/no-10-apologises-palace-parties-eve-prince-philip-funeral-queen-covid

36 Jessica Elgot, Aubrey Allegretti and Vikram Dodd, 'Frustration at Met as Boris Johnson not sent key Partygate questionnaire', *Guardian*, 5 May 2022, www.theguardian.com/politics/2022/may/05/frustration-at-met-as-boris-johnson-not-sent-key-partygate-questionnaire

37 Samuel Osborne, 'Boris Johnson fined: Prime minister apologises after receiving fixed penalty notice for lockdown-breaking party', Sky, 13 April 2022, news.sky.com/story/boris-johnson-fined-prime-minister-apologises-after-receiving-fixed-penalty-notice-for-lockdown-breaking-party-12588712

38 Andrew Rawnsley, 'Boris Johnson clings to office like chewing gum to a shoe but he is becoming unstuck', *Guardian*, 24 April 2022, www.theguardian.com/commentisfree/2022/apr/24/boris-johnson-clings-to-office-like-chewing-gum-on-shoe-becoming-unstuck

39 Harry Fletcher, 'Boris Johnson makes history by becoming first PM to have broken the law', indy100, 12 April 2022, www.indy100.com/politics/boris-johnson-first-pm-broken-law

40 Laura Keay, 'Sue Gray report key findings: Karaoke machine, drunkenness and panic button triggered', Sky, 26 May 2022, news.sky.com/story/sue-gray-report-all-the-key-criticisms-of-the-government-12621059

41 Ibid.

42 Heather Stewart and Aubrey Allegretti, 'Vomiting and partying until 4am: Sue Gray delivers damning verdict on Boris Johnson's No 10', *Guardian*, 25 May 2022, www.theguardian.com/politics/2022/may/25/sue-gray-law-breaking-no-10-parties-published-boris-johnson

43 Chloe Chaplain, 'Sue Gray report finds cleaners and security guards shown "lack of respect" by boozing No 10 staffers', inews, 25 May 2022, inews.co.uk/news/politics/sue-gray-report-cleaners-security-guards-lack-respect-1650285

44 'Partygate: PM criticised over treatment of No 10 cleaners and guards', BBC, 25 May 2022, www.bbc.co.uk/news/uk-politics-61582681

45 'Sexist of the year prize "handed out at No 10 lockdown-breaking Christmas party"', Sabrina Johnson, *Metro*, 2 May 2022, metro.co.uk/2022/05/02/sexist-of-the-year-prize-handed-out-at-no-10-christmas-party-16568545

46 Caroline Wheeler and Harry Yorke, 'Boris Johnson has cleared so many hurdles, but he may yet come a cropper', *The Times*, 16 April 2022, www.thetimes.co.uk/article/boris-johnson-has-cleared-so-many-hurdles-but-he-may-yet-come-a-cropper-dxqg77h28

47 Simon Kelner, 'Partygate is dismissible "fluff" according to Jacob Rees-Mogg, but the country disagrees', *iNews*, 21 March 2022, inews.co.uk/opinion/partygate-is-dismissible-fluff-according-to-jacob-rees-mogg-but-the-country-disagrees-1530665

48 Geneva Abdul, '"He was ambushed with cake" and other stories: Tories get creative to defend PM', *Guardian*, 19 April 2022, www.theguardian.com/politics/2022/apr/19/he-was-ambushed-with-cake-and-other-stories-tories-get-creative-to-defend-pm

49 'Minister compares PM party penalty to speeding fine', BBC, 19 April 2022, www.bbc.co.uk/news/uk-politics-61151734

50 Adam Bienkov [@AdamBienkov], Twitter, 21 April 2022, twitter.com/AdamBienkov/status/1517126166712360963

51 Tobi Thomas, 'Boris Johnson criticism of archbishop of Canterbury "a disgraceful slur"', *Guardian*, 20 April 2020, www.theguardian.com/world/2022/apr/20/boris-johnson-criticism-of-archbishop-of-canterbury-a-disgraceful-slur

52 Henry Dyer, 'Boris Johnson removes instruction to ministers to "uphold the very highest standards of propriety" in new Ministerial Code foreword', Business Insider, 27 May 2020, www.businessinsider.com/boris-johnson-cuts-highest-standards-propriety-instruction-ministerial-code-foreword-2022-5

53 Alix Culbertson, 'Boris Johnson changes ministerial code so those who breach it don't have to quit or face sack', Sky, 27 May 2022, news.sky.com/story/boris-johnson-changes-ministerial-code-so-those-who-breach-it-dont-have-to-quit-or-face-sack-12622599

54 Michael Savage, 'New Commons partygate inquiry poised to derail Tory conference' *Guardian*, 29 May 2022, www.theguardian.com/politics/2022/may/29/new-commons-party gate-inquiry-poised-to-derail-tory-conference

55 'Owen Paterson: Government faces backlash over new conduct rules plan', BBC, 4 November 2022, www.bbc.co.uk/news/uk-politics-59158469

56 Toby Helm, Phillip Inman and James Tapper, '"We got the big calls right" said Boris Johnson. But did he really?', *Guardian*, 30 January 2022, www.theguardian.com/politics/2022/jan/30/we-got-the-big-calls-right-said-boris-johnson-but-did-he-really

57 Kellyn F. Arnold, Mark S. Gilthorpe, Nisreen A. Alwan, Alison J. Heppenstall, Georgia D. Tomova, Martin McKee and Peter W. G. Tennant, 'Estimating the effects of lockdown timing on COVID-19 cases and deaths in England: A counterfactual modelling study', *Plos One Journals*, 14 April 2022, journals.plos.org/plosone/article?id=10.1371/journal.pone.0263432

58 'What Happened on the First Day of the Battle of the Somme?', IWM, www.iwm.org.uk/history/what-happened-on-the-first-day-of-the-battle-of-the-somme

59 Aubrey Allegretti, 'Dominic Cummings' timeline of the early days of the Covid crisis', *Guardian*, 26 May 2022, www.theguardian.com/politics/2021/may/26/dominic-cummings-timeline-of-coronavirus-crisis

60 Ian Sample, 'Covid timeline: the weeks leading up to first UK lockdown', *Guardian*, 12 October 2021,www.theguardian.com/world/2021/oct/12/covid-timeline-the-weeks-leading-up-to-first-uk-lockdown

61 Niamh McIntyre and Pamela Duncan, 'UK Covid death toll has passed 175,000, says ONS', *Guardian*, 11 January 2022, www.theguardian.com/world/2022/jan/11/uk-covid-death-toll-ons

62 'PM statement on the Sue Gray report: 31 January 2022', Gov.uk, 31 January 2021, www.gov.uk/government/speeches/pm-statement-on-the-sue-gray-report-31-january-2022

63 'The Seven Principles of Public Life', Gov.uk, 31 May 1995, www.gov.uk/government/publications/the-7-principles-of-public-life/the-7-principles-of-public-life--2

64 'Partygate: A timeline of the lockdown gatherings', BBC, 19 May 2021, www.bbc.co.uk/news/uk-politics-59952395

Part 4: A Perpetual Vortex of Agitation

1   'The Tamworth Manifesto: text', A Web of English History, Last modified: 4 March 2016, www.historyhome.co.uk/peel/politics/tam2.htm
2   'Diane Abbott "sorry" for drinking mojito on TfL train', Sky News, 20 April 2019, news.sky.com/story/diane-abbott-sorry-for-drinking-mojito-on-tfl-train-11698667
3   James Moore, 'Universal credit plunges kids into poverty and 120,000 have died because of austerity – but Jacob Rees-Mogg wants more cuts', Independent, 16 November 2017, www.independent.co.uk/voices/nhs-austerity-cuts-120000-deaths-universal-credit-only-get-worse-a8058231.html
4   Gemma Tetlow, 'Four theories to explain the UK's productivity woes', FT, 23 October 2017, www.ft.com/content/b6513260-b5b2-11e7-a398-73d59db9e399
5   Katharine Swindells, 'UK real wages will still be lower in 2026 than they were in 2008', New Statesman, 28 October 2021, www.newstatesman.com/chart-of-the-day/2021/10/uk-real-wages-will-still-be-lower-in-2026-than-they-were-in-2008
6   Patrick Collinson, 'Record numbers of young adults in UK living with parents', Guardian, 15 November 2019, www.theguardian.com/uk-news/2019/nov/15/record-numbers-of-young-adults-in-uk-living-with-parents
7   'Recovery of UK economy is the slowest since records began, say unions', Independent, 2 August 2015, www.independent.co.uk/news/uk/home-news/recovery-of-uk-economy-slowest-ever-say-unions-10432717.html
8   'Life expectancy falling in parts of England before pandemic – study', BBC, 13 October 2021, www.bbc.co.uk/news/uk-58893328
9   Valentina Romei, 'Falling business investment scars UK's long-term growth potential', FT, 30 September 2020, www.ft.com/content/c52fc1b5-3ef5-480c-8f7d-a62f943b8cf2
10   Robert Booth, 'Racism rising since Brexit vote, nationwide study reveals', Guardian, 20 May 2019, www.theguardian.com/world/2019/may/20/racism-on-the-rise-since-brexit-vote-nationwide-study-reveals
11   'Homelessness', Our World In Data, ourworldindata.org/homelessness-rise-england
12   D. Clark, 'Number of people receiving three days' worth of emergency food by Trussell Trust foodbanks in the United Kingdom from 2008/09 to 2021/22', Statista, 11 May 2022, www.statista.com/statistics/382695/uk-foodbank-users
13   Adam Bienkov, 'The Cost of Brexit: Brits say EU exit drove up prices, new poll finds', Byline Times, 27 May 2022, bylinetimes.com/2022/05/27/brexit-poll-cost-of-living-more-expensive-leaving-eu
14   Kevin Rawlinson, 'Charge … retreat! Boris Johnson's top U-turns in No 10', Guardian, 26 May 2022, www.theguardian.com/politics/2021/nov/04/charge-retreat-boris-johnsons-top-u-turns-in-no-10
15   'Government unveils levelling up plan that will transform UK', Gov.uk, 2 February 2022, www.gov.uk/government/news/government-unveils-levelling-up-plan-that-will-transform-uk

A Note on the Author

Russell Jones is the man behind @RussInCheshire on Twitter. He publishes regular breakdowns of the government's regular breakdowns under the hashtag #TheWeekInTory. *The Decade in Tory* is his first book.

Index

Unbound is the world's first crowdfunding publisher, established in 2011.

We believe that wonderful things can happen when you clear a path for people who share a passion. That's why we've built a platform that brings together readers and authors to crowdfund books they believe in – and give fresh ideas that don't fit the traditional mould the chance they deserve.

This book is in your hands because readers made it possible. Everyone who pledged their support is listed below. Join them by visiting unbound.com and supporting a book today.

A.C.H., Adam Abbott, Zahra Abdeali, Maarten Abele, Matthew Abercrombie, Christopher Abernethy, Peter Ablett, Joseph Michael Ablewhite, Bill Acres, Rebecca Acres, Alison Adams, Dan Adams, Luke Adams, Mark Adams, Gerald Adamson-Eadie, Daniel Addison, Liz Addison, Billy Addy, Lois Addy, Andy Agar, Phil Agius, Konstantinos Agrafiotis, Yuri Jazmin Aguilar, Kaitan Ahilan, Nisar Ahmed, Ameena Ahsan Pirbhai, John Ainsworth, Debbie Aitchison, Raad Al-Hamdani, Zoë Alderman, Phil Alderton, Jolanda Aldis, Trudy Alford, Imran Ali, Syeda Ali, Amanda Allan, Garry Allan, Julie Allan, Richard Allan, Adam Allen, Alex Allen, Heather MB Allen, Michael DJ Allen, NJ Allen, Oliver Allen, Richard Allen, Ross Allen, Nicola Alloway, Peter Allum, Sam Alner, Cerys Alonso, Henry Alston, Marta Alves Simões, James Amey, Nora Amin, Demi Amor, Leon Amos, Victoria Amsel, Analogueman, Adele Andersen, Alison Anderson, Carolyn B. Anderson, Elaine Jane Anderson, Jamie Anderson, Keith Anderson, Philip Anderson, Paul Anderson-Glew, Paul Anderton, Karl Andrew, Laura Andrew, Nicholas Andrew, Rhiann Andrew, Tjobbe Andrews,

Igor Andronov, Otto Aneirin, Aneta , Elaine Annable, Kirk Annett, Toby Anscombe, Kevin Ansfield, Ian Anstey, Matt Antley, M Anton, Stuart Appleby, Nigel Appleton, Ana Araujo, Rod Archer, James Ardouin, Peter Arfield, Marc Argent, Marion Argent, Rachel Armitage, Heather Armstead, Jonathan Armstrong, Lucy Armstrong, Rachel Armstrong, Rodger Armstrong, Julie Arnold, Peter J Arnold, Rosemary Arnold-Knights, Fiona Ashcroft, Nicola Ashdown, John Asher, Doug Ashley, Michael Ashley-Lahiff, Hilary Ashton, June Ashton, Nick Ashton, Paul Ashwin, Lisa & Lee Ashwood, Paul Ashworth, Richard Ashworth, Charlotte Aspden, Penny Asquith-Evans, Alexia Aston, Lou Atherton, Richard Atkin, Tim Atkin, Rob Atkinson, Varun Atre, MariaGabriella Atzori, Nathan Au, Ann Aubert, Mike Aubrey, Lisa Aubrey-Cosslett, Luke Austin, Lynne Austin, Jon Auty, Mark Avery, Andrew Aylett, James Aylett, Madeleine Ayling, Bazz B, Billy B, Cathryn B, Joanne B, Trevor Baden, Sina Bahrami, Ambreen Baig, Ali Bailey, Benato Bailey, Janice Bailey, Lauren Bailey, Liz Bailey, Marie Bailey, Stewart Bailey, Toby Bailey, Dorothy Baillie, Gordon Bain, Richard Bairwell, Donna Baker, Elizabeth Baker, James Baker, Paul Baker, Rebecca Baker, Steve Baker MP, Caroline Bald, James Baldry, Bernie Baldwin, Catherine Baldwin, Elizabeth Baldwin, Stephen Baldwin, Tanya Baldwin, Vince Baldwin, Carol Ball, Craig Ball, David Ball, Gemma Ball, Ian Ball, Michael Ball, Robin Ball, Sara Ball, Rachael Ball Risk, Fiona Ballantyne, James Ballantyne, Haydon Bambury, Jason Banham, John Banks, Philippa Banks, Martin Barber, Cheryl Barker, James Barker, Mark Barker, Charlotte Barker-Cox, Ben Barker-Street, Christopher Barlow, Peter Barlow, Andrew Barnard, Brian & Liz Barnard, Tom Barnard, Ariane Barnes, Chris Barnes, Iain Barnes, Mark Barnes, Richard Barnes, Ryan Barnes, Mary Barney, Caroline Barrass, Barbara Barrett, Lizzie Barrett, Dean Barron, Jen Barrow, Pete Barry, Felix Bartle, Rachael Bartlett, Richard Bartlett, James Bartoli, Kieron Barton, Sonia P Barzey, Shelley Bass, Yves Bastide, Andrew Batchelor, Kaye Batchelor, Michael Batchelor, Susie Batchelor, Ryan Bate, Doug Bates, Susannah Batstone, Thorsten Bausch, Belinda Bawden, Caroline Baxter, Robert Baylis, Gareth Bayliss, Tracy Bayly, Greg Bayne, Becky Beach, Dave Beal, Sue Bealing, Sam Beard, Mags Beardow, Stu Beattie, Bob Beaupre, Maureen Beckles, Nicola Bedford, Dave Beech, Greg Beech, Ruby Beech, Victoria Beecher, Nicola Beggs, Amy Begley, Andrew Belcher, Cath Belcher, David Bell, Jayne Bell, John Bell, Matt Bell, Richard Bellinger, Iain Bellingham-Smith, Ruth Bender, Carey Benn, Alex & Julie Bennett, Alison Bennett, David Bennett,

John Bennett, Jonathan Bennett, Kirsty Bennett, Steve Bennett, Phillip Bennett-Richards, Paula Bennetts, David Benson, Julie Benson, Shaun Bent, Matthew Bentley, Liam Bergin, Jon Berman, Lorna Bernard, Richard Bernau, Paul Berner, Eyvind Bernhardsen, Christopher Berry, Simon Berry, Rich Best, Ian Bevan, Kim Bevan, Louise Bevan, Margaret Bevan, K N Beveridge, Abi Beynon, Trevor Beynon, Simon Bezant, Roshni Bhogaita, Cathy Bickham, Frank Biederman, Julian Bigg, Phil Billingham, John K. Bilsbury, Steve Bindley, Simon Bingham, Simon Binks, Julia Birch, Matt Bird, Alex Birket, Jennifer Birtles, Chris Birtwhistle, Emily J Bishop, Jule Bishop, Sara Bishop, Heather Bithell, Amber Artemis Black, Kirsty Black, Matthew Black, Simon Blackham, Andrew Blackledge, Colin Blackman, Douglas Blaikie, Rosemary Blake, Rognvald Blance, Margaret Bland, Amy Blaney, Graham Blenkin, Anthony Blews, Paul Blinkhorn, Matt Blondek, Laura Bloomfield, Dennis Boella North, Sid Boggle, Matthieu Boisseau, Andy Bold, Paul Bolger, Catherine Bolt, Chris Bolt, Hannah Bolton, Paz Bombo, Caleb Bond, Bones, Maya Bonkowski, Alan Bonnyman, Alex Booer, Elisa Booker, Tom Booroff, Simon Booth, Tracey Booth, Nic Boothby, Wendy & David Boother, Phil & Chris Bosworth, Celia Botha, Cathy Bothwell, David Boughton, Joanna Bould, Kate Boulton, Oliver Boundy, James Bourke, John Bourke, Laura Bourne, Ruth Bourne, Dr and Mr Bournington, Abigail Bouwman, Jenny Bowden, Peter Bowden, Stuart Bowdler, James Bowker, Mike Bowker, Mark Boyle, Sarah Boyle, Adrian Brace, Richard J Brace, Clare Bracey, Graham Brack, Carolina Bracken, Samantha Bradbury, Charlie Bradford, Mark Bradford, Andrew D Bradley, Elizabeth Bradley, Lorraine Bradley, Sarah Bradley, Simon Bradley, Maryam Brady, Michael Brady, Daniel Brain, Douglas Brain, Caroline Braithwaite, Fiona Bramald, Donal Brannigan, Michael Brassington, Stephen Braund, Amanda Bray, Paul Bray, Bread and Circuses, Emma Breen, Mark Brennan, Noel Brennan, Lucy Brereton, Katrine Bretner, Julian Brewer, Jennifer Briant, Alan Brice, Julian Bridges, Christina Brien, Jess Briggs, Suzie Bright, Victoria Bright, Richard Brink, Dan Bristow, Adam Broadhurst, Michael Brockbanks, Natasha Broke, The Brollinsons, Alan Brook, Gavin Brook, Amy Brooke, Adrian Brooks, Claire Brooks, Matthew & Sarah Brooks, Paul Broom, Mike Brooman, Daniella Brotherton, Rachel Brougham, Elena Browett, Alison Brown, Anthony Brown, Ben Brown, Bill Brown, Carl Brown, David Brown, Dawn Brown, Denise Brown, Ed Brown, Hayley Brown, Heather Brown, Helen Brown, Jeff Brown, Joanna Brown, Julia Brown, Neil Brown, Robert Brown, Sara Brown, Tony &

Helen Brown, Brian Browne, Michelle Brownlee, Judy Brownsword, Courtney Brucato, Lesley Bruce, Tom Bruce, Jodie Bruce-Wright, Jane Brummitt, Darryn Brumwell, Rosie Brunger, Jamie Brunning, Vanessa Bryan, Christine Bryant, Paul Bryant, Craig Bryson, Danny Buchanan, Declan Buckley, Simon Buckner, Brian Budd, Lia Buddle, Jane Budge, Charles Budworth, Wendy Buggs, Christopher Bull, Tim Bull, Philly Bullens, Nim Bulteel, Alison Bunce, Cathy Bundy, Lesley Bunten, Lisa Burch, Liz Burcher, John Burdall, Andrea Burden, Carmela Burgess, Jo Burgess, Jon Burgess, Kevin Burgess, Matt Burgess, Sally Burgess, Bob Burgher, Paul G Burke, Sarah Burke, Simon Burley, Colin Burn-Murdoch, Paul Burnell, Tim Burnett, Rob Burney, Andrew Burns, Christine Burns, David Burns, Richard Burns, Margaret Burr, Clare Burrell, Deirdre Burrell, Lisa Burrell, Jane Bursnall, Daniel Burton, James Burton, Jeff Burton, Keith Burton, Tom Burton, Tamsin Bury, Dominic Bush, John Bushby, Aaron Butcher, Chris Butcher, David Butler, Joe Butler, Tim Butler, Adam Butler & Frederique Carrier, Lizzy Butterfield, David Buxton, Kit Byatt, Rik Byatt, Darren Byford, Gary Byrne, Matthew Byrne, Richard Bytheway, Joshua C, Michael C, Sara C, Steve C., Bideford, Sasha Caddell, Balvinder Cadoret, Emmeline Caines-Gooby, Maria-Elena Calderon, David Callaghan, Michael Callaghan, Anna Cameron, Cleo Cameron, Fiona Cameron, Tony Cameron, Fiona Cameron Coyle, Alan Campbell, Ashley Campbell, Cath Campbell, Catherine Campbell, Jutta Campbell, Kirsty Campbell, Neil Campbell, Glen Campey, Simon Camps, Jeffrey P Canning, Jo Cannon, Nigel Cansfield, Daniel Caple, Carlo Cappalonga, Mary Capron-Tee, Janet Carberry, Liz Carboni, Michael Card, Chris Carini, Kevin Carley, David Carlill, Miranda Carlson, Carol Carman, Jake Carman, Guy Carmichael, Jane Carnall, Christine Carr, Jonathan Carr, Leigh Carr, Paul Carr, Simon Carr, Micah Carr-Hill, Norman Carreck, Jon Carricker, Michael Carrington, Claire Carroll, Dan Carroll, Jeremy Paul Carroll, Damon Carter, Francis Carter, Joe Carter, Natalie Carter, Susan Carter, Tim Carter, Mike Cartmel, Stephen Carville, Jude Caryer, Sean Casely, Laura Casingena, Keith Cass, Richard Cassels, Kevin Caswell-Jones, Emma Catt, Andrew Cattanach, Ali Catterall, Matthew Catterall, Thomas Caullay, Alex Cauvi, William Cave, Gayle Cawson, Alessandro Cereda, Elaine Chadwick, Helen Chadwick, Martyn Chalk, Jack Challen, Debbie Challis, Jamie Chambers, Jenni Chambers, Sally Champion, Angela Chandler, Joanne Channon, Ang Chapman, Colin Chapman, Lindsay Chapman, Martin Chapman, Richard Chapman, Andy Charles, Kieran Chatham, Stuart Chatman, Rebecca Checkley, Donna Cheshire,

Ed Chester, Serena Chester, Sarah Cheung Johnson, David Childs, James Chiles, Ian Chilton, Robert Chilton, Rory Chilton, Michael Chilvers, Joseph Chipperfield, Sadia Chishti, Annie Cholewa, Monowara Choudhury, Nurul Islam Choudhury, Sadia Choudhury, Shamsul Choudhury, Michele Chowrimootoo, Alex Christie, Grant Christie, Jamie Christie, Kostis Christodoulou, Christopoulos, CHRONIC Campaign, Paul Chudleigh, Elaine Chung, Edward Churchill, Debby Claber, Peter Clapham, Guy Clapperton, Christine Clark, D Clark, Deb (Torys really are — — — — s aren't they?) Clark, Doug Clark, Gillian Clark, Mia Clark, Sean Clark, Simon Clark, Steve Clark, Alicia Clarke, Ben Clarke, Pauline Clarke, Russ Clarke, Stephen Clarke-Keating, Michael Clatworthy, Belle Claudi, Beth Claughton-Brown, Susannah Clay, Charlotte Cleave, Richard Clegg, Martin Clements, Richmond Clements, William Clements, Lesley Clemett, Gill Clifford, John Clifton, Graham Clouston, Liam CM, Mackenzie Cobbin, Felicity Cobbing, Jayne Coburn, Vaughan Cockell, Don Cockman, Graham Cockroft, Sean Coffey, Elliot Cohen, Sarah Jane Colclough, Michael Cole, Oliver Cole, Phil Coleman, Ady Coles, Deb Coles, Julia Coles, Stuart Coles, Lesley Collett, Cath Colley, Mark Colley, Ali Collier, Dave Collier, Ian L. Collier, Robert Collier, Alan Collins, Alison Collins, Caroline Collins, Chris Collins, Howard Collins, Katie Collins, Natasha Collins, Nick Collins, Oliver Collins, Ruth Collins, Kay Colquhoun, Paul Comis, Mike Compson, Floating Concrete, Jem Condliffe, DG Congalton, Liz Conmy, Leander Connaughton, Brian Connolly, John Connor, Clare Conroy, Gordon Conroy, Denny Conway, Nicola Conway, Sean Cooch, Lee Cook, Emma Cooke, John Cooke, Katazyna Cooke, Maria Cooke, Paul Cooke, Tim Coombe, Jan Coombs, Alison Cooper, Emma Cooper, Fiona Cooper, Jane Cooper, Matt Cooper, Paul Cooper, Tom Cooper, Sue Coorey, Mike Coote, Eleanor Cope, Richard Cope, Gary Copland, Kevin Copping, Allen Copsey, Fiona Corbett, Mary Corbett, Ian Corbishley, Suzanne Cordier, Adrian Cork, Ian Corke, Lisa Corkerry, Mike & Rosie Corlett, John Corney, Nicolas Corrarello, Cassandra Jules Corrigan, Nigel Corrigan, Paul Corrigan, Ian Corstorphine, John Corvesor, Joe Costigan, Tony Cottam, Claire Cotter, Sheena Cotter, David Cotterill, Philip, Beth, Daisy, Max and Sly Cotton, Chris Cottrell, Liz Coupland, Tom Coupland, Sarah-Jane Court, Richard Courtney, Christine Coutts, John Cowen, Christine Cowin, Angela Cox, Daniel Cox, Dondie Cox, Jim Cox, Karen Cox, Miranda Cox, Paul Cox, Sarah Cox, Andrew Coyle, John Coyle, Stella Coyle, Chris Coyne, Jennifer Coyne, John Coyne, Anthony Cozens, Biff Crabbe, Trevor Craddock, Nick

Craggs, Rachael Craggs, David Craig, Fiona Craig, Russell Craig, Malcolm Craik, Richard Cramb, Pete Crampton, Ellie Crane, Megan Crane, Nick Cranfield, Sean T.W. Craven, John Crawford, Michael Crawford, Adam Crawte, David Creasey-Benjamin, James Creedy, Lynda Creek, Robert Crerar, Ian Crighton, Andrew Crisp, James Crisp, Simon Crisp, Adam Critchley, Tom Crocker, Joe Crofts, Peter Crome, Paul Crompton, Deborah Crook, Nyssa Crorie, A W Crorkin, Jodi Croskerry, Debs Crosoer, Robert Cross, Susan Goose Cross, Annette Crossland, Louise Crossley, Adam Crowther, John Crowther, Mel Crowther, Jamie Cruickshank, Angela Cruz, David Cullen, Steven Culliford, James Cumberland, Graham Cumming, Jo Cundill, Brian Cunningham, Ian Cunningham, Jamie Cunningham, Neil Bigfoot Cunningham, Stewart Cunningham, Neil Curr, Carol Curran, Sarah Currant, Anna Cuzzy, Roman Czajkowski, Dan D, Samwise 'Garth' d'Artagnan, Julie Da Silva, Nicole Da Silva Oliveira, Martin Dabell, Phoebe Dace, Phillip Dack, Michelle Dale, Jennifer Daley, Eleanor Dalglish, Elena Dalla Vecchia, Peter Dalling, Edwin Dalmaijer, Ruth Dalton, Joann Daly, Ann Dalzell, Bob Damms, Andrew Dandilly, Danny Danger Castle, James Daniel, Amanda Daniels, John Daniels, Susan Daniels, Rich Darby, Kieron Darcy, Imre Darics, Jim Darrah, Judgement Dave, Ben Davenport, Sarah Davenport, Neil Davey, Stephen Davey, Mark Davias, David , Elizabeth Davidson, Barry Davies, Cathy Davies, Dave Ayerst Davies, Gareth Davies, Helen Davies, Jan Davies, Jude Davies, Nigel P Davies, Ollie Davies, Phil Davies, Rhiannon H M Davies, Russell Davies, Ryan Davies, Sally-Ann Davies, Sian Davies, Siwan Davies, Sophie Davies, Sue Davies, Christopher Davis, E R Andrew Davis, Mark Davis, Beverley Davison, Michael Davison, Stuart Davison, Alexandra Dawe, Colin Dawe, Matthew Dawkins, Darren Dawson, Pat Dawson, Lucy Day, Rachel Day, Robert Day, Dan Daymond, Giovanna De freitas Maalouf, Frank De Mita, Cecile de Toro Arias, Kor de Vries, Eimear Deady, Martin Dean, Clare Deans, Elizabeth Dearden, Dino Deasha, Sam Deasy, Christine Dee, Neil Deeley, Clare Deighton, Tony Deighton, Andreas Deimbacher, Valerie Delevan, Andy Delius, Johann Delport, Tracy Demianczuk, Nick Dempsey, Leif Denby, Alison Denham, Callan Denham, Mark Dennehy, Jim Dennett, Claire Denney, Louise Denney, Marc Denney, Jo Dennis, Simon Robert Harrison Dennis, Mark Dennison, Lisa Dent, Colin Dente, Stuart Denyer, Paul Devine, Gerry Devine-McGovern, Alex Dhawan, Julia Diamantis, Stephen Dick, Rob Dickens, Zoe Dickinson, Shuna Dicks, Claire Dickson, Maxwell Dickson, David Didau, Ian Diddams, Mark Diffenthal, Matt Diggins, Emily

Dillon, Rhiannon Dillon, Charlotte Disley, Lisa Diver, Stuart Dix, David Dixon, Michael Dixon, Stephen Dixon, DJG, Timothy Dobbs, Su Dobney, Adam Dobson, Robert Dobson, Tracy Dobson, Austin Docherty, John Docherty, Leo Docherty, Cory Doctorow, Adrian Doggett, Antony Doggwiler, Amy Doherty, Annie Doherty, Brian Doherty, Craig Doherty, Derek Doherty, Stephanie Doherty, Alan Doig, Chris Doig, Karen Donachie, Andrea Done, Michael Donnelly, Gary Donoghue, David Donohoe, Simon Donovan, Barry Dooley, Siobhan Dorai-Raj, Catherine Doran, Steve Dorans, Nessa Dorcey, Paul Dorset, Andy Doswell, Gill Douce, Caroline Doughty, Darren "SableDnah" Douglas, Mark Douglas, Tessa Douglas, Paul Douglass, Mark Dourish, Mark Dove, Tom Dowdle, Laura Dowell, Stephen Down, Richard Downer, Nathan Downing, Lakeisha Dowsey-Magog, Karen Doyle, Paul Drage, Gaynor Drake, Danny Draper, Dennis Drennan, Kinza Drewett, Mark Driver, Nicky Driver, Joe Drohan, Chelsea Drowley, Aoife Drumgoole, Gavin Drummond, Stuart Dryden, Miranda Dubner, Charlie Duboc, Tammy-Lyn and Richard Ducker, Tom Duffin, Michael Duffy, Brendan Duggan, Irvin Duguid, Gurj Dulai, Adrian Dummott, Tracy Dunbar, Cara Duncan, Joe Dunford, Gary Dunion, Richie Dunk, Chris Dunkley, Pam Dunn, Simon Dunn, Stuart Dunn, Gerald Dunne, Louise Dunne, David Dunning, Eoin Dunphy, Jim Dunphy, Jane Dunsmore, Ollie Dunthorne, Peter Durbin, Joanna H Durdey, Stuart James Durdey, Liam Durkin, Val Durow, Isobel Durrant, Nigel Dutson, DW, Karen Dyson, Neil Dyson, Sara Dyson, Tony Dyson, William Dyson, Sophie Eades, Stefanie Earle, Mark Earls, Lynne East, Dan "Stevie Wonder" Eastham, Barnaby Eaton-Jones, John Ebdon, Helen Eborall, Rich Eburne, Richard Eccles, Nicola Eckersall, Danielle Eckert, Rod Edbrooke, Emma Ede-Smith, Clive Edelsten, Suzanna Edey, Kate Edgar, Nicky Edmonds, Duncan Edmonstone, Michael Edmunds, Dan Edwards, Doreen Edwards, Ian Edwards, Mark Edwards, Paul Edwards, Rachel A Edwards, Nick Efford, Rose Egan, Rob Eggleshaw, Harriet Eisner, EJ, Arwen Elder, Craig Elder, Dr Sebastiaan Eldritch-Böersen, Hanna Eleri, Jane Elgar, E. Ellingsen, Chris Elliott, Debbie Elliott, Graham Elliott, Catriona Elliott Winter, Catherine Ellis, John R Ellis, Karen Ellis, Mervyn Ellis, Mike Ellis, Nick Ellis, John Ellison, Lesley Elrick, James Elsender, Mark Eltringham, John Emanuelli, Radical Embroiderer, Neil Emery, Louis Emmett, Jeannie Engela, Mark England, Russell England, Michael Englefield, Catherine English, Kate English, Cronan Enright, Richard Ensten, epredator, Arlene Esdaile, Nikki Espley, Keith Esson, Liz Etheridge, Keith Etherington, Alwyn & Zohrah

Evans, Anwen Evans, Darren Evans, David Evans, Gareth Evans, Gary Evans, Jake Evans, Mike Evans, Peter Evans, Simon Evans, Wendy Evans, Tom Evens, Christopher Everest, Glyn Everett, Simon Everett, Robert Eves, Jack Evetts, Brian Ewbank, Liam Eyers, Kerry Eyre, Stephen Eyre, Emer Fahy, Catheryne Fairbairn, Lisa Fairbairn, Conor Fairbrother, David Fairbrother, Marie Fairclough, Mark Fairclough, Stephanie Fairhurst, Inga Fairley, Mike Fallbrown, Lee Fallin, Tom Fallowfield, Miss Jane Fanghanel, David Farbey, Richard Farlie, Kit Farmer, Lindsay Farmer, Faizal Farook, Mrs M Farquhar, Finbarr Farragher, Cheryl Farrell, Christina Farrow, Gill Farthing, Simon Fathers, David Faulkes, Craig Faulkner, Ron Faulkner, Lucy Fawcett, Keith Fealy, A Fearn, Helen Featherstone, Roland Featherstone, Ian Fedden, Ciaran Fegan, Laura Feichter-Rowland, Robert Fell, Sam Fellows, SRob Felstead, Tony Fenn, Howard Fenton, Sue Fenton, Graham Fereday, Alex Ferguson, Mark Ferguson, Rafael Fernandez, Mairéad Fernández, Tiziana Ferri, Russ Ferriday, Joyce Ferrington, Jakob Fey, Patric ffrench Devitt, Cllr George Fielding, Shari Finch, Iain Findlay, Mimi Findlay, Fergus Finlay, Patrick Finlay, Richard Finlay, Paula Finn, Lindsey Firestone-Harvey, Suzanne Firth, David Fisher, Graeme Fisher, Lorna Fisher, Paul Fisher, James Fitt, Lisa Fitt, Geraldine Fitzgerald, Liam Fitzgerald, Rosemary Fitzhenry, Janice Thomas Fitzpatrick, Leah Fitzsimmons, Colum Fitzsimons, Nick Fitzsimons, Barbara Flaherty, Jean Flaherty, Roger Flatt, Claire Fleetneedle, Ralph Fleming, Catriona Fletcher, Daniel Fletcher, Jack Fletcher, Nicholas Fletcher, Emma Flint, Susie Flintham, Sean Flowerday, Adam Flynn, Rowenna Foggie, Mark Fogwill, Lauren Foley, Guy Foord-Kelcey, Kathryn Foot, Brian Forbes, Stuart Forbes, Daniel Ford, Professor Ford, Rob Ford, James Kenneth Ford Bannister , Del Fordham, Stephen Foreshew-Cain, Laura Lowe Forrest, Peter Forrest, Tuesday Forrest, Emily Forster, Gary Forster, Jemma Forte, G Foskett, James Foster, Janet Foster, Rob Foster, Ilka Föttinger, Henry Foulds, Sonya Foulds, Claire Fowler, Nicola Fowler, Scott Fowler, Martin Fowlie, Bridget Fox, Celia Fox, Dominic Fox, Michael Fox, Sarah Foxall, Andrew Foxcroft, Joanne Foxton, Chris Fraiel, Lena Frain-Atallah, Kelvin France, Stewart Francis, Joanna Franks, Oliver Franks, Elizabeth Fraser, Gwyn Fraser, Joanne Fraser, Lorraine Fraser, Neil Fraser, Stuart Fraser, Thomas Alexander Frederiksen, Daniel Fredriksson, Alison Freebairn, Rob Freeland, Emma Freeman, Jac Freeman, Jake Freeman, Louis Freeman, Matt Freeman, Paul Freeman, Rob Freeman, Lily French, Allison Frew, David Frew, Paul Frew, Kristian Frost, Paul Frost, Shirley Froud, Pauline Frow, Shaun

Fulham, Rhys Fullerton, Callum Furner, Mike Furness, Oliver "fuck the tories" Furness, Myles Furr, Adam Furse, Kirsten Fussing, Brian Gabriel, Colin Gaffney, Nick Gage, Caroline Gale, Jen Gale, Keir Gale, Keith Gale, Alison Gallacher, Mark Gallagher, Sam Gallagher, Helen Gallon, Stephanie Gallon, Dinah Gallop, Jane Gallop, Richard Galloway, Paddy Galvin, Mark Gamble, Stephen Game, Sean Gantly, Marg Gapper, Fiona Garden, Graham Gardiner, Joe Gardiner, Paul Gardiner, Roxy Gardiner, Sam & Adam Gardner, Iain Garioch, Lorna Garvey, Leanne Garvie, Ricardo Gaspar, Catherine Gasparini, Helen Louise Gateley, Sarah Gates, Carol Gault, Jeremy Gault, Luke Gawin, Peter Gay, Nikki Gearing, Marcus Gearini, Ronan Geary, Sveinn Geirsson, Amanda George, Fiona George, Geoff George, Jayne George, Jonathan George, Alex Gerrard, Caroline Gerrard, Paul Gerrard, Amanda Gerrish, Rich Gerrish, Lillian Geuken, Samantha Gibben, Rob Gibbins, Gerry Gibbon, Lisa Gibbons, Tom Gibbons, Steve Gibbs, Daniele Gibney, Claire Gibson, David Gibson, Philip Gibson, Samantha Gibson, Lucy Giddings, Steffan Giddins, Liam Gifford, Chris Gilbert, Sarah Gilburt, Joe T Giles, Robert Gilhooly, Matthew Gill, Richard Gill, Manda Gillard, Andrew John Gillespie, Karen Gillespie, Roy Gillett, Jacqui Gilliatt, Eric Gilligan, Rick Gillyon, Ben Gilman, Samantha Gilmore, Thea Gilmore, Geoff Ginns, NyLon Girl, Terry Girling, Caroline Gisbourne, Matt Gittins, Glad not to be led by these donkeys anymore…, David Gladman, Susan Glass, Chris Glencorse, David Glennie, Alex Glonek, Tony Glover, Daniel Glyn-Jones, Tom Godber, Matt Goddard, Tom Goddard, Deirdre Godfray, Roger (in his 50th year) Godfrey, Del Godfrey-Shaw, Andrew Godsell, Katie Goettlinger, Chris Goff, James Golding, Josh Golding, Laurence Golding, Sheila Golding, Amy Goldsmith, Sophie Goldspink, Sarah Gollin, Elma Goncalves, Mercedes Gonzalez, Jackie Good, Laurence Good, Hippo Goodall, Lindsay Goodall, Denise Goode, Julie Goodfellow, Chris Goodgame, Adam Gooding, Carly Goodman, Daniel Goodwin, Annette Goosey, Pravin Gorajala, Elizabeth Gordon, Pauline and Andrew Gordon, Frank Gorman, Will Gormley, Julia Gosling, Steph Gosling, Stephen Gosling, Evelyn Gothard, John Gotsell, Stathis Goudoulakis, M Gough, Fiona Govan, Andrew Gower, Lawrence Grady, Carola Graf, Jean Graham, Jennifer Graham, Y. Graignic, Steve Grainger, Ian Grant, James Grant, Jenny Grant, Russell Grant, H Grantham, Steve Grattage, Paul Grave, Adam Gray, Carolyn Gray, Ilona Gray, Oliver Gray, Great White Huntress, Peter Greatbanks, David Greaves, Dr Alan Greaves, Richard Greaves, Monica Greco, Anne Green, Gavin Green, Ian W. Green, Jen Green, Mark Green, Nick

Green, Simon Green, Ste Greenall, Wayne Greenfield, Cath Greenway, Louise Gregory, Andy Greig, Jo Grey, Patrick Grey, Dickie Greybeard, Martin Griffett, Clewin Griffith, Griff Griffith, Judith Griffith, Megan Griffith, Chloe Priest Griffiths, Mark Griffiths, Toby Griffiths, Tracy Griffiths, William Griffiths, Richard Grime, Ruth Grimes, Stuart Grist, James Grizzell-Jones, Philip Grobler, Julie Groom, Tarquin Grossman, Kenny Grue, Max Gruening, Andy Gubby, Dave Guerin, Katy Guest, Paul Guire, Barry Gunter, Ross Guy, Paula Gwinnett, Leonie H, Simon H, Neil Hadden, James Hadley, Hollie Haeney, Gill Hagemichael, Philip Haigh, Ros Haigh, Teresa Haigh, Luke Haines, Claire Hainstock, Steve Haith, David Hajas, Debra Halcrow, Cris Hale, David Hale, Jo Hales, Rebecca Halifax, Alan Duncan Hall, Alison Hall, Ana Hall, Angela Hall, Dave Hall, Kenton Hall, Matt Hall, Richard Hall, Sam Hall, Sophie Hall, William Hall, Greg Hallam, Neil Hallam, Norma Hallett, R Halliwell, Charlotte Halls, Dave Hallwood, Steven Halsall, Gareth Haman, Matthew Hambly, Viv Hamer, Kate Hames, James Hamill, Dave J Hamilton, David Hamilton, Jane Hamlet, Steve Hammonds, Helen Hampson, Julie Hampson, Peter Hampson, Jacquie Hampton, Russ Hancock, James Hancox, Melanie Hancox, Tim Handley, James Handscombe, Matt Haney, James Hanfrey, Phil Hangodi-Creek, Charlotte Hanna, Paul Hanna, Anthony Hannan, Ronan Hanrahan, Nick Hansard, Steve Hanson, Mary-Jane Harbottle, Jacqueline Harbour, Tamsin Hardacre, Giles Hardern, Andy Harding, Niki Harding, Tom Harding, Ben Hardwick, Gary Hardy, Joe Hardy, Sue Hardy, Anthony Hargreaves, David Hargreaves, Dominic Hargreaves, Andrew Harper, David Harper, Mel Harper, Stephen Harper, Sue Harper, Fergus Harradence, Ann Harries, Hayley Harrington, Jacqueline Harrington, Alex Harris, Danielle Harris, Denise Harris, Elayne Harris, Nigel Harris, Norman Harris, Paul Harris, Pete Harris, Robin Andrea Harris, Sean Harris, Steve Harris, Ben Harrison, Chris Harrison, Dr J Harrison, Lynne Harrison, Morven Harrison, Rhiannon Harrison, Simon Harrison, Nicholas Harrold, Carl Harrow, Liz Hart, Matthew Hart, Sarah Hart, Paul Hartley, Graham Hartstone, Nina Hartstone, Graham Harvey, Richard Harvey, Mark Harwood, Tim Harwood, Lucy Haskell, Gerri Hastings, Chris Hatcher, David Hathaway, Anja Hatlestad, Patrick Haveron, Rob Hawes, Ed Hawkins, Judith Hawkins, David Hawksworth, Andrew Hawley, Hannah Hawoldar, Martin Hay, Peter Haydon, Andy Hayes, Chris Hayes, Chris Haynes, Martin Haynes, Brad Hayward, James Hayward, Dr Stuart K Hazle, Alan Hazlie, Lawrence Head, Richard Head, Katy Heald, Damien Healey, Rebekkah

Healey, Jennie Heals, Lyn Healy, Joyce Heard, Charlotte Heathcote, Katherine Heathcote, Jay-Shelly Heathfield BA MA, Matthew Hebden, Mike Heckman, Andrew Hedges, Sue Heenan, Peter Hegarty, Jonny Heginbottom, David Heinersdorff, Helen (one of your Twitter harem), Charlie Helps FRSA, Annette Hemingway, Lloyd Hemming, Stuart Hemming, Alison Hemmings, Byron Hemmings, Matt Hemsworth, Helen Henderson, Ricky Henderson, Tracy Anne Henderson, Bill Hendry, Gary Hendry, Adam Henley, Elizabeth Henwood, Ruska Heppell, Luke Herbert, Mark Herbert, Mark Edward Herlihy, Edna Heron, Fiona Heron, Sarah Herring, Lee Herron, Robert Hewlett, Vincent Hibbard, Rupert Hibbert, James Hibbs, Ross Hibbs, Andy Hickey, Adam Hickin, Amanda Hickling, Jane Hickman, "Virtual" Colin Hicks, Gary Hicks, Judith Hider, Chris Higgins, Stephen Higginson, Graham Higgs, Davida Highley, James Highmore, David Hilary, Andy Hill, Craig Hill, Dave Hill, Giles Hill, Jim Hill, Matthew Hill, Mike Hill, Sam Hill, Andy Hillman, Suzanne Hillman, Samantha Hillock, Jenny Hina, Gina Hind, Graham Hind, John Hinder, Kieran Hines, James Hirst, Mark Hitchins, Martin Hobbs, John Hobson, Lydia Hocking, Steven Hodges, Kathryn Hodgson, Lorena Hodgson, Penny Hoffmann-Becking, Johanna Hogan, Sean Hogarty, Mick Hogben, Ben Holbrook, Mark Holbrook, William Holdaway, Diane Holden, Jill Holden, Philip Holden, Dave Hollands, Kirsty Hollingworth, Ian Holloway, Jack Holloway, Helen Holly, Hannah Holmes, Niall Holmes, Richard Holmes, Katherine Honan, Kerenza Hood, Stuart Hood, Kristina Hook, Anne Hopkins, Simon Horbury, Martha Horler, Amanda Horn, Julie Horncastle, Charlotte Horne, Chris Horner, Stephanie Horner, Rich Horsfall, Jerry Horsman, Patrick Horton, Tom Horton, Niall Hoskin, Gail Hotchkiss, Matt Houghton, Sean Houlihane, Jules Hoult, Jon Housley, Dave Houston, Jamie Houston, Alex Howard, Jonathan L. Howard, Paddy Howard, Peter Howard, Stephen Gwyn Howard, Claire Howarth, Dave Howarth, Karen Howat, Helen Howe, Katie Howe, Catherine Howell, Steven Howell, Dean Howells, Jennifer Howells, Michael Howes, Sarah Howes, Rodena Howes-Yarlett, David Howker, Tony Howse, Ed Hubbard, Sam Hubbard, Adam Huckerby, Jon Hudson, Josh Hudson, Tony Hudson, Alun Hughes, Andrew Hughes, Ben Hughes, George Hughes, Julianne Hughes, Nigel Hughes, Pete Hughes, Warren Hughes, Charlotte Hughes-Broughton, David Hughes-Payne, Chris Hulbert, Chris Hulme, Barbara Hulse, Herve Humbert, Michael Humphrey, Ian Hunneybell, Martin Hunnings, Rona Hunnisett, Andrew Hunt, Jon Hunt, Robin Hunt, Callum Hunter,

Carolyn Hurcom, Matthew Hurley, Shai Hussain, Martin Hussey, Kevin Hutchby, Sue Hutchings, Gavin Hutchinson, Kathryn Hutchinson, Dan Hutson, Peter Hutt, Desmond Hutton, Chris Hyde, Phil Hyde, Steve Hyde, David Hyett, Jessica Hyland, Mark Hymers, Mark Iliff, Maximilian Imm, Anthony in 't Veld-Brown, Steve Ingall, Sean Ingram, Maggie Innes, Niall Innes, Rob Innes, John Ireland, Natalie Irvin, Dean Irvine, Carole Irwin, Dave Irwing, Suzanne Isaacs, Isabelle, Kalli Isborne, Andy Ison, Jonathan Ison, Charis Isted, Brian Ives, Graham Ives, Rob Ives, Andy Ivory, Simon Iwaniszyn, Gwyn J (Part-time Legend, Fuck off Boris), Arthur Jackson, Ben Jackson, Declan Jackson, Frances Jackson, Jenna Jackson, Judith Jackson, Laura Jackson, Mike Jackson, Neil Jackson, Piers Jackson, Ross Jackson, Randall Jacobs, Phil Jaffray-Carr, Lisa Jain, Louise Jallow, David James, Jane James, Jonathan James, Mack James, Matt James, Matthew James, Philip James, Rob James, Stephen James, David Jameson, Stephen Jameson, Mark Jamieson, Francoise Jarvis, Simon Jarvis, Samuel Jasons, Sarah Jassal, Ravi Jayaram, JC, Leah Jeffery, Steve Jeffery, Jo Jeffries, Richard Jeffries, Betty Jenkins, Dai Jenkins, David S Jenkins, Matt Jenkinson, Jack Jennings, Logan Jensen, Jay Jernigan, Rigby Jerram, Ian Jespersen, Mark Jessett, Jill, Adam Jogee, Stephen John, Marjorie Johns, Andrea Johnson, Edward Johnson, JJ Johnson, Jon Johnson, Kim Johnson, Neil Johnson, Oliver Johnson, Philip Johnson, Rob Johnson, Jon Johnson ResistUK, Janie Johnson-Crossfield, Doug Johnston, Jo Johnston, Julie-Anne Johnston, Shereen Johnston, Ben Johnstone, Christine Jolley, Gina Jolliffe, Alf Jones, Becky Jones, Brian Jones, Cadi Jones, Catherine Jones, Chloe Jones, Claire Marie Jones, David Gareth Jones, Emma Jones, Gerin Jones, Graham Jones, Heather Jones, Jackie Jones, Jenny Jones, John Jones, Kate Jones, Kathryn Jones, Mark Jones, Matthew Jones, Mervyn Jones, Nick Jones, Nicola Jones, Rachael A Jones, Rachel Jones, Rosie Jones, Sandie Jones, Sarah Jones, Steve Jones, Susan Jones, Suzanne Jones, Thomas Jones, Victoria Jones, Andrew Jordan, Charlie Joseph, Ronan Jouffe, Jane Jowers, Helen Joy, Indra L Joyce, Kevin Joynes, JPL, Jason Judge, David Jurczyszyn, Nick Kaijaks, Bhavini Kalaria, Christos Kallinteris, Tom Kane, Zarina Kapasi, Andrew Katz, Jaskaran Deo Kaur, Ranjit Kaur, Suzanne Kavanagh, John Kay, Kayse & Jolz, Lesley Kazan-Pinfield, Mike Keal, Charmaine Keatley, Helen Keay, Richard Keay, Chris Keen, Frank Keenan, Jackie Keith, Alistair Kell, Colin Kelly, Janine Kelly, Jen Kelly, Paul Kelly, Stephen Kelly, Andrew Kemp, Ben Kemp, Edward Kemp, Simon Kempton, Paul Kendall, Pete Kennaugh-Gallacher, Annemarie Kennedy, Kathryn Kennedy, Robert Kennington,

Steven Kennington, Stephen Kent, Duncan Kerr, Frank Kerr, Neil Kerr, kerrymollymoon, Malcolm Kesterton, Claire Kettle, David Kettle, Rob Kevan, Tracy Kewley, Salman Khan, Fozia Khanam, Ifat Khawaja, Simon Kiddle, Karen Kidson, Dan Kieran, Ania Kierczynska, David Kiernan, Jessica Kill, Izzy Killeen, Lady (!) Lynn Killick, Heather Kincaid, Adam King, Alistair King, Daryl King, Derek King, E King, Jamie King, Joan King, Stephen King, Armand Kingsmill David, Michael & Deirdre Kinsella, Stephen Kinsella, Eleanor & Joseph Kinsella-Connolly, John C. Kirk, Mary Kirk, Tim Kirk, Jackie Kirkham, Jeff Kirkman, Chris Kirwan, Gary Kirwan, KitCatK, Victoria Kitchiner, Matthew Kitson, Tony Kitson, Nicolas Klaassen, Lars Klawitter, Thomas & Alexander Klima, Elizabeth Knight, Lindi Knight, Rebekka Knight, John Knowler, Gill Knowles, Howard Knowles, Alastair Knox, Arcadia Knox, Laura Knox, Lewis Knox, Peter Knox, Simon Knox, Alex Knudsen, Danay Koftori, Alison Konieczny, Evagelos Korais, Hendryk Korzeniowski, Melissa Kponou, Paul Kramer, Kerry Kriel, Alex Krondiras, Sunil Kumar, Mary Kuss, KZAaaam, Justin La Frenais, Paul La Planche, Joel Lacey, Nick Lacey, Tony Lacey, Anthony Lacny, Andrew Laing, Iain Laird, Caroline Lallis, Eileen Lambert, Graham Lambert, James Lambert, Sarah Lambeth, Julie Lambie, Steve Lambley, Alan Lamont, Nicholas Land, Frederick Lane, Liane Langdon, Dick Langford, Alex Langford-Smith, David Langlands, Rob Langley, Simon Langley, Anthony Larkin, James Larner, Larry & Paul, Katri Lassinen Walker, Rohan Latchman, Mike Latham, Ollie Latham-Jones, Tom Laughland, Michel Laurent-Regisse, Emily Law, I Law, Mark Lawfull, Kevin Lawlor, Cat Lawrence, Jody Lawrence, Leigh Lawrence, Lyn Lawrence, Nathan Lawrence, David Laws, Sharon Laws, Katherine Lawson, Lucy Lawson, Charlotte Lawthom, Peter Lax, Robin Layfield, Adam Le Boutillier, Gill Le Sage, Dean Lea, Debra Lea, Tonii Leach, Gillian Leake, Michael Leane, Andrew Leather, Marcel LeCocq, Robert Lecomber, Amanda Lee, Andy Lee, Diane Lee, Gordon Lee, James Lee, Janet Lee, Kevin Lee, Mark Lee, Michael Lee, Samantha Lee, Poppy Leeder, Mark Lees hates tories, Sarah Leeuwerke, Emma Leigh, Bryony Louise Leighton, Kate Leimer, Ian Leishman, Moonika Leisson, Chris Leith, Richard Lenderyou, Mark Lenel, Graham Lenton, Aidan Leonard, Claire Leonard, David Leonard, Niall Leonard, Ian Leroux, Simon Lester, Kirsty Levasseur, Jennifer Levesley, Rob Levine, Tracy Levitt, Rachel Levy, Fenella Lewin, Alison Sara Lewis, Damian Lewis, Emily Lewis, Marian Lewis, Neil Andrew Lewis, Paul Lewis, Philip Lewis, Rebecca Lewis, Clair Lewis-Hopkins, Paul Lewzey, Jacqueline Leyland,

Michael Leyton, Elaine Li-Koo, Agata Liberska, David Liddell, Archie Lievesley, Reena Life, Julia Lightfoot, Claire Lilly, Amanda Limbert, Michelle Lincoln, Mark Lindesay, Linda Lindsay, Steven Linnington, Andrew Lintern-Jones, Dean Lipscombe, Daniel Lister, Rob Lister, Adrian Liston, Lesley Little, Rachel Little, Sarah Little, Christie Rose Littlewood, Craig Lively, Jenny Livy, Stan Livy, Bizzie Lizzie, G Llewellyn, Katharina Lloyd, Kierion Lloyd, Mark Lloyd, Samantha Lloyd, Llygodenfawrdur, Charlotte Lo, George Lockley, Celia Lockwood, Charlotte Logan, Marion Logan, Gareth Logue, John Lohan, Keir Long, Linda Long, Andy Longshaw, Terry Loosley, Barbara Löster, Loz Lotz, Keith Loud, Joan Loughlin, Natalie Louise, Louise, Charlie Love, Mark David Love, Carol Lovegrove, Antony Loveless, Pippa Lovell, Samantha Loveridge, Gareth Lovett, Christopher Lowry, Steve Lucas, Stephen Ludlow, Maureen Luff, Min Luk, Shen Luk, Andy Lulham, Jose Miguel Vicente Luna, Christopher Lunt, Craig Lunt, Oliver Luton, Sally Luxmoore, Jonathan and Clare Lynas, Nicola Lynch, Sandeha Lynch, Carie Lyndene, Gareth Lynham, Dermot Lynott, Edward Lyon, Gerard Lyons, Adam Lyzniak, Tim M, Emma M #FBPE #FBPPR, Mel Macariou, Fiona Macaulay, Sam MacAulay, Lindsay Macdonald, Sharon Macdonald, Rebecca MacDougall, Bev Macfarlane, Robert Macfarlane, Steve E Mack, Andrew Mackay, Andrew & Lynn MacKay, Roderick Mackenzie, Siobhan Mackenzie, Dr Mackers, Helen Mackie, Jennifer Mackie, Lucy Mackie, Richard Mackie, Russell Mackintosh, Gareth Maclachlan, Deborah MacLaren-Smith, Rachel Maclean MP, Fiona MacLellan, Mhairi Maclennan, Neil Macnab, Sharon Macpherson, Maurice Macsweeney, Raymund MacVicar, MadameOvary, Ryan Maffey, Juliet Magee, Sharon Maguire, Chris Maidment, Grant Mainwaring, Graeme M Mair, Rachel Major, David Malcolm, John Malcolm, David Male, Dana Mallon, Tim Mallon, Fran Maloney, Jessica Maloney, Wendy Maloney, Cathy Maltby, Dale Maltby, Marie Man, Philippa Manasseh, Sabina Mangosi, Amardeep Singh Mann, Carol Mann, David Mann, Steven Mann, Eric Mannion, Janet Manser, Katrin Mansfeld, Mark Mansfield, Anna Mansourpour, Graeme Manuel-Jones, Deborah Manzoori, Alex Marchant, Rob Marcus, Ian Mardell, Chris Margetts, Gillian Marles, Gary Marlow, Katie Marlow, Andrew Marmot, Kevin Marnell, John Marr, A Marren, Milly Marrey, Jen Marsh, Richard Marsh, Stuart Marsh, Joseph Marshall, Mandy Marshall, Peter Marshall, Sam Marshall, Anthony Martin, Cory Martin, Dave Martin, David Martin, Deborah Martin, Ian Martin, Irene Martin, Jenny Martin, Jill Martin, Jude Martin, Leila Martin, Neil Martin, Russell Martin,

Valeria Martinelli, Paul Maslin, Christian Mason, Jacqueline Mason, Paula Mason, Rick Mason, Rowan Mason, Simon Mason, Kam Massey, Elaine Massung, AA Matar, Jane Matheson, Ian Mathewson, David Matkins, Susan Mattheus, Catherine Matthews, Keith Matthews, Indigo Maughn, James Maw, Stuart Maw, Andrew Mawby, Miranda Mawer, Simon Mawhinney, Peter and Karen May, Neil Maybin, Nicola Mayell, Ian Mayo, Charlotte Mayo-Evans, David Mazor, Duncan McAlister, Allan McAllister, LaToyah McAllister-Jones, Alex McAteer, Martina McAuley, Robin Mcauslan, Andrena McBain, Joanne McBride, Sharon McBride, Cecilia McBrinn, Paul McCafferty, Jacqueline McCallum, Rebecca McCarter, Susan McCarthy, Sarah McCartney, Ellen McClure, Peter McClure, Vaila McClure, Euan McCluskey, Carolyn McColm, Peter McConnell, Pam McCormac, Alison McCormick, Grant Mccourt, Dave McCraw, Scott McCrory, Lawrence McCrossan, John McCubbin, Eileen McCullagh, Emily McCullouch, Jason McCullough, Carol McCurdie, Rachael McCutcheon, Dipjoy McD, Fiona McDaid, Stuart McDermid, Christopher McDermott, Gerry McDermott, Kat McDonald, Kirsty Mcdonald, Matt McDonald, Simon McDonald, Conan McDonnell, Declan McDonnell, Maria McDonnell, Ian McDougall, Adam McDowall, Alexandra McEwan-Hannant, Odette McGahey, Helen McGarrity, Caron McGarvey, Ciaran Mcgechie, Kathleen McGee, Elizabeth McGhee, Andrew McGinnes, Mitch McGregor, Scott McGregor, Charlie McGrory, Brad McGuigan, Allison McGuinness, Sean McGuinness, Kathleen McGurl, Andrew McHardy, Samantha McHattie, Tracey McHugh, Shona Mcintosh, Vicky Mcintyre, Clare McIver, Martin McIver, Sheila McKeand, Bronagh McKee, John McKenzie, Andrew McKeown-Henshall, Chris McKibbin, Lucy McKillop, Denise McKinnell, Paul McKnespiey, Cameron McLaughlan, James Mclaughlin, Helen McLean, Michael McLean, Lenny McLenFace, Andy McLeod, Chris McLoughlin, Kerry McMahon, Stephen McMahon, Adrienne McMenamin, Paul McMenamin, Clare McMenemy, Andrew McMillan, Polly McMillan, Stephen Mcmillan, David McNab, Katie McNab, Susan McNaughton, Steve McNay, Lisa McNeice, Charlene McNeill, Graham McNeill, Hugo McNestry, Pete McPhee, Catherine McQueen, Andrew & Fiona McRait, Bryan McRell, Craig McVeigh, Mark McVitty, Lorna McWilliam, Stewart McWilliam, John Meacock, Jon Mead, Audrey Meade, Meader, Stephen and Michelle Medley-Daley, Sam Medrington, Elizabeth Meenagh, Jan Meikle, Helen Mellor, Kay Melmoth, Simon Melton, Noel Melvin, Clare Mendelle, Ms Mendelsohn, Jacqueline Menzies, Tabby Meow, Iain

Mercer, Luke Meredith, Alastair Merrill, Darryl Messer, Rachel Metcalf, Pamela Metcalfe, Simon Metheringham, David Mettham, John Mettham, Nicholas Mew, David Meyer, Patricia Meyer, Dai Michael, Sam Michel, Elaine Micklewright, Ali Middle, Barbara Middlemast-Neal, Ann Middleton, Fiona Middleton, Helen Middleton, Kenneth G Middleton, Adrian Midgley, Christine Midgley, Cecile Midrouillet, Birgit Mikus, Charlie Milano, Mandy Milano, James Milburn, Darren Miles, Sheila Miles, Gordon Millar, Maureen Millar, Robin Millar MP, Alexander Miller, Eleanor Miller, Gary Miller, John Miller, Liz Miller, Paul Miller, Ryan Miller, Tony Miller, Paul Milliken, Elizabeth Mills, Joan Mills, Rachel Mills, Alex Milne, Christine Milne, Tracey Milner, Christine Milson, Kathy Minah, Dominic Minghella, Ciara Minnitt, Luisa Kate Minter, Wade Minter, Gary Mitchell, Lorna Mitchell, Peter Mitchell, T Mitchell, Ian Mitchinson, John Mitchinson, Shaneez Mithani, Jane Moaveni, Virginia Moffatt, Erik Mogensen, Carolyn Moir, David Moncur, Paul Monks, Martin Monteiro, Aiden Montgomery, Pete Moody, Spike Moody, Paul Moogan, Marilyn Moolhuijzen, Andrew Moon, Ashton Moore, Brigid Moore, C Moore, Jacqueline Moore, Keziah Moore, Mark Moore, Michael Moore, Nigel Moore, Simon Moore, Steve Moore, Harriett Moore-Boyd, Marianne Moran, Mike Moran, Alice More O'Ferrall, Chris Morey, Fiona Morgan, Iain Morgan, Paul Morgan, Pete Morgan, Jen Morgana, Sue Morhall, Dorita Morito, Alec Morley, Jo Morley, Karen Morley, Rich 'Bisquash' Morley, Robert Morley, Tony Morley, David Morris, Gareth Morris, Gaz Morris, Richard C Morris, Ryan Morris, Siân Morris, Carrie Morrison, Kathleen Morrison, Jo Morse, Gail Mort, Sophie Mortimer, Alasdair Morton, Andy Morton, Clare Morton, Rob Morton, Sophie Morton, Andy Moseby, Rebecca Moses, Alex Mosley, David Moss, Emma Moss, Kathryn Moss, Brian Mottershead, Corrina Mottram, Kathryn Mottram, Peter Mounce, Stuart Mozley, @MrChrisClarkson, Hilary Mueller, Rob Mukherjee, Lydia Mulkeen, Dorothee Muller, Lee "Toryhater" Mullin, Patrick Mulvany, Graeme Mulvey, Robin Mulvihill, Lauren Mulville, Paul Mundy, Craig Munn, Guy Munnings, Paul Munro, Sarah M. T. Munro, Ebeth Murdoch, Sarah Murdoch, Caroline Murphy, Cat Murphy, Colin Murphy, Dan Murphy, Debbie Murphy, James Murphy, Jim Murphy, Niall Murphy, Ros Murphy, Sarah Murphy, Siobhan Murphy, Alison Murray, Bruno Murray, Campbell Murray, Caroline Murray, Claire Murray, Eti Murray, F Murray, Kevin Murray, Tracey Murray, Alex Murray-Brown, Nick Murza, Hannah & Cat Mycock-Overell, Vanessa

Mycroft-Ashun, Christine Myers, Malcolm Myles-Hook, Andy N @fintanbear, Natasha, Carlo Navato, Jonathan Naylor, Colin Neale, Jud Neale, Simon Nebesnuick, Kalpana Needham, Rhiannon Needham, Antony Nelson, Michael Nelson, Ritchie Nelson, Trevor Nelson, NeonFerret, Rob Nestor, Christopher Netherclift, Stella New, RS Newall, Joe Newbold, Lisa Newby, Andrea Newell, Sharon Newman, Chris Newsom and Jasmine Milton, John and Jen Newton, Deborah Newton-Cook, Tim Nice-But-Dim, Mark Nichols, Nick, Gary Nicol, Tony Nicol, Alan Nicolson, John Nield, Gary Nightingale, Jim Nightingale, Michael Nightingale, Máire NíGiollaBhríde, Juliane Niklaus, Michael Nimmo, Christine Nobbs, James Nocton, Karen Noice, Josselin Noirel, Charles Noirot, Liam Noonan, Linda Norman, Mark Norman, Steve Norman, Bex Norris, Andrew North, Matt North, Oliver North, Eric Northcote, Lesley Northfield, Daniel Northover, Thomas Nowacki, Emily O, Andrew O'Brien, Dan O'Brien, Marie O'Brien, Peta O'Brien-Day, Augusto O'Callaghan, Anthony O'Connell, Thomas O'Donnell, Greg O'Donoghue, Mark O'Donoghue, Joe O'Farrell, Jenny O'Gorman, Lynn O'Hara, Ciaran O'Hea, Conor O'Kane, Bruce O'Neil, Lindsey O'Neill, Nic O'Neill, Patrick O'Neill, Carole O'Reilly, Ann O'Shaughnessy, Timothy O'Sullivan, Louise O'Toole, Claire O'Brien, Kate O'Brien, Emma O'Connor, Benjamin O'Donovan, Michael O'Driscoll, Gregory O'Neill, P O'Neill, Paul O'Neill, Ann O'Shaughnessy, Ian Keith Oakeshott, Muriel Oatham, Hannah Obertelli, Mary Dolores ODonoghue, Sharon Odysseos, Denise Ogden, James Ogden, Peter OHanlon, Laura Ohara, Olav the Hairy, uncrowned King of Sidcup, Dave Old, Helen OLeary, Steve Oliver, Emma Oliver-Trend, Olle, Julie Ollerton, Susan Olney, Jon Olson, Pat Olver, Sarah Oma Davenport, Kobi Omenaka, Daniel Opitz, Marcel Opoko-Owusu, David Orchard, Jonathan Ord, Nir Oren-Woods, Paul Osborn, Terry Osborn, Claire Osborne, Karen Osborne, Cem Osken, Matt Osmont, Martin Otto, Luba Ovinnikova, Ben Owen, Dominic Owen, Elgan Owen, Emily and Axl Owen, James Owers-Bardsley, Peter Owlett, Rob P, Lucy Padget, Jeffrey Paffett, Chris Page, Deborah Page, Jane Page, Ryan Page, Sarah Paice, Dave Palmer, Jeremy Palmer, Phil Palmer, Tara Palmer, Gregory Panting, Nicola Pardy, Stephen Parker, Verity Parker, Ian Parker Heath, Leila Parker Heath, Andy Parkes, David Parkes, Susan Parkes, Philip Parle, David Parr, Duncan Parsons, Elisabeth Parsons, Nick Parsons, Mathew Partington, Briony Partridge, Mark Partridge, Matthew Pass, Simon Pass, Nadine Patefield, Suneet Patel, Jane Paterson, Lesley Paterson, Stephen Paterson, Carl Pates, Dominic Patmore, Andy Patrick, Lynne

Patrick, Rob Patrick, Adam Ross Patterson, Dr Roddy Pattison, Angela Paull, Nat Pawson, Cath Payne, Chris Payne, Louise Payne, Harry Payne and Omega, PDS, Dale Peakall, Russell Peaker, Debbie Pearce, James Pearce, Angela Pearsall, Richard Pearson, Rob Pearson, Adam Peasley, Richard Peck, Juliet Pedrazas, Professor Emeritus Nathaniel Pee, Christopher Pell, David Pell, Ruth Pellatt, Joanna Pellereau, Mary Pembleton, Louise Pengelly, Emily Penkett, Doug Penman, Alix Penn, Chris Pennell, Mike Pennell, Simon Pennell, Mike Pepper, Howard Perceval, Kathryn Percival, Antonio Pereira, Barry Perez, Nadia Permogorov, Randall Perrey, AJ Perrigo, Mark Perry, Michele Perry, Sue Perry, Nik Peters, Anne Petrie, Erik Pettersen, David Petterson, Nicki Pettitt, Matthew Phelps, Alex Phennah, Paul Philbert, David Phillipps, Ben Phillips, Jane Phillips, Jeremy Phillips, Jonathan Phillips, Mark Phillips, Rachel Phillips, Douglas Philp, Lisa Philpott, Andy Phippen, Nicola Phipps, Lucilla Piccari, Ryan Pickett, Phill Piddell, Daniel Piddock, Erin Pidsley, Richard Pierce, Clay Pilfold, Frankie Pilley, Barry Pilling, Alyson Pillinger, Seb Pillon, Joe Pina, Sarah Pineger, Colin Pink, Agnes Pinteaux, Matt Pitcher, Sandra Pither, Marcus Pitt, Paul Pittham, Alicia Pivaro, Janice Plant, Ben Platt, Philip Platt, Tom Pleasant, Claire Pockett, Steve Pocklington, Brian Pocock, Agnieszka Pokorska, Adam Poland-Goodyer, Justin Pollard, Steve Pont, Susie Poock, Kirsten Poole, Will Poole, Hazel Pope, Mark Pope, Kai Michael Poppe, Devon Pordage, Lee Porte, Graham Porter, Seth Porter, Christina Potter, Edward Potter, Steve Potz-Rayner, Mark Poulson, Katie Poulter, Ian Pouncey, Anthony Pounder, Adam Powell, Ellen Powell, Lynn Powell, Simon Powell, Annette Power, David Power, Samuel Joseph Power, Sue Power, Colin Powers, Leigh Poynter, Susan Pratley, Christiane Pratsch, Dean Pratt, Elaine Pratt, Russell Prebble, Trev Prellie RIP, Rebecca Prentice, Amber Prestidge, Charlene Price, Ian Price, Rob Price, Sarah Price, Sheila Price, Janine Price Lewis, Rachael Priddle, Anna Proctor, Sam Proctor, Sarah Profit, Dave Proudlove, Kate Psillou, Puckfarkinsons, Fran Puddick, Bill Pudney, Ann Pugh, Fi Pugh, Matthew Pumfrey, Richard Purcell, Polly Purvis, David Puttick, Vicky Pyne, Joris Quaatbloet, Samantha Quill, Sara & Simon Quin, Edwin Quinn, Jeremy Quinn, Kevin Quinn, Steven Quinn, Graham Quirke, Kieran Quirke, Omar Qureshi, Graham Race, Dan Rackham, Richard Rackham, Adam Radcliffe, Giles Radford, Sue Radford, Catherine Radley, Monika Radojevic, Kieran Rae, Dermot Rafferty, Paul Rainbow, Katy Raines-Rami, Marvin Rajaram, Dharmesh Rajput, Robyn Ramsay, Ben Randall, Peter Randazzo, Jen Rankine, Ben Ranson, Pekka

Rantanen, Michael Raraty, Naz Rasool, Francois Raulier, Robert Ravie, Heather Rawlin, Maggie Rawlings, Tomas Rawlings, Rauf Rawson, Colette Reap, Simon Reap, Simon Redican, Rupert Redington, Tom Redknap, Dave Rees, Patricia Rees, Sarah Rees, Heff Rees-Mogg, Vicki Reeve, Andrew Reeves-Hall, Colette Reid, Helen Reid, Justin Reid, Joe Reilly, Julian Rendall, Freya Rennie, Mark Rennison, Nitram Resrup, Liverpool Resurgent, Josh Reynolds, Matthew Reynolds, Megan Reynolds, Tina Reynolds, Gordon Rhind, Paul Rhodes, Barney Rhys Jones, Chris Richards, Daniel Richards, Ian Richards, James Norman Richards, Lindsay Richards, Michael Richards, Mike Richards, Mike & Mel Richards, Elaine Richardson, Mark Richardson, Paul Richardson, Peter Richer, Kirsten Riches-Suman, rick_the_framer, Simon Riden, Petra Rigby, Liam Riley, Ron Riley, Samantha Riley, Tracy Rimmer, Huw Ringer, Olwen Ringrose, Claire Riseborough, Derrick Ritchie, David Rivers, Andrew Rix, Jon Rix, Rob & Pam, Kate & Steve Robarts, Andrew Robb, Mike Robbins, Anthony Roberts, Claire Roberts, Dale Roberts, Danny Roberts, Hazel Roberts, James Roberts, Jean Roberts, Kate Roberts, Martin Roberts, Nick Roberts, Paul Roberts, Peter Roberts, Rebecca Roberts, S Roberts, Travis Roberts, Victoria Roberts, Alan Robertson, Graeme Robertson, Mark Robertson, Patrick Robertson, Stephen Robins, Abbie Keziah Robinson, Alison Robinson, Daniel Robinson, Jake Robinson, Jess Robinson, Mike Robinson, Shaun Robinson, Hannah Robinson-Smith, Carol Robson, Hannah Rocha-Leite, Eva Rode-Hilbert, John Roden, Alun Roderick, Jamie Rodger, Glen Rogers, Jane Rogers, Olly Rogers, Peter Rogers, Seb Rogers, Christian Rollinson, David Rollinson, Paul Rollinson, Lisa Ronan, Ian Roode-Orlin, Catherine Rooney, Jaime Rose, Malcolm Rose, Claire Ross, Duncan Ross, Ian Ross, Jo & Steve Ross, Matthew Ross, Sonja Ross, Sharon Rossiter, Samantha Rouse, Anna Route, James Routley, Louise Rowlands, Major Tom Rowlands, Peter Rowley, David Rowntree, Yvonne Rowse, Stu Rowson, Freddie Ruddick, Nicole Rugman, Lisa Rull, Redbeard Rum, Jon Rumfitt, Alistair Rush, Michael Rushton, Matty Rushworth, Andy and Sally Russell, Gordon Russell, Philip Russell, Stephen Russell, Amanda Rutter, Bruce Ryan, Vanessa Ryan, Yan Ryan, Charlotte Ryan-Fenton, Adam Ryder, James Scott Ryder, Chelsea Rye, David S, Feff S, Julian S, Louise S, Paul Sabourin, Matthew Sadler, Rebecca Sadler, Daniel Sage, Lucy Saint, Maria Sale, Jill Salisbury-Hughes, Timothy David Salt, Harry Salter, Katya Samoylova, Dave Sample, Chris Sampson, Jessica Samson, Barry Samuel, Jayne Samuel-Walker, Carlos Sanchez, Peter Sandbach, Kristy

Sansom, Louise Santa Ana, David Santamaria, Gavin Sargent, Dave Sarre, Jo Sastre, Deborah Saunders, Stuart Saunders, Tracy Saunders, Pierre Saveret, Shrikant Sawant, David Sawford, Paul Sawford, Rob Sawkins, Alistair Sawyer, David Saxon, Jane Scanlan, Maggie Scarisbrick, Jane Schaffer, Angela Schofield, Rob Sclater, Andrew Scott, Catriona Scott, Ffyonna Scott, Fiona Scott, Gemma Scott, Ian Scott, Peter Scott, Maria Scrivener, Michelle Scully, Kate Seaney, Matthew Searle, Pamela Seaton, Giovanni Sechi, Bekki Secker, Michael Sedlatschek, Andrea See, Antony Seedhouse, Marie Segar, Gill Selby, Pam Self, Torben Sell, Shaun Sellars, Karen Selley, Jonathan Senker, David Sercombe, Nigel Sergeant, Roland Serjeant, Helena Seth-Smith, Joseph Severn, Daniel Sewell, Suzanne Seyghal Buckingham, Mike Seymour, Neil Seymour, Cora Shafto, Rebecca Shannon, Raman Sharma, Vinoda Sharma, Steve Sharman, Thomas Sharp, Nick and Isabelle Sharples, Jamie Sharrock, Angus Shaw, Brigid Shaw, Claire Shaw, Colin Shaw, Darren Shaw, Fiona Shaw, Graham Shaw, Jonathan Shaw, Kate Sheerin, John Shelton, Andy Shepheard, David Shepherd, Laura Shepherd, Louise Shepherd, Paul Shepherd, Sianne Shepherd, Su Sheppard, Janet Sheppardson, Michelle Sheridan, Sue Sheridan, Jane Sherwood, Tina Shewring, Viv Shilton, Gavin Shinfield, Helen Shipley, Mike Shipp, Paul Shodimu, Kathy Shoemaker, Carol Short, Sam Short, Sally Shorthose, May Showell, Miles Showell, Shubhes Shrestha, Andy Shuker, Jean Shutt, Tanya Siann, Kevin Sides, Tim Siggs, Ian Silver, Miriam Silver, Iain Sim, James Sim, Andy Sime, Gareth Simkins, Andrew Simmonds, Jeremy Simmonds, Robin Simmonds, Jason Simpkin, Brian Simpson, Heva Simpson, Lisa Jayne Simpson, Neil "The bar never lies" Simpson, Alan Sims, Joan Sinclair, Katie Singer, Guru Singh, Divya Sinhal, Rebecca Sinker, Nimantha Siriwardana, Charlotte Emily Skardon, Graham Skeats, Harriet Skilbeck-Lewis, Leah Skipper, Steve Skyrme, Tim Slack, Neal Slateford, Michelle Slater, Thomas Slater, Nicholas Slattery, Gemma Slaughter, Ruth Slavin, Daniel Slee, Anthony Sleight, Matthew Sleight, Tony Sleight, Debbie Slevin, Stacia Smales Hill, Sharon Small, Rachel Smart, Peter Smeed, Daniel Smethurst, Edward Smiles, Adam Smith, Adrian Smith, Al Smith, Alan Smith, Alex Smith, Alice Smith, Alma Smith, Andrea Smith, Carl Smith, Christopher Smith, Craig Smith, Dave Smith, David Smith, David Leonard Smith, Dr Oliver Smith, Eleanor Smith, Gary Smith, Harry Smith, Heather Smith, Howard Smith, Ian Smith, Jane Smith, Jessica Smith, Jimmy Smith, John Kenneth Smith, Jude Smith, Kate Smith, Katie Smith, Kevin Smith, Leigh Smith, Lionel Smith, LJ Smith, Maria Smith, Martin Smith, Nicy Smith, Nory

Smith, Ollie Smith, Pam Smith, Richard Smith, Robert Smith, Ron Smith, Samara Smith, Simon Smith, Tanya Smith, Vicky Smith, Saskia Smith-Wells, James Smither, John Smyth, Martin Smyth, Jamie Snashall, Snook, Stephen Soars, Kirsty Softley, Koyeli Solanki, Joseph Somerville, Jiten Soni, Richard Soundy, Charlotte Soussan, Harry Souter, Nadine Southern, Greg Southey, Carrie Spacey, Eithne Spain, Darren Spalding, Frances Spall, Neil and Abigail Sparks, Jo Sparrey, Andrew Sparrow, Jane Speake, Chris Spear, Ruth Speare, Dominic Spencer, John Spencer, Sam Spencer, Mark Spencer-Scragg, David Spendlove, James Spibey, Paul Spicer, Liam Spinage, Helen Spires, Matteo Spreafico, Harald Sprengel, Dave Spring, Louise Squire, Tom Stables, Jon Stace, Simon Stacey, Jo Stafferton, Susan Stainer, Mark Stanford-Janes, Mike Stanislawski, Paula Stanton, Ann Stapleton, Andrew Stark, Annette Stark, Malcolm Starkey, Starling3232, Marios Stavridis, Jane Steed, Lisa Steel, Anne Steele, Dick Steele, Mark Steele, Ben Stephen, Nigel Stephens, Robert Stephens, Jessica Stephens QC, Donna Stephenson, Robin Stephenson, Annie Stevens, Emma Stevens, Kevin Stevenson, Craig Stewart, John Stewart, John Cadman Stewart, Robert Stewart, Tom Stewart, Catriona Stirling, Katie Stirling, Rebecca Stirling, Susan Stirzaker, Gaynor Stoddard, Lee Stoddart, Tina Stojko, Anthony Stokes, Toni Stokes, Wendy Stokes, Claire Stone, Quinnan Stone, Lauren Stoner, Jon Stones, Fiona Stops, Chris Storer, Lee Storey, Bekah Stott, Dan Stott, Frederick Stourton, Marin Stoychev, Callum Strachan, Davey Strachan, Iain Strachan, Paul Strawbridge, Martyn Stroud, Carolyn Stubbs, Cathy Stubbs, M.A. Stubbs, Chris Sturdy, Penelope Sturman, Pawan Subramaniam, JP Sullivan, Ross Sullivan, Aksa Sultan, Mike Sum, Naomi Sumpter, John Sunart, Ali Sunday, Amelie Surridge, Chris Suslowicz, Geraldine Sutcliffe, Rebecca Sutton, Emma Swaby, Rory Sweeney, Lucian Sweet, Stephen Swindley, Colin Sylvester, Felicity Szesnat, Helen Szewczyk, Iwona Szwedo-Wilmot, Faizah T, Jan T, Mads Taanquist, Jayesh Tailor, Anne Tait, Daniel Tait, Judith Talbot, Derek Tallent, Robert Tallis, Julia Tanner, Lucy Tapper Howe, Ben Target, George Tasker, Gillian Tate, Helen Tate, Maria Tate, Oliver Tate, Sarah Tate, Lucy Tatner, Tattooed_mummy, David Tausinger, Alex Taylor, Anna Taylor, Brian Taylor, Catriona Taylor, Chris Taylor, Jo Taylor, Kathy Taylor, Kev Taylor, Mark Taylor, Matthew Taylor, Melanie Taylor, Pam Taylor, Tim Taylor, Tina Taylor, Valerie Taylor, Wayne Taylor, Team Taylor-Hughes, Saffron Taylor-Sprakes, Jon Teall, Anton Teasdale, Quinton Tecza, Dr Philip Tee, Lorraine Templeton, Sue Thackeray, Margaret Thatcher, The Boyles in Pinner, The ghost of Margaret

Thatcher , The Lock Inn Crosby, The McCormacks in Harrow, @TheBrexitPartLy, thedweebster, Andrea Thiele, Alex Thomas, Amanda Thomas, Chris & Michelle Thomas, David Thomas, Gary Thomas, Jaymie Thomas, Josie Thomas, Judith Thomas, Michelle Thomas, Peter Thomas, Sandra Thomas, Stella-Maria Thomas, Stephen Thomas, Su Thomas, Amanda Thompson, Bob Thompson, Christine Thompson, David Thompson, Ian A Thompson, Lisa Thompson, Lynn Thompson, Mark Thompson, Richard Thompson, Rupert Doggy Thompson, Michael Thompson BA MA MBA DIC, Hugo Thomsen, John Thomson, Mark Thomson, James Thorne, Maria Cristina Thorne, Chris Thornley, Ann Thornton, Sian Thornton, Simon Thornton, Kevin Thorold, Lindsay Thorp, Sarah Thurmer, Jon Tickle, Kerry Tidd, Mark Tighe, Carl Tiivas, Theresa Tilley, Alison Tipper, Chris Tipping, David Tipping, Jo and Geoff Tipping, Alex Tischer, Rachel Titley, Mark Tittle, Mike Tobyn, Giles Todd, Andrew Toft, Cathy Togher, Becky Togneri, Alyx "sexy Alyx" Tole, David Tollitt, David Tomkins, John & Judy Tomlinson, Matt Tomlinson, Stu Tomlinson, Chris Tompkins, Stefano Tonelli, Andrew Tooke, Kris Tooke, @topicalcomedian , Keir Torrie, Jack Tovey, Emma Towler, Nancy Towler, Margaret Townsend, Chris Townsley-Gray, Victoria Tracey, Lucy Traves, Ian Travis, Scott Treacy, Stephen Treacy, Gareth Tregidon, Kathy Trevelyan, Dave Triffitt, Jo Trigg, Jonathan Trott, Mark Trotter, Tom Trower, Trudgin, Jill Trumper, Pem Tshering, Kerry Tucker, Ros Tucker, Andrew Tudor, Gail Tudor, Emma Tudor-Pratley, Aphra Tulip-Briggs, Ricki Tura, Andrew Turner, Barrie Turner, Dr. Andrew Turner, Harry Turner, Janice Turner, Martin Turner, Mike Turner, Richard Turner, Robbie Turner, Kyra Tweddle, Duncan Tweed, Ben Twemlow, Katie Twomey, Chris Tye, Dave Tyler, David Spinolli Tyler, Mike Tynan, Simon Tyrrell, Jorg Umbach, Andrew Underwood, Oscar Unwin, Amandeep Kaur Uppal, Mandeep Singh Uppal, David Urquhart, Sam Urquhart, Janet Valentine, Kate Valentine, Graham Vallance, Thomas Vallance, Hans van Baalen, Petra van der Heijden, Jake van Eijk, Valerie van Mulukom, Gary Vance, Eris Varga, Dr Dominic Varley, Adam Vaughan, Paul Vaughan, Zoe Veal, Veep, Lavan Velu, Mark Vent, Paul Verbinnen, P Vermoter, Christopher Vernon, Kerri Victoria, Joanna Vince, Viscountess Jeannie of Nouvelle Aquitaine, Bella Vivat, Fenna von Hirschheydt, Andy Wace, Matt Waddilove, Dr P D Wadey, Simon Wailling, John Wainwright, Lucy Wainwright, Paul Wainwright, Jamie Wakefield, Jonathan Wakeford, Tim Walford, Andy Walker, Antony Walker, Bridget Walker, Charlotte Walker, Conor Walker, David Walker, Dawn Walker,

Emma Walker, Geoff Walker, Mark Walker, Natalie Walker, Paul Walker, Robert Walker, Rosemary Walker, Zoe Walker, Phil Wall, William Wall, Elaine Wallace, Jane Walmsley, Alyson Walsh, Andrew Walsh, Clare Walsh, Daniel Walsh, Denise Walsh, Dr. Walsh, Catherine Walter, Steve Walter, Breda Walton, David Walton, Elizabeth Walton, Geoffrey Walton, John Walton, Kellie Walton, Carole-Ann Warburton, Philip Warburton, Becky Ward, David Ward, Ellie Ward, Eva Ward, Simon Warde, Charlie Wardrop, Anne Ware, Heather Wareing, Hannah Warman, Ellie Warmington, Caro Warner, Henna-Sisko Warner, Phil Warner, Stephen Warner, Ben Waterhouse, Andrew Waters, Martin Waters, Tony Waters, John Wates, Adam Watkins, James Watkins, Simon Watkins, Tom Watkins, Alex Watson, Allan Watson, Allison Watson, Diane Watson, Matt Watson, Paul Watson, Sam Watson, Emma Watson and David Milbourn, Colin Watt, Simon Watt, Bob Watts, Gwyneth Watts, Joseph Watts, Laura Watts, Paul Watts, Sam Watts, William Watts, Esther Watts-Nielsen, Ben Waugh, David Way, Tim Way, Pete Weaver, Ed Webb, Kelly Webb, Lin Webb, Michael Webb, Simon Webb, Jutta Weber, Ben Webster, Garry Webster, Kris Wedlake, Chris Weight, Simon Weightman, Andrew Weir, David Weir, Margaret Weir, Natalie Weir, Wayne Weir, John Wells, Michael Wells, Nicole Wells, Pete Wells, Michelle Wellsbury, Claire Welsh, WesDirk, Anthea West, Camilla West, Chris West, Clare West, Paul West, Sylvia West, Mig Weston, Chris Weston wb40podcast.com, Gill Westwood, Georgia Weyman, Paul Whateley, Andrew Wheatley, Mike Wheeler, Stephen Wheeler, Tim Wheeler, Claire Whelan, Mandy Whelan, Andrew Wheldon, Liz Whelen, Lori Whinn, Nicola Whitaker, Abigail Whitbread, Alistair White, Joanne White, John White, Karen White, Mike White, Miranda White, Nathan White, Nicholas White, Phill White, Sara White, Steven White, Adam White-Bower, Rhian Whitehead, Patricia Whitehouse, Nick Whiteside, Bryan Whitfield, Miranda Whiting, Jamie Whittam, Mark Whittingham, Andy Whittle, Ian Whittleworth, Peter Whitworth, Kel Wickett, Anna Wicks, Ben Wicks, Lawrence Widdicombe, Adrian Widdowson, Rysz Widelski, Julie Wiggins, Madelyn Wiggins, Eve Wigham, Patricia Wightman, Terry Wilcox, Mhairi Wild, Cat Wilde, Laura Wilkins, Rachel Wilkins, Alex Wilkinson, Dave Wilkinson, Geoffrey Wilkinson, Helen Wilkinson, Suzanne Wilkinson, Sean Wilks, Alex Raven Williams, Candy Williams, Carys Williams, Cassie Williams, Chris Williams, Christine Williams, Christopher Williams, Colin Williams, David Williams, Diane Williams, Donna Williams, Dyfrig Williams, Emma Williams, Gareth Williams, Gary Williams, George Williams, Heidi

Rees Williams, Helen Sian Williams, Jacquie Williams, Kate Williams, Mark Williams, Michael Williams, Michelle Williams, Oli Williams, Paul Williams, Sarah Williams, Shan Williams, Sophie Williams, Victoria Williams, Vikki Williams, Becca Williamson, Nicole Williamson, Rich Williamson, Steph Williamson, Julian Willis, Mark Willis, Fiona Willmott, Clara Willmott-Basset, Tom Willoughby, Helen Wills, Rachel Willshaw, Lucas Wilmshurst, Maurice Wilsdon, Adam Wilson, Alan Wilson, Angela Wilson, Drew Wilson, Jen Wilson, Keeley Wilson, Kevin Wilson, Lee Wilson, Martin Wilson, Peter Wilson, Robert Wilson, Shoshana YBH Wilson, Sian Wilson, Tracy Wilson, Yonni Wilson, Joanna Wincenciak, Nicky Windows, Craig Windsor, Jez Wingham, Michael Winiberg, Roger Winter, Chris Winters, Jayson Winters, Ross Winwood, Tom Wirschell, Rachel Wise, Trevor Wisker, Lyndsey Withers, Vanina Wittenburg, Theresa Witziers, Andy Wood, Chris Wood, Christopher Wood, Ian Wood, Liam Wood, Mark Wood, Matt J. Wood, Melanie Wood, Riley Wood, Tom Wood, Tracy Wood, Jon Woodcock, Stephen Woodcock, Mark Woodfield, Katherine Woodhouse, Stuart Woodington, Iona Woods, Jane Woods, John Woods, Paul Woods, Alison Woolcock, Alison Woolf, Jennet Woolford, Annette Woollam, Ian Woolley, The Woozle, Ben Worrall, Louise Worsfold, Peter Worth, Rita Worth, Ann Worthington, Diana Wraxall, Andrew Wren, Caroline Wren, Amy Wright, David Wright, Graham A. N. Wright, Guinevere Wright, Hazel Wright, Jane Wright, Jo Wright, Linda Wright, Suzanne Wright, Richard Wylie, David Wynn, Sarah Wynne, Stephanie Wynne McCoy, Alan Yates, Susan Yates, Caron Yeaman, Malinee Yindisiriwong, Mike Yorwerth, Anya Young, Brian Young, Helen Young, Kay Young, Martin Young, Tracie Young, Erica Youngman, Sara Yuen, Frances Yule, H Z, Victor Zanchi, Jane Zara, Barry Zubel, Maik Zumstrull, Ben Zurawel, קולופ קירטפ